Office 2010 Made Simple

Guy Hart-Davis

Apress®

Office 2010 Made Simple

Copyright © 2011 by Guy Hart-Davis

ISBN-13 (pbk): 978-1-4302-3575-0

ISBN-13 (electronic): 978-1-4302-3576-7

President and Publisher: Paul Manning
Lead Editor: Matthew Moodie
Technical Reviewer: Jennifer Kettell
Editorial Board: Steve Anglin, Mark Beckner, Ewan Buckingham, Gary Cornell, Jonathan Gennick, Jonathan Hassell, Michelle Lowman, James Markham, Matthew Moodie, Jeff Olson, Jeffrey Pepper, Frank Pohlmann, Douglas Pundick, Ben Renow-Clarke, Dominic Shakeshaft, Matt Wade, Tom Welsh
Coordinating Editor: Adam Heath
Copy Editor: Tracy Brown
Compositor: MacPS, LLC
Indexer: SPI Global
Artist: SPI Global
Cover Designer: Anna Ishchenko

Distributed to the book trade worldwide by Springer Science+Business Media, LLC., 233 Spring Street, 6th Floor, New York, NY 10013. Phone 1-800-SPRINGER, fax (201) 348-4505, e-mail orders-ny@springer-sbm.com, or visit www.springeronline.com.

For information on translations, please e-mail rights@apress.com, or visit www.apress.com.

Apress and friends of ED books may be purchased in bulk for academic, corporate, or promotional use. eBook versions and licenses are also available for most titles. For more information, reference our Special Bulk Sales–eBook Licensing web page at www.apress.com/bulk-sales.

Contents at a Glance

Contents

Chapter 5: Coauthoring in Real Time and Sharing Documents.................. 121

Chapter 6: Making the Office Programs Work Your Way............................ 141

About the Author

 **Guy Hart-Davis** is the author of more than 70 computer books, including *Beginning Microsoft Office 2010, Learn Office 2011 for Mac OS X*, and *Learn Excel 2011 for Mac*, all by Apress.

About the Technical Reviewer

Jennifer Ackerman Kettell has written and contributed to more than 30 computer books on topics such as Microsoft Office, Adobe Creative Suite, web design, and digital photography.

Acknowledgments

My thanks go to the many people who helped create this book:

- Steve Anglin for signing me to write the book
- Matthew Moodie for developing the manuscript.
- Jennifer Ackermann Kettell for reviewing the manuscript for technical accuracy and contributing helpful suggestions.
- Tracy Brown for editing the manuscript with care.
- Adam Heath for coordinating the book project and keeping things running.
- MacPS, LLC for laying out the chapters of the book.
- SPI Global for creating the index.

Part I

Quick Start Guide

To start using Microsoft Office, you need to log on to Windows, launch the program you want to use, and create documents in it. This Quick Start Guide shows you how to do just that.

You also learn what the major components of the Office programs' interface are and what they do, how to close a program when you finish using it, and where to look to find information about the topics you want to learn about.

Let's get started!

Logging On to Windows

First, get Windows up and running.

Start your PC by pressing its power button.

When the login screen appears, click your user name, type your password, and then press **Enter**, as shown in Figure 1.

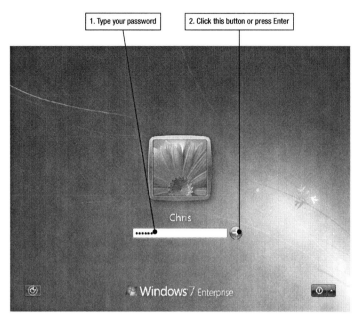

Figure 1. *To get started with Office, log in to Windows by typing your password and pressing **Enter**.*

Locating the Office Programs and Launching Word

Now that you've logged in to Windows, locate the Office programs and click Microsoft Word 2010 as shown in Figure 2. You'll normally find the Office programs in the **Microsoft Office** group on the **Start** menu.

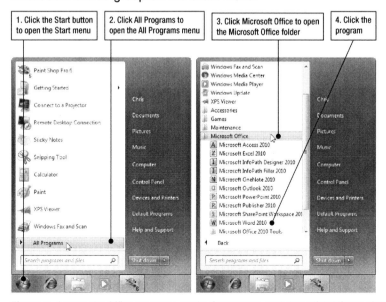

Figure 2. *Locate the Office programs on the **Start** menu, and then click **Microsoft Word 2010** to launch Word.*

Meeting the Major Components of the Word Window

When Word opens, it automatically creates a new document for you and displays it in a window. Figure 3 explains what you should be seeing at this point.

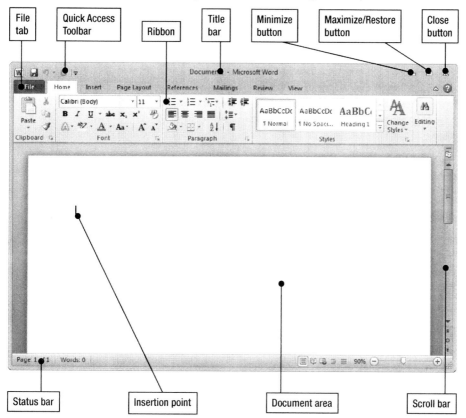

Figure 3. *Each of the Office programs has the same major components, including the **File** tab, Quick Access Toolbar, Ribbon, and status bar.*

Here's what the main elements of the Word window do:

- *Title bar.* Running across the top of the window, the title bar shows the name of the file open in the window (in this case, Document1) and the program's name.

- **File** *tab.* This tab, at the left end of the Ribbon, opens Backstage view, which you use to give commands for opening, printing, saving, and otherwise manipulating documents.

- *Quick Access Toolbar.* This bar at the left end of the title bar provides instant access to the commands you need most often.

- *Ribbon.* This control strip across the top of the program window contains tabs that hold groups of controls. The Ribbon is your main means of giving commands in the Office 2010 programs. (You can also give commands by right-clicking and using the context menus and by pressing keyboard shortcuts.)

- ***Minimize, Maximize/Restore,* and *Close* buttons.** At the right end of the title bar are (from left to right) the **Minimize** button, the **Maximize/Restore** button, and the **Close** button. Click the **Minimize** button to minimize the window to the taskbar; click the **Maximize** button to enlarge the window to full screen, or click the **Restore** button (which replaces the **Maximize** button) to return it to the size it was before you maximized it; or click the **Close** button to close the window.

- *Document area.* This is the main part of the window, where you enter the content of your document.

- *Insertion point.* This indicator shows where text you type on the keyboard will land in the document.

- *Status bar.* This bar at the bottom of the window shows readouts giving you information about the status of the file or the current object together with controls for changing the view and zooming in and out.

- *Scroll bar.* This bar at the right side of the window frame lets you scroll up and down through your documents.

As you'll see later in the book, the other Office programs also use most of these elements.

Closing a Document

As you saw a moment ago, Word automatically opens a new blank document for you when you launch the program. If you need such a document, you can start work by typing in it. If not, you can close it as shown in Figure 4.

When you click the File tab, Backstage view opens, as you can see in Figure 4, giving you access to commands for manipulating the document as a whole.

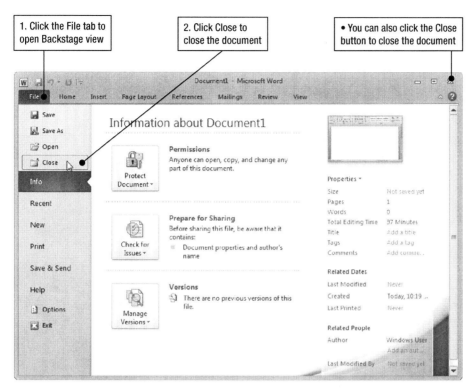

1. Click the File tab to open Backstage view

2. Click Close to close the document

• You can also click the Close button to close the document

Figure 4. *You can close a document by choosing* **File ➤ Close** *or by clicking the* **Close** *button at the upper-right corner of the window.*

Creating and Saving a New Document

To create a new document, you use Backstage view as well. When you click the **Open** button in the left column of Backstage view, as shown in Figure 5. Word displays the **New** pane. You can then use the controls in the **Available Templates** area to choose the template you want, and then click the **Create** button to create a new document based on that template.

NOTE: A *template* is a file that contains the framework for a new document. For example, a report template contains placeholders for items such as the report's title, author name, headings, and body text. Using a template helps you create consistently formatted documents quickly and easily.

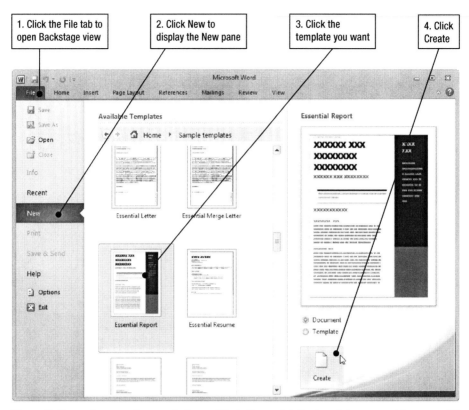

Figure 5. *To create a new document, choose **File ➤ New**, click the template you want to use, and then click the **Create** button.*

Now that you've created a document, save it as shown in Figure 6.

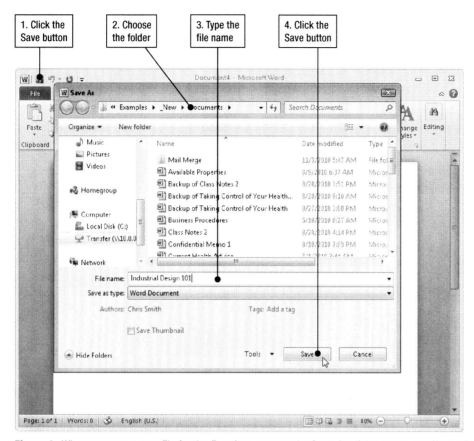

Figure 6. *When you save a new file for the first time, you use the* **Save As** *dialog box to specify the file name and choose the folder to save the file in.*

After saving and naming the document, you can add content to it—for example, by typing text or inserting pictures. To save the changes you make, click the **Save** button on the Quick Access Toolbar or press **Ctrl+S**.

Closing Word

When you finish using Word, close it as shown in Figure 7. If any of your open documents contain unsaved changes, Word prompts you to save them.

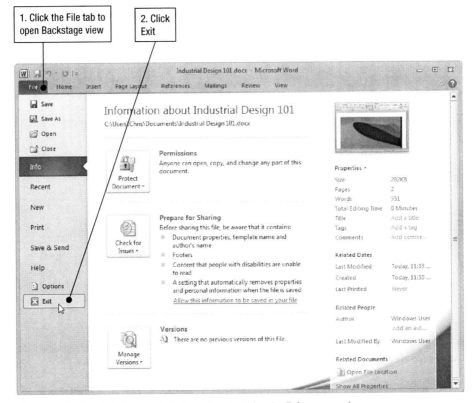

Figure 7. *To close Word, open Backstage view and give the **Exit** command.*

Where to Learn More

Table 1 lists the major Office topics this book discusses and where you'll find them.

Table 1: *Major Office Topics*

Topic	Where to Learn More (Chapter and Section)
Starting programs the easy way	Chapter 1, "Launching a Program"
Opening a recent file	Chapter 1, "Reopening a File You've Used Recently"
Giving commands with the Ribbon and keyboard	Chapter 2, "Using the Ribbon"

Topic	Where to Learn More (Chapter and Section)
Using the AutoCorrect feature	Chapter 2, "Entering Text Faster Using AutoCorrect"
Checking spelling and grammar	Chapter 2, "Checking Spelling and Grammar in Your Files"
Printing	Chapter 2, "Printing Your Documents"
Entering text and symbols	Chapter 3, "Entering Text in Your Documents"
Formatting text and objects	Chapter 3, "Applying Direct Formatting to Text and Objects"
Working with Cut, Copy, and Paste	Chapter 3, "Using Cut, Copy, and Paste"
Finding and replacing text	Chapter 3, "Using Find and Replace"
Creating tables	Chapter 3, "Laying Out Material with Tables"
Adding links	Chapter 3, "Inserting Hyperlinks in Your Documents"
Adding clip art items to documents	Chapter 4, "Inserting Clip Art Items in Your Documents"
Adding pictures to documents	Chapter 4, "Inserting Other Pictures in Your Documents"
Laying out graphical objects	Chapter 4, "Positioning Graphical Objects"
Adjusting picture color, style, and cropping	Chapter 4, "Making Your Pictures Look the Way You Want Them"
Creating diagrams	Chapter 4, "Creating Illustrations by Inserting SmartArt Graphics"
Working on the same document as your colleagues	Chapter 5, "Coauthoring in Real Time"
Sharing documents with your colleagues via a network	Chapter 5, "Sharing Documents on a Network"
Sharing documents via the Internet	Chapter 5, "Sharing Documents via E-mail, SkyDrive, and Electronic Documents"
Putting the buttons you need on the Quick Access Toolbar	Chapter 6, "Customizing the Quick Access Toolbar"

Topic	Where to Learn More (Chapter and Section)
Customizing the status bar	Chapter 6, "Customizing the Status Bar"
Changing the Ribbon	Chapter 6, "Customizing the Ribbon"
Choosing General options and Save options	Chapter 6, "Setting Essential Options"
Adding text to a Word document	Chapter 7, "Entering Text in Your Word Documents"
Selecting text and moving through documents	Chapter 7, "Selecting Text and Navigating Through Your Documents"
Seeing exactly the information you need to see	Chapter 7, "Working the Smart Way by Using Views and Windows"
Formatting a document using styles	Chapter 8, "Applying Styles to a Document"
Creating styles that look the way you want	Chapter 8, "Creating Custom Styles"
Adding further formatting to styled text	Chapter 8, "Applying Direct Formatting on Top of Styles"
Breaking up a document into sections	Chapter 9, "Using Sections to Create Complex Layouts"
Creating headers and footers	Chapter 9, "Adding Headers, Footers, and Page Numbers"
Creating tables in Word documents	Chapter 9, "Adding Tables to Your Documents"
Creating columns of text	Chapter 9, "Creating Newspaper-Style Columns of Text"
Using revision marks and comments	Chapter 10, "Revising a Document"
Creating a final version of a document	Chapter 10, "Finalizing a Document"
Printing only some pages of a document	Chapter 10, "Printing Your Documents"
Navigating the Excel interface	Chapter 11, "Navigating the Excel Interface, Worksheets, and Workbooks"

Topic	Where to Learn More (Chapter and Section)
Entering data in Excel	Chapter 11, "Entering Data in Your Worksheets"
Rearranging the worksheets in a workbook	Chapter 11, "Inserting, Renaming, Deleting, and Rearranging Worksheets"
Using views, splitting, and freezing	Chapter 11, "Displaying Worksheets the Way You Prefer to See Them"
Collaborating with your colleagues on a workbook	Chapter 11, "Sharing Your Workbooks and Tracking Changes"
Setting up the rows and columns in a worksheet	Chapter 12, "Working with Rows and Columns"
Formatting elements in worksheets	Chapter 12, "Formatting Cells and Ranges"
Creating headers and footers	Chapter 12, "Adding Headers and Footers to Your Worksheets"
Printing worksheets and workbooks	Chapter 12, "Printing Your Excel Worksheets and Workbooks"
Understanding the basics of formulas and functions	Chapter 13, "Referring to Cells and Ranges in Formulas and Functions"
Using formulas	Chapter 13, Performing Custom Calculations by Creating Formulas"
Using functions	Chapter 13, "Performing Standard Calculations by Inserting Functions"
Understanding how charts work in Excel	Chapter 14, "Learning the Essentials of Charts in Excel"
Creating a chart	Chapter 14, "Creating, Laying Out, and Formatting a Chart"
Creating a database in Excel	Chapter 15, "Creating Databases"
Sorting a database	Chapter 15, "Sorting a Database by One or More Fields"
Finding records in a database by criteria	Chapter 15, "Filtering a Database"
Solve business problems in Excel	Chapter 15, "Solving Business Problems with Scenarios and Goal Seek"
Getting started with OneNote	Chapter 16, "Meeting the OneNote User Interface"

Topic	Where to Learn More (Chapter and Section)
Working with notebooks and elements	Chapter 16, "Working with Notebooks, Section Groups, Sections, and Pages"
Taking notes in OneNote	Chapter 16, "Entering Notes on a Page"
Viewing your notes	Chapter 16, "Using Views, Windows, and Side Notes"
Searching your notes for information	Chapter 17, "Searching for Information in Your Notebooks"
Securing sensitive notes	Chapter 17, "Protecting Your Notes with Passwords"
Sharing a notebook with your colleagues	Chapter 17, "Sharing an Existing Notebook"
Customizing OneNote to work your way	Chapter 18, "Choosing the Most Important Options for OneNote"
Taking audio and video notes	Chapter 18, "Recording Audio and Video into Your Notebooks"
Printing your notes	Chapter 18, "Previewing and Printing Your Notebook Pages"
Using OneNote with Word, Excel, PowerPoint, and Outlook	Chapter 18, "Using OneNote with the Other Office Programs"
Starting a new presentation in PowerPoint	Chapter 19, "Creating a Presentation"
Getting around the PowerPoint interface	Chapter 19, "Navigating the PowerPoint Window"
Creating the slides for a presentation	Chapter 19, "Adding, Deleting, and Rearranging Slides"
Using PowerPoint's views	Chapter 19, "Using Views to Work on Your Presentation"
Outlining a presentation	Chapter 19, "Creating the Outline of a Presentation"
Planning a presentation	Chapter 20, "Planning the Slides in Your Presentation"
Choosing slide layouts	Chapter 20, "Choosing Slide Layouts to Suit the Contents"
Formatting text on slides	Chapter 20, "Formatting Text on Your Slides"

Topic	Where to Learn More (Chapter and Section)
Adding other objects to slides	Chapter 20, "Adding Tables, SmartArt, Charts, and Hyperlinks to Slides"
Adding pictures to slides	Chapter 21, "Adding Pictures to a Presentation"
Adding movies and sounds to slides	Chapter 21, "Adding Movies and Sounds to a Presentation"
Marking changeovers with transitions	Chapter 21, "Adding Transitions to Slides"
Enlivening slides with animations	Chapter 21, "Adding Animations to Slides"
Keeping extra information in reserve	Chapter 21, "Keeping Extra Information Up Your Sleeve with Hidden Slides"
Getting ready to deliver a presentation	Chapter 22, "Preparing to Deliver a Presentation in Person"
Giving a live presentation	Chapter 22, "Delivering a Presentation to a Live Audience"
Creating handouts	Chapter 22, "Creating a Handout for a Presentation"
Recording narration	Chapter 22, "Recording Narration into a Presentation"
Broadcasting a presentation or publishing slides	Chapter 22, "Exporting and Sharing a Presentation"
Set up e-mail accounts in Outlook	Chapter 23, "Setting Up Your E-mail Accounts in Outlook"
Changing an e-mail account's settings	Chapter 23, "Changing the Default Settings for an E-mail Account"
Learning the Outlook interface	Chapter 23, "Meeting the Outlook Interface"
Sending and receiving e-mail messages	Chapter 24, "Sending an E-mail Message"
Sending and receiving attachments	Chapter 24, "Sending and Receiving Attachments"
Organizing your e-mail messages	Chapter 24, "Deleting, Storing, and Organizing Messages"

Topic	Where to Learn More (Chapter and Section)
Dealing with junk mail	Chapter 24, "Dealing with Spam"
Creating contact records in Outlook	Chapter 25, "Creating Contacts"
Viewing, sorting, and communicating with your contacts	Chapter 25, "Working with Contacts"
Keeping your diary	Chapter 26, "Organizing Your Schedule with the Calendar"
Tracking your tasks	Chapter 26, "Working with Tasks"
Taking notes	Chapter 26, "Taking Notes"

Part II

Introduction

Do you need to get your work done with the Office programs—smoothly, easily, and quickly?

Do you prefer to pick up information graphically rather than by reading long explanations?

If so, you've picked up the right book.

Who Is This Book For?

This book is designed to help beginning and intermediate users get up to speed quickly with the Office 2010 programs and immediately become productive with them.

If you need to learn to use Word, Excel, OneNote, PowerPoint, and Outlook to accomplish everyday tasks, at work or at home, you'll benefit from this book's focused approach and detailed advice. You can either start from the beginning of the book and work through it, or use the table of contents or the index to find the topic you need immediately, and then jump right in there.

What Does This Book Cover?

This book contains six parts that cover the shared Office features and the five leading programs: Word, Excel, OneNote, PowerPoint, and Outlook.

Part III of the book brings you up to speed with the common features that the Office programs share.

- Chapter 1: "Meeting the Office Programs and Learning What They Do" introduces you to the five main Office programs and what you can do with them. You learn how to open and close the programs; you'll meet the key components of the programs; and you'll create, save, close and reopen documents.

▓ Chapter 2: "Using the Ribbon, Backstage, and Common Tools" shows you how to control the Office programs using the Ribbon and how to access Backstage and use its document-management features. It also explains Office's common ways of sharing a document with others, how to make the most of the AutoCorrect and AutoFormat features, and how to use the Spelling checker and Grammar checker. You'll also learn how to print documents.

▓ Chapter 3: "Working with Text" shows you how to do everything from entering text (using the keyboard or other means) to creating tables and hyperlinks. Along the way, you learn how to work with the Cut, Copy, and Paste tools, and how to use the Find and Replace features.

▓ Chapter 4: "Using Graphics in Your Documents" teaches you how to position graphical objects, insert clip art items or your own pictures, and make your pictures look the way you want them to. You also learn how to create illustrations by inserting SmartArt graphics in your documents and how to arrange graphical objects to control which ones are visible.

▓ Chapter 5: "Coauthoring in Real Time and Sharing Documents" explains how to use the coauthoring feature to work on a document at the same time as your colleagues in Word, Excel, PowerPoint, and OneNote. You also learn how to share a single copy of the document on a network drive so that your colleagues can work on it in turn, how to create multiple copies of documents so that people can work on them simultaneously, and how to share documents via e-mail and other means.

▓ Chapter 6: "Making the Office Programs Work Your Way" walks you through customizing the Quick Access Toolbar, the Ribbon, and the status bar to make them show the commands and information you need. You'll also learn how to set essential options in the programs, such as the General options and the Save options.

Part IV of the book covers using Microsoft Word, the powerful word processing program.

▓ Chapter 7: "Entering and Editing Text in Your Documents" shows you how to enter text quickly in Word documents, how to select text in advanced ways with the mouse and the keyboard, how to move around your documents, and how to tell Word where to find your custom templates. You'll also learn to create backup documents automatically, to make the most of Word's five different views of a document, and to work with multiple windows on the same document.

- Chapter 8: "Formatting Your Documents Easily and Efficiently" teaches you the right way to format a document quickly and consistently by using styles rather than by applying direct formatting one piece at a time. It also shows you how to get around your documents by using the Navigation pane.

- Chapter 9: "Adding Headers, Footers, Tables, and Columns" explains how to break a document into multiple sections; how to add headers, footers, and page numbers; and how to create newspaper-style columns of text.

- Chapter 10: "Revising, Finalizing, and Printing Your Documents" shows you how to use Word's powerful Track Changes feature to track exactly those changes that you want to be able to review, how to work in a document with Track Changes on, and how to integrate your colleagues' tracked changes into a single document. You also learn how to use comments in your documents, how to use the tools that Word gives you for comparing or combining different versions of the same document, and how to use Word's extra features for printing a document.

Part V of the book teaches you to create spreadsheets and charts with Excel.

- Chapter 11: "Creating Workbooks and Entering Data" covers creating different types of workbooks in Excel and entering data in them. You learn how to navigate the Excel interface, use workbooks and worksheets, and use Excel's assorted views and features to see the data you need.

- Chapter 12: "Editing Worksheets and Applying Formatting" explains how to insert, delete, and format rows and columns in worksheets, and how to format cells and ranges. This chapter also shows you how to use table formatting and styles, how to add headers and footers to worksheets, and how to print the parts of worksheets you want on paper.

- Chapter 13: "Performing Calculations with Formulas and Functions" lays out the difference between a formula and a function, then shows you first how to create custom formulas and then how to use Excel's built-in functions.

- Chapter 14: "Creating Charts to Present Your Data" teaches you how Excel's charts work and how to add them to your workbooks. You learn how to lay out a chart effectively, how to make it look good, and how to hide any components you don't want to display.

▨ Chapter 15: "Creating Databases and Solving Business Problems" shows you how to use Excel to create databases for storing and manipulating your information. You learn how to enter information in a database, how to sort the information, and how to filter it to find only the results you want. You also learn how to use Excel's scenarios feature to experiment with different values in a worksheet, and how to use the Goal Seek feature to make one cell's value reach a particular figure by changing one other value.

Part VI of the book teaches you to use OneNote, Office's program for recording, storing, and manipulating information.

▨ Chapter 16: "Getting Up to Speed and Taking Notes" shows you how to get around the OneNote interface and how to use its features to capture and view your information. You learn how to work with notebooks, sections, section groups, and pages; how to enter notes on a page; and how to use views, windows, and side notes.

▨ Chapter 17: "Organizing and Synchronizing Your Notes" explains how to organize your pages, sections, and notebooks so that you can find the information you need. Skills you pick up include searching for information, protecting your notes with passwords, and sharing your notebooks with other people.

▨ Chapter 18: "Customizing OneNote and Using It with Word, Excel, PowerPoint, and Outlook" first shows you how to choose settings for the options that make the most difference to your work in OneNote. The chapter then teaches you how to add audio and video to your notebooks, how to print your notebooks, and how to export data from OneNote to the other Office programs.

Part VII of the book takes you through creating good-looking, persuasive presentations with PowerPoint.

▨ Chapter 19: "Starting a Presentation" gets you started by creating a presentation document using either a design template or a content template. The chapter then shows you how to add, delete, and rearrange slides; how to use PowerPoint's four views effectively; how to develop the outline of a presentation; and how to break a presentation into separate sections.

▨ Chapter 20: "Building Effective Slides for Your Presentation" shows you how to create slides that convey your meaning clearly and powerfully. This chapter explains how to plan a presentation, choose suitable slide layouts (or create your own), and how to add text and other content—such as tables, charts, and hyperlinks—to your slides.

Chapter 21: "Giving a Presentation Life and Impact" suggests ways of adding life and interest to a presentation by using graphics, movies, sounds, animations, and transitions. You'll also learn how to hide slides to keep them up your sleeve.

Chapter 22: "Delivering a Presentation in Person or Online" explains how to deliver the presentation you've created. You can take the traditional approach and deliver the presentation in person, broadcast it across the Internet, or create a version of the presentation that you can share via e-mail or in other ways. You also learn how to use PowerPoint's Presenter view and how to create a handout for a presentation.

Part VIII of the book shows you how to manage your e-mail, schedule, contacts, and tasks with Outlook.

Chapter 23: "Setting Up Outlook and Meeting the Interface" tells you how to set up Outlook to work with your e-mail account or accounts. You also take a tour of the Outlook interface, learning how to use the host of controls that Outlook packs into its window to handle all its different roles and tasks.

Chapter 24: "Sending and Receiving E-mail" teaches you to send and receive messages and attachments; reply to messages and forward them to others; and delete the messages you don't want to keep and file those you do. You also learn how to quickly add standard closings to your messages by creating and using signatures and how to deal with spam, or unwanted email.

Chapter 25: "Managing Your Contacts with Outlook" covers creating contacts either from scratch or importing them from your address books. The chapter also shows you how to view and sort your contacts, add or update their contact information, and quickly create communications to your contacts.

Chapter 26: "Organizing Your Schedule, Tasks, and Notes" brings you up to speed with Outlook's Calendar interface, teaches you to use its views, and shows you how to create appointments and meetings. You also learn how to use the Tasks feature to track your commitments, doing everything from creating tasks yourself to delegating tasks to others. This chapter also explains how to use Outlook's Notes feature to jot down information as you work.

Conventions Used in This Book

This book uses several conventions to make its meaning clear without wasting words:

- *Ribbon commands.* The ➤ shows the sequence for choosing an item from the Ribbon. For example, "choose **Insert ➤ Illustrations ➤ Clip Art**" means that you click the **Insert** tab of the Ribbon (displaying the tab's contents), go to the **Illustrations** group, and then click the **Clip Art** button.

- *Special paragraphs.* Special paragraphs present information that you may want to pay extra attention to. Note paragraphs contain information you may want to know; Tip paragraphs present techniques you may benefit from using; and Caution paragraphs warn you of potential problems.

- *Check boxes.* The Office programs use many check boxes—the square boxes that can either have a check mark in them (indicate that the option is turned on) or not (indicating that the option is turned off). This book tells you to "select" a check box when you need to put a check mark in the check box, and to "clear" a check box when you need to remove the check mark from it. If the check box is already selected or cleared, you don't need to change it.

- *Keyboard shortcuts.* In the Office programs, you can often save time and effort by using a keyboard shortcut rather than a Ribbon command. This book uses + signs to represent keyboard shortcuts. For example, "press **Ctrl+S**" means that you hold down the **Ctrl** key, press the **S** key, and then release the **Ctrl** key. "Press **Ctrl+Alt+T**" means that you hold down the **Ctrl** key and the **Alt** key, press the **T** key, and then release the **Ctrl** key and the **Alt** key.

Part III

Chapter 1

Meeting the Office Programs and Learning What They Do

In this chapter, you get up to speed with the Office programs and learn what you can do with each of them. We'll go over how to launch the programs, look quickly at the user interface features they share, and then talk about how to create, save, and reopen documents.

We'll use Microsoft Word for most of the chapter, as most people find Word the most approachable of the programs and it's included in every edition of Office 2010.

If you're already familiar with the Office programs, feel free to skip straight ahead to Chapter 2.

Understanding the Office Programs

Office 2010 comes in several different editions, each with a different set of programs. The main editions are the Home and Student Edition, the Home and Business Edition, the Standard Edition, the Professional Edition, and the Professional Plus Edition. Microsoft also provides the Professional Academic Edition for college students and the Starter Edition, which comes preloaded on some PCs and features cut-down versions of Word and Excel.

In this section, we quickly review the Office programs and make sure you know what they do.

NOTE: This book covers the versions of the Microsoft Office programs that you install on your PC and run from it. Microsoft also provides an online version of Office, Office Web Apps, which is free but has very limited capabilities. To use Office Web Apps as a consumer, create an account (also free) with Windows Live SkyDrive; go to www.live.com to create the account and get started.

This book covers the five programs included in most versions of Office 2010:

- *Microsoft Word.* Word (see Figure 1–1) is a program for word processing and page layout. You can create many different kinds of documents in Word—a single-page memo or letter, a fully illustrated and indexed book of a thousand pages or more, or just about anything in between.

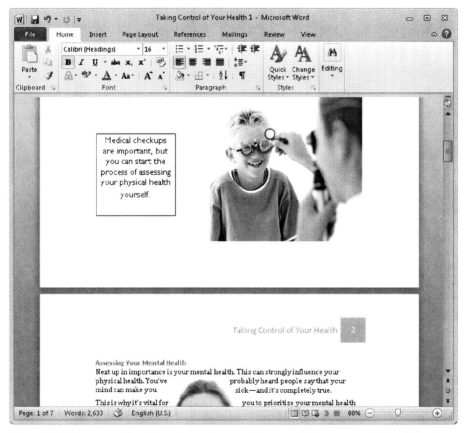

Figure 1–1. *You can use Word to create any document, from a short memo or note to a full-scale report or book.*

- *Microsoft Excel.* Excel (see Figure 1–2) is a spreadsheet program that you use for recording, calculating, and analyzing your data. Excel's files are called *workbooks* and consist of spreadsheets called *worksheets*.

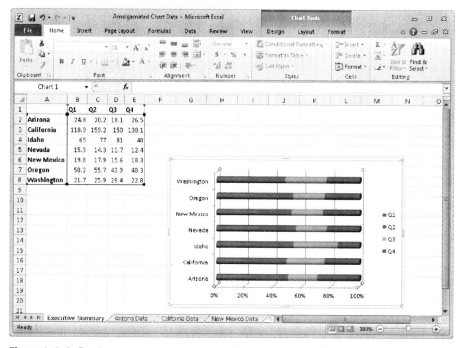

Figure 1–2. *In Excel, you create workbooks containing as many worksheets as you need to record, calculate, and analyze your data. You can easily create charts from your data.*

- *Microsoft OneNote.* OneNote (see Figure 1–3) is a program for taking all kinds of notes—you can store text notes, photos, audio, and even video in the same notebook, search for data, and share it with the other Office programs. For example, you can take notes in OneNote, and then start creating a Word document from them.

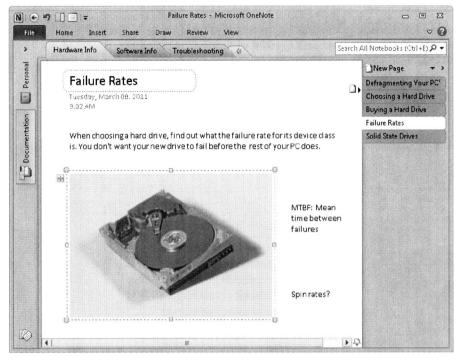

Figure 1–3. *You can use OneNote to record any kind of notes, from text and pictures to audio and video. You can then easily share your notes with the other Office programs.*

▨ *Microsoft PowerPoint.* PowerPoint (see Figure 1–4) is a program for creating presentations that you give either in person or via the Internet. Each presentation consists of one or more slides; each slide can contain text, pictures, or audio and video.

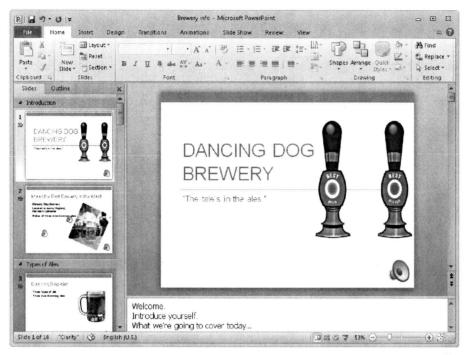

Figure 1–4. *PowerPoint makes it easy to create presentations that convey exactly the information you need.*

■ *Microsoft Outlook.* Outlook (see Figure 1–5) is a program for handling your e-mail, your contacts, and your schedule and tasks. You can send, receive, and manage e-mail messages; create and share contacts; and track your appointments and tasks. You can also assign tasks to other people—or receive tasks that other people assign to you.

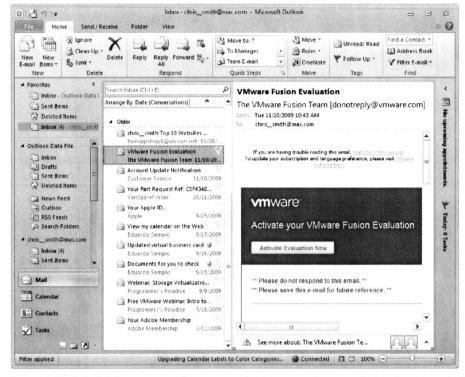

Figure 1–5. *Outlook brings your e-mail accounts, calendars, contacts, and tasks together into a single program.*

NOTE: Microsoft Office 2010 Home and Student Edition doesn't include Outlook.

As you can see, each of the programs has "Microsoft" at the beginning of its formal name. From here on, we'll use just the normal names—"Word" instead of "Microsoft Word," and so on.

Beyond these five core programs, some editions of Microsoft Office also include the following four programs, which this book doesn't cover:

- ▪ *Microsoft Publisher.* Publisher is a page-layout program for creating publications such as newsletters, brochures, and greeting cards. Publisher is included in Microsoft Office 2010 Standard Edition, Microsoft Office 2010 Professional Edition, Microsoft Office 2010 Professional Plus Edition, and Microsoft Office 2010 Professional Academic Edition.

- ▪ *Microsoft Access.* Access is a relational database program for building databases, storing data in them, and generating reports and queries based on the data. Access is included in Microsoft Office 2010 Professional Edition, Microsoft Office 2010 Professional Plus Edition, and Microsoft Office Professional Academic Edition.

- *Microsoft InfoPath.* InfoPath is a program for creating and filling in business forms. InfoPath is included in Microsoft Office 2010 Professional Plus Edition.

- *SharePoint Workspace.* SharePoint Workspace (formerly called Groove) is a program for connecting to Microsoft SharePoint Server, a server used by business and corporate users for sharing documents and keeping control of different versions. SharePoint Workspace is included in Microsoft Office 2010 Professional Plus Edition.

Launching a Program

Now that you've gotten an overview of the main programs in Microsoft Office, let's make sure you know how to perform five essential maneuvers with the programs. We'll start with launching a program; move on to creating new files, closing them, and reopening them; and then cover closing the program when you've finished using it.

We'll use Word for the examples, as you'll have Word no matter which edition of Office you have.

To launch Word, as shown in Figure 1–6, follow these steps:

- Click the **Start** button to open the **Start** menu.

- Click **All Programs** item to display the **All Programs** list.

- Click the **Microsoft Office** folder to display its contents.

- Click the **Microsoft Word** item.

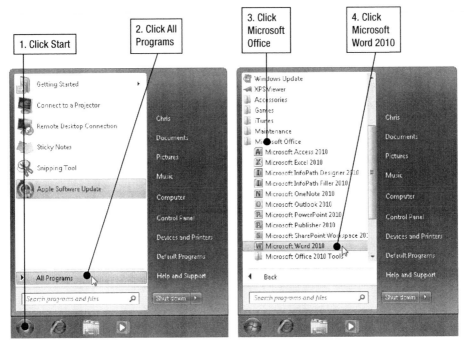

Figure 1–6. *To launch Microsoft Word from the Start menu, choose* **Start** ➤ **All Programs** ➤ **Microsoft Office** ➤ **Microsoft Word 2010**.

TIP: If you plan to use Word or another program frequently, pin it to the taskbar so that you can launch it with a single click. After opening the program, right-click its button on the taskbar, and then click **Pin this program to taskbar**, as shown in Figure 1–7. Alternatively, pin the program to the **Start** menu: Open the **Start** menu, right-click the program, and then click **Pin to Start Menu**; from here, you can also click **Pin to Taskbar** to pin the program to the taskbar.

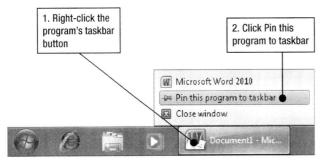

Figure 1–7. *You can quickly pin a running program to the taskbar so that you can launch it more easily in the future.*

CHOOSING WHETHER TO USE AUTOMATIC UPDATES

The first time you run one of the Office programs, Office may display the **Welcome to Microsoft Office 2010** dialog box (see Figure 1–8), which lets you choose which updates to receive. If someone else has already made this decision on your PC, you won't see the Welcome to **Microsoft Office 2010** dialog box.

If this dialog box appears, click the appropriate option button:

- ▓ *Use Recommended Settings*. Select this option button to allow Office, Windows, and other Microsoft software to automatically install updates, check online for solutions to problems the Office programs have, and update Office content such as clip art. Choose this setting if you're happy to have Microsoft update Windows, Office, and your other Microsoft programs automatically.

- ▓ *Install Updates Only*. Select this option button if you want to install updates for Office, Windows, and other Microsoft programs but not perform other actions. For many people, this is the best choice.

- ▓ *Don't make changes*. Select this option button if you don't want to get updates or you prefer to get updates manually at your convenience. The disadvantage to not getting updates is that your Microsoft software may remain exposed to security threats that the updates would reduce or eliminate.

After choosing the option button, click the **OK** button to close the dialog box and implement your choice. If a **User Account Control** dialog box opens, checking that you want to allow the program to make changes, click the **Yes** button. (If you are not an administrator-level user for your PC, you will need to get an administrator to enter a password in the **User Account Control** dialog box.)

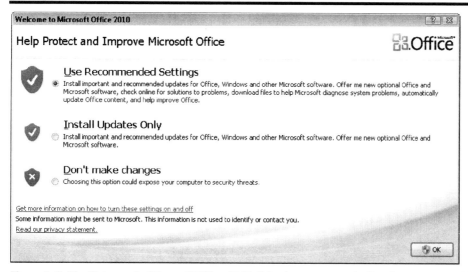

Figure 1–8. *The **Welcome to Microsoft Office 2010** dialog box may open the first time you run an Office program. If so, choose which updates to receive, and then click the **OK** button.*

When Word opens, you see the program window, shown in Figure 1–9 with a document open and its key features labeled.

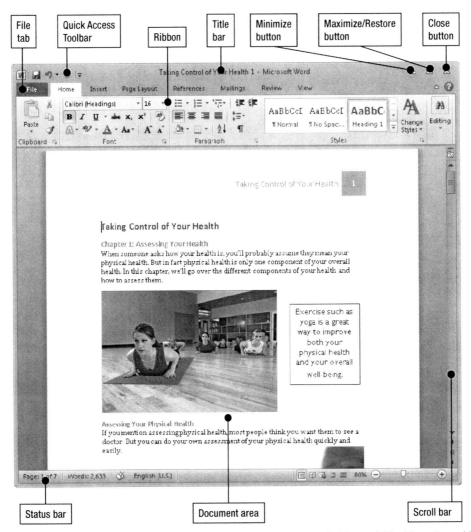

Figure 1–9. *The Office programs share essential components, shown in Microsoft Word here, to enable you to work quickly and easily in each program.*

Identifying the Standard Components of the Office Program Windows

Each of the Office programs has several standard components that you use for controlling the programs:

- *Title bar.* Like most programs, each of the Office programs has a title bar across the top of the window. The title bar shows the name of the file open in the window and the program's name—for example, when you're working on a document named Strategic Planning.docx in Word, the title bar displays "Strategic Planning – Microsoft Word" (the title bar omits the file extension unless you have set Windows to display file extensions).

- *Minimize, Maximize/Restore, and Close buttons.* At the right end of the title bar are (from left to right) the **Minimize** button, the **Maximize/Restore** button, and the **Close** button. As in most Windows programs, you click the **Minimize** button to minimize the window to the taskbar; click the **Maximize** button to enlarge the window to full screen, or click the **Restore** button (which replaces the **Maximize** button) to return it to the size it was before you maximized it; or click the **Close** button to close the window.

> **CAUTION:** When you have two or more documents open, clicking the **Close** button closes only the active document. When only one document is open, clicking the **Close** button closes Word as well as the document.

- *Quick Access Toolbar.* This bar at the left end of the title bar provides instant access to the commands you need most often. The Quick Access Toolbar contains just a few widely used commands at first, but you can customize it by adding the commands you need. See Chapter 6 for details.

- *Ribbon.* This control strip across the top of the program window contains tabs that hold groups of controls. The Ribbon is your main means of giving commands in the Office 2010 programs. (You can also give commands by right-clicking and using the context menus and by pressing keyboard shortcuts.)

- *File tab.* This tab, at the left end of the Ribbon, opens the Backstage view, which gives you access to commands for manipulating the document—for example, saving it, printing it, or closing it.

- *Document area.* This is the main part of the window, where you work on documents in Word; workbooks in Excel; presentations in PowerPoint; notebooks in OneNote; and messages, contacts, appointments, and tasks in Outlook.

- *Status bar.* This bar at the bottom of the window shows readouts giving you information about the status of the file or the current object together with controls for changing the view and zooming in and out. For example, the status bar in Word typically shows the current page number and the total number of pages, the word count, the proofing status (whether there are spelling or grammar errors), and the language.

- *Scroll bar.* This bar at the right side of the window frame lets you scroll up and down through your documents.

Creating, Saving, Closing, and Reopening Files

To get your work done in Word, Excel, PowerPoint, and OneNote, you create files. Each program uses a different type of files—Word creates documents, Excel creates workbooks, PowerPoint creates presentations, and OneNote creates notebook files— but you create and save them in the same way. When you finish working with a file, you close it; and when you need to work with a file again, you reopen it.

In this section, you learn to perform these essential moves.

Creating a File

To create a file, follow these steps. Again, we'll use Word as the example program, but you'll find Excel and PowerPoint work in just the same way. OneNote is a little different, as you'll see in Chapter 16.

If the Word window isn't already active, click the window to make it active. If you can't see the Word window because other windows are in the way, click the Word window's button on the taskbar instead.

1. Click the **File** tab on the left of the Ribbon to open the Backstage view.

2. Click the **New** item on the left side to display the New pane (see Figure 1–10).

> **NOTE:** A *template* is a kind of file that contains the skeleton or framework for a new document. For example, a letter template contains essential text such as the sender's address, the recipient's address, the greeting, and the signoff line. Using a template helps you create a document more quickly. The Blank document template we use in this section creates a plain document that you can turn into any kind of document. We'll look into using Word templates in Chapter 7, Excel templates in Chapter 11, and PowerPoint templates in Chapter 19.

3.   Click the template for the file type you want to create. In this example, click the **Blank document** item in the **Available Templates** list.

4.   Click the **Create** button. Word closes Backstage view and creates the new document.

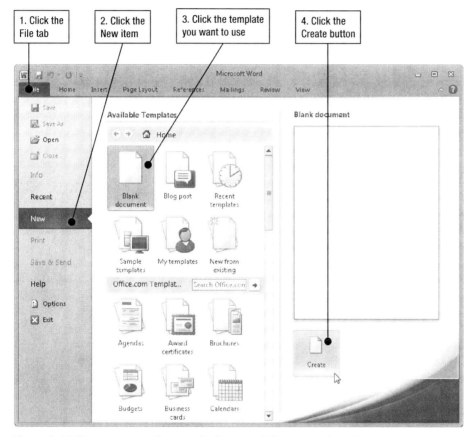

Figure 1–10. *To create a new file, open the New pane in Backstage view, choose the template, and then click the* **Create** *button.*

> ▨ **TIP:** When you need a new blank document in Word, a new blank workbook in Excel, or a new blank presentation in PowerPoint, you can also press the Ctrl+N keyboard shortcut.

Saving a File for the First Time

After creating a new file, save it to your PC's file system. Follow these steps:

1.   Click the **Save** button on the Quick Access Toolbar or press Ctrl+S. The **Save As** dialog box opens (see Figure 1–11).

NOTE: If the **Save As** dialog box opens at a smaller size than shown in Figure 1–11, click the **Show Folders** button to expand the dialog box to its full size.

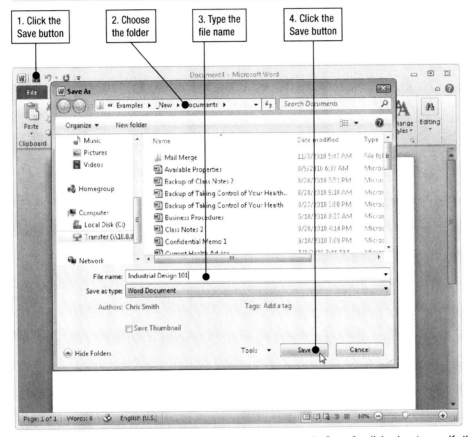

Figure 1–11. *When you save a new file for the first time, you use the **Save As** dialog box to specify the file name and choose the folder to save the file in.*

2. Navigate to the folder you want to save the file in. You can navigate in the address box at the top of the Save As dialog box or by using the folder pane on the left. Click the **Show Folders** button in the lower-left corner of the **Save As** dialog box if you need to display the folder area, or click the Hide Folders button (which replaces the **Show Folders** button) if you want to hide the folder area.

3. In the File name box, type the file name.

4. Click the **Save** button. The program closes the **Save As** dialog box and saves the file.

Closing a File

When you finish working with a file, close it. Follow these steps:

1. If the file contains unsaved changes, click the **Save** button on the Quick Access toolbar to save the changes.

> **TIP:** Always save your files before closing them. Even though the Office programs automatically prompt you to save unsaved changes in a file you're closing (see Figure 1–12), it's possible to click the wrong button and lose the changes. Saving the file before closing it avoids this problem.

Figure 1–12. *The Office programs prompt you to save unsaved changes to a file you're closing. Normally, you'll want to click the Save button when this dialog box appears.*

2. Click the **File** tab to open Backstage view.

3. Click the **Close** button on the left side.

> **TIP:** You can close the active document by pressing Ctrl+W.

Reopening a File You've Used Recently

Office's Backstage view keeps a list of the files you've recently used in each program. You can quickly reopen a recent file like this:

1. Click the **File** tab to open Backstage view. The program displays the Recent pane automatically (see Figure 1–13).

2. In the Recent list, click the file you want to open.

1. Click the File tab

2. Click the file you want to reopen

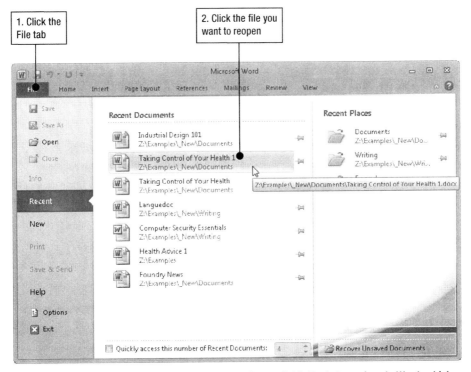

Figure 1–13. *You can quickly reopen a file from the Recent list in Backstage view. In Word, which you see here, the list is named Recent Documents.*

TIP: If you have pinned an Office program to the **Start** menu, you can click the right-arrow button next to it to display a list of recent documents, then click the document you want to open. Similarly, if you have pinned a program to the Taskbar, you can right-click the program to display a list of recent documents, and then click a document to open it.

Opening a File You Haven't Used Recently

To open a file that doesn't appear on the Recent list in Backstage view, follow these steps:

1. Click the **File** tab to open Backstage view.

2. Click the **Open** item in the left pane to display the **Open** dialog box (see Figure 1–14).

TIP: Press Ctrl+O to display the Open dialog box from the keyboard.

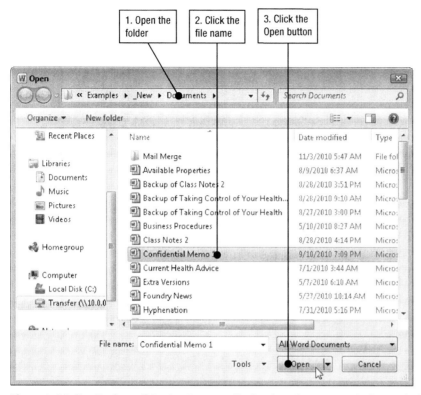

Figure 1–14. *Use the **Open** dialog box to open a file that doesn't appear on the Recent list in Backstage view.*

3. Navigate to the folder you want to save the file in. You can navigate in the address box at the top of the **Save As** dialog box or by using the folder pane on the left.

4. Click the file you want to open.

5. Click the **Open** button.

Closing a Program

When you have finished using a program for the time being, close it. Follow these steps:

1. Click the **File** tab to open Backstage view.

2. Click the **Exit** item.

> **NOTE:** If any files open in the program you're closing contain unsaved changes, the program prompts you to save them.

Instead of using the **File ➤ Exit** command to close a program, you can click the **Close** button at the right end of the title bar to close each open program window in turn. When you close the last window, the program closes too.

Summary

In this chapter, you met the five core Office programs that this book covers—Word, Excel, OneNote, PowerPoint, and Outlook—and learned which types of tasks they're designed for. You now know how to launch and close the programs; identify their main features, such as the Ribbon and the Quick Access toolbar; and create, save, close, and reopen files.

In the next chapter, I'll show you how to use the Ribbon, Backstage view, and other common tools.

Chapter 2

Using the Ribbon, Backstage, and Common Tools

In this chapter, you develop your Office skills by learning to use the Ribbon, Backstage view, and several other tools common to all the Office programs.

You'll learn to save time by using the AutoCorrect feature to enter text faster, to tame the AutoFormat As You Type feature's automatic formatting, and to add actions to the programs' context menus. You'll then learn how to check spelling in all the programs, check grammar if you want in Word and Outlook, and print your documents.

Using the Ribbon

The Ribbon is the main control interface for the Office programs. You can't miss the Ribbon; it runs straight across the top of the program window, as you can see in Figure 2–1, which shows Word's Ribbon.

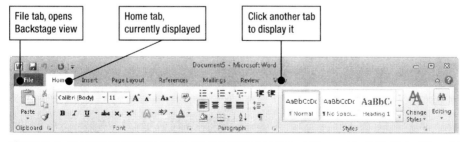

Figure 2–1. *The Ribbon appears across the top of the program window and is divided into different tabs. The active tab (here, the **Home** tab) has a different tab color. You click another tab to display it.*

Understanding the Ribbon's Tabs, Groups, and Controls

The Ribbon consists of a number of tabs, each of which contains controls divided into groups. Here's what those terms mean:

- *Tab.* A tab is one of the major divisions of the Ribbon. A tab takes up the whole width of the Ribbon, so you can display only one tab at a time. You switch from one tab to another by clicking the small tab at the top that bears the name of the tab you want to display. For example, you click the small **Insert** tab to bring the **Insert** tab as a whole to the front of the Ribbon and display the controls it contains.

- *Group.* A group is a vertical division of the Ribbon. For example, the **Home** tab in Word contains the **Clipboard** group, the **Font** group, the **Paragraph** group, the **Styles** group, and the **Editing** group, as you can see in Figure 2–2. The group name appears at the bottom of the group.

- *Control.* A control is one of the items that appears within a group. For example, Figure 2–2 shows the **Clipboard** group and **Font** group on the **Home** tab in Word with the groups and sample controls labeled.

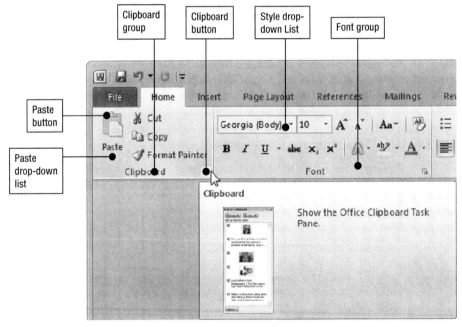

*Figure 2–2. A group is a vertical section of the Ribbon, such as the **Clipboard** group and **Font** group shown here. Each group contains one or more controls of different types, such as the buttons and drop-down lists shown here.*

TIP: If you're not sure what a Ribbon control does or what its icon represents, hold the mouse pointer over the control for a couple of seconds. The program displays a ScreenTip explaining the control, as shown in Figure 2–3. Move the mouse pointer away when you no longer need to see the ScreenTip.

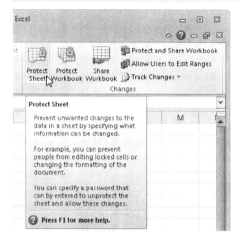

Figure 2–3. *To see a description of what a Ribbon control does, hold the mouse pointer over the control until a ScreenTip appears.*

Giving Commands Using the Ribbon

To give a command using the Ribbon, you click the control that represents the command. Depending on the Ribbon tab that's currently displayed, this process can take two or three steps:

1. Click the Ribbon tab to display it. (If the right Ribbon tab is already displayed, you don't need to do this.)

2. Go to the group that contains the command. You don't need to click the group.

3. Click the control that represents the command.

For Ribbon commands, this book uses the sequence tab–group–control. For example, "choose **Insert ➤ Illustrations ➤ Clip Art**" means that you click the **Insert** tab (if it's not already displayed), go to the **Illustrations** group, and then click the **Clip Art** button.

Minimizing the Ribbon

Chances are that you'll find the Ribbon an easy way to give commands—but even so, it takes up a hefty strip of the program window, especially if you're working on a low-resolution screen.

To recover most of the space the Ribbon takes up, minimize the Ribbon in one of these ways:

- Click the Minimize the Ribbon button to the right of the tab bar (see Figure 2–4).

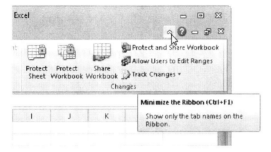

Figure 2–4. *You can quickly minimize the Ribbon by clicking the **Minimize the Ribbon** button. To expand the Ribbon again, click the **Expand the Ribbon** button that replaces the **Minimize the Ribbon** button.*

- Double-click the active tab.

- Right-click any tab and choose **Minimize the Ribbon** from the context menu.

- Press Ctrl+F1.

When you minimize the Ribbon, only its tab strip appears, as shown in Figure 2–5—not the main band of controls. Click a tab's name to display that tab so that you can give a command. The Ribbon then minimizes itself again automatically.

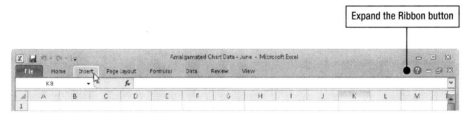

Figure 2–5. *After you minimize the Ribbon, only the tab strip appears. Click a tab to display the Ribbon temporarily so that you can give a command. Click the **Expand the Ribbon** button when you want the Ribbon displayed again permanently.*

When you want to display the Ribbon again permanently, take one of the following actions:

- Click the **Expand the Ribbon** button, which has replaced the **Minimize the Ribbon** button.

- Double-click the active tab.

- Right-click any tab and then click **Minimize the Ribbon** on the shortcut menu, removing the check mark next to this item.

- Press Ctrl+F1.

Giving Ribbon Commands Using the Keyboard

If you prefer to keep your hands on the keyboard as you work, you can give Ribbon commands using the keyboard. Follow these steps:

1. Press Alt to display letters on the tabs (see Figure 2–6).

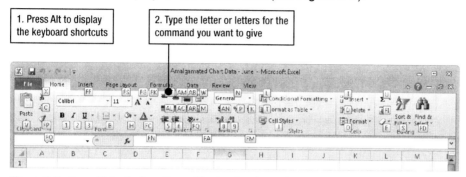

Figure 2–6. *Press Alt to display a ScreenTip showing the navigation letter for each Ribbon tab.*

2. Type the letter for the tab you want to display. The program displays letters for the controls on the tab (see Figure 2–7).

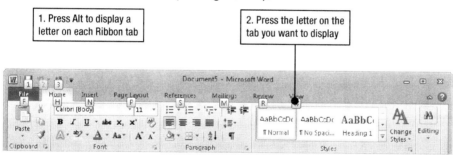

Figure 2–7. *You can give Ribbon commands using the keyboard by pressing Alt and then pressing the appropriate letters.*

3. Type the letter or letters for the command you want to give.

NOTE: At first, giving Ribbon commands using the keyboard may seem slow and awkward. But you will quickly learn the keyboard sequences for the commands you need to give often. You can then give the commands swiftly and accurately without even looking at the Ribbon.

Using Backstage View

Backstage view gives you access to commands that act on the active file as a whole rather than just part of it—for example, saving a file, printing it, or simply closing it.

> **NOTE:** If you're familiar with earlier versions of Microsoft Office, such as Office 2000 or Office 2003, the Backstage view takes the place of the **File** menu and various commands that appeared on other menus but affected the file as a whole rather than just part of it.

Backstage view is straightforward to work with. Open the file you want to affect, and then click the **File** tab to open Backstage view (see Figure 2–8). Backstage view opens at first with the Info pane displayed, showing you information about the active file, but you can quickly give one of the other commands by clicking the appropriate item in the left pane. For example:

- Click **Close** to close the active file.

- Click **Open** to display the **Open** dialog box and open another file.

- Click **Exit** to close the program (and the file).

> **NOTE:** Clicking the **Save & Send** button in the left pane in Backstage view opens the **Save & Send** pane, which contains commands for sharing the active file via e-mail, the Windows Live SkyDrive online storage site, or a SharePoint server, for saving the file in a different format, and for creating a PDF or XPS document from it. We'll look at how to use these features in Chapter 5.

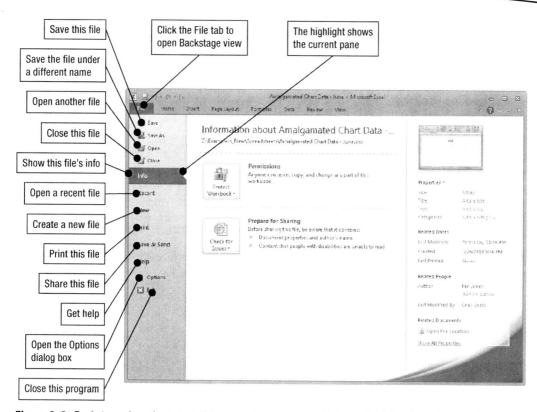

Figure 2–8. *Backstage view gives you quick access to the commands for manipulating the active file, for opening other files, for getting help, or for opening the program's* **Options** *dialog box. You can also exit the program.*

After you finish giving a command in Backstage view, the program automatically returns you to the regular view of the document. You can also close Backstage view manually:

- If you want to go back to the Ribbon tab that was displayed before, click the **File** tab again.

- If you want to display another Ribbon tab, click that tab.

Entering Text Faster Using AutoCorrect

The Office programs share a feature called AutoCorrect, which helps you to enter text faster and more accurately in your files. You'll probably want to create your own entries for AutoCorrect's Replace text as you type feature, and you'll do well to choose settings for AutoCorrect's other options, as the default settings can cause surprises.

Understanding How AutoCorrect Works

As you work in an Office program, AutoCorrect monitors the characters you type. When you type one of the entries in AutoCorrect's list of replacements, followed by a space or a punctuation character, AutoCorrect automatically replaces what you typed with its designated replacement text.

For example, if you type **abbout**, AutoCorrect automatically replaces it with **about**, the correct spelling. AutoCorrect contains hundreds of predefined corrections for common typos, spelling mistakes, and grammatical errors (such as changing "should of been" to "should have been").

These predefined corrections are helpful, but where you can really save time using AutoCorrect is by setting up your own AutoCorrect entries. You'll want to create AutoCorrect entries for your own special typos, of course, but you should also create an AutoCorrect entry for any lengthy item of text you need to enter regularly—for example, titles (such as Vice President of Human Resources), addresses, technical terms, or boilerplate text. Once you get the hang of AutoCorrect, you'll quickly find plenty of text items to create AutoCorrect entries for.

AutoCorrect also applies certain types of formatting when you enter text in particular ways. We'll look at the details of this after we see how to create AutoCorrect entries. But first, we need to open the AutoCorrect dialog box.

> **NOTE:** You can set up AutoCorrect separately in each of the Office programs. In this section, I'll show you how to set up AutoCorrect using Word, which has the most options. I'll point out where there are significant differences in the other programs.

Opening the AutoCorrect Dialog Box

To create AutoCorrect entries or configure AutoCorrect to work your way, first open the AutoCorrect dialog box like this:

1. Click the **File** tab to open Backstage view.

2. Click the **Options** item in the left pane to display the program's **Options** dialog box. For example, in Word, the **Word Options** dialog box opens (see Figure 2–9).

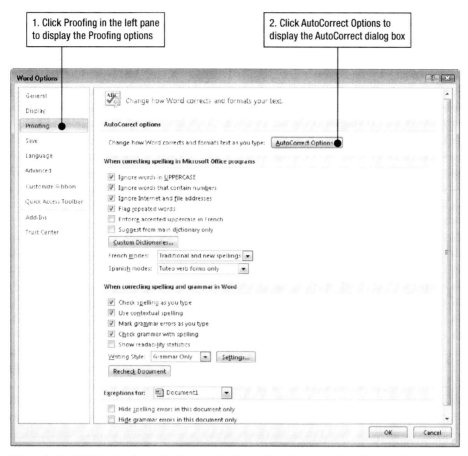

1. Click Proofing in the left pane to display the Proofing options

2. Click AutoCorrect Options to display the AutoCorrect dialog box

Figure 2–9. *Click the AutoCorrect Options button in the* **Proofing** *pane of the* **Options** *dialog box to display the* **AutoCorrect** *dialog box.*

3. Click the **Proofing** category in the left pane to display the proofing options.

4. Click the **AutoCorrect Options** button to display the **AutoCorrect** dialog box.

5. If the **AutoCorrect** tab isn't at the front, click it to display it.

Creating an AutoCorrect Entry

With the **AutoCorrect** dialog box open, you can create an AutoCorrect entry as shown in Figure 2–10. Briefly, you type the entry's short name in the **Replace** box, type or paste the entry's full text in the **With** box, and then click the **Add** button.

The **Replace text as you type** check box is the master switch for replacing entries on the list with their full text. So you need to make sure this check box is selected; clearing this check box turns off the replacement.

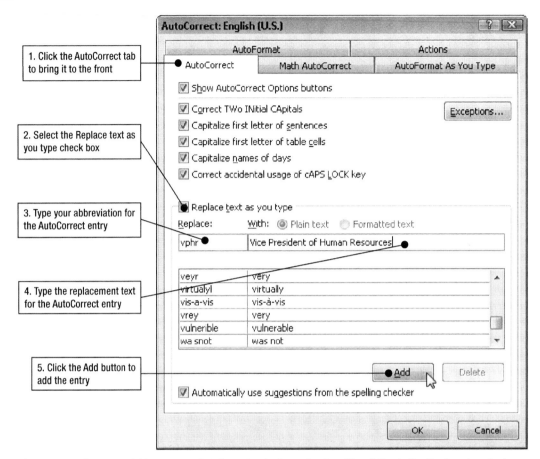

Figure 2–10. *You can quickly create an AutoCorrect entry by typing the abbreviation in the **Replace** box, typing the text in the **With** box, and then clicking the **Add** button.*

Setting AutoCorrect to Work Your Way

While you've got the AutoCorrect dialog box open, choose settings to control how AutoCorrect works. These settings are complex, but you need to understand them—so we'll go through them in detail.

Choosing Settings on the AutoCorrect Tab

Start on the AutoCorrect tab (shown in Figure 2–10) by choosing these settings:

- ▩ ***Show AutoCorrect Options buttons***. Select this check box to have the program display a small button under each item AutoCorrect changes. You can hold the mouse pointer over this button to make the program display a menu of AutoCorrect-related choices, such as stopping making this change. These buttons are usually helpful; clear this check box if you find them distracting.

- ▩ ***Correct TWo INitial CApitals***. Select this check box to have AutoCorrect apply lowercase to a second initial capital—for example, changing "THree" to "Three." This option is usually helpful.

- ▩ ***Capitalize first letter of sentences***. Select this check box if you want AutoCorrect to automatically start each sentence and paragraph with a capital. Clear this check box if you prefer to write in fragments and then fix them afterward.

- ▩ ***Capitalize first letter of table cells***. Select this check box if you want AutoCorrect to automatically capitalize the first letter of each entry in a table cell. How helpful this is depends on how you create tables and what their cells contain.

- ▩ ***Capitalize names of days***. Select this check box to have AutoCorrect automatically capitalize the first letter of the day names (for example, Tuesday). This option is usually helpful.

- ▩ ***Correct accidental use of cAPS LOCK key***. Select this check box to have AutoCorrect automatically turn off Caps Lock if you start a sentence with a lowercase letter and continue in caps. This option is usually helpful.

- ▩ ***Replace text as you type***. Keep this check box selected to use AutoCorrect's main feature, replacing misspellings and contractions with their designated replacement text.

- ▩ ***Automatically use suggestions from the spelling checker***. (Word only.) Select this check box to let the Replace text as you type feature use suggestions from the spelling checker as well as the entries in the list. This option is usually helpful, too.

> **NOTE:** The **Math AutoCorrect** tab contains controls for using AutoCorrect to enter math symbols in math areas in your documents. If you create math areas, make sure the **Replace text as you type** check box on the **Math AutoCorrect** tab is selected so that you can use this feature. You can create your own Math AutoCorrect entries by using the **Replace** box and the **With** box on the **Math AutoCorrect** tab.

Choosing Settings on the AutoFormat As You Type Tab

Now click the **AutoFormat As You Type** tab to display its contents (see Figure 2–11). This tab contains three sets of options: the **Replace as you type** options, the **Apply as you type** options, and the **Automatically as you type** options.

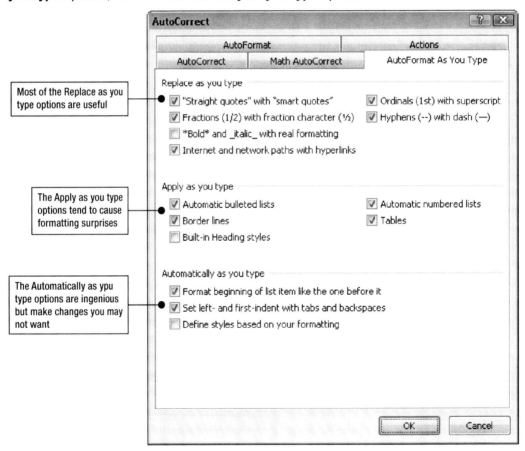

Figure 2–11. *Depending on how you work, you may want to turn off many of the **Apply as you type** options and **Automatically as you type** options on the **AutoFormat As You Type** tab of the **AutoCorrect** dialog box. This is the **AutoFormat As You Type** tab in Word.*

The options in the **Replace as you type** area are mostly helpful:

- ▨ ***"Straight quotes" with "smart quotes"***. Select this check box to have AutoCorrect replace straight-up-and-down quotes with smart or "curly" quotes.

- ▨ ***Fractions (1/2) with fraction character (½)***. Select this check box to have AutoCorrect insert real fraction characters in place of fractions you type.

- ▨ ****Bold* and _italic_ with real formatting***. Select this check box if you want to be able to apply boldface by typing an asterisk before and after a word, and apply italics by typing an underscore before and after a word. These are long-standing Internet conventions for designating formatting in plain text, but unless you're used to using them, it's easier to apply the boldface or italics using keyboard shortcuts or the Ribbon.

- ▨ ***Internet and network paths with hyperlinks***. Select this check box to have AutoCorrect insert a hyperlink when you type a URL (for example, www.yahoo.com) or a network path (for example, \\server1\users). If you don't want to have live hyperlinks in your documents, clear this check box.

- ▨ ***Ordinals (1st) with superscript***. Select this check box to have AutoCorrect apply superscript to the letters of ordinals (for example, 1st, 2nd).

- ▨ ***Hyphens (--) with dash (—)***. Select this check box to have AutoCorrect insert en dashes (–) in place of a hyphen preceded and followed by spaces, and em dashes (—) for two hyphens typed between words. This option tends to be the easiest way of inserting em dashes and en dashes.

The options in the Apply as you type area tend to cause formatting surprises. This means that either you need to understand how they work, so that you can use them intentionally, or you need to turn them off. Turning them off tends to be simpler.

Here's what the **Apply as you type** options do:

- ▨ ***Automatic bulleted lists***. Select this check box if you want AutoCorrect to automatically apply a bulleted list style when you start a paragraph with an asterisk, a hyphen, or a greater-than sign followed by a space or tab.

- ▨ ***Automatic numbered lists***. Select this check box if you want AutoCorrect to automatically apply a numbered list style when you start a paragraph with a number or letter followed by a period or closing parenthesis, and then type a space or tab.

- ▓ *Border lines*. Select this check box to have AutoCorrect apply border lines when you type three or more hyphens, underscores, asterisks, tildes, equal signs, or hash marks at the beginning of a paragraph and then press Enter. Try these out to see the types of lines they produce.

- ▓ *Tables*. Select this check box if you want to be able to create a table by typing a line of plus signs and hyphens. Each plus sign indicates a column border, so "+--+--+--+" produces a three-column table. The number of hyphens indicates the relative width of the columns—in the previous example, the columns are equal width.

- ▓ *Built-in Heading styles*. Select this check box if you want AutoCorrect to automatically apply Word's Heading styles when you create a short paragraph in the right way. For Heading 1 style, press Enter twice, type the heading, and then press Enter twice more. For Heading 2 style, press Enter twice, press Tab, type the heading, and press Enter twice more. For Heading 3 style, use two tabs, and for Heading 4 style, use three tabs. AutoCorrect removes the extra paragraphs and tabs when it makes the change.

The options in the **Automatically as you type** area try to apply more complex types of formatting. These are ingenious, but normally it's better to turn them off and format your documents conventionally, as explained in Chapter 8.

- ▓ *Format beginning of list item like the one before it*. Select this check box to have AutoCorrect format the second and subsequent items in a list using the same formatting you've added to the beginning of the first item—for example, italic or boldface. I recommend clearing this check box and formatting your lists using styles instead. Chapter 8 explains styles as well.

- ▓ *Set left- and first-indent with tabs and backspaces*. Select this check box to have AutoCorrect automatically move the left indent and first-line indent to the left when you press Backspace at the beginning of a blank paragraph, and move them to the right by pressing **Tab**. I recommend clearing this check box so that you can use Tab and Backspace normally.

- ▓ *Define styles based on your formatting*. Select this check box only if you want AutoCorrect to automatically create styles when it thinks you need one. I recommend clearing this check box and creating styles manually as needed (again, see Chapter 8 for details).

Choosing AutoFormat As You Type Options in Excel

In Excel, the **AutoFormat As You Type** tab (shown on the left in Figure 2–12) also contains these two options:

- *Include new rows and columns in table.* Select this check box to have Excel consider rows and columns you add to a table to be part of that table. This behavior is usually helpful.

- *Fill formulas in tables to create calculated columns.* Select this check box if you want Excel to automatically fill a whole column of a table with the formula you enter in one cell. Depending on the types of worksheets you create, this may be helpful. Clear this check box if you want to add the formulas manually.

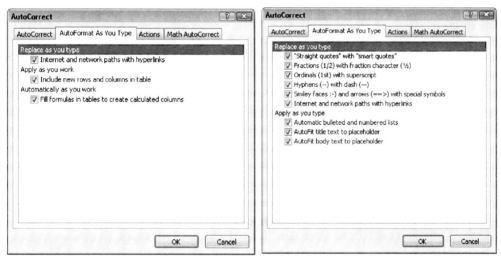

Figure 2–12. *The **AutoFormat As You Type** tab of the **AutoCorrect** dialog box in Excel (left) contains two Excel-specific options. Similarly, the **AutoFormat As You Type** tab of PowerPoint's **AutoCorrect** dialog box contains three PowerPoint-specific options.*

Choosing AutoFormat As You Type Options in PowerPoint

In PowerPoint, the **AutoFormat As You Type** tab (shown on the right in Figure 2–12) also contains these three options:

- *Smiley faces :-) and arrows (==>) with special symbols.* Select this check box if you want to be able to type in emoticons and arrows. (In Word, emoticons appear as AutoCorrect entries.)

- *AutoFit title text to placeholder.* Select this check box if you want PowerPoint to automatically reduce the point size of text when it becomes too long to fit in a title placeholder. This option is usually helpful unless you need to make sure your font sizes are regular.

■ *AutoFit body text to placeholder.* Select this check box if you want PowerPoint to automatically reduce the point size of text when it becomes too long to fit in a body placeholder. This option is often helpful, but you may prefer to edit the text down to size to keep it readable.

Choosing AutoFormat Settings in Word and Outlook

In Word and Outlook, the AutoCorrect dialog box also includes an **AutoFormat** tab. This tab contains options for controlling which types of items the AutoFormat feature applies when you use it to automatically format a document. In Word, you run this command manually when you need it. In Outlook, you can set AutoFormat to automatically format plain text e-mail documents.

Most of the options are similar to those on the **AutoFormat As You Type** tab. Select the **Styles** check box in the Preserve area if you want to preserve the document's existing styles. Select the **Plain text e-mail documents** check box in the Always AutoFormat area only if you want AutoFormat to spring into action every time you open a plain-text e-mail.

> **NOTE:** To display **the AutoCorrect** dialog box in Outlook, first choose File ➤ Options to display the **Outlook Options** dialog box. In the left column, click **Mail**, and then click the **Spelling and AutoCorrect** button to display the **Editor Options** dialog box. Then click the **AutoCorrect Options** button.

Adding Actions to the Context Menu

Like most Windows programs, the Office programs make extensive use of the context menu. You can right-click in any Office file to produce a menu of commands related to the item you clicked. You'll see the context menu in action later in this chapter when you learn how to check spelling.

> **NOTE:** The context menu is also called the *shortcut menu* and the *right-click menu.*

You can add extra actions to the context menu by clicking the Actions tab of the AutoCorrect dialog box (see Figure 2–13), selecting the **Enable additional actions in the right-click menu** check box, and then selecting the check box for each action you want. Most of the extra actions are quite specialized, so you may well not need to use them.

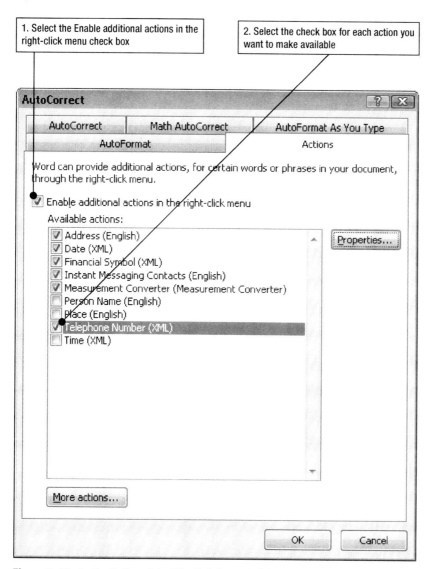

Figure 2–13. *On the **Actions** tab of the **AutoCorrect** dialog box, you can add actions to the program's context menu.*

Closing the AutoCorrect Dialog Box

When you have finished creating AutoCorrect entries and choosing settings in the **AutoCorrect** dialog box, click the **OK** button to close it.

The program then returns you to its **Options** dialog box. Click the **OK** button in this dialog box to close it, too.

Checking Spelling and Grammar in Your Files

To help you get the text in your documents into good shape, the Office programs include a Spelling checker. Word and Outlook also have a Grammar checker that works alongside the Spelling checker.

> **NOTE:** Computers are great at checking spelling, because in most cases, each word is either spelled correctly or incorrectly—there are few gray areas, and the Spelling checker doesn't need to understand what the text means to evaluate the spelling. So in most cases it's a good idea to use the Spelling checker to remove spelling mistakes from your documents. By contrast, grammar is far harder, and the Grammar checker is much less successful, especially with any writing that doesn't stick to rigid rules of grammar (such as fiction).

Checking Spelling

In Word, PowerPoint, Outlook, and OneNote, you can check spelling in two ways:

- *On the fly.* The Spelling checker checks spelling as you type. This enables you to fix mistakes as soon as you make them.

- *Full check.* When you're ready to sort out mistakes, you run the Spelling checker and go through each query in turn.

Excel doesn't offer on-the-fly checking, only full checking.

Checking Spelling As You Type

If you choose to check spelling as you type, the Spelling checker puts a wavy red underline beneath any word whose spelling it queries. You can then right-click an underlined word and choose how to deal with the problem. Figure 2–14 explains the main options this context menu contains.

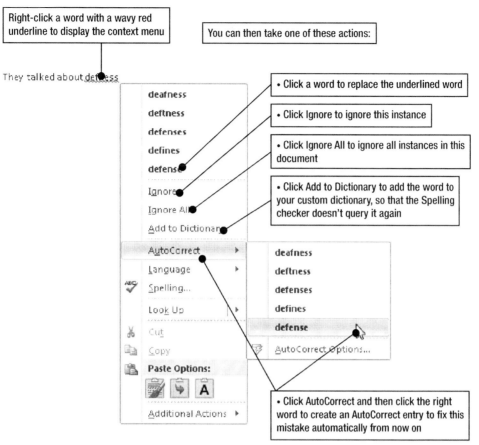

Figure 2–14. *In Word, PowerPoint, Outlook, and OneNote, you can check spelling on the fly by right-clicking a queried word and using the context menu.*

NOTE: From the on-the-fly spelling context menu, you can click the **Language** item to display the **Language** submenu, which you use to tell the Spelling checker that the queried word is in a different language. You can also click the **Spelling** item to launch a full spelling check, or click the **Look Up** item to open a submenu that gives you options for looking up the word online.

Checking Spelling in the Whole Document

When you want to check the spelling in an entire document, position the insertion point or selection where you want to start the check from. If you're checking the entire document for the first time, you'll usually want to place the insertion point or selection at the beginning of the document—for example, by pressing Ctrl+Home or by clicking at the beginning of the document. For subsequent checks, you may want to start at a point partway through the document.

Then start the Spelling checker or the Spelling and Grammar checker like this:

▪ *Word*. Choose **Review ➤ Proofing ➤ Spelling and Grammar**.

▪ *Excel.* Choose **Review ➤ Proofing ➤ Spelling**.

▪ *PowerPoint.* Choose **Review ➤ Proofing ➤ Spelling**.

▪ *OneNote.* Choose **Review ➤ Spelling ➤ Spelling**.

▪ *Outlook.* Choose **Review ➤ Proofing ➤ Spelling and Grammar** in a message window.

The Spelling checker or Spelling and Grammar checker displays its first query, and you can deal with it as explained in Figure 2–15. This figure shows the **Spelling and Grammar** dialog box from Word.

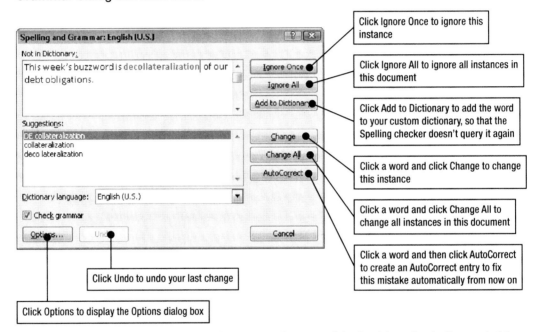

Figure 2–15. *The **Spelling** dialog box or the **Spelling and Grammar** dialog box (shown here) offers most of the same options as the spelling context menu.*

After you deal with the first query, the **Spelling** dialog box displays the next, and continues until you either click the Cancel button or deal with the final query.

> **TIP:** When you check spelling, create an AutoCorrect entry for any misspelling you think you may repeat. Each AutoCorrect entry may help only a little, but taken together, they can make a huge improvement in your typing speed and accuracy.

When you have dealt with every spelling query, the Spelling checker lets you know that the check is complete (see Figure 2–16). Click the **OK** button to close the dialog box.

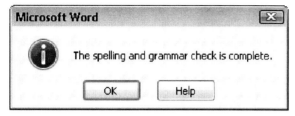

Figure 2–16. *When the program tells you that the spelling check is complete, click the **OK** button.*

Checking Grammar in Word and Outlook

For documents you create in Word or outgoing messages you write in Outlook, you can check the grammar as well as the spelling. As with spelling, you can check grammar either as you type or separately when you're ready to review your document.

> **CAUTION:** If you're going to use the Grammar checker, make sure you understand its limitations. The Grammar checker doesn't understand the meaning of the text, but it tries to identify the different parts of speech (nouns, verbs, and so on) and their relationship to each other. Many of the Grammar checker's suggestions will not improve your documents. Its best features are identifying minor problems such as unsuitable words or missing punctuation.

Checking Grammar on the Fly

If you leave on-the-fly grammar checking turned on, as it is by default, the Grammar checker puts a wavy green underline under any text that it queries. This may be a word, a phrase, or an entire sentence or more, depending on what the query is. You can then right-click the underlined text and choose what to do from the context menu (see Figure 2–17).

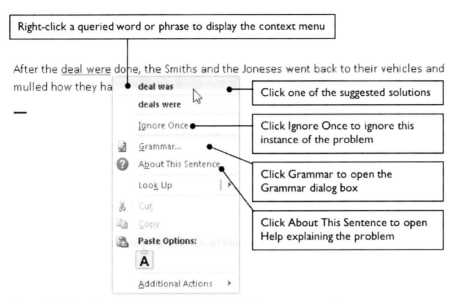

Figure 2–17 *Use the context menu to deal with on-the-fly grammar queries.*

Checking Grammar with Spelling

If you choose not to use on-the-fly grammar checking (or if you ignore the on-the-fly queries), you can check grammar at the same time as spelling. Figure 2–18 shows you how to handle grammar queries in the **Spelling and Grammar** dialog box.

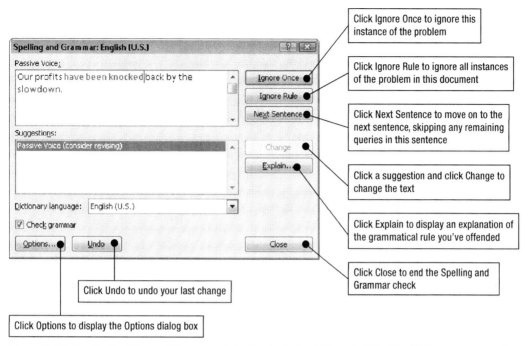

Figure 2–18. *Use the **Spelling and Grammar** dialog box to deal quickly and efficiently with the grammar queries in your Word documents and Outlook messages.*

Controlling How the Spelling Checker Works

Because the Spelling checker is a great way of reducing the number of errors in the documents you create using the Office programs, you'll normally want to leave it running. But you may well want to choose settings to make it run the way you prefer.

To control how the Spelling checker works, follow these steps:

1. Click the **File** tab to open Backstage view.

2. Click the **Options** item in the left pane to display the program's **Options** dialog box.

3. In the left pane, click the **Proofing** item to display the proofing options. Figure 2–19 shows the proofing options for Word, which has more options than the other programs.

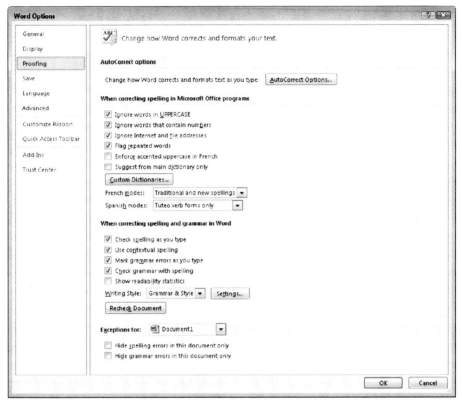

Figure 2–19. *In the* ***Proofing*** *pane of the* ***Options*** *dialog box for an Office program, you can choose options for checking spelling and make exceptions for the current document. For Word and Outlook, you can also turn off grammar checking either on the fly or altogether.*

> ⬛ **NOTE** In Outlook, click the **Mail** category in the left column to display the **Mail** pane. Then click the **Spelling and AutoCorrect** button to display the **Editor Options** dialog box. Click the **Proofing** category in the left column.

Once you've displayed the Proofing pane, you can choose settings for the following options in the When correcting spelling in Microsoft Office programs area:

- ⬛ ***Ignore words in UPPERCASE***. Select this check box if you want the Spelling checker to skip words that appear in uppercase. This is usually helpful, as it helps you avoid queries on technical terms.

- ⬛ ***Ignore words that contain numbers***. Select this check box to have the Spelling checker skip any word that includes numbers (for example, IPv6). Clear this check box if you tend to get number typos in words.

▨ *Ignore Internet and file addresses*. Select this check box to make the Spelling checker ignore any URLs (for example, www.apress.com) and file addresses (for example, \\server2\reference\manual.pdf). This option, too, is usually helpful. You'd turn it off only if you want the Spelling checker to query URLs and file address—for example, because the documents should contain only certain URLs and addresses that you've added to your custom dictionary.

▨ *Flag repeated words*. Select this check box to allow the Spelling checker to query a word that appears twice in succession. This option is good at picking up useless duplication, but you may occasionally need to approve a deliberate repetition.

▨ *Enforce accented uppercase in French*. Select this check box if your documents use a French dialect (such as Canadian French) that retains accents on uppercase letters rather than removing the accents (as in standard French).

▨ *Suggest from main dictionary only*. Select this check box if you want spelling suggestions only from Office's main dictionary file, not from custom dictionaries you create. Usually, you'll want to clear this check box so that the Spelling checker uses your custom dictionaries.

▨ *French modes*. In this drop-down list, choose which spelling type you want the Spelling checker to use: Traditional and new spellings, Traditional spelling, or New spelling.

▨ *Spanish modes*. In this drop-down list, choose whether to use the Tuteo verb forms, the Voseo verb forms, or both for the second person. The choices are Tuteo verb forms only, Tuteo and Voseo verb forms, and Voseo verb forms only.

▨ *Dictionary language*. (Excel only.) In this drop-down list, choose the language you want to use—for example, English (U.S.).

For all the programs except Excel, you can choose further options for correcting spelling in **Program** area (for example, the **When correcting spelling in OneNote** area). This area contains the following options:

▨ *Check spelling as you type*. Select the check box if you want the Spelling checker to check spelling continually as you type. The Spelling checker puts a wavy red underline under any word it queries. Clear this check box if you prefer to check spelling in a separate operation.

▨ *Use contextual spelling*. Select this check box if you want the Spelling checker to try to check words in their contexts rather than just on their own. The Spelling checker puts a wavy blue underline under a word that has a contextual spelling query. OneNote doesn't have this setting.

> **CAUTION:** Contextual spelling is worth using, but it doesn't work consistently because of the complexity of the English language, so don't rely on it. For example, if you write "She bought there car," the Spelling checker correctly suggests replacing "there" with "their." But the Spelling checker raises no query with "She wrecked there car," which has the same mistake.

- ***Mark grammar errors as you type***. (Word and Outlook only.) Select this check box if you want the Grammar checker to raise queries as you work. The Grammar checker puts a wavy green underline under items it queries. On-the-fly grammar checking tends to be distracting, especially if you tend to write several partial sentences and then sew them together, so you'll probably want to clear this check box.

- ***Check grammar with spelling***. (Word and Outlook only.) Select this check box if you want to use the Grammar checker. Otherwise, clear it.

- ***Hide spelling errors***. Select this check box if you want to hide spelling errors in the document. Outlook doesn't have this option. In Word, this option is called Hide spelling errors in this document only; Word also has a **Hide grammar errors in this document only** check box for hiding grammar queries.

- ***Show readability statistics***. (Word and Outlook only.) Select this check box if you want the Spelling checker to display the **Readability Statistics** dialog box when it finishes a spelling check.

> **TIP:** Don't bother with the readability statistics. The counts of words, characters, paragraphs, and sentences can be useful, but you can get the first three more easily in the Word Count dialog box (click the Words readout in the status bar or choose **Review ➤ Proofing ➤ Word Count**). The averages of sentences per paragraph, words per sentence, and characters per word have little relevance. The Passive Sentences, Flesch Reading Ease, and Flesch-Kincaid Grade Level are computed statistics that don't accurately assess how easy or hard the document is to read. If you want to know whether a document is hard to understand, ask a colleague to read it.

Choosing Grammar- and Style-Checking Options in Word and Outlook

In Word and Outlook, if you decide to use the Grammar checker, you can choose settings to control which errors it tries to identify.

In the When correcting spelling and grammar area of the Proofing pane of the program's **Options** dialog box, click the **Settings** button to display the **Grammar Settings** dialog box. You can then choose settings, as explained in Figure 2–20.

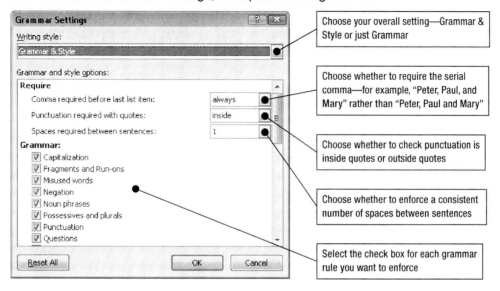

Choose your overall setting—Grammar & Style or just Grammar

Choose whether to require the serial comma—for example, "Peter, Paul, and Mary" rather than "Peter, Paul and Mary"

Choose whether to check punctuation is inside quotes or outside quotes

Choose whether to enforce a consistent number of spaces between sentences

Select the check box for each grammar rule you want to enforce

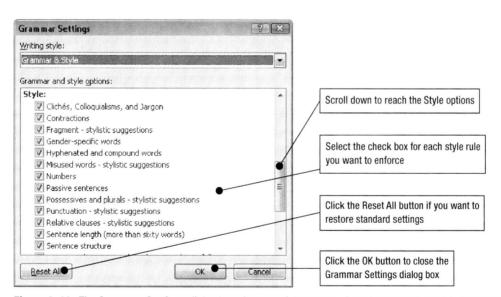

Scroll down to reach the Style options

Select the check box for each style rule you want to enforce

Click the Reset All button if you want to restore standard settings

Click the OK button to close the Grammar Settings dialog box

Figure 2–20. *The **Grammar Settings** dialog box gives you tight control of the Grammar checker in Word and Outlook.*

> **TIP:** Because of the complexities of the English language, the Grammar checker's strongest features are the most mechanical ones. The three options in the **Require** area are widely useful; in the **Grammar** area, options such as **Capitalization** and **Subject-verb agreement** can be helpful. The **Style** options tend to be less useful—but you may want to try them for yourself and see how helpful you find them.

After you close the **Grammar Settings** dialog box, click the **OK** button to close the program's **Options** dialog box. You can then start testing the settings you've chosen.

Printing Your Documents

To print your documents in Word, Excel, PowerPoint, and Outlook, you work in the **Print** pane in Backstage view. Click the **File** tab to open Backstage view, click the **Print** item in the left pane to display the **Print** pane, and then work as explained in Figure 2–21.

> **NOTE:** OneNote uses an old-style Print dialog box and has a separate Print Preview feature. We'll examine OneNote printing in Chapter 18.

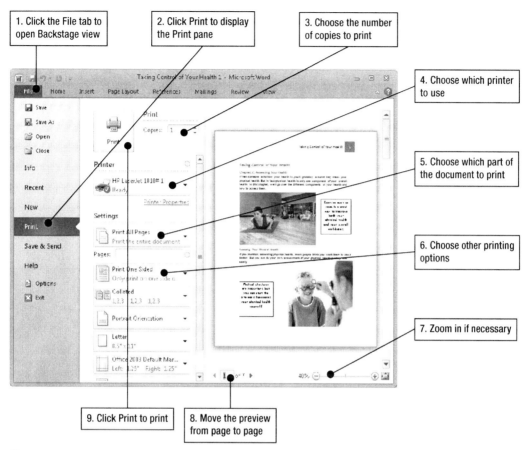

1. Click the File tab to open Backstage view

2. Click Print to display the Print pane

3. Choose the number of copies to print

4. Choose which printer to use

5. Choose which part of the document to print

6. Choose other printing options

7. Zoom in if necessary

9. Click Print to print

8. Move the preview from page to page

Figure 2–21. *The* **Print** *pane in Backstage view provides a full preview of the document, together with all the options you need to control which part of the document to print and which printer to use.*

Most of the options in the Print pane are straightforward, such as choosing the number of copies to print, selecting the printer, and choosing the page orientation. Other options vary depending on the program. We'll look at such options in detail in the chapters on using the individual programs.

When you choose a change that affects how the printout will look, the preview shows the change. (By contrast, the preview can't show changes such as the number of copies or whether they're set for collation.)

When you've finished choosing settings, click the **Print** button to print the document. The program sends it to the Windows print queue that serves the printer you chose, and Windows handles the print job from there.

Summary

In this chapter, you learned to use the Ribbon and Backstage view to give commands in your documents. You also learned how to enter text faster using AutoCorrect, how to configure AutoFormat, how to check spelling and grammar, and how to print.

In the next chapter, I'll show you how to work with text.

Working with Text

Even in this photo- and video-friendly world, most of your Office documents will contain text—and likely plenty of it. In this chapter, I'll show you how to work with text in the Office programs. Text is easy to work with, once you've learned some straightforward conventions, and the techniques you need are largely the same in all the programs.

First, we'll look at how you enter text using the keyboard or other means, such as having your PC transcribe the words you speak or read the text from a hardcopy document. Next, we'll cover navigating your documents with the keyboard, and applying direct formatting to text and other objects. We'll then dig into the Cut, Copy, and Paste tools and the Find and Replace features, all of which can save you considerable amounts of time and effort.

Toward the end of the chapter, I'll show you how to lay out complex document content clearly using tables. You'll learn how to create tables by using the Insert Table command or by drawing a table, how to adjust tables by merging and splitting cells, and how to add content to the resulting table and format it.

Finally, I'll show you how to create hyperlinks in your documents so that you can quickly direct a reader to a web site or other location.

Entering Text in Your Documents

In this section, I'll review the ways you can enter text in your documents.

Entering Text Using the Keyboard

The most straightforward way of entering text in your Office documents is by typing it using the keyboard. Position the insertion point or selection where you want the text to go—for example, click at the appropriate point in a Word document, make the right cell active in an Excel worksheet, or click a placeholder on a PowerPoint slide—and then type what's needed.

Entering Text Using Copy and Paste

If you already have the text you need to enter in the document, but it's in another document, copy the text from that document and paste it in. See the section "Using Cut, Copy, and Paste," later in this chapter.

ENTERING TEXT USING SPEECH RECOGNITION

If your version of Windows includes speech recognition, you can use it both to control the Office programs and to insert text in them.

Speech recognition can be a great way of entering text quickly, especially if you are good at dictating text or you are reading existing text. To get good results, use a headset microphone that lets you position the microphone consistently close to your mouth. Place the microphone to the side of your mouth rather than in front of it so that it doesn't pick up your breath stream.

To see whether your version of Windows includes speech recognition, click the **Start** button, click **Control Panel**, and then choose **View by ➤ Small icons** or click the **Switch to Classic view** link. If the **Speech Recognition** item appears, open it by clicking or double-clicking it (depending on the version of Windows), and then follow the instructions for connecting a microphone and setting up and training Speech Recognition. The more training you do, the more accurate the results you will get, so don't be discouraged if you get many mistakes at first.

Once you have set up speech recognition and trained it, you can dictate into the Office programs. If possible, watch the text that appears onscreen as you dictate, because this is the best time to catch the substitutions of words and phrases that speech recognition tends to make. If you leave them till later, you may find it hard to work out what the text should actually be.

If your version of Windows doesn't include speech recognition, you can buy a third-party speech-recognition program that works with Office—for example, Dragon NaturallySpeaking.

Entering Text Using Optical Character Recognition

If you have a hardcopy document that contains the text you need to put in an Office document, you can scan the text using a scanner, and then use optical character recognition (OCR) to get the text out of the picture file that the scanner produces. You can also use this technique to get text out of a picture file.

> **CAUTION:** To use the text from a hardcopy document or a picture created by someone else in a document of your own, you will typically need to get permission from the copyright holder.

If you have custom scanning software (for example, a program that came with your scanner), use that software. Otherwise, follow these general steps:

1. Open OneNote.

2. Choose **Insert ➤ Files ➤ Scanner Printout** to scan the document into OneNote.

3. Right-click the scanned picture and choose **Copy Text from Picture** (see Figure 3–1) to recognize the text in it.

4. Switch to the program you want to use the text in, and then paste the text in.

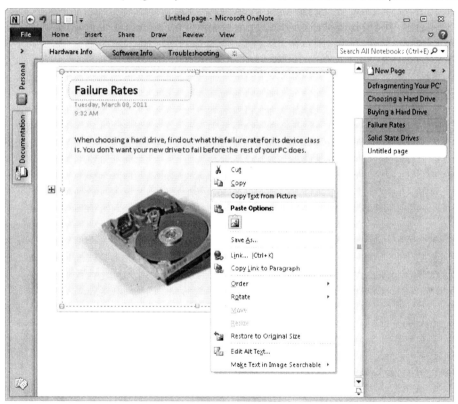

Figure 3–1. *You can use the **Copy Text from Picture** command in OneNote to quickly recognize the text in a picture and copy it to the Clipboard. From there, you can paste the text into any program.*

CAUTION: When you use OCR to get the text from a document, always read through the text and compare it to the original. While OCR does its best to recognize the text accurately, it often introduces errors—sometimes surprising ones.

Inserting Symbols in Your Documents

When a document needs a symbol that doesn't appear on the keyboard, you can insert it in either of two ways:

■ *Using the **Symbol** drop-down panel.* This panel appears in Word, Outlook (when you create an item such as an e-mail message), and OneNote, programs in which you arguably need symbols more often than in Excel or PowerPoint. As shown in Figure 3–2, choose **Insert ➤ Symbols ➤ Symbol**, and then click the symbol you want on the drop-down panel. The **Symbol** drop-down panel starts off with 20 common symbols, and then gradually swaps in the symbols you use most, so you end up with a quick way to insert your 20 most-needed symbols.

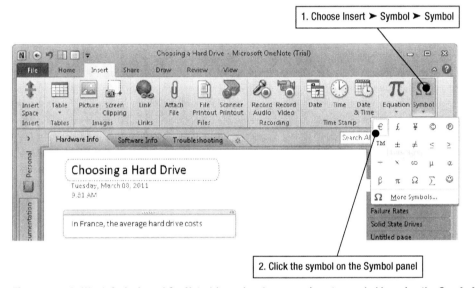

Figure 3–2. *In Word, Outlook, and OneNote (shown here), you can insert a symbol by using the **Symbol** drop-down panel in the **Symbol** group on the **Insert** tab of the Ribbon.*

■ *Symbol dialog box.* This dialog box appears in each of the Office programs. In Word, Outlook, and OneNote you open it by clicking the **More Symbols** button at the bottom of the **Symbol** drop-down panel. In Excel and PowerPoint, you choose **Insert ➤ Symbols ➤ Symbol**. Figure 3–3 shows you how to use the **Symbol** dialog box for Word and Outlook; this dialog box includes the **AutoCorrect** button and **Shortcut Key** buttons, which don't appear in the **Symbol** dialog box in Excel, PowerPoint, and OneNote.

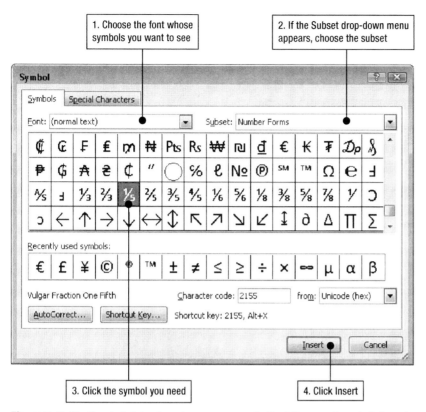

Figure 3–3. *The **Symbol** dialog box gives you access to the full range of symbol characters that the Office programs can use. The **Recently used symbol** box toward the bottom gives you quick access to the symbols you've used recently.*

When you insert a symbol, the **Symbol** dialog box stays open so that you can insert other symbols as needed.

The **Symbol** dialog box is straightforward to use, but there are three things you need to know to make the most of it:

■ The item named "(normal text)" that appears at the top of the **Font** drop-down list shows the symbol characters in the font you're using.

■ In Word, Outlook, and OneNote, you can continue to work in the document while the **Symbol** dialog box is open. For example, you can type some text in the document, or reposition the insertion point, then click in the **Symbol** dialog box and use it to insert another symbol character. In Excel and PowerPoint, you must close the **Symbol** dialog box before you can resume work in the document.

- In Word and Excel, the **Symbol** dialog box includes the "**Special Characters** tab (see Figure 3–4). Click this tab when you need to insert widely used symbols, such as the em dash (—), the paragraph symbol (¶), or special spaces such as the en space (the width of an *n* character in the font). As with the **Symbols** tab, click the item you want, and then click the **Insert** button.

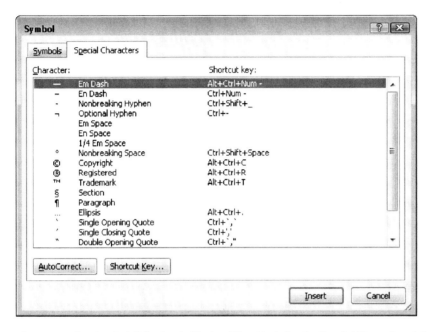

Figure 3–4. *The **Symbol** dialog box in Word and Excel includes the **Special Characters** tab, which gives you quick access to widely used symbols such as em dashes and en dashes, optional hyphens, and set-width spaces.*

When you have finished inserting symbols, click the **Close** button to close the **Symbol** dialog box.

Navigating with the Keyboard and Selecting Document Objects

In the Office programs, as in most Windows programs, the mouse is your main tool for moving around in documents, positioning the insertion point or selection, and selecting objects you want to work with. But you can also navigate using the keyboard by pressing the keyboard shortcuts shown in Table 3–1. These work the same way in most of the Office programs; most of the differences are in Excel, which uses cells rather than paragraphs.

Table 3–1. *Keyboard Shortcuts for Moving the Insertion Point in the Office Programs*

Press These Keys	To Move the Insertion Point Like This
Left arrow	One character to the left
Right arrow	One character to the right
Up arrow	Up one line, paragraph, or cell
Down arrow	Down one line, paragraph, or cell
Home	To the start of the line or object
End	To the end of the line or object
Ctrl+Left arrow	To the beginning of the current word (if the insertion point is in a word) or to the beginning of the previous word
Ctrl+Right arrow	To the beginning of the next word

You can also use the keyboard shortcuts shown in Table 3–1 for selecting text and objects. Move the insertion point to the beginning of what you want to select, hold down Shift, and then move the insertion point to the end of the selection. (Or, if you prefer, move the insertion point to the end of what you want to select, hold down Shift, and then move the insertion point back to the beginning.)

You may find it easier to select with the mouse. Just click at the start of what you want to select, hold down the mouse button, and then drag to the end, as shown in Figure 3–5.

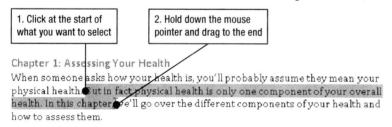

Figure 3–5. *Click and drag with the mouse to select text or other objects in your documents.*

When you're selecting larger amounts of material, you may find clicking and dragging awkward, especially when you need to scroll from screen to screen. If so, click to place the insertion point at the beginning of the selection, and then scroll so that you can see the end. Hold down Shift, and click at the end of the selection.

> **TIP:** In Word and Excel, you can also select multiple items at once. Select the first item as usual, using either the mouse or the keyboard. Then hold down Ctrl as you select each of the other items with the mouse.

Applying Direct Formatting to Text and Objects

To make text or objects appear the way you want them, you apply formatting to them. For example, to make text appear the way you want it, you can change the font it uses, change the font size, apply bold or italic, and so on.

Each of the Office programs provides a wide range of direct formatting—formatting that you apply directly to text or an object. Word, Outlook, Excel, an OneNote also provide styles, collections of formatting that you can apply in a single click.

> **TIP:** When working in Word, Outlook, Excel, or OneNote, use styles whenever possible instead of using direct formatting. By using styles, you can apply formatting far faster than by using direct formatting, and you can more easily keep the formatting consistent through your documents. You can also quickly make changes throughout the document, either by replacing one style with another style or by changing the formatting in the style. I show you how to use styles in Word in Chapter 8: "Formatting Your Documents Easily and Efficiently." Chapter 12: "Editing Worksheets and Applying Formatting" covers using styles in Excel, Chapter 16: "Getting Up to Speed and Taking Notes" explains styles in OneNote, and Chapter 24: "Sending and Receiving E-Mail" goes over styles in Outlook.

You can apply some direct formatting by using the Mini Toolbar that appears automatically when you make a selection. The formatting commands on the Mini Toolbar vary from one program to another, but those for Word (the Mini Toolbar is shown in Figure 3–6) are largely typical.

> **NOTE:** If the Mini Toolbar doesn't appear when you make a selection, you need to enable it. Click the **File** tab to open Backstage view, click **Options** to display the program's **Options** dialog box, and then select the **Show Mini Toolbar on selection** check box in the **General** category of options. Click the **OK** button to close the **Options** dialog box.

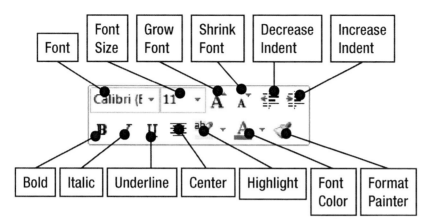

Figure 3–6. *You can apply widely used direct formatting from the Mini Toolbar, which appears automatically when you make a selection. This is the Mini Toolbar for Word, but those in the other Office programs have similar selections of commands.*

To apply formatting that the Mini Toolbar doesn't offer, use the Ribbon:

- *Word.* The **Home** tab includes the **Font** group and the **Paragraph** group.

- *Excel.* The **Home** tab includes the **Font** group and the **Alignment** group.

- *PowerPoint.* The **Home** tab includes the **Font** group and the **Paragraph** group.

- *OneNote.* The **Home** tab includes the **Basic Text** group.

- *Outlook.* Both the **Item** tab and the **Format** Text tab in an item window include the **Basic Text** group. For example, when you create an e-mail message, the **Message** tab and the **Format Text** tab both include the **Basic Text** group.

Figure 3–7 shows the **Font** group in Word. The **Font** group in Excel and PowerPoint and the Basic Text group in OneNote and Outlook contain most of the same formatting controls. To apply the formatting, you simply select the text, and then click the appropriate control.

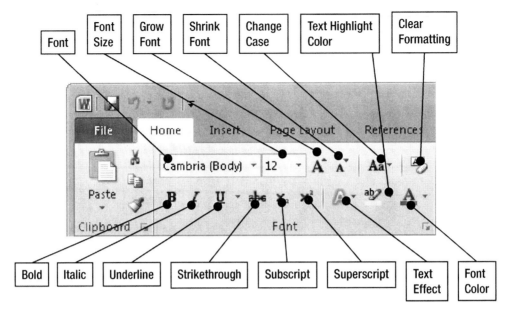

Figure 3–7. *The* ***Font*** *group on the* ***Home*** *tab in Word (shown here), Excel, and PowerPoint contains widely useful font-formatting commands. In OneNote and Outlook, the* ***Basic Text*** *group has similar commands.*

You can also apply widely used direct formatting by using keyboard shortcuts. Table 3–2 lists the most useful keyboard shortcuts for applying direct formatting.

Table 3–2. *Keyboard Shortcuts for Applying Direct Formatting*

Formatting Type	Keyboard Shortcut
Boldface	Ctrl+B
Italic	Ctrl+I
Underline	Ctrl+U
Subscript	Ctrl+=
Superscript	Ctrl++ (in other words, Ctrl+Shift+=)
Grow font by one increment	Ctrl+Shift+>
Shrink font by one increment	Ctrl+Shift+<
Align left	Ctrl+L
Align right	Ctrl+R
Center	Ctrl+E

Using Cut, Copy, and Paste

As in most Windows programs, you can cut, copy, and paste text and other objects in the Office programs. You can use either the standard Windows Clipboard or the Office programs' own Clipboard, and you can choose between pasting all the copied (or cut) content and pasting only part of it.

Using Standard Cut, Copy, and Paste in the Office Programs

The easiest way to give these commands is to use the **Clipboard** group, which appears on the **Home** tab of the Ribbon in Word, Excel, PowerPoint, and OneNote, and on both the **Message** tab and the **Format Text** tab in a message window in Outlook. Figure 3–8 explains how to use the Clipboard group.

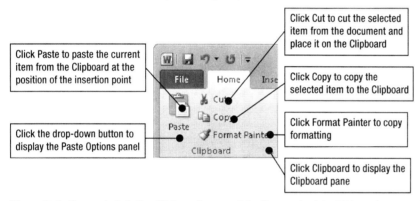

Figure 3–8. *The controls in the **Clipboard** group of the **Home** tab of the Ribbon give you quick access to **Cut**, **Copy**, and **Paste** commands. In an Outlook message window, the **Clipboard** group appears on the **Message** tab and the **Format Text** tab.*

> **TIP:** You can also cut, copy, and paste using the keyboard. Press Ctrl+X to cut, Ctrl+C to copy, and Ctrl+V to paste.

Cutting, Copying, Pasting with the Office Clipboard

Like other programs, the Office programs use the Windows Clipboard, which can contain only one item of a particular type at a time. So each time you cut or copy an item of a particular type, it overwrites the Clipboard's current contents. But when you copy or cut, the Office programs also put the copied or cut item on the Office programs' own clipboard. This Clipboard is separate from the Windows Clipboard and can store up to 24 items.

To use the Office Clipboard, click the Clipboard button, the tiny button in the lower-right corner of the Clipboard group. Figure 3–9 shows you how to use the Clipboard pane.

TIP: Most of the task panes in the Office programs appear *docked*—fixed to one side of to the program window. If you want to position such a task pane freely, click its title bar and drag it away from the side of the window. The task pane becomes free-floating, and you can move it to a different position and resize it by dragging its borders. To dock the task pane again, double-click its title bar.

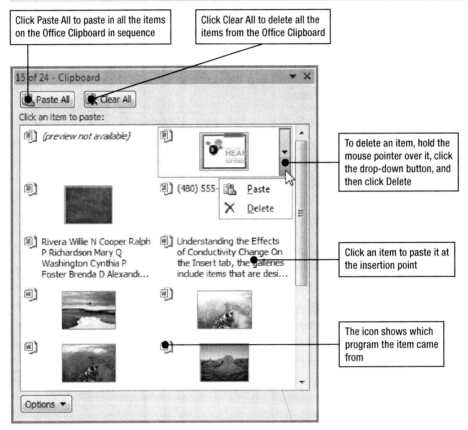

Figure 3–9. *Use the Office Clipboard when you need to paste in two or more items you've cut or copied. When you finish using the Office Clipboard, click the × button to close it.*

NOTE: You can copy text from most Office documents and from formats such as Portable Document Format (PDF), but not from pictures. To get text out of pictures, you need to use optical character recognition, as discussed in the section "Entering Text by Using Optical Character Recognition," earlier in this chapter.

CONTROLLING HOW THE OFFICE CLIPBOARD BEHAVES

To control how the Office Clipboard behaves, click the **Options** drop-down button at the bottom of the Clipboard pane, and then choose options on the drop-down list (see Figure 3–10). To turn an option on, click to place a check mark next to it. To turn an option off, click to remove the check mark next to it.

- **Show Office Clipboard Automatically**. Makes the Office programs display the Clipboard when you copy or cut an item.

- **Show Office Clipboard When Ctrl+C Pressed Twice**. Makes the Office programs display the Clipboard when you press the Ctrl+C shortcut for Copy twice in immediate succession.

- **Collect Without Showing Office Clipboard**. Prevents the Office programs automatically displaying the Clipboard when you cut or copy an item.

- **Show Office Clipboard Icon on Taskbar**. Makes the notification area of the Taskbar display an icon for the Office Clipboard. Click this icon to access the Office Clipboard.

- **Show Status Near Taskbar When Copying**. Makes the Office Clipboard icon in the notification area of the Taskbar display a message saying "Item collected" when you copy or cut an item in the Office programs.

Figure 3–10. *To control how the Office Clipboard behaves, click the **Options** drop-down button at the bottom of the Clipboard pane, and then place or remove check marks on the drop-down menu as needed.*

Pasting Exactly What You Want with Paste Options

When you paste material in by clicking in the **Paste** button, the program inserts the copied or cut material at the destination along with the material's current formatting. For example, if you copy an italic paragraph from an e-mail message and paste it into a document, the pasted text retains the italic formatting because it's included in what was copied.

If you want the formatting, this is fine. But other times, you'll want to paste only some of the information copied. To do so, the Office programs provide Paste Options, which lets you control whether the destination document receives both the pasted data and its formatting, just the data, just the formatting, or some other option (depending on the program involved).

The easiest way to use Paste Options is to paste in the material and see if the result is what you want. If not, click the **Paste Options** button that appears next to the pasted material, and then click a different button on the **Paste Options** panel. Figure 3–11 shows an example using Excel, which has many paste options.

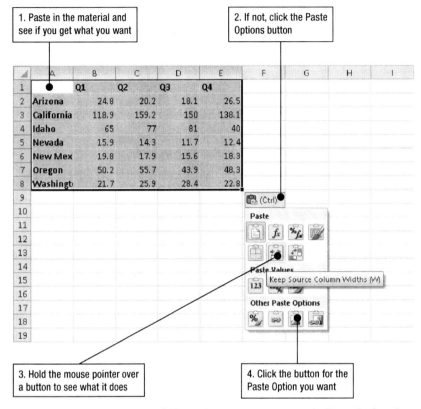

Figure 3–11. *After pasting material into a document, you can use the **Paste Options** button and panel to change the content or formatting of what you have pasted. This example uses Excel.*

If you know that you need a particular paste format, you can open the Paste Options panel and click the appropriate button on it instead of clicking the regular Paste button. Figure 3–12 shows the **Paste Options** panel, again for Excel.

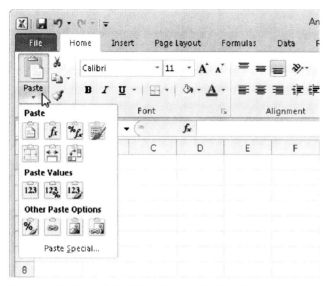

Figure 3–12. *Instead of clicking the main **Paste** button to perform a regular paste, you can click the **Paste** drop-down button and choose a type of paste on the **Paste Options** panel.*

> **TIP:** Word provides special options for controlling pasting. Choose **Home ➤ Clipboard ➤ Paste ➤ Set Default Paste** to display the **Cut, copy, and paste** area in the **Advanced** pane in the **Word Options** dialog box. You can then choose the default paste behavior for pasting within the same document, pasting between documents, pasting between documents that have styles with the same names but different formatting, and pasting from other programs. Click the **OK** button when you've made your choices.

Using Find and Replace

Often, when you're editing a document, you need to find specific text quickly. You can do this using the Find feature. Other times, you may need to replace specific text with other text. You can do this using the Replace feature.

In Word, Excel, and in Outlook's message windows, you access the Find and Replace features primarily through the **Find and Replace** dialog box, which lets you switch quickly between these two useful features. PowerPoint has a **Find** dialog box and a **Replace** dialog box that appear separate but are in fact different manifestations of the same dialog box.

> **NOTE:** Each Office program has different Find and Replace functionality to suit its needs. This section covers the common features and introduces you to the basics of using Find and Replace. As well as the **Find and Replace** dialog box, Word also includes the **Navigation Pane** for finding text and moving around your documents; see Chapter 7: "Entering and Editing Text in Your Documents" for details. OneNote handles Find differently (see Chapter 16: "Getting Up to Speed and Taking Notes" for details) and doesn't have a Replace feature.

Locating Text with Find

To locate text using the Find feature, open the **Find and Replace** dialog box or (in PowerPoint) the **Find** dialog box. Here are the commands you need:

- *Word.* Choose **Home ➤ Editing ➤ Find ➤ Advanced Find**.
- *Excel.* Choose **Home ➤ Editing ➤ Find & Select ➤ Find**.
- *PowerPoint.* Choose **Home ➤ Editing ➤ Find**.
- *Outlook.* Choose **Format Text ➤ Editing ➤ Find**.

Once you've opened the **Find and Replace** dialog box, work as explained in Figure 3–13.

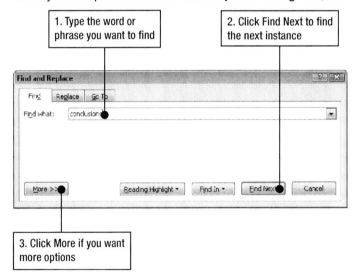

Figure 3–13. *Use the Find tab of the Find and Replace dialog box to quickly locate text in a document. This is Word's Find and Replace dialog box.*

To reach further options for find and replace, such as matching the case of the search text, click the **More** button in Word or the **Options** button in Excel. We'll look at the most useful of these features in the chapters on the individual programs.

Replacing Text with Replace

To replace text using the Replace feature, open the **Find and Replace** dialog box or (in PowerPoint) the **Replace** dialog box. Either press Ctrl+H (in Word, Excel, Outlook, or PowerPoint) or give the appropriate command from this list:

- *Word.* Choose **Home ➤ Editing ➤ Replace**.

- *Excel.* Choose **Home ➤ Editing ➤ Find & Select ➤ Replace**.

- *PowerPoint.* Choose **Home ➤ Editing ➤ Replace**.

- *Outlook.* Choose **Format Text ➤ Editing ➤ Replace**.

> **TIP:** If you already have the **Find and Replace** dialog box open, simply click the **Replace** tab at the top to display the Replace controls.

With the Replace tab of the **Find and Replace** dialog box displayed (Figure 3–14 shows the **Replace** tab in Excel), you can work like this:

1. Click in the **Find what** box, and then type your search term.

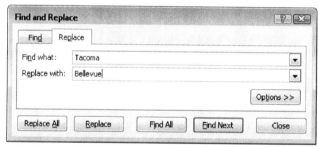

Figure 3–14. *Type your search term and replacement text on the **Replace** tab of the **Find and Replace** dialog box. This is Excel's **Find and Replace** dialog box.*

2. Click in the **Replace with** box, and then type the replacement text.

3. Click the appropriate button:

- ***Find Next.*** Click this button to find the next instance of the search term.

- ***Replace.*** Click this button to replace the current instance of the search term with the replacement term and find the next instance of the search term.

- ***Replace All.*** Click this button to replace every instance of the search term with the replacement term.

ind and **Replace** dialog box also contains the **Find All** button, which you can
nstances of the search term.

ı finish searching, click the **Close** button or the **Cancel** button to close
ınd **Replace** dialog box or the **Replace** dialog box.

Laying ∪ut Material with Tables

When you need to lay out data in a regular grid, create a table. A table consists of cells,
rectangular areas formed by the intersection of rows and columns. Each table can
contain one or more rows and one or more columns.

> **NOTE:** Excel uses the word *table* to mean a database created in a worksheet. Because Excel's
> worksheets have a grid structure, you don't need to create tables in them to lay out data the way
> you do in Word, PowerPoint, OneNote, and Outlook.

Inserting a Table

When you need to insert a regular table, use the **Table** button in the Insert group on the
Insert tab of the Ribbon. Figure 3–15 shows you what to do.

> **NOTE:** Instead of using the grid on the **Table** panel, you can click the **Insert Table** command to
> display the **Insert Table** dialog box, and then specify the number of columns and rows in this
> dialog box. In PowerPoint and OneNote, the **Insert Table** dialog box has no advantage over the
> table grid, but it Word and Outlook, the **Insert Table** dialog box contains options for setting the
> AutoFit behavior of the table—whether the column widths are fixed, automatically change to fit
> their contents, or automatically change to fit the window.

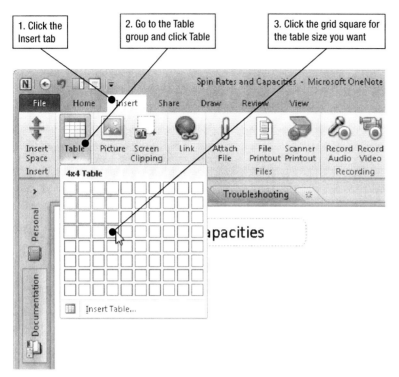

Figure 3–15. *The quick way to insert a regular table is to choose **Insert** ➤ **Table** ➤ **Table**, and then click the number of rows and columns you want.*

After the program inserts the table, you can work with it as described later in this chapter.

Drawing a Table

When you need a table that has different numbers of cells in different rows, or different numbers of cells in different columns, you can use the **Draw Table** command to create it. Word, PowerPoint, and Outlook have the Draw Table command, but OneNote doesn't.

To draw a table, choose **Insert** ➤ **Table** ➤ **Table** ➤ **Draw Table**, and then use the drawing cursor to draw the table layout you want (see Figure 3–16).

- ▨ *Draw a cell.* Click with the pen pointer and drag to draw a cell.

- ▨ *Erase a line.* Choose **Table Tools** ➤ **Design** ➤ **Draw Borders** ➤ **Eraser** to change the pen pointer to an eraser, and then click the line you want to erase. Choose **Table Tools** ➤ **Design** ➤ **Draw Borders** ➤ **Draw Table** when you want to switch back to the pen for drawing more cells.

■ *Stop drawing.* Choose **Table Tools ➤ Design ➤ Draw Borders ➤ Draw Table** to un-press the **Draw Table** button and turn off the pen pointer.

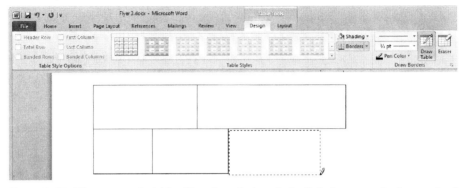

Figure 3–16. *When you need a table with an irregular layout of cells in its rows and columns, give the* **Draw Table** *command, and then use the pen pointer to draw the table layout you need.*

Merging and Splitting Cells in a Table

To change the layout of the table you've created, you can either merge two or more cells to form a larger cell or split an existing cell into several smaller cells.

To merge cells, select the cells, and then choose **Table Tools ➤ Layout ➤ Merge ➤ Merge Cells**, as shown in Figure 3–17. The program turns the selected cells into a single cell. Any contents of the previous cells appear as separate paragraphs in the merged cell.

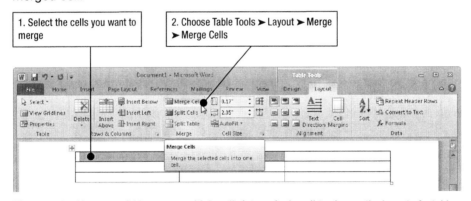

Figure 3–17. *You can quickly merge multiple cells into a single cell to change the layout of a table.*

To split a single cell into multiple cells, follow these steps:

1. Click in the cell you want to split.

2. Choose **Table Tools ➤ Layout ➤ Merge ➤ Split Cells** to display the **Split Cells** dialog box (see Figure 3–18).

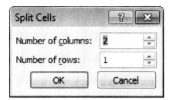

Figure 3–18. *Use the **Split Cells** dialog box to split one existing cell into two or more new cells.*

3. Set the number of columns and rows you want to create within the cell.

4. Click the **OK** button. The program splits the cell. If the cell contains one paragraph, it goes into the first of the new cells. If the cell contains multiple paragraphs, the program distributes them among the new cells.

Adding Content to a Table

You can add content to a table in several easy ways:

- **Type the text**. Click in the destination cell, and then type as usual. If you have AutoCorrect set to automatically capitalize the first letter of table cells, it will make this change for you.

- **Paste text or other material**. Copy the material from its source, click in the destination cell, and then give the Paste command. For example, choose **Home ➤ Clipboard ➤ Paste**.

> **TIP:** In Word and Outlook, you can copy text that's laid out with a tab between each separate item, and then paste it into multiple cells at once. Copy the text from the source, switch to Word or Outlook, select the appropriate number of cells in the table, and then give the Paste command.

- **Insert an object**. Click in the cell, and then insert the object as usual. For example, choose **Insert ➤ Illustrations ➤ Picture** to insert a picture.

> **NOTE:** Press the Tab key to move the insertion point to the next cell, or press Shift+Tab to move the insertion point to the previous cell. If you need to type a tab into a cell, press Ctrl+Tab.

Formatting a Table

To make a table look the way you want, you format it. You can apply formatting either quickly by using a table style or manually by applying only the formatting the table needs.

To apply a table style, work as explained in Figure 3–19.

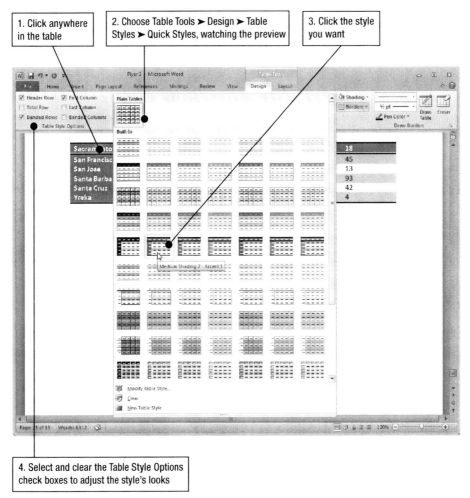

1. Click anywhere in the table

2. Choose Table Tools ➤ Design ➤ Table Styles ➤ Quick Styles, watching the preview

3. Click the style you want

4. Select and clear the Table Style Options check boxes to adjust the style's looks

Figure 3–19. *You can quickly give a table a colorful, coordinated look by applying a style from the* **Quick Styles** *box or* **Quick Styles** *drop-down palette on the* **Design** *tab of the Ribbon.*

If you prefer not to use a table style, you can format a table manually. These are the main techniques you'll need:

- *Borders.* Click the table, choose **Table Tools ➤ Design ➤ Table Styles ➤ Borders**, and then click the border style you want.

- *Shading.* Click the table, choose **Table Tools ➤ Design ➤ Table Styles ➤ Shading**, and then click the shading color.

- *Font formatting.* Select the cell or cells you want to format, and then use the controls in the **Font** group of the **Home** tab of the Ribbon as for other text.

Inserting Hyperlinks in Your Documents

A *hyperlink* is text or an object on a web page that's linked to another location—for example, to another web page or to another place on the same web page. You can insert hyperlinks as needed in your Office documents.

You can create both text hyperlinks and object hyperlinks. A text hyperlink appears as underlined text. An object hyperlink appears as just the object—for example, a picture or a shape. For either type of hyperlink, you can display a ScreenTip when the user holds the mouse pointer over the hyperlink, as in the text hyperlink shown in Figure 3–20. Many users find ScreenTips helpful.

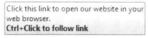

Click this link to open our website in your web browser.
Ctrl+Click to follow link
To find out how you can help, visit the Learn More page on our website.

Figure 3–20. ***When you create a hyperlink, you can include a ScreenTip that appears when the user holds the mouse pointer over the hyperlink.***

Figure 3–21 shows you how to insert a text hyperlink in a document.

> **NOTE:** To create a text hyperlink that displays text that already appears in your document, select that text before opening the **Insert Hyperlink** dialog box. To create an object hyperlink, insert the object and select it before opening the **Insert Hyperlink** dialog box.

After inserting the hyperlink, Ctrl+click it to test that it works. If you need to edit the hyperlink, right-click the hyperlink's text or object, and then click **Edit Hyperlink** on the context menu.

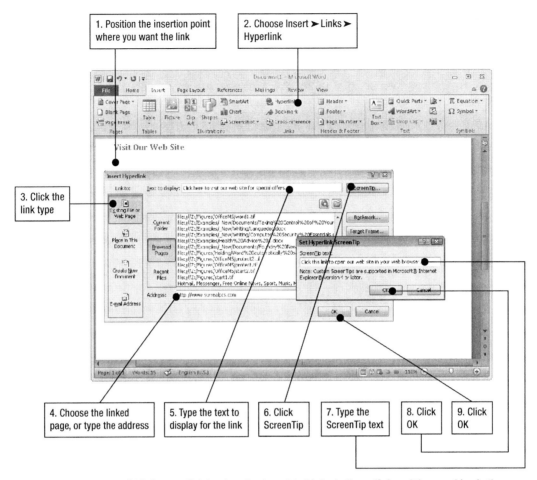

Figure 3–21. *You can quickly insert a link by choosing* **Insert ➤ Links ➤ Hyperlink** *and then working in the* **Insert Hyperlink** *dialog box.*

Summary

In this chapter, you learned how to work with text in the Office programs. We started by looking at how to enter text in your documents, using every means from the keyboard to optical character recognition and speech recognition. We moved on to navigating with the keyboard and applying direct formatting, then covered using the Cut, Copy, and Paste tools and the Find and Replace features.

You also learned to create tables by using the **Insert Table** command or by drawing a table, how to adjust tables by merging and splitting cells, and how to add content to the resulting table and format it. And I showed you how you can easily insert hyperlinks in your documents.

In the next chapter, you'll learn to work with pictures and graphics.

Chapter 4

Using Graphics in Your Documents

To illustrate your Word documents and PowerPoint presentations—and maybe your Excel worksheets and your outgoing e-mail messages in Outlook—you can add graphics. In OneNote, too, you can store graphics with your other notes in your notebooks.

In this chapter, you'll learn how to work with graphics in the Office programs. We'll start by looking at how to position graphical objects in documents, because you need to understand this in order to get the objects where you want them.

We'll then start working with graphics by inserting clip art items, which provide a handy way to get quick illustrations in your documents. After that, we'll look at how to insert your own pictures and shapes, move on to positioning graphical objects, and then examine how to make your pictures look the way you want them to.

At the end of the chapter, I'll show you how to create illustrations by inserting SmartArt graphics in your documents and how to arrange graphical objects to control which ones are visible.

Understanding How You Position Graphical Objects in Documents

Each Office document appears to be flat on screen, but to give you flexibility in how you position objects, it actually consists of multiple layers. You can position objects on different layers as needed, which enables you to place one object in front of another so that it obscures part of it.

For example, in Figure 4–1, you can see a chunky arrow and a picture of three penguins arguing geopolitics. The arrow appears in front of the penguins because it is in a layer above the picture, so it obscures part of the birds.

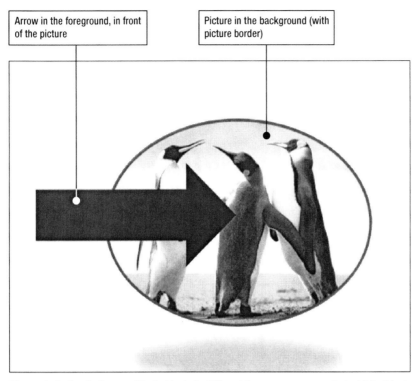

Figure 4–1. *By placing graphical objects in different layers, you can control which object appears in front of which. For example, the arrow appears in front of the penguins.*

This is straightforward enough—it's just like making a collage and sticking one picture on top of another.

Word documents and Outlook messages have a text layer, which contains the document's text, just as you'd expect. But you can also place graphical objects in the text layer if you want. When you place a graphical object in the text layer, it's anchored in place like a text character and behaves as part of the stream of text, even if it's much larger. So inserting text before the graphical object moves it down the document, and deleting text before it moves it up the document. Figure 4–2 shows an example of how a graphic moves when placed inline with text. We'll look at this in more detail later in this chapter.

Figure 4–2. *When you place a graphical object inline in a Word document or an Outlook message, it moves when you edit the text.*

The other thing you need to do when adding a graphical object is to choose where it goes in your document. To do this, you place the insertion point or selection before inserting the object:

- *Word, OneNote, or Outlook.* Place the insertion point where you want to insert the object.

- *Excel.* Click the cell where you want to place the upper-left corner of the object.

- *PowerPoint.* Click the slide on which you want to insert the object, or select the placeholder in which you want to place the object.

Okay, enough background. Let's look at what this means in practice.

Illustrating Your Documents with Clip Art Items

The quick way to illustrate your documents is by inserting clip art items—a picture or photograph, a video snippet, or an audio clip. Office comes with a selection of clip art items, and you can easily download other items from the Office.com website.

The advantage to using clip art is that you can quickly find high-quality images, videos, and audio that you can use freely in your documents without needing to seek permissions or pay royalties. The disadvantage is that you're limited to the selection of clip art that Office and Office.com provide, and that the items you use are available for use by every other Office user on the planet. (So if you need an original look to your documents, you may be better off using your own photos, as described later in this chapter.)

> **NOTE:** You can sometimes use other people's copyrighted items, such as photos or illustrations, without getting permission under the "fair use" exemption. This exemption covers uses such as commentary, news reporting, education, and parody. Fair uses tend not to be clear-cut, and lawyers love arguing about them. If you're not sure whether your use of an item would be fair use, consult a lawyer who specializes in copyright law.

Inserting a Clip Art Item in a Document

What you'll probably want to do first with clip art is find a suitable item and insert it straight into a document. To do this, position the insertion point or selection where you want the item to go, choose **Insert ➤ Illustrations ➤ Clip Art** to display the **Clip Art** task pane, and then work as shown in Figure 4–3.

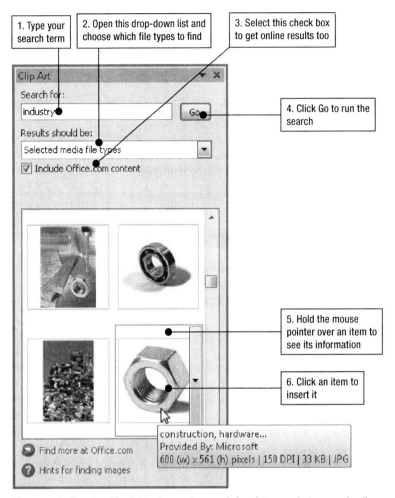

Figure 4–3. *Use the Clip Art task pane to search for pictures, photos, movie clips, or sounds and insert them in your Office documents.*

Adding a Clip Art Item to a Collection

When you're browsing clip art, you may find items that you want to keep for future use rather than put straight into your documents. When you find such an item, you can add it to a collection in the **Clip Organizer** program so that you can easily access it later.

> **NOTE:** To open the **Clip Organizer** program for managing your clip art, choose **Start ➤ All Programs ➤ Microsoft Office ➤ Microsoft Office Tools ➤ Microsoft Clip Organizer**. You can then browse the existing items, organize them into collections, and insert items in your documents.

To add an item to a collection, work as shown in Figure 4–4.

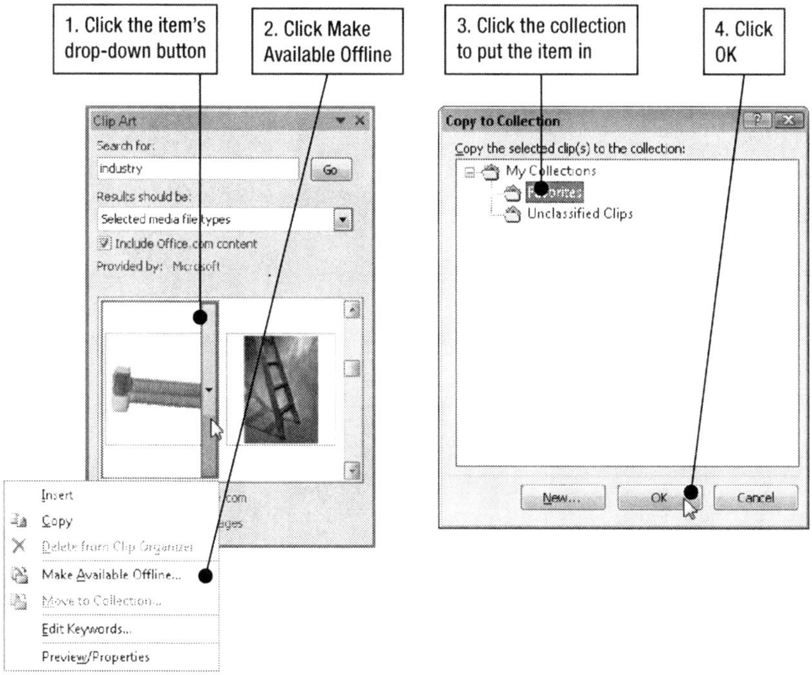

Figure 4–4. *To keep a clip art item for later use, click the **Make Available Offline** command to display the **Copy to Collection** dialog box, and then choose the collection to put the item in.*

> **NOTE:** You can create a new collection by clicking the **New** button in the **Copy to Collection** dialog box and then working in the **New Collection** dialog box. By creating multiple collections, you can sort your clip art items into different categories by their content (for example, Animals, Buildings, Corporate) or by their use (for example, Work, Home, Other). You can also create a new collection by working in **Clip Organizer**.

Previewing a Clip Art Item

When you need to see more detail about a clip art item than you can see in the **Clip Art** pane, click its drop-down button and then click **Preview/Properties** to display the **Preview/Properties** dialog box (see Figure 4–5).

Figure 4–5. *Open the **Preview/Properties** dialog box when you want to get a closer look at a clip art item. You can click the **Previous** button or the **Next** button to move through the clip art items while keeping the Preview/Properties dialog box open.*

On the right side of the **Preview/Properties** dialog box, you can see the item's details, including its type (for example, JPEG image), its resolution, and its file size. The **Keywords** box shows the keywords already associated with the item.

From the **Preview/Properties** dialog box, you can take these three actions:

- *Browse other clip art items.* Click the **Next** button or the **Previous** button.

- *Open the Keywords dialog box.* Click the **Edit Keywords** button. We'll look at the **Keywords** dialog box shortly.

- *Close the dialog box.* Click the **Close** button when you finish previewing or checking properties.

Examining and Adding Keywords

Each clip art item contains one or more keywords to enable searches to find it. To see which keywords an item contains, open the **Keywords** dialog box (see Figure 4–6) by either clicking the item's drop-down button in the **Clip Art** pane and then clicking **Edit Keywords** on the drop-down menu, or clicking the **Edit Keywords** button in the **Preview/Properties** dialog box.

> **NOTE:** You can change the keywords only for items you've added to the **Clip Organizer**, not for Office's items. But you may find it helpful to view an Office item's keywords so that you know which keywords to search for to find similar items.

You can add a keyword to a clip art item as shown in Figure 4–6, or click an existing keyword in the **Keywords for current clip** list, and then click the **Modify** button to change the keyword or the **Delete** button to delete it. When you finish working with keywords, click the **OK** button to close the **Keywords** dialog box.

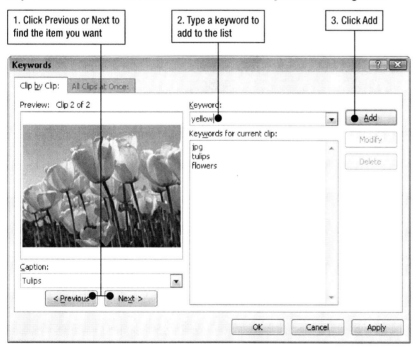

Figure 4–6. *You can edit the keywords for a clip art item you've added to the **Clip Organizer** by using the **Keywords** dialog box.*

Inserting Other Pictures in Your Documents

Office's clip art is handy, but anyone who has Office or an Internet connection can use the same pictures. To make your documents look unique, you'll probably want to use your own pictures to illustrate the documents.

To insert a picture in a document, position the insertion point or selection, choose **Insert** ➤ **Illustrations** ➤ **Picture**, and then work as shown in Figure 4–7.

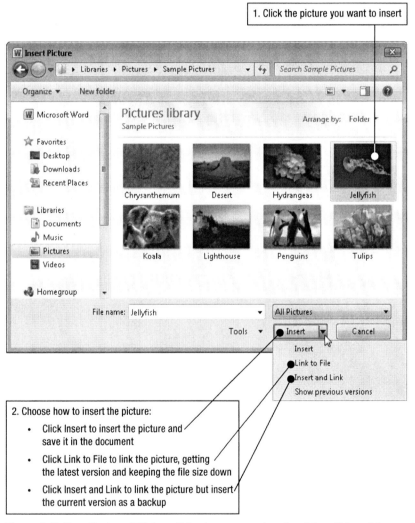

1. Click the picture you want to insert

2. Choose how to insert the picture:
   - Click Insert to insert the picture and save it in the document
   - Click Link to File to link the picture, getting the latest version and keeping the file size down
   - Click Insert and Link to link the picture but insert the current version as a backup

Figure 4–7. *From the **Insert Picture** dialog box, you can insert a picture, link a picture, or insert and link a picture.*

UNDERSTANDING INSERTING, LINKING, AND INSERTING AND LINKING PICTURES

The normal way of putting a picture in a document is by inserting it. When you do this, the program adds a copy of the picture to the document. The program saves the picture in the document, so even if you move the document, the picture stays in it.

If you need to keep the document's file size down, or if you need to be able to update the picture easily, you can link the picture instead. In the **Insert Picture** dialog box, click the drop-down button on the **Insert** button, and then click **Link to File** on the drop-down menu instead. Instead of inserting a copy of the picture in the document, the program adds a link to the picture file. When you open the document, the program loads the current version of the picture from the file. But if you move the document to a different computer, the link will no longer work, because the program will be unable to find the picture file.

To solve the problem of broken links, the **Insert** drop-down menu also contains the **Insert and Link** command. This command both inserts a copy of the picture in the document *and* links it back to the original picture. When you open the document, the program checks to see if the linked version is available. If so, the program loads the linked picture; if not, it displays the version saved in the document.

Inserting Shapes in Your Documents

To add an illustration to a document, you can insert one or more of Office's shapes by choosing **Insert ➤ Illustrations ➤ Shapes**, and then working as shown in Figure 4–8.

After inserting a shape, you can resize it by dragging its handles:

- *Drag a square side handle to resize the shape only in one dimension*. For example, drag the right side handle to the left to make the shape narrower.

- *Drag a round corner handle diagonally to resize the shape in two dimensions*. For example, drag the lower-right corner handle out and down to make the shape bigger.

> **TIP:** Shift+drag a corner handle to resize the shape proportionally.

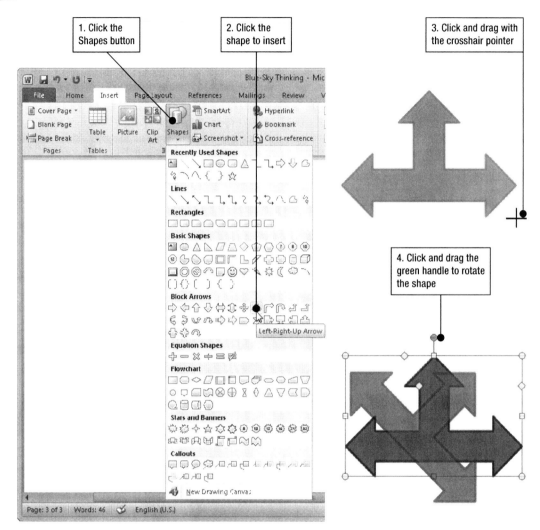

Figure 4–8. *You can quickly insert any of a wide variety of shapes by using the **Shapes** drop-down panel. After you insert a shape, you can rotate it by dragging its green handle.*

To make a shape appear the way you want it to, you can use the controls in the **Shape Styles** group on the **Drawing Tools ➤ Format** tab of the Ribbon (see Figure 4–9). The **Drawing Tools** section appears in the Ribbon when you have selected a shape.

Figure 4–9. *The **Drawing Tools ➤ Format** tab appears on the Ribbon when you have selected a shape. You can use the controls in the **Shape Styles** group to format a shape quickly.*

The quick way to format a shape is to apply a style from the **Shape Styles** box or drop-down panel, as shown in Figure 4–10. The color options shown depend on the theme the document uses.

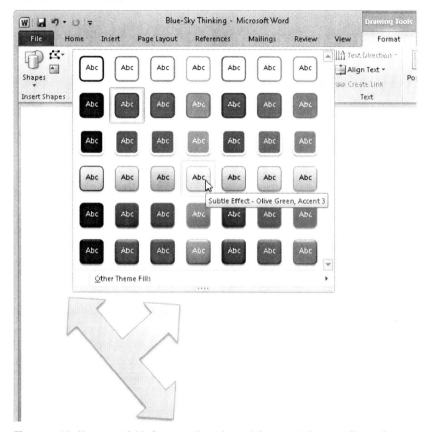

Figure 4–10. *You can quickly format a shape by applying a style from the **Shape Styles** drop-down panel on the **Drawing Tools ➤ Format** tab of the Ribbon. Hold the mouse pointer over a style to preview how it will look.*

Instead of applying a shape style, you can use the **Shape Fill** drop-down panel to apply a fill to a shape, use the **Shape Outline** drop-down panel to apply an outline, and use the **Shape Effects** drop-down panel to apply an effect (such as a reflection or a shadow).

Positioning Graphical Objects

To move a graphical object after inserting it, use one of these two techniques:

- *Click and drag.* To move the object quickly, click it and drag it to where you want it.

▧ *Nudge.* To move the object a short distance, click the object, and then press the Up arrow key, the Down arrow key, the Left arrow key, or the Right arrow key, as needed.

Wrapping Text Around Graphical Objects in Word and Outlook

As mentioned earlier in this chapter, in Word and Outlook, you can place a graphical object either inline with the text, so that it moves with the text, or in the graphics layers.

To change how the object appears in Word, click the object, and then use the **Format ➤ Arrange ➤ Position** command and the **Format ➤ Arrange ➤ Wrap Text** command, as shown in Figure 4–11.

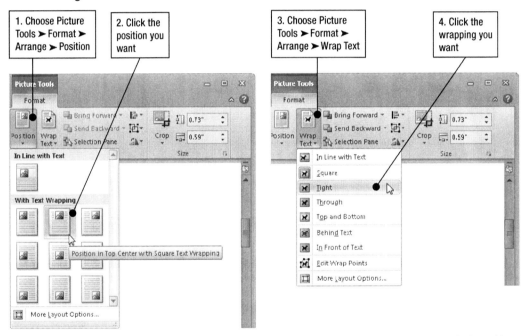

Figure 4–11. *In Word, first use the **Position** drop-down panel to control whether an object appears in line with text or with text wrapping. You can then use the **Wrap Text** panel to control the wrapping.*

To change how the object appears in an Outlook message, click the object, choose **Format ➤ Arrange ➤ Wrap Text**, and then click the appropriate option: **In Line with Text**, **Square**, **Top and Bottom**, **Behind Text**, or **In Front of Text**.

In either Word or Outlook, you can also click **More Layout Options** at the bottom of the **Wrap Text** panel to display the **Text Wrapping** tab of the **Layout** dialog box (see Figure 4–12), which provides controls for wrapping the text exactly as you need it.

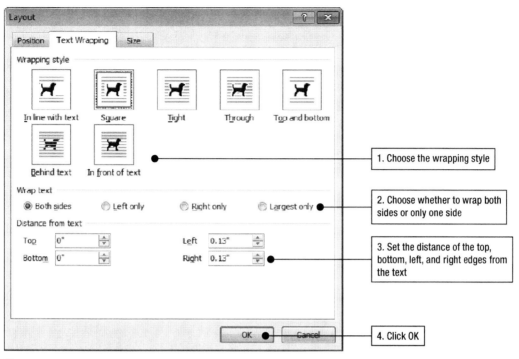

Figure 4–12. *Use the* ***Text Wrapping*** *tab of the* ***Layout*** *dialog box to take precise control of how Word or Outlook wraps text around an object.*

Making Your Pictures Look the Way You Want Them

After you insert a picture, you can use the controls that appear on the **Format** tab of the **Picture Tools** section of the Ribbon to make the picture look the way you want it. You can adjust the picture's colors, apply a picture style to the picture, or crop the picture so that only part of it shows.

Adjusting a Picture's Sharpness, Brightness, Contrast, and Colors

To adjust the sharpness, brightness, or contrast in a picture, click the picture to select it, and then use the **Corrections** drop-down panel, as shown in Figure 4–13.

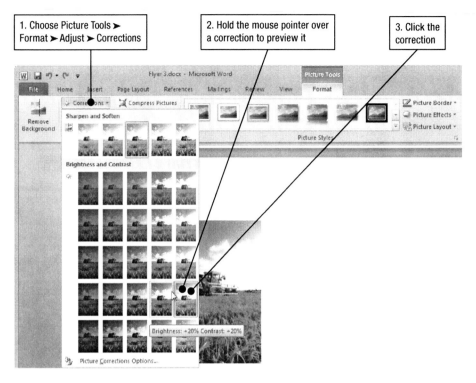

1. Choose Picture Tools ➤ Format ➤ Adjust ➤ Corrections

2. Hold the mouse pointer over a correction to preview it

3. Click the correction

Figure 4–13. *To fix problems with a picture's sharpness, brightness, or contrast, open the **Corrections** drop-down panel and choose the look you want.*

Similarly, you can use the **Color** drop-down panel in the **Adjust** group on the **Picture Tools ➤ Format** tab of the Ribbon to adjust a picture's coloring. The **More Variations** panel provides color options using the document's theme. Figure 4–14 shows an example.

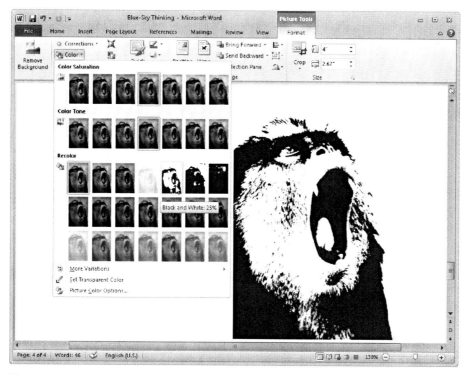

Figure 4–14. *Use the **Picture Tools ➤ Format ➤ Adjust ➤ Color** command to change a picture's color saturation or color tone, or to recolor it (as shown here).*

To apply an effect such as paint strokes or a light screen to a picture, click the picture, choose **Picture Tools ➤ Format ➤ Adjust ➤ Artistic Effects**, and then click the effect you want.

To reset a picture to its original look, choose **Picture Tools ➤ Format ➤ Adjust ➤ Reset Picture**. Resetting a picture is useful when you take your changes too far and need to start over.

> **TIP:** If you need to replace a picture you've worked on with another picture, choose **Picture Tools ➤ Format ➤ Adjust ➤ Change Picture**, and then use the **Insert Picture** dialog box to pick the replacement picture. The program retains any cropping or effects you've applied to the picture in the document, which saves you from having to reapply them.

Applying a Picture Style to Give a Particular Look

To give a picture a particular look, such as a bevel perspective or snip diagonal corners, you can apply a picture style to it by clicking the picture, choosing **Picture Tools ➤ Format ➤ Picture Styles**, and then clicking the style you want either in the **Quick Styles** box or on the drop-down panel (see Figure 4–15).

Figure 4–15. *Choose the picture style from the **Quick Styles** box or drop-down panel in the **Picture Styles** group of the **Format** tab of the Ribbon.*

Cropping a Picture

When you want the document to show only part of a picture, you can crop off the parts you don't want. Follow these steps:

1. Click the picture to select it and to add the **Picture Tools** section to the Ribbon

2. Choose **Picture Tools ➤ Format ➤ Size ➤ Crop**, clicking the top part of the **Crop** button rather than the drop-down button. The program displays crop handles on the picture (see Figure 4–16).

Figure 4–16. *To crop a picture, choose* **Picture Tools** ➤ **Format** ➤ **Size** ➤ **Crop**, *and then drag the crop handles until they encompass the part of the picture you want to keep.*

3. Drag the crop handles to make the cropping area contain the part of the picture you want to show:

   ▧ Shift+drag to crop the image proportionally.

   ▧ Ctrl+drag to crop the image evenly about its center point.

   ▧ Ctrl+Shift+drag to crop the image proportionally about its center point.

   TIP: After making the crop area exactly the size you need, you can click and drag within the crop area to make a different part of the picture appear in it.

4. Click the **Crop** button again to turn off the **Crop** tool, or click elsewhere in the document to deselect the picture. The program applies the cropping to it.

> **NOTE:** For more cropping options, choose **Picture Tools ➤ Format ➤ Size ➤ Crop**, clicking the **Crop** drop-down button rather than the top part of the button. On the drop-down menu that appears, choose **Crop to Shape** if you want to make the picture fit into a shape; choose **Aspect Ratio** if you want to crop the picture to a specific aspect ratio, such as 4:3 or 3:5.

Creating Illustrations by Inserting SmartArt Graphics

When you need to create an illustration such as an organization chart, a flow chart, or a Venn diagram, use Office's SmartArt feature. Follow these steps:

1. Position the insertion point or the selection where you want to put the SmartArt object.

2. Choose **Insert ➤ Illustration ➤ SmartArt** to display the **Choose a SmartArt Graphic** dialog box.

3. Choose the category and type of graphic as shown in Figure 4–17, and then click the **OK** button.

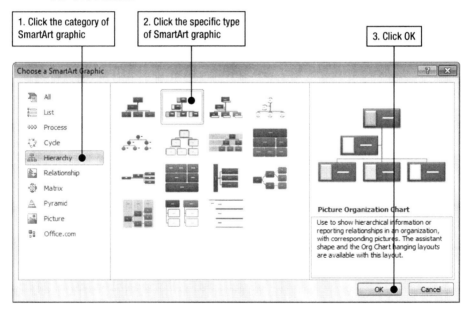

Figure 4–17. *In the **Choose a SmartArt Graphic** dialog box, choose the type of SmartArt graphic you want to create.*

When you click the **OK** button, the program inserts the SmartArt graphic, displays the text pane (the window called **Type your text here**) next to it, and adds the **SmartArt Tool**s section to the Ribbon (see Figure 4–18).

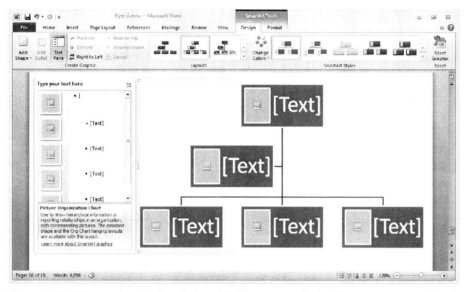

Figure 4–18. *When you insert a SmartArt graphic, the program displays the text pane next to it and adds the* **SmartArt Tools** *section to the Ribbon.*

You can now add text and other objects to the SmartArt graphic as shown in Figure 4–19.

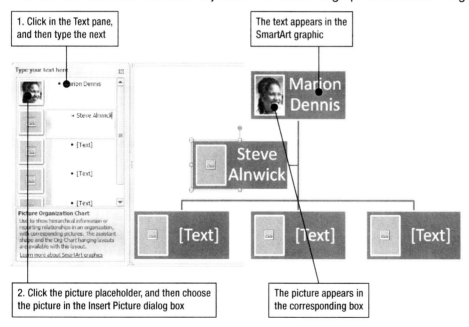

Figure 4–19. *Add the text to the SmartArt graphic by typing in the text pane. To add other items, such as the pictures shown here, click the placeholder and use the dialog box that opens.*

After entering all the text, you can finish up the SmartArt graphic quickly by resizing it and applying a style:

▨   *Resize the SmartArt graphic.* Click to select the SmartArt graphic, and then drag a side handle or a corner handle.

▨   *Apply a style.* Click the SmartArt graphic, choose **SmartArt Tools ➤ Design ➤ SmartArt Styles**, and then click the style you want. The color options come from the document's theme.

> **TIP:** If you need to change the layout of the SmartArt graphic, choose another layout from the **Change Layout** box or **Change Layout** drop-down panel in the **Layout** group of the **Design** tab on the **SmartArt Tools** section of the Ribbon.

Arranging Graphical Objects to Control Which Are Visible

When you have placed multiple graphical objects in the same area of a document, you may need to arrange the order in which they appear in the document's layers to control how they appear in relation to each other. For example, you may need to move a particular object to the front of the stack of document layers, so that it appears on top of the other objects, or move another object back so that it appears behind one of its companion objects.

To change where an object appears in the layers, select the object by clicking it. If the object is obscured, click another object to add the **Tools** section to the Ribbon, then choose **Format ➤ Arrange ➤ Selection Pane** to display the **Selection and Visibility** pane (see Figure 4–20). You can then click the object in the **Selection and Visibility** pane to select it.

After selecting the object, use the **Bring Forward** controls and **Send Backward** controls in the **Arrange** group on the **Format** tab to move it forward or backward:

▨   **Bring Forward**. Click this button to bring the object forward by one layer. To bring it all the way to the front, click the **Bring Forward** drop-down button, and then click **Bring to Front** (see Figure 4–21).

Figure 4–20. *You can use the **Selection and Visibility** pane to quickly select an object that's obscured by other objects.*

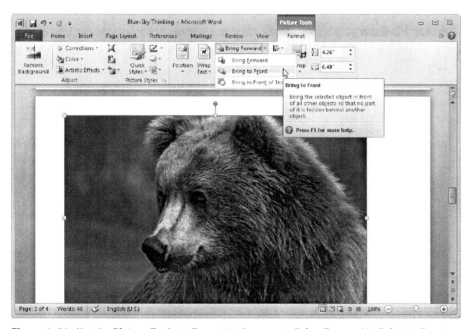

Figure 4–21. *Use the **Picture Tools ➤ Format ➤ Arrange ➤ Bring Forward ➤ Bring to Front** command to bring the selected object to the front of the stack.*

NOTE: In Word, the **Bring Forward** drop-down list includes the **Bring in Front of Text** command for bringing the selected object in front of the text. Similarly, the **Send Backward** command includes the **Send Behind Text** command.

▪ *Send Backward.* Click this button to send the object backward by one layer. To send the object all the way to the back, click the **Send Backward** drop-down button, and then click **Send to Back**.

NOTE: You can also move an object forward or back by right-clicking it and using the **Bring to Front** command and submenu and the **Send to Back** command and submenu on the context menu. For example, to send an object backward, right-click it and choose **Send to Back ➤ Send Backward**.

Summary

In this chapter, you learned to use graphics in your documents. You now know how graphical objects fit in the layers of your documents and how to put the different kinds of graphical objects there—clip art, pictures of your own, shapes, and SmartArt objects. You know how to position and resize objects, how to improve your pictures by using the corrections and color tools, and how to arrange objects to make the right ones visible.

In the next chapter, I'll show you how to work on documents with your colleagues in real time.

Chapter 5

Coauthoring in Real Time and Sharing Documents

To get your documents created and edited as quickly and as smartly as possible, you will likely need to work on them with your colleagues. The Office programs give you several different ways of sharing your documents with others. This chapter shows you how to use these different ways and explains which way to use when.

In Word, Excel, PowerPoint, and OneNote, you can work on a document at the same time as your colleagues, using a feature that Microsoft calls *coauthoring*. This can be a great way to get a document finished quickly, as long as you and your colleagues can avoid working on the same part of the document simultaneously and creating conflicting changes that you then need to resolve. In this chapter, we'll look at coauthoring in Word, PowerPoint, and OneNote, leaving Excel's coauthoring—which is different—for the Excel part of the book.

Instead of coauthoring, you can share a single copy of the document on a network drive and work on it in turn, or create multiple copies of the document so that people can work on them simultaneously, producing different versions that you then need to integrate.

The Office programs also make it easy to share your documents with others. In the second half of this chapter, I'll show you how to send a document via e-mail, how to save a document to Windows Live SkyDrive, and how to share a document as an electronic printout in the PDF or XPS document format.

Working on Documents with Your Colleagues

In the Office programs, you can work on documents with your colleagues either together or separately:

▓ *Work on the same copy of the document simultaneously.* If you have a SharePoint site or you store documents on Windows Live SkyDrive, you and your colleagues can store the document on the site, each open it at the same time, and work on it together.

▓ *Work on the same copy of the document in turn.* Instead of coauthoring, you can take turns to open the same copy of the document, make your changes, and then close the document. The Office programs help you by warning you when the document you want is already open and alerting you when the current user stops using it.

▓ *Work on separate copies of the document.* Another option is to work on separate copies of the same document and then integrate the changes into a single document. This tends to be more laborious, but you may sometimes need to do it—for example, when you need to get a document finished in a hurry, and you can parcel out responsibility for different parts of it to your colleagues.

Which approach is most practical depends on you, your colleagues, and the type of document you're creating:

▓ Coauthoring is most effective when you give different people responsibility for separate parts of the document. For example, when you're creating a presentation in PowerPoint, having several people try to edit the same slide tends to cause conflicts. But if one person works on the five slides in the introductory section, a second works on the remaining slides, and a third steps in to build custom animations— preferably liaising closely with the first two people—it's easy to avoid conflicts.

▓ Working on the same copy of the document in turn is the best choice when you have plenty of time to create the document, when people need to work on it at different times, or if each person is performing a different role on the document (for example, creating the document, editing it, reviewing it, and so on).

▓ Working on separate copies of the same document tends to be a last resort when neither of the other options is workable. The downside is that you end up with multiple documents containing changes that you then need to integrate into a single document. Word, Excel, and PowerPoint include tools for helping you integrate changes, but it's still more work than the other approaches.

NOTE: Using separate copies is also useful when you need to gather input from multiple people without them seeing (and perhaps being influenced by) each other's changes.

Coauthoring in Real Time

The fastest way to get a document finished is usually by coauthoring it. *Coauthoring* means that you and your colleagues simultaneously work on the same copy of the document rather than working on the document in turn or working on separate copies.

Word, Excel, PowerPoint, and OneNote all support coauthoring. Coauthoring works in a similar way in Word, PowerPoint, and OneNote, so we'll cover those three programs together here. Excel's coauthoring works differently, and we'll cover it in Chapter 11.

NOTE: To use coauthoring, you must store the document either on a SharePoint site or on Windows Live SkyDrive (which runs on SharePoint). You cannot use coauthoring with documents stored on a regular network drive. SharePoint is a Microsoft server technology that many companies use, but you can also rent SharePoint space from SharePoint hosting sites online. Windows Live SkyDrive is a document-storage site owned by Microsoft. You can sign up for a free account on SkyDrive by going to `http://skydrive.live.com`.

Preparing a Document for Coauthoring

Beyond saving the document to a SharePoint site or Windows Live SkyDrive, there's no special preparation for coauthoring. Once you save the document to SharePoint or SkyDrive, other people who can access the folder it's stored in can open the document. If someone else already has the document open at that point, coauthoring begins.

Opening a Document for Coauthoring

Open the document as usual from the SharePoint site or from SkyDrive. When coauthoring starts, the Authors readout appears on the status bar, showing how many people are editing the document. Each person with the document open sees a pop-up message from the status bar notifying them about the other authors. Figure 5–1 shows an example.

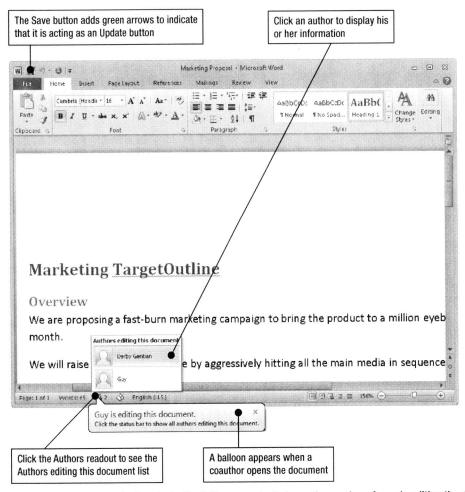

Figure 5–1. *When coauthoring starts, the **Authors readout** shows the number of people editing the document. A pop-up balloon appears to draw your attention to the change.*

Editing a Document During Coauthoring

When coauthoring, you can edit the document, presentation, or notebook as usual. The big difference is that only one person can edit a particular paragraph, placeholder, or other element at a time. As you work, the program shows you which parts of the document other authors are working on by placing a line to the left of the items and displaying a box containing the author's name (see Figure 5–2). Similarly, your coauthors see lines and boxes indicating which parts of the document you're working on.

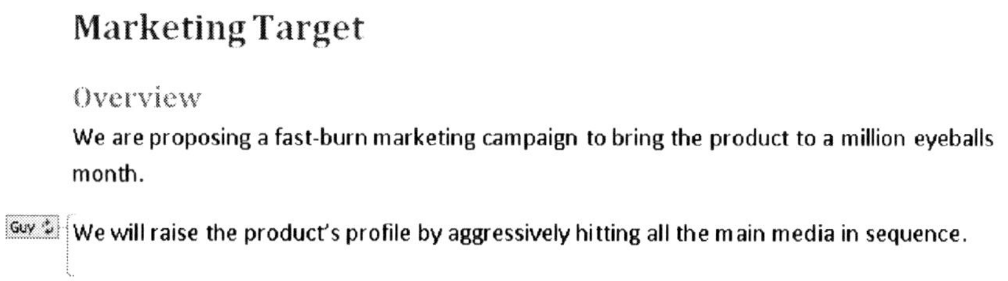
Marketing Target
Overview
We are proposing a fast-burn marketing campaign to bring the product to a million eyeballs
month.
Guy
We will raise the product's profile by aggressively hitting all the main media in sequence.

Figure 5–2. *A line indicates that a coauthor is working on that part of the document. The box shows the coauthor's name.*

Saving Your Changes and Getting Others' Saved Changes

When you've made changes you want to save, click the **Save** button on the Quick Access Toolbar or press Ctrl+S as usual to save them. You may also want to save the document when you haven't made changes but when the **Updates Available** button appears on the status bar (see Figure 5–3) to let you know your coauthors have saved changes; this will refresh the document with the latest changes.

Page: 1 of 1
Words: 69
2
English (U.S.)
Updates Available
130%

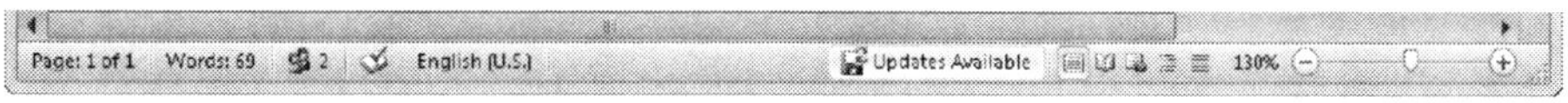

Figure 5–3. *When the **Updates Available** button appears in the status bar, save your document to get the latest changes your coauthors have saved.*

> **TIP:** Clicking the **Updates Available** button in the status bar displays the **Info** pane in **Backstage** view, which contains a **Save** button you can click to save the document and get the updates. But usually it's easier to press Ctrl+S or click the Save button on the Quick Access Toolbar as usual to save the document.

Changes that others have made to the document appear highlighted, so that you can easily identify them. At first, the program displays a dialog box telling you that it has refreshed the document with changes made by other authors, as you see in Figure 5–4. Normally, you will want to select the Don't show this message again check box before dismissing this dialog box—you don't need to have it appear each time you get updates.

Figure 5–4. *When you update a document, others' changes appear highlighted.*

TIP: When coauthoring a document, save your changes even more frequently than when working normally. Saving frequently is vital for two reasons: first, it makes your changes available to your coauthors, and their changes available to you, so you can track the document's development more closely. Second, it helps you avoid getting conflicting changes that you then need to resolve (as discussed later in this chapter).

Resolve Conflicts During Coauthoring

Even though Word, PowerPoint, and OneNote try to show you and your coauthors who's working where, it's possible for two or more of you to change the same part of a document during the same cycle of saving and updating.

When this happens, whichever coauthor first saves his or her changes gets them saved to the document—just as you'd expect. When another coauthor tries to save changes that conflict with those changes that have been saved, the program displays the **Upload Failed** bar (see Figure 5–5). Click the **Resolve** button to start dealing with the conflicts.

> **TIP:** When you run into the **Upload Failed** bar, resolve your conflicts as soon as possible. The longer you wait, the more changes your coauthors can make to the document that may conflict with other changes you've made but haven't saved.

The Upload Failed bar appears when there are conflicting changes

Click the Resolve button to start resolving the conflicts

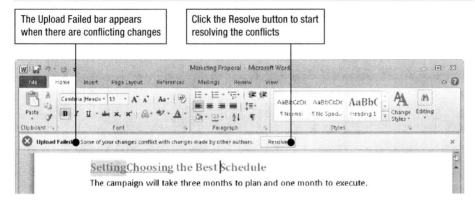

Figure 5–5. *Click the **Resolve** button on the **Upload Failed** bar to start dealing with the conflicts between the changes you've made and the changes your coauthors have already saved to the document.*

When you click the **Resolve** button, the program displays the **Conflicting changes** pane. Use this pane and the Ribbon controls to work through the conflicting changes, as shown in Figure 5–6. Usually, it's a good idea to discuss the conflicting changes with your coauthors—for example, via instant messaging.

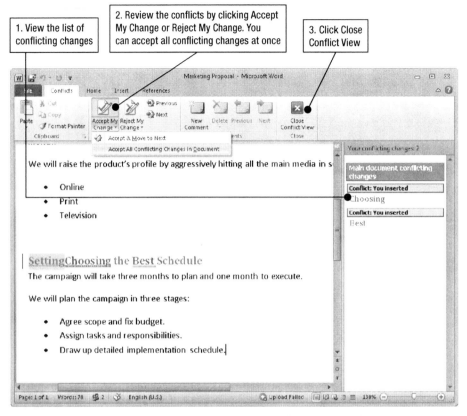

Figure 5–6. *Use the **Conflicting changes** pane and the **Conflicts** tab of the Ribbon to resolve the conflicts between the changes you've made and the changes saved in the coauthored document.*

Sharing Documents on a Network

Coauthoring can be great, but it doesn't work for everyone. You may find it easier to have people take turns at working on your documents, so that only one person has any given document open at a particular time. To make the documents available to all the people who need to work them, you put the documents on a network drive or a SharePoint site.

The advantage to sharing documents this way is that whoever has a particular document open can work freely in it without having to worry about running into changes other authors or editors are making.

The disadvantages are that creating and editing the document tend to take longer than in coauthoring, and you may need to chase laggard authors or editors.

You will also likely run into two or more people trying to open the same document at the same time. When this happens, Word or Excel displays the **File in Use** dialog box, which lets you decide what to do. The upper screen in Figure 5–7 shows the Word version of the **File in Use** dialog box; the lower screen shows the Excel version.

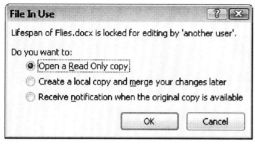

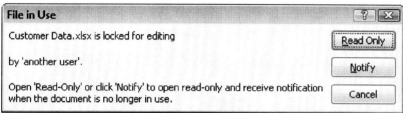

Figure 5–7. *When you try to open a document that another person has already opened, the program warns you that the document is locked for editing, and gives you choices about how to proceed.*

NOTE: If you try to open a presentation that someone else has opened, PowerPoint opens the presentation in read-only mode without offering you alternatives. In OneNote, you cannot open a notebook that someone else has already opened and that is not stored on SharePoint or SkyDrive.

From here, you have four choices in Word or three choices in Excel:

- ▓ *Cancel opening the document.* Click the **Cancel** button to cancel your request to open the document. You can then try again at a convenient time.

- ▓ *Open a read-only copy of the document.* In Word, select the **Open a Read-Only Copy** option button and click the **OK** button; in Excel, click the **Read Only** button. The program opens the document in a read-only state. Read-only means that you can't save changes to the network copy of the document, but you can save it under a different name. If you want to integrate those changes into the network copy, you'll need to do so either manually or by using the **Document Combine** feature in Word (see Chapter 10) or the **Track Changes** feature in Excel (see Chapter 11).

- *Create a local copy and merge your changes later.* In Word, select **Create a local copy** and merge your changes later option button and click the **OK** button if you need to go ahead and make changes to the document now rather than waiting. When the document becomes available for editing, Word offers to merge your changes into it; click the **Merge** button to do so.

- *Have Word or Excel tell you when the document becomes available.* In Word, select the **Receive notification when the original copy is available** option button and click the **OK** button. In Excel, click the **Notify** button. This makes Word or Excel keep checking the document's status and tell you when the other person has finished with it. When Word or Excel displays the **File Now Available** dialog box (see Figure 5–8), click the **Read-Write** button to open the document for editing.

Figure 5–8. *When the document for which you've requested notification becomes available, click the **Read-Write** button to open it for editing.*

Working on Separate Copies of the Same Document

Either coauthoring or working in turn on a single copy of a document allows you and your colleagues to get a document finished without complications. But other times, you may need to have people work simultaneously on separate copies of the same document.

The advantage to doing this is that you can have multiple people working on the document at once. The disadvantage is that someone—typically you—then has to integrate the changes from the separate copies into a single document.

When you're working manually, such integrating can be a slow and thankless task—but fortunately it's a task that your PC can help you with. Word, Excel, PowerPoint, and OneNote provide different tools for integrating multiple copies of the same document into a single document. We'll cover the techniques you use in the chapters on the individual programs rather than covering them here.

Sharing Documents via E-mail, SkyDrive, and Electronic Documents

Word, Excel, and PowerPoint all enable you to share a document with other people in several different ways. This section covers the three ways common to all three programs:

- Send via e-mail
- Save to Web
- Save as PDF or XPS

NOTE: If your company or organization has a SharePoint site, you can save documents to it to share them with your colleagues. Choose **File ➤ Save & Send ➤ Save to SharePoint**, click the folder, and then click the **Save As** button.

Sending a Document via E-mail

You can send a document by e-mail by starting a message in Outlook and then attaching the document. But when you have the document open in Word, Excel, or PowerPoint, you can start a message directly from the program. This saves you from having to switch to Outlook, and it eliminates the risk of you attaching the wrong document—for example, a version with the same name stored in a different folder.

Figure 5–9 shows you how to send the active document via e-mail.

NOTE: If the document is saved on a SharePoint site or on Windows Live SkyDrive, you can send a link to the document instead of sending the entire document. Send a link when whoever you are sending the message to has access to the shared location. The recipient can then click the link to open the document from there. Sending a link avoids creating multiple copies of the same document and having to integrate the changes later. To send the link, click the **Send a Link** button in the **Send Using E-mail** pane.

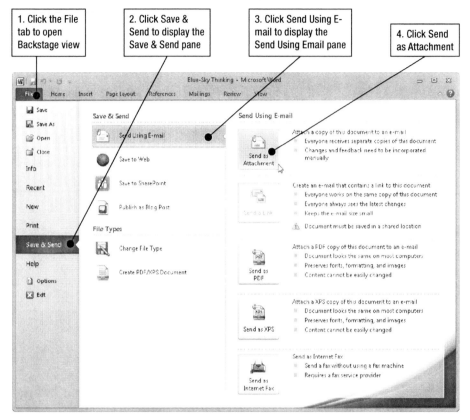

Figure 5–9. *You can quickly send the open document via e-mail from Word, Excel, or PowerPoint by choosing* **File ➤ Save & Send ➤ Send Using E-mail ➤ Send as Attachment.**

When you click the **Send as Attachment** button, the program (in this case, Word) hands off the document to Outlook, which creates a new e-mail message with the document attached. You can then address and send the message, as shown in Figure 5–10.

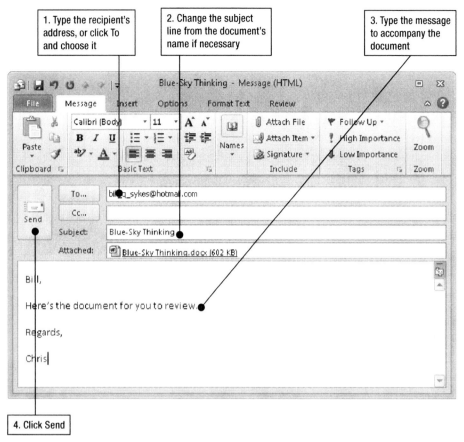

1. Type the recipient's address, or click To and choose it

2. Change the subject line from the document's name if necessary

3. Type the message to accompany the document

4. Click Send

Figure 5–10. *After Outlook automatically creates a new message with the document attached, address the message and send it.*

Sending a Document to the Web

If you have a Windows Live account (including a Hotmail account or an MSN account), you can save documents to SkyDrive, Microsoft's online document service. You can use SkyDrive either to share documents with other people who have Windows Live accounts or to access and work on your documents from other computers.

> **NOTE:** You can sign up for a free Windows Live account at the Windows Live website (http://home.live.com).

To save the open document to SkyDrive, work as shown in Figure 5–11.

1. Click the File tab to open Backstage view

2. Click Save & Send to display the Save & Send pane

3. Click Save to Web to display the Save to Windows Live pane

4. Click Sign In to sign in to Windows Live

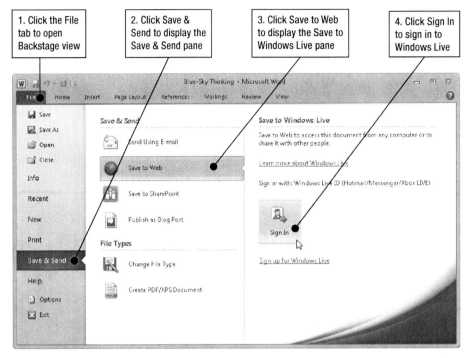

Figure 5–11. *To save the open document to SkyDrive from Word, Excel, or PowerPoint, choose **File ➤ Save & Send ➤ Save to Web**, and then click the **Sign In** button.*

The first time you go to use SkyDrive, the **Sign In** button appears in the **Save to Windows Live** pane, because you haven't yet set up SkyDrive. Click the **Sign In** button, provide your Windows Live user name and password in the **Connecting** dialog box that opens (see Figure 5–12), and then click the **OK** button.

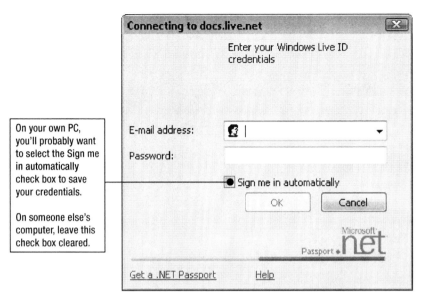

On your own PC, you'll probably want to select the Sign me in automatically check box to save your credentials.

On someone else's computer, leave this check box cleared.

Figure 5–12. *The first time you connect to Windows Live SkyDrive, you need to provide your e-mail address and password. After that, you can save the credentials on your PC so that you don't need to type them again.*

Once you've provided your credentials, the **Save to Windows Live** pane changes to the **Save to Windows Live SkyDrive** pane and displays your folders, as shown in Figure 5–13. You can then click the folder you want to put the document in, and then click the **Save As** button.

> **NOTE:** At first, SkyDrive gives you a Public folder (which you share with everyone) and a private **My Documents** folder. You can create other folders as needed either by clicking the **New** button or by working in a web browser.

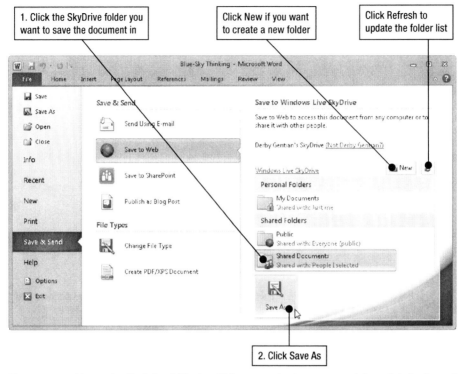

1. Click the SkyDrive folder you want to save the document in

Click New if you want to create a new folder

Click Refresh to update the folder list

2. Click Save As

*Figure 5–13. Choose the **SkyDrive** folder in which to save the document, and then click the **Save As** button.*

Sharing a Document as a PDF or XPS File

When you need to share the document in a format that people can easily read but cannot change, or when you need to make sure the document retains its layout perfectly, you can create a PDF file or an XPS file. Each of these is a kind of electronic printout of the document. PDF is the abbreviation for the widely used Portable Document Format, while XPS is short for XML Paper Specification.

TIP: PDF is much more widely used than XPS and is often the better choice. Use XPS when you're sure the person you're sharing the document with has Windows 7 or Windows Vista on their PC; these operating systems include XPS reader programs, whereas Mac OS X does not. Use PDF when you're not sure which operating system the recipients' computers use, when you know the recipient uses a Mac, and when you're preparing a document for wide distribution.

To start creating a PDF file or XPS file, open the document, and then work as explained in Figure 5–14.

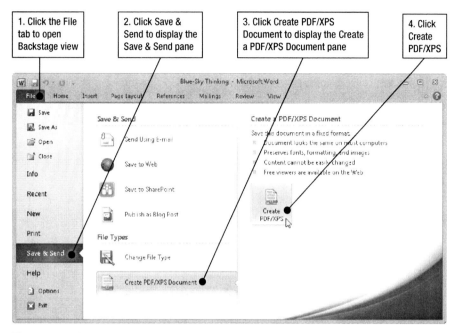

Figure 5–14. *Choose* **File ➤ Save & Send ➤ Create PDF/XPS Document ➤ Create PDF/XPS** *to start creating a PDF file or XPS file from the active document.*

When you click the **Create PDF/XPS** button, the program displays the **Publish as PDF or XPS** dialog box. Figure 5–15 shows you how to work with this dialog box.

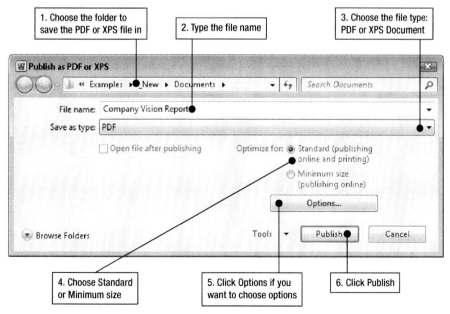

Figure 5–15. *In the* **Publish as PDF or XPS** *dialog box, choose whether to create a PDF file or an XPS file, choose the file name and location, and choose how to optimize the file.*

When you just need to create a PDF file or XPS file quickly, you can try using the default options. But when you want to control the details of the PDF file or XPS file, click the **Options** button, and then work in the **Options** dialog box. Figure 5–16 shows the **Options** dialog box for creating PDF files; the **Options** dialog box for creating an XPS document has the same controls except for the options section at the bottom.

> **NOTE:** Select the **Open file after publishing** check box in the **Publish as PDF or XPS** dialog box if you want to open the PDF or XPS document automatically after creating it. This lets you check that the document has come out as you intended, so it's often a good idea. This check box is available only if your PC has a PDF reader program or XPS reader program installed.

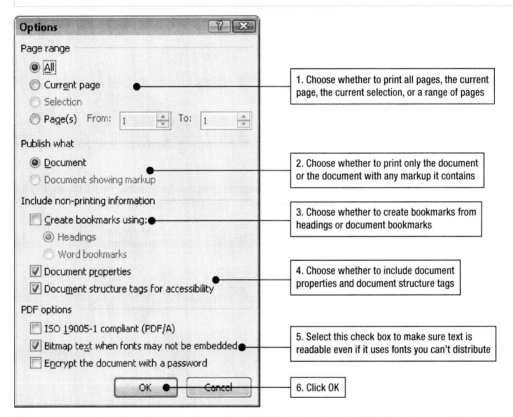

Figure 5–16. *In the **Options** dialog box for creating PDF files (shown here) or XPS files, choose which pages to publish, whether to include markup, and which non-printing information to include.*

When you click the **OK** button to close the **Options** dialog box, the program returns you to the **Publish as PDF or XPS** dialog box. You can then click the **Publish** button to create the PDF file or XPS document.

NOTE: If you have Adobe Acrobat installed on your PC, you can create PDFs either from Acrobat itself or by using the tools that Acrobat installs into the Office programs.

Summary

In this chapter, you learned how to share your documents with your colleagues. We started by reviewing the different ways of sharing documents and covering which works best when. We then examined the powerful coauthoring feature, which lets you and your colleagues work on the same copy of a document at the same time, before moving on to cover working on a shared document in turns and working on separate copies of a shared document.

In the second half of the chapter, you learned how to send a document quickly via e-mail, how to save a document to Windows Live SkyDrive, and how to turn a document into a PDF file or XPS document file that you can share with others.

Chapter 6

Making the Office Programs Work Your Way

In this chapter, I'll show you how to make the Office programs work your way. You can put the commands you use most frequently on the Quick Access Toolbar, customize the toolbar, and customize the status bar so that it contains the items you find most useful. In Word, you can also create custom keyboard shortcuts so that you can give commands from the keyboard without having to reach for the mouse.

You can customize the Office programs further by setting the many options they offer. In this chapter, we'll look at how to set the most widely useful options shared among the programs. These are the **General** options and the options for controlling where and how you save your Office files.

Customizing the Quick Access Toolbar

The easiest way to start customizing the Office programs is the Quick Access Toolbar, the short row of buttons that appears at the left end of the title bar in the program window, just to the right of the control-menu icon. Figure 6–1 shows the Quick Access Toolbar with just a few buttons.

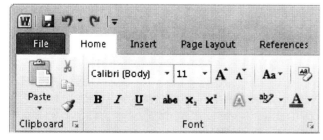

Figure 6–1. *The* Quick Access Toolbar *at the left end of the program's title bar contains just a few buttons at first, but you can add as many other controls as you need.*

You can customize the Quick Access Toolbar in several ways. We'll start with the easiest.

Using the Customize Quick Access Toolbar Menu

The quick way to customize the Quick Access Toolbar is to click the **Customize Quick Access Toolbar** button and work as explained in Figure 6–2. The **Customize Quick Access Toolbar** menu contains a short list of common commands for the program. To add a command from the list, click it; to remove a command that's currently displayed, click it. Either way, the menu closes, and the change appears immediately on the Quick Access Toolbar.

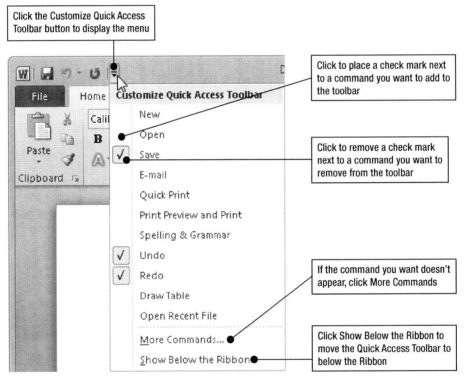

Figure 6–2. *You can quickly customize the* Quick Access Toolbar *opening the **Customize Quick Access Toolbar** menu and placing check marks next to the commands you want on it. To add other commands, click **More Commands.***

To add a command that isn't on the **Customize Quick Access Toolbar** menu, you can click **More Commands** to display the **Quick Access Toolbar** pane in the program's **Options** dialog box. I'll show you how to add commands to the Ribbon this way in a moment—but first, we'll look at an easier way to add them.

Adding Commands to the Quick Access Toolbar from the Ribbon

The second easiest way to add commands to the Quick Access Toolbar is to use the Ribbon. When you find a command you want to put on the Quick Access Toolbar, add it as explained in Figure 6–3.

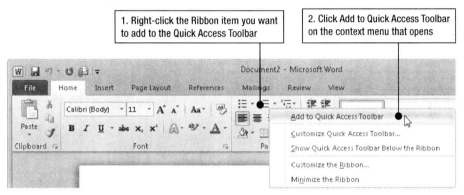

Figure 6–3. *You can quickly add a Ribbon item to the* Quick Access Toolbar *by right-clicking it and then clicking* **Add to Quick Access Toolbar** *on the context menu.*

What's neat about this technique is that you can add not only an individual command to the Quick Access Toolbar but also a whole group of commands. For example, if you right-click the label at the bottom of the **Paragraph** group, and then click **Add to Quick Access Toolbar**, you end up with a button on the Quick Access Toolbar that you can click the display the whole **Paragraph** group (see Figure 6–4).

Figure 6–4. *You can add a complete Ribbon group to the* Quick Access Toolbar *so that you can always reach it easily.*

Customizing the Quick Access Toolbar Using the Options Dialog Box

When you need to reach the full range of commands the program offers, use the **Quick Access Toolbar** pane in the program's **Options** dialog box to customize the Quick Access Toolbar. Follow these steps to display the **Quick Access Toolbar** pane in the **Options** dialog box:

1. Click the **Customize Quick Access Toolbar** button to display the menu.

2. Click the **More Commands** item to display the **Quick Access Toolbar** pane.

You can now work as explained in Figure 6–5, which shows the Word Options dialog box.

> **TIP:** If you want to divide the controls on the Quick Access Toolbar into different groups, click the **<Separator>** item at the top of the left list box and then click **Add** to add it to the Quick Access Toolbar. You can then move the separator up or down as needed to create groups.

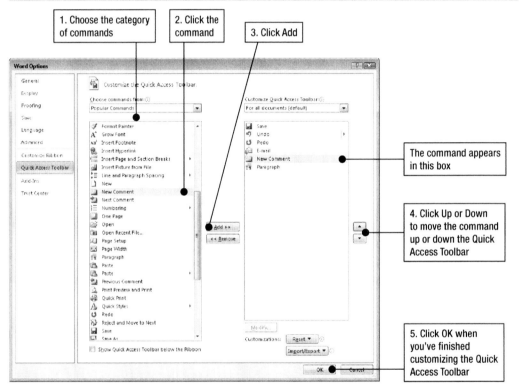

Figure 6–5. *Use the **Quick Access Toolbar** pane in the **Options** dialog box to add other commands to the* Quick Access Toolbar.

Here are the extra details you need to know about adding commands using the **Quick Access Toolbar** pane in the **Options** dialog box:

- *Choose which documents you want to affect.* In Word, Excel, and PowerPoint, you can make the customization for either the active document or all documents. Click the **Customize Quick Access Toolbar** drop-down list in the upper-right corner of the **Options** dialog box, and then click **For all documents** (default) or For *document*, where *document* is the active document's name.

TIP: Normally, you'll want to make your Quick Access Toolbar customizations for all documents, so that they're always available. Making the customizations in either of the other ways described earlier in this chapter makes them for all documents. But when you want to provide a particular set of commands in only one document, use the **Customize Quick Access Toolbar** drop-down list to restrict the changes to only that document. For example, you might do this with a document or workbook you intend to distribute to your colleagues, who probably have their own Quick Access Toolbar customizations on their own PCs.

- *Find the commands you need*. The **Choose** commands from drop-down list breaks up the program's commands into several different categories:

  - **Popular Commands**. These are the commands that appear on the **Customize Quick Access Toolbar** menu. So if you've already used that menu to customize the Quick Access Toolbar, you'll probably want to select a different category.

  - **Commands Not in the Ribbon**. This choice gives you access to commands that don't appear in the Ribbon, which is what you'll often want—any command that is on the Ribbon, you can quickly add to the Quick Access Toolbar directly from the Ribbon, as described in the previous section.

  - **All Commands**. This choice gives you the full range of commands available. The list is awkwardly long to navigate, but you can be sure the command you need is somewhere on it.

  - **Macros**. If you record or write your own macros, select this category when you want to put buttons on the Quick Access Toolbar that run the macros. (A *macro* is a sequence of commands that you create. Macros are beyond the scope of this book.)

  - **File Tab**. This category gives you access to the **Backstage** commands.

  - **Home Tab and other tabs**. These categories display all the commands associated with these tabs.

NOTE: To remove an item from the Quick Access Toolbar, click it in the right list box, and then click the **Remove** button.

■ ***Show Quick Access Toolbar below the Ribbon.*** If you want to position the Quick Access Toolbar below the Ribbon rather than in the title bar, select this check box. Putting the Quick Access Toolbar below the Ribbon gives you space for many more buttons on the Quick Access Toolbar, as you can see in Figure 6–6.

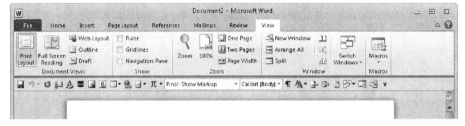

Figure 6–6. *Move the* Quick Access Toolbar *to appear below the Ribbon when you need space for more buttons without crowding the title bar.*

■ ***Rearrange the existing buttons on the Quick Access Toolbar.*** If you want to rearrange the buttons on the Quick Access Toolbar, click a button in the right list box, and then click the up arrow button or the down arrow button until the button appears where you want it.

Remove a Button from the Quick Access Toolbar

To remove a button from the Quick Access Toolbar, right-click the button, and then click **Remove from Quick Access Toolbar** on the context menu.

Resetting the Quick Access Toolbar to Its Default Buttons

If you need to reset the Quick Access Toolbar to its default buttons, follow these steps:

1. Click the **Customize Quick Access Toolbar** button to display the menu.

2. Click the **More Commands** item to display the **Quick Access Toolbar** pane of the program's **Options** dialog box.

3. Click the **Reset** drop-down button in the lower-right corner (see Figure 6–7).

Figure 6–7. *In the **Quick Access Toolbar** pane of the program's **Options** dialog box, click the **Reset** drop-down list, and then click **Reset Only Quick Access Toolbar**.*

4. Click **Reset only Quick Access Toolbar** on the drop-down menu. The program displays the **Reset Customizations** dialog box (see Figure 6–8).

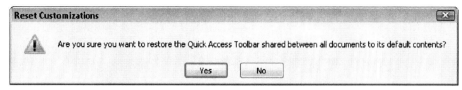

Figure 6–8. *In the **Reset Customizations** dialog box, click the **Yes** button to confirm that you want to erase the customizations you've made to the **Quick Access Toolbar**.*

5. Click the **Yes** button. The program resets the Quick Access Toolbar to its standard buttons.

Customizing the Status Bar

The status bar at the bottom of each program window gives you quick information about the current document and the part of it you're working in, and provides controls for changing views and zooming in and out.

> **NOTE:** This section doesn't apply to OneNote, which has no status bar.

You can customize the status bar to show only the information and controls you find most helpful. Figure 6–9 shows you how to customize the status bar.

> **NOTE:** Even when you select their check boxes, many of the items that you can display in the status bar appear only when the circumstances are right. For example, the **Signatures** item appears only if the document has a digital signature applied to it, and the **Information Management Policy** item appears only if the document has **Information Rights Management (IRM)** applied. To learn about IRM, choose **File ➤ Info**, click the **Protect Document** button, and click the **Restrict Editing** item. In the **Restrict Formatting and Editing** pane that opens, click the **Restrict permission** link.

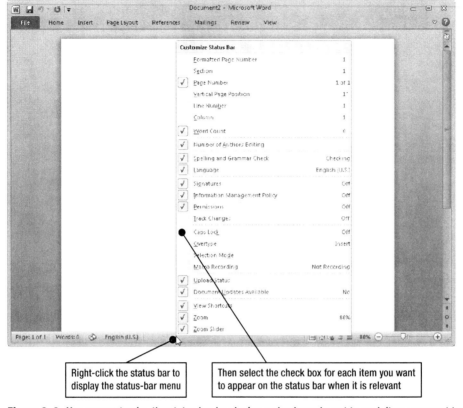

Right-click the status bar to display the status-bar menu

Then select the check box for each item you want to appear on the status bar when it is relevant

Figure 6–9. *You can customize the status bar by placing a check mark next to each item you want to see. Some items appear on the status bar only when they are relevant to the document.*

Customizing the Ribbon

To put commands where you need them, you can customize the Ribbon in several ways:

- *Create new tabs.* You can create new Ribbon tabs as needed.

- *Create new groups.* You can create new groups either on the existing tabs or on new tabs you create.

- *Rearrange existing tabs.* You can rearrange the existing tabs into an order that suits you better.

- *Rearrange existing groups.* You can rearrange the existing groups within the tabs.

- *Add controls to new groups.* When you create a custom group, you can add individual controls to it. You can't add individual controls to an existing group.

> **TIP:** The Ribbon's customization possibilities can be confusing—so here's a quick example. You probably use a number of commands from various tabs, but seldom or never use other controls on those tabs. So what you may want to do is create a custom tab with custom groups in which you can put all your frequently-used controls together.

If you feel the Ribbon could suit you better, go through this section's examples of changing it, and then make further changes along these lines. As you'll see at the end of this section, you can quickly restore the Ribbon to its default settings, so there's no harm in experimenting. (Or minimal harm, anyway—restoring the Ribbon to its default settings also restores the Quick Access Toolbar to its defaults, so you lose any Quick Access Toolbar customizations you've made.)

> **CAUTION:** Customizing the Ribbon can be a great help in putting commands where you find them most useful—but the instructions in this book assume that you're using the Ribbon in its default state. So if you do customize the Ribbon, you may need to find the commands in different places than described.

Opening the Customize Ribbon Pane in the Options Dialog Box

First, open the **Customize Ribbon** pane in the program's **Options** dialog box like this:

1. Right-click anywhere on the Ribbon or on the Quick Access Toolbar to display the context menu.

2. Click **Customize the Ribbon**. The program's **Options** dialog box opens with the **Customize Ribbon** pane at the front. Figure 6–10 shows the **Customize Ribbon** pane in the **Word Options** dialog box with its main features labeled.

Choose the category of commands

Choose the command to add

Choose Main Tabs to work with the tabs that appear all the time

Click + to expand a tab or group

Click – to collapse a tab or group

Click Up or Down to move the selected item

Click New Tab to create a new tab

Click New Group to create a new group

Click Rename to rename the selected tab or group

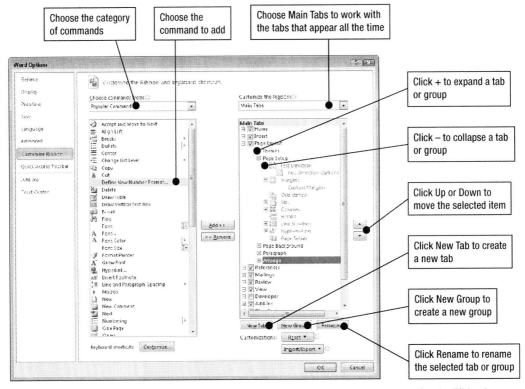

Figure 6–10. *From the Customize Ribbon pane in the Options dialog box, you can customize the Ribbon's existing tabs or create new tabs of your own.*

Choosing the Tab You Want to Affect

With the **Customize the Ribbon** pane displayed in the **Options** dialog box, choose which tab to affect. To work with an existing tab, open the **Customize the Ribbon** drop-down list, and then click **Main Tabs**, All **Tabs**, or **Tool Tabs**. Here's what these terms mean:

- *Main Tabs.* These are the tabs that appear on the Ribbon all the time—the **Home** tab, the **Insert** tab, the **View** tab, and so on. This is usually the best place to start with your customization unless you want to create a new tab.

- *All Tabs.* Choose this item when you want to see the full list of tabs.

- *Tool Tabs.* Choose this item to display the list of tool tabs, such as the **SmartArt Tools** tab, the **Chart Tools** tab, and the **Picture Tools** tab.

If you want to create a new tab, work as explained in Figure 6–11.

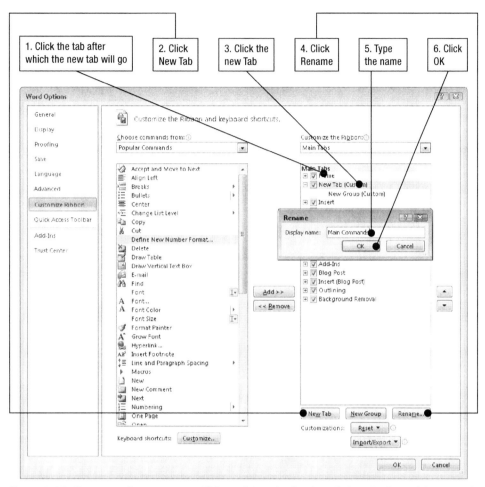

Figure 6–11. *You can easily create a new Ribbon tab by selecting the existing tab after which to place it, clicking the **New Tab** button, and then using the **Rename** dialog box to rename the tab.*

Creating a New Group

To create a new group, follow these steps:

1. In the right box in the **Customize Ribbon** pane in the **Options** dialog box, click the **+** sign to expand the tab you will put the group on.

2. Under that tab, click the group after which the new group will go.

3. Click the **New Group** button. A new group named **New Group (Custom)** appears.

4. With the new group still selected, click the **Rename** button to display the **Rename** dialog box (see Figure 6–12).

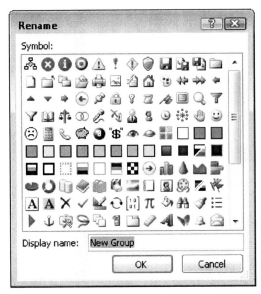

Figure 6–12. *In this **Rename** dialog box, click the **Symbol** for the group when it's collapsed, type the name for the group, and then click the **OK** button.*

5. In the upper box, click the icon you want the group to have when the Ribbon is narrow enough to make it appear collapsed rather than at its full width.

6. Type the new name.

7. Press **Enter** or click the **OK** button.

Adding Commands to a New Group

After you create a new group, add commands to it like this:

1. In the right box in the **Customize Ribbon** pane in the **Options** dialog box, click the + sign to expand the tab that contains the group.

2. Click the group to select it.

3. On the left side of the dialog box, open the **Choose commands from** drop-down list, and then click the item you want—for example, **Commands Not in the Ribbon**, **All commands**, or **File** tab. The list of commands appears in the left box.

4. In the left box, click the command you want to add.

5. Click the **Add** button.

6. If necessary, click the button you've added, and then click the **Up** button or the **Down** button to move the button to where you want it.

7. Repeat this process to add each other command you need.

Figure 6–13 shows a custom Ribbon tab with three custom groups added and populated with useful commands.

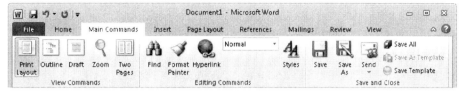

Figure 6–13. *By creating a custom Ribbon tab, you can put exactly the commands you need where they're most useful.*

Moving an Existing Group

Another Ribbon customization you may want to make is moving a group, either from one position to another on its current tab or to another tab. For example, if you use formulas a lot in Excel, you may want to move the **Function Library** group from the **Formulas** tab to the **Home** tab to make it handier. (You may need to move one of the **Home** tab's default groups to another tab to make room.)

To move a group, select it in the right box in the **Customize Ribbon** pane in the **Options** dialog box, and then click the **Up** button or the **Down** button as needed.

Moving an Existing Tab

You can also move an existing tab to a different position. For example, if you use the commands on the **View** tab in Word frequently, you may want to move the **View** tab so that it appears next after the **Home** tab rather than on the right of the window.

To move an existing tab, click it in the right box in the **Customize Ribbon pane** in the **Options** dialog box, and then click the **Up** button or the **Down** button as needed.

> **TIP:** You can rename an existing tab if you want. Click the tab in the right box in **OK** the **Customize Ribbon** pane, click the **Rename** button, type the new name in the **Rename** dialog box, and then click the button.

Resetting the Ribbon to Its Default Settings

If you don't want to keep your Ribbon customizations, you can reset either a tab or all customizations. All customizations include changes you've made to the Quick Access Toolbar, so be prepared to lose these as well when you reset all of the Ribbon.

To reset the Ribbon, follow these steps:

1. Right-click anywhere in the Ribbon to display the context menu.

2. Click **Customize Ribbon** to display the program's **Options** dialog box, with the **Customize Ribbon** item selected in the left column.

3. To reset a tab, click it in the right list box, click the **Reset** drop-down button in the lower-right corner, and then click **Reset only selected Ribbon** tab. The program resets the tab without confirmation.

4. To reset the whole of the Ribbon and the Quick Access Toolbar, click the **Reset** drop-down button in the lower-right corner, and then choose **Reset all customizations**. In the confirmation dialog box that the program displays (see Figure 6–14), click the **Yes** button.

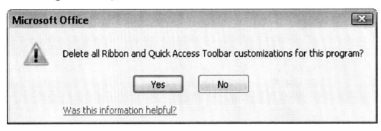

Figure 6–14. *You can quickly reset the Ribbon to its default settings, removing your customizations. But doing so also resets the Quick Access Toolbar.*

5. Click the **OK** button to close the **Options** dialog box.

Sharing Quick Access Toolbar and Ribbon Customizations with Other PCs

After customizing the Quick Access Toolbar and Ribbon on one PC, you can easily share the customizations with another PC. To do so, follow these steps:

1. In the program that contains the customizations, right-click anywhere in the Ribbon, and then click **Customize Ribbon** on the context menu. The program opens the **Options** dialog box and selects the **Customize Ribbon** item in the left column.

2. In the lower-right corner, click the **Import/Export** drop-down button, and then click **Export All Customizations**. The program opens the **File Save** dialog box.

3. Either accept the suggested name (for example, PowerPoint Customizations) or type another name over it.

4. Click the **Save** button. The program saves the file.

5. Click the **Cancel** button to close the **Options** dialog box.

6. Transfer the customizations file to the other computer. For example, put it on a network drive or a USB stick, or send it via e-mail.

7. On the other computer, open the same program, and then open the **Customize Ribbon** pane, as described in step 1.

8. Click the **Import/Export** drop-down button, and then choose **Import Customization File**. The program displays the **File Open** dialog box.

9. Choose the customizations file, and then click the **Open** button. The program displays a confirmation message box (see Figure 6–15).

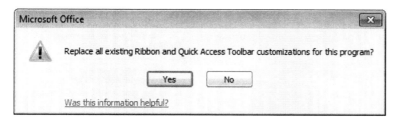

Figure 6–15. *You can quickly import customizations on another PC.*

10. Click the **Yes** button. The program imports the customizations.

11. Click the **OK** button to close the **Options** dialog box.

Creating Custom Keyboard Shortcuts in Word

In Word, you can create custom keyboard shortcuts to supplement the built-in keyboard shortcuts. Creating your own keyboard shortcuts to give the commands you need the most can be a great help in working fast and smoothly in Word.

To create custom keyboard shortcuts, open the **Customize Keyboard** dialog box like this:

1. Right-click any Ribbon tab to display its context menu.

2. Click **Customize the Ribbon** to display the **Ribbon** pane in the **Word Options** dialog box.

3. Click the **Customize** button next to **the Keyboard Shortcuts** label at the bottom.

You can then work in the **Customize Keyboard** dialog box, as explained in Figure 6–16.

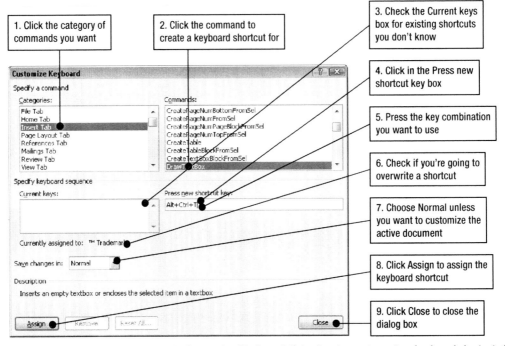

Figure 6–16. *In Word, you can use the **Customize Keyboard** dialog box to create custom keyboard shortcuts for the commands you need to give from the keyboard.*

Setting Essential Options

Each Office program contains hundreds of options that you can set to customize the program's appearance and behavior. In this section, we'll look at settings that are common to several (or all) of the programs and that make a big difference in the way that the programs behave. We'll look at some of the most important program-specific settings in the chapters that cover the individual programs.

Opening the Options dialog box

Open the Options dialog box for the program you want to configure. With the program running, click the **File** tab to open **Backstage** view, and the click the **Options** button to display the **Options** dialog box.

Choosing General Options

The best place to start is with the general options, so click the **General** category in the left column to display the **General** pane. Figure 6–17 shows the **General** pane for PowerPoint.

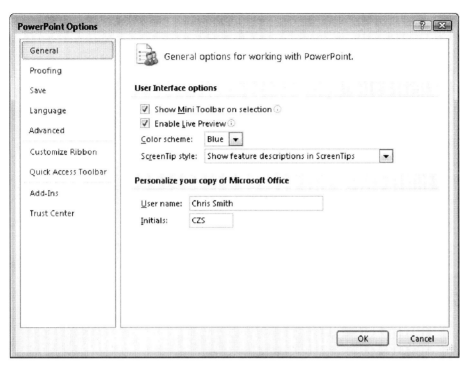

Figure 6–17. *The **General** pane in the **Options** dialog box lets you choose whether to display the Mini Toolbar and ScreenTips, whether to use Live Preview, and which color scheme to use. This is the **General** pane for PowerPoint.*

These are the common features you can set here:

- **Show Mini Toolbar on selection.** Select this check box if you want the program to display the floating Mini Toolbar when you make a selection. This toolbar shows buttons for working with the selection and is often useful. Figure 6–18 shows the Mini Toolbar for PowerPoint.

Figure 6–18. *If you find the pop-up Mini Toolbar unhelpful or intrusive, you can turn it off in the **General** pane of the **Options** dialog box.*

▓   ***Enable Live Preview***. Select this check box to have the program display previews of formatting changes so that you can see them in place before you actually apply them. This is a great feature. The only reason to turn it off is if it makes your PC run slowly.

▓   ***Color scheme***. In this drop-down list, select the overall color scheme you want the Office applications to have: Blue, Silver, or Black. Office uses this color scheme for all the programs—you can't have different programs use different colors.

▓   ***ScreenTip style***. In this drop-down list, choose how you want ScreenTips to appear. To start with, you'll probably want to use the **Show feature descriptions in ScreenTips** setting, which shows the feature's name and a short description of what the feature does. Once you know your way around, you may prefer the **Don't show feature descriptions in ScreenTips** setting, which shows just the feature's name. Or you can choose the **Don't show ScreenTips** setting to turn ScreenTips off altogether.

▓   ***User name***. Make sure your name appears they way you want it in this text box. Office uses this setting, and the Initials setting, for each of the programs, so changing your name or initials in one program changes them for the other programs too.

▓   ***Initials***. Check that this text box shows your initials. (Excel doesn't have this text box, so you need to set the initials in one of the other programs.)

Choosing Save Options in Word, Excel, and PowerPoint

When you're customizing Word, Excel, and PowerPoint, spend a few minutes setting the programs' **Save** options. This section shows you how to set the most important **Save** options, leaving the more esoteric options that you probably won't need to set.

In the left column of the **Options** dialog box, click the **Save** category to display the **Save** pane. Figure 6–19 shows the **Save** pane of the **Word Options** dialog box; in Excel and PowerPoint, the **Save** pane also has the options discussed here, but it has some other program-specific options as well.

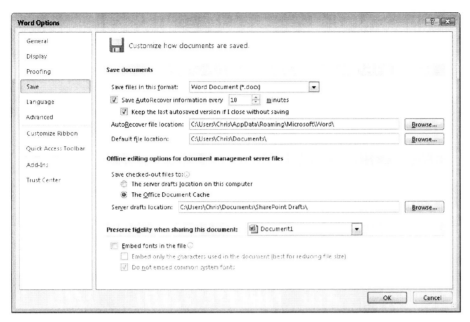

Figure 6-19. *In the **Save** pane of the **Options** dialog box, choose the default format for saving documents, the default folder in which to save them, and choose whether to save AutoRecover files.*

Choosing the Default Format for Saving Documents

Word, Excel, and PowerPoint can each save documents in several different formats. Each program comes set to save documents in its preferred format—for example, PowerPoint uses the latest PowerPoint Presentation format by default. But to make sure that other people can open the documents you share with them, you may need to change the format. For example, you may need to use a Word document format that colleagues using the old but widely used Office 2003 can open.

To change the default format, open the **Save file in this format** drop-down list, and then choose the format you want.

These are the formats you're most likely to need for Word:

- *Word Document*. Use this format if your colleagues have Office 2010, Office 2007 for Windows, or Office 2011 or Office 2008 for Mac. Anyone with Office 2003 for Windows or Office 2004 for Mac will need to install converter filters to be able to open the documents.

- *Word 97–2003 Document*. Use this format if your colleagues have Office 2003 for Windows, Office 2004 for Mac, or an earlier version of Office. You can also use this format for greater compatibility with other word processors, such as OpenOffice.org Write or Google Docs.

- *Rich Text Format*. Use this format if you're creating text-based documents that you need to ensure are fully readable in almost any word processor.

These are the formats you're most likely to need for Excel:

- *Excel Workbook*. Use this format if your colleagues have Office 2010, Office 2007 for Windows, or Office 2011 or Office 2008 for Mac. Anyone with Office 2003 for Windows or Office 2004 for Mac will need to install converter filters to be able to open the workbooks.

- *Excel Macro-Enabled Workbook*. Use this format if you need to include macros in your workbooks—for example, to perform custom actions. Again, your colleagues will need to have Office 2010, Office 2007 for Windows, Office 2011 for Mac, Office 2008 for Mac, or Office 2003 or Office 2004 with filters installed to open these workbooks.

- *Excel Binary Workbook*. Use this format if you create large and complex workbooks and need to improve performance. Once more, your colleagues will need to have Office 2010, Office 2007 for Windows, Office 2011 for Mac, Office 2008 for Mac, or Office 2003 or Office 2004 with filters installed to work with these workbooks.

- *Excel 97–2003 Workbook*. Use this format if your colleagues have Office 2003 for Windows, Office 2004 for Mac, or an earlier version of Office. You can also use this format for greater compatibility with other spreadsheet programs, such as OpenOffice.org Calc or Google Docs.

These are the formats you're most likely to need for PowerPoint:

- *PowerPoint Presentation*. Use this format if your colleagues have Office 2010, Office 2007 for Windows, Office 2011 for Mac, or Office 2008 for Mac. Anyone with Office 2003 for Windows or Office 2004 for Mac will need to install converter filters to be able to open the workbooks.

- *PowerPoint Presentation 97–2003*. Use this format if your colleagues have Office 2003 for Windows, Office 2004 for Mac, or an earlier version of Office. You can also use this format for greater compatibility with other presentation programs, such as OpenOffice.org Impress, Google Docs, or Apple Keynote.

NOTE: If you need to change the format only for a particular document, you can change it when you're saving that document. But if you need to create all your documents in a different format, change the default format in the **Options** dialog box.

Choosing AutoRecover Settings

Next, choose whether to keep AutoRecover files and (if so) where to save them. AutoRecover is a safety feature that automatically saves a copy of each open document every few minutes in case the program crashes and loses the changes you've made. After the program restarts automatically, or you restart it manually, the program opens the latest AutoRecover files for you so that you can choose which versions to keep. If you save your documents and then exit the program, it gets rid of the AutoRecover files it has saved.

> **CAUTION:** Never rely on AutoRecover as protection against disasters. When AutoRecover works, it can save your bacon. But you should always save your documents frequently while working on them, just in case AutoRecover doesn't work. You can save a document at any time by pressing Ctrl+S or clicking the **Save** button on the Quick Access Toolbar.

To use AutoRecover, select the **Save AutoRecover information every *N* minutes** check box, and then set the number of minutes in the text box. The default setting is 10 minutes, but if you work quickly and prefer not to save your documents manually, it's a good idea to reduce the interval to 2 or 3 minutes.

Select the **Keep the last Auto Recovered file if I close without saving** check box if you want to prevent the program from deleting the last AutoRecover file it has saved when you close a program without saving changes. This setting is usually helpful.

The AutoRecover file location text box shows the folder in which the program is storing your AutoRecover files. This is usually a folder buried deep in your AppData folder, which itself is normally hidden. You don't need to open AutoRecover files manually, as the program automatically opens them for you, so normally there's no need to change this folder.

> **NOTE:** For Excel, you can select the **Disable AutoRecover for this workbook only** check box to turn off AutoRecover for the current workbook. You may want to do this when you're working on an especially large workbook and you find that AutoRecover takes so long that it interrupts your work.

Choosing the Default File Location

Last, check the folder shown in the **Default file location** text box. This is the folder in which the program suggests saving your documents. If you find you frequently need to change to a different folder in the **Save As** dialog box, you may want to change the default location. Click the **Browse** button to display the **Modify Location** dialog box, click the folder, and then click the **OK** button.

Summary

In this chapter, you learned how to make the Office programs work your way. You now know how to put the commands you use most frequently on the Quick Access Toolbar and Ribbon, create custom keyboard shortcuts for commands you prize in Word, and customize the status bar with the controls and information you find most useful. You also learned to set essential **General** options and **Save** options.

Part **IV**

Chapter 7

Entering and Editing Text in Your Documents

In this chapter, we'll look at how to work quickly with text in your Word documents by using the extra features that Word provides. We'll start by creating a document. We'll then go over three ways to enter text quickly in documents: by inserting the contents of a file, by using the AutoText feature, and by creating formatted AutoCorrect entries. We'll move along to selecting text and navigating through your documents before delving into how to tell Word where to find your templates and how to make Word automatically create backups of your documents in case things go wrong.

Toward the end of the chapter, I'll show you how to work the smart way by using Word's five views to suit the work you're doing and by opening extra windows as needed. You'll also learn how to split a single document window into two panes so that you can see different parts of the same document in them, and how to use the Navigation pane to move quickly through a document.

Creating and Saving a New Document

To create a new document in Word, you use the **New** pane in **Backstage** view as you learned in Chapter 1: "Meeting the Office Programs and Learning What They Do." As you can see in Figure 7–1, you can create a document in six main ways using the templates on your PC:

- *Blank document.* This document has no contents, so you can create whichever type of document you need. But often, you can create a document quicker by using one of Word's templates to insert part of the content for you.

- *Blog post.* This document is set up to help you quickly create a blog post and publish it to your blog.

- *Document based on a template you've used recently.* Clicking **Recent templates** gives you quick access to templates you've used for your last few documents.

- *Document based on one of Word's sample templates.* Clicking **Sample templates** opens the list of templates that come with Word.

- *Document based on one of your templates.* Clicking **My templates** opens the **New** dialog box, which shows the templates in your templates folders.

- *Document based on an existing document.* Clicking **New from existing** opens the **New from Existing Document** dialog box. You can then pick the document on which you want to base the new document. This gives you an easy way to reuse an existing document without the risk of overwriting its existing contents. You run this risk if you open the document intending to use the **File ➤ Save As** command to save it under a new name, but give the Save command instead.

> **NOTE:** If you don't have a suitable template on your PC, see if you can find one on the Office.com website. Use the **Office.com Templates** area in the **New** pane in **Backstage** view to browse or search for a template. To browse, double-click the category of templates you want to see. To search, click in the Search box, type a search term (for example, **resume** or **report**), and then press Enter. If you find a suitable template, download it to your PC so that you can base a document on it.

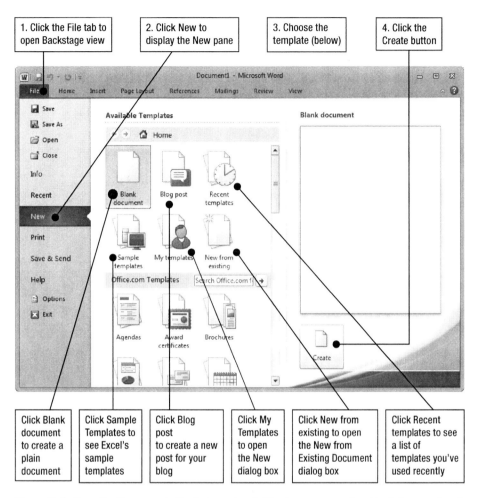

1. Click the File tab to open Backstage view

2. Click New to display the New pane

3. Choose the template (below)

4. Click the Create button

Click Blank document to create a plain document

Click Sample Templates to see Excel's sample templates

Click Blog post to create a new post for your blog

Click My Templates to open the New dialog box

Click New from existing to open the New from Existing Document dialog box

Click Recent templates to see a list of templates you've used recently

Figure 7–1. *From the **New** pane in **Backstage** view in Word, you can create a blank document, a document based on a template, or a document based on an existing document.*

After creating a new document, save it like this:

1. Click the **Save** button on the Quick Access Toolbar or press **Ctrl+S** to display the **Save As** dialog box.

2. Select the folder in which you want to save the document.

3. Type the name you want to give the document.

4. If colleagues using versions of Word that cannot open the new Word Document format will need to use the document, open the **Save As Type** drop-down list and click **Word 97–2003 Document**.

5. Click the **Save** button. Word saves the document.

TIP: The Word Document format uses the `.docx` file extension. Word 2010 for Windows, Word 2007 for Windows, Word 2011 for Mac, and Word 2008 for Mac can all open this format with you needing to add any file converter software. Word 2003 for Windows and Word 2004 for Mac can open this format if you install converter files. Older versions of Word cannot open this format.

Entering Text in Your Word Documents

Most Word documents you create will need text—usually plenty of it. To create the documents quickly, you'll want to enter text as quickly and efficiently as possible.

You can enter text using the techniques explained in Chapter 3: "Working with Text." They are:

- Type the text.

- Paste the text in from another source.

- Scan a hard-copy document and use optical character recognition (OCR) to get the text from it.

- Use voice recognition to transcribe what you dictate.

- Use AutoCorrect to turn short entries into longer replacement text.

You can also use three Word-only features to enter text quickly:

- *Insert a file.* You can insert a whole file or document in another document.

- *Use AutoText.* AutoText is a tool for inserting preexisting blocks of text or other objects, such as shapes or graphics.

- *Use formatted AutoCorrect entries.* Word shares the text-only AutoCorrect entries with the other Office programs, but you can also create formatted AutoCorrect entries that belong only to Word. Formatted AutoCorrect entries enable you to insert larger sections of text at once, with or without formatting. You can also include other objects, such as tables, equations, or graphics.

Inserting the Contents of a File in a Document

If another document contains the text (and other objects) you need in a document you're creating, you can open that document, select and copy the contents, and then paste them into the new document. But using the Text from File command is even easier. Follow these steps:

1. Place the insertion point where you want to insert the text.

TIP: Needs vary, but inserting a file tends to be most useful in two particular circumstances. First, when you've created the individual sections of a report or chapters of a book in separate documents, and you then need to put the whole report or book together. Second, when you create structured documents built up of existing chunks that you deliberately save in separate documents.

2. Choose **Insert ➤ Text**, click the **Object** drop-down button, and then select Text from File from the drop-down menu, as shown in Figure 7–2. Word displays the **Insert File** dialog box.

Figure 7–2. *To quickly insert the entire contents of a file, position the insertion point, and then choose **Insert ➤ Text ➤ Object ➤ Text from File**.*

3. Navigate to the document you want to insert, and then click on it.

4. Click the **Insert** button. Word inserts the document's contents.

Inserting Preexisting Blocks of Text with AutoText

The next feature for inserting preexisting blocks of text in your documents is AutoText. This feature provides an easy way to store chunks of text and other objects so that you can quickly reuse them in your documents. Rather than replacing text automatically as AutoCorrect does, AutoText inserts items only when you tell it to—but you can have Word automatically prompt you to insert available AutoText entries.

An AutoText entry consists of as much text as needed, plus any other objects, such as graphics or tables. Word includes various AutoText entries as part of its Building Blocks that lets you quickly insert elements such as headers and footers, tables, cover pages, and text boxes. You can also create your own AutoText entries to insert exactly the content you need. We'll start by looking at how to create your own AutoText entries and then look at how to insert them in documents.

Creating Your Own AutoText Entries

To create an AutoText entry, select the text or other objects, and then choose **Insert ➤ Text ➤ Quick Parts ➤ AutoText ➤ Save Selection to AutoText Gallery**, as shown in Figure 7–3.

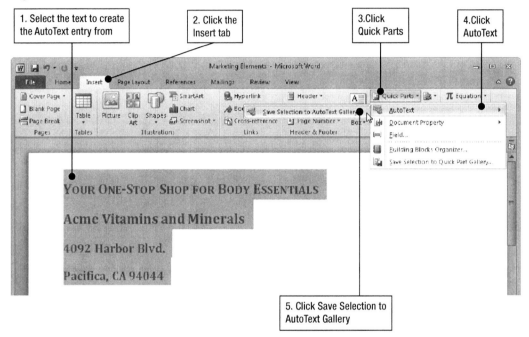

Figure 7–3. You can quickly create an AutoText entry from selected text or other objects.

When you click **Save Selection to AutoText Gallery**, Word displays the **Create New Building Block** dialog box. Set up the entry as explained in Figure 7–4, and then click the **OK** button.

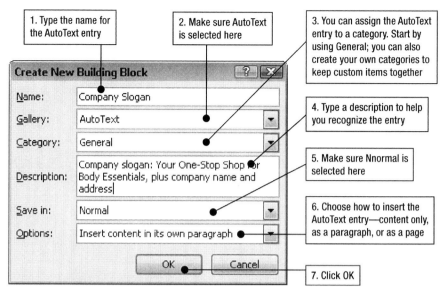

Figure 7–4. *In the **Create New Building Block** dialog box, name the new entry, choose where to store it and how to insert it, and give it a description to make it easily identifiable.*

TIP: When creating an AutoText entry, pay most attention to the name, description, and options settings. The **Name** gives you a quick way to enter the entry, as you'll see in a minute, so make it memorable. Use the **Description** field to make clear what the AutoText entry contains and to differentiate it from other, similar entries. The **Options** drop-down list lets you choose among the **Insert content only**, **Insert content in its own paragraph**, and **Insert content in its own page settings**. Choose **Insert content only** when you want the AutoText entry to drop into the existing paragraph. Choose **Insert content in its own paragraph** when you want the entry to go in as its own paragraph always; this is useful for separate chunks of boilerplate. Choose **Insert content in its own page** when the AutoText entry contains one or more full pages.

Inserting an AutoText Entry

The quickest way to insert an AutoText entry is by using the keyboard. Position the insertion point where you want to insert the entry, and then start typing the entry's name. When Word displays a ScreenTip containing the first part of the AutoText entry (see Figure 7–5), press **Enter** to insert it.

Manifold Media Consulting Inc....
4481 Main Street (Press ENTER to Insert)
      oura|

Figure 7–5. *You can insert an AutoText entry by typing the first few letters of its name and then pressing **Enter** when Word displays a ScreenTip showing the entry's details.*

NOTE: If Word doesn't display a ScreenTip prompting you to press **Enter** to insert the AutoText entry, type the whole name (or enough to identify it uniquely) and then press **F3** to enter it.

If you don't remember the name of the AutoText entry you want to insert, insert it using the **Quick Parts** gallery, as shown in Figure 7–6.

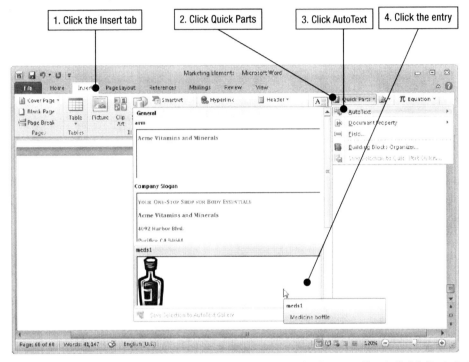

Figure 7–6. *You can browse the list of AutoText entries by choosing **Insert** ➤ Text ➤ **Quick Parts** ➤ AutoText. Click the entry you want to insert.*

Creating Formatted AutoCorrect Entries

As well as creating text-only AutoCorrect entries using the technique you learned in Chapter 2: "Using the Ribbon, Backstage, and Common Tools," you can create AutoCorrect entries that contain formatted text, graphics, tables, or other objects. Formatted AutoCorrect entries are a great tool for entering standard content quickly in your documents.

NOTE: Formatted AutoCorrect entries are available to Word only, whereas text-only AutoCorrect entries are shared among all the Office programs.

To create a formatted AutoCorrect entry, follow these steps:

1. Enter the text or other objects in your document, and format them as you want them to be.

2. Select the text or other objects you want to include in the AutoCorrect entry.

3. Click the **File** tab to open **Backstage** view.

4. Click the **Options** item in the left pane to display the **Word Options** dialog box.

5. Click the **Proofing** category in the left pane to display the **Proofing** options.

6. Click the **AutoCorrect Options** button to display the **AutoCorrect** dialog box.

7. If the **AutoCorrect** tab isn't at the front, click it to display it.

8. Make sure the **Formatted text** option button is selected.

9. In the **Replace** box, type the text you will use to trigger the replacement.

10. Click the **Add** button.

11. Click the **OK** button to close the **AutoCorrect** dialog box.

12. Click the **OK** button to close the **Word Options** dialog box.

Selecting Text and Navigating Through Your Documents

In this section, we'll look at how you can select text quickly with the mouse, move through your documents using keyboard shortcuts, and navigate using the powerful but little-known browse object. You'll also learn the secrets of the vertical scroll bar.

Selecting Text Quickly with the Mouse

Before you can edit, format, or otherwise manipulate text, you usually need to select it. You can select text using the standard Office techniques you learned in Chapter 3: "Working with Text," but Word also provides several shortcuts that are worth knowing.

To select text quickly with the mouse, move the mouse pointer to the left of the text area so that the pointer changes to an arrow pointing up and to the right, as shown in Figure 7–7.

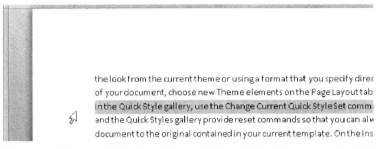

Figure 7–7. *You can select text quickly by clicking, double-clicking, or triple-clicking in the area to the left of the text, where the mouse pointer changes to an arrow pointing up and to the right.*

You can then use this selection pointer like this:

- *Select a line.* Click next to the line you want to select, as in Figure 7–7.

- *Select multiple lines.* Click to place the insertion point anywhere in the line at which you want to begin the selection. Then **Shift+click** in the left margin at the line on which you want to end the selection.

- *Select a paragraph.* Double-click next to the paragraph you want to select.

- *Select the whole document.* Triple-click or **Ctrl+click**.

- *Select a column of text.* When you need to select only part of several lines, such as selecting the first few blank characters at the beginning of several lines, **Alt+drag** with the mouse (see Figure 7–8). When you've selected the text you want, you can format it or delete it.

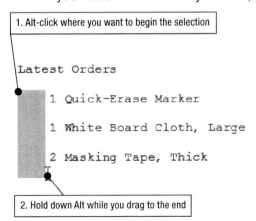

Figure 7–8. *Alt+drag* when you need to select part of the text on each of several lines—for example, to delete unwanted blank space.

| **MEETING THE EXTEND SELECTION FEATURE** |

For selecting text, Word provides an odd feature called Extend Selection. You put Word into Extend mode by pressing **F8**, and you can then continue selecting like this:

- *Keep pressing **F8**.* Press once more to select the current word. Press twice more to select the current sentence. Press three more times to select the current paragraph. Press four more times to select the whole document.

- *Press the character to which you want to extend the selection.* For example, press **M** to extend the selection to the next letter *m*; press **.** (the period key) to extend the selection to the end of the sentence, or press **Enter** to extend the selection to the end of the paragraph.

- *Use the arrow keys.* Press **Right Arrow** to extend the selection by a single character, or press **Left Arrow** to reduce the selection by a single character. Press **Down Arrow** to extend the selection by a line, or press **Up Arrow** to reduce the selection by a line.

- *Use the mouse.* Click or right-click at the point to which you want to extend the selection.

- *Stop selecting.* Press **Esc** when you've finished selecting and want to work with the selection.

Give the Extend Selection feature a try, and see if you find it useful. If not, file it away in the back of your brain for when Word starts selecting text unexpectedly as you type. If this happens, you may have pressed **F8** by accident; if so, press **Esc** to turn off Extend mode and restore normality.

Moving with Keyboard Shortcuts

When you're working in a document, keyboard shortcuts can be the easiest way to move the insertion point quickly and accurately. You can use the standard keyboard shortcuts explained in Table 3-1, earlier in this book; for example, press **Home** to move the insertion point to the beginning of the line, press **End** to move the insertion point to the end of the line, or press **Ctrl+Right arrow** to move the insertion point to the beginning of the next word. But to get the most out of keyboard shortcuts, you'll also want to use the extra ones that Word provides. Table 7–1 has the details.

Table 7–1. *Keyboard Shortcuts for Moving the Insertion Point in Word*

Press These Keys	To Move the Insertion Point Like This
Ctrl+Up Arrow	If the insertion point is in a paragraph, to the start of that paragraph. If the insertion point is at the start of a paragraph, to the start of the previous paragraph.
Ctrl+Down Arrow	To the start of the next paragraph.
Ctrl+Home	To the start of the document.
Ctrl+End	To the end of the document.
Ctrl+Page Down	To the next page (or the next browse object; see the next section).
Ctrl+Page Up	To the previous page (or the previous browse object).

Moving with the Browse Object Panel

To move about a document with the mouse, you can click the scroll arrows or drag the scroll box as usual, but you can also use the three buttons that appear below the vertical scroll bar on the right side of the Word window (see Figure 7–9).

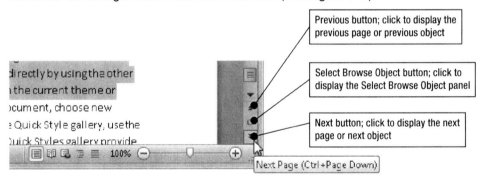

Figure 7–9. *You can navigate quickly around a document by using the **Previous** button, **Next** button, and **Select Browse Object** button at the bottom of the vertical scroll bar.*

You click the **Previous** button to display the next page or next object, or click the **Next** button to display the next page or next object.

At first, when you open a document, the **Previous** button and **Next** button take you to the previous page or next page. To start browsing by another object, click the **Select Browse Object** button to open the **Select Browse Object** panel (see Figure 7–10), and then click the object. For example, click **Table** to start browsing by tables, so when you click the **Next** button, Word takes you to the next table.

NOTE: When you use **Find** or **Replace**, Word automatically changes the browse object to **Find**.

Most of the browse objects are straightforward—tables, graphics, headings, and so on. Here are quick notes on the five that are less obvious:

- *Footnote.* A footnote is a note that appears at the bottom of the page that refers to it.

- *Endnote.* An endnote is a note that appears at the end of a section or of a document.

- *Field.* A field is a placeholder you use to have Word automatically insert a piece of information in the document—for example, the current date.

- *Edits.* The **Edits** browse object lets you move back and forth among the last four edits you've made. You can also move the insertion point to your last four edits by pressing **Shift+F5** once, twice, thrice, or four times.

- *Go To.* The **Go To** browse object lets you move among pages, sections, lines, bookmarks, comments, footnotes, endnotes, fields, tables, graphics, equations, objects, and headings. Choose **Home ➤ Editing ➤ Find ➤ Go To** to display the **Go To** tab of the **Find and Replace** dialog box.

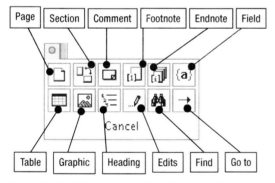

Figure 7–10. *When you need to switch to another browse object, click the **Select Browse Object** button, and then click the object you want on the **Select Browse Object** panel.*

TIP: You can also change the browse object using the keyboard. Press **Ctrl+Alt+Home** to open the **Select Browse Object** panel from the keyboard, press the arrow keys to select the browse object, and press **Enter** to close the panel and start browsing by that object. You can then press **Ctrl+Page Down** to move to the next instance of the browse object or **Ctrl+Page Up** to move to the previous instance.

Learning the Secrets of the Vertical Scroll Bar

The vertical scroll bar at the right side of the Word window looks pretty standard, but it has several extra tricks up its sleeve. First, as you click and drag the scroll box (also called the *thumb*) up or down, Word displays a ScreenTip showing the current page number and the nearest heading, to help you navigate. Figure 7–11 shows an example.

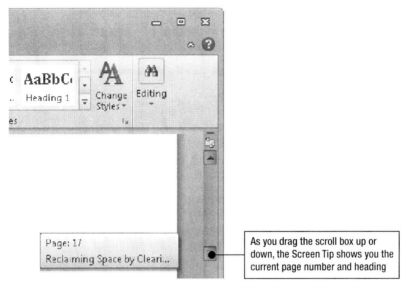

As you drag the scroll box up or down, the Screen Tip shows you the current page number and heading

Figure 7–11. *To help you navigate long documents, Word displays a ScreenTip containing the current page number and heading.*

Second, instead of dragging the scroll box, you can also navigate by clicking the buttons, clicking in the scroll bar above or below the box, or right-clicking the scroll bar and using the context menu. Figure 7–12 explains what you can do.

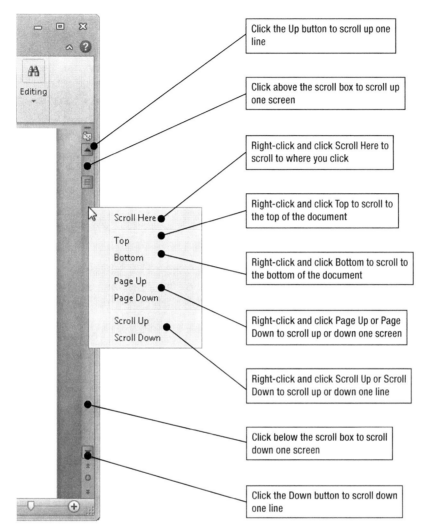

Figure 7–12. *You can navigate quickly up and down a document by clicking or right-clicking the vertical scroll bar.*

Creating Your Own Templates

As you saw at the beginning of this chapter, you use a template to jump-start creating the type of document you want. Word comes with various templates that appear in the **New** pane when you open **Backstage** view, but you will likely want also to develop your own templates for letters, reports, and so on. You may also want to use templates your colleagues create.

In this section, we'll look first at creating a template. I'll then show you how to tell Word where to find your templates if you store them in a different folder than the **Templates** folder Word provides for you.

Creating a Template

To create a template, create a new document as described earlier in this chapter. If you want complete freedom of action in the template, create a blank document; if you can save time by basing the new template on an existing template, create a document based on the most suitable template.

Set up the new document with the content and formatting the template needs. This depends on what the template is for, but here's a quick example: for a memo template, you'll typically add fields such as To, From, Subject, and Date, lay them out with plenty of space, and format them so that they're easy to read.

When you're ready to save the template, click the **Save** button on the Quick Access Toolbar to display the **Save As** dialog box. You can then work as explained in Figure 7–13.

> **NOTE:** Figure 7–13 shows you how to save a template in the **Templates** folder that Word provides. This is usually the easiest place to store templates you create for your own use. If you prefer to store your templates in another folder, follow the procedure described in the next section to tell Word where to find the templates.

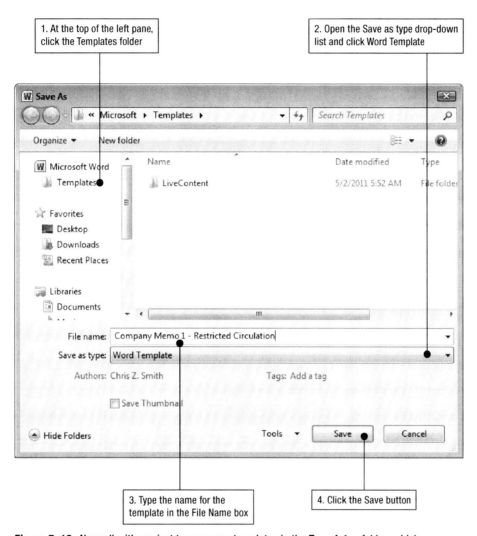

1. At the top of the left pane, click the Templates folder

2. Open the Save as type drop-down list and click Word Template

3. Type the name for the template in the File Name box

4. Click the Save button

Figure 7–13. *Normally, it's easiest to save your templates in the **Templates** folder, which you can access under the Microsoft Word item at the top of the left pane in the **Save As** dialog box.*

Telling Word Where to Find Your Templates

Word uses two template folders, the User templates folder and the Workgroup templates folder. When you install Office, the installer automatically sets the **User templates** folder for you to a folder on your PC. This is the folder that appears as **Templates** in the left pane of the **Save As** dialog box. If you choose to store your templates elsewhere, you can change the folder that Word uses. You need to do this to make your custom templates appear in the **New** dialog box, where you can easily start documents based on them.

For a normal installation, the installer normally does not set the **Workgroup templates** folder. If you share templates with others on your network, you can set the Workgroup templates folder manually to point to this folder by using the technique described in this section.

To change your templates folders, follow these steps:

1. Click the **File** tab to open **Backstage** view.

2. Click the **Options** item in the left column to display the **Word Options** dialog box.

3. In the left column, click the **Advanced** category to display the **Advanced** pane.

4. Scroll down all the way to the bottom of the pane.

5. Click the **File Locations** button to display the **File Locations** dialog box (see Figure 7–14).

6. In the **File types** list box, click the **User templates** item.

7. Click the **Modify** button to display the **Modify Location** dialog box.

> **TIP:** If you need to open the folder in a Windows Explorer window so that you can move your templates to it, click the address box in the **Modify Location** dialog box. Word displays the folder path (for example, `C:\Users\Jan\AppData\Roaming\Microsoft\Templates`) and selects it. Press **Ctrl+C** or right-click and choose **Copy** to copy the address to the Clipboard. Click the **Start** button, right-click the **Search** box and choose **Paste**, and then press **Enter** to open a Windows Explorer window showing the folder.

8. Select the folder you want to use.

9. Click the **OK** button to close the **Modify Location** dialog box.

10. Click the **OK** button to close the **File Locations** dialog box.

11. Click the **OK** button to close the **Word Options** dialog box.

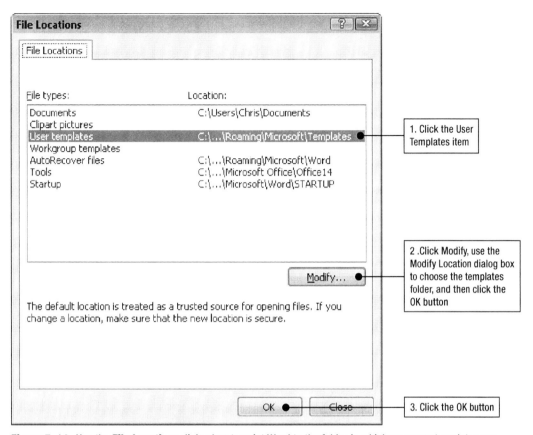

Figure 7–14. *Use the* **File Locations** *dialog box to point Word to the folder in which your user templates are stored. You can also set the* **Workgroup Templates** *folder.*

Setting Word to Create Backup Documents Automatically

When you're working fast in Word, it's easy to delete large amounts of text by mistake. For example, if you select text inadvertently instead of moving the insertion point, you can then type over the text, deleting it. If you save the document before you notice the problem, the text is gone.

To help you recover from such disasters, Word can automatically back up the active document each time you save it. For safety, you should turn on this feature. Click the **File** tab to open **Backstage** view, click the **Options** item to display the **Word Options** dialog box, and then follow the steps shown in Figure 7–15.

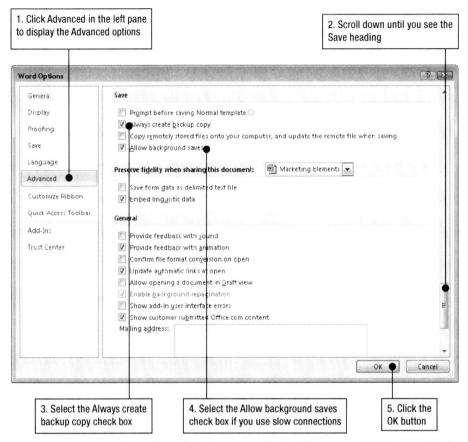

1. Click Advanced in the left pane to display the Advanced options

2. Scroll down until you see the Save heading

3. Select the Always create backup copy check box

4. Select the Allow background saves check box if you use slow connections

5. Click the OK button

Figure 7–15. *For protection against editing disasters, select the Always create backup copy check box in the Save category of the Word Options dialog box.*

> **NOTE:** If you work with documents on SkyDrive or another drive you access across an Internet connection, you may also want to select the **Copy remotely stored files onto your computer, and update the remote file when saving** check box. This setting makes Word store a working copy of the file on your PC and save changes to it there, then copy the updated file back to the remote drive, instead of saving changes directly to the remote drive. This maneuver helps you avoid losing changes because of interruptions to the Internet connection.

Now that you've selected the **Always create backup copy** check box, Word keeps one backup of each document. Here's how it does it:

- The first time you save, Word saves the document as normal. There's no backup.

▓ Each time you save the document after that, Word changes the name of the latest saved version of the document to the backup name, and then saves the current version under the document name.

Word names the backup file *Backup of* and the document's name, gives it the `.wbk` file extension (which Windows associates with the Microsoft Word Backup Document file type), and keeps it in the same folder as the document. So if you create a document named Merlot Tasting.docx, Word names the backup file Backup of Merlot Tasting.wbk.

RECOVERING YOUR WORK FROM A BACKUP DOCUMENT

If a document becomes corrupted, or if you delete a vital part of it and save the change, you can recover your work by opening the backup document. To open the backup document, follow these steps:

1. Click the **File** tab to open **Backstage** view.

2. Click the **Open** button to display the **Open** dialog box.

3. In the drop-down list above the **Open** button, choose **All Files**.

4. Click the backup document.

5. Click the **Open** button.

After opening the document, you can copy the parts you need, or choose **File ➤ Save As** to save the backup document under a different name.

Working the Smart Way by Using Views and Windows

To work quickly and comfortably in your documents, you need to understand the five different views that Word provides and know when to use each of them. You may also need to open multiple windows on the same document so that you can work in different parts of it. Or you may want to split a single document window into two panes so that you can view the document differently in each.

Choosing the Best View for Your Writing or Editing Tasks

As you'll see in the next few pages, each of Word's five views has a distinct purpose: laying out text and other elements, developing the outline of the document, reading a document, and so on. You can switch freely from view to view as you need for the documents you're working on and the tasks you're performing on them.

Switching Views

You can switch views in three ways:

■ *Status bar*. Click the five View Shortcuts buttons on the status bar (see Figure 7–16).

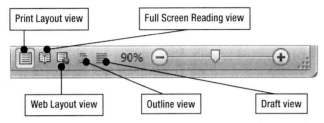

Figure 7–16. *Click the **View Shortcuts** buttons at the right end of the status bar to change view quickly using the mouse.*

■ *Ribbon.* Click the **View** tab, go to the **Document Views** group, and then click the button for the view you want (see Figure 7–17).

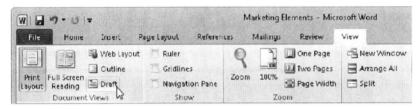

Figure 7–17. *You can also change views by using the buttons in the **Document Views** group on the **View** tab of the Ribbon.*

■ *Keyboard.* Press **Ctrl+Alt+P** for Print Layout view, **Ctrl+Alt+O** for Outline view, and **Ctrl+Alt+N** for Draft view (which used to be called Normal view).

Laying Out a Document with Print Layout View

When you first open a document, Word usually displays it in Print Layout view. This view (see Figure 7–18) shows you the document as it will appear on paper. You can see each printable element in the document—text, tables, graphics, equations, and so on—in the positions they occupy on the page, along with the white space of the page margins. If you have added headers or footers to the document, you see them too.

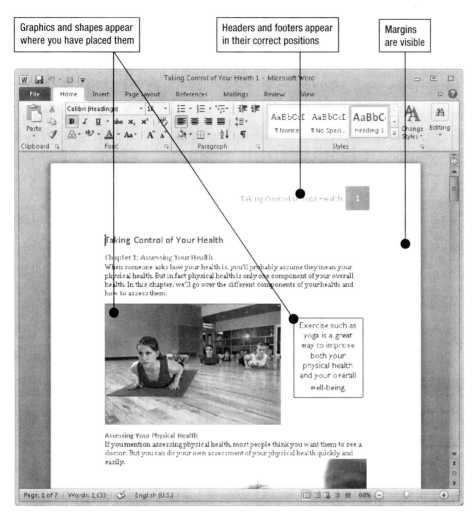

Graphics and shapes appear where you have placed them

Headers and footers appear in their correct positions

Margins are visible

Figure 7–18. *Print Layout view shows the document with headers and footers, margins, and graphics all in the positions they occupy on paper.*

Viewing a Document Easily with Full Screen Reading View

When you need to see as much of a document as possible, either for reading it or for editing it, switch to Full Screen Reading view. In Full Screen Reading view (see Figure 7–19), Word maximizes the window and hides the Ribbon and displays only essential controls on the Quick Access Toolbar, dedicating as much space as possible to the document. Word displays two screens of the document as large as they will go, shifting elements as needed to make the text readable and the elements visible.

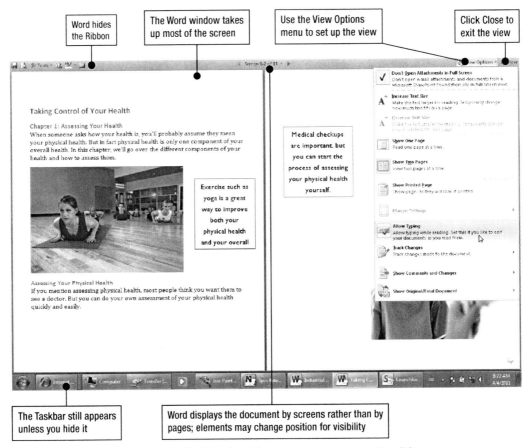

Word hides the Ribbon

The Word window takes up most of the screen

Use the View Options menu to set up the view

Click Close to exit the view

The Taskbar still appears unless you hide it

Word displays the document by screens rather than by pages; elements may change position for visibility

Figure 7–19. *You can use Full Screen Reading view either to read a document or to edit it.*

Use the View Options drop-down menu to set Full Screen Reading view up so that it's comfortable for you. These are the changes you'll most likely need:

- *Change the font size.* Use the Increase Text Size command or the Decrease Text Size command to make the font bigger or smaller as needed. You may need to give the same command several times in sequence to get the effect you want.

- *Switch between one page and two pages.* Click the Show One Page button or the Show Two Pages button.

- *View the document as it will print.* Click the Show Printed Page command. Unless you have a large monitor, the text may be too small to read comfortably (this is why Full Screen Reading view changes the layout).

- *Enable typing.* In Full Screen Reading view, typing is disabled at first. Click the Allow Typing button if you want to turn it on.

When you finish using Full Screen Reading view, click the Close button in the upper-right corner of the screen. Word returns the document to the view you were using before.

Using Web Layout View to Get a Preview of Web Pages

Web Layout view (see Figure 7–20) shows you how the document will look if you save it as a web page. Word hides all the items that don't appear on web pages—headers and footers, margins, and page breaks—and wraps the lines to the width of the window, just as a web browser does.

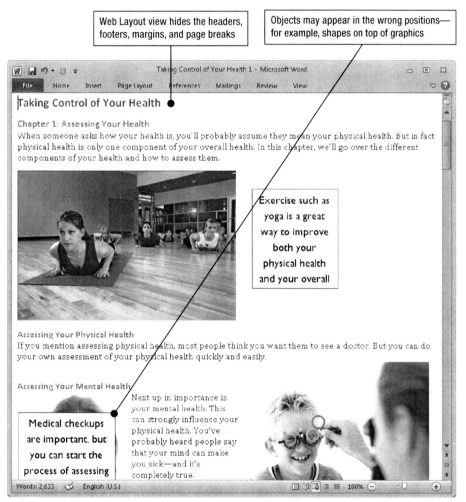

Figure 7–20. *Web Layout view displays the page as if it were in a web browser, with no headers and footers, margins, or page breaks. Objects may shift to unsuitable positions.*

> **TIP:** Although Word can save documents as web pages, Word is not really designed for creating web pages. If you are planning to create a web site, seriously consider using a web-design program rather than Word.

Developing a Document in Outline View

Outline view (see Figure 7–21) is a powerful tool for developing the outline and structure of a document. Outline view displays the document as a structure of headings, each of which you can collapse or expand as needed. See Chapter 9: "Adding Headers, Footers, Tables, and Columns" for instructions on using Outline view.

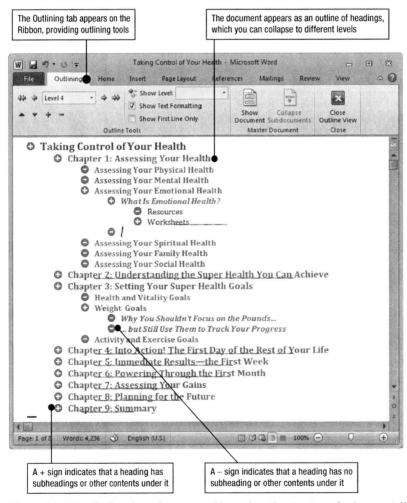

The Outlining tab appears on the Ribbon, providing outlining tools

The document appears as an outline of headings, which you can collapse to different levels

A + sign indicates that a heading has subheadings or other contents under it

A – sign indicates that a heading has no subheading or other contents under it

Figure 7–21. *Use Outline view when you need to work on the structure of a document. You can expand different sections of the document to different levels as needed.*

Entering and Editing Text Quickly in Draft View

Draft view, which used to be called Normal view, is the best view for entering or editing the body text of a document. In Draft view, Word displays all the text but hides headers and footers, margins, and objects. Figure 7–22 shows a sample document in Draft view.

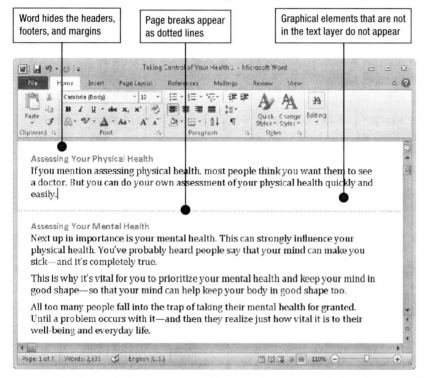

Figure 7–22. *Use Draft view when you need to concentrate on the text of the document without seeing the page's layout or elements such as headers and footers.*

Opening Extra Windows to See More of the Same Document

At first, Word displays a single window of each document. For short documents, this is all you need, but for long or complex documents, you can work faster by opening extra windows so that you can see two or more parts of the document at once or use different views at the same time.

Opening Another Window Showing the Same Document

To open a new window, choose **View ➤ Window ➤ New Window**. Word adds **: 1** to the document's name in the title bar of the original window to indicate that it's now the first window of the document. The second window's name includes : 2—for example, **Linguistics Report: 2**.

Arranging the Windows of a Document

To arrange the windows of a document, click and drag the windows to where you need them.

> **TIP:** To arrange a document's windows side by side, minimize all other windows, right-click the notification area, and then choose **Show Windows Side by Side** from the context menu. Don't use Word's **View ➤ Window ➤ Arrange All** command, because it tiles the windows horizontally, which is seldom helpful.

To switch to another window, click the window if you can see it. If not, choose **View ➤ Window ➤ Switch Windows**, and then click the window you want.

> **TIP:** Press **Ctrl+F6** or **Alt+F6** to display the next window (of any open Word document, not just the one that has multiple windows open). Press **Ctrl+Shift+F6** or **Alt+Shift+F6** to display the previous window.

Closing a Window of a Document

To close a window, click its **Close** button (the x button). The document remains open until you close its last window; if the document contains unsaved changes at that point, Word prompts you to save them.

Splitting the Document Window into Two Panes

Another way of working in two parts of the same document at once is to split the document window into two panes. Splitting the document window is like opening a new window except that you don't need more space, so it's good when you're short of space—for example, when you're using a netbook.

To split the document window, click the split box above the vertical scroll bar, and then drag it down until the window is split as you want (see Figure 7–23). You can also double-click the split box to split the window into two equal parts, and then adjust the split by dragging the split bar up or down as needed.

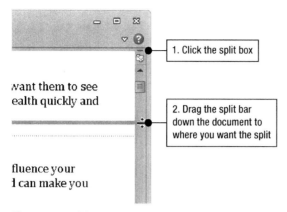

1. Click the split box

2. Drag the split bar down the document to where you want the split

vant them to see ealth quickly and

fluence your 1 can make you

Figure 7–23. *Click the split box above the vertical scroll bar and drag it down to split the window.*

> **TIP:** You can also split the window by choosing **View ➤ Window ➤ Split** or by pressing **Ctrl+Alt+S**. Press the **Up arrow** or **Down arrow** to move the split bar to where you want it, and then press **Enter** to lock it in place.

Once you've split the window (as shown in Figure 7–24), you can scroll each pane separately, so you can display a different part of the document in each pane. You can also use a different view in each pane—for example, display the document's outline in Outline view in one pane while you write the introduction or summary in Normal view in the other pane.

To switch to the other pane, click in it. You can also press **F6** to move the insertion point to the next pane.

> **TIP:** You can also zoom out in one pane to get an overview of the document as a whole, and zoom in using the other pane so that you can see the detail of a section.

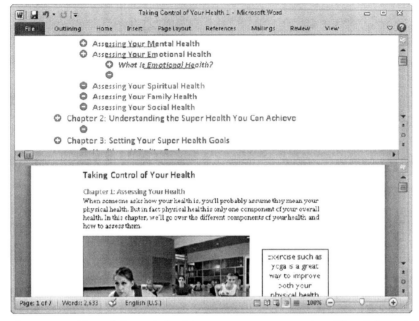

Figure 7–24. *After splitting a window into two panes, you can use two different views at once or work in different parts of the document.*

When you want to remove the split, take one of these actions:

- *Mouse.* Double-click the split bar. Alternatively, drag it to the top (to keep the lower pane) or to the bottom (to keep the upper pane).

- *Keyboard.* Press **Ctrl+Alt+S**.

- *Ribbon.* Choose **View ➤ Window ➤ Remove Split**.

Navigating Your Documents Quickly with the Navigation Pane

To move quickly around your documents, you can use the **Navigation** pane. Choose **View ➤ Show ➤ Navigation Pane**, selecting the **Navigation Pane** check box, to display the **Navigation** pane (see Figure 7–25).

> **NOTE:** At first, the **Navigation** pane appears at the left side of the Word window, docked to the window. If you prefer to have the **Navigation** pane on the right side of the window, simply drag it there. If you want to position the Navigation pane freely, drag it off the side of the window, so that it appears as a floating pane. You can then drag it to where you need it.

Selected the Navigation Pane check box to display the Navigation pane

Hold the mouse pointer over a heading to display a Screen Tip showing the full text

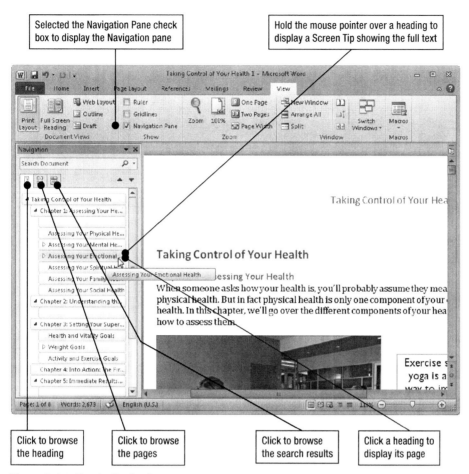

Click to browse the heading

Click to browse the pages

Click to browse the search results

Click a heading to display its page

Figure 7–25. *Use the* **Navigation** *pane to move around your documents quickly. You can navigate by headings, by pages, or by search results.*

Click the **Pages** tab near the top of the **Navigation** pane if you want to browse your document by pages, as shown on the left in Figure 7–26.

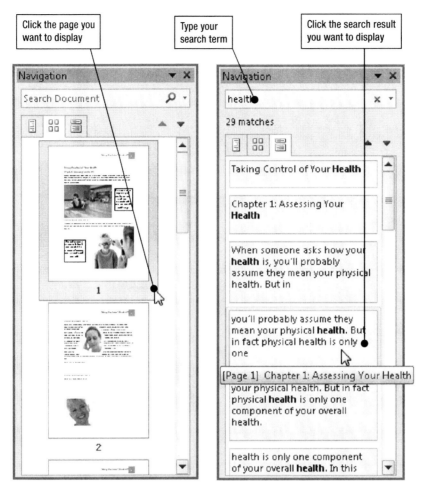

Figure 7–26. *To browse the document's pages, click the **Pages** tab in the **Navigation** pane. To browse by search results, click the **Search Results** tab, and then type your search term in the **Search** box.*

TIP: You can search using any of the tabs in the **Navigation** pane. After you search, the **Headings** tab highlights any headings that match the search, and the **Pages** tab shows only the pages that match the search. Click the **X** button in the **Search** box when you want to clear the search.

When you have finished using the **Navigation** pane, click the **Close** button (the × button) to close it.

> **TIP:** You can quickly cycle through the last three edits in the document by pressing **Shift+F5** one, two, or three times. Press a fourth time to go back to the last position of the insertion point before you pressed **Shift+F5**.

Summary

In this chapter, you learned how to work quickly with text in your documents by using Word-specific features. You now know how to enter text quickly by inserting the contents of a file, by using the AutoText feature, and by using formatted AutoCorrect entries.

We examined how to set up Word to display your custom templates in the **New** pane in **Backstage** view; how to make Word automatically create backups of your documents as a safety measure; and how to use views, windows, and splitting to work quickly and efficiently in your documents. You also know how to use the Navigation pane to move through your documents.

In the next chapter, I'll show you how to format your documents.

Chapter 8

Formatting Your Documents Easily and Efficiently

To make your documents look professional or persuasive, you'll need to format them. In this chapter, you learn how to format your documents easily and efficiently by using Word's styles, how to create custom styles of your own, and how to modify existing styles. You'll also learn how to apply direct formatting on top of styles to create special effects where you need them.

When you simply need a minimal amount of formatting to change the look of a document, you can use direct formatting without worrying about styles. For example, if you're writing a short menu, you may just need to apply italics to a product name to make it stand out. In this case, you can apply the direct formatting using the tools you meet in the section "Creating Custom Styles" in this chapter.

Why You Should Use Styles Rather Than Direct Formatting

In Word, the best and fastest way to format your documents is by using styles rather than by applying direct formatting such as boldface or a font. A *style* is a collection of formatting that you can apply with a single click of a mouse or with a keystroke. For example, Figure 8–1 shows a short section of text that uses four styles:

- *Heading 1*. This style uses 20-point Cambria font, dark blue color, and boldface to stand out. The paragraph has 24 points of space before it, which helps to draw the reader's eye to it. You'd use this style for the top-level headings in the document.

- *Body Text.* This style uses 11-point Calibri font in black, so it looks like standard text. The paragraph has 6 points of space after it, so that the paragraphs don't touch each other. You'd use this style for the body text paragraphs of the document.

- *List Bullet.* This style uses the same font formatting as the Body Text style, but has a bullet point applied to each paragraph, with a hanging indent that keeps the bullet out to the left of the text. The paragraph has no extra space between paragraphs of the same style but extra space when the next paragraph has a different style, as you can see if you look at the extra space after the second bulleted paragraph. You'd use this style for first-level bulleted lists (there are other styles for bulleted sub-lists that have larger indents to indicate they're subordinate)

- *Heading 2.* This style has 14-point Cambria font, light blue color, and boldface, so it looks related to the Heading 1 style, but is subordinate to it. The paragraph has 10 points of space after it. You'd use this style for the second-level headings in the document.

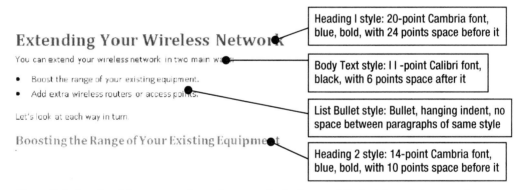

Figure 8–1. *By using styles, you can give each paragraph of a document the look it needs in moments.*

Word's Normal template, which is the template on which Word bases blank documents, and most other templates contain a wide variety of built-in styles. You can either use these styles as they are to format your documents quickly and consistently or customize the styles so that they look exactly as you want them to.

> ## UNDERSTANDING WORD'S FIVE TYPES OF STYLES
>
> Word has five different types of styles:
>
> 1. *Paragraph style.* This is a style you apply to a whole paragraph at a time. A paragraph style contains a full range of formatting for that paragraph—everything from the font name, size, and color through to the indentation and spacing for the paragraph, and the language used.
>
> 2. *Character style.* This is a style that you apply to individual characters within a paragraph, usually to make it look different from the style of the rest of the paragraph. For example, within a paragraph that uses the Body Text style, you can apply an Emphasis character style to a word to make it stand out.
>
> 3. *Linked paragraph and character style.* This is a style that works either for a paragraph as a whole or for individual characters within a paragraph. Word applies the linked style as a paragraph style if you either place the insertion point in the paragraph or select the whole of the paragraph. If you select just part of the paragraph, Word applies the style as a character style. Both the paragraphs formatted with the paragraph style and the text formatted with the character style appear at the same level in the table of contents. (Word uses styles to control which paragraphs or other text appear in the table of contents.)
>
> 4. *Table style.* This is a style you can apply to a Word table. Like a paragraph style, the style can contain font and paragraph formatting, but it can also contain table formatting such as borders and shading.
>
> 5. *List style.* This is a style you can apply to one or more paragraphs to make them into a list—a numbered list, a bulleted list, or a multilevel list. A list style usually contains font formatting and numbering formatting.

When you have applied styles to the paragraphs and other elements in your documents, you can quickly make three types of changes:

- *Apply the same style from a different set.* Some Word templates include different sets of styles called Quick Styles. Each set contains styles with the same names but different looks. You can change the set of Quick Styles the document is using, changing the look of each styled paragraph or element in moments.

- *Modify the style.* If the style doesn't look right, you can modify it. Each paragraph to which you've applied the style takes on the changes you make immediately. You don't have to reapply the style.

- *Replace one style with another style.* You can replace every instance of one style with another style in moments, making sweeping changes right through a document.

Applying Styles to a Document

The easiest way to get started with styles is to apply styles by using the **Quick Styles** gallery on the **Home** tab of the Ribbon as shown in Figure 8–2. Click in a paragraph to apply the style only to that paragraph, or click and drag through several paragraphs to apply the style to them all. Then choose the style from the **Quick Styles** gallery.

> **NOTE:** If the style you need appears in the **Quick Styles** box, you can simply click it there instead of opening the **Quick Styles** gallery. You can also click the up button or the down button to display other styles in the **Quick Styles** box without opening the **Quick Styles** gallery.

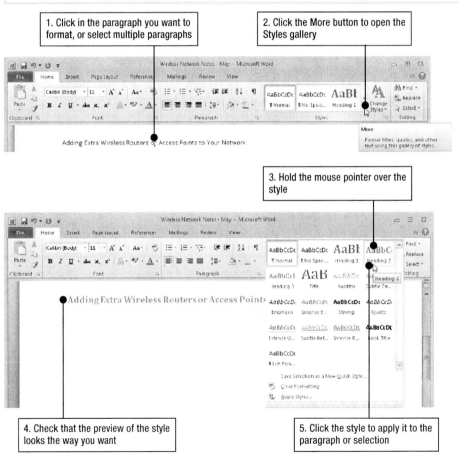

1. Click in the paragraph you want to format, or select multiple paragraphs

2. Click the More button to open the Styles gallery

3. Hold the mouse pointer over the style

4. Check that the preview of the style looks the way you want

5. Click the style to apply it to the paragraph or selection

Figure 8–2. *You can quickly apply a style to a paragraph or selected paragraphs by using the **Quick Styles** gallery on the **Home** tab of the Ribbon.*

NOTE: If Word doesn't display a preview of the style when you hold the mouse pointer over the style name, click the **File** tab to open **Backstage** view, and then click **Options**. In the **General** pane of the **Word Options** dialog box, select the **Enable Live Preview** check box, and then click the **OK** button.

Changing to a Different Set of Quick Styles

Once you have given each paragraph the style it needs, and applied character styles, list styles, and table styles as needed, you've defined what the different parts of the text are—headings, body text, lists, and so on. You can now quickly change the whole look of the document by applying a different set of quick styles, as shown in Figure 8–3.

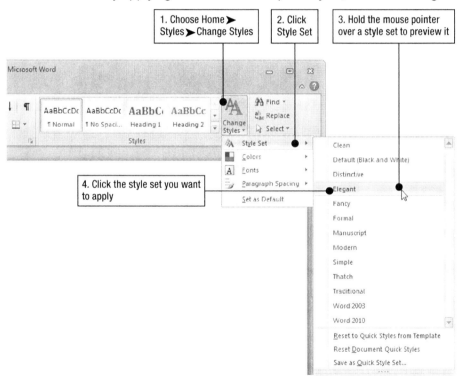

Figure 8–3. *Use the **Home ➤ Styles ➤ Change Styles ➤ Style Set** command to change to a different set of quick styles, giving the document a different look.*

NOTE: If you want to use the Quick Style look you've chosen as your standard look, choose **Home ➤ Styles ➤ Change Styles ➤ Set as Default**.

Changing the Colors, Fonts, or Paragraph Spacing

When you want to change the document's look without going as far as to switch to a different set of quick styles, you can change the colors, fonts, or paragraph spacing used by the styles. Choose **Home ➤ Styles ➤ Change Styles**; click **Colors**, **Fonts**, or **Paragraph Spacing** on the **Change Styles** gallery, and then use the **Colors** gallery (shown on the left in Figure 8–4), the **Fonts** gallery (shown in the center in Figure 8–4), or the **Paragraph Spacing** gallery (shown on the right in Figure 8–4) to make the changes you want.

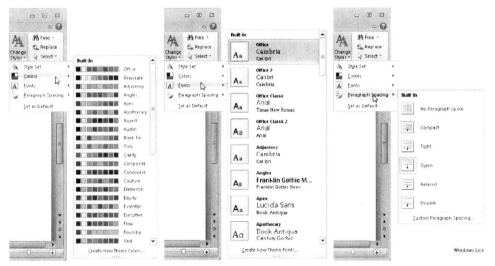

Figure 8–4. *From the Change Styles gallery, you can quickly change the document's color set (left), the font families (center), or the paragraph spacing (right).*

Putting the Styles You Need in the Quick Styles Gallery

By default, the **Quick Styles** gallery contains widely useful styles, such as **Heading 1**, **Heading 2**, **Heading 3**, **Title**, and **Emphasis**. You can remove styles you don't need and add other styles you find useful.

Removing a Style from the Quick Styles Gallery

To remove a style from the Quick Style gallery, right-click the style, and then click **Remove from Quick Styles Gallery** on the context menu, as shown in Figure 8–5. This just removes the style from the **Quick Styles Gallery**, not from the template as a whole. You can still access the style using the other style tools, which you'll meet shortly.

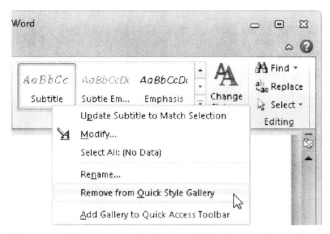

Figure 8–5. *To remove a style from the **Quick Styles** gallery, right-click the style, and then click **Remove from Quick Styles Gallery**.*

Adding an Existing Style to the Quick Styles Gallery

To add an existing style to the Quick Styles gallery, open the Styles pane, right-click the style, and then click **Add to Quick Styles Gallery**. Figure 8–6 shows you how to do this.

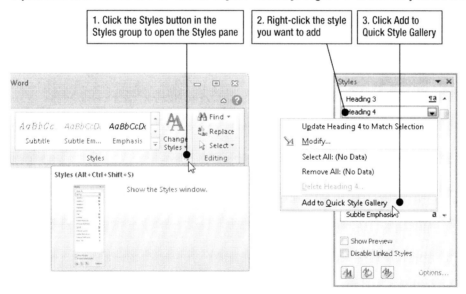

Figure 8–6. *You can quickly add an existing style to the **Quick Style** gallery from the **Styles** pane.*

Creating a New Style and Adding It to the Quick Styles Gallery

When none of the existing styles suits your needs, you can create a new style and add it to the **Quick Styles** gallery. Follow these steps:

1. Format some text with the formatting you want the new style to have.

2. Choose **Home ➤ Styles ➤ More ➤ Save Selection as a New Quick Style**. Word displays the **Create New Style** from **Formatting** dialog box shown in Figure 8–7.

*Figure 8–7. Use this **Create New Style** from Formatting dialog box to create a **Quick Style** from formatting and add the style to the **Quick Style** gallery.*

3. In the **Name** text box, type the name for the style.

4. Click the **OK** button. Word creates the style and adds it to the **Quick Style** gallery.

NOTE: This is the quick way to create a style. I'm showing it to you now because it enables you to add a style to the **Quick Style** gallery easily. Later in the chapter, you'll learn the full way to create a style.

Applying Styles Using the Apply Styles Pane

If you find the **Quick Style** gallery awkward to use, or if you like to keep the Ribbon hidden, you may prefer to use the **Apply Styles** pane (see Figure 8–8) to apply styles. To open this pane, click the **Styles** drop-down button, and then click **Apply Styles** at the bottom of the **Styles** pane.

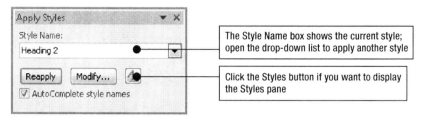

Figure 8–8. *The **Apply Styles** pane can be a handy tool for applying styles if you prefer to keep the Ribbon hidden. You can click the **Styles** button to display the **Styles** pane when you need to manipulate styles.*

Here's how to use the **Apply Styles** pane:

- *Check the style name.* The **Style Name** box in the **Apply Styles** pane shows the style applied to the current paragraph. If you have selected multiple paragraphs with different styles, the **Style Name** box shows the style applied to the last paragraph.

- *Apply another style.* Open the **Style Name** drop-down list, and then click the style you want to apply. To jump quickly to a style name, type its first letters.

- *Reapply the same style, removing any extra formatting.* Click the **Reapply** button.

- *Open the Styles pane.* Click the **Styles** button (the button with the **AA** icon).

- *Close the Apply Styles pane.* Click the **Close** button (the × button).

Applying Styles Using Keyboard Shortcuts

You can also apply styles by using keyboard shortcuts, which is useful when you want to keep your hands on the keyboard as you work. Table 8–1 shows standard keyboard shortcuts, which work in Word's Normal template and in many other templates.

Table 8–1. *Standard Keyboard Shortcuts for Applying Styles in Word*

Style	Keyboard Shortcut
Normal	Ctrl+Shift+N
Heading 1	Ctrl+Alt+1
Heading 2	Ctrl+Alt+2
Heading 3	Ctrl+Alt+3
List Bullet	Ctrl+Shift+1

> **TIP:** If you want to apply other styles from the keyboard, create keyboard shortcuts for them as discussed in Chapter 6: "Making the Office Programs Work Your Way."

Using the Style Area to See Which Styles the Paragraphs Use

When you need to see which style is applied to each paragraph, you can open the style area. This is a vertical strip on the left side of the **Word** window that shows the style names (see Figure 8–9). You can display the style area only in **Draft** view and **Outline** view, not in any of the views that displays the page as it will appear when laid out.

The style area shows the name of the style applied to each paragraph

Click and drag the divider bar to change the width of the style area; drag all the way left to close it

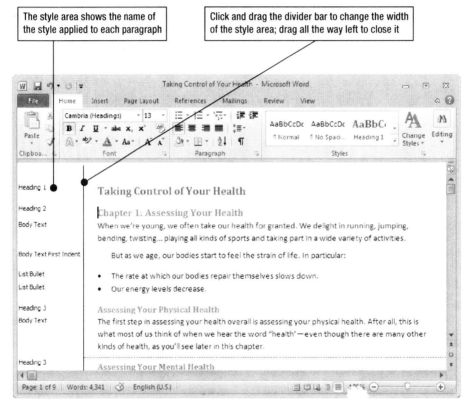

Figure 8–9. *In* ***Draft*** *view and* ***Outline*** *view, you can display the style area on the left side of the window to see the style applied to each paragraph.*

To display the style area, follow these steps:

1. Click the **File** tab to open **Backstage** view.

2. Click the **Options** item to display the **Word Options** dialog box.

3. Click the **Advanced** item in the left pane to display the **Advanced** category.

4. Scroll down to the **Display** heading, about halfway down.

5. In the **Style** area pane within the **Draft** and **Outline** views text box, type a width such as **1"** for the style area. (The default setting, **0"**, hides the style area.)

6. Click the **OK** button to close the **Word Options** dialog box.

Now click the **Draft** button in the **View Shortcuts** area on the status bar to switch to **Draft** view. The style area appears on the left of the screen, and you can easily see which style each paragraph has.

Managing Styles with the Styles Pane and the Manage Styles Dialog Box

As you've seen so far in this chapter, you can quickly apply styles from the **Quick Style** gallery, and you can customize the gallery with the styles you need most. To perform other aspects of managing styles, you can use either the **Styles** pane or the **Manage Styles** dialog box. In this section, we'll look quickly at what you can do with each of these tools.

Managing Styles with the Styles Pane

The Styles pane (see Figure 8–10) is a tool you can for applying styles, changing styles, and managing styles. To open the **Styles** pane, choose **Home ➤ Styles ➤ Styles**, clicking the tiny button with the arrow in the lower-right corner of the Styles group (look back to Figure 8–6).

At first, the **Styles** pane shows only the selection of styles that Word recommends for frequent use. If you need other styles, click the **Options** link in the lower-right corner of the **Styles** pane to display the **Style Pane Options** dialog box, and then choose settings as explained in Figure 8–11.

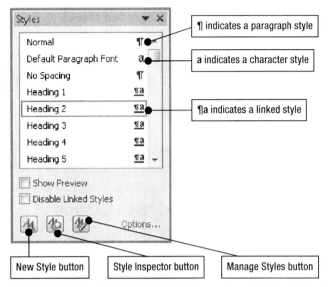

¶ indicates a paragraph style

a indicates a character style

¶a indicates a linked style

New Style button

Style Inspector button

Manage Styles button

*Figure 8–10. From the **Styles** pane, you can apply a style, inspect a style, start creating a new style, or manage your styles.*

1. Choose All Styles if you want to see all the styles

2. Choose Alphabetical if you want an alphabetical list of styles rather than the recommended order

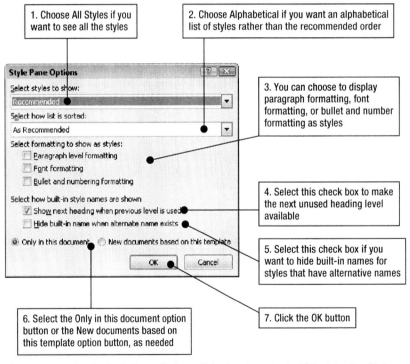

3. You can choose to display paragraph formatting, font formatting, or bullet and number formatting as styles

4. Select this check box to make the next unused heading level available

5. Select this check box if you want to hide built-in names for styles that have alternative names

6. Select the Only in this document option button or the New documents based on this template option button, as needed

7. Click the OK button

*Figure 8–11. Use the **Style Pane Options** dialog box to control which styles the **Styles** pane displays.*

▓ *Apply a style.* Click in the paragraph or select the text, and then click the style in the Styles pane.

▓ *View a preview of your styles.* Select the **Show Preview** check box to make the **Styles** pane show the styles with their font formatting rather than as a plain list. This makes the styles easier to identify.

▓ *Unlink linked styles.* Select the **Disable Linked Styles** check box to turn off the linkage between paragraph and character styles, so that character styles don't appear in the outline.

▓ *Start creating a new style.* Click the **New Style** button to display the larger version of the **Create New Style** from **Formatting** dialog box, which you'll meet later in this chapter.

▓ *Open the Style Inspector.* Click the **Style Inspector** button.

▓ *Open the Manage Styles dialog box.* Click the **Manage Styles** button.

▓ *Change all instances of one style to another.* Right-click the style, and then click the **Select All** command. Word selects all the instances of the style. Click the style you want to apply instead of the current style.

▓ *Modify a style.* Right-click the style, and then click **Modify** to display the **Modify Style** dialog box. You can then modify the style, as discussed later in this chapter.

TIP: If you need to change heading styles to different heading levels, you may find it easier to promote or demote the headings in Outline view rather than change the styles as described here. See Chapter 9: "Adding Headers, Footers, Tables, and Columns" for instructions on using **Outline** view.

Managing Styles with the Manage Styles Dialog Box

When you need to take advanced actions with styles, open the **Manage Styles** dialog box (see Figure 8–12) by clicking the **Manage Styles** button in the **Styles** pane.

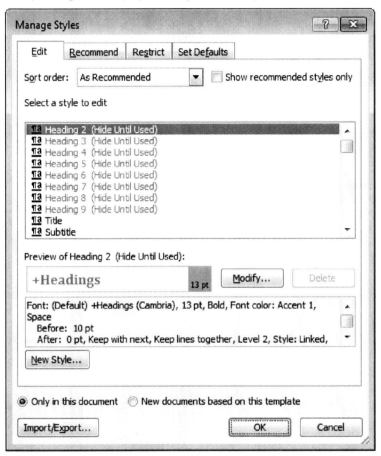

Figure 8–12. *You use the **Manage Styles** dialog box to edit existing styles, start creating new styles, recommend styles for use or restrict them from use, and to set default styles.*

Of the many actions you can take in the **Manage Styles** dialog box, these six tend to be the most useful:

- *Change the sort order.* On the **Edit** tab, click the **Sort order** drop-down list, and then choose the sort order you want—for example, **Alphabetical** or **By type**.

▥ *Open a style to modify it.* On the **Edit** tab, click the style, and then click the **Modify** button to display the **Modify Style** dialog box. The **Modify Style** dialog box is almost exactly the same as the larger **Create New Style** from **Formatting** dialog box, which you'll meet in Figure 8–21, later in this chapter.

▥ *Recommend styles.* On the **Recommend** tab, build a list of the styles you want Word to display in the Recommended list. Clear the **Show recommended styles only** check box if you want to make the full list of styles available. You can then click a style in the main list box and click the **Show** button to make it appear in the **Recommended** list. Similarly, you can use the **Move Up** button and **Move Down** button to rearrange the styles in the **Recommended** list.

> **NOTE:** A typical Word template has so many styles that wading through the full list is awkward. By setting up the **Recommended** list with the styles you normally use, you can apply styles faster and more easily.

▥ *Restrict styles.* On the **Restrict** tab, build a list of the styles to restrict when you protect a document for formatting changes. This topic is beyond this book, but briefly, you can permit your colleagues to use only certain styles when they're editing a document you've applied restrictions to.

▥ *Set the default font, size, color, paragraph position, and paragraph spacing.* Use the controls on the **Set Defaults** tab to choose the default settings.

▥ *Export or import styles.* To import styles from or export styles to another document or template, click the **Import/Export** button at the bottom of any tab in the **Manage Styles** dialog box, and then work on the **Styles** tab of the **Organizer** dialog box that Word opens.

Creating Custom Styles

If you find that Word's styles don't meet your needs, you can either create custom styles of your own or customize the built-in styles to make them suitable.

In this section, I'll show you the easiest way to create a custom style, which is called *by example*—you set up text with the formatting you want, and then create the style from it. In passing, I'll show you how to create a new style by specifying its formatting in the **Create New Style from Formatting** dialog box.

Creating a Custom Style by Example

To create a custom style by example, choose an existing paragraph or type a sample paragraph, and then apply formatting to it as discussed in the following sections.

> **TIP:** If Word has an existing style that's similar to the style you want to create, apply that style first, so you don't need to make as many formatting changes.

Setting the Font Formatting for the Style

Usually, it's best to start by setting the font formatting for the style. You can apply font formatting by using the controls in the Font group on the Home tab of the Ribbon or the controls on the Mini Toolbar, as discussed in Chapter 2: "Using the Ribbon, Backstage, and Common Tools," but when you really need to dig into font formatting, you may find it easier to use the Font dialog box as shown in Figure 8–13.

To open the **Font** dialog box, click the **Home** tab, go to the **Font** group, and click the small button with the arrow at the lower-right corner. You can also press Ctrl+D.

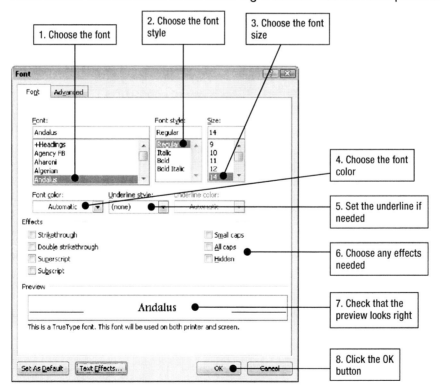

Figure 8–13. *Use the **Font** tab of the **Font** dialog box when you want to adjust various details of the font formatting.*

NOTE: On the **Advanced** tab of the **Font** dialog box, you can change the scaling, spacing, and position of fonts. For example, you can change the spacing to spread the letters farther apart, or choose the **Raised** position to create a superscript raised exactly as far as you want it rather than the standard distance applied by the **Superscript** setting on the **Font** tab. You can also work with features such as ligatures (two letters joined together), which you'll normally need only if you're typesetting a document.

Setting the Paragraph Formatting for the Style

To set the style's paragraph formatting, such as its alignment and indentation, you can use either the controls in the **Paragraph** group on the **Home** tab of the Ribbon (see Figure 8–14) or the **Paragraph** dialog box.

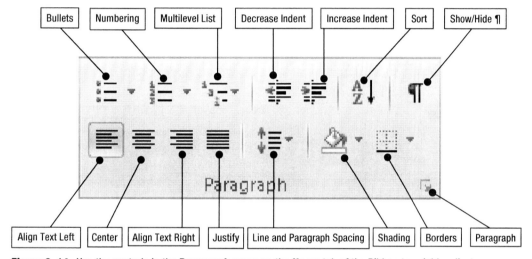

Figure 8–14. *Use the controls in the **Paragraph** group on the **Home** tab of the Ribbon to quickly adjust alignment, spacing, or indentation. Click the **Paragraph** button in the lower-right corner when you need to open the **Paragraph** dialog box.*

When you need to make sweeping changes to the paragraph formatting, or when you need to use the full range of paragraph formatting, choose **Home ➤ Paragraph ➤ Paragraph** to display the **Paragraph** dialog box.

Figure 8–15 shows you how to set alignment, indentation, and line spacing on the **Indents and Spacing** tab of the **Paragraph** dialog box. After you do this, you can click the **OK** button to close the dialog box, click the **Line and Page Breaks** tab to display its controls, or click the **Tabs** button to display the Tabs dialog box.

NOTE: A point (pt) is 1/72 inch. Try 6 points after single-spaced paragraphs if you want a small gap, or 12 points for a larger gap. Body text doesn't usually need space before it, but you will probably want to add 12–24 points of space before a heading to separate it from the text above it, and around 12 points to separate it from the text below.

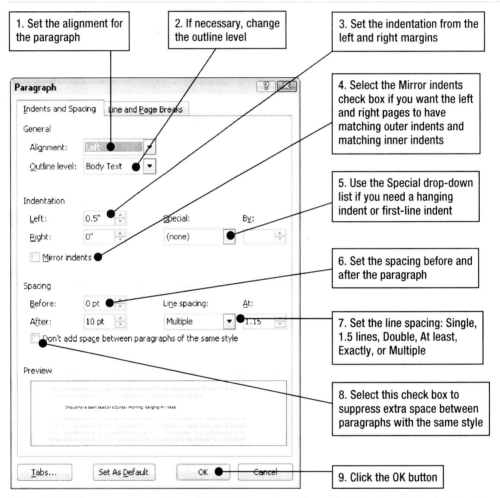

1. Set the alignment for the paragraph

2. If necessary, change the outline level

3. Set the indentation from the left and right margins

4. Select the Mirror indents check box if you want the left and right pages to have matching outer indents and matching inner indents

5. Use the Special drop-down list if you need a hanging indent or first-line indent

6. Set the spacing before and after the paragraph

7. Set the line spacing: Single, 1.5 lines, Double, At least, Exactly, or Multiple

8. Select this check box to suppress extra space between paragraphs with the same style

9. Click the OK button

Figure 8–15. *Choose paragraph alignment, indentation, and spacing on the **Indents and Spacing** tab of the **Paragraph** dialog box.*

NOTE: A *hanging indent* is where the first line of a paragraph extends to the right of the following lines. A first-line indent is where the first line of a paragraph is indented further than the following lines.

Figure 8–16 shows you how to use the controls on the **Line and Page Breaks** tab to control how Word handles line and page breaks.

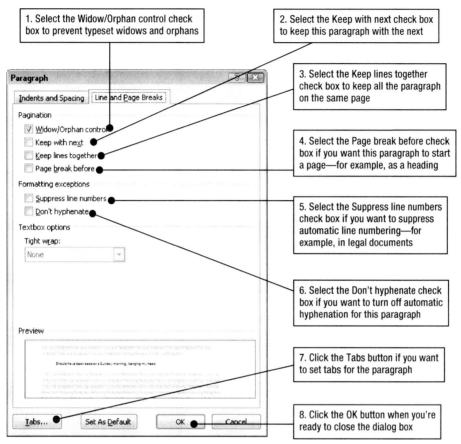

1. Select the Widow/Orphan control check box to prevent typeset widows and orphans

2. Select the Keep with next check box to keep this paragraph with the next

3. Select the Keep lines together check box to keep all the paragraph on the same page

4. Select the Page break before check box if you want this paragraph to start a page—for example, as a heading

5. Select the Suppress line numbers check box if you want to suppress automatic line numbering—for example, in legal documents

6. Select the Don't hyphenate check box if you want to turn off automatic hyphenation for this paragraph

7. Click the Tabs button if you want to set tabs for the paragraph

8. Click the OK button when you're ready to close the dialog box

Figure 8–16. *Choose pagination options and formatting exceptions on the **Line and Page Breaks** tab of the **Paragraph** dialog box.*

NOTE: In typesetting terms, a *widow* is a single line that appears at the top of a page, separated from the rest of its paragraph; an *orphan* is a single line that appears at the end of a page, likewise separated from the rest of its paragraph. Normal typesetting practice is to suppress both widows and orphans to make the text easier to read.

Setting the Tabs for the Style

If you want to set tabs for the style, click the **Tabs** button at the bottom of the **Paragraph** dialog box to display the **Tabs** dialog box. You can then set tabs as shown in Figure 8–17, and then click the **OK** button to close first the Tabs dialog box and then the **Paragraph** dialog box.

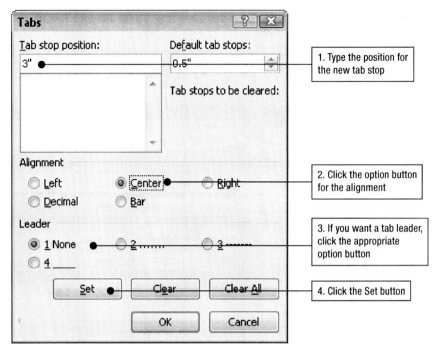

Figure 8–17. *You can quickly set any tabs the style needs by using the **Tabs** dialog box.*

> **NOTE:** A bar tab is a vertical bar that appears at the position of the tab stop. In earlier versions of Word, bar tabs were useful for creating vertical lines; now, Word's drawing tools make it easy to create lines. A decimal tab is a tab aligned on a decimal point. You'd typically use a decimal tab to align columns of figures. For example, by using a decimal tab, you can align 12345.67 and 1.23 at the decimal point, which makes the figures easy to read.

To get rid of a tab, click it in the list of tabs, and then click the **Clear** button. To get rid of all the tabs, click the **Clear All** button.

Adding Bullets or Numbering to the Style

When you're creating a list style, your next move is to add the bullets or numbering it needs. Select the text, and then use the **Bullets** button, **Numbering** button, or **Multilevel List** button in the **Paragraph** group on the **Home** tab, as needed. Figure 8–18 shows an example of using the **Bullets** button.

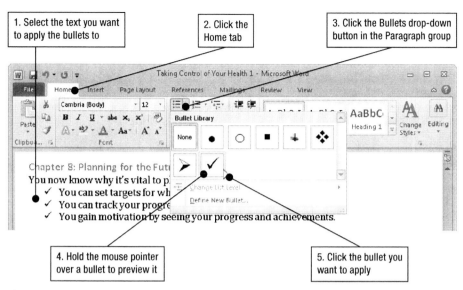

1. Select the text you want to apply the bullets to

2. Click the Home tab

3. Click the Bullets drop-down button in the Paragraph group

4. Hold the mouse pointer over a bullet to preview it

5. Click the bullet you want to apply

Figure 8–18. *You can quickly apply bullets, numbering, or a multilevel list by using the **Bullets** drop-down button, the **Numbering** drop-down button, or the **Multilevel List** drop-down button in the **Paragraph** group of the **Home** tab.*

NOTE: You can also apply the default style of bullets, numbering, or multilevel list by clicking the button itself (for example, the **Bullets** button) rather than the drop-down button.

Adding Borders and Shading to the Style

If the style needs borders or shading, add them by using either the **Home ➤ Paragraph ➤ Borders** drop-down panel or the **Borders and Shading** dialog box. Generally, the **Borders and Shading** dialog box gives you better control over the borders and shading, so it's a better choice.

NOTE: The ScreenTip for the **Borders** button shows the name of the last border type you used— for example, **Top Border**—rather than the word **Borders**.

To open the **Borders and Shading** dialog box, choose **Home ➤ Paragraph ➤ Borders ➤ Borders and Shading**. You can then work as explained in Figure 8–19.

NOTE: To move the borders closer to the text or farther away from it, click the **Options** button. In the **Borders and Shading Options** dialog box that opens, adjust the **Top**, **Bottom**, **Left**, and **Right** measurements, and then click the **OK** button.

To apply shading to a style, click the **Shading** tab in the **Borders and Shading** dialog box, and then follow these steps:

1. In the **Apply to** drop-down list, choose **Paragraph** if you want to apply the shading to the whole paragraph. Choose **Text** if you want to apply the border only to the text.

2. In the **Fill** drop-down list, choose the shading color you want.

3. In the **Style** drop-down list, choose the shading style—for example, **25%** shading or **Dk Trellis** shading.

4. In the **Color** drop-down list, choose the pattern color.

5. Click the **OK** button to close the **Borders and Shading** dialog box.

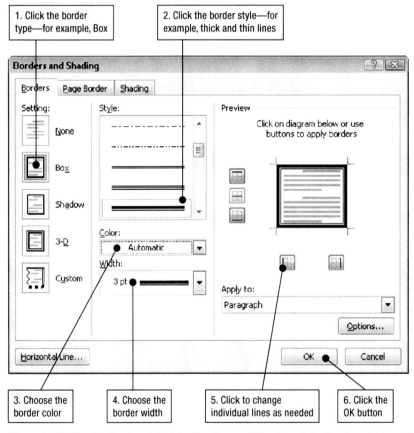

Figure 8–19. *Use the **Borders** tab of the **Borders and Shading** dialog box to quickly apply borders to a paragraph.*

Adding Language Formatting to the Style

If the style you're creating will contain text in a different language than the standard language you use for checking spelling, you can add language formatting to the style. Language formatting tells Word to treat the text as being in a particular language. For example, if you're writing a paper on German Romanticism, you could create a style for block quotes and set its language to German. This would stop the Spelling checker from querying the words as not being in the language you're normally using.

To apply language formatting, select the text, and then choose **Review ➤ Language ➤ Language ➤ Set Proofing Language**. The **Language** dialog box opens, and you can then work as shown in Figure 8–20.

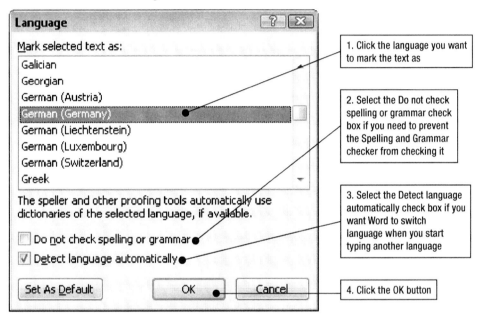

Figure 8–20. *In the **Language** dialog box, you can specify the language used for the text. You can also turn off spelling and grammar checking for the style—for example, for programming code or other non-words.*

Creating a Style from the Text You Have Formatted

You can now create a style from the text you have formatted. Follow these steps:

1. Select the paragraph.

2. Choose **Home ➤ Styles ➤ More ➤ Save Selection as a New Quick Style**. Word displays the **Create New Style** from **Formatting** dialog box.

3. Click the **Modify** button to display the larger version of the **Create New Style** from **Formatting** dialog box.

4. Set up the style as explained in Figure 8–21. Make sure you select the **Add to Quick Style** list check box if you want the style to appear in the **Quick Style** gallery.

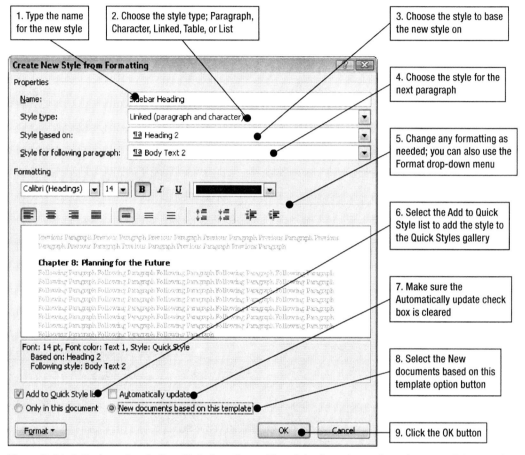

1. Type the name for the new style

2. Choose the style type; Paragraph, Character, Linked, Table, or List

3. Choose the style to base the new style on

4. Choose the style for the next paragraph

5. Change any formatting as needed; you can also use the Format drop-down menu

6. Select the Add to Quick Style list to add the style to the Quick Styles gallery

7. Make sure the Automatically update check box is cleared

8. Select the New documents based on this template option button

9. Click the OK button

Figure 8–21. *In the large* **Create New Style from Formatting** *dialog box, choose the style type and the style for the next paragraph. Select the* **New documents based on this template** *option button if you want to make the style available to other documents.*

5. Click the **OK** button. Word closes the **Create New Style from Formatting** dialog box and creates the style.

TIP: Clear the **Automatically update** check box when creating a style. Otherwise, when you change the formatting of text that uses that style, Word automatically applies that change to the style. This makes all the other items to which the style is applied change as well. Normally, it's easiest to turn off automatic updating and update styles manually, as discussed in the next section.

Modifying an Existing Style

Instead of creating a new style, you can modify an existing style—either one of Word's built-in styles or a style you've created yourself. The quick way to modify a style is by updating it to match formatting you've applied, but you can also open the style in the **Modify Style** dialog box and change its formatting there.

Updating a Style with New Formatting

To change a style quickly, update it with new formatting as explained in Figure 8–22.

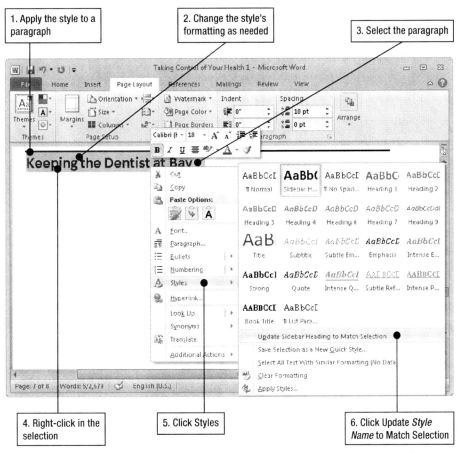

Figure 8–22. *You can quickly update a style with new formatting by using the **Update Style Name to Match Selection** command.*

Changing a Style Using the Modify Style Dialog Box

When you need to modify a style with many changes, you can open the style in the **Modify Style** dialog box and work on it there. The **Modify Style** dialog box has the same controls as the **Create New Style from Formatting** dialog box (shown in Figure 8–21).

You can open the **Modify Style** dialog box from the **Styles** pane, the **Quick Style gallery**, or the **Apply Styles** pane:

- *Styles pane.* Right-click the style name, and then click **Modify** on the context menu.

- *Quick Style gallery.* Right-click the style name, and then click **Modify** on the context menu.

- *Apply Styles pane.* Select the style, and then click the **Modify** button.

Applying Direct Formatting on Top of Styles

After you've applied the style each paragraph needs, and you've applied list styles and character styles as needed, you can finish off the formatting by applying direct formatting to any parts of the document that need it. For example, you may need to apply different font formatting to pick out special display elements or add more space before some paragraphs.

> **NOTE:** It's fine to use direct formatting when you need to make only a few changes to a document. But to get the most out of Word's automatic formatting features, use direct formatting as little as possible. If you need to apply the same direct formatting to several different items, create a style with that formatting so that you can apply it instantly in future. If you will need to use the same direct formatting and text, save it as an AutoText entry (see Chapter 7: "Entering and Editing Text in Your Documents" for instructions).

To apply direct formatting, use the tools you've met earlier in this chapter for setting up font formatting, paragraph formatting, bullets and numbering, and so on. For example:

- *Font formatting.* Use the controls in the **Font** group on the **Home** tab of the Ribbon, on the **Mini Toolbar**, or in the **Font** dialog box.

- *Paragraph formatting.* Use the controls in the **Paragraph** group on the **Home** tab of the Ribbon or in the **Paragraph** dialog box.

- *Bullets and numbering.* Use the controls in the **Paragraph** group on the **Home** tab of the Ribbon.

> **TIP:** To remove direct formatting from text, select the text, and then press **Ctrl+spacebar**.

Copying and Pasting Formatting Using the Format Painter

When you have applied direct formatting to text or another object, you can quickly reuse the formatting by using the **Format Painter**. This feature enables you to pick up the formatting for a selection and then "paint" it on other text or another object. Follow these steps:

1. Select the text or object that contains the formatting you want to copy.

2. Choose **Home ➤ Clipboard ➤ Format Painter** (the brush icon) or press **Ctrl+Alt+C** to copy the formatting. Word changes the mouse pointer to a brush icon.

> **TIP:** If you want to apply the formatting to multiple items, double-click the **Format Painter** button in the **Clipboard** group. The mouse pointer then stays as the **Format Painter** brush until you turn it off by clicking the **Format Painter** button again or pressing **Esc**.

3. Drag the brush over the text or object to which you want to apply the formatting. Word applies the formatting and restores the normal mouse pointer.

Seeing Which Formatting You've Applied to Text

Because Word uses both styles and direct formatting, you'll often need to check exactly what formatting a paragraph or some text uses—especially if you've received the document from someone else rather than formatting it yourself.

To see which style a particular paragraph uses, you can click in it, and then look at the style name displayed in whichever formatting tool you're using—for example, the **Apply Styles** pane or the **Styles** pane. In **Draft** view and **Outline** view, you can also display the style area on the left of the Word window to see at a glance which style each paragraph uses, as you saw earlier in this chapter.

But to really dig into the details of the formatting, you need to use two other tools that Word provides: the **Style Inspector** and the **Reveal Formatting** pane.

Using the Style Inspector to Examine a Style

To see whether a paragraph uses only style formatting or has direct formatting applied to it as well, open the Style Inspector (see Figure 8–23) by clicking the Style Inspector button in the Styles pane.

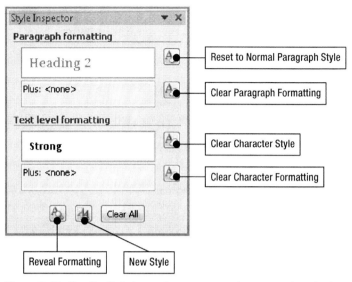

Figure 8–23. *Use the **Style Inspector** pane to see the paragraph style, the text level formatting, and any additional formatting added.*

You can quickly change the formatting of the paragraph and text by using the four buttons on the right side of the Style Inspector:

- ***Reset to Normal Paragraph Style.*** Click this button only if you want to apply the **Normal** style to the paragraph. Doing this is usually not helpful. It's best to give each paragraph a style that defines its role in the document—for example, **Heading 1** or **Body Text**—rather than using the **Normal** style.

- ***Clear Paragraph Formatting.*** Click this button to remove from the paragraph all the extra paragraph formatting listed in the **Plus** box. For example, if you've applied double line spacing or indents to the paragraph manually, clicking this button removes them, restoring the style's usual paragraph formatting.

- ***Clear Character Style.*** Click this button to remove character styles from the paragraph. Doing this is sometimes helpful, but what you'll frequently want to do is leave the character styles in place but remove direct formatting, as discussed next.

- ***Clear Character Formatting.*** Click this button to remove any extra formatting you've applied to the paragraph's text (as opposed to the paragraph as a whole). For example, if you've changed the font or font color using direct formatting, clicking this button restores the default font.

NOTE: Click the **Clear All** button if you want to wipe out all the paragraph, style, and direct formatting and apply the **Normal** style to the paragraph. This isn't usually a good idea. It's better to remove the formatting using the **Clear Paragraph Formatting** button, **Clear Character Style** button, and **Clear Character Formatting** button, as needed, leaving the style in place. Or, if you need another style, apply that style.

As you can see in the figure, the Style Inspector contains two more buttons:

- ▓ *Reveal Formatting.* Click this button to open the **Reveal Formatting** pane (discussed in the next section).

- ▓ *New Style.* Click this button to open the large **Create New Style from Formatting** dialog box (which you've met earlier in this chapter).

Using the Reveal Formatting Pane to Examine Which Formatting Is Applied

To see exactly what formatting a paragraph uses, and perhaps sort out problems with it, open the **Reveal Formatting** pane by clicking the **Reveal Formatting** button in the **Style Inspector**.

Figure 8–24 shows the **Reveal Formatting** pane with different views of the same formatting information:

- ▓ The screen on the left shows the **Reveal Formatting** pane as it normally opens, showing the details of the font formatting and paragraph formatting (in expanded lists) and offering details of the section formatting (in a collapsed list).

- ▓ The screen on the right shows the **Reveal Formatting** pane with the **Distinguish style source** check box selected. Selecting this check box makes the **Reveal Formatting** pane break down each list to show which formatting comes from styles and which comes from direct formatting. For example, here you can see that the **Subtle Emphasis** character style provides italics and a font color, but that the underline, dark blue font color, and shadow effect come from direct formatting applied on top of the style.

Click a – sign to collapse a category

Click a + sign to expand a category

Click a link to open the relevant dialog box

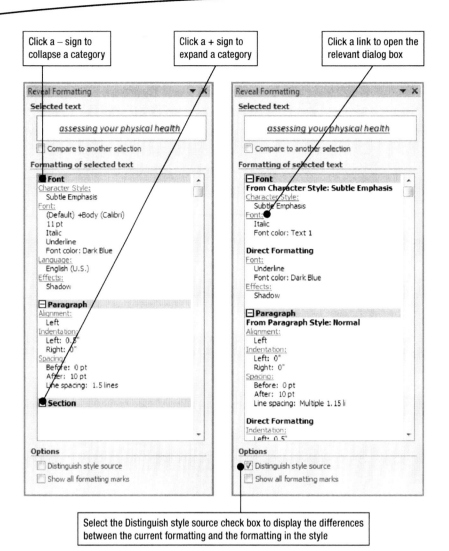

Select the Distinguish style source check box to display the differences between the current formatting and the formatting in the style

Figure 8–24. *Use the **Reveal Formatting** pane to see exactly what formatting a selection uses (left) or to see how that formatting differs from the styles applied (right).*

TIP: To see how the formatting of your current selection compares to other text, you can select the **Compare to another** selection check box. Next, click in or select the text that you want to compare it with. The **Reveal Formatting** pane displays a list of the formatting differences, which you can use to remove unwanted formatting from the selection.

Summary

In this chapter, you learned the best way to format your documents quickly and consistently—by using styles. You now know how to apply styles, how to create custom styles with exactly the look you need, and how to modify existing styles. You can also apply direct formatting where it's needed, and you can navigate quickly through your documents by using the **Navigation** pane.

In the next chapter, I'll show you how to add headers, footers, tables, and columns to your documents. Turn the page when you're ready to start.

Chapter 9

Adding Headers, Footers, Tables, and Columns

In this chapter, you'll learn how to add four types of widely useful elements—headers, footers, complex tables, and columns—to your documents.

We'll cover headers and footers first, which are great both for documents you print and for documents you distribute as PDF files or XPS documents. We'll then move on to look at the extra features that Word brings to tables, both in terms of adding them to your documents and formatting them to look the way you want. And after that, I'll show you how to create newspaper-style columns of text in documents such as newsletters and reports.

To use columns and complex headers and footers effectively, you need to split your documents up into different sections. So we'll look first at what sections are and how you use them.

Using Sections to Create Complex Layouts

When you need to create documents that use multiple layouts, you have to put each layout in a separate section. For example:

- A newsletter may need different numbers of columns on different pages.

- A report may require different headers and footers for different chapters.

- A business letter may need to contain an envelope page as well, as in the example shown in Figure 9–1.

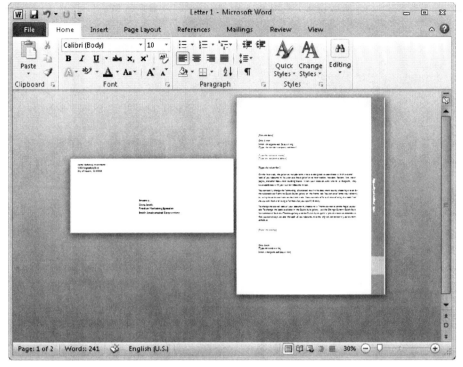

Figure 9–1. *When you create a document that has two or more different layouts, such as the envelope and letter here, you need to put each layout in a different section.*

Word's sections give you great flexibility in your documents, but they're tricky both to see and to grasp. Word makes matters worse by automatically creating sections when your documents need them—for example, when you apply columns to part of a document, as discussed later in this chapter—but not making clear what it's doing.

Here's what you need to know to use sections successfully:

- *Each new blank document has a single section to start.* When you create a new blank document, Word creates it as a single section until you add further sections. By contrast, documents you create based on a template contain however many sections the template has.

- *When you need to give part of the document a different layout, you create a new section.* For example, if you need to create a landscape page in a document that uses portrait orientation, you put the landscape page in a separate section so that you can change the layout.

- *A section can start on the same page or on a different page.* Word uses four kinds of section breaks:

▓ *Continuous.* The new section starts on the same page as the previous section. This type of break is useful for creating multi-column layouts on part of a page.

▓ *Next page.* The new section starts on the next page after the previous section ends. This is the kind of break you use for putting a new chapter on a new page or for changing layout from portrait to landscape.

▓ *Even page.* The new section starts on the next even page after the previous section ends. This may mean having a blank page in the printed document.

▓ *Odd page.* The new section starts on the new odd page after the previous section ends. This too may mean a blank page appears in the printed document.

▓ *A section break divides one section from the next.* When you create a section (or Word creates one automatically for you), you add a section break to the document. A section break is normally hidden, but if you display paragraph marks and other invisible characters, it appears as a dotted double line with the words Section Break and the type in the middle—for example, Section Break (Continuous). Figure 9–2 shows an example of a section break.

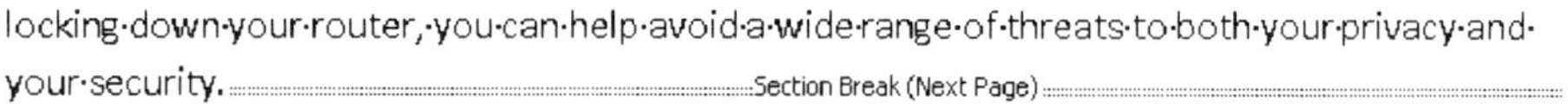

locking·down·your·router,·you·can·help·avoid·a·wide·range·of·threats·to·both·your·privacy·and·
your·security. ··Section Break (Next Page)··

Figure 9–2. *Like paragraph marks, section breaks are hidden until you display invisible characters. A section break then appears as a double dotted line with the section break type in the middle.*

With that in mind, you can easily insert a section break, as shown in Figure 9–3.

TIP: When you start using sections in a document, add the Section readout to the status bar so you can easily see which section you're working in. Right-click any blank part of the status bar to display the **Customize Status Bar** menu, click to place a check mark next to the Section item, and then click outside the menu to hide it. You'll then see the Section readout saying **Section: 2** (or whatever the section number is) at the left end of the status bar.

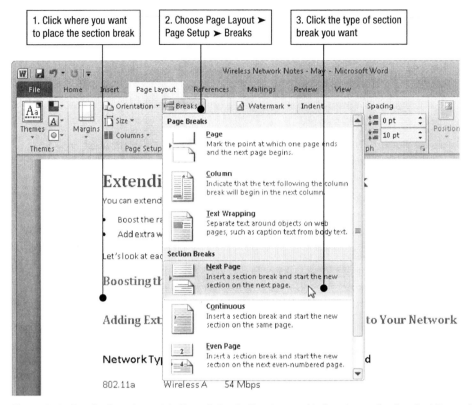

Figure 9–3. *Use the **Page Layout** ➤ **Page Setup** ➤ **Breaks** panel to insert a section break at the position of the insertion point.*

Adding Headers, Footers, and Page Numbers

To make your documents easy to identify, both on screen and on paper, you can add headers and footers to them. You can also add automatic page numbering, which makes Word place a page number on each page and adjust it automatically.

Adding Headers and Footers to a Document

A *header* appears across the top of a page, and a *footer* appears across the bottom of a page. You can use headers and footers to add information such as the document name and file name, author name, date, and page numbers—or any other information that you need to make available to the reader.

NOTE: Don't confuse headers with headings or footers with footnotes. A *heading* is the title of a division of a document or section; for example, this section's heading is "Adding Headers and Footers to a Document." A *footnote* is a note that appears at the bottom of the same page as the text it refers to. The text has either a number or a decorative character after it to indicate the footnote reference.

You can use the same header or footer all the way through a document if that's what you need. But you can also use different headers or footers on the odd pages of the document to the even pages, use different headers and footers from one section of the document to the next, or prevent the header or footer from appearing on the first page of a document.

Adding a Header to a Document

To insert a header, choose **Insert ➤ Header and Footer ➤ Header**, and then click the header you want on the **Header** panel (see Figure 9–4). You can hold the mouse pointer over a header type to display a ScreenTip describing the header and suggesting when it's useful.

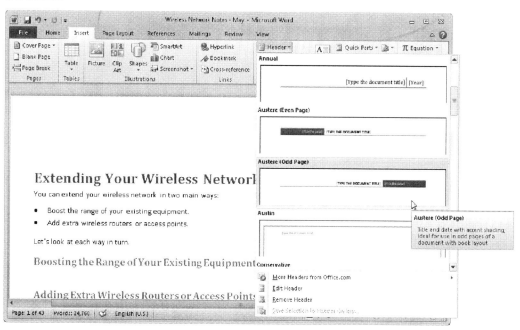

Figure 9–4. *You can quickly insert a built-in header by using the* **Header** *panel on the* **Insert** *tab of the Ribbon. Scroll the main part of the panel down to see further headers.*

TIP: The headers and footers available for a document depend on the template the document uses. Some templates already have headers and footers in place to help you create a finished document more quickly. So have a look at the header and footer areas of the page before inserting a header or footer.

When you click a header, Word inserts it in your document, opens it for editing, and adds the **Header & Footer** section to the toolbar. You can then fill in the header, as shown in Figure 9–5.

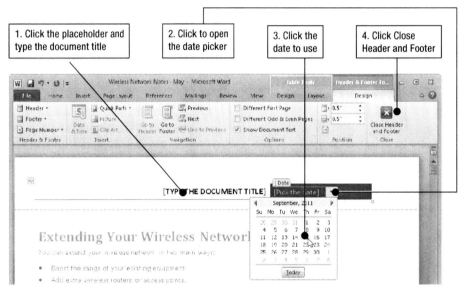

Figure 9–5. *After inserting a built-in header or footer, complete it by filling in its placeholders with suitable information. You can also add text or other elements outside the placeholders if you want.*

TIP: You can adjust the header's position relative to the top of the page by changing the value in the **Header from Top** box in the **Position** group of the **Design** tab on the **Header & Footer Tools** section of the Ribbon (see Figure 9–6). Similarly, you can adjust the footer's position relative to the bottom of the page by changing the **Footer from Bottom** value.

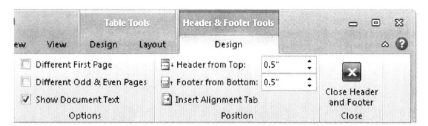

Figure 9–6. *Use the* **Header from Top** *box to adjust the distance of the header from the top of the page and the* **Footer from Bottom** *box to adjust the distance of the footer from the bottom of the page.*

If you need to change the alignment of the header, click in it, and then choose **Header & Footer Tools ➤ Design ➤ Position ➤ Insert Alignment Tab**. You can then set up the alignment tab, as shown in Figure 9–7.

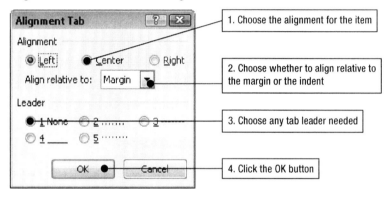

Figure 9–7. *Use the* **Alignment Tab** *dialog box to change the alignment of a an item in the header.*

Adding a Footer to a Document

To insert a footer, choose **Insert ➤ Header and Footer ➤ Footer**, and then click the footer you want on the **Footer** panel. Footers work in the same way as headers, so you can set up the footer by working as described in the previous section.

Creating Different Headers and Footers for Different Pages or Different Sections

Many documents either don't need a header (or footer) on the first page or need a different one there. Likewise, many documents need a different header or footer on their odd pages than on their even pages. You may also need to set up different headers or footers for different sections of a document—for example, the chapters of a report or book.

To set up different headers and footers for the first page, for odd and even pages, or for different sections, double-click the header or footer you want to affect, and then work as shown in Figure 9–8.

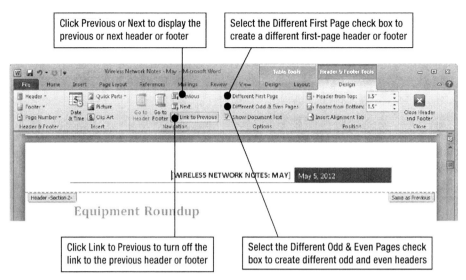

Figure 9–8. *Use the controls in the* **Navigation** *group and* **Options** *group of the* **Design** *tab to set up different headers and footers for different pages or different sections.*

Delete a Header or Footer

When you want to get rid of a header or footer, you can open it for editing and then delete its contents. This is easy if the header or footer is only text, but may take longer if the header or footer contains various types of objects.

Instead, choose **Insert ➤ Header & Footer ➤ Header ➤ Remove Header** or **Insert ➤ Header & Footer ➤ Footer ➤ Remote Footer** to get rid of the header or footer in one move. Alternatively, double-click in the header area or footer area, press **Ctrl+A** to select it all, and then press **Delete**.

Adding Page Numbers to a Document

To make clear which page belongs where, you can easily add page numbers to your documents, as shown in Figure 9–9.

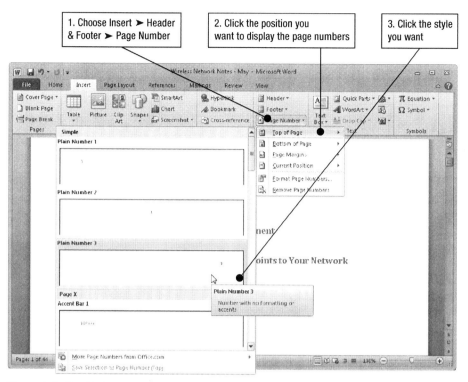

Figure 9–9. *Use the* ***Insert ➤ Header & Footer ➤ Page Number*** *panel to insert automatic page numbers in a document.*

The page number then appears on each page in your document.

If you need to change the way the page number appears, or change the numbering used, choose **Insert ➤ Header & Footer ➤ Page Number ➤ Format Page Numbers**, and then work in the **Page Number Format** dialog box (see Figure 9–10).

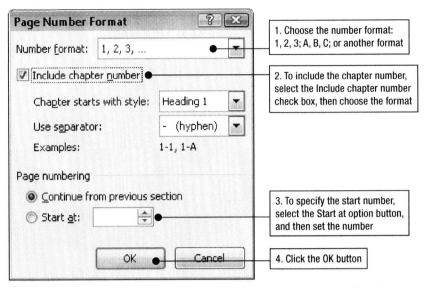

Figure 9–10. *Use the* **Page Number Format** *dialog box to change the formatting of a page number you've already inserted in a document.*

NOTE: To remove the page numbers from a document, choose **Insert ➤ Header & Footer ➤ Page Number ➤ Remove Page Numbers**.

Adding Tables to Your Documents

In Word, you can create tables in three ways:

- *Insert a table.* When you need a regular table—one that has the same number of rows in each row—you can use the standard method of creating a table discussed in Chapter 3. Choose **Insert ➤ Tables ➤ Table**, and then click the table arrangement you want on the **Insert Table** grid. For example, if you want a table with five rows of four columns each, click the 4×5 square on the **Insert Table** grid.

- *Draw a table.* Also as discussed in Chapter 3, choose **Insert ➤ Tables ➤ Table ➤ Draw Table**, and then use the drawing cursor to draw the table layout you want. Drawing a table is good for creating irregular tables.

- *Convert existing text to a table.* If the document already contains the text you want to create the table from, you can convert the text into a table, as discussed next.

Converting Existing Text to a Table

If you already have the text you want to create a table from, you can quickly convert it to a table. Converting existing material is almost always quicker than creating a new table and moving some existing material into it.

To convert existing material to a table, follow these steps:

1. Make sure the material is laid out using a separator character Word can recognize:

   ▓ *Tabs.* Make sure that only one tab separates each item that needs to go into a different column, as in the example table in Figure 9–11. If two or more tabs separate the items, you'll get the wrong number of columns.

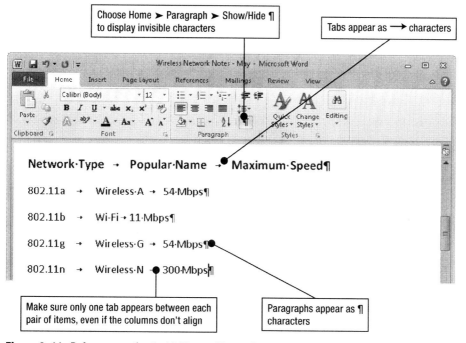

Figure 9–11. *Before converting text laid out with tabs into a table, check that there's only one tab between each item.*

   ▓ *Paragraph marks.* If each cell's data appears in a separate paragraph, you can quickly convert it to a table. Figure 9–12 shows some of the same source data laid out as paragraphs.

Network·Type¶
Popular·Name¶
Maximum·Speed¶
802.11a¶
Wireless·A¶
54·Mbps¶
¶
802.11b↵
Wi-Fi¶
11·Mbps¶
802.11g¶
Each paragraph will become a separate cell in the table
Delete any extra paragraphs, or the table will have empty cells
Replace any line breaks (↵ characters) with paragraphs; select the line break and press Enter

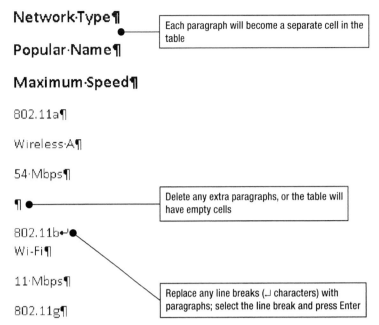

Figure 9–12. ***Before converting tabs laid out as paragraphs into a table, delete any extra paragraphs, and replace any line breaks with paragraphs.***

> **NOTE:** When converting paragraph-separated text into a table, check for line breaks, the ↵ characters that you can enter by pressing **Shift+Enter** to break text from line to the next. You need to replace any line breaks that are acting as paragraph breaks—otherwise, the table will have the wrong cell layout. But you can leave any line breaks that you want to carry through to the table as line breaks within cells.

- *Commas.* If you have data separated by commas, such as a comma-separated values export from a spreadsheet, you can use a comma as the separator character for a table. Figure 9–13 shows the same source data laid out with commas.

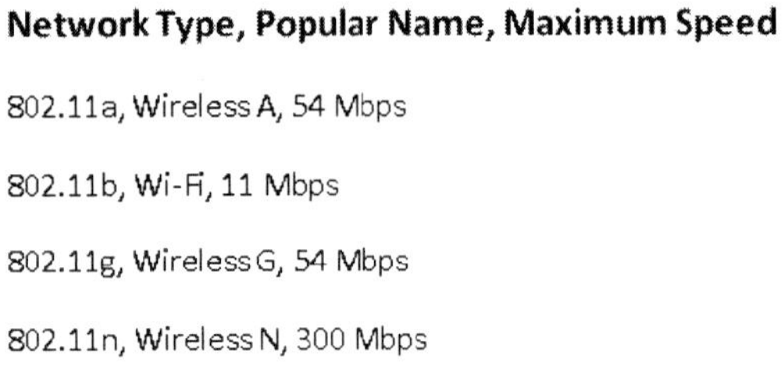

Network Type, Popular Name, Maximum Speed
802.11a, Wireless A, 54 Mbps
802.11b, Wi-Fi, 11 Mbps
802.11g, Wireless G, 54 Mbps
802.11n, Wireless N, 300 Mbps

Figure 9–13. *You can also convert data that's laid out with a comma where you want each cell division.*

■   *Other character.* If your data is separated consistently by another character (for example, * or |), you can specify that character as the separator character. You need to make sure that this character doesn't appear as part of the regular text, only as the separator character.

2.   Select the data you will turn into the table. Make sure you select the paragraph mark at the end of the last paragraph. This is easier to do if you have clicked the **Show/Hide ¶** button to reveal paragraph marks.

3.   Choose **Insert ➤ Tables ➤ Table ➤ Convert Text to Table**. Word displays the Convert Text to Table dialog box.

4.   Set up the conversion as explained in Figure 9–14, and then click the **OK** button.

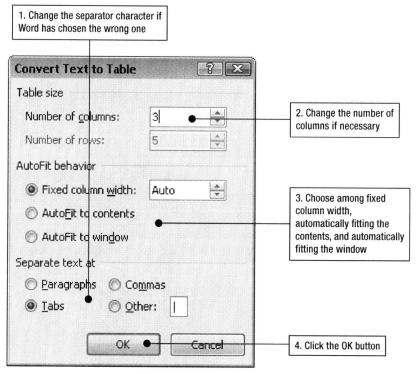

Figure 9–14. *In the **Convert Text to Table** dialog box, make sure that Word has chosen the right separator character (for example, tabs), and choose the **AutoFit** behavior you want.*

TIP: The **AutoFit** behavior area of the **Convert Table to Text** dialog box lets you choose whether to fit the column widths automatically to their contents. Select the **Fixed column width** option button if you want each column to have a fixed width; you can then choose **Auto** to have Word allocate the space equally among the columns, or type the fixed width you want. Select the **AutoFit to contents** option button to let Word adjust each column's width to fit its contents. Select the **AutoFit to window** option button have Word make the table automatically fit the window's width.

Figure 9–15 shows a table converted from the sample data using the **AutoFit to contents** setting.

Network Type	Popular Name	Maximum Speed
802.11a	Wireless A	54 Mbps
802.11b	Wi-Fi	11 Mbps
802.11g	Wireless G	54 Mbps
802.11n	Wireless N	300 Mbps

Figure 9–15. *Using the **AutoFit to contents** setting produces a table with columns just wide enough to contain their data.*

Nesting One Table Inside Another Table

When you need to create a complex layout, you can nest one table inside another, so that one cell of the outer table contains however many cells the inner table has. Figure 9–16 shows an example of a nested table.

To nest a table, click in the cell in which you want to nest the table, and then insert the table as usual. For example, choose **Insert ➤ Tables ➤ Table**, and then click the size of nested table you want.

Department	Coverage		Contact Information
Anthropology	Biological Anthropology	1-8	
	Cultural Anthropology	1-4	
	Linguistic Anthropology	5-12	
	Social Anthropology	1-12	
Biology			
Chemistry			

Figure 9–16. *You can nest one table inside another table to create complex layouts.*

TIP: You can nest tables several levels deep if necessary, but the further you nest tables, the more confusing working with them tends to become. If you're considering several levels of nesting, see if merging and splitting cells could give you a similar result with less fuss.

Converting a Table to Text

Sometimes it's useful to convert a table back to text—for example, when you've received material in a table that you need to convert to a different layout. To convert a table back to text, work as shown in Figure 9–17.

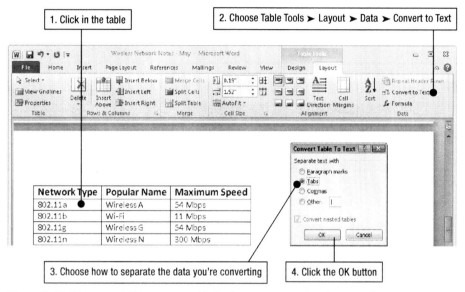

Figure 9–17. *You can quickly convert a table back to text, separating the cells with paragraph marks, tabs, commas, or another character that you type in the **Other** box.*

Creating Newspaper-Style Columns of Text

If you create publications such as newsletters, you may want to use multicolumn layouts to get a suitable look. You can set up a multicolumn layout quickly by selecting the text you want to include and working as shown in Figure 9–18.

TIP: If you want to change the number of columns in the whole document, just click anywhere in the document rather than selecting part of it.

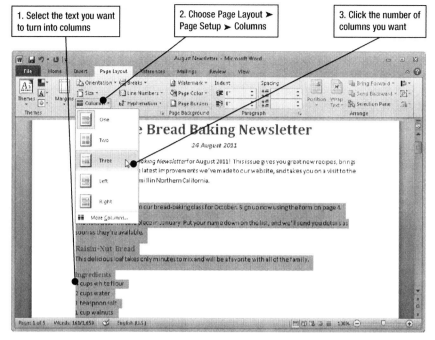

Figure 9–18. *You can quickly set up a multicolumn layout from selected text by choosing* **One**, **Two**, *or* **Three** *columns. Choose* **Left** *for a narrow left column and a wide right column, and* **Right** *for wide left and narrow right. Click* **More Columns** *for further options.*

After you set the number of columns, the Word window displays the columns you've created. Figure 9–19 shows an example.

Figure 9–19. *The sample document with a basic three-column layout applied*

If you need to create four or more columns, or set up your columns with custom spacing or lines between them, click the **More Columns** item on the **Columns** panel to display the **Columns** dialog box. Then choose settings as explained in Figure 9–20.

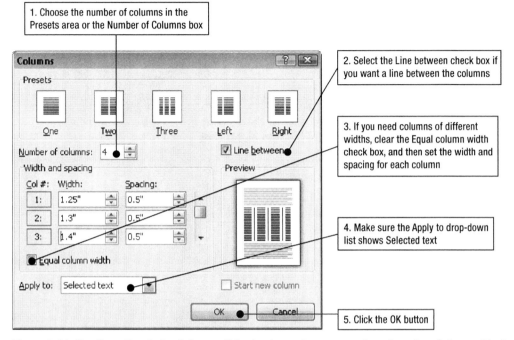

Figure 9–20. *Use the options in the* **Columns** *dialog box to create more complex column layouts in your Word documents.*

Breaking Your Columns with Column Breaks

After you've created the columns, Word automatically flows the text down each column as you enter it. When the first column reaches the bottom of the text area on the page, Word flows it to the start of the second column, and so on.

To end a column early, you can insert a column break. Position the insertion point where you want the break, then choose **Page Layout ➤ Page Setup ➤ Breaks ➤ Column**. Word inserts the column break and moves the insertion point to the top of the next column.

If you need to remove a column break, delete it. Choose **Home ➤ Paragraph ➤ Show/Hide ¶** or press **Ctrl+*** to display invisible characters so that you can see the column break, which appears as a row of dots with the words Column Break in the middle. Position the insertion point before the column break, and then press **Delete** to delete it.

Removing Multiple Columns from a Section or Document

If you want to change a multiple-column section or document back to a single column, click in the section or document, and then choose **Page Layout ➤ Page Setup ➤ Columns ➤ One**. Word restores the text to a single column.

Summary

In this chapter, you learned how to use headers, footers, complex tables, and columns in your documents. You also learned how to divide your documents up into different sections so that you can use different layouts in different parts of the documents.

In the next chapter, I'll show you how to revise, finalize, and print your Word documents. Turn the page when you're ready to start.

Chapter 10

Revising, Finalizing, and Printing Your Documents

In this chapter, I'll show you how to use Word's features for revising and finalizing your documents—plus I'll explain some useful printing features Word offers.

You'll learn first how to use Word's powerful Track Changes feature to track exactly those changes that you want to be able to review, how to work in a document with Track Changes on, and how to integrate your and your colleagues' tracked changes into a single document. We'll then go through how to use comments in your documents, and then move on to the tools that Word gives you for comparing or combining different versions of the same document.

After that, I'll show you how to finalize a document by removing sensitive information from it, marking it as final, encrypting it with a password, and signing it with a digital signature.

At the end of the chapter, we'll also look at the extra features that Word provides for printing your documents—for example, printing just particular pages of a document or pages including tracked changes.

Revising a Document

To create documents, you'll often need to work with other people. As you saw in Chapter 5: "Coauthoring in Real Time and Sharing Documents," you can use Word's coauthoring feature to work on a document with your colleagues in real time. But it's often easier for you and your colleagues to work on documents individually at a time convenient for each of you.

To do so, you can track changes using the Track Changes feature or insert comments in the document. You can then review the changes and, if necessary, compare or combine different edits of the same document.

Tracking Revisions with the Track Changes Feature

When you need to work with other people on creating or revising a document, use Word's Track Changes feature. Track Changes can automatically track almost all the changes in the document so that you can review them, see who made which changes and when, accept the changes you want to keep, and reject the rest. You can choose whether to track all the types of changes that Word can track or track only some types of changes.

Setting Word to Track the Changes You Want to See

First, set Word to track the changes you're interested in seeing. Choose **Review ➤ Tracking ➤ Track Changes** (clicking the drop-down arrow button) ➤ **Change Tracking Options** to display the **Track Changes Options** dialog box, and then work as explained in Figure 10–1.

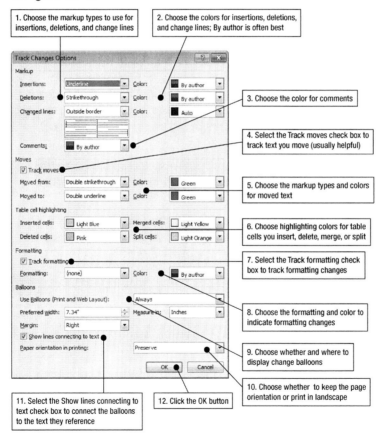

Figure 10–1. *In the **Track Changes Options** dialog box, choose how to show markup, track moves, and handle changes to table cells and formatting. You can also choose whether to use balloons to display changes, where to display them, and whether to connect them to the text.*

Here's what you need to know about the options in the **Track Changes Options** dialog box:

- *Insertions and deletions.* Word can track text that's inserted and text that's deleted. Word offers various options for marking up insertions and deletions, but usually it's clearest to mark up insertions with **Underline** or **Double Underline** and deletions with **Strikethrough** or **Double Strikethrough**. In the **Color** drop-down lists, you can either choose **By author** to have Word give each author a different color or pick the color to use for all insertions or all deletions.

- *Changed lines.* To help draw your eye to lines that have changed, Word can display a vertical line next to each line in a document that contains changes. In the left drop-down list, choose where to put this line: **Left border**, **Right border**, or **Outside border**. Choose the **"(none)"** item to turn off changed lines.

- *Moves.* Word can track text or other items you move within the document (by dragging or by using **Cut** and **Paste**). Tracking moves is usually helpful; if you don't track moves, the moved text appears to have been deleted from its original position and inserted in its new position.

- *Table cell highlighting.* Word uses different highlight colors to show which cells have been inserted, deleted, merged, or split. These colors are for the table structure only; changes to the contents of cells appear as insertions, deletions, and so on.

- *Formatting.* Word can track formatting changes—for example, when someone applies a different style or direct formatting (such as italics).

- *Balloons.* As you'll see in a moment, Word can display the tracked changes either in balloons in the markup area at the side of the page or within the text. In the **Use Balloons** drop-down list, choose **Always** if you want to display all changes in balloons; this is usually the best way to view changes unless there are too many balloons to fit on the page. You can also choose **Only for comments/formatting** if you want to use balloons for comments and formatting but not for other tracked changes, or choose **Never** to turn off balloons.

NOTE: If you display markup in balloons, set the width of the markup area using the **Preferred width** box and the **Measure in** drop-down list. For example, choose **Inches** in the **Measure in** drop-down list and enter **2"** in the **Preferred width** box to make the markup area two inches wide, or choose **Percent** in the Measure in drop-down list and enter **25%** in the **Preferred width** box to make the markup area 25 percent of the window's width.

Turning On Track Changes for a Document

After choosing which changes to track and how to track them, turn Track Changes on by choosing **Review ➤ Tracking ➤ Track Changes**, as shown in Figure 10–2. The button then takes on orange shading to indicate that Track Changes is on; click the button again when you need to turn Track Changes off again.

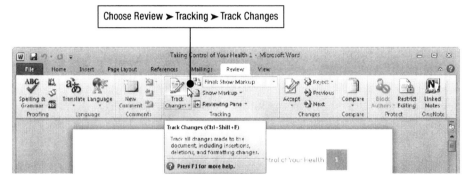

Figure 10–2. *Click the main part of the **Track Changes** button to turn Track Changes on or off.*

If you want to be able to turn Track Changes on or off without displaying the **Review** tab of the Ribbon, use these two ways:

- *Keyboard.* Press **Ctrl+Shift+E**.

- *Status bar.* Right-click blank space on the status bar to display the **Customize Status Bar** menu. Click the **Track Changes** item to put a check mark next to it, then click the status bar to close the menu. The status bar then displays a **Track Changes** readout that you can click to toggle Track Changes on or off, as shown in Figure 10–3.

Figure 10–3. *Adding the **Track Changes** button to the status bar lets you both see whether **Track Changes** is on or off and turn it off or on quickly.*

Working in a Document with Track Changes On

After you turn on Track Changes for a document, you can work in it much as normal. Word tracks your insertions, deletions, and other changes and displays such markup as you've chosen to show.

For example, in **Print Layout** view, **Web Layout** view, and **Full Screen Reading** view, Word normally displays the markup area and balloons, as shown in Figure 10–4. Which changes appear in the text and which appear in balloons depends on what you choose to view, as you'll see in a moment, but you'll normally see the insertions in the text and the deletions in the markup area.

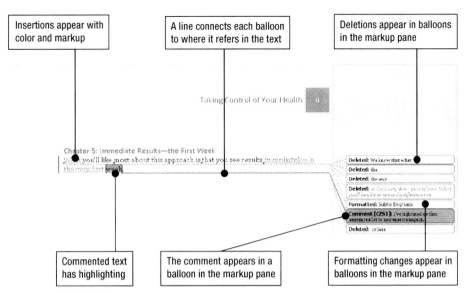

Insertions appear with color and markup

A line connects each balloon to where it refers in the text

Deletions appear in balloons in the markup pane

Commented text has highlighting

The comment appears in a balloon in the markup pane

Formatting changes appear in balloons in the markup pane

Figure 10–4. *In **Print Layout** view, **Web Layout** view, and **Full Screen Reading** view, Word displays the markup area with balloons detailing the changes.*

In **Draft** view and **Outline** view, Word shows the changes inline, using the markup specified in the **Track Changes Options** dialog box—for example, applying an underscore to each insertion and strikethrough to each deletion, as shown in Figure 10–5. This figure also shows a comment in the markup area; you'll learn to work with comments later in this chapter.

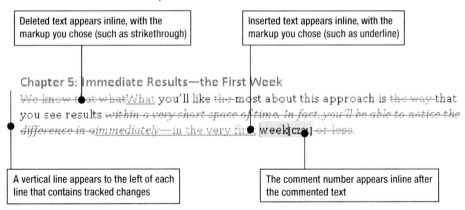

Deleted text appears inline, with the markup you chose (such as strikethrough)

Inserted text appears inline, with the markup you chose (such as underline)

A vertical line appears to the left of each line that contains tracked changes

The comment number appears inline after the commented text

Figure 10–5. *Depending on the markup options you've chosen and the view you're using, Word can mark insertions and deletions inline.*

To see the details of a change, you can hold the mouse pointer over the text. Word displays a ScreenTip showing the change (see Figure 10–6). This move works in all views, but it's most useful when you're not using balloons.

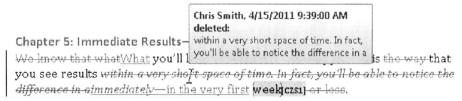

Figure 10–6. *Hold the mouse pointer over a tracked change to display a ScreenTip showing the details.*

Choosing How to View the Document's Changes and Markup

As you work with Track Changes on, you may find it helpful to change how Word displays the markup for review. For example, you can show the document as it will appear with all the markup accepted, or show the document's original version to see how it was.

To choose how to view the document's markup, go to the **Review ➤ Tracking ➤ Display for Review** drop-down menu, and then click the setting you want :

- *Final: Show Markup.* Choose this item to see the document's final text with all the markup displayed. This is the default setting, and the one you'll probably want to use most of the time while marking up the document. Inserted items appear inline, and deleted items appear in balloons. Figure 10–7 shows sample text using the **Final: Show Markup** view.

Figure 10–7. *Use the **Final: Show Markup** display setting when you want to see the final text with the insertions that produce it.*

- *Final.* Choose this item to see the document's final text with no markup appearing—the way you would see it if you were to accept all the revisions marked. Use this view when you want to read the document without the visual distraction of markup. It's especially helpful for picking up errors that are hard to spot when markup is displayed—for example, because the document is heavily marked up. Figure 10–8 shows the same sample text using the **Final** view.

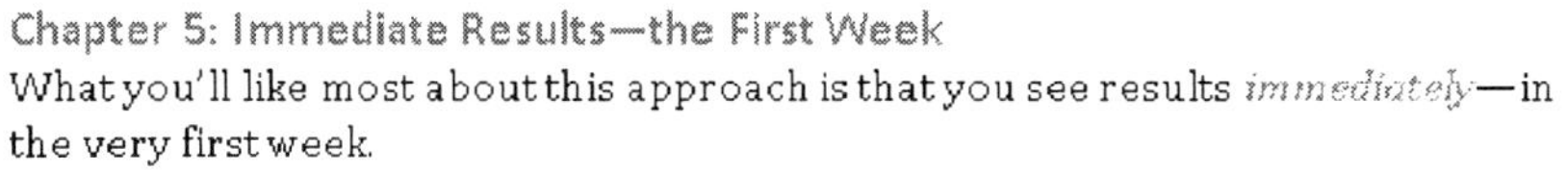

Chapter 5: Immediate Results—the First Week
What you'll like most about this approach is that you see results *immediately*—in the very first week.

Figure 10–8. *Use the **Final** display setting when you want to see the final text without any markup at all.*

- ***Original: Show Markup****.* Choose this item to see the document's original text with the markup displayed. Use this view when you want to focus on the changes made to the original text. Deleted items appear inline, and inserted items appear in balloons. This view is the opposite of the **Final: Show Markup** view. Figure 10–9 shows the same sample text using the **Original: Show Markup** view.

Chapter 5: Immediate Results—the First Week
We know that what you'll like the most about this approach is the way that you see
results within a very short space of time. In fact, you'll be able to notice the
difference in a week or less.
Inserted: What
Formatted: Subtle Emphasis
Comment [CZS1]: I've tightened up this sentence a lot to increase its impact.
Inserted: immediately—in the very first

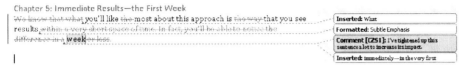

Figure 10–9. *Use the **Original: Show Markup** display setting when you want to see the changes made to the original text.*

- ***Original****.* Choose this item to see the document's original text before any of the changes were made. Figure 10–10 shows the same sample text using the **Original** view.

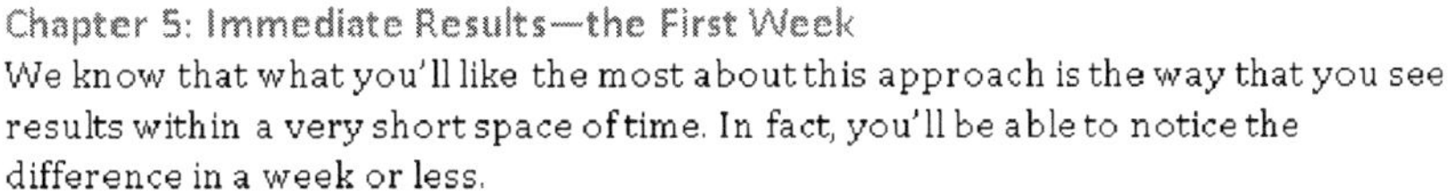
Chapter 5: Immediate Results—the First Week
We know that what you'll like the most about this approach is the way that you see
results within a very short space of time. In fact, you'll be able to notice the
difference in a week or less.

Figure 10–10. *Use the **Original** display setting when you want to switch back to the document's original text. Word displays the document without any markup or tracked changes.*

Controlling Which Changes Word Displays

When a document contains many changes, or when you want to focus only on one aspect of the changes, you may want to turn off the display of some changes so that you see only others. To control which changes Word displays, choose **Review ➤ Tracking ➤ Show Markup**. On the **Show Markup** drop-down menu (see Figure 10–11), select the check box for each item you want to see, and clear the check box for each item you want to hide: **Comments**, **Ink** (annotations using digital handwriting—for example, using a drawing tablet), **Insertions and Deletions**, **Formatting**, **Markup Area Highlight**, **Highlight Updates**, and **Other Reviewers**.

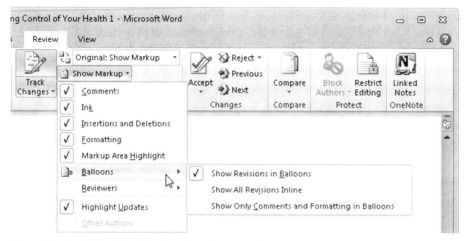

Figure 10–11. *On the **Show Markup** drop-down panel, you can choose which tracked changes to display.*

To switch among using balloons for all revisions, showing all revisions inline, and showing only comments and formatting in balloons, click the **Balloons** submenu, and then click the view you want.

To control which reviewers' changes Word displays, click the **Reviewers** submenu, and then clear the check box for each reviewer you don't want to see.

> **CAUTION:** Hiding some reviewers can sometimes make extra words appear in your document—for example, both the word deleted by a reviewer you've hidden and the word that reviewer inserted as a replacement. If the way the text reads is clearly wrong with some reviewers hidden, display all reviewers and switch to **Final** view to work out which words are really there and which aren't.

Integrating Tracked Changes into a Document

When everyone has made their edits to the document, you can go through the changes and accept those you want to keep and reject the others.

Click the **Previous** button and **Next** button in the **Changes** group on the **Review** tab of the Ribbon to move from one change to another; use the **Accept** button to accept the current change or the commands on the **Accept** drop-down list to accept multiple changes at once (see Figure 10–12); and use the **Reject** button to reject the current change or the commands on the **Reject** drop-down list to reject multiple changes at once. After you accept or reject a tracked change using the **Previous** button or **Next** button, Word displays the next tracked change.

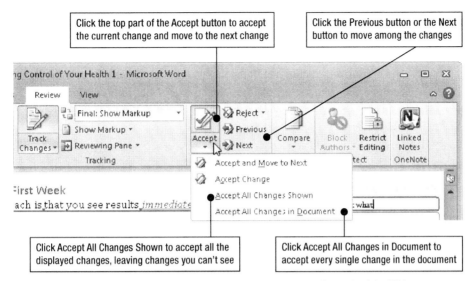

Figure 10–12. *Use the commands in the **Changes** group on the **Review** tab of the Ribbon to accept or reject the changes in the document.*

When you're reviewing many changes, it's usually easiest to go through them in the order in which they appear in the document. But when a document has only a few changes, or you don't need to review all the changes, you may find it faster to use the context menu, as shown in Figure 10–13.

NOTE: The **Accept All Changes Shown** option in the **Accept** drop-down list accepts all the changes that are currently displayed on screen. For example, if you've displayed changes from only some reviewers, choosing **Accept All Changes Shown** accepts only those changes—not those from the reviewers whose changes are not displayed.

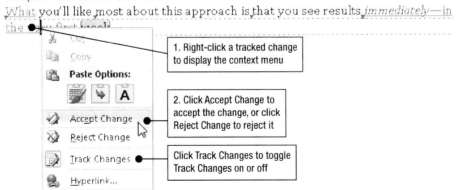

Figure 10–13. *You can quickly review individual changes by right-clicking the change and then clicking **Accept Change** or **Reject Change** on the context menu.*

> **TIP:** When working in **Full Screen Reading** view, you can work with Track Changes by clicking the **View Options** button and using the **Track Changes** submenu, the **Show Comments and Changes** submenu, and the **Show Original/Final Document** submenu at its bottom. For example, choose **View Options ➤ Show Original/Final Document ➤ Final with Markup** to switch to showing the final document with its markup.

Working with Comments

When you're editing a document, it's often useful to add a comment to the text—for example, to provide information that your colleagues should bear in mind, or to recommend a way of improving the document.

Figure 10–14 shows you how to insert a comment in a document in **Print Layout** view, with comments displayed in balloons in the markup area.

> **TIP:** Use comments when you want to suggest changes or add information to a document but want to make sure that your colleagues don't unthinkingly incorporate unsuitable text into the document. A colleague can copy the text from a comment and insert it in the document if necessary, but doing so takes conscious effort, whereas simply accepting all changes in the document is the work of a moment.

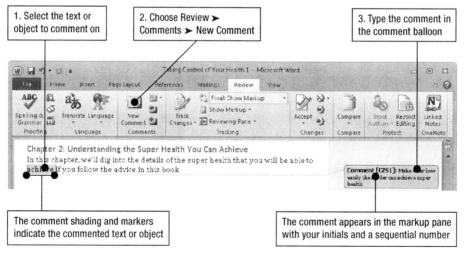

Figure 10–14. In **Print Layout** view, **Web Layout** view, or **Full Screen Reading** view, Word displays comments in the markup area to the side of the document

> **TIP:** Comments are plain text at first, but you can select text in a comment and format it (for example, by using the controls on the Home tab of the Ribbon). You can also insert elements such as tables and graphics in comments.

You can also insert comments in **Draft** view and **Outline** view, which don't show the markup area. In these views, Word opens the **Reviewing** pane automatically when you insert a comment, and you type the comment in the pane (see Figure 10–15). The **Reviewing** pane shows a list of all the tracked changes and comments in the document; you can click an item in the **Reviewing** pane to jump to that point in the document so that you can see it in context.

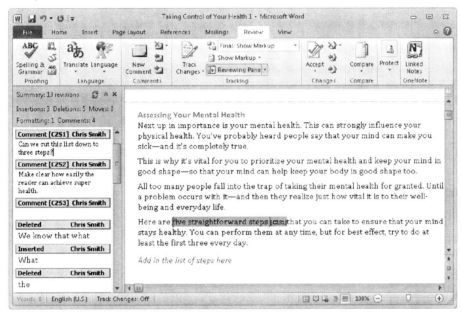

Figure 10–15. *In **Draft** view and **Outline** view, Word displays comments in the **Reviewing** pane and shows the commenter's initials and the comment number in brackets after the commented item.*

The easiest way to close the **Reviewing** pane is to click the **Close** button (the × button) at its upper-right corner of the **Reviewing** pane. You can also toggle the display of the Reviewing pane by choosing **Review ➤ Tracking ➤ Reviewing Pane**.

> **TIP:** If you find it awkward to have **Reviewing** pane at the side of the Word window, choose **Review ➤ Tracking ➤ Reviewing Pane ➤ Reviewing Pane Horizontal** to switch it to horizontal placement. Choose **Review ➤ Tracking ➤ Reviewing Pane ➤ Reviewing Pane Vertical** to put it back.

Viewing and Reviewing the Comments in a Document

Usually the best way to review the comments in a document is by using comment balloons in the layout views or the **Reviewing** pane in **Draft** view and **Outline** view. You can also hold the mouse pointer over commented text or the comment mark to display a ScreenTip showing the text of the comment, as shown in Figure 10–16.

> Chris Smith, 4/20/2011 3:32:00 PM
> commented:
> Can we cut this list down to three steps?

Here are five straightforward steps [czsi] that you can take
stays healthy. You can perform them at any time, but for l

Figure 10–16. *Hold the mouse pointer over commented text or a comment mark to display a ScreenTip showing the text of the comment.*

> **TIP:** If there are too many tracked changes in balloons for you to see the comments easily, choose **Review ➤ Tracking ➤ Show Markup ➤ Balloons ➤ Show Only Comments and Formatting in Balloons**. If there are too many comments to see them fully, choose **Review ➤ Tracking ➤ Reviewing Pane** to display the **Revisions** pane.

Deleting Comments

The most straightforward way to delete a comment is to right-click it and then click **Delete Comment** on the context menu. You can right-click the comment in text, as shown in Figure 10–17, in the markup area, or in the **Reviewing** pane.

Figure 10–17. *You can quickly delete a comment by right-clicking it and then choosing the **Delete Comment** command on the context menu.*

As you'd imagine, you can also delete one or more comments from the Ribbon. To delete one comment, select it, and then choose **Review ➤ Comments ➤ Delete**, clicking the top part of the **Delete** button rather than the drop-down part.

To delete all the comments from a document, choose **Review ➤ Comments ➤ Delete ➤ Delete All Comments in Document**, as shown in Figure 10–18. If you have some comments displayed but others not displayed, this drop-down list also offers the **Delete All Comments Shown** command, which deletes the visible comments but leaves the comments that aren't displayed in place.

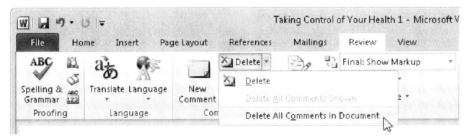

Figure 10–18. *Use the **Delete All Comments in Document** command to strip a document clean of comments.*

Comparing or Combining Different Versions of the Same Document

When you need to follow and review the changes in a document, the best approach is to use Track Changes (as described earlier in this chapter) on a single document that each reviewer works on in turn. This way, Track Changes records all the information you need about the changes made to a document and gives you the tools to review the changes and incorporate them easily.

Other times, you may need to circulate a document to various colleagues at the same time—for example, to get the review done more quickly. Using this approach, you end up with multiple copies of the same document containing their different edits marked by Track Changes. To incorporate all the different edits into a single copy of the document, you can use Word's Document Combine feature to combine or compare two documents at a time. You can then repeat the combining or comparing process for other documents as needed.

> **NOTE:** You may also need to compare two copies of a document in which the changes haven't been tracked. For this, you can use the Document Compare feature. This feature isn't as good as Track Changes used consistently, but it's a huge improvement over spending hours poring over different document files and trying to integrate the best changes into a single version.

To compare or combine two documents, make sure you haven't got either document open. (If either is open, close it.) Then give the command for comparing or combining, as needed:

- *Compare.* Choose **Review** ➤ **Compare** ➤ **Compare** to display the **Compare Documents** dialog box.

- *Combine.* Choose **Review** ➤ **Compare** ➤ **Combine** to display the **Combine Documents** dialog box, which is almost identical to the **Compare Documents** dialog box apart from the title.

After opening the dialog box, you can work as shown in Figure 10–19, which shows the **Compare Documents** dialog box expanded to display all its settings. To expand the dialog box, you click the **More >>** button, which Word then replaces with the **<< Less** button so that you can shrink the dialog box again.

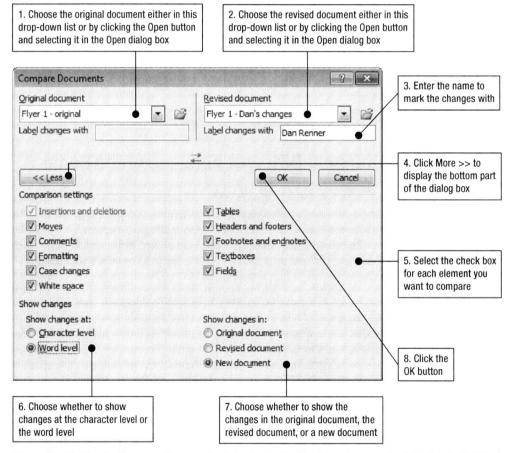

Figure 10–19. *Use the **Compare Documents** dialog box or the **Combine Documents** dialog box (which is almost identical) to identify the changes between two documents based on the same document.*

Most of the comparison settings are straightforward, but here are three tips:

- *Comparison settings.* Normally, you'll want to keep most of these check boxes selected so that you can see all the changes. But if there are particular changes you don't want to see, clear the appropriate check box. For example, if the header or footer contains a date field, each author will appear to have changed the date. To avoid seeing these changes, you could clear the **Headers and footers** check box.

- *Show changes at.* Select the **Word level** option button to make Word analyze changes at the word level—looking at each word to see if it has changed. If you need to dig deeper, you can select the **Character level** option button instead, but for many documents this produces more detail than you need.

- *Show changes in.* Select the **New document** option button if you want to merge the changes into a new document. This is usually clearest, but you can select the **Original document** option button or the **Revised document** option button instead if you prefer.

If Word displays the dialog box shown in Figure 10–20, warning you that it will treat the tracked changes in the documents as having been accepted so that it can make the comparison, click the **Yes** button. (The alternative is to click the **No** button, go back into the documents, and accept or reject the revisions before you compare or combine the documents.)

Figure 10–20. *If Word displays this dialog box when you're comparing or combining documents, click the **Yes** button to proceed.*

Word then displays the result of the comparison or combination—for example, a new compare document together with the source documents that produced it, with the **Reviewing** pane showing a list of the differences (see Figure 10–21).

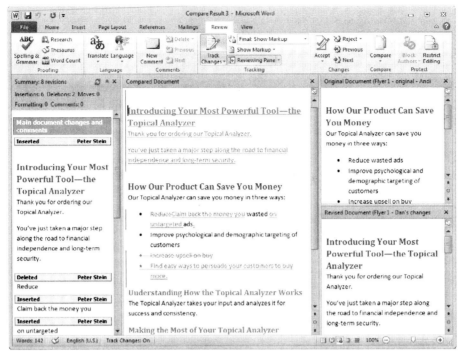

Figure 10–21. *After you compare documents, Word displays the resulting document (the document named* **Compare Result 3** *in this example) plus the source documents. The* **Reviewing** *pane shows a list of the changes.*

If you don't need to see the source documents as you review the result of the comparison, click the **Close** button (the × button) button on each of the source document panes or choose **Review ➤ Compare ➤ Compare ➤ Show Source Documents ➤ Hide Source Documents**. The **Show Source Documents** submenu also gives you commands for opening the compared document's source documents again if you need them.

If you want to keep the changes made to the compared document or combined document, save the document as usual. For example, click the **Save** button on the Quick Access Toolbar.

Finalizing a Document

When you have finished creating, editing, and reviewing a document, you can make it final. Finalizing a document has three main parts:

- Removing sensitive or surplus information from the document.

- Marking the document as being final.

- Signing the document with a digital signature to prove it hasn't been altered.

NOTE: Whether you need to make a document final depends on what the document is for. When you're creating documents for a company or organization that follows formal procedures, you'll probably need to produce a final version of a document for distributing electronically, archiving, or providing to regulators. When you're creating a document for your own use, or that you will print and distribute as hard copies, you probably don't need to finalize it.

Removing Sensitive Information from a Document

Even if its contents aren't secret or confidential, a Word document can include sensitive information about who worked on it, who last saved it, and who added and deleted which parts of it. Before you distribute a document, use Word's tools for cleaning up a document to make sure it doesn't contain anything that will come back to bite you.

To remove potentially sensitive information from a document, take the steps shown in Figure 10–22 to open the **Document Inspector** dialog box.

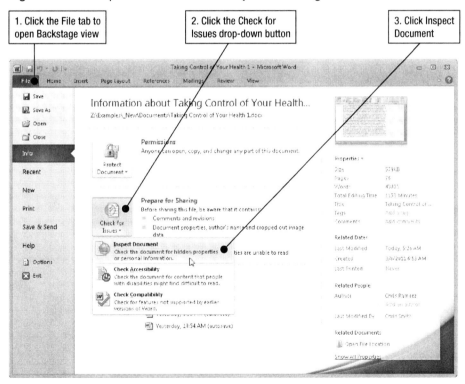

Figure 10–22. *Open* **Backstage** *view and choose* **Check for Issues** ➤ **Inspect Document** *to open the* **Document Inspector** *dialog box.*

With the **Document Inspector** dialog box open (see Figure 10–23), select the check box for each content type you want to scan the document for (see the following list). Usually, it's best to scan for all the content types unless you're sure you don't want to know about particular ones.

- **Comments, Revisions, Versions, and Annotations.** Select this check box to scan for comments, tracked changes, earlier versions of the document, and ink annotations.

- **Document Properties and Personal Information.** Select this check box to scan for potentially sensitive document properties and personal information about you or other people who have worked on the document.

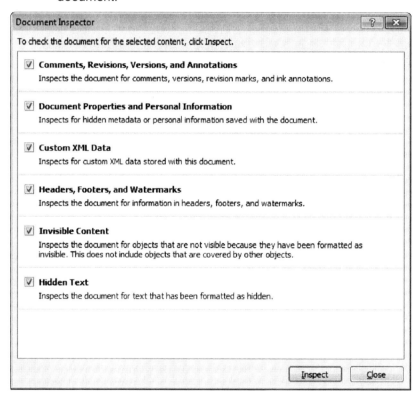

Figure 10–23. *In the **Document Inspector** dialog box, choose the types of metadata and hidden content for which you want to scan the document.*

- *Custom XML Data*. Select this check box to scan for custom XML tags and mappings. (XML is an advanced feature used for manipulating data automatically.)

- *Headers, Footers, and Watermarks*. Select this check box to have Word check the headers, footers, and any watermarks you've applied. These may contain information that you want to remove or update before sharing the document. For example, you may need to remove a Draft watermark or add a Confidential watermark.

■ *Invisible Content.* Select this check box to scan for items that have been formatted as invisible.

■ *Hidden Text.* Select this check box to scan for text formatted to be hidden from view using hidden font formatting. Hidden text is easy to miss when you're looking through a document, but anyone you share the document with can display the hidden text.

When you've made your choices, click the Inspect button to run the inspection. Word examines the document and then updates the **Document Inspector** with details of the items it found in the document (see Figure 10–24). The **Document Inspector** shows a red exclamation point next to each category of items that it found; read the details, and then click the **Remove All** button if you want to remove the items.

After removing the items you want to remove, click the **Reinspect** button, and then click the **Inspect** button. Again, Word checks the document and displays its findings.

When you are satisfied with the results the Document Inspector shows, click the **Close** button to close the **Document Inspector** dialog box.

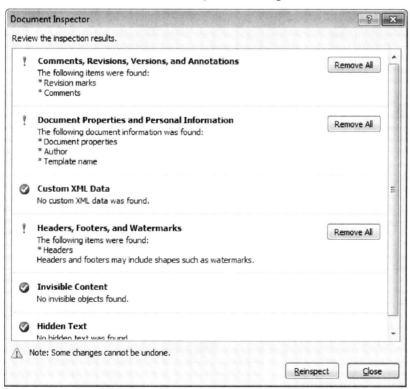

Figure 10–24. *After the **Document Inspector** has inspected the document, click the **Remove All** button for each item you want to remove.*

> **TIP:** After closing the **Document Inspector** dialog box, look through your document to make sure that the items you've removed haven't caused any problems with it. If all is well, you can then save the document and mark it as final, as discussed in the next section.

Marking a Document as Final

When you have finished revising a document, you can mark it as final to indicate that it is no longer a draft. Marking a document as final makes the document read-only, so nobody can make changes to the document without deliberately changing its status from final.

To mark a document as final, work as shown in Figure 10–25.

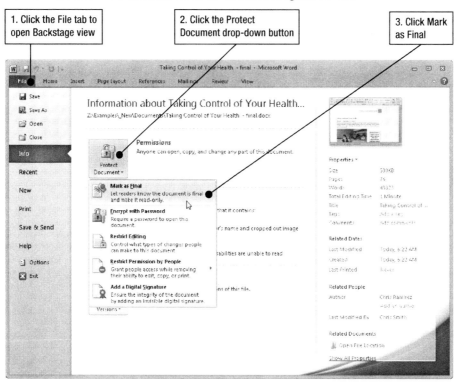

Figure 10–25. *You can mark a document as final to ensure that nobody edits it further without knowing that it's finished.*

When Word displays the confirmation dialog box shown in Figure 10–26, click the **OK** button. Word marks the document as final and read-only, and then saves it.

Figure 10-26. *Click the **OK** button in the confirmation dialog box to finalize the document.*

Word displays a yellow bar across the top of the window to warn you that the document is marked as final (see Figure 10–27). Click the **Edit Anyway** button if you want to open the document for editing anyway. When you've finished editing the document, repeat the above process to mark it as final again.

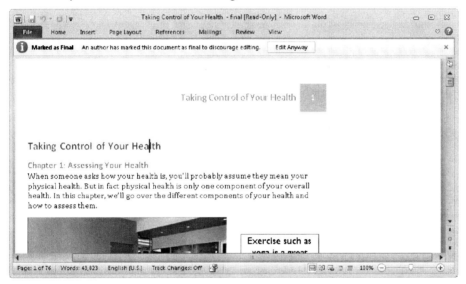

Figure 10-27. *After you mark a document as final, Word makes it read-only so that you cannot change it unless you click the **Edit Anyway** button.*

Encrypting a Document with a Password

If you need to keep other people out of a document, or let only approved people open it, you can encrypt the document with a password. Follow these steps:

1. Click the **File** tab to open **Backstage** view.

2. Click the **Protect Document** drop-down button, and then click **Encrypt with Password** to display the **Encrypt Document** dialog box (see Figure 10–28).

Figure 10–28. *You can encrypt a document with a password. Doing so provides moderate protection against conventional snoopers but not against determined attackers.*

> **TIP:** To create a strong password, use eight or more characters, using both capitals and lowercase, and including numbers and symbols. Memorize the password, or write it down somewhere safe.

3. Click the **OK** button. Word displays the **Confirm Password** dialog box, which is almost exactly the same as the **Encrypt Document** dialog box.

4. Type the password again (to make sure you've typed what you intended), and then click the **OK** button. Word closes the dialog box and changes the **Permissions** readout in the **Info** pane in **Backstage** to show that the document is protected.

5. Click the **Save** button on the Quick Access Toolbar or press **Ctrl+S** to save the document.

> **CAUTION:** Word's encryption is effective only against casual snoopers. An attacker who uses a password-cracking program (which are widely available on the Internet) can open an encrypted document with minimal effort.

Signing a Final Document with a Digital Signature

When you need to prove that a document is a final and approved version, apply a digital signature to the document. A *digital signature* is encrypted data saved in the document that verify that the document hasn't been changed since the signature was applied. To create a digital signature, you use a digital certificate, which is a file containing encrypted data that identifies you or your company or organization.

WHERE TO GET A DIGITAL CERTIFICATE

To get a digital certificate, you apply to a certificate authority (CA). Commercial CAs, such as VeriSign (www.verisign.com) or Comodo (www.comodo.com), issue certificates to both companies and individuals. Your company or organization may also run its own CA to provide digital certificates to its employees.

If you need to see how digital certificates work before deciding whether to get one, create a digital certificate of your own for testing by using the Digital Certificate for VBA Projects tool (see Figure 10–29), which you'll find in the **Microsoft Office\Microsoft Office 2010 Tools** folder on the **Start** menu. This tool crates self-signed certificates that work as examples, but because you have created these certificates, other people will have no reason to trust them.

Figure 10–29. *You can create a test digital certificate by running the Digital Certificate for VBA Projects tool and entering a suitable name in the Create Digital Certificate dialog box.*

Signing a document with a digital signature authenticates the final document, but doesn't protect it; to protect the document, you need to use a password, as discussed earlier in this chapter. If somebody changes the document, Word removes the digital signature. If you're the one who changes the document, you can sign it again once you've finalized it.

To sign a document with a digital signature, follow these steps:

1. Click the **File** tab to open **Backstage** view. The **Info** screen appears.

2. Click the **Protect** dialog box, and then click **Add a Digital Signature** to display the Sign dialog box (see Figure 10–30).

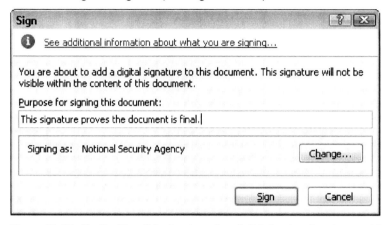

Figure 10–30. *Use the* **Sign** *dialog box to apply a digital signature to a document to prove it remains unchanged since you last worked on it.*

3. If you need to use a different digital certificate than the one that appears in the **Signing as** box, click the **Change** button, click the digital certificate in the **Windows Security: Select a Certificate** dialog box (see Figure 10–31), and then click the **OK** button.

Figure 10–31. *If necessary, use the* **Windows Security: Select a Certificate** *dialog box to choose the digital certificate to sign the document with.*

4. Click the **Sign** button. Word displays the **Signature Confirmation** dialog box (see Figure 10–32).

Figure 10–32. *Word displays the **Signature Confirmation** dialog box to confirm that you have applied a digital signature to the document.*

5. Click the **OK** button to close the **Signature Confirmation** dialog box. You can select the **Don't show this message again** check box first if you want to suppress this dialog box in future, but usually it's useful to see.

NOTE: If you open the signed document for editing, Word warns you that editing will remove the signature. Click the **Yes** button if you want to do this. Word removes the signature, saves the document, and then displays the **Signature Removed** dialog box. Click the **OK** button, and you can then edit the document.

Printing Your Documents

You can print your documents by using the standard techniques explained in Chapter 2: "Using the Ribbon, Backstage, and Common Tools," but Word also offers extra features that you may want to use, such as printing a custom range of pages, printing markup with its document or without its document, or printing a document's properties, styles, or custom key assignments.

Printing a Custom Range of Pages

When you need to print just a custom range of pages in a document, work as shown in Figure 10–33. Use the conventions shown in Table 10–1 to specify which pages you want.

Table 10–1. *Specifying a Custom Range of Pages to Print*

To Print These Pages	Type This	Example
Consecutive pages	Starting page number, hyphen, ending page number	**8-10**
Individual pages	Page number, comma, page number	**7,11,15**
Sections	**s** and section number	**s1,s3**
Range of sections	**s** and starting section number, hyphen, **s** and ending section number	**s1-s3**
Pages within sections	**p** and page number, **s** and section number	**p3s5-p8s7**

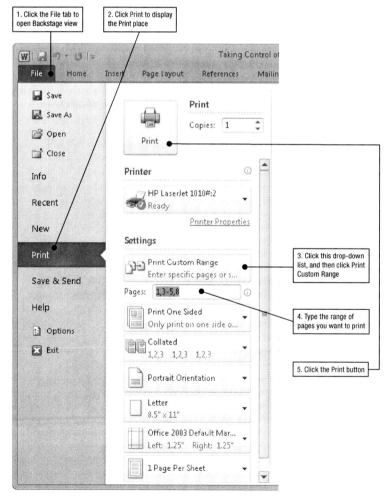

Figure 10–33. *Use the **Print Custom Range** setting in the **Print** page in **Backstage** view to print only some of the pages in the document.*

Choosing Whether to Print Markup—Or Only Markup

When you print a document, you can choose whether to print any markup and comments it contains or whether to print the document as it appears without the markup and comments.

To tell Word which you want, open the **Print What** drop-down menu in the **Print** pane in **Backstage** (the **Print What** drop-down menu usually shows **Print All Pages** at first). At the bottom, click the **Print Markup** item, placing a check mark next to it, if you want to print the markup. If you don't want the markup, make sure the **Print Markup** item has no check mark next to it.

> **NOTE:** Sometimes it's useful to print only the markup for a document. To do so, open the **Print What** drop-down menu in the **Print** pane in **Backstage**, click **List of Markup**, and then click the **Print** button.

Printing Document Properties, Styles, AutoText Entries, and Key Assignments

In the same way that you can print only the markup in a document, you can also print four other items by choosing them on the **Print What** drop-down menu in the **Print** pane in **Backstage**:

- *Document Properties.* Select this item to print a page showing the document's properties—the filename, directory (folder), template, title, subject, author, and so on.

- *Styles. Select* this item to print pages listing the styles used in the document and their formatting.

- *AutoText Entries.* Select this item to print a list of the AutoText entries stored in the document's template.

- *Key Assignments.* Select this item to print a list of the custom key assignments in the document (there may not be any).

Summary

In this chapter, you learned how to use Word's features for revising, finalizing, and printing your documents. You now know how to mark and review revisions with the Track Changes feature; how to create, review, and delete comments; and how to finalize a document.

This is the end of the part of the book that covers Word. In the next part of the book, we'll tackle Excel.

Part **V**

Chapter 11

Creating Workbooks and Entering Data

In this chapter, I'll show you how to get up and running with Excel.

We'll start with creating a new workbook—either a blank one or one based on a template or an existing workbook—and saving it. We'll then examine the components of the Excel user interface and how you navigate them, and go through the various ways you can to enter data in your worksheets. We'll then move on to inserting, renaming, deleting, and rearranging worksheets, and setting them up so that you can see your data easily. Finally, I'll show you how to share your workbooks with others, track changes in your workbooks, and review and integrate changes to produce a final version of a workbook.

Creating and Saving a New Workbook

To create a new workbook in Excel, you use the **New** pane in **Backstage** view, as you learned in Chapter 1: "Meeting the Office Programs and Learning What they Do." As you can see in Figure 11–1, you can create a workbook in five ways:

- *Blank workbook.* This workbook has no contents, so you can turn it into whichever type of workbook you want.

- *Workbook based on a template you've used recently.* Clicking the **Recent Templates** button gives you quick access to templates you've used for your last few workbooks.

- *Workbook based on one of Excel's sample templates.* Clicking the **Sample Templates** button opens the list of templates that come with Excel.

- *Workbook based on one of your templates.* Clicking the **My templates** button opens the **New** dialog box, which shows the templates in your folders.

■ *Workbook based on an existing workbook.* Clicking the **New from existing** button opens the **New from Existing Workbook** dialog box. You can then pick the workbook on which you want to base the new workbook. This is the best way to reuse an existing workbook.

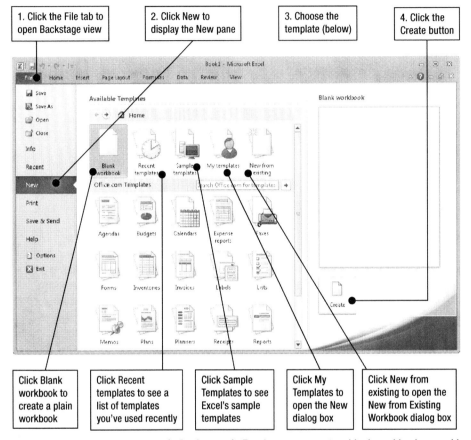

1. Click the File tab to open Backstage view

2. Click New to display the New pane

3. Choose the template (below)

4. Click the Create button

Click Blank workbook to create a plain workbook

Click Recent templates to see a list of templates you've used recently

Click Sample Templates to see Excel's sample templates

Click My Templates to open the New dialog box

Click New from existing to open the New from Existing Workbook dialog box

Figure 11–1. *From the **New** pane in **Backstage** in Excel, you can create a blank workbook, a workbook based on a template, or a workbook based on an existing workbook.*

After creating a new workbook, save it immediately:

1. Click the Save button on the Quick Access Toolbar or press Ctrl+S to display the Save As dialog box.

2. Select the folder in which you want to save the workbook.

3. Type the name you want to give the workbook.

4. If colleagues using versions of Excel that cannot open the Excel Workbook format will need to use the workbook, open the **Save as** type drop-down list and click **Excel 97–2003 Workbook**. Otherwise, leave **Excel Workbook** selected in the **Save as type** drop-down list.

5. Click the **Save** button. Excel saves the workbook.

> **TIP:** The Excel Workbook format uses the .xlsx file extension. Excel 2010 for Windows, Excel 2007 for Windows, Excel 2011 for Mac, and Excel 2008 for Mac can all open this format without you needing to add any file converter software. Excel 2003 for Windows and Excel 2004 for Mac can open this format if you install converter files. Older versions of Excel cannot open this format.

Navigating the Excel Interface, Worksheets, and Workbooks

With a workbook open, you see the worksheets it contains. Figure 11–2 shows a workbook that has data entered on various worksheets. The labels on the figure indicate what the main elements of the Excel user interface do.

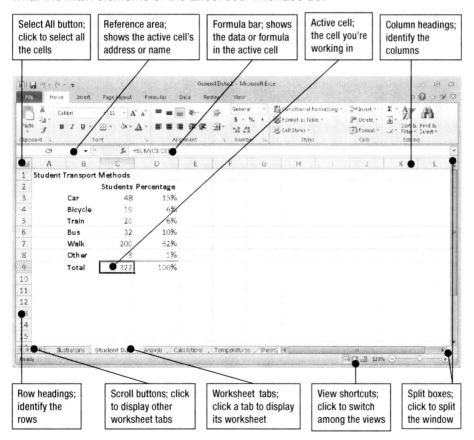

Select All button; click to select all the cells

Reference area; shows the active cell's address or name

Formula bar; shows the data or formula in the active cell

Active cell; the cell you're working in

Column headings; identify the columns

Row headings; identify the rows

Scroll buttons; click to display other worksheet tabs

Worksheet tabs; click a tab to display its worksheet

View shortcuts; click to switch among the views

Split boxes; click to split the window

Figure 11–2. *The main elements of the Excel program window and a workbook*

NOTE: Selecting a column heading selects that whole column, enabling you to format all the cells in the column or enter data in them all at once. Similarly, selecting a row heading selects the whole row, enabling you to work with it as a whole.

Understanding Workbooks, Worksheets, Columns, and Rows

Each workbook consists of one or more worksheets or other sheets, such as chart sheets or macro sheets. To display the worksheet you want to use, you click its tab in the worksheet tab bar (see Figure 11–3). If the worksheet's tab isn't visible in the worksheet tab bar, you click the scroll buttons to display it.

TIP: You can drag the divider bar to the right to make the worksheet tab bar wider so that more tabs appear at once. Excel makes the horizontal scroll bar smaller to compensate.

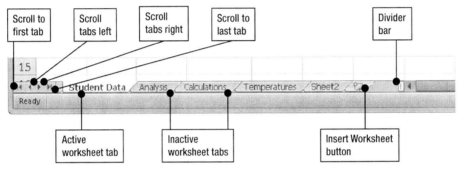

Figure 11–3. *Use the worksheet tab bar to display the worksheet you want or to insert a new worksheet. You can drag the divider bar left or right to change the length of the tab bar.*

Each worksheet contains 16,384 columns and 1,048,576 rows, giving a grand total of 17,179,869,184 cells. Normally, you'll use only a small number of these cells—perhaps a few hundred or a few thousand—but there's plenty of space should you need it for large data sets.

TIP: You can quickly move to the next worksheet by pressing **Ctrl+Page Down** or to the previous worksheet by pressing **Ctrl+Page Up**.

Each column is identified by one, two, or three letters:

1. The first 26 columns use the letters A to Z.

2. The next 26 columns use AA to AZ, the following 26 BA to BZ, and so on.

3. When the two-letter combinations are exhausted, Excel uses three letters: AAA, AAB, and so on.

Each row is identified by a number, from 1 up to 1048576.

Each cell is identified by its column lettering and its row number. For example, the cell at the intersection of column A and row 1 is cell A1, and the cell at the intersection of column ZA and row 2256 is ZA2256.

Moving the Active Cell

In Excel, you usually work in a single cell at a time. That cell is called the *active cell* and receives the input from the keyboard.

You can move the active cell easily using either the mouse or the keyboard:

- *Mouse.* Click the cell you want to make active.

- *Keyboard.* Press the arrow keys to move the active cell up or down by one row or left or right by one column at a time. You can also press the keyboard shortcuts shown in Table 11–1 to move the active cell further.

Table 11–1. *Keyboard Shortcuts for Moving the Active Cell*

To Move the Active Cell Like This	Press This Keyboard Shortcut
First cell in the row	Home
First cell in the active worksheet	Ctrl+Home
Last cell used in the worksheet	Ctrl+End
Down one screen	Page Down
Up one screen	Page Up
Right one screen	Alt+Page Down
Left one screen	Alt+Page Up
To the last row in the worksheet	Ctrl+Down arrow
To the last column in the worksheet	Ctrl+Right arrow
To the first row in the worksheet	Ctrl+Up arrow
To the first column in the worksheet	Ctrl+Left arrow or Home

Selecting a Range of Cells

When you want to affect multiple cells at once, you select the cells using the mouse or the keyboard. Excel call a selection of cells a *range*. A range can consist of either a rectangle of contiguous cells or various cells that aren't next to each other.

The easiest way to select a range of contiguous cells is to click the first cell in the range and then drag to select all the others, as shown in Figure 11–4.

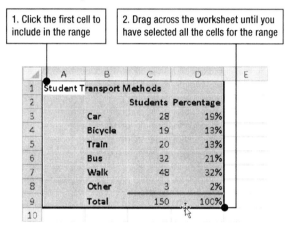

Figure 11–4. *The easiest way to select a range of contiguous cells is to click and drag. You can drag in any direction from the cell you first click.*

> **TIP:** You can also select a range of contiguous cells by clicking the first cell and then **Shift+clicking** the last cell. Alternatively, move the active cell to the first cell you want to select, then hold down **Shift** while you press the arrow keys to extend the selection across the rest of the range.

Figure 11–5 shows you how to select a range of noncontiguous cells.

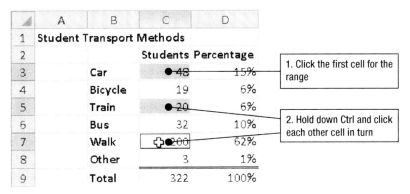

Figure 11–5. *To select a range of noncontiguous cells, click the first cell, and then hold down **Ctrl** while you click each other cell in turn.*

Excel uses a colon to separate the beginning cell and ending cell in a contiguous range. For example, the range A1:E3 starts at cell A1 and runs to cell E3.

For a continuous range, Excel uses commas to separate the individual cells. For example, the range D3,E5,F7 consists of the three individual cells (D3, E5, and F7).

> **NOTE:** You can include a range of contiguous cells in a range of noncontiguous cells. For example, the range E5,F7,G1:G13 consists of two individual cells (E5 and F7) and one range of contiguous cells (G1 through G13).

You can quickly select rows, columns, or all the cells in the active worksheet:

- *Select a column.* Click the column heading, or click in the column and press **Ctrl+spacebar**.

- *Select multiple contiguous columns.* Click and drag through the column headings.

- *Select multiple noncontiguous columns.* Click the first column heading, then **Ctrl+click** each of the other column headings you want to include.

- *Select a row.* Click the row heading, or click in the row and press **Shift+spacebar**.

- *Select multiple contiguous rows.* Click and drag through the row headings.

- *Select multiple noncontiguous rows.* Click the first row heading, then **Ctrl+click** each of the other row headings you want to include.

- *Select all the cells in the worksheet.* Click the **Select All** button. Or press **Ctrl+spacebar** followed by **Shift+spacebar** (or the other way around).

To deselect a range you've selected, click anywhere outside the range.

Entering Data in Your Worksheets

You can enter data in your worksheets by typing it, by pasting it, or by using drag and drop to move or copy it. Excel also includes a feature called AutoFill that automatically fills in series data for you based on the input you've provided.

Typing Data in a Cell

To enter data in a cell, first make the cell active by clicking in it or moving the selection rectangle to it. Then start typing in the cell. As you start typing, Excel displays an insertion point in the cell, and what you type appears in the cell.

When you've finished typing the contents of the cell, move to another cell in any of these ways:

- *Press **Enter**.* Excel moves the active cell to the next cell below the current cell.

- *Press **Tab**.* Excel moves the active cell to the cell in the next column to the right.

- *Click another cell.* Excel moves the active cell to the cell you click.

- *Press an arrow key.* Excel moves the active cell to the next cell in the direction of the arrow. For example, press the right arrow key to move the active cell to the next cell to the right.

> **TIP:** If you want, you can change the direction Excel moves the active cell when you press **Enter**. Choose **File ➤ Options** to display the **Excel Options** dialog box, then click the **Advanced** item in the left column to display the **Advanced** options. In the **Editing** options area at the top, open the **Direction** drop-down list, and then choose **Down**, **Right**, **Up**, or **Left**, as needed. Click the **OK** button to close the **Excel Options** dialog box.

Editing a Cell

You can edit a cell's existing contents either within the cell itself or in the formula bar (see Figure 11–2 for a reminder on what the formula bar is).

The easiest way to edit within the cell is to double-click the cell. Excel opens the cell for editing, and you can then change its contents, as shown on the left in Figure 11–6. You can also open a cell for editing by making it the active cell and then pressing F2.

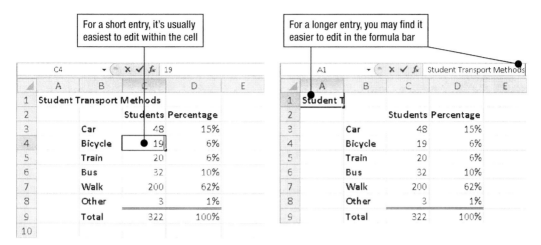

Figure 11–6. *You can edit a cell's contents in the cell itself (left) or in the formula bar (right).*

To edit in the formula bar, click the cell, and then click the cell's contents in the formula bar, as shown on the right in Figure 11–6.

When you're editing a cell in the cell, pressing an arrow key moves the insertion point within the cell rather than finishing the entry and moving to another cell:

- *Left arrow key.* Moves left by one character.

- *Right arrow key.* Moves right by one character.

- *Down arrow key.* Moves to the end of the cell's contents.

- *Up arrow key.* Moves the insertion point back to where it was before you moved to the end of the cell's contents.

To finish editing a cell, press **Enter**, click the check mark on the formula bar, or click another cell. You can also press **Tab** to select the cell in the next column or **Shift+Tab** to select the cell in the previous column. To cancel editing a cell and restore its previous contents, press **Esc** or click the cross on the formula bar.

> **NOTE:** Instead of editing a cell's existing contents, you can simply replace them by making the cell active and then typing new contents over the existing contents. Replacing tends to be faster than editing when a cell contains a short entry that you can easily retype.

Entering Data Quickly Using AutoFill

When you need to fill in a series of data, see if Excel's AutoFill feature can enter the data for you and save time and effort.

To use AutoFill, you enter the base data for the series in one or more cells, then select them and drag the AutoFill handle in the direction you want to fill. AutoFill checks your base data, works out what the other cells should contain, and fills it in for you.

Using AutoFill's Built-in Capabilities

Open a test workbook, or press **Shift+F11** to add a test worksheet to your current workbook, and then try AutoFill. The easiest way to learn is by putting AutoFill to use. First, try the example shown in Figure 11–7.

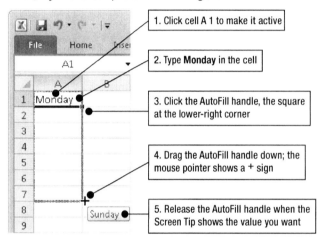

Figure 11–7. *Drag the **AutoFill** handle down or across to fill in a series of data derived from one or more existing entries. In this case, AutoFill fills in the days of the week, and repeats the series if you drag further.*

Next, drag through the range on which you used AutoFill, and press **Delete** to clear the cells. Then try the example shown in Figure 11–8.

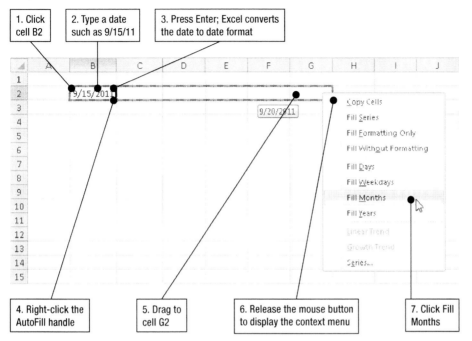

Figure 11–8. *Right-click and drag the **AutoFill** handle to reveal the context menu with further options for automatically filling the cells. Click the **Fill Months** item on the context menu to enter the months.*

Next, clear your data again, and then try the example shown in Figure 11–9, which uses two starting values instead of a single starting value.

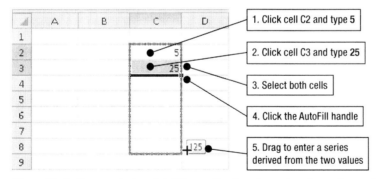

Figure 11–9. *You can start an AutoFill operation from two values to create a series based on their relationship. Here, AutoFill increments each number by 20, because the second value (25) is 20 more than the first value (5).*

Finally, click the **Undo** button on the Quick Access Toolbar to undo the AutoFill operation. Then try the example shown in Figure 11–10, which creates a growth trend from the values 5 and 25. Because the second value (25) is 5 times the first value (5), Excel multiplies each value by 5, giving the sequence, 5, 25, 125, 625, 3125, and so on.

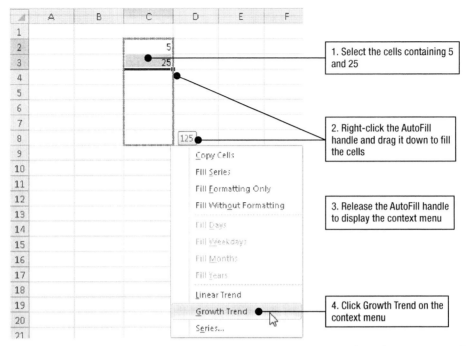

Figure 11–10. *To create a series based on a growth trend or a linear trend, right-click and drag the AutoFill handle, and then click the appropriate option on the context menu.*

TIP: The AutoFill context menu also contains items for filling the cells with formatting only (copying the formatting from the first cell), filling the cells without formatting (ignoring the first cell's formatting), and filling in days, weekdays, and years. All of these tricks can save you time and effort.

Creating Your Own Custom AutoFill Lists

If you need to enter the same series of data frequently, you can create your own AutoFill lists. Follow these steps:

1. Click the **File** tab to open **Backstage** view.

2. In the left column, click **Options** to display the **Excel Options** dialog box.

3. In the left column, click **Advanced** to display the **Advanced** options.

4. Scroll all the way down to the bottom, and then click the **Edit Custom Lists** button in the **Options** area to display the **Custom Lists** dialog box (shown in Figure 11–11 with settings chosen).

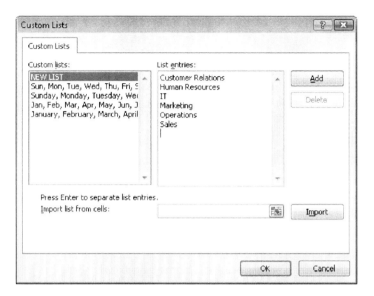

Figure 11–11. *You can supplement Excel's built-in AutoFill lists by creating your own data series that you need to enter frequently in your worksheets.*

5. In the **Custom lists** box, click the **NEW LIST** item.

6. Click in the **List** entries box, and then type your list, putting one item on each line by pressing **Enter**.

> **TIP:** If you've already entered your list on cells in the worksheet, you don't need to retype it— instead, import it from the worksheet. Click the **Collapse Dialog** button to the left of the Import button to collapse the **Custom Lists** dialog box to a shallow **Options** dialog box, then drag through the list on the worksheet. Click the **Collapse Dialog** button to restore the **Custom Lists** dialog box, and then click the **Import** button.

7. Click the **Add** button to add the list to the **Custom lists** box.

8. When you've finished creating custom lists, click the **OK** button to close the **Custom Lists** dialog box.

9. Click the **OK** button to close the **Excel Options** dialog box.

You can now use your custom list like any other AutoFill list. To try the custom list, click a cell, type the first item in the list, and then drag the **AutoFill** handle to expand it.

Pasting Data into a Worksheet with Paste, Paste Options, and Paste Special

If the data you need to add to a worksheet is already in another document, you can copy it and paste it into the worksheet using the techniques explained in Chapter 3: "Working with Text."

- *Paste an item with all its formatting.* Choose **Home** ➤ **Clipboard** ➤ **Paste**, clicking the top part of the **Paste** button.

- *Change a pasted item.* Click **the Paste Options** drop-down button that appears below and to the right of material you've pasted. Then click the **Paste Option** you want on the drop-down list, as shown on the left in Figure 11–12.

- *Paste using a paste option.* Choose **Home** ➤ **Clipboard** ➤ **Paste**, clicking the drop-down part of the **Paste** button. On the panel that appears, click the button for the paste option you want to use, as shown on the right in Figure 11–12.

> **TIP:** Hold the mouse pointer over a button on the **Paste Options** panel to see a preview of the paste result you'll get from clicking the button.

Figure 11–12. *You can choose a paste option either for an item you've already pasted (left) or an item you're about to paste (right). For other options, click the **Paste Special** item on the **Paste** drop-down panel to open the **Paste Special** dialog box.*

The **Paste Options** panel shows a useful selection of **Paste Options**. But when you want to reach the full range of options, you can use the **Paste Special** dialog box instead. The **Paste Special** dialog box is also good if you find text descriptions of options easier to understand than the graphical buttons on the Paste Options panel,

To use the **Paste Special** dialog box, follow these steps:

1. Choose Home ➤ Clipboard ➤ Paste ➤ Paste Special to open the Paste Special dialog box (see Figure 11–13).

Figure 11–13. *Use the **Paste Special** dialog box when you need to paste only some of the data, when you need to perform an operation on the data, or when you need to transpose its rows and columns.*

2. In the **Paste** area, choose the option button you want:

   ▓ *All.* Pastes in all the data and all its formatting. Normally, you'll want to do this only if you're using the **Skip blanks** check box, the **Transpose** check box, or the **Paste Link** button.

   ▓ *Formulas.* Pastes in all the formulas and constants without formatting.

   ▓ *Values.* Pastes in formula values instead of pasting in the formulas themselves. Excel removes the formatting from the values.

   ▓ *Formats.* Pastes in the formatting without the data. This option is surprisingly useful once you know it's there.

   ▓ *Comments.* Pastes in only comments. This option is handy when you're integrating different colleagues' takes on the same worksheet.

   ▓ *Validation.* Pastes in only data-validation criteria.

- **All using Source theme.** Pastes in all the data using the theme from the workbook the data came from.

- **All except borders.** Pastes in all the data and formatting but removes the cell borders.

- **Column widths.** Pastes in only the column widths—no data and no other formatting. This option is useful when you need to lay one worksheet out like another existing worksheet.

- **Formulas and number formats.** Pastes in formulas and number formatting but no other formatting.

- **Values and number formats.** Pastes in values (rather than formulas) and number formatting.

- **All merging conditional formats.** Pastes all data and formatting and merges in any conditional formatting. See Chapter 12: "Editing Worksheets and Applying Formatting" for details on conditional formatting.

- If you need to perform a mathematical operation on the data you're pasting, go to the **Operation** area of the **Paste Special** dialog box and select the **Add** option button, the **Subtract** option button, the **Multiply** option button, or the **Divide** option button, as needed. Otherwise, leave the **None** option button selected to paste the data without performing math on it.

3. In the bottom section of the **Paste Special** dialog box, select or clear the two check boxes as needed:

   - **Skip blanks.** Prevents Excel from pasting blank cells.

   - **Transpose.** Transposes columns to rows and rows to columns. This option is much quicker than retyping data laid out the wrong way.

4. Click the **OK** button to paste the data, formatting, or other item you chose.

NOTE: To link the data you're pasting back to its source, click the **Paste Link** button in the **Paste Special** dialog box instead of the **OK** button. This makes Excel create a link to the source data, so that when the source data changes, the linked data changes, too. If the source data is in the same workbook, Excel updates the links automatically. If the source data is in another workbook, Excel updates the data when you open the workbook that contains the links.

Copying and Moving Data with Drag and Drop

When you need to copy or move data within Excel, you can use drag and drop.

Normal drag and drop moves or copies all of the data and all of its formatting, much like pasting the material. To use this kind of drag and drop, follow these steps:

1. Select the range of cells you want to move.

2. Move the mouse pointer over an edge of the selection so that it turns to a four-headed arrow, as shown on the left in Figure 11–14.

3. Drag the range to its destination, and then drop it.

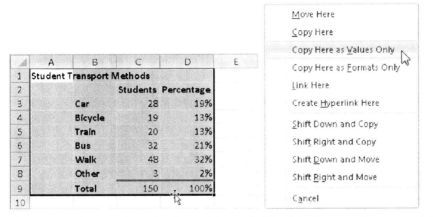

Figure 11–14. *To move data using drag and drop, select the data, then move the mouse pointer over one of its edges. When the drag-and-drop pointer appears (left), drag the data to its destination. You can also right-drag and then click an option on the context menu (right).*

To reach more options, such as copying only the values or the formats, or creating a link or a hyperlink to the source, right-click and drag instead of left-clicking and dragging. When you release the mouse button, Excel displays a context menu of options, as shown on the right in Figure 11–14. Click the option you want.

Inserting, Renaming, Deleting, and Rearranging Worksheets

When you create a workbook, Excel puts three worksheets in it by default. You can add extra worksheets as needed, or delete any of these default worksheets you don't need. You can also give the worksheets custom names and rearrange their order.

> **TIP:** To change the number of worksheets that Excel includes in a blank workbook, click the **File** tab to open **Backstage**, and then click **Options**. In the Excel Options dialog box, change the number in the **Include this many sheets** box to the number of worksheets you want, and then click the **OK** button.

Inserting a Worksheet

The quick way to insert a worksheet is to activate the worksheet after which you want to insert the new worksheet, and then press **Shift+F11**.

You can also insert a worksheet by following these steps:

1. Right-click the tab of the worksheet before which you want to insert the new worksheet.

2. On the context menu, click **Insert** to display the **Insert** dialog box.

3. On the **General** tab, click the **Worksheet** item. (This item may already be selected.)

4. Click the **OK** button to close the dialog box and insert the worksheet.

Renaming a Worksheet

To rename a worksheet, follow these steps:

1. Double-click its tab to select the current name.

2. Type the name you want to give the worksheet. You can use up to 31 characters in the name.

3. Press **Enter** or click elsewhere in the worksheet.

> **TIP:** If you want to make the tab stand out, right-click the tab again, click or highlight **Tab Color**, and then click the color for the tab.

Deleting a Worksheet

You can easily delete any worksheets you don't need. Follow these steps:

1. Click the worksheet's tab, and double-check that the worksheet doesn't contain any data you need.

2. Right-click the worksheet's tab, and then click **Delete** on the context menu.

3. If the worksheet contains any data, Excel displays a dialog box (see Figure 11–15) to double-check that you're prepared to delete it.

Figure 11–15. *When you go to delete a worksheet that contains data, Excel double-checks that you're prepared to lose the data on the worksheet.*

> **NOTE:** If the worksheet is blank, Excel deletes it without double-checking that you want to delete it.

   4.   Click the **Delete** button to delete the worksheet.

Rearranging the Worksheets in a Workbook

You can rearrange the worksheets in a workbook into the order you need. Figure 11–16 shows the quick way to move a worksheet. You simply click the worksheet's tab, drag it left or right until Excel displays a downward arrow between the worksheets where you want to place it, and then drop it.

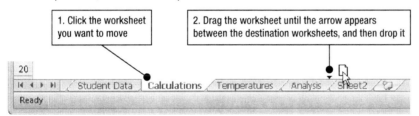

Figure 11–16. *The quick way to move a worksheet is to click its tab in the worksheet tabs bar and drag it to where you want it to appear.*

> **TIP:** To move two or more worksheets, select them first. Click the first worksheet's tab, then **Ctrl+click** each other worksheet's tab in turn. To select a range of worksheets that appear next to each other, click the first worksheet's tab, and then **Shift+click** the tab for the worksheet at the other end of the range.

This method works well for moving a worksheet a short distance along the tab bar, but for moving larger distances, you may prefer to use the **Move or Copy** dialog box. Follow these steps:

   1.   Right-click the worksheet's tab to display the context menu. To move multiple worksheets, select them, and then right-click one of the selected tabs.

2. On the context menu, click **Move or Copy** to display the **Move or Copy** dialog
    box (see Figure 11–17).

Figure 11–17. *Use the **Move or Copy** dialog box to move one or more worksheets further than you can comfortably drag within a workbook or to move or copy worksheets to another open workbook.*

3. In the **To book** drop-down list, make sure the current workbook is selected
    unless you want to move the worksheet to another workbook—in which case,
    select that workbook.

4. In the **Before sheet** list box, click the worksheet before which you want to
    position the worksheet you're moving.

5. Select the **Create a copy** check box if you want to copy the worksheet to the
    destination rather than move it. Copying tends to be most useful when the
    destination is another workbook, but you can copy within a workbook as well.

6. Click the **OK** button to close the dialog box. Excel moves or copies the worksheet
    to the destination you chose.

Displaying Worksheets the Way You Prefer to See Them

Excel lets you display worksheets in several different ways:

- You can choose among three different views and **Full Screen** view.

- You can split the window into two or four parts.

- You can hide windows you don't need to see.

- You can use freezing to keep important parts of the window in view.

Using Excel's Views Effectively

Excel gives you three different views for working in your workbooks:

- *Normal view*. This is the view in which workbooks normally open, and the view in which you'll do most of your data entry, formatting, and reviewing. **Normal** view is the view in which you've seen Excel so far in this chapter.

- *Print Layout view*. This view shows your worksheets as they will look when laid out on paper. Normally, you use this view to adjust the page setup, but you can also enter data, edit, and so on. You'll learn how to adjust the page setup in the next chapter.

- *Page Break Preview*. This view shows where the page breaks will fall when you print the workbook. You use this view to make sure the page breaks are in suitable positions and to move them if they're not. You'll learn how to do this too in the next chapter.

The easiest way to switch views is to click the **View Shortcuts** button at the right end of the status bar (see Figure 11–18). You can also click the **View** tab of the Ribbon, go to the **Workbook Views** group, and then click the **Normal** button, the **Page Layout** button, or the **Page Break Preview** button.

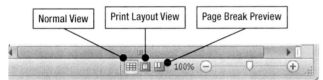

Figure 11–18. *Use the **View Shortcuts** buttons on the status bar to change views quickly.*

TIP: When you want to see as much of a worksheet as possible, choose **View ➤ Workbook Views ➤ Full Screen**. Excel hides the Ribbon and displays the worksheet full screen. You can use **Full Screen** view in any of the three views. Press **Esc** when you want to return from **Full Screen** view to a window.

Viewing Two or Four Separate Parts of a Worksheet at the Same Time

When you need to view separate parts of a worksheet at the same time, you can split the window into two or four panes. You can then display a different part of the worksheet in each pane as needed.

Figure 11–19 shows you how to split a window into two or four panes the size you want.

1. Click the split box at the top of the vertical scroll bar

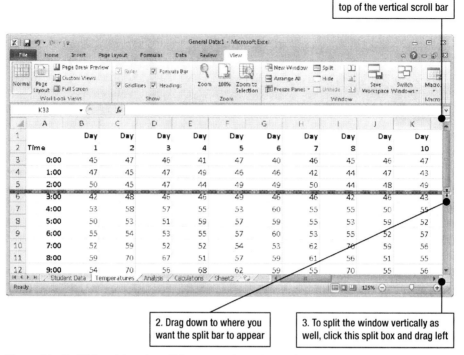

2. Drag down to where you want the split bar to appear

3. To split the window vertically as well, click this split box and drag left

Figure 11–19. *Click and drag the split boxes to split the Excel window into two or four panes when you need to work in separate areas of the worksheet at the same time.*

> **TIP:** You can also split the window into four panes by choosing **View ➤ Window ➤ Split**.

Figure 11–20 shows how the window looks when split into four panes and explains how to adjust the splits and the panes.

> **NOTE:** When you split the window, you may find it helpful to freeze certain rows and columns, as discussed later in this chapter, to keep them visible even when you scroll to other areas of the worksheet.

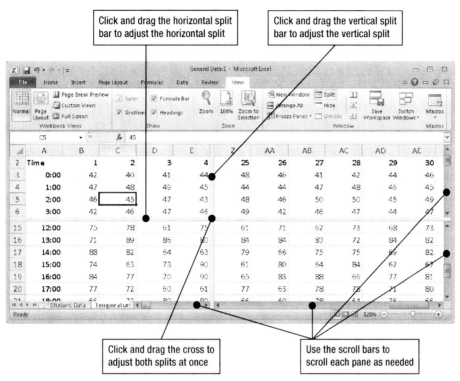

Click and drag the horizontal split bar to adjust the horizontal split

Click and drag the vertical split bar to adjust the vertical split

Click and drag the cross to adjust both splits at once

Use the scroll bars to scroll each pane as needed

Figure 11–20. *You can adjust the splits as needed and scroll the panes to show the parts of the worksheet you want to see.*

You can remove the split in any of these ways:

▧ Double-click the split bar or the cross of both split bars.

▧ Click the vertical split bar and drag it all the way to the left of the window.

▧ Click the horizontal split bar and all the way to the top of the window.

▧ Choose **View ➤ Window ➤ Split**.

Opening Extra Windows to Show Other Parts of a Workbook

Instead of splitting a window, you can open one or more extra windows to show other parts of the workbook. Figure 11–21 shows you how to open an extra window and arrange the windows.

NOTE: The **Cascade** arrangement puts the windows in a stack so you can see each one's title bar. This is good for choosing the window you want when you have many windows open. The **Tiled** arrangement resizes all the nonminimized windows to roughly even sizes. This can make the windows too small for use, but it's useful for seeing which windows are open and closing ones you no longer need. To close a window, click its **Close** button (the ✕ button) as usual.

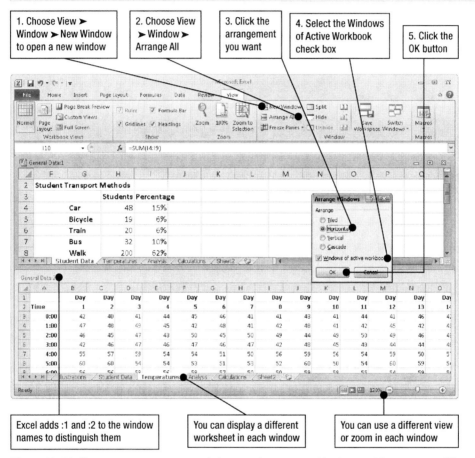

1. Choose View ➤ Window ➤ New Window to open a new window

2. Choose View ➤ Window ➤ Arrange All

3. Click the arrangement you want

4. Select the Windows of Active Workbook check box

5. Click the OK button

Excel adds :1 and :2 to the window names to distinguish them

You can display a different worksheet in each window

You can use a different view or zoom in each window

Figure 11–21. *You can open two or more windows on the same workbook to enable you to see different parts of the workbook at the same time.*

NOTE: Opening extra windows has two advantages over splitting a window. First, you can display other worksheets (or workbooks) in the windows if you want rather than just other parts of the same worksheet. Second, you can zoom each window by a different amount as needed.

When you don't need to see a particular window, you can hide it to get it out of the way. Click the window, and then choose **View ➤ Window ➤ Hide Window**. To display the window again, choose **View ➤ Window ➤ Unhide** window, click the window in the **Unhide** dialog box, and then click the **OK** button.

After displaying a window, you can double-click its title bar to maximize it within the Excel window.

Zooming In or Out to Show the Data You Need to See

You can zoom in or out on your worksheets to make the data easier to read or to display more of a worksheet at once. The easiest way to zoom in or out is by using the **Zoom** buttons and **Zoom** slider on the status bar. Click the **–** button or the **+** button to change the zoom by 10 percent per click, or drag the **Zoom** slider to make larger changes or to set a custom zoom percentage.

When you need to zoom just the right amount to display a particular area of the worksheet as large as it will fit in the window, select the area, and then choose **View ➤ Zoom ➤ Zoom to Selection**.

Comparing Two Windows Side by Side

When you need to compare the contents of two open windows, use the **View Side by Side** command. You can also set the windows to scroll in sync, which makes it easier to compare them. Follow these steps:

1. Click one of the windows you want to compare.

2. Choose **View ➤ Window ➤ View Side by Side**. If you have only two windows open, Excel arranges them side by side. If you have more windows open, Excel displays the **Compare Side by Side** dialog box (see Figure 11–22).

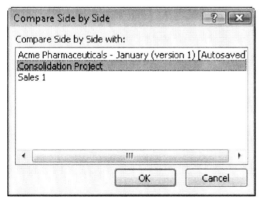

Figure 11–22. *In the* ***Compare Side by Side*** *dialog box, select the window you want to compare with the active window.*

3. Click the window you want to compare with the active window.

4. Click the **OK** button to close **the Compare Side by Side** dialog box. Excel positions the windows side by side, sizing them to share the space in the Excel window, and turns on synchronous scrolling. You'll see that the Vi**ew Side by Side** button and the **Synchronous Scrolling** button in the **Window** group both appear pressed in.

You can now compare the data in the two windows as needed. When you scroll one window, Excel automatically scrolls the other window too by the same amount, keeping them synchronized.

If you need to turn off synchronous scrolling, choose **View ➤ Window ➤ Synchronous Scrolling** (un-pressing the button).

When you have finished the comparison, choose **View ➤ Window ➤ View Side by Side** to un-press the **View Side** by Side button and restore the windows to their previous sizes and positions.

Freezing Rows and Columns So That They Stay on Screen

To keep your data headings on screen when you scroll down or to the right on a large worksheet, you can freeze the heading rows and columns in place. For example, if you have headings in column A and row 1, you can freeze column A and row 1 so that they remain on screen.

Figure 11–23 shows you how to freeze the rows and columns you want to fix. You can also choose **View ➤ Window ➤ Freeze Panes ➤ Freeze Top Row** to quickly freeze the worksheet's top row or **View ➤ Window ➤ Freeze Panes ➤ Freeze First Column** to freeze the first column.

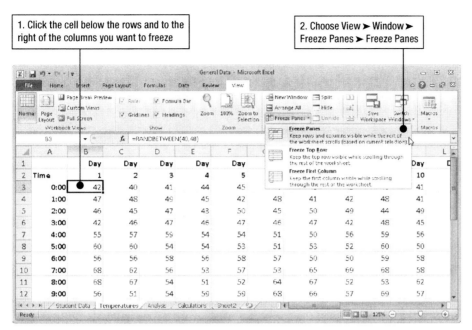

1. Click the cell below the rows and to the right of the columns you want to freeze

2. Choose View ➤ Window ➤ Freeze Panes ➤ Freeze Panes

Figure 11–23. *You can freeze the rows above and the columns to the left of the selected cell.*

Excel displays a black line along the gridlines of the frozen cells. Once you've applied the freeze, the frozen columns and rows don't move when you scroll down or to the right. Figure 11–24 shows the same worksheet with rows 1 and 2 and column A frozen.

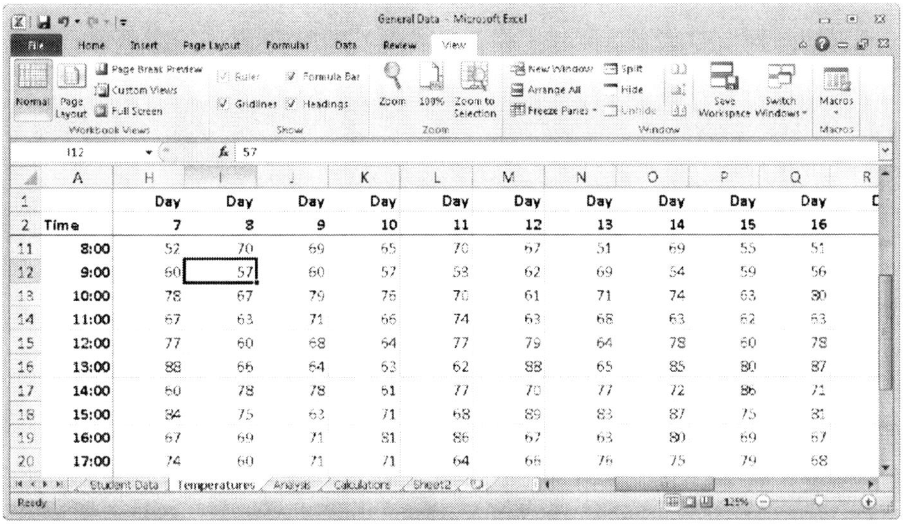

Figure 11–24. *After you freeze the heading rows and columns, they stay in place when you scroll down or across the worksheet.*

When you no longer need the freezing, choose **View ➤ Window ➤ Freeze Panes ➤ Unfreeze Panes** to remove the freezing.

Sharing Your Workbooks and Tracking Changes

Unless you work on your own, you'll probably need to share some workbooks with your colleagues. Before you share a workbook, you can set Excel to track the changes your colleagues make so that you can easily review them without having to compare old and new versions of each worksheet.

Tracking Changes to a Workbook

To track the changes your colleagues make to a workbook, turn on the Track Changes feature. Excel then automatically shares the workbook for you.

To turn on Track Changes and share a workbook, follow these steps:

1. Choose **Review ➤ Changes ➤ Track Changes ➤ Highlight Changes** to display the **Highlight Changes** dialog box (see Figure 11–25).

Figure 11–25. *In the **Highlight Changes** dialog box, select the **Track changes while editing** check box, and then choose which changes to save and whether to highlight them on screen.*

2. Select the **Track changes while editing** check box. Excel then enables the other controls in the dialog box.

3. To specify the time period over which to track the changes, select the **When** check box, open the pop-up menu, and then click the appropriate item:

   ▪ *Since I last saved.* Tracks only the changes since you last saved the workbook. If you save the workbook only after reviewing the changes, this can be a good way of keeping the number of changes down to a manageable level.

   ▪ *All.* Tracks all the changes.

■ *Not yet reviewed.* Tracks changes only until you review them. This is another approach to keeping down the number of changes that remain in the workbook.

■ *Since date.* Lets you specify the date at which to begin tracking the changes. Excel suggests the current date, but you can change it as needed.

4. To choose whose changes Excel tracks, select the **Who** check box, open the pop-up menu, and then click the **Everyone** item or the **Everyone but me** item, as needed. (The idea is that you may not need to see the changes you yourself have made.)

5. To specify the range for which to track the changes, select the **Where** check box, and then drag through the range in the worksheet to enter it in the text box. If you need to get the **Highlight Changes** dialog box out of the way, click the **Collapse Dialog** button, but usually it's easier just to work around it.

6. Select the **Highlight changes on screen** check box if you want Excel to highlight the changes on screen. This is usually helpful.

7. Select the **List changes on a new sheet** check box if you want Excel to create a new worksheet and put a list of the changes on it. Creating this list can be a handy way of reviewing the changes, as you can add comments next to them if you need to.

> **NOTE:** Excel makes the **List changes on a new sheet** check box available only when you've turned on **Track Changes** and the workbook contains at least one tracked change. This means that you'll need to close the **Highlight Changes** dialog box, make some tracked changes, and then open the dialog box again before you can select the **List changes on a new sheet** check box.

8. Click the **OK** button to close the **Highlight Changes** dialog box. Excel prompts you to save the workbook (see Figure 11–26).

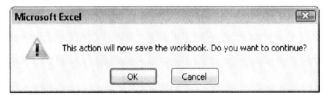

Figure 11–26. *After turning on Track Changes, Excel prompts you to save the workbook. Click the **OK** button.*

9. Click the **OK** button. Excel saves the workbook and shares it. You'll see **"[Shared]"** appear in the window's title bar after the workbook's name.

After sharing a workbook by turning on Track Changes, you may need to adjust the sharing. To do so, follow the instructions in the next section.

Sharing a Workbook So That Your Colleagues Can Edit It

When you need to be able to work on a workbook with your colleagues, turn on sharing. Follow these steps:

1. Open the workbook.

2. Choose **Review ➤ Changes ➤ Share Workbook** to display the **Share Workbook** dialog box. The left screen in Figure 11–27 shows the **Editing** tab of the **Share Workbook** dialog box, which is where you start the sharing process.

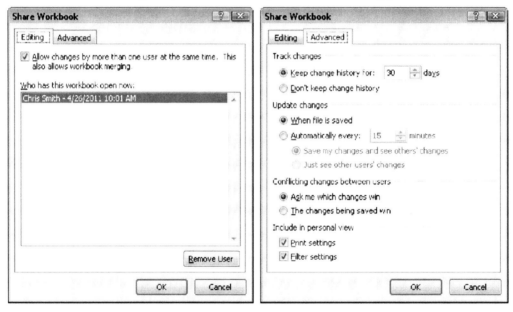

Figure 11–27. *On the Editing tab (left) of the Share Workbook dialog box, select the Allow changes by more than one user at the same time check box. You can then choose options on the Advanced tab (right).*

3. Select the **Allow changes by more than one user at the same time** check box on the Editing tab.

4. Check the **Who has this workbook open now** list box. If you haven't shared the workbook yet (for example, by turning on Track Changes) this list will show only your name and should include the word *Exclusive* to indicate that you've got sole access to the workbook.

5. Click the **Advanced** tab to display its contents (shown on the right in Figure 11–17).

6. In the **Track Changes** area, hoose how long to keep the change history for the workbook:

▧ Normally, you'll want to select the **Keep change history for** option button and set the number of days in the days box.

▧ The default setting is 30 days, but if you develop your workbooks quickly, you may want to reduce the interval to 7 days or 14 days to prevent Excel from keeping large amounts of history you don't need.

▧ The alternative is to select the **Don't keep change history** option button, but usually it's best to keep change history so that you can unravel any mysterious changes.

7. In the **Update changes** area, choose when to update the changes to the workbook:

▧ The default setting is the **When file is saved** option button, which usually works well.

▧ The alternative is to select the **Automatically every** option button and set the number of minutes in the minutes box. The default setting is 15 minutes. If you work fast, you may want to shorten the interval to 5 or 10 minutes.

▧ If you select the **Automatically every** option button, you can choose between the **Save my changes and see others' changes** option button (usually the better choice) and the **Just see other users' changes** option button.

8. In the **Conflicting change between users** area, choose how to handle conflicting changes to the workbook. Normally, you'll want to select the **Ask me which changes win** option button so that you can decide which of the conflicting changes to keep. The alternative is to select the option button called **The changes being saved win**, which tells Excel to overwrite the conflicting changes with the latest changes.

9. In the **Include in personal view** area, select the **Print settings** check box if you want to include print settings in your view of the workbook. Select the **Filter settings** check box if you want to include filter settings for a database table.

10. Click the **OK** button to close the **Share Workbook** dialog box. Excel then displays a dialog box telling you that it will save the workbook.

11. Click the **OK** button. Excel sets up the sharing and adds **"[Shared]"** to the workbook's title bar so that you can easily see it's shared.

Working in a Shared Workbook

Once you've shared a workbook or someone else has shared it, you can perform basic editing in it much as normal. You can enter data and formulas in cells or edit their existing contents, format cells, and use both drag and drop and cut, copy, and paste. You can also insert rows, columns, and even whole worksheets.

Beyond these basics, Excel prevents you from making changes that may cause problems with the sharing. These are the main restrictions:

- *Apply conditional formatting.* If your workbook needs conditional formatting, apply it before sharing the workbook.

- *Insert objects.* You can't insert pictures, SmartArt, charts, hyperlinks, or various other objects.

- *Insert or delete blocks of cells.* You can insert or delete a whole row or column, but you can't insert or delete a block of cells. You also can't merge cells together.

- *Delete a worksheet.* You can't delete a worksheet from the shared workbook.

- *Protect a sheet with a password.* Any protection you've applied before sharing the workbook remains in force, but you can't apply protection to a sheet in a shared workbook.

- *Outline the workbook.* Excel's advanced capabilities include creating a collapsible outline from a worksheet. (This book does not cover outlining; look at the Help files or a book such as *Beginning Microsoft Office 2010*, also from Apress, to learn about outlining.) You can't create an outline in a shared workbook.

Reviewing Tracked Changes in a Shared Workbook

When you've tracked changes in a shared workbook, you can review them, accepting the changes you want to keep and rejecting the other changes.

To review the tracked changes, follow these steps:

1. Open the shared workbook if it's not already open.

2. Choose **Review ➤ Changes ➤ Track Changes ➤ Accept/Reject Changes** to display the **Select Changes to Accept or Reject** dialog box (see Figure 11–28).

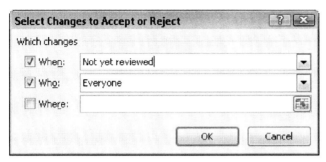

Figure 11–28. *In the **Select Changes to Accept or Reject** dialog box, choose which changes you want to review, and then click the **OK** button.*

3. Use the controls in the **Which changes** area to choose which changes Excel presents for your review:

   ▪ **When.** Select this check box to specify a date range. Then open the pop-up menu and choose the **Not yet reviewed** item if you want to review all the changes you haven't yet reviewed, or select the **Since date** item and enter the date in the text box.

   ▪ **Who.** Select this check box if you want to specify whose changes you'll review. Then open the pop-up menu and choose **Everyone**, **Everyone but Me**, or a user name.

   ▪ **Where.** Select this check box if you want to see the changes in only part of the workbook. Then click in the text box and drag through the range in the worksheet.

4. Click the **OK** button to close the **Select Changes to Accept or Reject** dialog box. Excel displays the **Accept or Reject Changes** dialog box (see Figure 11–29), which shows the number of changes and the details of the first change.

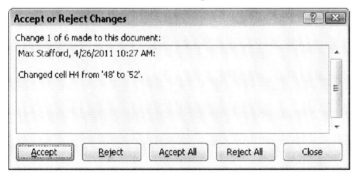

Figure 11–29. *Use the **Accept or Reject Changes** dialog box to work your way through the tracked changes in a shared workbook.*

5. Work through the changes using the **Accept** button and the **Reject** button. You can click the **Accept All** button if you decide all the changes are worthwhile or the **Reject All** button if they're worthless; if you click either button, Excel closes the **Accept or Reject Changes** dialog box for you.

6. When you've worked your way through the changes, click the **Close** button to close the **Accept or Reject Changes** dialog box.

Summary

In this chapter, you learned how to create and save workbooks, how to get around the user interface, and how to set up a workbook with the worksheets you need. You learned how to enter data; use views, splitting, and freezing to enable yourself to see exactly what you need to; and you met the tools for sharing your workbooks, tracking changes others make to them, and reviewing those changes.

In the next chapter, I'll show you how to edit your worksheets and apply formatting to them.

Chapter 12

Editing Worksheets and Applying Formatting

In this chapter, I'll show you how to lay out your worksheets and apply formatting to them.

First, we'll cover how to insert, delete, and format rows and columns so that your worksheet's data appears the way you want it. You'll learn how to insert and delete cells, set row height and column width, and hide columns and rows you don't want to see.

Next, we'll go over formatting cells and ranges. You'll meet the three main tools for applying formatting; learn how to control the way data appears by applying number formatting; and format a workbook using a theme, alignment, font formatting, and borders and fills.

After that, we'll move on to fast formatting. Instead of formatting cells painstakingly one attribute at a time, you can format an entire table in one move—or you can use styles to apply complete sets of formatting to cells in moments.

At the end of the chapter, I'll show you how to add headers and footers to worksheets and how to print the parts of worksheets you need on paper.

Working with Rows and Columns

To arrange the data in your worksheets, you can insert and delete rows, columns, and cells. To make the data visible and easy to read, you can change the width of columns and the height of rows. And when you don't need to see particular rows or columns, you can hide them.

Inserting and Deleting Columns, Rows, and Cells

You can quickly insert columns or rows in a worksheet to give yourself more space to work in.

> **TIP:** To tell Excel how many columns or rows you want to insert, select the same number of existing columns or rows.

Inserting Columns and Rows

Figure 12–1 shows you the quickest and easiest way to insert columns in a worksheet: select the column or columns before which you want to insert the new columns, then right-click the selection and choose **Insert**.

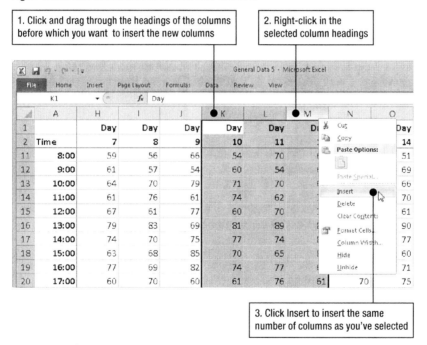

Figure 12–1. *To insert columns, select the same number of existing columns as you want to insert new columns. Then right-click the column heading and click **Insert** on the context menu.*

You can use the same technique for inserting rows: select the headings of the rows above which you want to insert the new rows, then right-click in the selected row headings and click **Insert** on the context menu.

To insert just a single column or row, right-click the heading of the column or row before which you want to place the new one, then click **Insert** on the context menu.

If you prefer to use the Ribbon, you can insert columns or rows by choosing **Home ➤ Cells ➤ Insert ➤ Insert Sheet Columns** or **Home ➤ Cells ➤ Insert ➤ Insert Sheet Rows**. If you select multiple columns or rows beforehand, these commands insert the same number of new columns or rows. Otherwise, the commands insert a single column or row.

Deleting Columns and Rows

To delete a column or a row, right-click its heading, and then click **Delete** on the context menu.

To delete multiple columns or rows at once, drag through their headings, then right-click in the selection and click **Delete** on the context menu.

Inserting Cells

You can also insert one or more cells without inserting an entire column or row. When you insert cells like this, you can choose which way to shift the existing cells—to the right, or downward—to make room for the new cells.

Figure 12–2 shows you how to insert a block of cells.

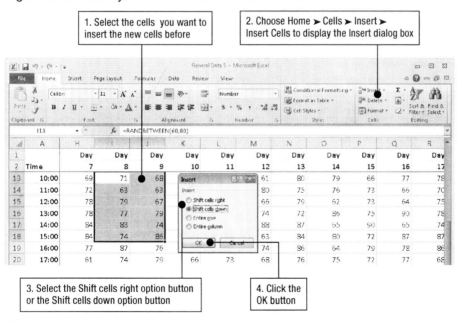

Figure 12–2. *When you insert a block of cells, click the **Shift cells right** option button or the **Shift cells down** option button in the **Insert** dialog box to tell Excel which way to move the existing cells.*

Deleting Cells

To delete just some cells, select them, and then choose **Home ➤ Cells ➤ Delete ➤ Delete Cells**. In the **Delete** dialog box (see Figure 12–3) that Excel displays, select the **Shift cells left** option button or the **Shift cells up** option button, as appropriate, and then click the **OK** button.

Figure 12–3. *When you delete a block of cells, click the **Shift cells left** option button or the **Shift cells up** option button in the **Delete** dialog box to tell Excel which cells to use to fill the gap in the worksheet.*

Setting Row Height

By default, Excel sets the row height automatically to accommodate the tallest character or object in the row. For example, if you type an entry in a cell, then select the cell and click the **Increase Font Size** button in the **Font** group of the **Home** tab a few times, Excel automatically increases the row height so that there's enough space for the tallest characters.

When you need to set row height manually, drag the lower border of the row heading up or down, as shown in Figure 12–4.

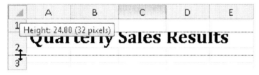

Figure 12–4. *Drag the lower border of the row heading up or down to change the row height. The ScreenTip shows the exact measurement in points (a point is 1/72 inch).*

If you need to set a precise measurement, right-click the row heading, and then click **Row Height** to display the **Row Height** dialog box (see Figure 12–3). Type the row height you want in points, and then click the **OK** button.

Figure 12–5. *Use the **Row Height** dialog box when you need to set a row's height precisely in points.*

Setting Column Width

Excel doesn't automatically adjust column width as you enter data in a worksheet. This is because in a typical spreadsheet, many cells may need entries wider than their columns. But you can quickly set column width, as shown in Figure 12–6.

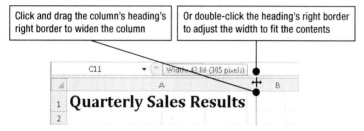

Figure 12–6. *You can quickly change a column's width by dragging the right border of its heading. To automatically fit the column's contents, double-click the heading's right border.*

To automatically adjust the width of multiple columns to fit their contents, select cells in all the columns you want to affect, and then double-click the right border of any of the selected column headings. You can also select the cells and then choose **Home ➤ Cells ➤ Format ➤ AutoFit Column Width**.

> **TIP:** AutoFit is usually the best way to resize a worksheet's columns. But if some cells have such long contents that AutoFit will create huge columns, set the column width manually and hide parts of the longest contents. You can also wrap the contents of a cell, making it deeper rather than wider to accommodate longer entries; see the section "Setting Alignment," later in this chapter, for details.

If you need to resize a column precisely, right-click the column heading, and then click **Column Width** on the context menu to display the **Column Width** dialog box (see Figure 12–7). Type the cell width (measured in standard characters in the font you're using), and then click the **OK** button.

Figure 12–7. *Use the **Column Width** dialog box when you need to set column width precisely.*

Hiding Rows and Columns

Sometimes it's helpful to hide particular columns and rows so that they're not visible in the worksheet. You may want to do this to hide sensitive data from your printouts, or simply to make the part of the worksheet you're actually using fit on the screen all at once.

To hide a column or row, work as shown in Figure 12–8.

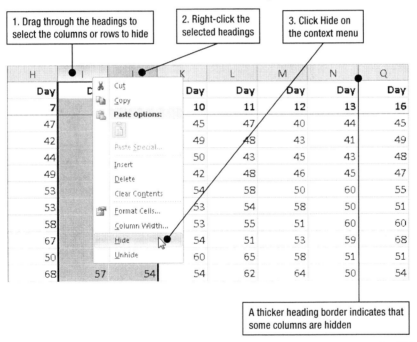

Figure 12–8. *To hide selected columns or rows, right-click the heading and then click **Hide** on the context menu.*

TIP: To quickly hide the active row or selected rows, press **Ctrl+9**. To hide the active column or selected columns, press **Ctrl+0**.

To unhide a column or row, select the columns on either side of it or the rows above and below it. Then right-click the selected column headings or row headings and click **Unhide** on the context menu.

> **NOTE:** You can also hide and unhide items by using the **Home ➤ Cells ➤ Format ➤ Hide & Unhide** submenu. But usually it's easier to right-click the column heading or row heading.

Formatting Cells and Ranges

In Excel, you can format cells in a wide variety of ways—everything from choosing how to display the borders and background to controlling how Excel represents the text you enter in the cell. This section shows you how the most useful kinds of formatting work and shows you how to apply them.

Each cell comes with essential formatting applied to it—the font and font size to use, and usually the General number format, which you'll meet shortly. So when you create a new workbook and start entering data in it, Excel displays the data in a normal-size font.

> **TIP:** To control the font and font size Excel uses for new workbooks, choose **File ➤ Excel Options**. In the **General** category, go to **the When creating new workbooks** area. Set the font in the **Use this font drop-down** list and the font size in the **Font size** drop-down list. Then click the **OK** button.

Meeting the Three Main Tools for Applying Formatting

Excel gives you three main tools for applying formatting to cells and ranges: the Mini Toolbar, the **Home** tab of the Ribbon, and the **Format Cells** dialog box.

Formatting with the Mini Toolbar

Excel has two versions of the Mini Toolbar. The smaller version (see Figure 12–9) appears when you select text within a cell and provides widely used font-formatting commands. As usual, click the formatting you want to apply.

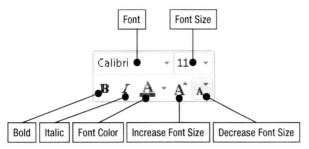

Figure 12–9. *The smaller Mini Toolbar gives you quick access to essential font formatting when you're editing in a cell.*

The larger version of the Mini Toolbar (see Figure 12–10) appears when you right-click a cell or selection. This Mini Toolbar provides a wider selection of formatting tools.

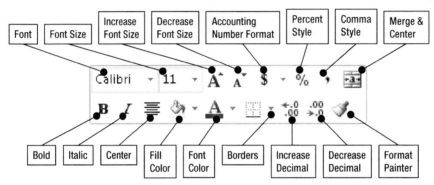

Figure 12–10. *The larger Mini Toolbar gives you a wider range of formatting commands.*

Formatting with the Home Tab of the Ribbon

The **Home** tab of the Ribbon contains three groups of formatting controls:

- The **Font** group provides widely used font formatting.

- The **Alignment** group offers horizontal and vertical alignment, orientation, indentation, wrapping, and merging.

- The **Number** group gives you a quick way to apply essential number formatting.

Figure 12–11 shows the **Font** group. Figure 12–12 shows the **Alignment** group and the **Number** group.

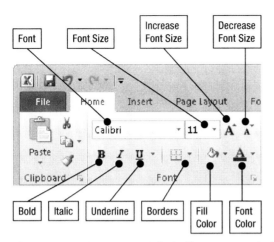

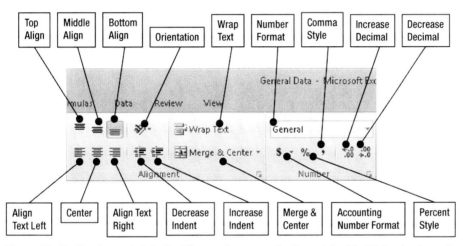

Figure 12–11. *Use the controls in the **Font** group on the **Home** tab of the Ribbon to apply formatting quickly.*

Figure 12–12. *Use the controls in the **Alignment** group on the **Home** tab of the Ribbon to align cell contents horizontally and vertically and for effects such as wrapping text or centering it across cells. Use the controls in the **Number** group to apply styles and increase or decrease the number of decimal places.*

Formatting with the Format Cells Dialog Box

When you need to apply formatting types that don't appear on the Mini Toolbar or on the **Home** tab of the Ribbon, open the **Format Cells** dialog box and work on its six tabs, which you'll meet later in this chapter.

The easiest way to display the **Format Cells** dialog box is right-click a cell or a selection and then click **Format Cells** on the context menu. Other ways (there are many) include pressing **Ctrl+1** and choosing **Home ➤ Cells ➤ Format ➤ Format Cells**.

Setting the Workbook's Overall Look by Applying a Theme

To control the overall look of a workbook, apply a suitable theme to it, as shown in Figure 12–13.

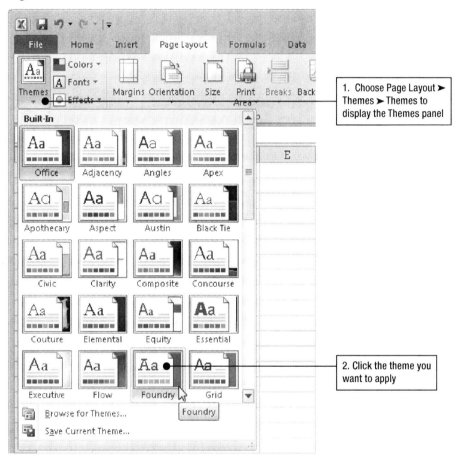

Figure 12–13. *Apply a theme to set the overall look of a workbook. You can then use the **Colors** drop-down panel, **Fonts** drop-down panel, and **Effects** drop-down panel to fine-tune the look.*

Controlling How Data Appears by Applying Number Formatting

When you enter a number in a cell, Excel displays it according to the number formatting applied to that cell. For example, if you enter **40900** in a cell formatted with **General** formatting, Excel displays it as **40900**. If the cell has **Currency** formatting, Excel displays a value such as **$40,900.00** (depending on the details of the format). And if the cell has **Date** formatting, Excel displays a date such as **23 December 2011** (again, depending on the details of the formatting). In each case, the number stored in the cell remains the same—so if you change the cell's formatting to a different type, the display changes.

Table 12–1 explains Excel's number formats and tells you the keyboard shortcuts for applying them. You can also apply number formatting by using the buttons on the larger Mini Toolbar, the **Number Format** drop-down list and buttons in the **Number** group of the **Home** tab of the Ribbon, and the **Number** tab of the **Format Cells** dialog box (see Figure 12–14).

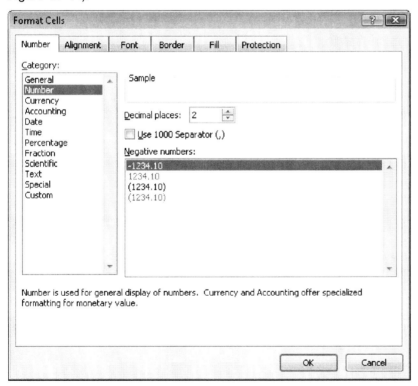

Figure 12–14. *Use the **Number** tab of the **Format Cells** dialog box when you need access to the full range of number formatting.*

Table 12–1. *Excel's Number Formats*

Number Format	Explanation	Examples	Keyboard Shortcut
General	Excel's default format for all cells in new worksheets. No specific format, but displays up to 11 digits per cell and uses no thousands separator.	1234567 Industry	Ctrl+Shift+~ (tilde)
Number	Displays the number of decimal places you choose. You can choose whether to use the thousands separator and how to display negative numbers.	1000 1,000 1,000.00	Ctrl+Shift+!
Currency	Displays the number of decimal places you choose, using the thousands separator. You can choose which currency symbol to display (for example, $) and how to display negative numbers.	$2,345.67 –$2,345.67	Ctrl+Shift+$
Accounting	Displays the number of decimal places you choose, using the thousands separator. You can choose which currency symbol to use. The symbol appears aligned at the left edge of the cell. Negative numbers appear with parentheses around them.	$ 1,000,000 $ (99.999.00)	—
Date	Displays any of a variety of date formats.	12/24/2011 Saturday, December 24, 2011	—
Time	Displays any of a variety of date formats.	11:59:59 PM 23:59:59	—
Percentage	Displays a percent sign and the number of decimal places you choose.	78.79% 200%	Ctrl+Shift+%

Number Format	Explanation	Examples	Keyboard Shortcut
Fraction	Displays the number as a fraction. Fractions tend to be visually confusing, so use them only if you must—for example, for betting charts.	1/2 1 1/4	—
Scientific	Displays the number in exponential form, with E and the power to which to raise the number. You can choose how many decimal places to use.	1.2346E+08 −9.8765E+07	Ctrl+Shift+^
Text	Displays and treats the data as text, even when it appears to be another type of data (for example, a number or date).	Champions of Breakfast 18	—
Special	Displays the data in the format you choose: Zip Code, Zip Code + 4, Phone Number, or Social Security Number.	10013 10013-8295 (212) 555-9753 722-86-8261	—
Custom	Displays the data in the custom format you choose. Excel provides dozens of custom formats, but you can also create your own formats.	[Various]	—

UNDERSTANDING HOW EXCEL STORES DATES AND TIMES

Excel stores dates as serial numbers starting from 1 (Sunday, 1 January 1900) and running way into the future. To give you a couple of points of reference, Saturday, 1 January 2011 is 40544, and Sunday, 1 January 2012 is 40909.

You can enter a date by typing either the serial number (if you know it or care to work it out) or a date in most conventional formats. For example, if you type **1/1/2011**, Excel converts it to **40544** and displays the date in whichever format you've chosen.

Excel stores times as decimal parts of a day. For example, 40544.25 is 6 AM (one quarter of the way through the day) on 1 January 2011.

Setting Alignment

To align the contents of cells, use the buttons in the **Alignment** group of the Ribbon or the controls on the **Alignment** tab of the **Format Cells** dialog box (see Figure 12–15):

▪ *Horizontal alignment.* You can align the text **Left**, **Center**, **Right**, or **Justify**; apply **General** alignment, which depends on the data type (left for text, right for numbers); choose **Center Across Selection** to center the text across multiple cells; or choose **Distributed (Indent)** to distribute the text across the cell (using wider spaces between words).

NOTE: The **Fill** horizontal alignment fills the cell with the character you specify.

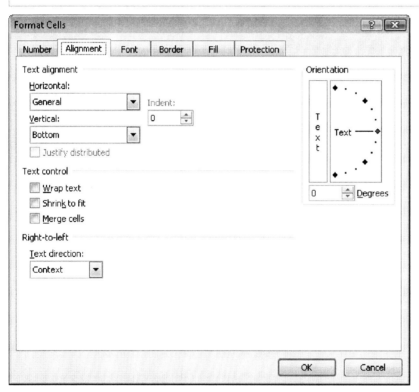

Figure 12–15. *The **Alignment** tab of the **Format Cells** dialog box lets you rotate text to precise angles when needed.*

▪ *Vertical alignment.* You can align text **Top**, **Center**, **Bottom**, or **Justify**. You can also choose **Distributed** to distribute the text vertically, which can be useful when you rotate the text so that it runs vertically.

- *Rotate text.* Use the **Orientation** box on the **Alignment** tab of the **Format Cells** dialog box or the **Orientation** drop-down list in the **Alignment** group.

- *Indentation.* You can indent the text as far as is needed.

- *Wrap.* You can wrap the text to make a long entry appear on several lines in a cell rather than disappear where the next cell's contents start. You may need to increase the row height to accommodate the wrapped text.

- *Shrink to fit.* Select this check box on the **Alignment** tab of the **Format Cells** dialog box to shrink the text so that it fits in the cell.

- *Merge cells.* Use the **Merge & Center** drop-down list in the **Alignment** group to merge selected cells together into a single cell. You can also center an entry across a merged cell.

Choosing Font Formatting

You can quickly format either the contents of a cell or the selected part of a cell's contents by using the controls in the **Font** group on the **Home** tab or the **Font** tab of the **Format Cells** dialog box (see Figure 12–16).

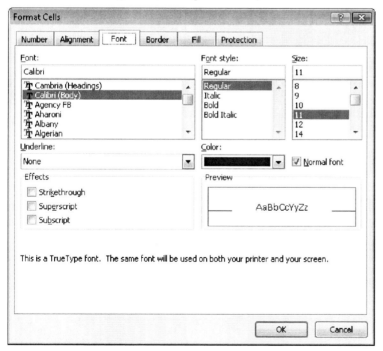

Figure 12–16. *The **Font** tab of the **Format Cells** dialog box gives you a full range of font formatting for the current selection.*

Applying Borders and Fills

The quick way to apply a border to the active cell or selected cells is to use the **Borders** drop-down list in the **Font** group on the **Home** tab of the Ribbon as shown in Figure 12–17.

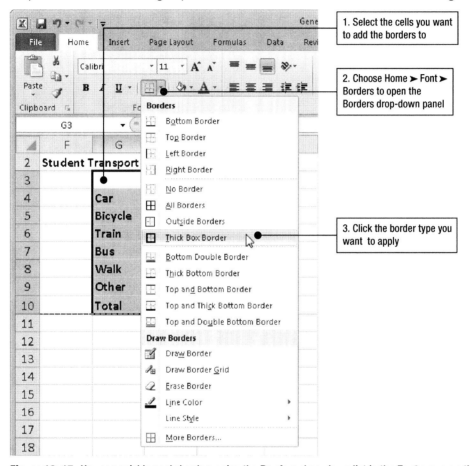

Figure 12–17. *You can quickly apply borders using the **Borders** drop-down list in the **Font** group on the **Home** tab of the Ribbon. To draw a border, click the appropriate item in the **Draw Borders** section of the list, and then draw with the resulting pointer.*

When you want to reach the full range of border options, click the **More Borders** item at the bottom of the list to display the **Borders** tab of the **Format Cells** dialog box. Use its controls to set up the borders you want, as explained in Figure 12–18, and then click the **OK** button.

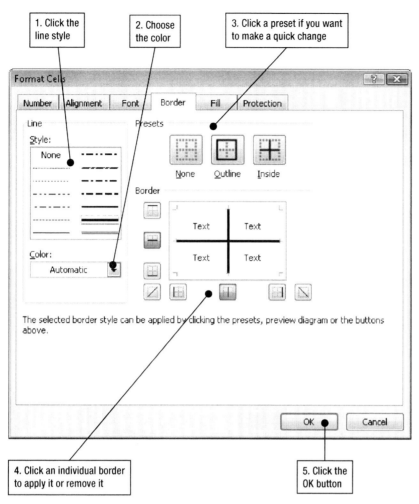

Figure 12–18. *For full control over the borders, use the controls on the **Border** tab of the **Format** Cells dialog box.*

To apply a fill to the active cell or selected cells, use the **Fill Colors** drop-down list in the **Font** group on the **Home** tab of the Ribbon or work on the **Fill** tab of the **Format Cells** dialog box.

> **NOTE:** The **Protection** tab of the **Format Cells** dialog box contains two controls: the **Locked** check box and the **Hidden** check box. You can select the Locked check box to lock a cell against changes, or select the **Hidden** check box to hide a formula the cell contains while leaving the result visible. But neither setting takes effect until you apply protection to the worksheet by using the **Review ➤ Changes ➤ Protect Sheet** command. I'll show you how to create formulas in the next chapter.

Formatting Quickly with Table Formatting and Styles

To save you time with formatting, Excel provides preset formatting that you can apply to a table to give it an overall look. And to save you the effort of applying many different types of formatting over and over again to different cells, Excel includes styles, collections of formatting that you can apply all at once.

Formatting with Table Formatting

When you need to format a table quickly, see if Excel's preset table formatting will do the trick. Select the table, then choose **Home ➤ Styles ➤ Format as Table** and click the style you want (see Figure 12–19).

> **NOTE:** See Chapter 15: "Creating Excel Databases and Analyzing Data" for instructions on creating and working with Excel tables.

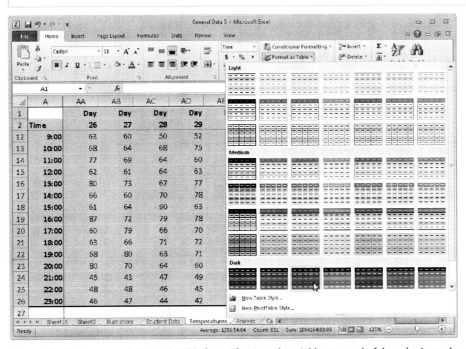

Figure 12–19. *You can quickly apply table formatting to make a table more colorful, easier to read, or (sometimes) both.*

Formatting with Styles

To save time and ensure your formatting is consistent, you can use Excel's styles. If you're familiar with Word's styles (discussed in Chapter 8: "Formatting Your Documents Easily and Efficiently"), you'll find Excel's styles easy, as they work in much the same way.

Each style is a collection of formatting that you can apply to one or more cells. The style contains six types of formatting, one for each tab of the **Format Cells** dialog box:

- *Number.* For example, **General**, **Currency**, or **Percentage**.

- *Alignment.* Horizontal alignment (for example, **General**, **Center**, or **Justify**), vertical alignment (for example, **Top**, **Center**, or **Bottom**), and any trimmings (such as wrapping the text to the window).

- *Font.* The font, font size, font color, and so on.

- *Border.* Any borders you've applied to the style, or **No Borders** if it has no borders.

- *Fill.* Any fill you've applied to the style, or **No Shading** if it's plain.

- *Protection.* **Locked**, **Hidden**, both, or **No Protection**.

Most Excel templates contain plenty of styles to get you started, but you can create your own custom styles as well if you need to.

Applying a Style

To apply a style, choose **Home** ➤ **Styles** ➤ **Cell Styles**, and then click the style on the **Cell Styles** panel (see Figure 12–20). This panel lists the styles in the following categories:

- *Custom.* This category appears only when you have created one or more custom styles in the workbook.

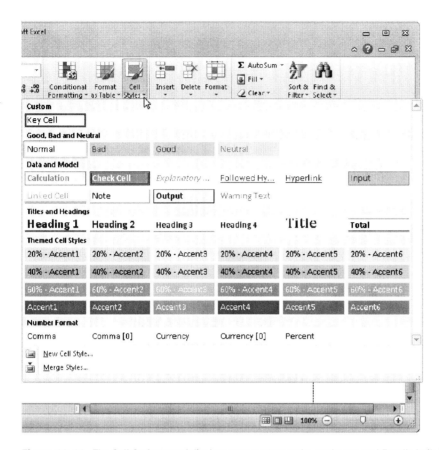

Figure 12–20. *The **Cell Styles** panel displays your custom styles at the top and Excel's built-in styles in different categories.*

- *Good, Bad and Neutral.* This category has **Good**, **Bad**, and **Neutral** styles that you can use to apply color coding to cells. Here is also where you will find the **Normal** style that Excel applies to any cell that doesn't have another style.

- *Data and Model.* This category contains the **Calculation**, **Check Cell**, **Explanatory**, **Followed Hyperlink**, **Hyperlink**, **Input**, **Linked Cell**, **Note**, **Output**, and **Warning Text** styles. Most of these styles are used for data modeling. Excel automatically applies the **Hyperlink** style to cells containing hyperlinks you have not clicked yet, changing their style to **Followed Hyperlink** once you have clicked them.

- *Titles and Headings.* This category contains four styles for descending levels of headings (**Heading 1**, **Heading 2**, **Heading 3**, and **Heading 4**), the **Title** style for giving a worksheet a title, and the **Total** style for easily formatting cells that contain totals.

▪ *Themed Cell Styles.* This category contains six Accent styles (**Accent 1** through **Accent 6**) featuring six of the theme colors, with four degrees of shading for each.

▪ *Number Format.* This category contains five number formats: **Comma** (thousands separator, two decimal places), **Comma [0]** (thousands separator, no decimal places), **Currency** (currency symbol, thousands separator, two decimal places), **Currency [0]** (currency symbol, thousands separator, no decimal places), and **Percent** (percent symbol, multiplies the number by 100).

TIP: You can also apply the **Currency** style, the **Percent** style, and the **Comma** style from the **Number** group on the **Home** tab of the Ribbon.

Creating Custom Styles

If none of Excel's styles meets your needs, you can create your own styles. To create a style, format a cell with the formatting you want the style to have, choose **Home ➤ Styles ➤ Cell Styles ➤ New Cell Style** to display the Style dialog box, and then work as shown in Figure 12–21.

TIP: To jump-start your formatting, apply the existing style that's nearest to the look and formatting you want.

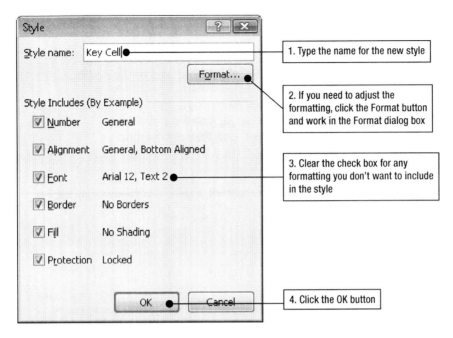

Figure 12–21. *In the* **Style** *dialog box, you can quickly create a new style based on the formatting of the selected cell. You can change the formatting as needed by clicking the* **Format** *button and working in the* **Format Cells** *dialog box.*

After you close the **Style** dialog box, Excel adds the style to the **Custom** area at the top of the **Cell Styles** panel.

> **TIP:** Instead of creating a new style, you can modify one of the built-in styles. Choose **Home ➤ Styles ➤ Cell Styles** to display the **Cell Styles** panel, right-click the style you want to change, and then click the **Modify** button. In the **Style** dialog box, click the **Format** button to display the **Format Cells** dialog box, and make the changes you need. When you have finished, click the **OK** button to return to the **Style** dialog box, and then click the **OK** button.

Copying Styles from One Workbook to Another

If you have styles in one workbook that you want to use in another workbook, you can copy the styles across. Excel calls this *merging styles*. When you merge the styles, the destination workbook receives all the styles from the source workbook—you can't pick and choose (but see the Tip after the instructions below).

To merge the styles, follow these steps:

1. Open the source workbook (the workbook that contains the styles) and the destination workbook.

2. Switch to the destination workbook by clicking in it.

3. Choose **Home ➤ Styles ➤ Cell Styles ➤ Merge Styles** to display the **Merge Styles** dialog box (see Figure 12–22).

Figure 12–22. *Use the **Merge Styles** dialog box to copy all the styles from one workbook into another workbook.*

4. In the **Merge styles from** list box, click the source workbook.

5. Click the **OK** button to close the **Merge Styles** dialog box. Excel copies the styles into the destination workbook, and you can then start using them.

> **TIP:** If you need to copy just one style from one workbook to another, apply that style to a cell. Then copy that cell and switch back to the destination workbook. Right-click a cell you don't mind changing, go to the **Paste Options** section of the context menu, and click the **Formatting** icon. Excel pastes the style onto the cell, and you can then use the style in the workbook.

Deleting Styles You Don't Need

If you no longer need a style, you can delete it. Choose **Home ➤ Styles ➤ Cell Styles**, right-click the style on the **Cell Styles** panel, and then click **Delete** on the context menu.

> **NOTE:** Excel prevents you from deleting the **Normal** style, because workbooks need this style.

Adding Headers and Footers to Your Worksheets

Before printing a worksheet or creating a PDF or XPS file from it, you'll probably want to add headers, footers, or both to identify the pages. Excel gives each worksheet a separate header and footer, which you can fill with either preset text or custom text. Each header and footer area consists of a left section, a center section, and a right section.

To add headers and footers to the active worksheet, follow these steps:

1. Choose **Insert ➤ Text ➤ Header & Footer** to display the header area and reveal **Header & Footer Tools** section of the Ribbon, which contains the **Design** tab (see Figure 12–23). Excel switches to **Page Layout** view (unless you're already using this view).

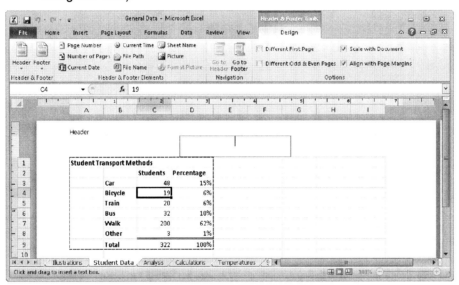

Figure 12–23. *To work with headers and footers, you display the **Header & Footer Tools** section of the Ribbon. Each header and footer consists of three sections—left, center, and right.*

2. To insert a preset header that contains workbook information such as the page number, worksheet title, or filename, choose **Header & Footer Tools ➤ Design ➤ Header & Footer ➤ Header**, and then click the preset header you want. Similarly, you can insert a preset footer by clicking the **Footer** button in the **Header & Footer** group, and then clicking the one you want.

3. To move from the header area to the footer area, choose **Header & Footer Tools ➤ Design ➤ Navigation ➤ Go to Footer**. To go back, choose **Header & Footer Tools ➤ Design ➤ Navigation ➤ Go to Header**.

4. To add text to the header or footer, click in the section in which you want to place the text—for example, the middle section—and then type the text.

5. To add a predefined element to the current section, click the appropriate button—**Page Number**, **Number of Pages**, **Current Date**, **Current Time**, **File Path**, **File Name**, or **Sheet Name**—in the **Header & Footer Elements** group.

6. To add a picture to the current section, click the **Picture** button in the **Header & Footer Elements** group, select the picture in the **Insert Picture** dialog box, and then click the **Insert** button. To format the picture, click the **Format Picture** button in the **Header & Footer Element**s group, and then work on the **Size** tab and **Picture** tab of the **Format Picture** dialog box. For example, set the picture's height and width on the **Size** tab. Click the **OK** button when you've finished.

7. Choose options for the header and footer in the **Options** group:

   a. *Different First Page.* If the printout will occupy two or more pages, you can select this check box to put a different header or footer on the first page. When you're working in this header or footer, Excel displays **First Page Header** or **First Page Footer** so that you can easily tell which one you're editing.

   b. *Different Odd & Even Pages.* If the printout needs different headers and footers on odd pages than on even pages, select this check box. When you're working in these headers and footers, Excel displays **Odd Page Header**, **Odd Page Footer**, **Even Page Header**, or **Even Page Footer**, as appropriate.

   c. *Scale with Document.* Select this check box to have Excel resize the header or footer if you resize the worksheet to fit it on paper when printing. Clear this check box if you want the header or footer to print at full size each time.

   d. *Align with Page Margins.* Select this check box to make Excel align the edges of the header and footer with the page's left and right margins. Alignment usually makes for a tidy look, but you may sometimes need to clear this check box to accommodate wider headers or footers.

8. When you finish creating the header or footer, click a cell in the worksheet to return to the worksheet.

Printing Your Excel Worksheets and Workbooks

To print from Excel, you use the Print pane in Backstage, as with the other programs. But before you print, you need to tell Excel which part of the workbook to print. You may also want to check the page setup to make sure that your printout looks the way you intend it to.

Telling Excel Which Part of the Worksheet to Print

Usually, you want to print only the range of cells you've used on a worksheet, or perhaps only a small subset of that range. So when you're printing, the first thing to do is tell Excel which part of the worksheet you want to print. Excel calls this setting the *print area*. You can set a separate print area for each worksheet.

> **CAUTIONL** Until you set the print area, Excel assumes you want to print all the cells you've used on the worksheet—even if there are huge amounts of blank space between them. So it's a good idea always to set the print area before printing.

To set the print area, follow these steps:

1. Click the worksheet whose print area you want to set.

2. Select the range of cells you want to print.

3. Choose **Page Layout ➤ Page Setup ➤ Print Area ➤ Set Print Area**. Excel displays a dotted line around the print area to indicate that it is set.

If you need to change the print area afterward, repeat the above steps. If you need to clear the print area so that the worksheet has no print area set, click the worksheet, and then choose **Page Layout ➤ Page Setup ➤ Print Area ➤ Clear Print Area**.

Checking the Page Layout and Where the Page Breaks Fall

After setting the print area, check the page layout of the worksheet and adjust it as needed. Follow these steps:

1. Switch to **Page Layout** view in either of these ways:

   - Click the **Page Layout View** button in the **View Shortcuts** area in the status bar.

   - Choose **View ➤ Workbook Views ➤ Page Layout**.

2. Click the **Page Layout** tab of the Ribbon to show its controls. Figure 12–24 shows a worksheet in **Page Layout** view with the **Page Layout** tab displayed.

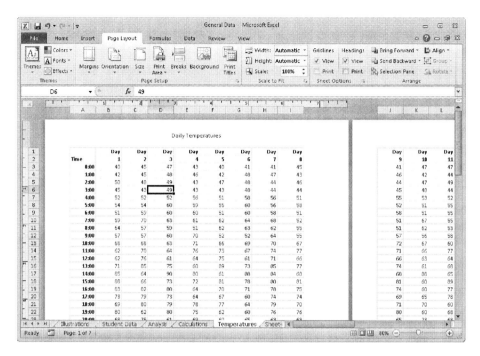

Figure 12–24. *To see a worksheet's pages laid out, switch to **Page Layout** view. You can then use the controls on the **Page Layout** tab of the Ribbon to refine the layout.*

3. Use the controls in the **Page Setup** group to change the page setup as needed:

    a. Change the margins. Click the **Margins** button, and then click **Normal**, **Wide**, or **Narrow**. Or click **Custom Margins**, work on the **Margins** tab of the **Page Setup** dialog box, and then click the **OK** button.

    b. Change the orientation. Click the **Orientation** button, and then click **Portrait** or **Landscape**.

    c. Change the paper size. Click the **Size** drop-down list, and then click the paper size.

    d. Insert a page break. Click the column before which you want to insert a manual page break. Click the **Breaks** button, and then click **Insert Page Break**.

> **NOTE:** If you put a page break in the wrong place, click the **Undo** button on the Quick Access Toolbar to remove it, and then replace it where it's needed. If you get several page breaks wrong, click the column after one of them, and then choose **Page Layout ➤ Page Setup ➤ Breaks ➤ Remove Page Breaks**. To restore all page breaks to where Excel had placed them, choose **Page Layout ➤ Page Setup ➤ Breaks ➤ Reset Page Breaks**.

4. To get an overall view of where page breaks fall, and to adjust them, click the **Page Break Preview** button in the **View Shortcuts** area of the status bar to switch to **Page Break Preview**.

5. In **Page Break Preview** (see Figure 12–25), click and drag the page breaks as needed. A dotted blue line indicates a page break that Excel has placed, and a solid blue line indicates a page break you've placed.

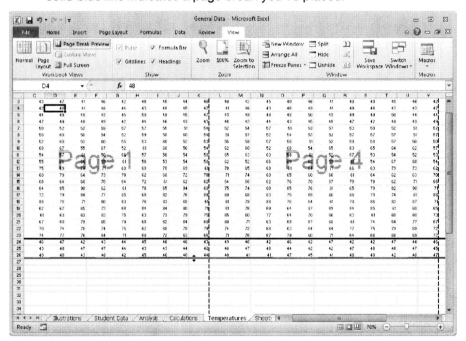

Figure 12–25. *In Page Break Preview, you can drag a page break to move it to a new position.*

When you have finished laying out the pages, click the **Save** button on the Quick Access Toolbar to save your workbook.

Printing a Worksheet or Workbook

After you've set the print area for each worksheet you want to print, you can print a worksheet or workbook as shown in Figure 12–26.

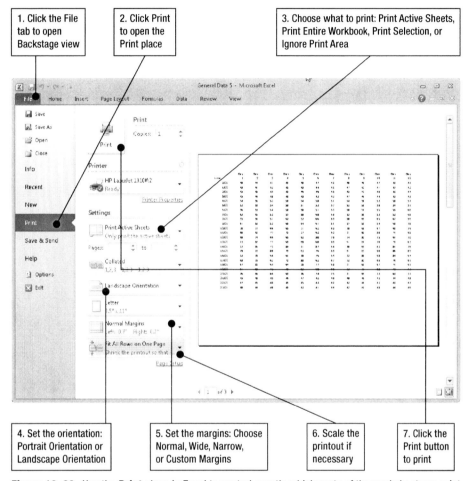

1. Click the File tab to open Backstage view

2. Click Print to open the Print place

3. Choose what to print: Print Active Sheets, Print Entire Workbook, Print Selection, or Ignore Print Area

4. Set the orientation: Portrait Orientation or Landscape Orientation

5. Set the margins: Choose Normal, Wide, Narrow, or Custom Margins

6. Scale the printout if necessary

7. Click the Print button to print

Figure 12–26. *Use the **Print** place in Excel to control exactly which parts of the worksheet you print.*

Summary

In this chapter, you learned how to lay out you your worksheets and apply formatting to them. You now know how to insert, delete, and format rows and columns; use table formatting and styles, and create headers and footers that help to identify the worksheet pages that you then print.

In the next chapter, I'll show you how to perform calculations with formulas and functions. Turn the page when you're ready to start.

Chapter 13

Performing Calculations with Formulas and Functions

In this chapter, you'll learn to use formulas and functions to perform calculations with your data.

First, you'll learn what functions and formulas are and what the difference between them is. Then we'll go over how you refer to cells and ranges in formulas and functions. After that, I'll show you how to create your own formulas, using Excel's calculation operators. You'll find it easy to get started, as Excel provides plenty of help, but we'll also look at how to troubleshoot common problems that occur with formulas.

In the second half of the chapter, I'll show you how to insert functions in your worksheets using the various tools that Excel provides, how to find the functions you want, and how to give the functions the data they need for the calculations.

Understanding the Difference Between Formulas and Functions

In Excel, you can perform calculations by using formulas and functions:

- *By using a formula.* A *formula* is a custom calculation that you create when none of Excel's functions (discussed next) does what you need. The word *formula* tends to sound imposing, but a formula can be a simple calculation; for example, to subtract 50 from 100, you can type **=100-50** in a cell (the equal sign tells Excel you're starting a formula). Formulas can also be more complex, as you'll see later in this chapter.

■ *By using a function.* A *function* is a preset calculation that performs a standard calculation. For example, when you need to add several values together, you use the **SUM( )** function—for instance, =**SUM(A1:A6)**, which is simpler than =**A1+A2+A3+A4+A5+A6,** but has the same effect. You can use functions only in formulas, either as the main part of a formula (as in the **SUM** example there) or as constituent parts of formulas (for example, =**SUM(A1:A6)*0.25)**.

I'll show you how to use formulas first, and then functions. But before we start on formulas, let's go over the ways of referring to cells and ranges in formulas and functions.

Referring to Cells and Ranges in Formulas and Functions

To make your formulas and functions work correctly, you need to refer to the cells and ranges you want. You can create references to cells and ranges in different locations:

■ On the same worksheet as the formula

■ On a different worksheet than the formula

■ In a different workbook than the formula

Referring to a Cell or Range on the Same Worksheet

To refer to a cell on the same worksheet, enter its column lettering and its row number. For example, use =**A10** to refer to cell A10.

You can either type in the reference or click the cell—whichever you find easier. You'll see examples of this shortly.

Similarly, to refer to a range, enter the range's address. For example, use =**A10:A20** to refer to the range A10:A20.

Referring to a Cell or Range on a Different Worksheet

To refer to a cell or range on a different worksheet, enter the worksheet's name followed by an exclamation point and the cell or range reference. For example, use =**Supplies!A10** to refer to cell A10 on the worksheet named Supplies, or use =**'Sales Results'!BB20:BB25** to refer to the range BB20:BB25 on the worksheet named Sales Results.

> **NOTE:** If the worksheet's name contains any spaces, you must put the name inside single quotes—for example, =`'Sales Results'!A10` rather than =`Sales Results!A10`. You can use the single quotes on worksheet names that don't have spaces too if you find it easier to be consistent.

You can type in the reference, but using the mouse is usually easier. Figure 13–1 shows you how to create the reference using the mouse.

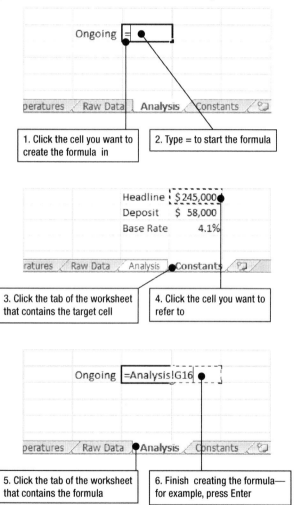

Figure 13–1. *You can quickly create a reference to a cell on another worksheet by using the mouse.*

Referring to a Cell or Range in a Different Workbook

To refer to a cell or range in a different workbook, enter the workbook's path, then the file name in brackets, then the worksheet's name, and then the cell reference or range reference. For example, the reference `='Shared:Spreads:[Results.xlsx]Sales!'AB12` refers to cell AB12 on the worksheet named Sales in the workbook Results.xlsx in the Shared:Spreads folder.

Unless you happen to know the path, file name, worksheet name, and cell or range, it's usually easiest to set up the reference by using the mouse. Follow these steps:

1. Open the workbook you want to refer to.

2. In the workbook that will contain the reference, start creating the formula. For example, type = in the cell.

3. Switch to the other workbook.

    ▓ If you can see the other workbook, click it.

    ▓ If you can't see the other workbook, open the **Window** menu on the menu bar, and then click the appropriate window.

4. Navigate to the worksheet that contains the cell, and then click the cell or select the range.

5. Switch back to the workbook in which you're creating the reference, and then complete the formula.

When you create a reference to a cell or range in another workbook, Excel keeps the value of the referring cell updated. If you move or delete the other workbook, Excel displays a dialog box warning you that it cannot find the workbook and asking if you want to locate it manually.

Referring to Ranges

To refer to a range that consists of a block of cells, give the cell addresses of the first cell and the last cell, separating them with a colon. For example, to refer to the range from cell P10 to cell Q12, use `=P10:Q12`.

To refer to a range that consists of individual cells, give the address of each cell, separating the addresses with commas. For example, to refer to cell J14, cell K18, and cell Z20, use `=J14,K18,Z20`.

To refer to a range on a different worksheet or in a different workbook, use the techniques explained in the previous section. For example, if you need to refer to the range P10 to Q12 on the worksheet named Stock Listing, use `='Stock Listing'!P10:Q12`. (You'll need a worksheet named Stock Listing for this to work.)

UNDERSTANDING ABSOLUTE REFERENCES,
RELATIVE REFERENCES, AND MIXED REFERENCES

Using cell addresses or range addresses is straightforward enough, but when you start using formulas, there's a complication. When you copy a formula and paste it, you need to tell Excel whether the pasted formula should refer to the cells it originally referred to, or the cells in the same relative positions to the cell where the formula now is, or a mixture of the two. (If you move a formula to another cell by using drag and drop or Cut and Paste, Excel keeps the formula as it is.)

To make references clear, Excel uses three types of references:

- *Absolute reference.* A reference that always refers to the same cell, no matter where you copy it. Excel uses a dollar sign ($) to indicate that each part of the reference is absolute. For example, B3 is an absolute reference to cell B3.

- *Relative reference.* A reference that refers to the cell by its position relative to the cell that holds the reference. For example, if you select cell A3 and enter =B5 in it, the reference means "the cell one column to the right and two rows down." So if you copy the formula to cell C4, Excel changes the cell reference to cell D6, which is one column to the right and two rows down from cell C4. To indicate a relative reference, Excel uses a plain reference without any dollar signs; for example, B5.

- *Mixed reference.* A reference that is absolute for either the column or the row and relative for the other. For example, $B4 is absolute for the column (B) and relative for the row (4), while B$4 is relative for the column and absolute for the row. When you copy and paste a mixed reference, the absolute part stays the same, but the relative part changes to reflect the new location.

If you're typing a reference, you can type the **$** signs into the reference to make it absolute or mixed. If you're entering references by selecting cells, click in the reference in cell you're editing or in the formula bar, and then press **F4** repeatedly to cycle a reference through its absolute, relative, column-absolute, and row-absolute versions.

If a formula refers to multiple cells, you need to alter the reference for each cell separately—you can't change the whole lot in one fell swoop.

Referring to Named Cells and Ranges

To make your references easier to enter in your worksheets and easier to identify in formulas, you can give a name to any cell or range. You can then refer to the cell or range by the name instead of by its cell reference or range reference.

Figure 13–2 shows you how to assign a name to a cell or range. The process is straightforward apart from these two details:

- The name must start with a letter or an underscore. The rest of the name can be any mix of letters, numbers, and underscores, but you can't use spaces or symbols.

■ The name can have either workbook scope or worksheet scope.
Workbook scope means that the name is unique within the whole
workbook, so no matter which worksheet you use the name on, it
refers to the same cell. Worksheet scope means that the name is
unique only on a particular worksheet. Worksheet scope enables you
to use the same range names on different worksheets in the same
workbook. Sometimes this is helpful, but other times it's confusing.

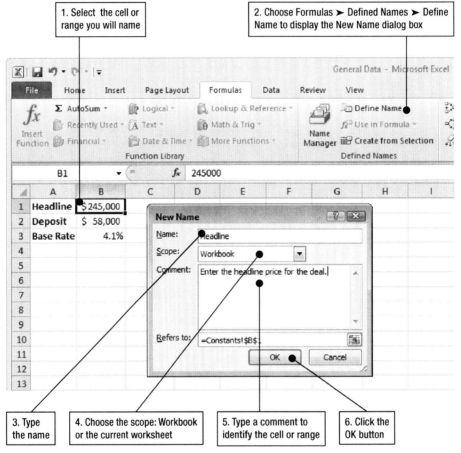

Figure 13–2. *Use the **New Name** dialog box to create a name for a cell or range so that you can refer to it easily
and recognize it immediately in formulas.*

When you need to change or delete a name, choose **Formulas ➤ Defined Names ➤
Name Manager**, and then work in the **Name Manager** dialog box (see Figure 13–3).

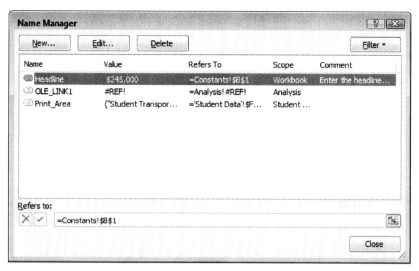

Figure 13–3. *In the **Name Manager** dialog box, click the existing range name you want to work with. You can then click the **Edit** button to change its name, comment, scope, or reference, or click the **Delete** button to delete it.*

Performing Custom Calculations by Creating Formulas

When you need to perform a custom calculation in a cell, use a formula rather than a function. All you need to do is type in a simple formula using the appropriate calculation operators, such as + signs for addition and – signs for subtraction. In this section, you'll meet the comparison operators, try using them in a worksheet, and learn the order in which Excel applies them—and how to change that order.

Meeting Excel's Calculation Operators

To perform calculations in Excel, you need to know the operators for the different operations—addition, division, comparison, and so on. Table 13–1 explains the full set of calculation operators you can use in your formulas in Excel.

Table 13–1. *Calculation Operators You Can Use in Excel*

Calculation Operator	Operation	Explanation or Example
Arithmetic Operators		
+	Addition	=1+2
–	Subtraction	=1–2
*	Multiplication	=2*2
/	Division	=A1/4
%	Percentage	=B1%
^	Exponentiation	=B1^2 raises the value in cell B2 to the power 2.
Comparison Operators		
=	Equal to	=B2=15000 returns TRUE if cell B2 contains the value 15000. Otherwise, it returns FALSE.
<>	Not equal to	=B2<>15000 returns TRUE if cell B2 does not contain the value 15000. Otherwise, it returns FALSE.
>	Greater than	=B2>15000 returns TRUE if cell B2 contains a value greater than 15000. Otherwise, it returns FALSE.
>=	Greater than or equal to	=B2>=15000 returns TRUE if cell B2 contains a value greater than or equal to 15000. Otherwise, it returns FALSE.
<	Less than	=B2<15000 returns TRUE if cell B2 contains a value less than 15000. Otherwise, it returns FALSE.
<=	Less than or equal to	=B2<=15000 returns TRUE if cell B2 contains a value less than or equal to 15000. Otherwise, it returns FALSE.

Calculation Operator	Operation	Explanation or Example
Reference Operators		
[cell reference]:[cell reference]	The range of cells between the two cell references	=A1:G5 returns the range of cells whose upper-left cell is cell A1 and whose lower-right cell is cell G5.
[cell reference],[cell reference]	The range of cells listed	=A1,C3,E5 returns three cells: A1, C3, and E5.
[cell or range reference][space][cell or range reference]	The range (or cell) that appears in both cells or ranges given.	=A7:G10 B10:B12 returns the cell B10, because this is the only cell that appears in both the ranges given.
Text Operator		
&	Concatenation (joining values as text)	=A1&B1 returns the values from cells A1 and B1 joined together as a text string. For example, if A1 contains "New York " (including a trailing space) and B1 contains "Sales", this formula returns "New York Sales." If A1 contains 100 and B1 contains 50, this formula returns 10050.

Using the Calculation Operators

Now that you know what the calculation operators are, try the following example of creating a simple worksheet that uses the four most straightforward operators—addition, subtraction, multiplication, and division.

First, create a new workbook (for example, press **Ctrl+N**) and enter the labels shown in the first column, as explained in Figure 13–4.

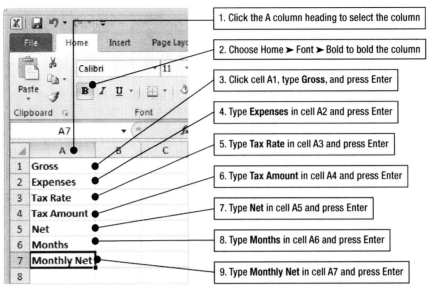

1. Click the A column heading to select the column

2. Choose Home ➤ Font ➤ Bold to bold the column

3. Click cell A1, type **Gross**, and press Enter

4. Type **Expenses** in cell A2 and press Enter

5. Type **Tax Rate** in cell A3 and press Enter

6. Type **Tax Amount** in cell A4 and press Enter

7. Type **Net** in cell A5 and press Enter

8. Type **Months** in cell A6 and press Enter

9. Type **Monthly Net** in cell A7 and press Enter

Figure 13–4. *Start the example worksheet by applying boldface to column A and entering labels in it.*

Next, format the second column and start entering data in it, as explained in Figure 13–5.

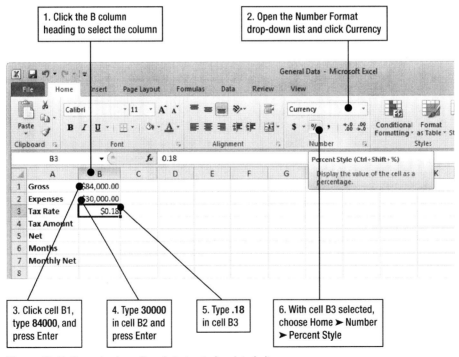

1. Click the B column heading to select the column

2. Open the Number Format drop-down list and click Currency

3. Click cell B1, type **84000**, and press Enter

4. Type **30000** in cell B2 and press Enter

5. Type **.18** in cell B3

6. With cell B3 selected, choose Home ➤ Number ➤ Percent Style

Figure 13–5. *Format column B and start entering data in it.*

After that, follow the steps in Figure 13–6 to enter in cell B4 a formula that calculates the tax amount by multiplying the **Gross** value in cell B1 by the **Tax Amount** value in cell B3 (=B1*B3).

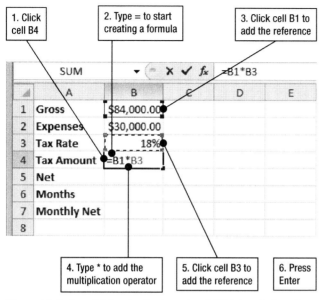

Figure 13–6. *In cell B4, enter the formula =B1*B3 to calculate the tax amount.*

Now enter the formula =B1-(B2+B4) in cell B5 as shown in Figure 13–7. The parentheses create what's called a *nested expression*, a part of the formula that is evaluated separately from the rest. You'll learn about nested expressions later in this chapter.

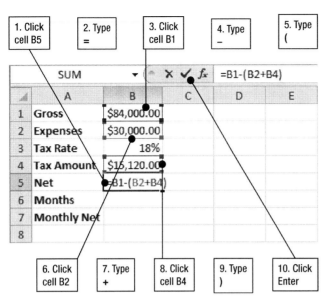

Figure 13–7. *Enter the formula =B1-(B2+B4) in cell B5. This time, click the **Enter** button on the formula bar to enter the formula in the cell.*

Now finish the worksheet by entering **12** in cell B6 and the formula **=B5/B6** in cell B7, as shown in Figure 13–8.

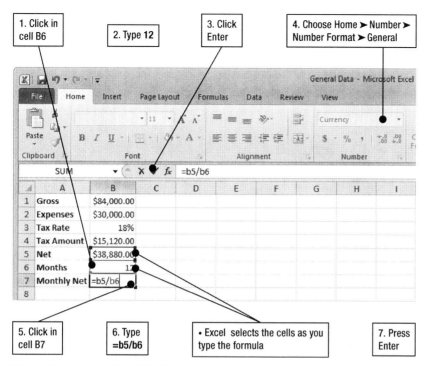

Figure 13–8. *Type 12 in cell B6, then type the formula =B5/B6 in cell B7 to divide the Net amount by the Months value, producing the Monthly Net value.*

Figure 13–9 shows the worksheet with all the formulas in place. Now that you've created it, press **Ctrl+S** to save your workbook. Then try changing the figures in cells B1, B2, and B3. You'll see the results of the formulas in cells B4, B5, and B7 change accordingly. Excel recalculates the formulas each time you change a value in a cell, so the formula results remain up to date.

	A	B	C
1	Gross	$84,000.00	
2	Expenses	$30,000.00	
3	Tax Rate	18%	
4	Tax Amount	$15,120.00	
5	Net	$38,880.00	
6	Monts	12	
7	Monthly Net	$ 3,240.00	
8			

Figure 13–9. *After entering all the formulas, save your workbook. You can then try entering different figures in the Gross cell, the Expenses cell, and the Tax Rate cell. Excel recalculates the worksheet after each change.*

NOTE: If you create a workbook with huge amounts of data, automatic recalculation may make Excel run slowly. If this happens, choose **Formulas ➤ Calculation ➤ Calculation Options ➤ Manual** to turn off automatic recalculation. You can recalculate manually when necessary by pressing **Shift+F9** or choosing **Formulas ➤ Calculation ➤ Calculate Sheet** (to recalculate just the active worksheet), or pressing **F9** or choosing **Formulas ➤ Calculation ➤ Calculate Now** to recalculate the whole workbook.

Understanding the Order in Which Excel Evaluates Operators

In the previous example, you entered the formula =B1-(B2+B4) in cell B5. The parentheses are necessary because the calculation has two separate stages—one stage of subtraction and one stage of addition—and you need to control the order in which they occur.

Try changing the formula in cell B5 to =B1-B2+B4 and see what happens. Follow these steps:

1. Click cell B5.

2. Click in the formula bar to start editing the formula there. (You can also edit in the cell by double-clicking the cell or pressing F2, but editing in the formula bar gives you more space, so it's often easier.)

3. Delete the opening and closing parentheses.

4. Click the **Enter** button on the formula bar.

You'll notice that the Net amount (cell B5) jumps substantially. This is because you've changed the meaning of the formula:

▨ =B1-(B2+B4). This formula means "add the value in cell B2 to the value in cell B4, then subtract the result from the value in cell B1."

▨ =B1-B2+B4. This formula means "subtract the value in cell B2 from the value in cell B2, then add the value in cell B4 to the result."

Click cell B5 and press F2 to open the cell for editing. Position the insertion point before B2 and type **(,** then position the insertion point after B4 and type **)**. As you type the closing parenthesis, notice that the opening parenthesis momentarily darkens to make the pairing clear. In this case, you can easily see the opening parenthesis because the cell's contents are short and simple. But when a cell has complex contents, and contains other nested items, having the corresponding parenthesis darken like this helps you to identify it.

The order in which Excel evaluates the operators is called *operator precedence*, and it can make a huge difference in your formulas—so it's vital to know both how it works and how to override it. Table 13–2 shows you the order in which Excel evaluates the operators in formulas.

Table 13–2. *Excel's Operator Precedence in Descending Order*

Precedence	Operators	Explanation
1	–	Negation
2	%	Percentage
3	^	Exponentiation
4	* and /	Multiplication and division
5	+ and –	Addition and subtraction
6	&	Concatenation
7	=, <>, <, <=, >, and >=	Comparison operators

When two operators are at the same level, Excel performs the operator that appears earlier in the formula first.

Nesting Parts of Formulas to Override Operator Precedence

You can override operator precedence in any formula by nesting one or more parts of the formula in parentheses. For example, as you just saw, using `=B1-(B2+B4)` makes Excel evaluate B2+B4 before the subtraction.

You can nest parts of the formula several levels deep if necessary. For example, the following formula uses three levels of nesting and returns 180.

`=10*(5*(4/(1+1))+8)`

> **TIP:** Nested formulas can quickly become hard to read. If you find a formula is becoming too complex, break it up into intermediate stages, and place each in a separate cell. Excel gives you almost unlimited space, and it's much better to use more cells than to get the wrong result by creating a formula that's impressively complex but wrong.

Entering Formulas Quickly by Copying and Using AutoFill

In many worksheets, you'll need to enter related formulas in several or many cells. For example, say you have the worksheet shown in Figure 13–10, which lists a range of products with their prices and sales. Column D needs to show the total revenue derived by multiplying the **Units** figure by the **Price** value.

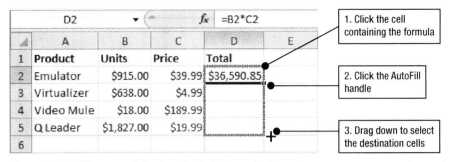

Figure 13–10. *When a worksheet needs similar formulas in a column or row, you can enter one formula manually and then use AutoFill or Copy and Paste to enter it quickly in the other cells.*

Each cell in column D needs a different formula: Cell D2 needs **=B2*C2**, Cell D3 needs **=B3*C3**, and so on. Because the formula is the same except for the row number, you can use either AutoFill or Copy and Paste to enter the formula from cell D2 into the other cells as well.

To enter the formula using AutoFill, click the cell that contains the formula (here, cell D2), and then drag the AutoFill handle down through cell D5. Excel automatically fills in the formulas, adjusting each for the change in row.

To enter the formula using Copy and Paste, click the cell that contains the formula, and then give the Copy command (for example, press **Ctrl+C**.). Select the destination cells, and then give the Paste command (for example, press **Ctrl+V**).

> **NOTE:** If you need to copy a formula to a different row or column but have it refer to the original location, create the formula using mixed references. If you need to keep the column the same, make the column absolute (for example, **=$B2**); if you need to keep the row the same, make the row absolute (for example, **=B$2**).

Troubleshooting Common Problems with Formulas

Formulas are great when they work, but a single-letter typo or a wrong reference can prevent a formula from working correctly. This section shows you how to deal with common problems with formulas, starting with solutions to the error messages you're most likely to produce.

Understanding and Resolving Common Errors

Excel includes an impressive arsenal of error messages, but some of them appear far more frequently than others. Table 13–3 shows you eight errors you're likely to encounter, explains what they mean, and tells you how to solve them.

Table 13–3. *How to Solve Excel's Eight Most Common Errors*

Error	What the Problem Is	How to Solve It
#####	The formula result is too wide to fit in the cell.	Make the column wider—for example, double-click the column head's right border to AutoFit the column width.
#NAME?	A function name is misspelled, or the formula refers to a range that doesn't exist.	Check the spelling of all functions; correct any mistakes. If the formula uses a named range, check that the name is right, and that you haven't deleted the range.
#NUM!	The formula tries to use a value that is not valid for it—for example, returning the square root of a negative number.	Give the function a suitable value.
#VALUE!	The function uses an invalid argument—for example, using =FACT( ) to return the factorial of text rather than a number.	Give the function the right type of data.
#N/A	The function does not have a valid value available.	Make sure the function's arguments provide values of the right type.
#DIV/0	The function is trying to divide by zero (which is mathematically impossible).	Change the divisor value from zero. Often, you'll find that the function is using a blank cell (which has a zero value) as the argument for the divisor; in this case, enter a value in the cell.
#REF!	The formula uses a cell reference or a range reference that's not valid—for example, because you've deleted a worksheet.	Edit the formula and provide a valid reference.
#NULL!	There is no intersection between the two ranges specified.	Change the ranges to produce an intersection.

Seeing the Details of an Error in a Formula

When Excel identifies an error in a formula, it displays a green triangle at the upper-left corner of the cell that contains the formula. Click the cell to display an action button that you can hold the mouse over to display a ScreenTip explaining the problem (see Figure 13–11) or click to display a menu of actions you can take to resolve the problem.

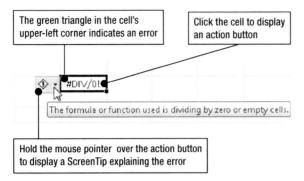

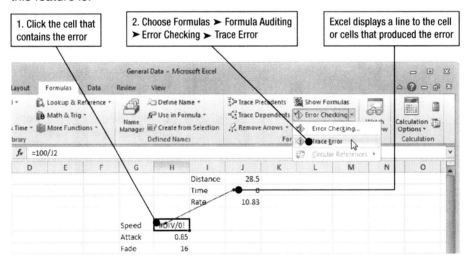

Figure 13–11. *Hold the mouse pointer over the action button for an error cell to display a ScreenTip explaining what's wrong.*

Tracing an Error Back to Its Source

To see which cell is causing an error, work as shown in Figure 13–12. This shows a simple example of tracing an error; the more complex the worksheet, the more helpful this feature is.

Figure 13–12. *Use the* **Formulas ➤ Formula Auditing ➤ Error Checking ➤ Trace Error** *command to identify the cell that's causing an error.*

Displaying All the Formulas in a Worksheet

When you need to review or check all the formulas in a worksheet, choose **Formulas ➤ Formula Auditing ➤ Show Formulas**. Excel displays the formulas and automatically widens the worksheet columns to give you more space (see Figure 13–13).

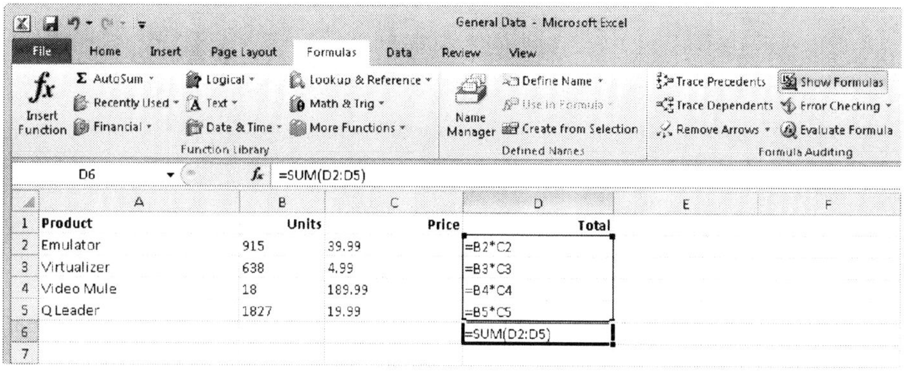

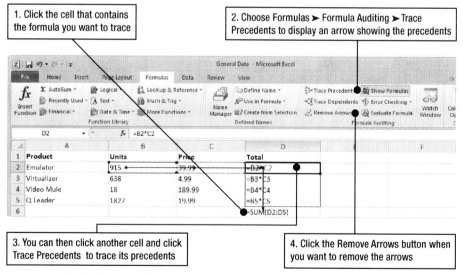

Figure 13–13. *Click the* **Show Formulas** *button in the* **Formula Auditing** *group of the* **Formulas** *tab of the Ribbon when you need to see all the formulas in a worksheet.*

When you've finished viewing the formulas, choose **Formulas ➤ Formula Auditing ➤ Show Formulas** again to un-press the **Show Formulas** button. Excel automatically restores the columns to their former widths.

Seeing Which Cells a Formula Uses

To see which cells a formula uses, work as shown in Figure 13–14.

Figure 13–14. *Use the* **Trace Precedents** *command to see which cells you're using to produce a formula result. In this example, cells B2 and C2 go to make up the formula in cell D2, which in turn appears in the* **=SUM(D2:D5)** *formula in cell D6.*

When you need to look at the problem the other way and see which formulas use a particular cell, click the cell, and then choose **Formulas ➤ Formula Auditing ➤ Trace**

Dependents. Again, Excel displays arrows, this time from the cell going to each of the formulas that use it.

> **TIP:** You can use the **Trace Precedents** command and the **Trace Dependents** command either with formulas displayed or with formula results displayed—whichever you find most useful.

When you've finished tracing precedents and dependents, choose **Formulas ➤ Formula Auditing ➤ Remove Arrows** to remove the arrows from the screen. To remove all the arrows, click the main part of the button. To remove just precedent arrows or dependent arrows, click the **Remove Arrows** drop-down button, and then click **Remove Precedent Arrows** or **Remove Dependent Arrows**, as needed.

Performing Standard Calculations by Inserting Functions

When you need to perform standard calculations in your worksheets, use Excel's built-in functions. The functions are predefined calculations that you drop into your formulas and provide with the data they need.

You can enter functions using either the **Function** drop-down list in the **Editing** group of the **Home** tab of the Ribbon or by using the controls in the **Function Library** group on the **Formulas** tab. We'll look at each approach in turn. But first, we'll examine the components of a function so that you know what's what.

Understanding Function Names and Arguments

In Excel, a function has a name written in capitals followed by a pair of parentheses. For example:

- *SUM( )*. This widely used function adds together two or more values that you specify.

- *COUNT( )*. This function counts the number of cells that contain numbers (as opposed to text, blanks, or other data types) in the range you specify.

- *TODAY( )*. This function enters the current date in the cell.

Most functions take *arguments*—pieces of information that tell the function what you want it to work on. Excel prompts you to provide the arguments each function needs. For example, when you enter the function in a cell, Excel displays a ScreenTip showing the arguments needed. Figure 13–15 shows an example using the *SUM( )* function.

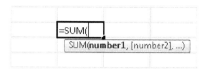

Figure 13–15. *When you enter a function in a cell, Excel prompts you to supply the arguments it needs.*

The ScreenTip shows that the SUM() function has one required argument, one optional argument. and that you can add further arguments as needed:

- *Required argument.* Each required argument appears in boldface, like the argument number1 in the ScreenTip. You separate the arguments with commas. For example, you can use SUM() to add the values of cells in a range: SUM(C1:C10).

- *Optional argument.* Each optional argument appears in brackets, like the argument [number2] in the ScreenTip. For example, you can use SUM() to add the values of two cells: SUM(C1,C3).

- *Extra arguments.* The ellipsis (...) shows that you can enter extra arguments of the same type. For example, you can use SUM() to add the values of many cells: SUM(C1,C3,D4,D8,E1,XF202).

> **NOTE:** A few functions take no arguments. For example, you don't need to tell the TODAY() function which day you're talking about. Similarly, the NOW() function needs no arguments to return the current date and time, and the NA() function enters #(N/A) in a cell to indicate that the information is not available.

Inserting Functions with the Function Drop-Down List

The quickest and easiest way to enter any of five widely used functions—SUM(), AVERAGE(), COUNT(), MAX(), or MIN()—in your worksheets is to use the **Function** drop-down list in the **Editing** group of the **Home** tab of the Ribbon, as shown in Figure 13–16.

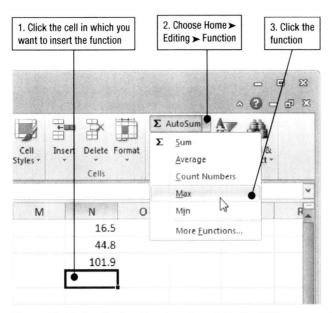

1. Click the cell in which you want to insert the function

2. Choose Home ➤ Editing ➤ Function

3. Click the function

Figure 13–16. *Use the **Function** drop-down list in the **Editing** group of the **Home** tab when you need to insert the SUM(), AVERAGE(), COUNT(), MAX(), or MIN() function quickly.*

Excel inserts the function in the cell you chose and selects the range it thinks you may want to use as the argument. Figure 13–17 shows an example with the MAX() function. Adjust the range if necessary, and then press **Enter** to enter the function in the cell. The cell then displays the result of the formula.

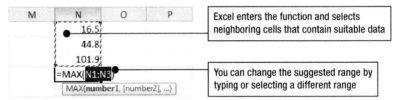

Excel enters the function and selects neighboring cells that contain suitable data

You can change the suggested range by typing or selecting a different range

Figure 13–17. *After inserting a function, you may need to change the range that Excel suggests. Press **Enter** when the range is right.*

Finding the Functions You Need with the Insert Function Dialog Box

Excel includes more than 500 functions that cover a wide variety of needs—everything from calculations that almost everyone uses (such as the SUM() function) to highly specialized functions for statistics (such as the CHISQ.DIST.RT() function for returning the right-tailed probability of the chi-squared distribution) and engineering (such as the various Bessel functions).

When you need to find a function but don't know its name, use the **Insert Function** dialog box to search for the function. Follow these steps:

1. Click the cell in which you want to insert the function.

2. Choose **Formulas ➤ Function Library ➤ Insert Function** to open the **Insert Function** dialog box (see Figure 13–18).

> **NOTE:** You can also open the **Insert Function** dialog box by choosing **Home ➤ Editing ➤ Function ➤ More Functions** or by clicking the **More Functions** item at the bottom of most of the drop-down lists in the **Function Library** group on the **Formulas** tab of the Ribbon.

3. Type your search terms in the **Search for a Function** box, and then press **Enter** or click the **Go** button.

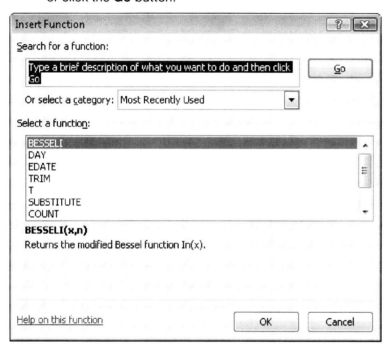

Figure 13–18. *Use the **Insert Function** dialog box when you need to search for a function by name or description.*

4. In the **Select a Function** list box, click the function you want. Excel displays details of what the function does.

5. Click the **OK** button. Excel closes the **Insert Function** dialog box and displays the **Function Arguments** dialog box. You can then enter the arguments for the function as discussed in the section "Providing the Arguments for the Function," later in this chapter.

NOTE: You can also browse for a function by opening the **Or select a category** drop-down list and choosing the category of function you want. This is sometimes useful, but if you want to view functions by category, the drop-down lists in the **Function Library** group on the **Formulas** tab of the Ribbon are usually faster and easier.

Inserting Functions with the Function Library

The third way of inserting functions is to use the controls in the **Function Library** group on the **Formulas** tab of the Ribbon. The **Function Library** group (see Figure 13–19) breaks the functions down into the following categories:

- *AutoSum.* Open this drop-down list when you want to insert one of the five frequently used functions that appears in the **Function** drop-down list in the **Editing** group of the **Home** tab: SUM(), AVERAGE(), COUNT(), MAX(), or MIN().

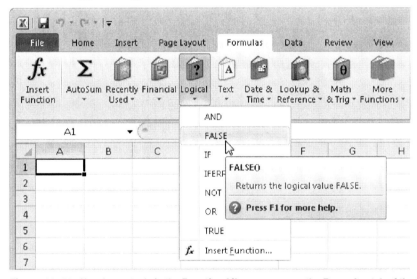

Figure 13–19. *Use the controls in the **Function Library** group on the **Formulas** tab of the Ribbon to insert functions by category.*

- *Recently Used.* Open this drop-down list when you need a function you've used recently. Many spreadsheets need only a small number of different functions, so this list can be a great time-saver if you use it whenever possible.

- *Financial.* Open this drop-down list to insert financial functions—for example, to calculate the payments on your mortgage or the depreciation on an asset.

▓ *Logical.* Open this drop-down list to insert the AND(), FALSE(), IF(), IFERROR(), NOT(), OR(), and TRUE() functions.

▓ *Text.* Open this drop-down list to insert functions for manipulating text, such as the TRIM() function (for trimming off leading and trailing spaces) and the LEFT() function, which returns the leftmost part of the value.

▓ *Date & Time.* Open this drop-down list to insert date and time functions—everything from returning the current date with the TODAY() function to using the WEEKDAY() function to return the day of the week for a particular date.

▓ *Lookup & Reference.* Open this drop-down list to insert functions for looking up data from other parts of a worksheet or referring to other cells in it.

▓ *Math & Trig.* Open this drop-down list to insert mathematical functions, such as the SQRT() function for returning a square root, and trigonometric functions, such as the COS() function for calculating a cosine.

▓ *More Functions.* Open this drop-down menu to reach submenus for the following:

> ▓ *Statistical.* Open this submenu to reach Excel's statistical functions, such as those for calculating standard deviations based on a population or a sample.

> ▓ *Engineering.* Open this submenu to get to the engineering functions, such as the DEC2HEX() function (for converting a decimal number to hexadecimal) and the HEX2OCT() function (for converting a hexadecimal number to octal, base 8).

> ▓ *Cube.* Open this submenu to access functions for working with data cubes.

> ▓ *Information.* Open this submenu to reach functions for returning information about the current selection. For example, you can use the ISBLANK() function to determine whether the cell is blank or the ISNUMBER() function to find out whether it contains a number.

> ▓ *Compatibility.* Open this submenu to find functions included for compatibility with Excel 2007 (Windows), Excel 2008 (Mac), and earlier versions. It's best to use these functions only for compatibility with these older versions; if you're developing worksheets for Excel 2010 or Excel 2011 (Mac), use the newer functions that these versions support—for example, use the new POISSON.DIST() function rather than the old POISSON() function.

You can hold the mouse pointer over a function's name to see a ScreenTip explaining briefly what the function does. When you've found the function you want, click it. Excel then displays the **Function Arguments** dialog box, in which you work as described in the next section.

Providing the Arguments for the Function

Whether you use the **Insert Function** dialog box or one of the drop-down lists in the **Function Library** to identify the function you want to insert, Excel displays the **Function Arguments** dialog box. Figure 13–20 shows the **Function Arguments** dialog box for the NETWORKDAYS() function, which you use to calculate the net number of working days between two dates. The figure explains how to use the **Function Arguments** dialog box.

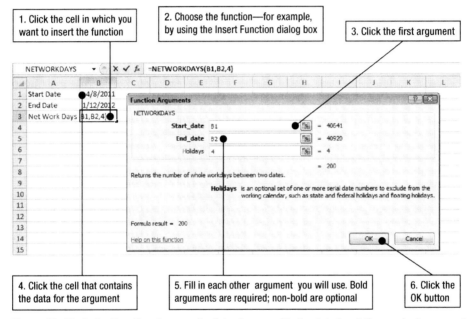

Figure 13–20. *In the Function Arguments dialog box, provide the data for all the required arguments and for each optional argument you want to use. The boldface arguments are required, whereas those in regular font are optional.*

> **TIP:** You can also type references or values into the argument boxes in the **Function Arguments** dialog box if you want. When you need to get the **Function Arguments** dialog box out of the way so that you can select a cell, click the **Collapse Dialog** button at the right of the argument box to minimize the dialog box.

To edit a function you've inserted in the worksheet, click the cell, and then choose **Formulas ➤ Function Library ➤ Insert Function**. Excel displays the **Function**

Arguments dialog box, and you can edit the function as before. For quick fixes, you can also double-click the cell that contains the function, and then edit it right in the cell.

Inserting Functions by Typing Them Into a Worksheet

You can also enter a function by typing it directly into a cell, as shown in Figure 13–21.

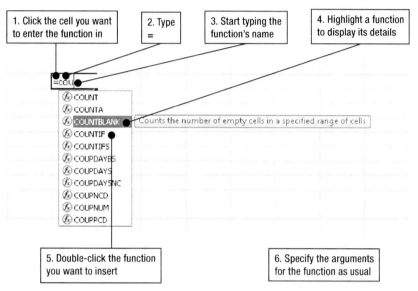

Figure 13–21. *When you start typing a function name into a cell, Excel lists matching functions. Select a function to display a ScreenTip explaining it.*

Summary

In this chapter, you learned to perform calculations with formulas and functions. You know that a formula is the recipe for a calculation, and you know how to assemble it from its various components—an equal sign, cell or range references, operators, and more. You know how to create the formulas you need, and how to troubleshoot them when they go wrong.

You're now also familiar with functions. You know that a function is a preset calculation built into Excel, how to insert functions from the Ribbon or by typing them into cells, and how to give functions the arguments they need to work.

In the next chapter, I'll show you how to create powerful and persuasive charts from your data.

Chapter 14

Creating Charts to Present Your Data

In this chapter, I'll show you how to create clear and compelling charts that present your data exactly as you want it to appear.

We'll start by making sure you understand the ways you can place charts in your workbooks, what the components or charts are, and which types of charts you can create in Excel. We'll then look in detail at how you create a chart from your data, lay it out the way you want, and then give it the look it needs—everything from adding a chart title and axis titles to adding a picture to the chart wall for visual appeal.

Learning the Essentials of Charts in Excel

In this section, we'll look at the two ways you can place charts in your workbooks, identify the different components of charts and examine what they show, and go over the many different types of charts that Excel offers you.

Understanding Embedded Charts and Chart Sheets

In Excel, you can either place a chart on a worksheet (for example, with its data) or on its own chart sheet:

- *Chart on a worksheet.* Excel calls a chart on a worksheet an *embedded chart*—the chart object is embedded in the worksheet. Usually, the worksheet is the one that contains the chart's data, but you can embed a chart on a different worksheet if necessary. Create an embedded chart when you want to look at the chart alongside its data or alongside other information, including other charts. Figure 14–1 shows an embedded chart.

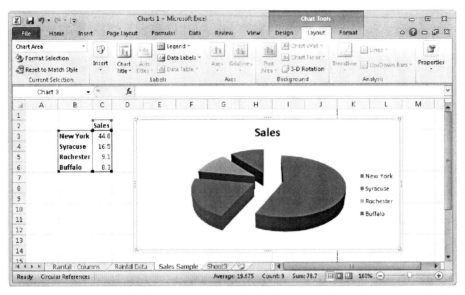

Figure 14–1. *Create an embedded chart on a worksheet when you want to work on or view the chart alongside its data.*

> ▪ *Chart on chart sheet.* When you need more space for a chart, create it
> on a *chart sheet*—a separate sheet in the workbook that contains only
> a chart. The chart sheet doesn't contain the source data, but you can
> add a data table showing the source data if you don't mind sacrificing
> some of the chart sheet's space for the table. Figure 14–2 shows a
> chart on a chart sheet, with a legend but without the source data.

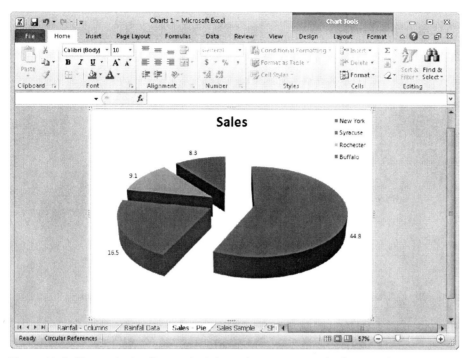

Figure 14–2. *Place a chart on its own chart sheet when you want to give it plenty of space.*

NOTE: You can change an embedded chart to a chart on its own chart sheet, or a chart on a chart sheet to an embedded chart, as needed.

Understanding the Components of a Chart

Excel's charts vary widely in looks and use, but most of them use the same set of components. Figure 14–3 shows a typical type of chart — a 3-D column chart — of rainfall data for six months for seven weather stations, with the main parts of the chart labeled.

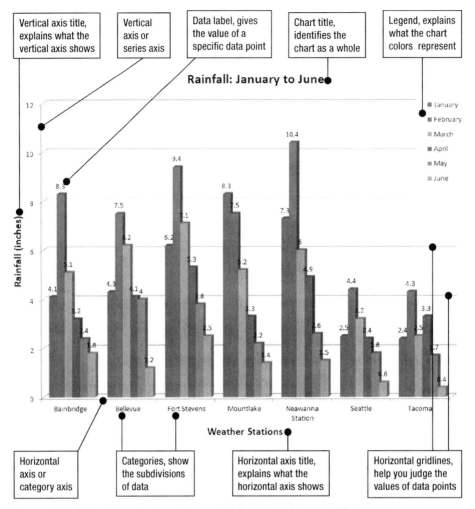

Figure 14–3. *This column chart contains most of the typical elements of Excel charts.*

Apart from the chart elements shown in Figure 14–3, you need to know the following three elements:

- *Chart area.* The chart area is the whole area occupied by the chart. If the chart has a white background, the easiest way to see the extent of the chart area is to click the chart so that Excel displays a border around it.

- *Plot area.* The plot area is the area of the chart that contains the plotted data—in other words, the main part of the chart area, excluding the areas occupied by the chart title, the axis titles, and the legend (if it appears outside the plot area).

- *Depth axis.* In 3-D charts, this is the axis that provides the third dimension. The depth axis is also called the Z-axis.

Understanding Excel's Chart Types and Choosing Which to Use

Excel enables you to create many different types of charts. Some of the chart types are widely useful, like the column chart shown in Figure 14–3; other chart types are highly specialized. Table 14–1 describes the types of charts that Excel provides and suggests typical uses for them. The table lists the charts in the same order as Excel's **Insert Chart** dialog box, which you'll meet shortly and which puts the most widely used chart types first.

Table 14–1. *Excel's Chart Types and Suggested Uses*

Chart Category	Description	Suggested Uses
Column	Displays data in vertical bars.	Comparing equivalent items (such as sales results) or sets of data that change over time (such as rainfall).
Line	Displays each series in a line.	Showing evenly spaced values that change over time, such as temperatures.
Pie	Displays a single data series as a pie divided up by the contribution of each data point.	Showing how much each item contributes to the whole—for example, breaking down expenses by department.
Bar	Displays data in horizontal bars.	Comparing similar items or indicating progress.
Area	Displays data as lines but with the areas between them shaded.	Showing how values have changed over time, especially the contribution of different data points in the series.
X Y (Scatter)	Displays each data point as a point (or cross, or similar marker) on the plot area.	Showing values sampled at different times or that are not directly related to each other.
Stock	Displays each data series as a vertical line or bar indicating three or more prices or measurements (for example, high, low, and closing prices).	Showing the daily prices of stocks. Also suitable for some scientific data.
Surface	Displays the data points as a three-dimensional surface.	Comparing two sets of data to find a suitable combination of them.

Chart Category	Description	Suggested Uses
Doughnut	Displays the data series as a sequence of concentric rings.	Showing how much each item contributes to the whole—like a pie chart, but it works with two or more data series.
Bubble	Displays the data points as bubbles of different sizes depending on their values.	Showing the relative importance of each data point.
Radar	Displays the combined values of different data series.	Showing how the combined values of separate data series compare to each other—for example, the sales contributions of several different products over several periods of time.

Creating, Laying Out, and Formatting a Chart

In this section, we'll look at how to create a chart from your data, lay it out with the components and arrangement you want, and apply the most useful types of formatting.

Creating a Chart Using the Chart Category Buttons

The quickest way to create a chart is by using the chart category buttons, as shown in Figure 14–4. Briefly, you select the range that contains the data, and then choose the chart type by using the controls in the **Charts** group on the **Insert** tab of the Ribbon.

> **TIP:** You can create a chart from either a block range or from a range of separate cells. To use separate cells, select them as usual—for example, click the first, and then **Ctrl+click** each of the others.

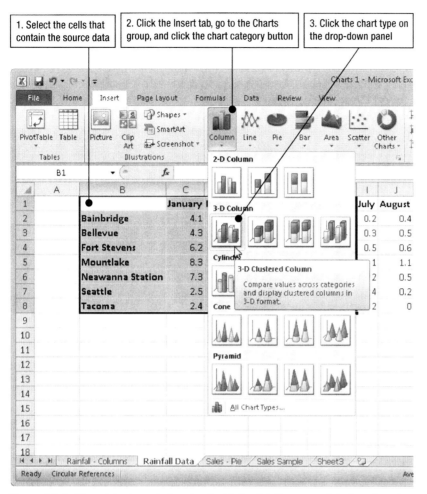

Figure 14–4. *The quickest way to insert a chart is to click the appropriate drop-down button in the* **Charts** *group on the* **Insert** *tab of the Ribbon, and then click the chart type you want.*

When you create a chart this way, Excel creates it as an embedded chart in the current worksheet.

TIP: If the chart doesn't turn out the way you want it, you can change to another chart type. Right-click the chart, and then click **Change Chart Type** on the context menu to display the **Change Chart Type** dialog box, which is like the **Insert Chart** dialog box. Click the chart category, click the chart type, and then click the **OK** button. Excel changes the chart to the new type.

Creating a Chart Using the Insert Chart Dialog Box

If you prefer to browse through the various types of chart that Excel offers, use the **Insert Chart** dialog box instead of the **Charts** group on the Ribbon. Figure 14–5 shows you how to use the **Insert Chart** dialog box. The **Create Chart** button is the tiny button at the lower-right corner of the **Charts** group; the button shows an arrow pointing down and to the right.

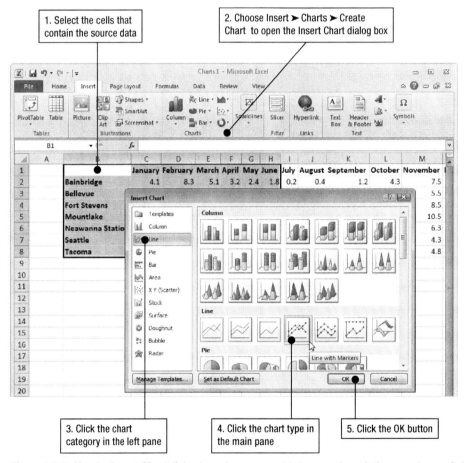

1. Select the cells that contain the source data

2. Choose Insert ➤ Charts ➤ Create Chart to open the Insert Chart dialog box

3. Click the chart category in the left pane

4. Click the chart type in the main pane

5. Click the OK button

Figure 14–5. *Use the **Insert Chart** dialog box when you want to browse through the many types of charts that Excel offers. To see what a chart type is called, hold the mouse pointer over it until the ScreenTip appears.*

Resizing or Repositioning an Embedded Chart

Whether you use the controls in the **Charts** group or the **Insert Chart** dialog box, Excel inserts the chart as an embedded chart on the active worksheet. You can then resize it or reposition it, as shown in Figure 14–6.

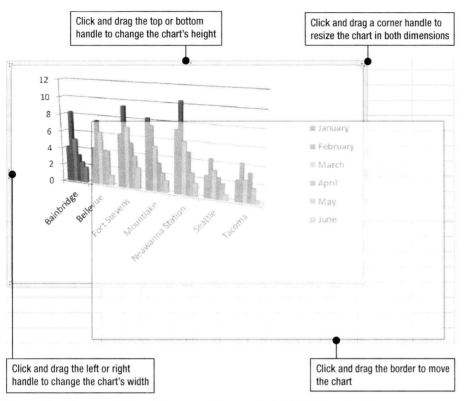

Figure 14–6. *You can quickly resize or reposition an embedded chart by using the mouse.*

Changing a Chart from an Embedded Chart to a Chart Sheet

You can change a chart from being embedded in a worksheet to being on its own chart sheet like this:

1. Click the chart on the worksheet it's embedded in.

2. Choose **Chart Tools ➤ Design ➤ Location ➤ Move Chart** to display the **Move Chart** dialog box (see Figure 14–7).

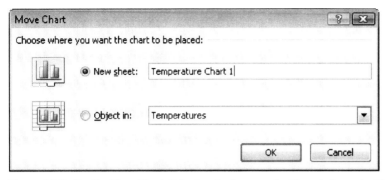

Figure 14–7. *Use the **Move Chart** dialog box to change a chart from being embedded to being on its own chart sheet.*

3. Select the **New sheet** option button.

4. Type the name for the new chart sheet in the **New sheet** text box.

5. Click the **OK** button. Excel creates the new chart sheet and moves the chart to it.

> **NOTE:** You can also use the **Chart Tools ➤ Design ➤ Location ➤ Move Chart** command to move a chart from a chart sheet to an embedded chart on a worksheet, or to move an embedded chart from one worksheet to another.

Switching the Rows and Columns in a Chart

When Excel displays the chart, you may realize that the data series are in the wrong place—for example, the chart is displaying months by rainfall instead of rainfall by months.

To fix the problem, switch the rows and columns by choosing **Chart Tools ➤ Design ➤ Data ➤ Switch Row/Column**. Excel displays the chart with the series the other way around.

Changing the Source Data for a Chart

After creating the chart, you may find you need to change the source data. For example, you may need to remove some data because there's too much, or add data you left out.

To change the source data for the chart, follow these steps:

1. Choose **Chart Tools ➤ Design ➤ Data ➤ Select Data** to display the **Select Data Source** dialog box (see Figure 14–8).

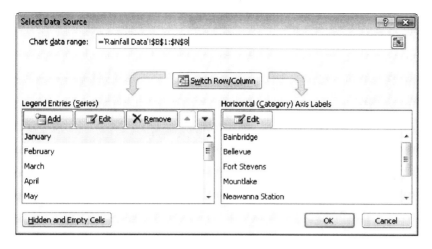

Figure 14–8. *Use the **Select Data Source** dialog box to change the source data the chart is using.*

2. Click in the **Chart data range** box.

3. Click the **Collapse Dialog** button to collapse the dialog box.

4. Drag on the worksheet to select the right data range.

5. Click the **Collapse Dialog** button again to restore the dialog box.

> **TIP:** You can also type the data range in the **Chart data range** box. This is easy when you just need to change a column letter or row number to fix the data range.

6. If you need to switch the rows and columns as well, click the **Switch Row/Column** button.

7. Click the **OK** button to close the **Select Data Source** dialog box. Excel updates the chart with the new source data.

Choosing the Layout for the Chart

After selecting the chart type and the source data, you can choose which preset layout to use for the chart. The layout controls where the title, legend, and other chart elements appear. After applying a layout, you can reposition the elements as needed.

Figure 14–9 shows you how to apply a chart layout.

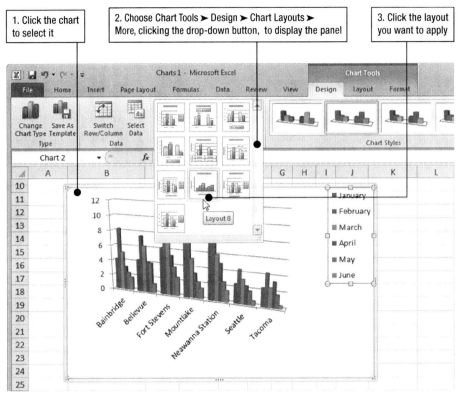

Figure 14–9. *To set the overall layout of chart elements, such as the chart title and legend, open the* **Quick Layout** *panel and click the layout you want.*

Applying a Style to a Chart

To control the overall graphical look of a chart, apply one of Excel's styles to it from the **Quick Styles** box in the **Chart Styles** group on the **Design** tab of the **Chart Tools** section of the Ribbon.

Click the chart to select it, and then click the **More** button on the **Quick Styles** box to display the **Quick Styles** panel (see Figure 14–10). Click the style you want to apply.

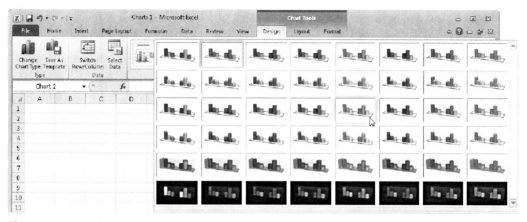

Figure 14–10. *To give the chart an overall graphical look, apply a style from the **Quick Styles** panel in the **Chart Styles** group of the **Design** tab.*

Adding a Title to a Chart

To let viewers know what your chart shows, add a descriptive title to it. Add the title as shown in Figure 14–11, triple-click the placeholder text to select it all, and then type the text you want.

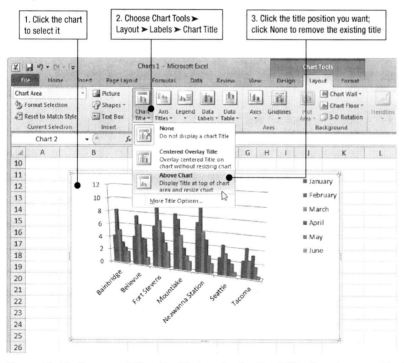

Figure 14–11. *You can quickly add a title by using the **Chart Title** drop-down panel in the **Labels** group on the **Layout** tab of the Ribbon.*

After adding the title, you can drag it to a different position if necessary.

Adding Axis Titles to the Chart

To make clear what the chart shows, you'll usually want to add titles to the axes. To do so, use the **Axis Titles** button in the Labels group on the **Layout** tab of the Ribbon. Figure 14–12 shows you how to add a title to the vertical axis.

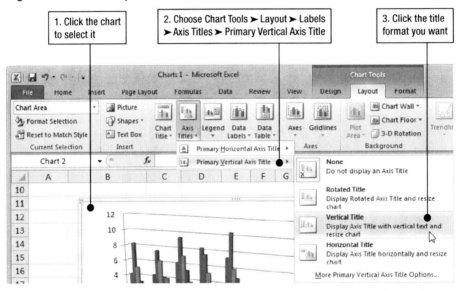

Figure 14–12. *You can quickly add vertical axis titles and horizontal axis titles by using the **Axis Titles** drop-down panel in the **Labels** group on the **Layout** tab of the Ribbon.*

After adding the title, select the placeholder text, and then type your title over it. If you want to reposition the title, drag it to the new location.

> **NOTE:** For the vertical axis title, you can choose among **Horizontal Title**, **Rotated Title**, and **Vertical Title**. **Horizontal Title** makes the axis title appear horizontally, so it's easy to read, but it takes up more space. **Rotated Title** rotates the axis title 90 degrees counterclockwise so that it runs upward along the axis. **Vertical Title** makes the axis title appear vertically, with the letters placed horizontally one above the other.

Similarly, you can add a title to the horizontal axis by clicking the chart and choosing **Chart Tools ➤ Layout ➤ Labels ➤ Axis Titles ➤ Primary Horizontal Axis Title ➤ Title Below Axis**. Type the title text over the placeholder that Excel adds.

NOTE: If the chart has a Z axis, you can add the axis title by choosing **Chart Tools ➤ Layout ➤ Labels ➤ Axis Titles ➤ Depth Axis Title**, and then clicking the **Rotated Title** item, the **Vertical Title** item, or the **Horizontal Title** item, as needed.

Changing the Scale or Numbering of an Axis

When you insert a chart, Excel automatically numbers the vertical axis to suit the data range. If you need to change the scale or numbering, follow these steps:

1. Right-click the vertical axis, and then click Format Axis on the context menu. The Format Axis dialog box opens with the Axis Options category at the front (see Figure 14–13).

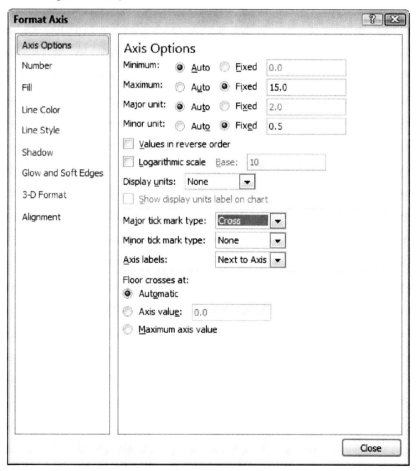

Figure 14–13. *You can format an axis to control its values, major and minor units, and where the tick marks appear. Excel applies the changes as you work in the* **Axis Options** *category of the* **Format Axis** *dialog box.*

2. Use the controls at the top to set up the values on the axis:

- *Minimum, Maximum, Major unit, and Minor unit.* To have Excel set the value, select the **Auto** option button. To set it yourself, select the **Fixed** option button, and then type the value in the box.

> **TIP:** Depending on how big your chart is, you'll probably want between five and ten major units on the scale you've set by choosing the **Minimum** value and **Maximum** value. Similarly, try using four and ten minor units per major unit, depending on what the chart shows.

- *Values in reverse order.* Select this check box if you want the values to run in reverse order—for example, lowest values at the top instead of the highest.

- *Logarithmic scale.* If you need the chart to use a logarithmic scale rather than an arithmetic scale, select the **Logarithmic scale** check box, and then enter the logarithm base in the **Base** box. For example, enter **10** to have the scale use the values 1, 10, 100, 1000, 10000, and so on at regular intervals.

- *Display units.* If you want the chart to show units—**Hundreds**, **Thousands**, **Millions**, and so on—select the unit in this drop-down list. Excel reduces the figures shown accordingly; for example, **1000000** appears as **1**, with **Millions** next to the scale. This helps make the axis easier to read.

3. In the second section, set up the positioning of the tick marks:

- *Major tick mark type.* In this drop-down list, choose **Inside** to have the tick marks appear inside the chart, **Outside** to have them appear outside (on the axis side), or **Cross** to have them appear on both sides. Choose **None** if you do not want major tick marks.

- *Minor tick mark type.* In this drop-down list, choose how you want minor tick marks to appear—**Outside**, **Inside**, **Cross**, or **None**.

- *Axis labels.* Choose **Next to Axis** to have the labels appear next to the axis. Choose **High** to have the labels appear on the high side of the chart, or choose **Low** to have them appear on the low side. Choose **None** to suppress the labels.

4. In the bottom section, choose where to have the horizontal axis cross the vertical axis:

- *Automatic.* Select this option button to have Excel decide. If your chart looks right with Excel's choice, there's no reason to change it.

- *Axis value.* Select this option button if you need to control where the axis crosses. Type the value in the box. For example, for some charts, it's helpful to have the horizontal axis cross at a negative value.

- *Maximum axis value.* Select this option button to make Excel place the horizontal axis at the maximum value.

5. When you're satisfied with the axis, click the **Close** button to close the **Format Axis** dialog box.

Adding a Legend to a Chart

Many charts benefit from having a legend that summarizes the colors used for different data series. You can add a legend by working as shown in Figure 14–14. Whichever placement you use for the legend, you can drag it to a better position as needed. You can also resize the legend by clicking it and then dragging one of the handles that appear around it.

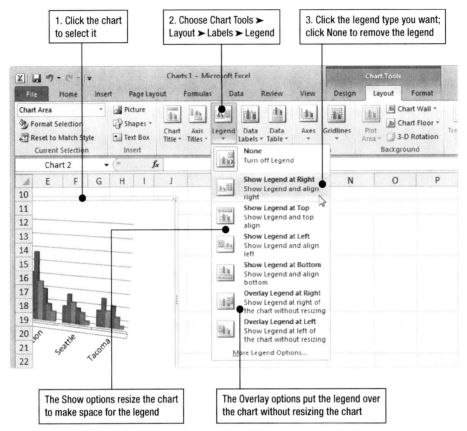

Figure 14–14. *When adding a legend from the Labels group, you can select a **Show** placement to resize the chart to make space for the legend or an **Overlay** placement to place the legend on the chart.*

Adding Data Labels to the Chart

If viewers will need to see the precise value of data points rather than just getting a general idea of their value, add data labels to the chart. To do so, click the chart, and then choose **Chart Tools ➤ Layout ➤ Labels ➤ Data Labels ➤ Show**.

> **CAUTION:** Use data labels sparingly. Only some charts benefit from data labels—other charts may become too busy, or having the details may distract the audience from the overall thrust of the chart.

When you add data labels to a chart, Excel displays a data label for each data marker. If you want to display only some data labels, delete the ones you don't need. To delete a data marker, click it, and then either press **Delete** or right-click the selection and click **Delete** on the context menu.

Choosing Which Gridlines to Display

On many types of charts, you can choose whether to display horizontal and vertical gridlines to help the viewer judge how the data points relate to each other and to the axes.

To control which gridlines appear, work as shown in Figure 14–15.

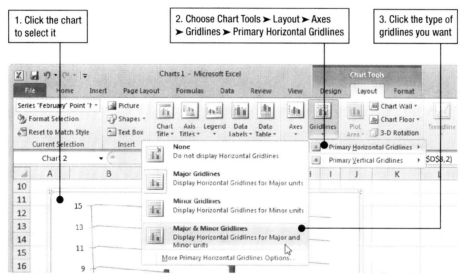

Figure 14–15. *Use the* **Gridlines** *drop-down panel in the* **Axes** *group on the* **Layout** *tab of the Ribbon to control whether Excel displays major gridlines, minor gridlines, both, or neither for the chart.*

> **NOTE:** To change the values at which the gridlines appear, format the axis, as described earlier in this chapter.

Formatting the Chart Wall and Chart Floor

Some charts look fine with a plain background, but for others you may want to decorate the chart walls and the chart floor. The *chart wall* is the vertical area at the back of a chart; if the chart is three-dimensional, it has a side chart wall and a chart floor as well. You can add a solid color, a gradient, a picture, or a texture to the walls, the floor, or both, to give the chart a meaning or context, or simply to make it more visually appealing. Figure 14–16 shows a chart that uses a picture for the walls.

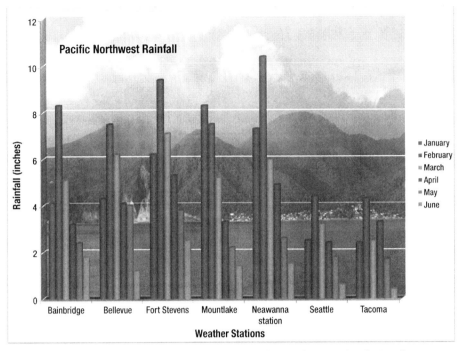

Figure 14–16. *You can give a chart a themed look by applying a picture to the chart walls.*

> **TIP:** Usually, the chart walls and floors are the elements that look best with a custom fill (such as a picture). But you can apply a custom fill to many other chart elements as well. To do so, display the **Format** dialog box for the element, click the **Fill** category in the left pane, and then make your choices.

To format the chart wall or the chart floor, first open the Format dialog box for the wall or the floor. Figure 14–17 shows you how to do this.

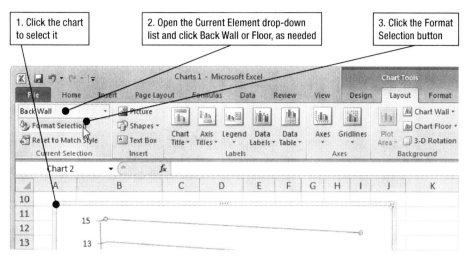

Figure 14–17. *Select the* **Back Wall** *element or the* **Floor** *element in the* **Chart Elements** *drop-down list in the* **Current Selection** *group on the* **Layout** *tab of the Ribbon. Then click the* **Format Selection** *button to display the* **Format** *dialog box for the element.*

Clicking the **Format Selection** button opens the **Format** dialog box for the element you chose—in this case, the **Format Wall** dialog box. Use the controls in this dialog box to choose the picture or specify the fill you want. Figure 14–18 shows you how to choose a picture from a file on your PC.

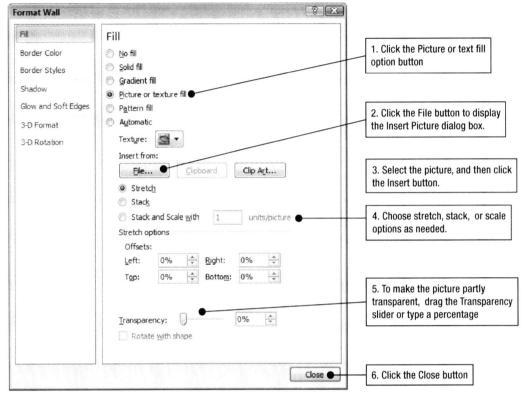

Figure 14–18. *Use the Fill pane in the Format dialog box to apply a picture fill to objects such as the chart wall or floor.*

Formatting Individual Chart Elements

You can format any of the individual elements of a chart—for example, the legend, the gridlines, or the data labels—by selecting it and then using its **Format** dialog box. This dialog box includes the name of the element it affects: the **Format Data Labels** dialog box, the **Format Plot Area** dialog box, and so on.

You can display the **Format** dialog box in either of these ways:

- Right-click the element, and then click the Format item on the context menu. This is usually the easiest way of opening the **Format** dialog box.

▨ *Select the element in the Chart Elements drop-down list, and then click the Format Selection button.* If you're finding it difficult to right-click the element on the chart (for example, because the chart is busy), choose **Chart Tools ➤ Format ➤ Current Selection ➤ Chart Elements**, and then click the element you want on the drop-down list. You can then click the **Format Selection** button (also in the **Current Selection** group) to open the **Format** dialog box for the element.

The contents of the **Format** dialog box vary depending on the object you've selected, but for mast objects, you'll find categories such as these:

▨ *Fill.* You can fill in a solid shape with a solid color, color gradient, picture, or texture.

▨ *Border Color.* You can give a shape a color border, gradient border, or no line.

▨ *Border Styles.* You can choose among different border styles, change the border width, and pick a suitable line type.

▨ *Shadow.* You can add a shadow to the shape, set its color, and adjust its transparency, width, and other properties.

▨ *Glow and Soft Edges.* You can make an object stand out by giving it a glow, choosing a color that contrasts with the object's surroundings, and choosing how wide the glow should be. You can also apply soft edges to a shape.

▨ *3-D Format.* You can apply a 3-D format to different aspects of a shape—for example, setting a different bevel for the top and bottom of the shape.

▨ *3-D Rotation.* You can apply a 3-D rotation to the object.

▨ *Alignment.* For text objects, you can choose how to align text and whether to rotate it.

If the chart element contains text, you can format it by using the controls on the **Home** tab of the Ribbon or keyboard shortcuts. For example, to apply boldface to the data labels, click the data labels, and then choose **Home ➤ Font ➤ Bold** (or press **Ctrl+B**).

TIP: To restore an element to its original formatting, select the element either by clicking it on the chart or by using the **Chart Elements** drop-down list. Then choose **Chart Tools ➤ Format ➤ Current Selection ➤ Reset to Match Style**.

Summary

In this chapter, you learned to create charts that present your data in a clear and compelling way. You know the difference between embedded charts and charts on chart sheets, you can identify the components of charts, and you're familiar with the different types of charts you can create in Excel. You know how to create a chart from your data, change its layout, and apply formatting as needed.

In the next chapter, I'll show you how to create databases in Excel and solve business problems using what-if analysis.

Chapter 15

Creating Databases and Solving Business Problems

In this chapter, I'll show you how to create databases and solve business problems in Excel.

Each Excel worksheet contains sixteen thousand columns and more than a million rows, so it has space to store huge amounts of data. By using each column to contain a data field (such as a customer's last name) and each row to contain a customer record (with all the customer's data), you can quickly build a straightforward database in which you can store data, sort it, and filter it. Similarly, you can create a database for a home inventory by using the columns to contain the data fields (such as the item, its value, and when you bought it) and the rows to contain the items (with all their details).

Excel refers to such databases as *tables*, and they can be great for either home use or small business use; in this chapter, I'll refer to them as "databases" for simplicity. (Larger businesses are better off with full-scale databases. More on this in a moment.)

Excel is also great for solving business problems. In the second half of this chapter, I'll show you how to use Excel's scenarios feature to experiment with different values in a worksheet, and how to use the Goal Seek feature to make one cell's value reach a particular figure by changing one other value.

Creating Databases

When you need to store a large amount of data that consists of related records, you can create a database. For example, you can create a database that records all your business' sales, your customers' contact details, or the ups and downs of your stock-trading transactions.

To create a database, you first enter the fields that will contain the data. You then tell Excel that you're creating a database rather than a regular worksheet. After that, you add your data to the database, either by typing it into the cells as usual or by using a data-entry form (which is usually more convenient).

Once the data is in the database, you can sort the database to reveal different aspects of its contents, or filter it to identify items that match the criteria you specify.

Understanding the Type of Databases You Can Create in Excel

The type of database you can create in an Excel worksheet is called a *flat-file database*. All the data in the database is stored in a single table rather than in separate tables that are linked to each other.

- Each row contains a *record*—an item that holds all the details of a single entry. For example, in a database that records your sales to customers, a record would contain the details of a purchase.

- Each column contains a *field* in the database—a column for the purchase number, a column for the date, a column for the customer's last name, and so on. Figure 15–1 shows part of an Excel database for tracking sales to customers.

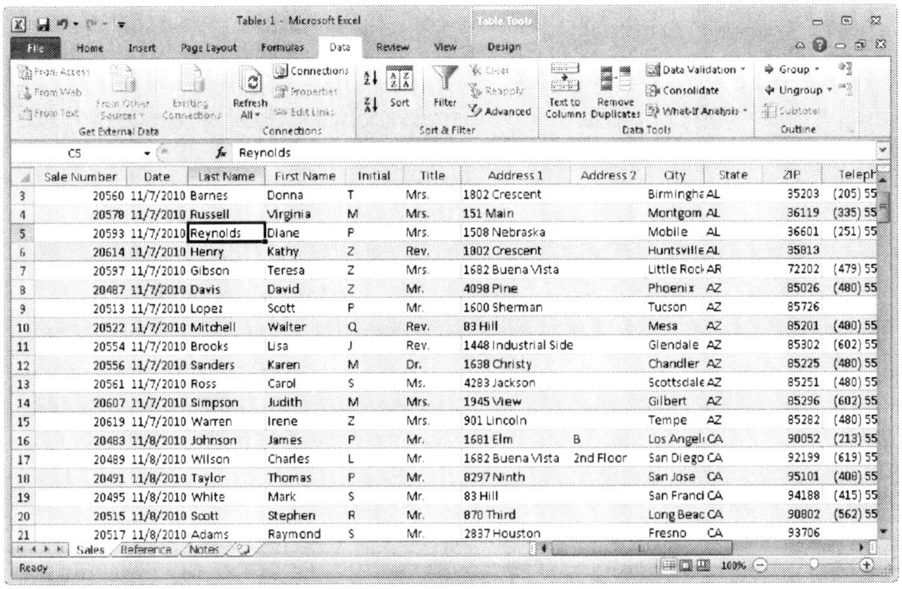

Figure 15–1. *An Excel database consists of a table, with each row forming a record and each column containing a field.*

This means that you can use Excel to create any database for which you can store all the data for a record in a single row. Because each worksheet has a million rows, you can create large databases if necessary, but they may make Excel run slowly.

What you can't do with Excel is create *relational databases*—ones that store the data in linked tables. A relational database is the kind of database you create with full-bore database programs such as Microsoft Access. In a relational database, every record has a unique ID number or field that the program uses to link the data in the different tables. For example, a relational database might include a table of customer names and addresses, a table of purchases by those customers, and similar tables.

Creating a Database and Entering Data

You can quickly create a database in an Excel worksheet by setting up the columns with the fields the database needs. You can then enter data in the database either directly or by using a data-entry form.

Creating a Database

Open the workbook you want to put the database in, or create a new workbook (for example, press **Ctrl+N**). Then work as shown in Figure 15–2.

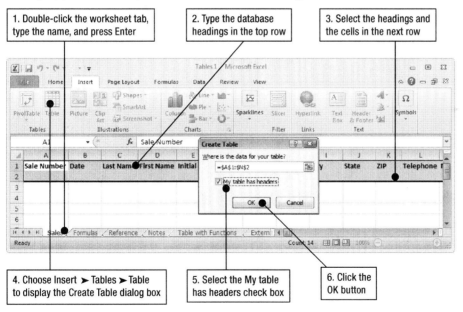

Figure 15–2. *To create a database, open the workbook, name the worksheet, and enter the headings. With the headings and the next two rows selected, choose* **Insert ➤ Tables ➤ Table***, select the* **My table has headers** *check box, and click the* **OK** *button.*

When you click the **OK** button to close the **Create Table** dialog box. Excel does the following:

- Creates the database and displays the **Table Tools** section of the Ribbon. This section appears whenever the active cell or selection is in the database, so you can display it at any time by clicking in the database.

- Names the database with a default name, such as Table1 or Table2. You can rename the table as shown in Figure 15–3.

- Turns the header row into headers with drop-down buttons. Excel keeps these headers displayed when you scroll further down the database—you don't have to freeze the panes the way you do with a regular worksheet.

- Applies a table style with banded shading based on the workbook's theme. You can change these colors later as needed.

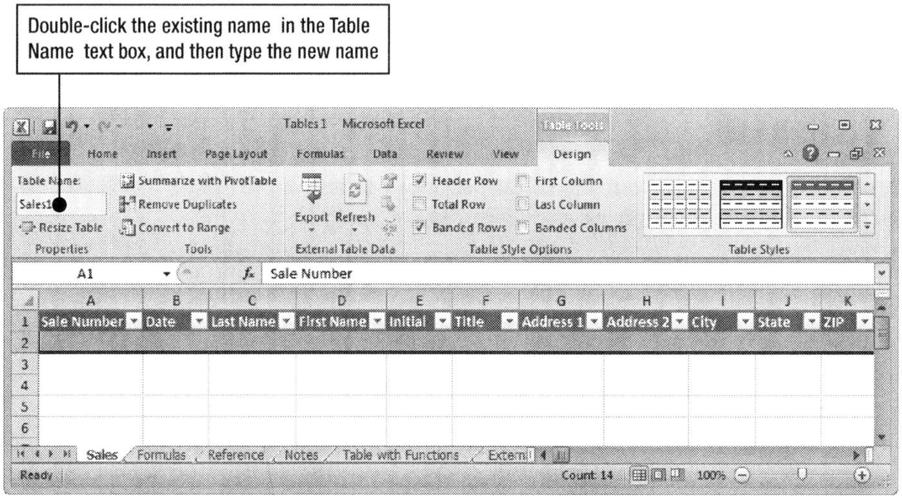

Double-click the existing name in the Table Name text box, and then type the new name

Figure 15–3. *You can change the table's default name by typing the new name in the* **Table Name** *text box in the* **Properties** *group on the* **Table Tools ➤ Design** *tab of the Ribbon.*

Making the Database Look the Way You Want

To make the database look the way you want, you can use the options on the **Design** tab of the **Table Tools** section of the Ribbon. You may find this easier to do after you've entered a few rows of data in the database, so you can see how the table styles look.

First, give your table an overall look by applying a table style, as shown in Figure 15–4.

1. Choose Table Tools ➤ Design ➤ Table Styles ➤ Quick Styles ➤ More, clicking the drop-down button at the right end of the Quick Styles box

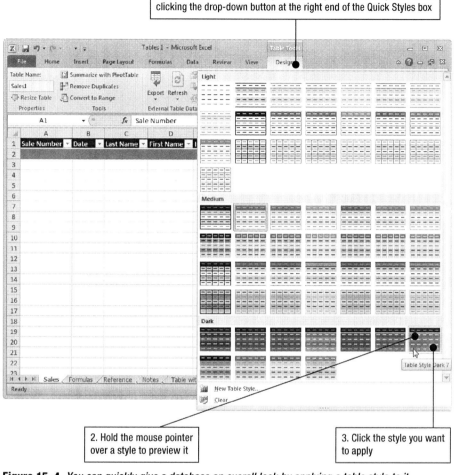

2. Hold the mouse pointer over a style to preview it

3. Click the style you want to apply

Figure 15–4. *You can quickly give a database an overall look by applying a table style to it.*

After applying the style, choose from the options in the **Table Style Options** group on the **Design** tab. These are the options:

- *Header Row.* Select this check box to display the header row. This is almost always useful.

- *Total Row.* Select this check box to add a row labeled **Total** straight after the database's last row. This is useful when you need to add a total formula or another formula in the last row. To add a formula, click a cell, click the drop-down button that appears (see Figure 15–5), and then click the formula you want on the drop-down list. Even though the word Total initially appears in the row's first column, you can apply a different formula to the cell.

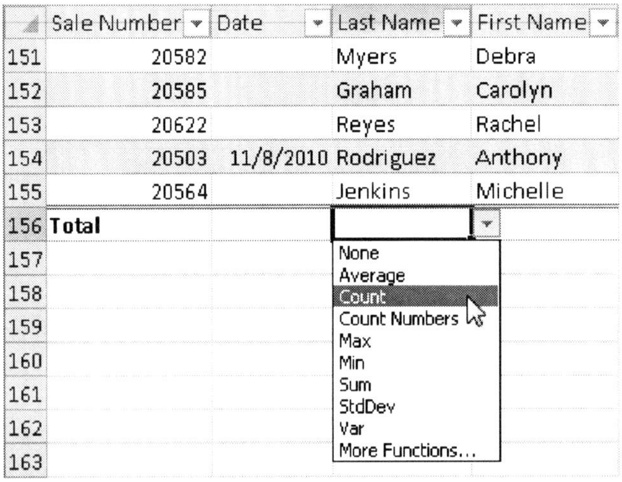

Figure 15–5. *Adding a **Total** row to a database lets you quickly insert functions in the row's cells.*

> **TIP:** The drop-down list in the **Total** row of a database gives you instant access to the most widely used functions in databases—**Average, Count, Count Numbers, Max, Min, Sum, StdDev** (Standard Deviation), or **Var** (calculating variance based on a sample). You can also click the **More Functions** item at the bottom of the drop-down list to display the **Insert Function** dialog box, from which you can access the full range of Excel's functions. For example, you can insert the **COUNTBLANK()** function to count the number of blank cells in a column. You might do this to ensure that a column of essential data contains no blanks.

* *Banded Rows.* Select this check box to apply a band of color to every other row. This helps you read the rows of data without your eyes wandering to another row.

* *First Column.* Select this check box if you want the first column to have different formatting. You may want to do this if the first column contains the main field for identifying each record (for example, a unique number).

* *Last Column.* Select this check box if you want the last column to have different formatting. Usually, you'll want this only if the last column contains data that is more important in some way than the data in the other columns.

* *Banded Columns.* Select this check box to apply a band of color to every other column. This is sometimes helpful, but usually less helpful than banded rows.

Entering Data in a Database

You can enter data in a database either by typing it in directly or by using a data-entry form. In most cases, the data-entry form is the easier option, as you'll see in a moment.

Entering Data Directly in a Database

To enter data directly in a database, click the target cell, and then type the data into it.

> **TIP:** You can quickly select a row, column, or an entire database with the mouse. To select a row, move the mouse pointer to the left part of a cell in the database's leftmost column, and then click with the horizontal arrow that appears. To select a column, move the mouse pointer over a column heading, and then click with the downward arrow that appears. To select the whole database, move the mouse pointer over the upper-left cell in the database, and then click with the diagonal arrow that appears.

Entering Data Using a Data-Entry Form

Typing directly into the database works for small databases, but for larger databases, it's easier to use the data-entry form that Excel includes. The only problem is that you need to add the Form command to the Quick Access Toolbar before you can use it. See the "Adding the Form Command to the Quick Access Toolbar" sidebar for instructions.

ADDING THE FORM COMMAND TO THE QUICK ACCESS TOOLBAR

To add the Form command to the Quick Access Toolbar, follow these steps:

1. Click the Customize Quick Access Toolbar drop-down button to display the Customize Quick Access Toolbar menu.

2. Click the More Commands item to display the Quick Access Toolbar category in the Excel Options dialog box.

3. In the Customize Quick Access Toolbar drop-down list in the upper-right corner of the Excel Options dialog box, choose For all documents to make this customization available for all your Excel workbooks. (If you want the Data Form command to be available only in your database workbook, open the Customize Quick Access Toolbar drop-down list and click the For [*workbook*] item, where *workbook* is the database workbook's name.)

4. Open the Choose commands from drop-down list, and then click Commands Not in the Ribbon to display the list of commands that don't appear on the Ribbon in the left list box.

5. Scroll down to the Form command, click it, and then click the Add button to add it to the bottom of the list in the right box.

6. If you want to move the Form button up the list in the Quick Access Toolbar, click the Move Up button as many times as needed.

7. Click the OK button to close the Excel Options dialog box. The Form button now appears on the Quick Access Toolbar.

When you have added the **Form** button to the Quick Access Toolbar, click the **Form** button to display the **Form** dialog box. Figure 15–6 shows you how to use this dialog box, whose title bar shows the name of the worksheet you're using (here, **Sales**) rather than the word "Form". As you enter the data in the data-entry form, Excel enters it in the database for you.

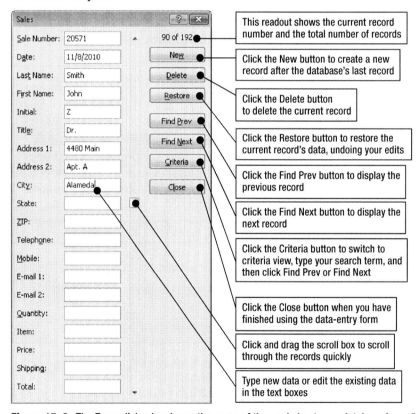

Figure 15–6. *The **Form** dialog box bears the name of the worksheet your database is on (here, **Sales**), and shows each field in the order they appear in the header row. After entering data in a record, click the **New** button or the **Close** button to enter the data.*

> **NOTE:** When you need to find a record using particular criteria, click the **Criteria** button. Excel switches the **Form** dialog box to **Criteria** view, and you can type the term by which you want to search. Click the **Find Next** button to find the next instance of the term or the **Find Prev** button to find the previous instance.

Resizing a Database

When you've created a database, Excel normally resizes it for you automatically when you add or delete rows. For example, when you add a record by using the data-entry form, Excel expands the database to include it.

Excel also expands the database automatically if you add data to the row after the current last row in a database that doesn't have a totals row. Excel calls this feature Table AutoExpansion. If you don't want Excel to do this, click the **AutoCorrect** smart tag that appears below and to the right of the first cell in the added row, and then click **Undo Table AutoExpansion** (see Figure 15–7). Click the smart tag again, and then click **Stop Automatically Expanding Tables**.

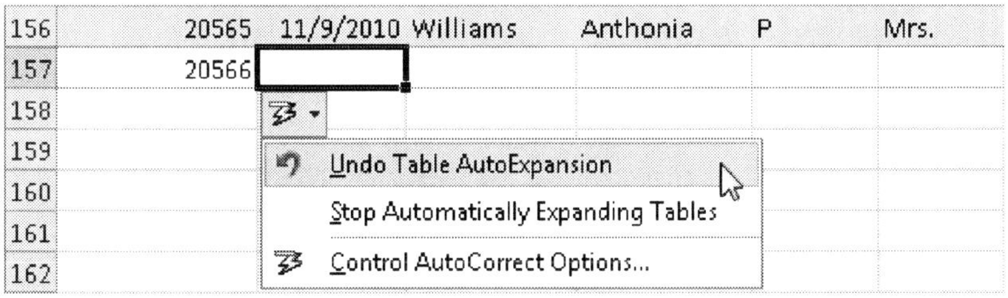

Figure 15–7. *You can use the **AutoCorrect** smart tag both to undo **Table AutoExpansion** and to turn it off.*

> **NOTE:** To turn **Table AutoExpansion** back on, click the **File** tab to open **Backstage** view, then click **Options**. In the **Excel Options** dialog box, click **Proofing** in the left column, and then click the **AutoCorrect Options** button. In the **AutoCorrect** dialog box, click the **AutoFormat As You Type** tab. Select the **Include new rows and columns in table** check box, and then click the **OK** button to close the **AutoCorrect** dialog box. Click the **OK** button to close the **Excel Options** dialog box.

Sorting a Database by One or More Fields

When you need to examine the data in your database, you can sort it either by a single field or by using multiple fields.

> **TIP:** If you need to be able to return a database to its original order, include a column with sequential numbers in it. These numbers may be part of your records (for example, sequential sales numbers for transactions) or simply ID numbers for the records; in either case, you can use AutoFill to enter them quickly (see Chapter 11: "Creating Worksheets and Entering Data" for instructions on using AutoFill). To return the database to its original order, you can then sort it by this column.

Sorting Quickly by a Single Field

To sort a database by a single field, click the column you want to sort, then click the **Sort A to Z** button or the **Sort Z to A** button (see Figure 15–8).

- *Sort A to Z.* Click this button to produce an ascending sort—from A to Z, from low values to high, or from earlier dates to recent dates.

- *Sort Z to A.* Click this button to produce a descending sort—from Z to A, from high values to low, or from recent dates to earlier dates.

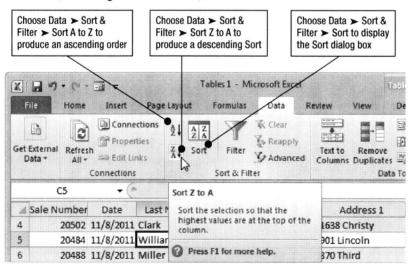

Figure 15–8. *Use the **Sort A to Z** button or the **Sort Z to A** button in the **Sort & Filter** group of the **Data** tab when you need to sort quickly by the column you've selected.*

After you sort, the database remains sorted that way until you change it.

Sorting a Database by Multiple Fields

Often, it's useful to sort your database by two or more fields at the same time. For example, in a customer database, you may need to sort your customers first by state, and then by city within the state.

1. Choose **Data ➤ Sort & Filter ➤ Sort** to display the **Sort** dialog box. Figure 15–9 shows the **Sort** dialog box with two criteria entered and a third criterion underway.

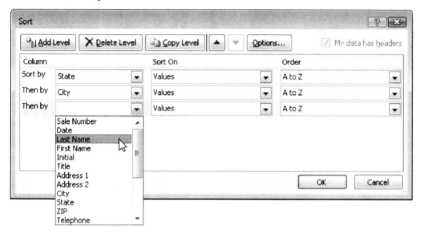

Figure 15–9. *In the **Sort** dialog box, you can set up exactly the sort criteria you need to identify data in your database.*

2. Set up your first sort criterion using the controls on the first row of the main part of the Sort dialog box. Follow these steps:

   a. Open the **Sort by** drop-down list, and then click the column you want to sort by first. For example, click the **State** column.

   b. Open the **Sort On** drop-down list, and then click what you want to sort by: **Values**, **Cell Color**, **Font Color**, or **Cell Icon**. In most cases, you'll want to use **Values**, but the other three items are useful for tables to which you've applied conditional formatting.

   c. Open the **Order** drop-down list, and then click the sort order you want. If you choose **Values** in the **Sort On** drop-down list, you can choose **A to Z** for an ascending sort, **Z to A** for a descending sort, or **Custom List**. Choosing **Custom List** opens the **Custom List** dialog box, in which you can choose a custom list by which to sort the results. For example, you could use a custom list of your company's products or offices to sort the database into a custom order rather than being restricted to ascending or descending order.

    d. If you need the sort to be case sensitive (so that "smith" appears before "Smith," and so on), click the **Options** button. In the **Sort Options** dialog box (see Figure 15–10), select the **Case sensitive** check box, and then click the **OK** button.

Figure 15–10. *Select the **Case sensitive** check box in the **Sort Options** dialog box if you want to treat lowercase letters differently than their uppercase versions.*

3. Click the **Add Level** button to add a second line of controls to the main part of the **Sort** dialog box.

4. Set up the criterion for the second-level sort using the same technique. The only difference is that the first drop-down list is called **Then by** rather than **Sort by**. For example, set up a second-level sort using the **City** column in the database.

5. Set up any other criteria needed by repeating steps 3 and 4.

6. Click the **OK** button to close the **Sort** dialog box. Excel sorts the data using the criteria you specified.

Filtering a Database

When you need to find records in a database that match the terms you specify, you can *filter* it quickly using Excel's AutoFilter feature. Filtering makes Excel display only the records that match your search terms, hiding all the other records.

> **NOTE:** You can also search for records by using Excel's Find feature. Choose **Home ➤ Editing ➤ Find & Select ➤ Find** or press **Ctrl+F** to display the **Find and Replace** dialog box, type your search term in the **Find what** box, and then click either the **Find Next** button or the **Find All** button. But because filtering displays all the matching records together rather than spread out in the database, it's often more convenient than using **Find**.

Figure 15–11 shows you the most straightforward way to filter a database using AutoFilter—by selecting the check boxes for the items you want to include in the filter.

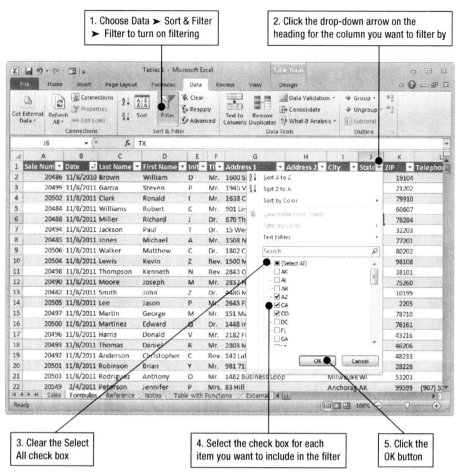

1. Choose Data ➤ Sort & Filter ➤ Filter to turn on filtering

2. Click the drop-down arrow on the heading for the column you want to filter by

3. Clear the Select All check box

4. Select the check box for each item you want to include in the filter

5. Click the OK button

Figure 15–11. *To apply filtering, click the drop-down arrow on a column heading (here, the* **State** *column), and then click the filtering type you want. After you apply a filter, the column heading shows a filter icon rather than the down-arrow icon.*

The filtering choices available depend on the data the column contains. Here are three examples:

■ *Text Filters.* Click this item to display a submenu containing comparisons you can apply (see Figure 15–12). Click the type of comparison you want to use. For example, choose **Equals** to set a filter that picks particular states, or choose **Begins With** to set a filter than selects cities that start with text you specify. Use the fields in the **Custom AutoFilter** dialog box (see Figure 15–13) to set up the rest of the comparison.

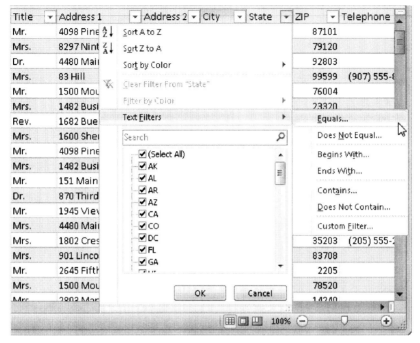

Figure 15–12. *From the **Text Filters** submenu, choose the type of comparison you want to use for the filter—for example, **Equals**.*

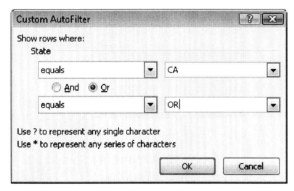

Figure 15–13. *In the **Custom AutoFilter** dialog box, set up the details of the filter. You can use one criterion or two—for example, the **State** column contains **CA** or **OR**.*

■ *Number Filters.* Click this item to display a submenu containing comparisons you can apply (see Figure 15–14), and then click the type of comparison you want to use. For the **Above Average** and **Below Average** items, you need specify no more information; for the other comparisons, use the **Custom AutoFilter** dialog box to set up the rest of the comparison—for example, **Greater Than 5000**.

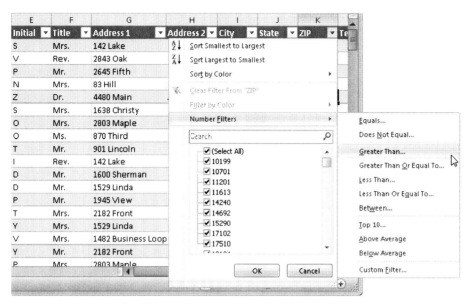

Figure 15–14. *The **Number Filters** submenu provides comparisons suited to numbers, including **Greater Than** and **Less Than**, **Between**, **Top 10**, and **Above Average** and **Below Average**.*

- *Date Filters.* Click this item to display a submenu containing comparisons you can apply (see Figure 15–15), and then click the type of comparison you want to use. Comparisons that show no ellipsis, such as **Yesterday** or **Last Week**, need no further information. For comparisons that do show an ellipsis, you use the **Custom AutoFilter** dialog box to specify the details.

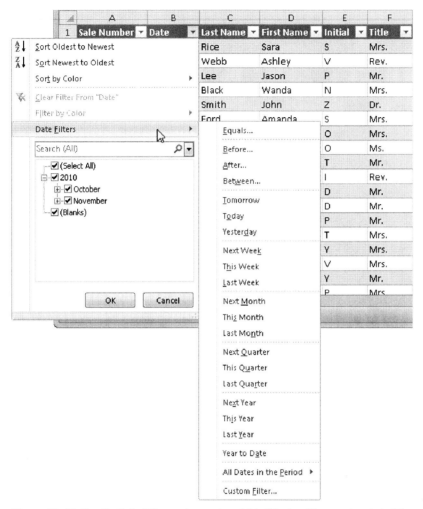

Figure 15–15. *Use the **Date Filters** submenu to quickly filter by either a set period of time, such as a week or a quarter, or by specific dates.*

When you've specified the details of the filter, Excel applies it to the database and reduces the display to those rows that match the filter. Excel displays a filter symbol in place of the drop-down button on the column that contains the filtering (as on the State column heading in Figure 15–16).

H	I	J	K	L
Address 2 ▼	City ▼	State ⥯	ZIP ▼	Telephone ▼
B	Los Angeli	CA	90052	(213) 555-0834
2nd Floor	San Diego	CA	92199	(619) 555-0201
	San Jose	CA	95101	(408) 555-8201
	San Franci	CA	94188	(415) 555-5028
	Long Beac	CA	90802	(562) 555-8882

Figure 15–16. *The filter symbol (shown here on the **State** column heading) indicates that you're filtering the database by that column.*

To remove filtering from a single column, click the filter symbol on the column heading, and then click the **Clear Filter** item on the drop-down list. This item includes the column's name—for example, **Clear Filter from "State"** for the **State** column.

To remove filtering from the database as a whole, choose **Data ➤ Sort & Filter ➤ Filter**, un-pressing the **Filter** button in the **Sort & Filter** group.

Solving Business Problems with Scenarios and Goal Seek

In this section, I'll show you how to use two tools for solving business problems:

- *Scenarios*. **Scenarios** give you an easy way to experiment with different values without changing the existing data in your worksheet.

- *Goal Seek*. **Goal Seek** computes the change you need to make to one value in order to make another cell's value reach your target value—working backward from your goal, as it were.

Examining Different Scenarios in a Worksheet

Often, when you've built a worksheet, you'll want to experiment with different data in it. Instead of changing the actual figures in the worksheet itself, you can use Excel's scenarios, which give you a way to assign multiple values to each key cell and then switch among the sets of values.

Creating the Worksheet for Your Scenarios

Start by creating the workbook and worksheet you'll use for your scenarios. If you have an existing workbook with the data in it, open it up. Set up the data and formulas in your worksheet as usual.

Figure 15–17 shows the sample worksheet this section uses as an example. The worksheet summarizes the financial returns from five rental properties.

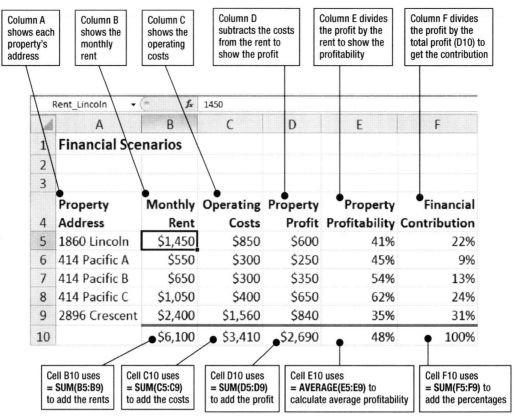

Figure 15–17. *To start using scenarios, create a worksheet containing your existing data and the formulas needed for the calculations.*

Times are bad, and the total profit is too low. So we'll use scenarios to see how we can improve matters by raising rents and shaving costs.

TIP: To make your scenarios easy to set up and adjust, define a name for each cell that you will change in the scenario. Click the cell, choose **Insert ➤ Name ➤ Define** to display the **Define Name** dialog box, and then work as described in the "Referring to Named Cells and Ranges" section in Chapter 13: "Performing Calculations with Formulas and Functions." If you look at Figure 15–17, you can see that cell B5 (the active cell) has the name **Rent_Lincoln**, making it easy to identify. (The name appears in the Reference box at the left end of the Formula bar.)

Opening the Scenario Manager Dialog Box

After creating your worksheet, choose **Data** ➤ **Data Tools** ➤ **What-If Analysis** ➤ **Scenario Manager** to display the **Scenario Manager** dialog box. At first, when the workbook contains no scenarios, the **Scenario Manager** dialog box appears as shown in Figure 15–18.

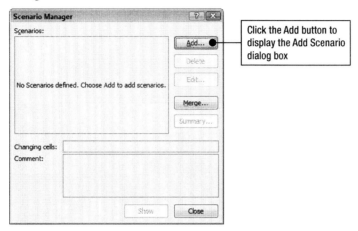

Click the Add button to display the Add Scenario dialog box

Figure 15–18. *At first, the Scenario Manager dialog box contains nothing but a prompt telling you to click the Add button.*

Creating Scenarios

To get started with scenarios, click the **Add** button in the **Scenario Manager** dialog box to display the **Add Scenario** dialog box. Then work as shown in Figure 15–19.

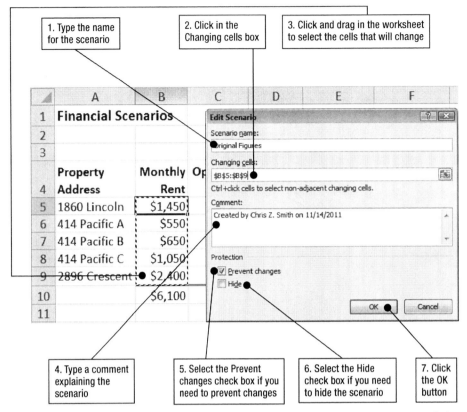

Figure 15–19. *Use the **Add Scenario** dialog box to set up each scenario. First create a scenario for your original data so that you can easily return to it.*

As you can see in Figure 15–19, creating a scenario is straightforward. But here are three quick notes:

- It's a good idea to start by creating a scenario containing your original data. This gives you an easy way to go back to the original data when you've finished testing scenarios.

- When you enter a cell or a range of cells in the **Changing cells** text box by clicking in the worksheet, Excel changes the name of the dialog box from **Add Scenario** to **Edit Scenario**. Odd though this seems, it's normal.

- If you select the **Prevent changes** check box or the **Hide** check box, you need to apply protection to the worksheet. Until you apply protection, these check boxes have no effect. I'll show you how to apply protection in the next section.

When you click the **OK** button to close the **Add Scenario** dialog box or **Edit Scenario** dialog box. Excel displays the **Scenario Values** dialog box (see Figure 15–20). This dialog box shows a text box for each of the changing cells in the scenario, so its shape and size depends on the number of changing cells. Here's where you see the benefit of naming the changing cells—each text box is easy to identify. If you haven't named the changing cells, the cell addresses appear, and you may need to refer to the worksheet to see which cell is which.

When you've entered your values in the **Scenario Values** dialog box, click the **Add** button if you want to add another scenario. Click the **OK** button if this is the last scenario you want to create for the time being.

NOTE: When you're creating a scenario for your original values, you won't need to change the values in the **Scenario Values** dialog box.

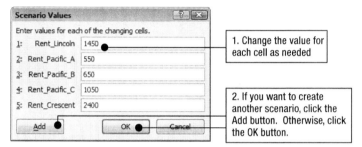

Figure 15–20. *In the **Scenario Values** dialog box, enter the values to use for the new scenario you're creating. The cell names produce the labels (Rent_Lincoln and so on), which are much easier to refer to than cell addresses (for example, B5).*

TIP: You can type formulas into the text boxes in the **Scenario Values** dialog box. For example, to increase the Rent_Lincoln value in Figure 16-14 by 25 percent, you could change the 1450 value to the formula **=1.25*1450**. After you enter formulas like this, Excel displays the dialog box shown in Figure 15–11 when you close the **Scenario Values** dialog box, telling you that it has converted names and results of formulas to values.

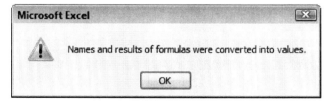

Figure 15–21. *After you enter formulas in the **Scenario Values** dialog box, Excel automatically converts them to values for you.*

Applying Protection to Your Scenarios

If you selected either the **Prevent changes** check box or the **Hide** check box in the **Protection** area of the **Add Scenario** dialog box or the **Edit Scenario** dialog box, you need to protect the worksheet to make the protection take effect.

To protect the worksheet, click the **Close** button to close the **Scenario Manager** dialog box if it's open, and then work as shown in Figure 15–22.

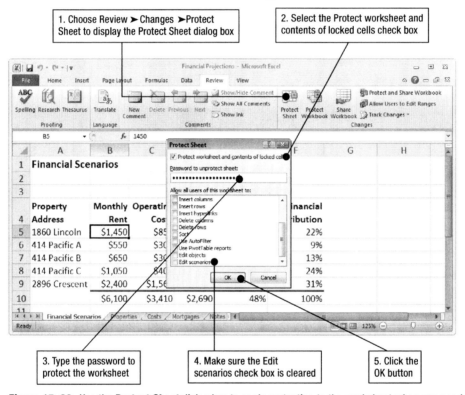

Figure 15–22. *Use the **Protect Sheet** dialog box to apply protection to the worksheet when you need to prevent changes to scenarios or hide scenarios from your colleagues.*

After protecting the worksheet, save the workbook. For example, press **Cmd+S** or click the **Save** button on the Quick Access toolbar.

When you have protected the scenarios in the worksheet like this, you'll need to turn off the protection before you can edit the scenarios. To turn off the protection, choose **Review ➤ Changes ➤ Unprotect Sheet**, type the password in the **Unprotect** dialog box, and then click the OK button.

Editing and Deleting Scenarios

From the **Scenario Manager** dialog box, you can quickly edit a scenario by clicking it in the **Scenarios** list box, clicking the **Edit** button, and then working in the **Edit Scenario** dialog box. Excel automatically updates the scenario's comment for you with details of the modification (for example, "Modified by Jack Cunningham on 11/18/2011"), but you'll often want to type in more details, such as what you're trying to make the scenario show.

When you no longer need a scenario, delete it by clicking the scenario in the **Scenarios** list box and clicking the **Delete** button. Excel doesn't confirm the deletion; but if you delete a scenario by mistake, and recovering it is more important than losing any other changes you've made since you last saved the workbook, you can recover the scenario by closing the workbook without saving changes (assuming the scenario was already saved in the workbook).

Switching Among Your Scenarios

Once you've created multiple scenarios for the same worksheet, you can switch among them by clicking the scenario you want in the **Scenarios** list box in the **Scenario Manager** dialog box (see Figure 15–23) and then clicking the **Show** button. Excel displays the scenario's figures in the worksheet's cells. The **Scenario Manager** dialog box stays open, so you can quickly switch to another scenario.

Figure 15–23. *To switch to another scenario, click the scenario in the **Scenarios** list box in the **Scenario Manager** dialog box, and then click the **Show** button.*

TIP: If you need to be able to switch quickly among scenarios, add the **Scenario** control to the Quick Access Toolbar. Click the **Customize Quick Access Toolbar** drop-down button, and then click **More Commands** to display the **Excel Options** dialog box. Open the **Choose commands from** drop-down list, and then click **Commands Not in the Ribbon**. Click **Scenario**, and then click **Add** to add it to the Quick Access Toolbar. Click the **OK** button. You can then click the **Scenario** drop-down button on the Quick Access Toolbar and choose the scenario you want to display (see Figure 15–24).

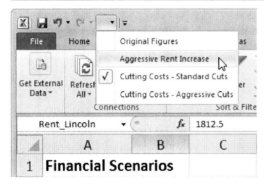

Figure 15–24. *Add the **Scenario** control to the Quick Access Toolbar to enable you to switch instantly among scenarios.*

Merging Scenarios into a Single Worksheet

If you develop and share your scenarios in a single workbook, you can keep them all together. But other times you may need to develop your scenarios in separate workbooks and then combine them. You can do this easily by using the **Merge** command in the **Scenario Manager** dialog box.

To merge scenarios, follow these steps:

1.   Open all the workbooks containing the scenarios you will merge.

2.   Make active the workbook and worksheet you will merge the scenarios into.

3.   Choose **Data ➤ Data Tools ➤ What-If Analysis ➤ Scenario Manager** from the Ribbon to display the **Scenario Manager** dialog box.

4.   Click the **Merge** button to display the **Merge Scenarios** dialog box (see Figure 15–25).

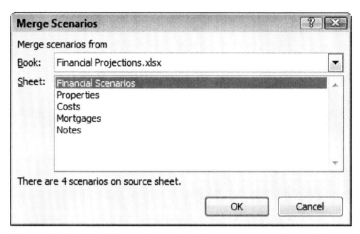

Figure 15–25. *In the **Merge Scenarios** dialog box, choose the workbook and worksheet that contain the scenarios you want to merge into the active workbook.*

5. Open the **Book** pop-up menu, and choose the open workbook that contains the scenarios you want to merge in. The **Sheet** list box shows a list of the worksheets in the workbook.

6. In the **Sheet** list box, click the worksheet that contains the scenarios. The readout at the bottom of the **Merge Scenarios** dialog box shows how many scenarios the worksheet contains, which helps you pick the right worksheet.

7. Click the **OK** button. Excel closes the **Merge Scenarios** dialog box, merges the scenarios, and then displays the **Scenario Manager** dialog box again.

NOTE: If any scenario you merge into the active worksheet has the same name as an existing scenario in the worksheet, Excel adds the current date to the incoming scenario to distinguish it.

Creating Reports from Your Scenarios

Sometimes you can make the decisions you need by simply creating scenarios and looking at them in the worksheet. Other times, it's helpful to create a report from the scenarios so that you can compare them. Excel gives you an easy way to create either a summary report or a PivotTable report straight from the **Scenario Manager** dialog box.

To create a report from your scenarios, open the **Scenario Manager** dialog box (choose **Data ➤ Data Tools ➤ What-If Analysis ➤ Scenario Manager**). Click the **Summary** button to display the **Scenario Summary** dialog box, and then work as shown in Figure 15–26.

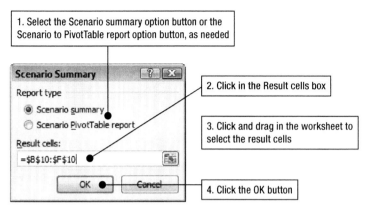

Figure 15–26. *In the **Scenario Summary** dialog box, choose between a scenario summary and a scenario PivotTable, and then select the result cells for the summary.*

Figure 15–27 shows a sample of a summary report, which Excel places on a new worksheet named **Scenario Summary** at the beginning of the workbook.

	Current Values:	Original Figures	Aggressive Rent Increase	Cutting Costs - Standard Cuts	Cutting
Changing Cells:					
Rent_Lincoln	$1,813	$1,450	$1,813	$1,813	
Rent_Pacific_A	$688	$550	$688	$688	
Rent_Pacific_B	$813	$650	$813	$813	
Rent_Pacific_C	$1,313	$1,050	$1,313	$1,313	
Rent_Crescent	$3,000	$2,400	$3,000	$3,000	
Costs_Lincoln	$750	$750	$750	$750	
Costs_Pacific_A	$250	$250	$250	$250	
Costs_Pacific_B	$240	$240	$240	$240	
Costs_Pacific_C	$300	$300	$300	$300	
Costs_Crescent	$1,280	$1,280	$1,280	$1,280	
Result Cells:					
B10	$7,625	$6,100	$7,625	$7,625	
C10	$2,820	$2,820	$2,820	$2,820	
D10	$4,805	$3,280	$4,805	$4,805	
E10	65%	57%	65%	65%	
F10	100%	100%	100%	100%	

Notes: Current Values column represents values of changing cells at time Scenario Summary Report was created. Changing cells for each scenario are highlighted in gray.

Figure 15–27. *Excel places a summary report on a new worksheet named **Scenario Summary** at the beginning of the workbook.*

Using Goal Seek

When you're planning or forecasting, you'll often need to work backward from your target to derive the figures you need. For example, when planning your next financial year, you may need to find out how many widgets you need to sell in order to reach $300,000 in sales.

To work this out, you can try increasing the number of widgets until your revenue figure reaches or exceeds the target. But you can save time and effort by using Excel's Goal Seek feature to derive the required price automatically by working backward from the revenue figure.

To derive values using Goal Seek, work as shown in Figure 15–28.

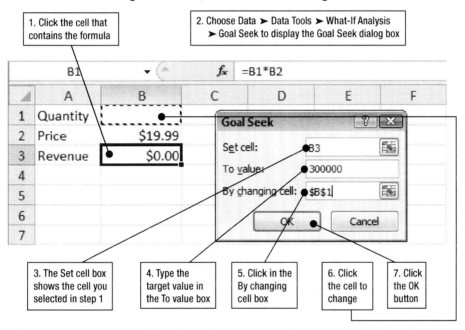

Figure 15–28. *Use the **Goal Seek** dialog box to work backward from your desired result to the figure you need.*

When you click the **OK** button in the **Goal Seek** dialog box, Goal Seek calculates the answer, enters it in the worksheet, and then displays the **Goal Seek Status** dialog box (see Figure 15–29).

Look at the value in the target cell. Click the **OK** button if you want to keep it. Click the **Cancel** button if you want to go back to the previous value.

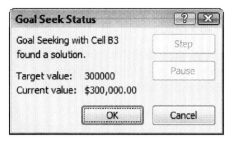

Figure 15–29. *When Excel displays the **Goal Seek Status** dialog box, look at the value in the target cell in the worksheet. Click the **OK** button if you want to keep the value. Click the **Cancel** button if you want to revert to the previous value.*

> **NOTE:** If the calculation is straightforward, Goal Seek finds a solution quickly. But if the calculation is more complex, Goal Seek may take a while. If this happens, you can click the **Pause** button to pause the calculation to see which value Goal Seek is trying at the moment. If you want to follow the individual values Goal Seek is trying, click the **Step** button to display the next value but keep the calculation paused; keep clicking the **Step** button as needed to see further values. Click the **Resume** button when you want Goal Seek to resume the calculation at full speed.

Summary

In the first half of this chapter, you learned how to create a flat-file database in an Excel worksheet, enter data in it either directly or by using a data-entry form, and how to format the database to look the way you want. You also learned to sort and filter the data in the database.

In the second half of the chapter, you learned to use Excel to solve business problems. You now know how to use Excel's scenarios to enter different sets of values in a worksheet and switch quickly among the sets, and you can use the Goal Seek feature to work backward from the desired result of a calculation to derive a value required to produce that result.

This is the end of the part of the book that covers Excel. In the next chapter, we'll get started with OneNote.

Part **VI**

Chapter 16

Getting Up to Speed and Taking Notes

In this chapter, I'll show you how to get started with OneNote, Office's powerful program for recording, storing, and manipulating information. With OneNote, you can record many types of information—from text and pictures to audio and video—in notebooks, organize it however you need, and then export finished notes to other programs.

This chapter brings you up to speed with OneNote, showing you how to get around the OneNote interface and how to capture and view your information. The following two chapters explain how to organize your information, share it with other people, and export it for use with the other Office programs.

Meeting the OneNote User Interface

In OneNote, you store your notes in a file called a notebook. OneNote's user interface shows the notebook using an easy-to-use interface based on a physical notebook, the ring-binder kind of notebook to which you can add ever more sections and pages.

Launching OneNote and Creating Your First Notebook

To launch OneNote and create your first notebook, follow these steps:

1. Choose Start ➤ All Programs ➤ Microsoft Office ➤ Microsoft OneNote 2010. The first time you run OneNote, the Microsoft OneNote: Opening first notebook dialog box opens (see Figure 16–1).

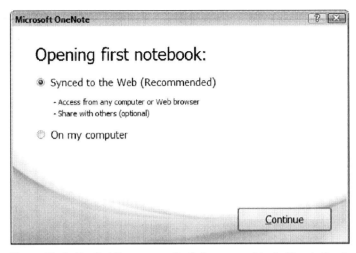

Figure 16–1. *The first time you run OneNote, you need to decide whether to sync your first notebook to the Web or store it on your computer.*

2. Select the appropriate option button:

   ▪ **Synced to the Web**. Select this option button if you want to synchronize the notebook to the Web. This enables you to access the notebook from any computer or Web browser, so it's great for being able to get to your notes anywhere. You can also share the notebook with other people via the Web. Syncing a notebook to the Web is slower than storing on your PC and may have privacy implications. We'll use this option for this example.

   NOTE: To store your OneNote notebooks on the Web, you must have a Windows Live SkyDrive account. If you don't yet have an account, you can create one from the next dialog box.

   ▪ **On my computer**. Select this option button if you prefer to keep the notebook on your computer. Storing the notebook on your computer gives better performance and is more secure.

3. Click the Continue button. If you selected the Synced to the Web option button, OneNote displays the Microsoft OneNote: Notebook synced to Web dialog box (see Figure 16–2).

Figure 16–2. *In the **Microsoft OneNote: Notebook synced to Web** dialog box, click **the Sign In** button. If you don't yet have a Windows Live SkyDrive account, click the **Sign up for Windows Live SkyDrive** link first.*

4. Click the Sign In button. OneNote displays the Connecting to docs.live.net dialog box (see Figure 16–3).

Figure 16–3. *After typing your e-mail address and password in the **Connecting to docs.live.net** dialog box, select the **Sign me in automatically** check box if you want to sign in automatically in future. Then click the **OK** button.*

5. Type your e-mail address and password.

6. Select the **Sign me in automatically** check box if you want the Office programs to sign you in automatically in the future. If you sync your notebooks with the Web, signing in automatically is usually a good idea.

7. Click the **OK** button. OneNote then automatically creates a sample notebook named Personal for you so that you can see how things work. The notebook contains sample data that you can either use to try out OneNote or simply delete so that you can use the notebook. Or, if you prefer, you can simply create a new notebook from scratch (you'll see how to do this later in this chapter). Figure 16–4 shows this default notebook as it'll look the first time you launch OneNote.

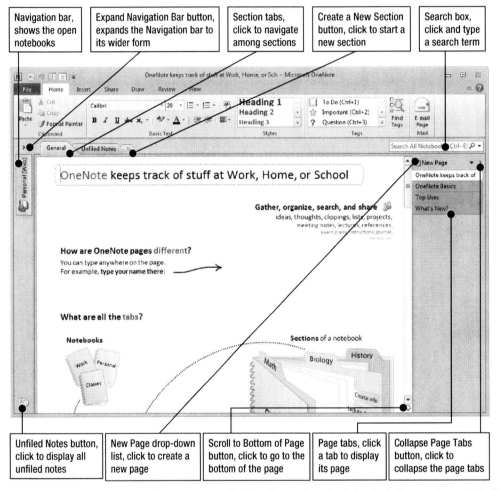

Figure 16–4. *OneNote automatically starts you off with a Personal notebook that includes sample contents. You can either adapt these contents to suit your needs or delete them.*

NOTE: Pin OneNote to the Taskbar or to the **Start** menu so that you can open it easily. Or set OneNote to launch automatically when you log in so that your notes are always just the click of a mouse away.

You use the Navigation bar at the left side of the OneNote window to move among your notebooks and sections. As you can see in Figure 16–4, at first the Navigation bar appears as a narrow strip containing a vertical button showing the notebook's name. When you click the Expand Navigation Bar button, the Navigation bar grows to a pane in which each notebook appears as a horizontal bar under which you can display its sections. Figure 16–5 shows the Navigation bar expanded with several notebooks open.

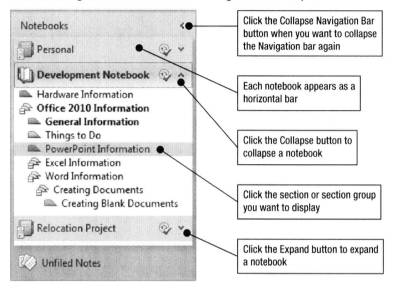

Figure 16–5. *Expand the Navigation bar to a pane when you want to use it to access the section groups and sections in the workbooks.*

Working with Notebooks, Section Groups, Sections, and Pages

In this section, we'll examine the major elements that you use in OneNote—notebooks, section groups, sections, and pages—and see how to create them.

Working with Notebooks

The documents you create in OneNote are called *notebooks*. Each notebook can contain as many section groups, sections, and pages as you need to store your notes.

As you saw earlier in this chapter, when you first launch OneNote, it creates the Personal notebook for you. You can choose whether to sync the Personal notebook to the Web, so that you can access it from any computer or Web browser, or store it only on your PC.

You can also create as many other notebooks as you need.

Looking Around in the Personal Notebook

If you've just launched OneNote for the first time, OneNote will have opened the Personal notebook that it creates for you. You'll see that the **Personal** tab in the Navigation bar is selected, and then section tabs named **General** and **Unfiled Notes** appear below the Ribbon.

Take a few minutes to explore the Personal notebook. Click a page tab in the Page Tabs bar on the right of the window to display the page's contents. You can then scroll down to view more of the page's contents, or click the **Scroll to Bottom of Page** button to scroll all the way down.

You may want to keep the default pages in the Personal notebook for a while so that you can refer to them. When you want to get rid of them, delete them as discussed later in this chapter.

Deciding How to Divide Your Notes Among Notebooks

When you're starting to use OneNote, you may find it hard to decide how to split your notes among different notebooks. But this isn't a problem, because OneNote lets you quickly move sections or pages from one notebook to another as needed.

At first, you may want to put all of your notes into a single notebook so that no matter which information you need, it's always there for you. Once you see which categories of information you gather, you'll probably want to break it up differently. At that point, you can create each other notebook you need, and then move the information around to where it belongs.

> **TIP:** If you know you'll need to share some data with colleagues, create a separate notebook for that type of data. That way, you can share some notes with your colleagues without sharing irrelevant or private notes.

Creating a New Notebook

To create a new notebook, work as shown in Figure 16–6.

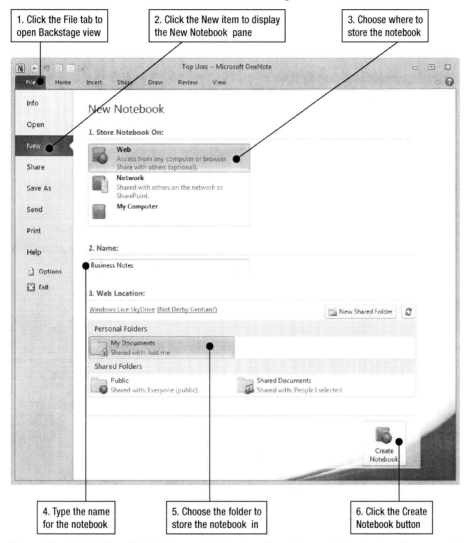

1. Click the File tab to open Backstage view

2. Click the New item to display the New Notebook pane

3. Choose where to store the notebook

4. Type the name for the notebook

5. Choose the folder to store the notebook in

6. Click the Create Notebook button

Figure 16–6. *In the **New Notebook** pane in Backstage view, choose whether to store the new notebook on your PC, on your local network, or on the Web.*

> **NOTE:** If you choose **My Computer** in the **Store Notebook On** area, OneNote suggests saving the notebook in the folder specified in the **Save & Backup** pane in the **OneNote Options** dialog box. (See Chapter 18: "Using OneNote with Word, Excel, PowerPoint, and Outlook" for instructions on setting the OneNote options.) The first time you choose Network, you will need to use the **Select Folder** dialog box to identify the network location.

If you store your new notebook on the Web or on the network, OneNote displays the dialog box shown in Figure 16–7, asking if you want to e-mail someone about the notebook. Click the **E-mail a Link** button if you want to start creating a message in your default e-mail program (for example, Outlook). Otherwise, click the **No, Thanks** button.

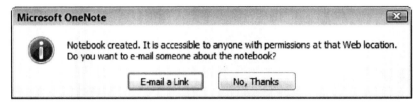

Figure 16–7. *When you store a new notebook on the Web or on the network, Outlook offers to create an e-mail to tell others about the notebook.*

Working with Sections and Section Groups

Inside a notebook, you create your notes on pages that take roughly the same role as sheets of paper within a ring binder. The main differences are that the pages can be as long as you want, and you can add subpages to a page. You can even add subpages to a subpage.

As in a ring binder with tabs, you divide your pages into different sections. The Personal notebook that OneNote creates for you contains only the **General** section and the **Unfiled Notes** section, but you can add other sections as needed.

Creating a Section

To create a section, work as shown in Figure 16–8.

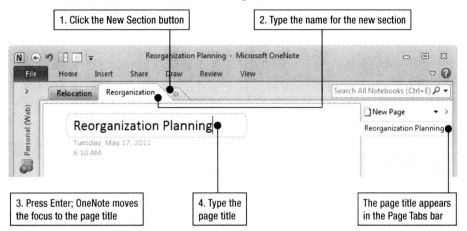

1. Click the New Section button

2. Type the name for the new section

3. Press Enter; OneNote moves the focus to the page title

4. Type the page title

The page title appears in the Page Tabs bar

Figure 16–8. *You can quickly create a new section in a notebook by clicking the **New Section** button and typing the section name. You can then press **Enter** and carry on to type the name of the page that OneNote automatically adds to the section—and then press **Enter** again to insert a container in which to start typing text.*

Deleting a Section

To delete a section, right-click the section's tab, and then click **Delete** on the context menu. In the confirmation dialog box that OneNote displays (see Figure 16–9), click the **Yes** button.

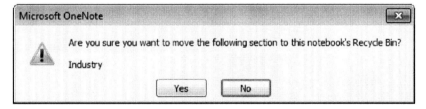

Figure 16–9. *To avoid mishaps, OneNote makes you confirm that you want to delete a section.*

NOTE: When you delete a page, section, or section group, OneNote places it in the **Notebook Recycle Bin** for the notebook that contained it. If necessary, you can retrieve items from the Notebook Recycle Bin. See Chapter 18: "Using OneNote with Word, Excel, PowerPoint, and Outlook" for details.

Renaming and Reorganizing Sections

To rename a section, right-click its tab and choose **Rename** from the context menu (see Figure 16–10). OneNote selects the current name. Type the new name and press Enter to apply it.

Figure 16–10. *You can quickly rename a section by right-clicking its tab, clicking* **Rename***, and then typing the new name. The context menu also contains other commands for manipulating the section—for example, deleting it, moving it, or copying it.*

To move a section to a different position in the notebook, drag it as shown in Figure 16–11.

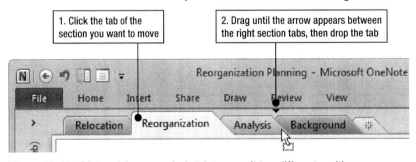

Figure 16–11. *Click and drag a section's tab to move it to a different position.*

Creating a Section Group

When a notebook contains just a few sections, it's easy to keep them organized. But when you've added a couple of dozen sections, you may find you need to break them up further. You can divide the sections up into different categories by using section groups.

> **NOTE:** You can create a section group within another section group as needed, so you can give yourself a whole hierarchy of section groups.

To create a section group, work as shown in Figure 16–12.

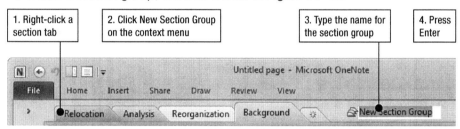

Figure 16–12. *Create a section group when you need to organize your sections into groups.*

Adding Sections to a Section Group

After creating a section group, you can add sections to it by dragging them to it in the Navigation bar. Click the section, drag it until the section group's name is highlighted, and then release it.

To create a new section within a section group, click the section group, and then create the section as described earlier.

Placing One Section Group Inside Another

When you need to organize many section groups, you can create a hierarchy of section groups by placing one section group inside another. To nest one section group inside another, click the section group in the Navigation bar and drag it to the section group in which you want to nest it.

> **NOTE:** You can also nest sections and groups by dragging the tabs within the section bar.
> Working in the Navigation bar tends to be easier, as there's more space.

To take a section group back to the top level in the workbook, either drag the tab from the section bar to the notebook's name, or follow these steps:

1. Right-click the section group you want to move, and then click **Move** on the context menu to display the **Move Section Group** dialog box (see Figure 16–13).

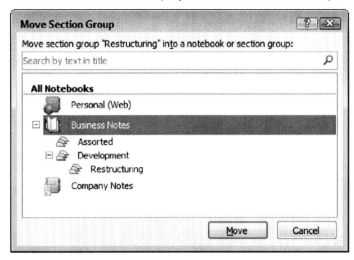

Figure 16–13. *Use the **Move Section Group** dialog box to move a section group from being nested up to the top level of a notebook.*

2. Click the notebook's name in the **All Notebooks** list. Click the – sign to the left of an item to collapse it, or click the + sign to the left of an item to expand it.

3. Click the **Move** button to close the dialog box and move the section group.

TIP: OneNote keeps the section groups in alphabetical order in the notebook.

Merging One Section into Another

When you need to put all the contents of one section into another section, you can merge the sections as shown in Figure 16–14. This is quicker and easier than moving one section's pages into the other section.

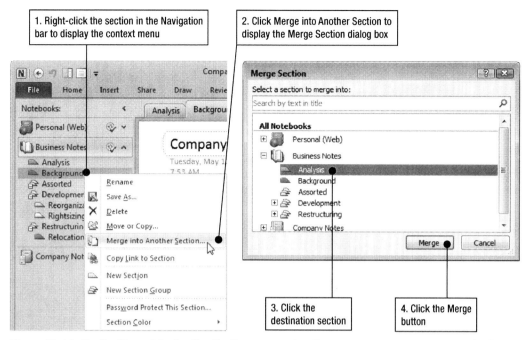

Figure 16–14. *Use the **Merge into Another Section** command on the context menu to merge one section into another. Choose the destination section in the **Merge Section** dialog box.*

Splitting a Section into Two

At other times, you may need to split a section into two separate sections. OneNote doesn't provide a command for automating this process, so just create a new section, and then drag into it the pages that you want it to contain.

Merging Two Notebooks into a Single Notebook

If you find you've created two notebooks with overlapping content areas, you can merge them into a single notebook. OneNote doesn't provide a command for merging, so you need to do it manually: open both notebooks, and then move all the sections from one notebook into the other notebook.

Splitting a Notebook into Two or More Notebooks

If a notebook becomes too big, or you realize you need to have an entire notebook for a particular topic that's currently within a notebook, you can split the notebook. Open the notebook, create another notebook, and then move the appropriate sections from the original notebook to the new notebook.

Changing the Display Name for a Notebook

Sometimes you may want to change the name that OneNote displays for a notebook—for example, because the original name is too short, too long, or not descriptive enough. You can change the display name without changing the file name.

To change the display name, right-click the notebook in the Navigation bar and choose **Rename** from the context menu to open the **Notebook Properties** dialog box. Then work as shown in Figure 16–15.

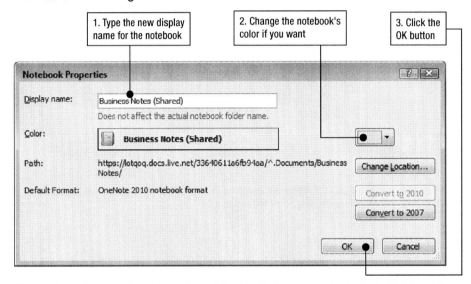

Figure 16–15. *You can change the active notebook's display name and color in the **Notebook Properties** dialog box.*

Navigating Among Sections and Section Groups

You can navigate among your sections and section groups by using either the Navigation bar or the section tabs bar. If your OneNote window has plenty of space to keep the Navigation bar expanded, the Navigation bar is usually the easiest way to get around. Figure 16–16 shows you how to navigate by double-clicking and clicking in the Navigation bar.

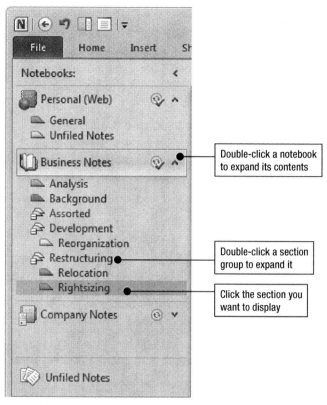

Figure 16–16. *You can navigate among section groups and sections quickly by double-clicking and clicking in the Navigation bar.*

You can also navigate among sections by using the section bar. When you've displayed the contents of a section group, the section bar displays the **Navigate to parent section group** button (a curling up arrow) to the left of the section group at its left end (see Figure 16–17). Click this button to display the *parent section group*, the section group that contains this section or section group.

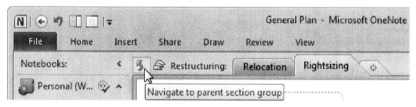

Figure 16–17. *Click the **Navigate to parent section group** button to move up to the section group that contains the current section group.*

Working with Pages

When you've organized your sections and section groups to be going on with, you can add pages and create notes on them. This section shows you the main moves for working with pages.

> **NOTE:** When you create a new section, OneNote automatically adds a page to it. After typing the section name, press **Enter** to move to the page title container. You can then type the page name, press **Enter**, and start taking notes in the container that OneNote automatically places on the page for you.

Creating a New Blank Page

You can create a new page in the current section in several ways, as I'll show you in this and the next section.

To add a new page at the end of the section, click the **New Page** button in the **Page Tabs** pane or press **Ctrl+N**. You can leave the page there, or drag it further up the list of page tabs as needed.

The easiest way to insert a new page between existing pages is to use the floating **New Page** button, as shown in Figure 16–18.

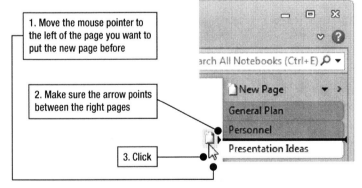

Figure 16–18. *The floating **New Page** icon is the easiest way to insert a new page between existing pages.*

> **TIP:** You can also insert a new page between existing pages by using the context menu. Right-click the page after which you want to insert the new page, and then click **New Page**.

Creating a New Page Based on a Template

When you need a particular type of page rather than a blank page, you can insert a page based on a template. Figure 16–19 shows you how to do this.

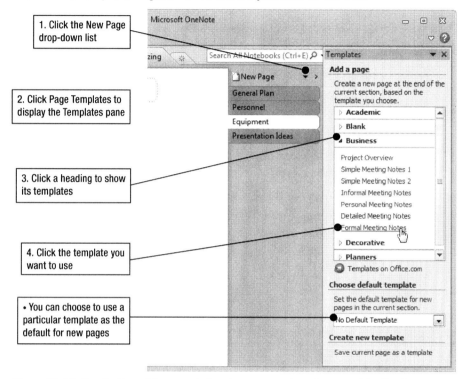

Figure 16–19. *Use the **Templates** pane to insert a new page based on one of OneNote's templates.*

NOTE: To get further templates, click the **Templates on Office.com** link in the Templates **pane**. OneNote opens a browser window to the Office website, which contains a wide variety of templates you can download.

Creating a Custom Page Template

If you frequently take the same kinds of notes, you can save time and effort by creating a custom page template for them. For example, you can create a page for lecture notes, including placeholders for the class name, lecturer's name, and topic, and perhaps containers for audio and video notes.

To create a custom page template, follow these steps:

1. Set up a page that contains the existing information and the containers you need.

2. With this page active, click the **New Page** drop-down list and choose **Page Templates** to open the **Templates** pane.

3. Click the **Save current page as a template** link at the bottom of the **Templates** pane to display the **Save As Template** dialog box (see Figure 16–20).

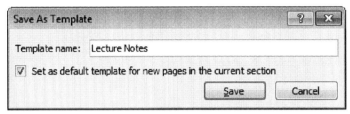

Figure 16–20. *You can create a custom page template and use it as the default for new pages in the current section.*

4. In the **Template name** text box, type a descriptive name for the template.

5. If you want to use this template as the default for this section of the notebook, select the **Set as default template for new pages in the current section** check box. This setting can be a great time-saver if the section contains mostly pages of the same type.

6. Click the **Save** button to close the **Save As Template** dialog box and save the template.

> **NOTE:** Your templates appear under a heading called **My Templates** at the top of the **Templates** pane.

Renaming a Page

To rename a page, first click its tab to display the page. Then click in the page name container at the top and either edit the existing name or simply type the new name over it. Press **Enter** when you're done.

Moving a Page

When you need to move a page to a different position in the notebook, drag it as shown in Figure 16–21.

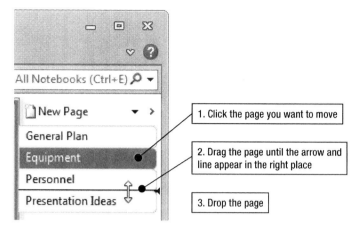

Figure 16–21. *You can quickly move a page within a section by dragging it up or down the **Page Tabs** pane.*

To move the page to another section with the mouse, follow these steps:

1. Expand the **Page Tabs** pane if it's collapsed.

2. Drag the page's tab to the section tab for the destination section.

3. Keep holding down the mouse button while OneNote displays that section in place of the one previously displayed.

4. Drag the page's tab back to the **Page Tabs** pane, which now shows the destination section's page tabs.

5. Move the line and arrow till they're between the destination tabs.

6. Drop the page where you want it to appear.

> **TIP:** If you expand the Navigation bar, you can drag the page's tab to another section in the Navigation bar rather than in the Section Tab bar. Sometimes it's easier to find the tab in the Navigation bar than in the Section Tab bar.

To move the page to another section or notebook, follow these steps:

1. Right-click the page's tab, and then choose **Move or Copy** to display the **Move or Copy Pages** dialog box (see Figure 16–22).

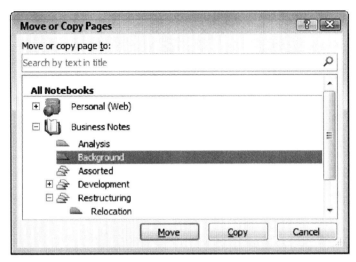

Figure 16–22. *You can use the **Move or Copy Pages** dialog box to move or copy a page to a different section or to a different notebook.*

2.   Click the section you want to move the page to.

3.   Click the Move button.

> **TIP:** To move a page, you can also drag the page tab to a section tab and drop it there.

Working with Subpages

When you need to add extra information to a page without it becoming so long it's hard to navigate, you can add one or more subpages to it. You can even add subpages to subpages if necessary. Figure 16–23 shows several subpages and the buttons you use to display and hide them.

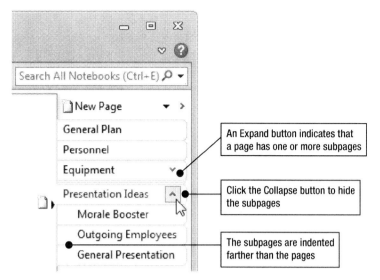

Figure 16–23. *You can add subpages to a page to organize your information more neatly.*

To add a subpage, follow these steps:

1. Click the page's tab to display the page.

2. Click the **New Page** drop-down button, and then choose **New Subpage** from the drop-down list. OneNote inserts a subpage and names it Untitled page as usual.

3. Type the name for the subpage, and then press **Enter** to create a container on the subpage so that you can start taking notes.

> **TIP:** To create a subpage based on a page template, create the subpage as a normal page, and then use the **Make Subpage** command to turn it into a subpage.

You can also turn an existing page into a subpage by right-clicking its page tab and then clicking **Make Subpage** on the context menu. Similarly, you can turn a subpage into a regular page by right-clicking its pane tab and then clicking **Promote Subpage** on the context menu.

TIP: You can drag a page tab to the right to turn the page into a subpage, or drag it to the left to promote the subpage to a page.

Navigating from Page to Page

In OneNote, you can navigate to any page with just a few clicks of the mouse, as shown in Figure 16–24.

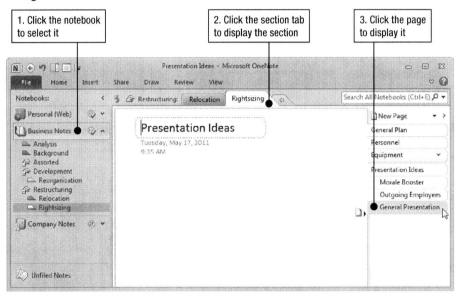

Figure 16–24. *You can navigate from page to page by displaying the notebook, displaying the section, and then clicking the page tab.*

Entering Notes on a Page

When you've created a page, you can quickly enter notes on it. This section teaches you the main techniques for entering notes, leaving audio and video notes for the next chapter.

WHAT TYPES OF INFORMATION CAN YOU SAVE IN ONENOTE?

You can save a wide variety of different types of information in a OneNote notebook:

- *Text.* You can store any amount of text, either leaving it plain or formatting it using styles or direct formatting.

- *Tables.* You can create either simple tables (ones with a regular structure) or complex tables (ones that include other tables nested inside cells). Your tables can include text, pictures, and other objects.

- *Equations.* Like Microsoft Word, OneNote includes a full set of equation tools that you can use to construct a wide range of equations, including binomials, Fourier series equations, and quadratic equations.

- *Pictures.* You can add pictures to your notebooks and position them as needed.

- *Screen clippings.* OneNote includes a built-in feature for capturing parts of the screen and including them in your notebooks. This feature is great for documenting computer procedures, but it's also good for quickly capturing information that you want to store. For example, you can capture a screen clipping of a web page for a product you're thinking of buying.

- *Document printouts.* You can print documents from the other Office programs straight to pages in OneNote. This is a great way of pulling together all the information you need in a notebook.

- *Scanner printouts.* If you want to include paper documents in your OneNote workbooks, you can scan them straight in.

- *Audio.* You can record audio straight into OneNote. For example, you can record audio of a lecture to supplement the notes you take.

- *Video.* If your PC has a video camera, you can record video straight into a notebook.

- *Files.* You can attach just about any type of file to a OneNote notebook so that you have it available. For example, you can attach an Excel workbook or a PowerPoint presentation to a workbook. You can't open these files in OneNote, but you can open them from it in the programs associated with them.

Adding Text to a Page

To add text to a page, click the point in the page at which you want to start entering the text. OneNote adds a container for the text where you click, and puts the insertion point in the container. You can then enter the text and format it as shown in Figure 16–25.

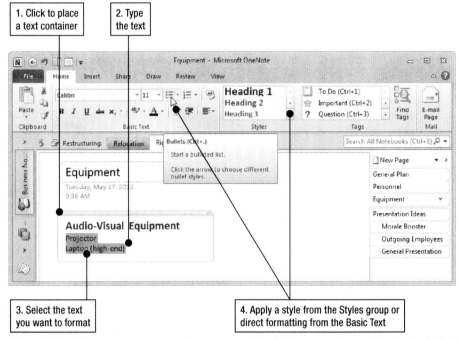

Figure 16–25. *You can enter text anywhere on a page by placing a container and then typing in it. You can then apply formatting to the text from the Home tab of the Ribbon.*

NOTE: You can enter text by typing it, by pasting it, or by dragging it in from another program and dropping it. When you drag and drop text (or another object) from one of the other Office programs, OneNote automatically creates a link back to the source document so that you can easily see where the text came from.

Use styles wherever possible when formatting text-based notes. When you export notes to Word, the text keeps the styles, and you can snap in a different set of formatting in moments by attaching a different template to the resulting Word document.

TIP: Press **Ctrl+down arrow** to move from the end of one container to the beginning of the next container. Press **Ctrl+up arrow** to move from the start of one container to the end of the previous container.

Adding Graphics to Pages

To illustrate your notes, you can quickly add a graphic to a page. Choose **Insert ➤ Images ➤ Picture** to open the **Insert Picture** dialog box, navigate to the graphic and select it, and then click the **Open** button.

After inserting a graphic, you can resize it by selecting the graphic and then dragging one of the placeholders that OneNote displays. Drag a corner placeholder to resize the graphic proportionally, so that the ratio of height to width remains constant. Drag a side placeholder to resize the graphic only in that dimension, distorting the image.

> **TIP:** You can also drag a graphic from a Windows Explorer window to a OneNote page. This method is handy when you're working in Windows Explorer and need to get a graphic into OneNote instantly.

Capturing Screen Clippings in Your Notebooks

If you need to store information displayed on screen, you'll find OneNote's Screen Clipping feature useful. You can insert a full screen or any part of it on the current page. Choose **Insert ➤ Images ➤ Screen Clipping**, and then drag the resulting crosshair to capture the area you want (see Figure 16–26).

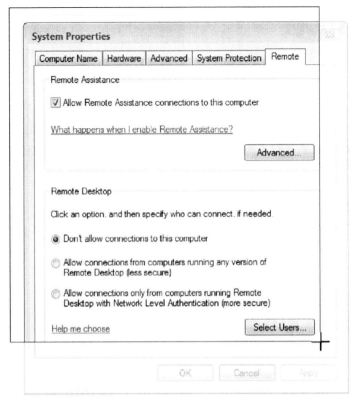

Figure 16–26. *To capture part of the screen, choose **Insert ➤ Images ➤ Screen Capture**, and then drag with the crosshair to select what you want.*

NOTE: To control where OneNote places your screen clippings, choose a setting in the **Screen Clippings** drop-down list in the **Send to OneNote** pane in the **OneNote Options** dialog box. See Chapter 18: "Using OneNote with Word, Excel, PowerPoint, and Outlook" for details.

Creating Drawings on Pages

If you need to create drawings in OneNote, click the **Draw** tab on the Ribbon and use the tools it provides. See Chapter 4: "Working with Graphics" for an introduction to these tools.

Creating Tables

You can add tables to your pages by using the standard technique you learned in Chapter 3: "Working with Text." Choose **Insert ➤ Tables ➤ Table**, and then click the gird square for the table layout you want (for example, five rows of four columns each).

> **TIP:** You can also create a table by starting typing in a container and then pressing **Tab** when you want a column break. Press **Tab** until you have as many columns as you want. Then press **Enter** to create a new row.

Sending Printouts to OneNote

You can also send data to OneNote by printing from another program, as shown in Figure 16–27. This is a great way to insert a final copy of a document right into a OneNote notebook so that you can keep it to hand.

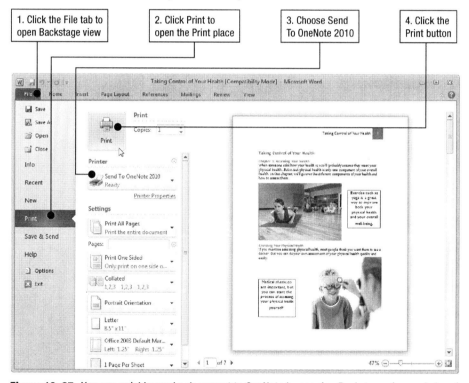

Figure 16–27. *You can quickly send a document to OneNote by opening Backstage view and choosing **Send To OneNote 2010** in the **Printer** drop-down list in the **Print** place.*

When OneNote receives the incoming printout, it displays the **Select Location in OneNote** dialog box (see Figure 16–28). Choose the notebook and section you want to put the printout in. Select the **Always send printouts to the selected location** check box if you want to use the same location for all printouts. Then click the **OK** button.

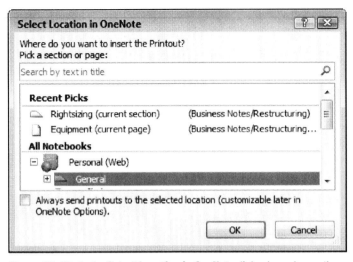

Figure 16–28. *In the Select Location in OneNote dialog box, choose the section or page to add the printout to. Select the Always send printouts to the same location check box if you want to use the same location for all your printouts.*

NOTE: You can specify a different default location for printouts in the **Print to OneNote** drop-down list in the **Send to OneNote** pane in the **OneNote Options** dialog box.

Sending Outlook Items to OneNote

You can instantly send a copy of a selected Outlook item to OneNote by giving the appropriate command:

- *Mail.* Choose **Home ➤ Move ➤ OneNote**.
- *Contacts.* Choose **Home ➤ Actions ➤ OneNote.**
- *Calendar.* Choose **Appointment ➤ Actions ➤ OneNote**.
- *Tasks.* Choose **Home ➤ Move ➤ OneNote**.

If Outlook displays the **Select Location in OneNote** dialog box, click the section in which you want to put the item you're sending, and then click the **OK** button.

NOTE: If you always want to put this type of item in the same section in OneNote, select the **Always send *item* to the selected location** check box in the **Select Location in OneNote** dialog box before you click the **OK** button.

Sending Web Content to OneNote

When you find a web page you want to remember, you can quickly send it from Internet Explorer to OneNote by using the **Send To OneNote** command, as discussed earlier in this chapter. Click the **Print** button on the command bar to open the **Print** dialog box, click the **Send To OneNote 2010** button, and then click the **Print** button.

Inserting a Scanner Printout

If you need to add a paper document into OneNote, you can scan it in directly, as shown in Figure 16–29. OneNote calls this inserting a scanner printout.

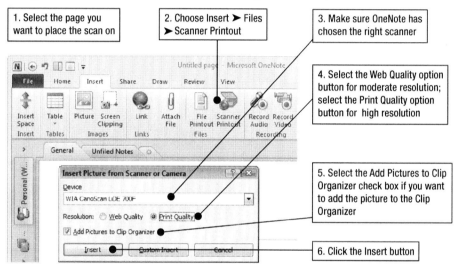

Figure 16–29. *You can quickly insert a scanned document by using the* **Insert ➤ Files ➤ Scanner Printout** *command.*

NOTE: Click the **Insert** button in the **Insert Picture from Scanner or Camera** dialog box if you want to insert a scan of the whole item. If you want just part of the item, click the **Custom Insert** button. You then get to select which part of the item to scan.

Performing Calculations

OneNote has an automatic calculation feature, sometimes called "napkin math," that lets you perform calculations quickly and easily in your notes. This feature is great both for informal calculations and for math notes.

To perform a calculation, click in a container, type the calculation followed by an equal sign, and press **Enter**. For example, type **$.75*23=** and then press **Enter**. OneNote enters the result.

Here are the characters and text to use for calculations:

- *Addition.* Type a **+** sign.

- *Subtraction.* Type a **–** sign (hyphen).

- *Multiplication.* Type an asterisk, a lowercase x, or an uppercase X—all work.

- *Division.* Type a forward slash, as in Excel—for example, 5/4=.

- *Percentage.* Type the % sign.

- *Exponentiation.* Type a **^** (caret) followed by the power—for example, $3^4=$.

- *Factorial computation.* Type the number followed by an exclamation point—for example, 6!=.

- *Pi and Phi.* Type **pi** or **phi** as needed—for example, 5*pi=.

- *Functions.* OneNote supports the ABS, ACOS, ASIN, ATAN, COS, DEG, LN, LOG, LOG2, LOG10, MOD, PMT, RAD, SIN, SQRT, and TAN functions. Type the function name (lowercase is fine) followed by the argument or arguments in parentheses. For example, type **sqrt(225)=** **or 200 mod 8=**.

NOTE: If the automatic calculation feature isn't working, choose **File ➤ Options**, click the **Advanced** category, and select the **Calculate mathematical expressions automatically** check box.

Using Views, Windows, and Side Notes

To make the most of OneNote, you will need to use the different views it offers. You may also find it helpful to open more than one window at once so that you can view or edit two or more pages of notes at the same time.

Using Normal View, Full Page View, and Dock to Desktop View

At first, OneNote opens in Normal view, which shows the Navigation bar, the Ribbon, the Section Tabs, and the Page Tabs pane so that you can navigate easily among notebooks, sections, and pages.

Using Full Page View to See More of Your Notes

When you plan to stay on the page that's currently displayed, and you need as much space as possible to take or work with your notes, switch to Full Page view (see Figure 16–30). You can switch in any of these ways:

- *Quick Access Toolbar.* Click the **Full Page View** button, so that it appears pressed in.

- *Ribbon.* Choose **View ➤ Views ➤ Full Page View**.

- *Keyboard.* Press F11.

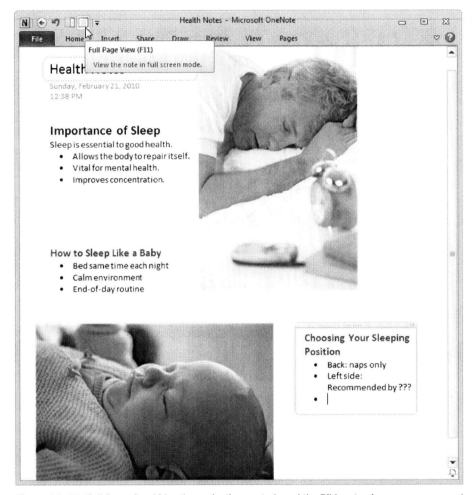

Figure 16–30. *Full Page view hides the navigation controls and the Ribbon to give you more space to concentrate on your notes.*

To switch back from Full Page view to Normal view, click the **Full Page View** button on the Quick Access Toolbar again (to un-press it), press **F11** again, or choose **View ➤ Views ➤ Normal View**.

Docking the OneNote Window to the Desktop

When you're working in another program and you want to keep OneNote handy for taking notes, you may dock OneNote to the desktop. Docking positions the OneNote window at the right side of the desktop and hides the Ribbon, the Navigation bar, and the page tabs, as you can see in Figure 16–31.

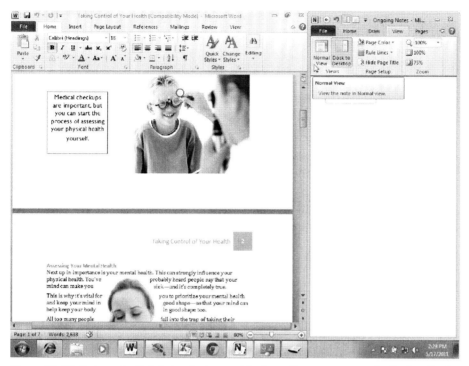

Figure 16–31. *To keep OneNote to hand when working in another program, use the* **Dock to Desktop** *command to position the OneNote window at the side of the desktop and hide the Ribbon, Navigation bar, and page tabs.*

You can dock the OneNote window to a different side of the desktop by clicking its title bar and dragging it there. For example, drag it to the top of the screen to dock it across the top of the window. OneNote remembers the docked position and uses it again next time.

To dock the OneNote window, click the **Dock to Desktop** button on the Quick Access Toolbar or press **Ctrl+Alt+D**. You can also choose **View ➤ Views ➤ Dock to Desktop** if you prefer.

To undock the OneNote window, click the **Dock to Desktop** button on the Quick Access Toolbar or press **Ctrl+Alt+D** again. You can also choose **View ➤ Views ➤ Normal View** from the Ribbon.

NOTE: When you dock the OneNote window, Backstage becomes unavailable. OneNote turns the **File** tab gray to indicate that it is not available.

Opening Extra Windows

To take down notes about two or more different topics, to compare different pages, or to transfer data from one page to another, it's often helpful to open two or more OneNote windows at once rather than switching back and forth between pages in the same window.

To open a new window, choose **View ➤ Window ➤ New Window**. OneNote opens the new window to the same page as the current window, but you can then navigate to whichever page you need.

> **TIP:** To give yourself space to work in two OneNote windows at once on a small screen, open a new docked window by choosing **View ➤ Window ➤ New Docked Window**.

Working with Side Notes

When you need to take a quick note, use a side note rather than starting a new page.

Side notes can be handy and save time, because they enable you to take a note without opening OneNote (if you don't keep it open the whole time) or without moving away from the page you're working on (or opening a new window).

When OneNote isn't open, you can create a new side note by pressing Windows **Key+N** or by clicking the **Open New Side Note** icon in the notification area (see Figure 16–32).

Figure 16–32. *Click the **Open New Side Note** icon in the notification area to quickly start a new side note when OneNote isn't open. You can also press **Windows Key+N**.*

When OneNote is open, you can create a side note by choosing **View ➤ Window ➤ New Side Note** or pressing **Ctrl+Alt+M**.

When you give one of these commands, OneNote opens a new side note window, which is a OneNote window in Full Page view. You can start taking notes as usual, as in Figure 16–33. When you've finished, click the **Close** button (the × button) to close the window.

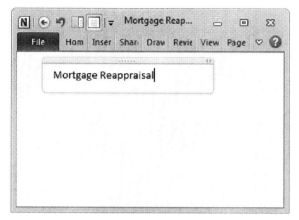

Figure 16–33. *Open a side note window when you need to take a quick note either without opening OneNote fully or without moving from the page you're working on.*

OneNote adds the side note as a new page in the **Unfiled Notes** section. You can display this section by clicking the **Unfiled Notes** button at the bottom of the Navigation bar, and then edit the page, copy the information from it, or move the page to the section it belongs to.

Summary

In this chapter, you got up to speed with OneNote. You met the OneNote user interface, learned to capture notes using everything from the keyboard to a scanner, and got the hang of docking the OneNote window and taking quick notes with side notes.

In the next chapter, I'll show you how to organize and synchronize your notes using OneNote.

Searching, Protecting, and Synchronizing Your Notes

To find the information you need, you can search any part of your notebooks, from a single page to every notebook. And to prevent other people from finding information you don't want them to see, you can protect sections of your notebooks with passwords.

To get the most out of OneNote, you'll probably want to share some of your workbooks with other people. In this chapter, you'll learn how to do this, view older versions of pages, recover the versions you need, and clear out old page versions that you no longer require.

Searching for Information in Your Notebooks

To search quickly for information, work as shown in Figure 17–1.

> **NOTE:** To activate the Search box, press the **Ctrl+E** rather than the **Ctrl+F** keyboard shortcut that most of the Office programs use for Find. This shortcut is different because OneNote also uses **Ctrl+F** for Find—but it's for searching on a page rather than for searching through your workbooks.

1. Click in the Search box or press Ctrl+E

2. Type your search term

3. Hold the mouse pointer over a result to display a ScreenTip showing where it is

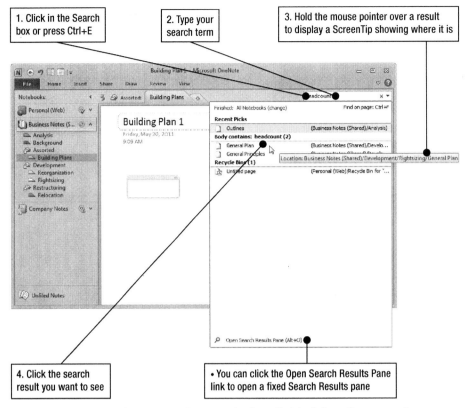

4. Click the search result you want to see

• You can click the Open Search Results Pane link to open a fixed Search Results pane

Figure 17–1. *You can quickly search all your notebooks to find the information you need.*

When you need to work with multiple search results rather than a single one, open a fixed **Search Results** pane by pressing **Alt+O** or by clicking the **Open Search Results Pane** link at the bottom of the pop-up search pane. Figure 17–2 shows the **Search Results** pane open, with instructions on how to use it.

Searching, Protecting, and Synchronizing Your Notes

To find the information you need, you can search any part of your notebooks, from a single page to every notebook. And to prevent other people from finding information you don't want them to see, you can protect sections of your notebooks with passwords.

To get the most out of OneNote, you'll probably want to share some of your workbooks with other people. In this chapter, you'll learn how to do this, view older versions of pages, recover the versions you need, and clear out old page versions that you no longer require.

Searching for Information in Your Notebooks

To search quickly for information, work as shown in Figure 17–1.

> **NOTE:** To activate the Search box, press the **Ctrl+E** rather than the **Ctrl+F** keyboard shortcut that most of the Office programs use for Find. This shortcut is different because OneNote also uses **Ctrl+F** for Find—but it's for searching on a page rather than for searching through your workbooks.

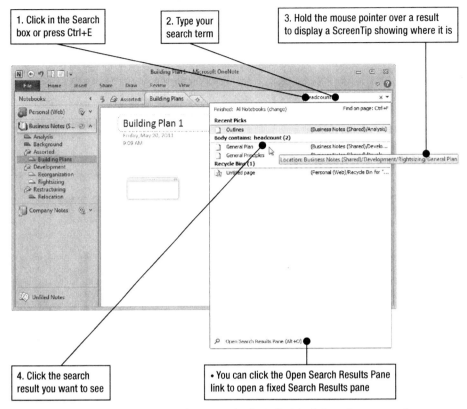

Figure 17–1. *You can quickly search all your notebooks to find the information you need.*

When you need to work with multiple search results rather than a single one, open a fixed **Search Results** pane by pressing **Alt+O** or by clicking the **Open Search Results Pane** link at the bottom of the pop-up search pane. Figure 17–2 shows the **Search Results** pane open, with instructions on how to use it.

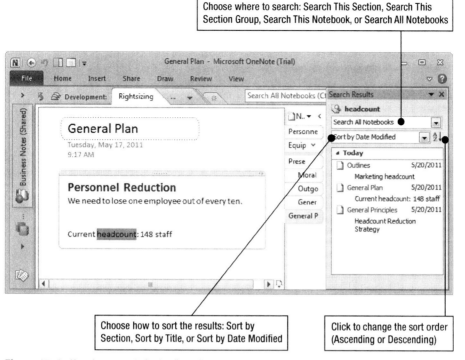

Choose where to search: Search This Section, Search This Section Group, Search This Notebook, or Search All Notebooks

Choose how to sort the results: Sort by Section, Sort by Title, or Sort by Date Modified

Click to change the sort order (Ascending or Descending)

Figure 17–2. *Use the controls in the fixed **Search Results** pane to filter the results, sort them, and reverse the sort order.*

> **CAUTION:** If you password-protect a section (as described later in the next section), OneNote excludes that section from searches. To include the section in searches, you must unprotect it before you begin the search.

When you finish using the Search Results pane, click its **Close** button (the × button) to close it.

Protecting Your Notes with Passwords

When you need to keep a section of a notebook secret, you can protect it with a password. Figure 17–3 shows you how to do this.

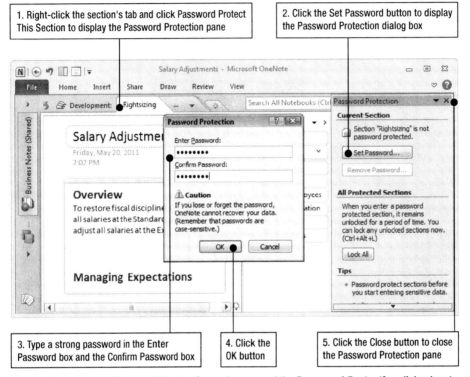

1. Right-click the section's tab and click Password Protect This Section to display the Password Protection pane

2. Click the Set Password button to display the Password Protection dialog box

3. Type a strong password in the Enter Password box and the Confirm Password box

4. Click the OK button

5. Click the Close button to close the Password Protection pane

Figure 17–3. *Use the **Password Protection** task pane and the **Password Protection** dialog box to protect notes with a strong password.*

CAUTION: Remember your password. Without it, you will not be able to recover your notes.

Unlocking a Password-Protected Section to Work in It

To work in a password-protected section, you need to unlock it, as shown in Figure 17–4.

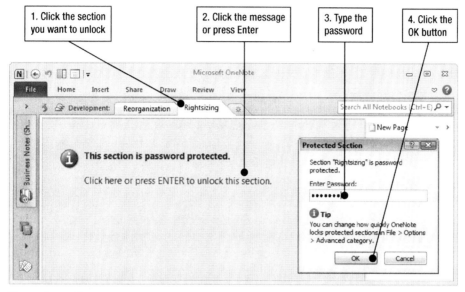

Figure 17–4. *You must unlock a password-protected section before you can work in it.*

> **NOTE:** OneNote has several settings that let you control when your passwords take effect and how long you unlock a password-protected section for. See Chapter 18: "Using OneNote with Word, Excel, PowerPoint, and Outlook" for details on these settings.

Locking Password-Protected Sections Manually

You can lock all password-protected sections of a notebook manually if necessary. Right-click the section's tab and choose **Password Protect This Section** to display the **Password Protection** task pane, and then click the **Lock All** button.

Removing Password Protection from a Section of a Notebook

To remove password protection from a section of a notebook, follow these steps:

1. Right-click the section's tab and choose **Password Protect This Section** to display the **Password Protection** task pane.

2. Click the **Remove Password** button. OneNote displays the **Remove Password** dialog box.

3. Type the password, and then click the **OK** button. (You need to type the password to prove that the person removing the protection is you.)

Sharing an Existing Notebook

As you saw in Chapter 16: "Getting Up to Speed and Using Notes," when you create a new notebook stored on Windows Live SkyDrive or on a network, OneNote gives you the opportunity to e-mail a link to the notebook to other people who share that folder. If you share the notebook, you and other people can work on it at the same time, using the coauthoring features explained in Chapter 5: "Coauthoring in Real Time and Sharing Documents."

If you want to share an existing notebook rather than create a new notebook, open the notebook and work as shown in Figure 17–5.

After OneNote creates the shared notebook, it displays a dialog box telling you that the notebook is shared with anyone who has permission to access the network folder. If you want to e-mail your colleagues a link to the notebook, click the **E-mail a Link** button, and then address and send the message that OneNote creates for you in Outlook. Otherwise, click the **No, Thanks** button.

> **TIP:** If you need to let other people know about a notebook you shared earlier, click the **File** tab to open Backstage view, and then click **Share** in the left column. On the **Share Notebook** screen, which shows that the notebook is already shared, click the **E-mail Others About the Notebook** link, and then fill in and send the e-mail message that OneNote causes Outlook to create.

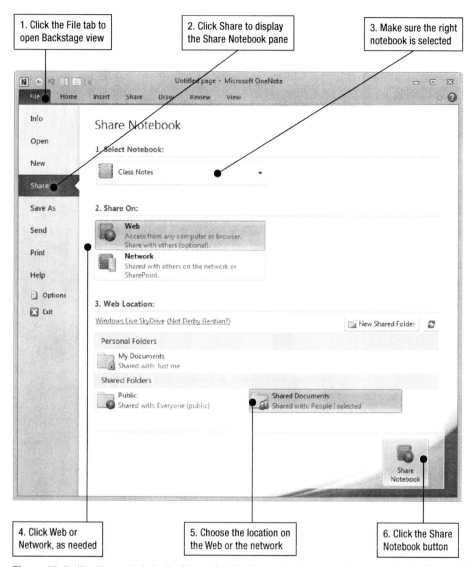

1. Click the File tab to open Backstage view

2. Click Share to display the Share Notebook pane

3. Make sure the right notebook is selected

4. Click Web or Network, as needed

5. Choose the location on the Web or the network

6. Click the Share Notebook button

Figure 17–5. *Use the controls in the **Share Notebook** pane to share an existing notebook either on Windows Live SkyDrive or on your local network.*

Opening a Shared Notebook

To open a shared notebook, choose **File ➤ Open ➤ Open Notebook**, select the notebook in the **Open Notebook** dialog box, and then click the **Open** button.

After that, you can normally open the notebook from the **Recently Closed Notebooks** list in the **Open Notebook** pane, unless you've opened many other notebooks since you last opened this one.

> **TIP:** The easiest way to see if a notebook is shared is to check whether the **Sync Status** icon—a circle with two curving arrows inside it—appears on the notebook's heading in the Navigation Bar. This icon appears only on shared notebooks. See the next figure for an example.

Choosing How to Update a Shared Notebook

As long as your PC is online, OneNote automatically synchronizes each shared notebook and updates it with the latest changes. Normally, you'll want to keep getting the updates so that you don't waste time doing work someone else has done—but you may sometimes need to turn off synchronization or force immediate synchronization.

The **Sync Status** indicator on the notebook's name bar in the Navigation Bar shows whether the notebook is currently synchronized or not. Figure 17–6 shows the **Sync Status** indicators and explains what they mean.

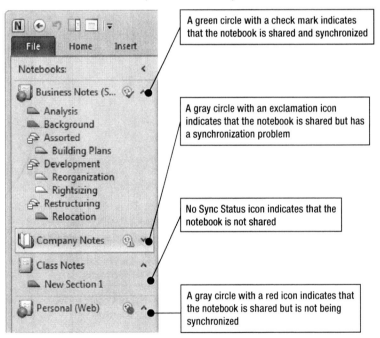

Figure 17–6. *The Sync Status icon shows each notebook's synchronization status. If a notebook has no Sync Status icon, you're not sharing it online.*

Turning Off Synchronization for a Notebook

If you want to turn off synchronization so that you can work without interruptions, follow these steps:

1. Right-click any notebook in the Navigation Bar and choose **Notebook Sync Status** from the context menu to display the **Shared Notebook Synchronization** dialog box (see Figure 17–7).

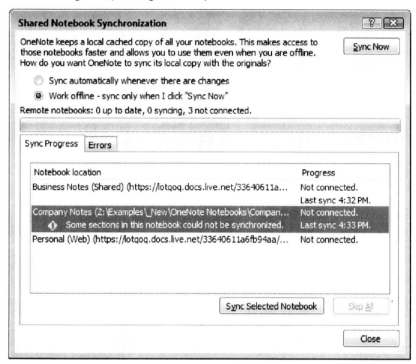

Figure 17–7. *Select the* **Work offline – sync only when I click "Sync Now"** *option button in the* **Shared Notebook Synchronization** *dialog box to take your notebooks offline for editing in peace.*

2. Select the Work offline – sync only when I click "Sync Now" option button.

3. Click the Close button.

When you want to return to automatic synchronization, open the **Shared Notebook Synchronization** dialog box again, select the **Sync automatically whenever there are changes** option button, and then click the **OK** button.

Forcing Immediate Synchronization of a Notebook

If you've taken your notebooks offline, or if you're about to disconnect your PC from the network, you can force synchronization by right-clicking the notebook in the Navigation bar and then clicking **Sync This Notebook Now** on the context menu (see Figure 17–8). You can also press **Shift+F9** to sync the active notebook.

Figure 17–8. *Right-click a notebook in the Navigation bar and click* **Sync This Notebook Now** *to force immediate synchronization of a notebook.*

TIP: To force synchronization of all notebooks, open the **Shared Notebook Synchronization** dialog box, and then click the **Sync Now** button.

Using Different Versions of Pages

OneNote stores different versions of the pages it contains, so you can go back to an earlier version of a page as needed. This feature is useful when you find a colleague has deleted material that you need to keep in the notebook—or when you delete material yourself by accident.

NOTE: OneNote keeps the versions of a page for 60 days and then discards them automatically. If necessary, you can get rid of them sooner, as discussed later in this chapter.

Viewing or Recovering an Earlier Page Version

To view or recover an earlier version of a page, work as shown in Figure 17–9.

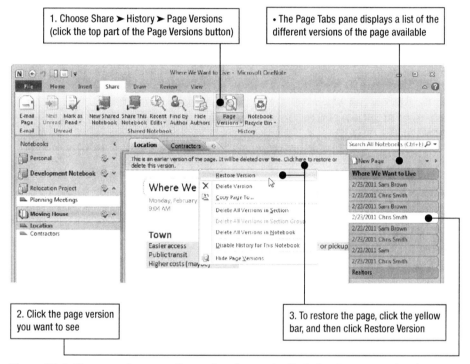

1. Choose Share ➤ History ➤ Page Versions (click the top part of the Page Versions button)

• The Page Tabs pane displays a list of the different versions of the page available

2. Click the page version you want to see

3. To restore the page, click the yellow bar, and then click Restore Version

Figure 17–9. *You can restore an earlier version of a page by displaying the page versions in the Page Tabs pane, clicking the version you want, and then using the yellow bar to restore it. The gray tabs in the Page Tabs pane indicate other versions of the currently selected page.*

NOTE: From the menu that appears when you click the message at the top of a page version, you can also click the **Delete Version** command to delete this version or click the **Copy Page To** command to copy it to a different location. Copying the page to a different location enables you to edit the page and use it further without overwriting the current page version.

Getting Rid of Old Page Versions to Save Space

Keeping the old page versions can greatly increase the amount of space a notebook takes up on a drive and the length of time it takes to load across the Internet. You can clear out old material by using the three Delete commands on the **Share ➤ History ➤ Page Versions** menu:

- **Delete All Versions in Section**. Deletes all the page versions in the current section.

- **Delete All Versions in Section Group**. Deletes all the page versions in the current section and its section group. This command is available only if the current section is in a section group.

- **Delete All Versions in Notebook**. Deletes all the versions in the whole notebook. Review the whole notebook quickly before giving this command, or at least make sure you have a recent backup of the notebook.

> **NOTE:** If you find that a notebook is growing too big and unwieldy, you can turn off history in it by choosing **Share ➤ History ➤ Page Versions ➤ Disable History for This Notebook** or **Share ➤ History ➤ Notebook Recycle Bin ➤ Disable History for This Notebook**. OneNote then gets rid of old versions and deleted material immediately rather than keeping them in case you need to recover material.

Summary

In this chapter, you learned how to search, protect, and synchronize your notes using OneNote.

You can search for information, sort and filter search results, and protect your notes with passwords. You also learned how to share existing workbooks with other people and how to open workbooks other people have shared. You can view older versions of pages, recover the versions you need, and clear out old page versions that you no longer require.

In the next chapter, we'll look at how to use OneNote with Word, Excel, PowerPoint, and Outlook.

Chapter 18

Customizing OneNote and Using It with Word, Excel, PowerPoint, and Outlook

In this chapter, we'll look at how to customize OneNote to suit the way you work, add audio and video to your notebooks, print your notebooks, and export data from OneNote to Word, Excel, PowerPoint, and Outlook.

Choosing the Most Important Options for OneNote

To customize OneNote, you choose settings for the many options in the **OneNote Options** dialog box. In this section, we'll look at the settings that make the most difference to the way you work in OneNote; I'll leave you to investigate the other settings at your leisure.

Start by clicking the **File** tab to open Backstage view, and then clicking the **Options** button to display the **OneNote Options** dialog box. When the dialog box opens, the **General** pane appears at the front. Set the **General** options as discussed in Chapter 6: "Making the Office Programs Work Your Way." You can then set other options as discussed in this section.

> **NOTE:** Chapter 2: "Using the Ribbon, Backstage, and Common Tools" explains how to set the **Proofing** options.

Choosing Display Options

Use the options in the **Display** pane in the **OneNote Options** dialog box (see Figure 18–1) to control how OneNote looks:

- **Place OneNote icon in the notification area of the taskbar.** Select this check box to make OneNote include a OneNote icon in the notification area. This icon lets you open a new side note, so you'll want the icon if you find side notes useful. Chapter 16: "Getting Up to Speed and Taking Notes" explains side notes.

- **Create all new pages with rule lines.** Select this check box if you want OneNote to display rule lines on each new page you create. If you clear this check box, you can display rule lines by choosing **View ➤ Page Setup ➤ Rule Lines**, and then clicking the type of lines you want: **Narrow Ruled**, **College Ruled**, **Standard Ruled**, **Wide Ruled**, **Small Grid**, **Medium Grid**, **Large Grid**, or **Very Large Grid**.

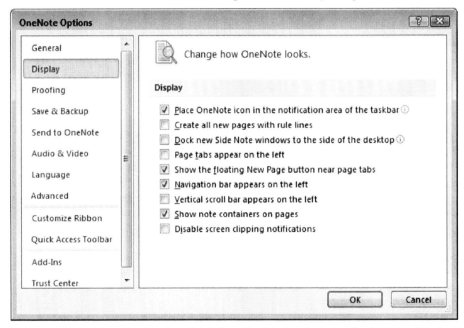

*Figure 18–1. The **Display** options include placing a OneNote icon in the notification area of the taskbar and controlling the placement of the navigation bar.*

- **Dock new Side Note windows to the side of the desktop.** Select this check box if you want OneNote to automatically dock each new Side Note window you open to the side of the desktop. This option can be helpful for keeping your Side Notes organized. Clear this check box if you prefer to be able to position Side Note windows manually.

- **Page tabs appear on the left.** Select this check box if you want to display page tabs on the left rather than on the right, where they normally appear. Even when you do this, the Navigation bar appears on the far left of the OneNote window.

- **Show the floating New Page button near page tabs.** Select this check box if you want OneNote to display the New Page button when you move the mouse pointer over the page tabs. The New Page button tends to be the quickest way to insert a page, so it's useful. Clear this check box if you prefer to insert pages in other ways.

- **Navigation bar appears on the left.** Select this check box (which is selected by default) to display the Navigation bar; clear it to hide the Navigation bar and give yourself more space to work in.

- **Vertical scroll bar appears on the left.** Select this check box if you want the vertical scroll bar to appear on the left rather than on the right, where it normally appears.

- **Show note containers on page.** Select this check box (which is selected by default) to have OneNote display a container around each note you place on a page. Clear this check box if you want to hide the containers, so that notes appear simply as text (or whatever they contain) on the page.

- **Disable screen clipping notifications.** Select this check box if you want to prevent Windows from displaying a ScreenTip above the OneNote icon in the notification area when you're using the Screen Clipping feature.

Choosing Save & Backup Options

In the **Save & Backup** pane (see Figure 18–2) in the OneNote Options dialog box, choose where to save and how to back up your notebooks. It's worth spending a few minutes setting these options, because they're vital to keeping your valuable information safe—and they can reduce the amount of space your notebooks take up on disk.

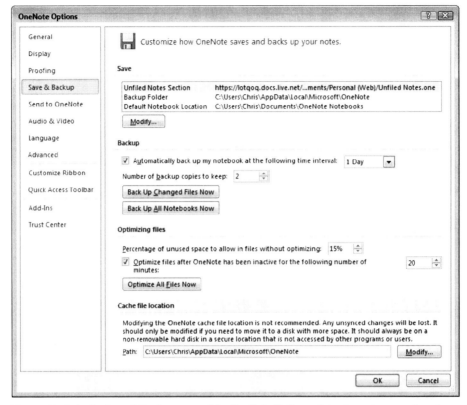

Figure 18–2. *In the **Save & Backup** pane of the **OneNote Options** dialog box, choose options for saving, backing up, and optimizing your notebooks.*

In the **Save** list box, you can choose where to save each of the items that appears: the **Unfiled Notes Section**, the **Backup Folder**, and the **Default Notebook Location**. To change one of these:

1. Click the item in the **Save** list box.

2. Click the **Modify** button to display the **Select File** dialog box (for the **Unfiled Notes** Section) or the **Select Folder** dialog box (for the **Backup Folder** item and the **Default Notebook Location** item).

3. Choose the file or folder.

4. Click the **Select** button to close the dialog box and apply your choice.

In the **Backup** area, you can choose the following options:

- **Automatically back up my notebook at the following time interval.** Select this check box if you want to make automatic backups—which is usually a good idea. In the drop-down list, choose the time interval between backups. Your choices range from 1 Minute to 6 Weeks; the default setting of 1 Day is a reasonable medium, but if you use OneNote heavily, you may want to shorten the interval to 12 Hours, 6 Hours, or less.

- **Number of backup copies to keep.** In this text box, choose how many backups of your OneNote notebooks to keep. The default setting is 2, but you may want to increase this to a number in the 5–10 range to give you a better chance of recovering data if you find that your current notebook and the latest backups have been corrupted.

- **Back Up Changed Files Now.** Click this button to back up the OneNote files you've changed.

- **Back Up All Notebooks Now.** Click this button to force a backup of all your OneNote notebooks—for example, because you've had a premonition of impending data loss.

> **NOTE:** To open a backup file, choose **File ➤ Info ➤ Open Backups**. OneNote displays the **Open Backup** dialog box, showing the backup folder set in the **Save & Backup** pane. Select the backup you want (usually the most recent), and then click the **Open** button.

In the **Optimizing files** area, choose how to optimize your OneNote notebooks:

- **Percentage of unused space to allow in files without optimizing.** In this text box, set the amount of unused space you're prepared to tolerate before OneNote optimizes the file. The default setting is 15 percent. Increase this setting if OneNote seems to spend too long optimizing your files.

- **Optimize files after OneNote has been inactive for the following number of minutes.** Select this check box if you want OneNote to run optimization automatically after you've left it alone for a period of time. Set the number of minutes in the text box. The default setting is 30 minutes, but if you tend to leave your PC for shorter breaks, reduce the interval to start optimization sooner.

- **Optimize All Files Now.** Click this button to run optimization immediately. This button is especially useful if you clear the previous check box, but you can also use it to force optimization at any convenient time (for example, when you're heading off to a lengthy meeting).

In the **Cache file location** area, you can click the **Modify** button to choose a different folder for the OneNote cache file location. Normally, you should leave the cache folder in its default place unless your PC's hard disk is running out of space and you need to move the folder to another hard drive. Even then, you should place the folder on an internal hard drive rather than on a removable hard drive (such as a USB hard drive).

Choosing Send to OneNote Options

Next, click the **Send to OneNote** category in the left pane in the **Send to OneNote** pane of the **Options** dialog box (see Figure 18–3), you can streamline your work by telling OneNote how to deal with content you send to it from other programs.

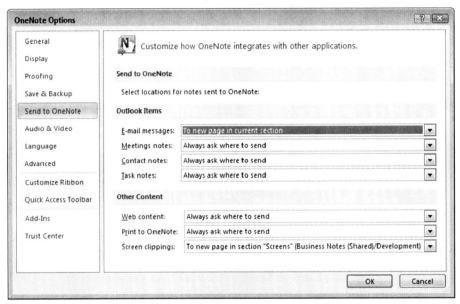

Figure 18–3. In the **Send to OneNote** pane, tell OneNote how to handle content you send to it from Outlook and other programs.

In the **Outlook Items** area, open the **E-mail messages** drop-down list, the **Meetings notes** drop-down list, the **Contact notes** drop-down list, and the **Task notes** drop-down list in turn, and choose the destination for each item you send to OneNote using the Send to OneNote command. These are your choices:

- **Always ask where to send.** Outlook displays the **Select Location in OneNote** dialog box (shown in Figure 18–4) to let you choose where to send the item. You can select the **Always send *item* to the selected location** check box if you want to choose a standard location.

Figure 18–4. *When you use the **Always ask where to send** option in OneNote, Outlook prompts you to choose the notebook and section in which to insert the item you're sending.*

- ▣ **To current page.** Outlook inserts the item on the page you're working on in OneNote.

- ▣ **To new page in current section.** Outlook creates a new page in the current section and inserts the item on it. This setting is good for e-mail messages, especially if you send multiple messages at once to OneNote.

- ▣ **Set default location.** Click this item to open the **Select Location in OneNote** dialog box. Choose the notebook and section, and then click the **OK** button.

In the **Other Content** area, use the **Web content** drop-down list, the **Print to OneNote** drop-down list, and the **Screen clippings** drop-down list to choose where to place these items . The destinations are the same as for the **Outlook Items** discussed previously, except that the **Screen clippings** drop-down list offers the choice **To Clipboard only** instead of the **To current page** choice. Select this item if you want to place a screen clip on the Clipboard so that you can insert it wherever it belongs.

Choosing Audio & Video Options

If you put audio and video items in your notebooks (we'll look at how to do this later in this chapter), click the **Audio & Video** category in the left column of the **OneNote Options** dialog box, and then choose suitable settings in the **Audio & Video** pane (see Figure 18–5).

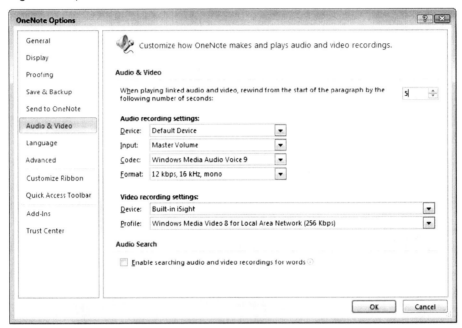

Figure 18–5. *Make sure that OneNote is using suitable settings for the audio and video you add to your notebooks.*

At the top of the pane, set the **When playing linked audio and video, rewind from the start of the paragraph by the following number of seconds** setting as needed. The default setting is 5 seconds, but you may need to rewind by more seconds or fewer seconds.

Next, make your choices in the Audio recording settings area:

- **Device.** In this drop-down list, make sure that OneNote has selected your PC's audio input device. If your PC has multiple input devices, such as a microphone and a USB headset, pick the right one.

- **Input.** In this drop-down list, choose the audio input—for example, **Master Volume**.

▓ **Codec.** In this drop-down list, choose the codec (the *coder/decoder* software) to use for compressing audio you record. Use **Windows Media Audio Voice 9** for recording of spoken audio. Use **Windows Media Audio 10 Professional** for high-quality recordings within OneNote.

> **NOTE:** The higher the quality setting you choose in the **Format** drop-down list, the larger the resulting audio files are, and the larger your OneNote notebook grows. So you need to strike a balance between good enough audio quality and file size. The more audio you record, the more important it is that you strike this balance, especially if you keep the audio notes in the long term (as opposed to creating written notes of the good parts and jettisoning the audio files).

▓ **Format.** In this drop-down list, choose the quality at which you want to record. For the **Windows Media Audio Voice 9** codec, start with the **8 Kbps, 8 kHz, mono** setting, and test to see if it gives you high enough quality. If not, increase the setting to **12 Kbps, 16 kHz, mono** and test again; again, move to one of the higher quality settings if necessary. For the **Windows Media Audio 10 Professional** codec, experiment with the **128 Kbps, 44 kHz, stereo (A/V) CBR** setting for recording music, and choose a higher setting if necessary.

> **NOTE:** CBR is the abbreviation for *constant bit rate*, recording the same amount of data for each second of audio rather than recording more data for more complex audio than for less complex audio (or silence). 44 kHz is the sampling rate used for CD-quality audio; normally, it's not worth using the higher 48 kHz sampling rate, as it takes up more space for very little gain.

Now choose settings in the **Video recording** settings area:

▓ **Device.** In this drop-down list, make sure that OneNote has chosen the right video camera. Unless you have multiple cameras attached, the choice will usually be right.

▓ **Profile.** In this drop-down list, choose the setting at which you want to record video. Start with the **Windows Media Video 8 for Local Area Network (256 Kbps)**, test it, and see if the quality is high enough. If not, choose a higher setting, such as **Windows Media Video 8 for Local Area Network (384 Kbps)**.

In the **Audio Search** area, select the **Enable searching audio and video recordings for words** check box if you want OneNote to search your audio recordings and the audio in your video recordings and try to index the words it finds. You can then search for particular words and phrases in the audio recordings and video recordings. This feature gives mixed results, but it's worth testing to see if it's useful to you.

NOTE: If you turn on searching for audio recordings, you will normally need to use relatively high audio quality to get useful search results. The audio quality on any of the **Windows Media Video 8 for Local Area Network** choices is usually high enough for searching, provided that you position the microphone close to the speaker.

Choosing Advanced Options

The **Advanced** pane in the **OneNote Options** dialog box (see Figure 18–6) contains many options. But because these options make a huge difference to the way OneNote behaves, you'll benefit from knowing what they do.

Figure 18–6. *Take a few minutes to set OneNote's **Advanced** options, because they make a big difference to how easy the program is to use.*

Start by choosing options in the **Editing** area at the top of the pane:

- **Show Paste Options button when content is pasted.** Select this check box to make OneNote display a **Paste Options** button when you paste in content. The **Paste Options** button lets you choose among different ways of pasting the item—for example, as unformatted text instead of formatted text. This button is usually useful.

- **Include link to source when pasting from the Web.** Select this check box to make OneNote automatically build in a link to the Web page from which you pasted in information. You can click the link to display the Web page.

- **Apply numbering to lists automatically.** Select this check box if you want OneNote to automatically create a numbered list when you start typing a paragraph with a number followed by a period, a closing parenthesis, or a tab. Some people find this helpful; others don't.

> **NOTE:** The **Apply numbering to lists automatically** feature and **Apply bullets to lists automatically** feature are like the **AutoFormat As You Type** features in the other programs, discussed in Chapter 3: "Working with Text."

- **Apply bullets to lists automatically.** Select this check box if you want OneNote to automatically create a bulleted list when you start a paragraph with a bullet-like character (such as an asterisk) followed by a tab. If you don't find this feature helpful, clear this check box.

- **Calculate mathematical expressions automatically.** Select this check box if you want to use OneNote's automatic calculation feature, also called "napkin math." You can simply type a sum such as **$218*365=** and press **Enter** to have OneNote calculate the formula and fill in the result. This feature is usually helpful.

- **Enable link creation by typing [[ ]] around a phrase.** Select this check box if you want to be able to create a link by typing two brackets before and after a word or phrase. If you type the name of an existing page, OneNote creates a link to it; if not, OneNote creates a new page in the current section and gives it the name you typed. Try this feature and see if you find it useful.

- **Automatically switch keyboard to match language of surrounding text.** Select this check box if you want OneNote to try to detect changes of language and automatically change the keyboard layout to match.

In the **Linked Notes** area, choose how to handle Linked Notes:

- **Allow creation of new Linked Notes.** Select this check box if you want to use Linked Notes—notes linked to the program next to which you're working in a docked OneNote window. For example, if you're developing a worksheet in Excel, you can keep notes in OneNote that are linked to the worksheet. Linked Notes are usually helpful.

- **Save document snippets and page thumbnail for better linking to the right place in the document.** Select this check box to save this additional information in each Linked Note. Saving this information is usually helpful.

- **Remove Links from Linked Notes.** Click this button if you want to remove the links from Linked Notes. You won't usually need to do this.

In the **Pen** area, choose how OneNote should respond to pen input:

- **Disable the scratch-out gesture while inking.** Select this check box to turn off the scratch-out gesture (for deleting an item) when you're using ink. This setting helps you to avoid deleting things by mistake and is usually helpful.

- **Use pen pressure sensitivity.** Select this check box if you want OneNote to register pen pressure as well as movements. This is useful when you're drawing, but you'll probably want to clear this check box when you're just using a pen for input.

- **Automatically switch between inking, selecting, typing, and panning.** Select this check box if you want OneNote to automatically switch among different types of pen input depending on what you're doing. This feature is intended to save time, but if you find it doesn't work satisfactorily with the way you use pen input, clear this check box.

In the **E-mail sent from OneNote** area, choose options for e-mail you send starting from OneNote:

- **Attach a copy of the original notes as a OneNote file.** Select this check box only if you want to include a OneNote file containing the original notes when you send an e-mail from OneNote. This feature is sometimes useful, but it's not what you'll usually want.

- **Attach embedded files to the e-mail message as separate files.** Select this check box to have OneNote include separate files of any embedded files that the OneNote notes contain. This is usually a good choice, as receiving separate files enables the recipient to work with the individual files.

> ▧ **Add the following signature to e-mail messages and Web pages created in OneNote.** Select this check box only if you want to add a specific signature to e-mail messages you've started from OneNote. If you do use this feature, customize the text rather than including Microsoft's marketing information.

The **Battery Options** area contains just one setting, the **Optimize for the following battery life** drop-down list. For a laptop, select the setting for the amount of battery life you want. The choices are **Maximum performance**, **Short**, **Medium**, **Long**, and **Maximum battery life**. OneNote reduces its demands by doing fewer background operations such as indexing, text recognition, and synchronization when running on battery life. For a desktop computer, you don't need to worry about this setting.

In the **Tags** area, choose settings for handling tags when creating a summary:

> ▧ **When using the Tags Summary task pane to create a summary page.** In this area, select the **Show original tagged notes as dimmed** area if you want original tagged notes to appear dimmed so that you can distinguish them from notes that weren't tagged. The alternative is to select the **Leave original tagged notes unchanged** option button to leave the notes as they were.

> ▧ **Show dimmed tagged notes in the Tags Summary task pane.** Select this check box to have OneNote display the dimmed tagged notes. Clear this check box to have OneNote suppress the dimmed tagged notes.

In the **Passwords** area, choose how to handle password-protected sections of your notebooks:

> ▧ **Lock password protected sections after I have not worked in them for the following amount of time.** Select this check box to have OneNote automatically lock password-protected sections after the length of time you specify in the drop-down list. This setting usually works well once you've chosen the length of time that suits you. Your choices range from **1 Minute** to **12 Hours** or **1 Day**; the default setting is 10 Minutes.

> ▧ **Lock password protected sections as soon as I navigate away from them.** Select this check box if you want OneNote to automatically lock password-protected sections the moment you leave them. This makes for tight security but is awkward if you often need to return to protected sections to make further changes.

> ▧ **Enable add-in programs to access password protected sections when they are unlocked.** Select this check box if you want to give OneNote add-ins access to the password-protected sections you've unlocked. This setting is normally helpful.

In the **Search** area, you can click the **Install Instant Search** button to download and install the Microsoft Windows Desktop Search component. This component adds instant search to OneNote.

In the **Text recognition in pictures** area, select the **Disable text recognition in pictures** check box if you don't want OneNote to try to recognize text in pictures so that you can search for it. Whether you should use text recognition in pictures depends on the types of pictures you store in your OneNote notebooks. If you include text-heavy diagrams, having OneNote recognize the text is usually helpful. But if you include mainly illustrative pictures, it's not worth having OneNote devote time and effort to trying to pick out the text in them.

In the Other area, you can choose your preferred measurement unit in the Measurement unit's drop-down list. Your choices are **Inches**, **Centimeters**, **Millimeters**, **Points**, and **Picas**. A point is 1/72 inch, and a pica is 12 points, or 1/6 inch.

Also in the **Other** area, you can select the **Show add-in user interface errors** check box if you want OneNote to display errors caused by add-ins. Normally, OneNote suppresses these errors, but you may want to see them if you're trying to troubleshoot problems with add-ins.

Recording Audio and Video into Your Notebooks

When you need to take multimedia notes, you can record audio and video straight into a notebook.

> **NOTE:** Before recording audio or video into a notebook, make sure you've chosen suitable quality settings in the **Audio & Video** pane of the **OneNote Options** dialog box, as discussed earlier in this chapter.

Recording Audio into a Notebook

To record audio into a notebook, start recording as shown in Figure 18–7.

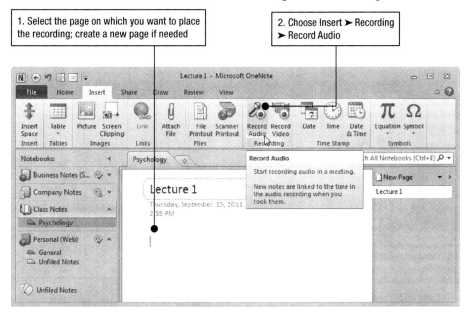

Figure 18–7. *You can quickly start recording audio into the current page by giving the **Insert ➤ Recording ➤ Record Audio** command.*

When you click the **Record Audio** button, OneNote does the following:

- Reveals the **Audio & Video** section of the Ribbon and displays the **Recording** tab.

- Creates a container for the audio recording.

- Starts recording the audio.

Figure 18–8 shows an audio recording taking place.

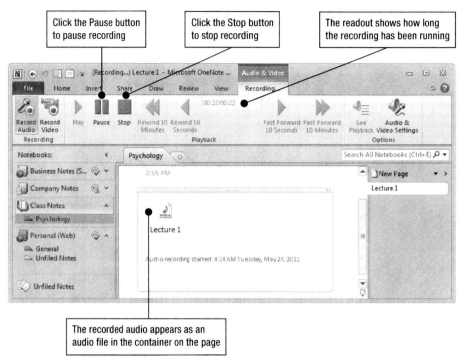

Click the Pause button to pause recording

Click the Stop button to stop recording

The readout shows how long the recording has been running

The recorded audio appears as an audio file in the container on the page

Figure 18–8. *OneNote displays the* **Recording** *tab on the* **Audio & Video** *section of the Ribbon when you start a recording. The readout under the* **View** *tab shows how long the recording has been running.*

> **TIP:** While the recording runs, you can continue working in OneNote as needed. OneNote automatically links the notes you take during the recording to the recording as it goes along, so that when you play back the recording, OneNote can automatically display the relevant section of your written notes, as long as it's on the same page. This is great for patching the holes in lecture notes after you were unable to keep up with written notes.

After you end recording by clicking the **Stop** button, OneNote displays the **Playback** tab of the **Audio & Video** section of the Ribbon (see Figure 18–9). This tab is similar to the Recording tab but has playback controls instead of recording controls.

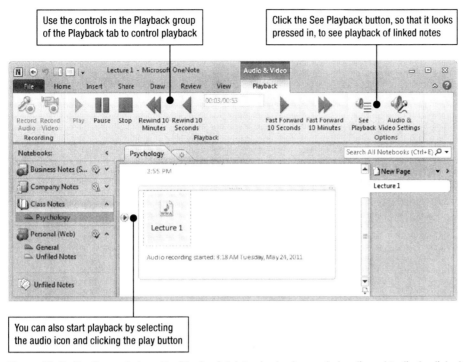

Use the controls in the Playback group of the Playback tab to control playback

Click the See Playback button, so that it looks pressed in, to see playback of linked notes

You can also start playback by selecting the audio icon and clicking the play button

Figure 18–9. *Use the controls on the* **Playback** *tab to play back recorded audio and to display linked notes.*

Recording Video into a Notebook

To record video into a notebook, click the page on which you want to place the video, and then work as shown in Figure 18–10.

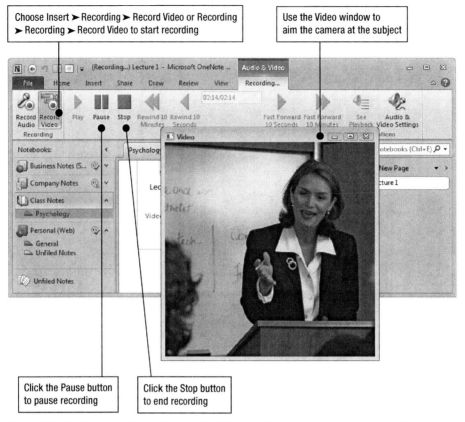

Choose Insert ➤ Recording ➤ Record Video or Recording ➤ Recording ➤ Record Video to start recording

Use the Video window to aim the camera at the subject

Click the Pause button to pause recording

Click the Stop button to end recording

Figure 18–10. *When recording video, use the **Video** window to make sure you're capturing your subject rather than the scenery.*

> **TIP:** You can minimize the **Video** window if you want to get it out of the way so that you can take notes, but don't close it—closing the window stops the recording.

To play back a video file, click it, and then click the **Play** button on the **Playback** tab of the Ribbon.

Exporting or Removing an Audio or Video File

To export an audio file or a video file, right-click the file in its container and choose **Save As** from the context menu. In the **Save As** dialog box, choose the folder in which to save the file and the filename to use, and then click the **Save** button.

If you no longer need an audio or video file, delete it by clicking it in its container, and then pressing **Delete**.

Searching for Words in Audio and Video Recordings

If you selected the **Enable searching audio and video recordings for words** check box in the **Audio & Video** pane in the **OneNote Options** dialog box, OneNote searches through the recordings when the program is idle and your PC is not busy with other tasks. Depending on how heavily you use your PC, it may be several hours or days before you can search for words in the recordings.

If you haven't turned on searching through audio and video, OneNote displays the **Audio Search** dialog box (see Figure 18–11) when you stop your first recording, to give you the chance to turn it on. Click the **Enable Audio Search** button if you want to turn audio search on; otherwise, click the **Keep Audio Search Disabled** button to leave it off.

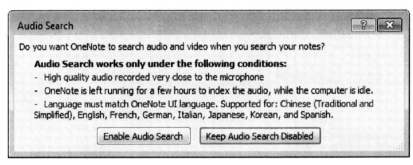

Figure 18–11. *When you stop your first recording, OneNote checks whether you want to enable audio search if it is currently disabled.*

Previewing and Printing Your Notebook Pages

Unlike the other Office programs, OneNote doesn't have a print preview feature integrated into Backstage. If you want to preview a document, you need to launch the separate **Preview** feature. As this feature has its own **Print** button for printing directly from it, you may well prefer this means of printing to printing without previewing the document.

Previewing a Notebook Page

To preview a notebook page, select the page and then choose **File ➤ Print ➤ Print Preview**. You can then work in the **Print Preview and Settings** dialog box, as shown in Figure 18–12.

1. Click to move from page to page

2. Choose what to print: Current Page, Page Group, or Current Section

3. Choose the paper size

4. Choose whether to scale the content to the paper width—often a good idea

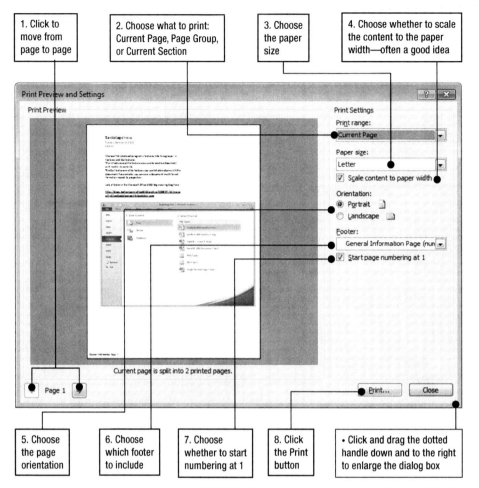

5. Choose the page orientation

6. Choose which footer to include

7. Choose whether to start numbering at 1

8. Click the Print button

• Click and drag the dotted handle down and to the right to enlarge the dialog box

Figure 18–12. *Use the **Print Preview and Settings** dialog box to make sure your document is set up to print the way you want. Then click the **Print** button to display the **Print** dialog box.*

If you're ready to print the document, click the **Print** button to display the **Print** dialog box, and then choose settings as described in the next section, starting at step 4. If you want to return to the notebook to make changes before printing, click the **Close** button.

Printing Notebook Pages

To print without previewing, follow these steps:

1. Click the File tab to open Backstage view.

2. Click **Print** to display the Print place.

3. Click **Print** to display the **Print** dialog box.

4. Choose the printer you want to use.

5. Choose the number of copies to print.

6. Click the **Print** button to close the **Print** dialog box and start printing.

Using OneNote with the Other Office Programs

You can quickly share the notes you've taken with the other Office programs. For example, you can export a page or a notebook section to a Word document, or create an e-mail message in Outlook using the content of a notebook page.

Exporting a Page or Section to a Word Document

When you need to get information into Word, you can export either a page or a section of a OneNote notebook to a Word document. You can put the Word document anywhere in your PC's file system.

To export part of a notebook to a Word document, select the page or section, and then work as shown in Figure 18–13.

> **NOTE:** If you choose to export the whole notebook, you can save it as a PDF, a OneNote package, or an XPS file.

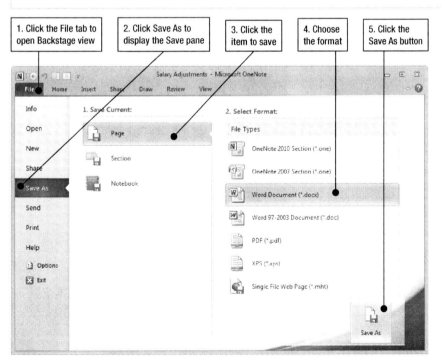

Figure 18–13. *Use the* **Save As** *screen to save a page or a section of a OneNote workbook to a Word document.*

When you click the **Save A**s button, OneNote displays the **Save As** dialog box. Choose the folder and type the name for the Word document as usual, and then click the Save button to save the document.

You can then open the document and work with it in Word, or share it with another Word user.

Exporting Data to an Excel Worksheet or a PowerPoint Presentation

OneNote doesn't provide any special commands for exporting data from a notebook to an Excel worksheet or a PowerPoint presentation, but you can use copy and paste or drag and drop freely. For example:

- **Excel.** Right-click anywhere in a table in a OneNote page, choose **Table ➤ Select Table** from the context menu, and then copy the selection. Switch to Excel, right-click the upper-left cell of the destination area, and then give one of the **Paste** commands (for example, **Match Destination**). Excel puts the contents of each table cell in a separate cell.

- **PowerPoint.** Select a picture in OneNote and drag it to the slide on which you want to place it.

Creating an Outlook Message from OneNote

If you have information in OneNote that you want to send in an e-mail message using Outlook, you can quickly create a message like this:

1. In OneNote, open the page that you want to send.

2. Choose **Share ➤ E-mail ➤ E-mail Page**. OneNote makes Outlook create a new message containing the page.

3. If you want to remove any part of the page, select it, and then press **Delete** to delete it.

4. Address the message, adjust the subject line as needed, and then click the **Send** button to send it.

> **NOTE:** When you need to send just a single item from a OneNote page, you may find it easier to select the item, copy it, start a message in Outlook manually, and then paste the item into the message.

When Creating an Outlook Task from OneNote

When you need to create a task in Outlook from a note in OneNote, work as shown in Figure 18–14.

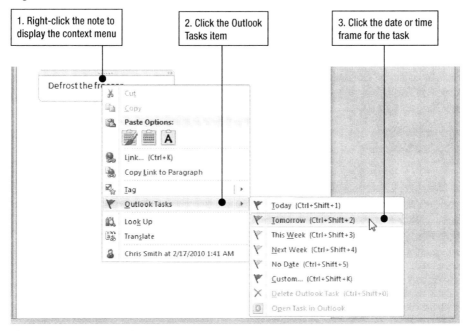

Figure 18–14. *You can quickly create a task in Outlook from a note in OneNote.*

If you choose **Custom**, Outlook displays the task in a window so that you can choose the date; otherwise, OneNote simply adds the task to Outlook, linking it back to the note. OneNote adds a flag icon to the note so that you can see a task is attached to it.

You can also use the keyboard shortcuts shown in Table 18–1 to quickly create tasks in Outlook.

Table 18–1. *Keyboard Shortcuts in Outlook*

Create a Task	Keyboard Shortcut
Today	Ctrl+Shift+1
Tomorrow	Ctrl+Shift+2
This Week	Ctrl+Shift+3
Next Week	Ctrl+Shift+4
No Date	Ctrl+Shift+5
Custom Date	Ctrl+Shift+K

> **NOTE:** After creating a task from OneNote, you can choose the **Delete Outlook Task** from the **Outlook Tasks** submenu on the context menu to delete an Outlook task directly from OneNote. You can also choose **Open Task in Outlook** to open the task so that you can work with it.

Retrieving Material from the Notebook Recycle Bin

When you delete material from a notebook, OneNote doesn't get rid of the material in the same way that the other programs do. Instead, OneNote places deleted material in the Notebook Recycle Bin.

Material stays in the Notebook Recycle Bin for 60 days unless you remove it sooner. After 60 days, OneNote deletes the material, and it's gone for good (unless you have backups of it).

To open the Notebook Recycle Bin (see Figure 18–15), right-click the notebook's name in the navigation bar and choose **Notebook Recycle Bin** from the context menu. You can also choose **Share ➤ History ➤ Notebook Recycle Bin**, clicking the upper part of the **Notebook Recycle Bin** button in the **History** group (the lower part of the button displays a drop-down list).

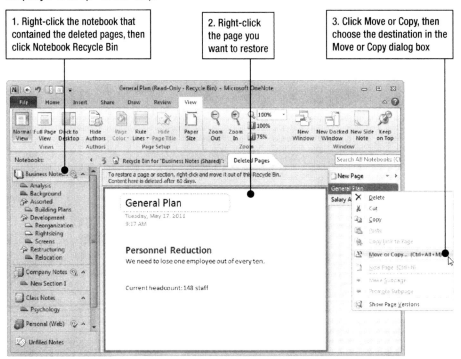

Figure 18–15. *When you need to retrieve material you've deleted, open the Notebook Recycle Bin, and then use the **Move or Copy** command to put the page back in a notebook.*

TIP: When you need to reduce the amount of space a notebook is taking up, empty **the Notebook Recycle Bin**. Choose **Share ➤ History ➤ Notebook Recycle Bin ➤ Empty Recycle Bin**, and then click the **Yes** button in the confirmation dialog box that OneNote displays.

To leave the Notebook Recycle Bin, click a notebook in the Navigation bar.

Summary

In this chapter, you learned how to set options to make OneNote behave the way you prefer, how to record audio and video into your notebooks, and how to print from OneNote. You also know how to export notes from OneNote to the other Office programs easily.

This is the end of our coverage of OneNote. In the next part of the book, I'll show you how to create compelling presentations with PowerPoint.

In this chapter, you learned how to use OneNote with Word, Excel, PowerPoint, and Outlook.

Part **VII**

Chapter 19

Starting a Presentation

In this chapter, I'll show you how to start building a presentation in PowerPoint.

First, you create the presentation file. PowerPoint gives you a wide range of choices, from colorful design templates called themes to sample templates with canned content that can give your presentation a kick start. You can change the look, colors, or fonts, and you can also customize the slide size and orientation as needed.

Next, you add slides to the presentation or customize the sample slides it contains. A PowerPoint presentation consists of a series of slides that you normally play from start to finish. Each slide can contain any of a wide variety of different types of content, from text titles and bullet points to charts, diagrams, and even movies. You'll learn how to add straightforward content in this chapter and how to add more entertaining content types in the next two chapters.

When you've created slides, you can rearrange them as needed, or delete slides you don't need. I'll show you how to use PowerPoint's four views to work efficiently on a presentation, how to develop the outline of a presentation quickly, and how to organize a presentation's slides into different sections for convenience.

Creating a Presentation

When you launch PowerPoint, it creates a new blank presentation, just as Word creates a blank document and Excel creates a blank workbook. You can use this presentation, but you're usually better off starting a new presentation based on a template.

To create a presentation, use the **New** pane in Backstage view, as shown in Figure 19–1.

TIP: PowerPoint offers so many templates that the **Recent templates** category can be a real timesaver when you need to create a presentation similar to one you've created before. If the previous presentation wasn't based on a template, use the **New from existing** command instead to create a new presentation based on the previous one.

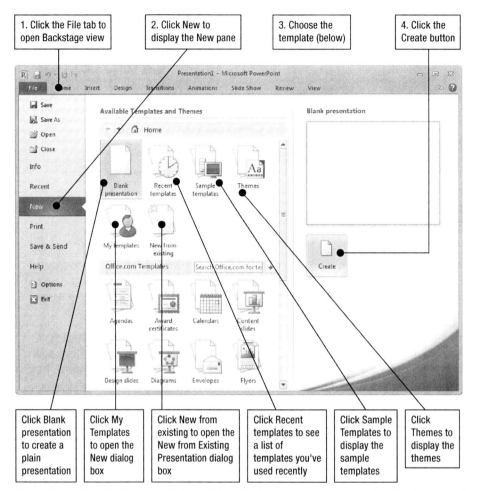

1. Click the File tab to open Backstage view

2. Click New to display the New pane

3. Choose the template (below)

4. Click the Create button

Click Blank presentation to create a plain presentation

Click My Templates to open the New dialog box

Click New from existing to open the New from Existing Presentation dialog box

Click Recent templates to see a list of templates you've used recently

Click Sample Templates to display the sample templates

Click Themes to display the themes

Figure 19–1. *From the **New** pane in PowerPoint's Backstage view, you can create a blank presentation or a presentation based on a template, a theme, or on an existing presentation.*

For example, if you click the **Themes** button in the **New** pane, you see the available themes, as shown in Figure 19–2. A *theme* is an overall look for a presentation, including a slide background design, a set of colors, a set of fonts, and a set of visual effects for graphical objects such as arrows. You can browse through the themes, click the one you want, and then click the **Create** button.

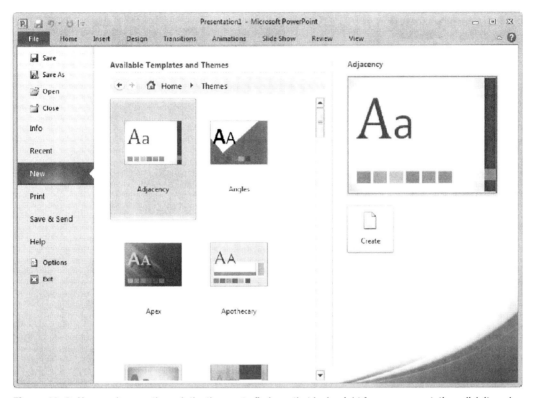

Figure 19–2. *You can browse through the themes to find one that looks right for your presentation, click it, and then click the **Create** button to create the presentation.*

> **NOTE:** A presentation template includes sample contents that you can use as the basis of your presentation. A presentation theme is a coordinated look for the slides in a presentation but does not contain sample contents.

Changing the Presentation's Theme, Colors, Fonts, and Effects

When you create a presentation based on a theme, the presentation receives the theme's look. When you create a presentation based on a template, the presentation receives the look of the theme used for the template. In either case, you can change the way the presentation looks by applying a different theme to it, as shown in Figure 19–3.

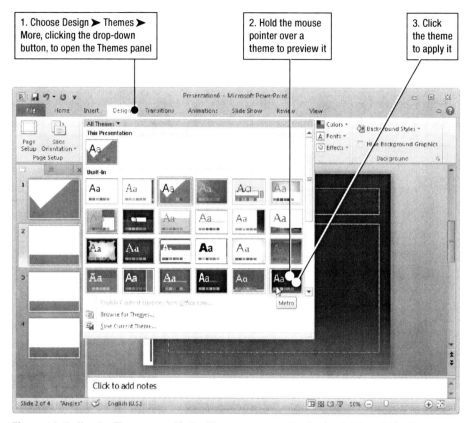

Figure 19–3. *Use the **Themes** panel in the **Themes** group on the **Design** tab to quickly change your presentation's theme. For smaller changes within the theme, use the **Colors** panel, the **Fonts** panel, or the **Effects** panel.*

After applying the theme you want, you can make changes within it:

- *Change the colors.* Choose **Design ➤ Themes ➤ Colors**, and then click the color set you want to use.

- *Fonts.* Choose **Design ➤ Themes ➤ Fonts**, and then click the fonts set.

- *Effects.* Choose **Design ➤ Themes ➤ Effects**, and then click the effects set.

Changing the Slide Size or Orientation

For some presentations, you may also need to change the size or orientation of the slides. Most PowerPoint templates start you off with slides sized for displaying on a regular-format screen in a landscape (wider than high) orientation, which is what you'll most often need. But if you need to create widescreen slides, slides sized for printing on paper, or slides in a portrait orientation, you'll need to change the setup.

> **TIP:** If you just need to change the slide orientation, choose **Design ➤ Page Setup ➤ Slide Orientation**, and then select **Landscape** or **Portrait**.

To change the size or orientation, choose **Design ➤ Page Setup ➤ Page Setup**, and then work in the **Page Setup** dialog box as shown in Figure 19–4.

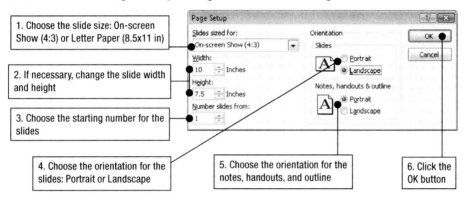

1. Choose the slide size: On-screen Show (4:3) or Letter Paper (8.5x11 in)

2. If necessary, change the slide width and height

3. Choose the starting number for the slides

4. Choose the orientation for the slides: Portrait or Landscape

5. Choose the orientation for the notes, handouts, and outline

6. Click the OK button

Figure 19–4. *Use the **Page Setup** dialog box to change slide size or orientation. You can also switch the notes, handouts, and outline from portrait orientation to landscape if necessary, although usually you will lay these items out for printing on paper, where portrait orientation is often the best choice.*

> **TIP:** In the **Page Setup** dialog box, you'll normally want to leave the **Number slides from** setting at 1. But when you're creating a presentation that you will run immediately after another presentation, you can set whichever number is needed to continue the numbering in the previous presentation.

Navigating the PowerPoint Window

When you first open a presentation, PowerPoint usually displays it in Normal view. In this view, the PowerPoint window contains three panes: the **Navigation** pane, the **Slide** pane, and the **Notes** pane. Figure 19–5 explains these three panes and the other main elements of the PowerPoint interface.

> **TIP:** You can resize the **Slide** pane, **Navigation** pane, and **Notes** pane by dragging the borders that separate them. For example, you may want to widen the **Slides** pane to make the thumbnail pictures larger so that you can identify the slides more easily.

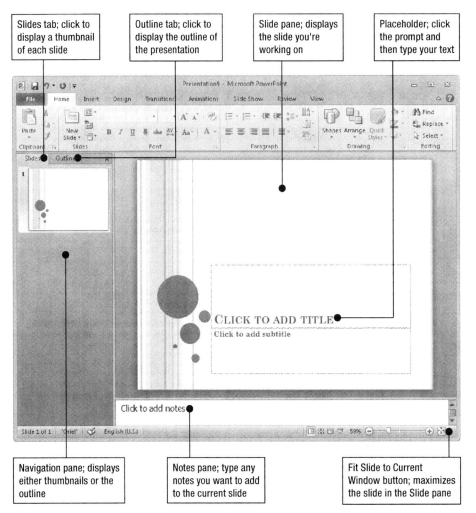

Figure 19–5. *In Normal view, the **Navigation** pane appears on the left and the **Notes** pane at the bottom of the window, leaving the **Slide** pane taking up most of the space.*

TIP: If you want more room to work on your slide, close the **Navigation** pane by clicking its **Close** button (the ✕ button) or by dragging its right border all the way to the left side of the window. The **Navigation** pane closes, but the border remains visible. To display the **Navigation** pane again, drag the border back to the right. Similarly, you can hide the **Notes** pane by dragging its border down to the bottom of the window and reveal it again by dragging the border back up.

Adding, Deleting, and Rearranging Slides

When building your presentation, you will likely need to add slides to it (depending on the theme or template you started with). When editing your presentation, you may need to delete slides or arrange them into a different order.

Adding a Slide

To add a new slide, work as shown in Figure 19–6.

THREE QUICK WAYS OF ADDING SLIDES TO A PRESENTATION

You can also add slides quickly by duplicating them, by inserting them from an outline, or by copying them from another presentation:

- *Duplicate slides from the presentation.* To create new slides based on ones already in your presentation, select those slides, and then choose **Home ➤ Slides ➤ New Slide ➤ Duplicate Selected Slides**. You can quickly duplicate a slide by right-clicking it in the **Slides** pane or in Slide Sorter view and then clicking **Duplicate slide** on the context menu. Alternatively, select the slide, and then press **Ctrl+D**.

- *Insert slides from an outline in a document.* If you've created an outline in a Word document, a rich text format (RTF) document, or a text document, you can create slides based on it. Choose **Home ➤ Slides ➤ New Slide ➤ Slides from Outline** to open the Insert **Outline** dialog box, click the document that contains the outline, and then click the **Insert** button.

- *Copy slides from another presentation.* You can insert slides from another presentation by choosing **Home ➤ Slides ➤ New Slide ➤ Reuse Slides**, using the controls in the **Reuse Slides** pane that opens to choose the source of the slides, and then picking the slides to insert.

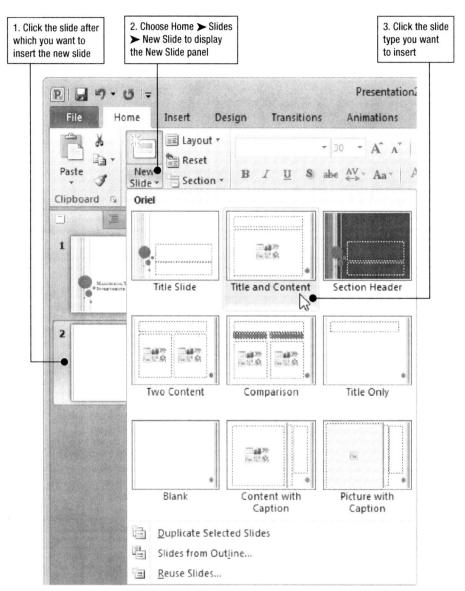

Figure 19–6. *Insert a slide by opening the **New Slide** panel on the **Home** tab of the Ribbon and clicking the slide layout you want.*

Deleting a Slide

You can delete a slide in the **Slides** pane or the **Outline** pane in Normal view or in the main pane in Slide Sorter view (which you'll meet shortly). Use either of these techniques:

- *Context menu.* Right-click the slide, and then click **Delete Slide** on the context menu.

- *Delete key.* Click the slide, and then press **Delete**.

NOTE: You can also delete a slide by selecting it in the **Outline** pane in Normal view or in the main pane in Slide Sorter view, and then giving a **Cut** command—for example, choosing **Home ➤ Clipboard ➤ Cut**. Cutting the slide removes it from the presentation and places it on the Clipboard, from which you can paste it somewhere else if you want to.

Rearranging Slides

In Normal view, you can rearrange slides quickly in the **Navigation** pane. In either the **Slides** pane or the **Outline** pane, drag a slide up or down as needed (see Figure 19–7).

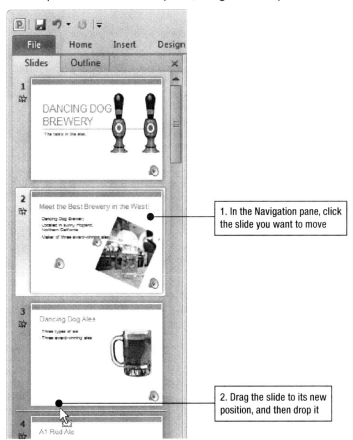

Figure 19–7. *Drag a slide up or down in the **Slides** pane (shown here) or the **Outline** pane to move it to a different position in the presentation.*

The **Navigation** pane is good for moving a slide (or a few slides) a short distance. When you need to move more slides, or you need to move a slide a long way, it's usually easier to work in Slide Sorter view, as explained in Figure 19–8.

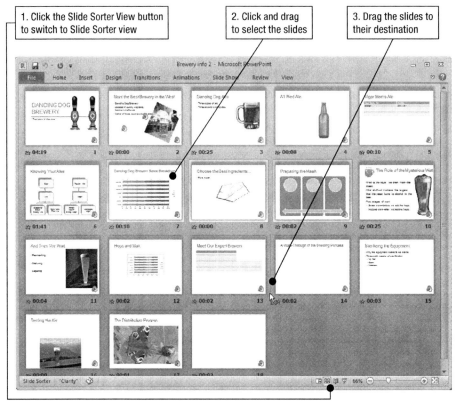

Figure 19–8. *When you need to move multiple slides, switch to Slide Sorter view, select the slides, and then drag them to their destination.*

Add Content to a Slide

Once you've created a slide, you can add content to it. As you'll see in the next couple of chapters, PowerPoint slides can contain a wide variety of types of content, from text to audio and movies.

Most slides come with one or more placeholders for adding content, such as the title placeholder (where it says **"Click to add title"**) and a subtitle placeholder (**"Click to add subtitle"**) in Figure 19–5. Other slides contain placeholders for other types of content, such as tables or graphics.

To add text to a text placeholder, and resize the placeholder if necessary, work as shown in Figure 19–9.

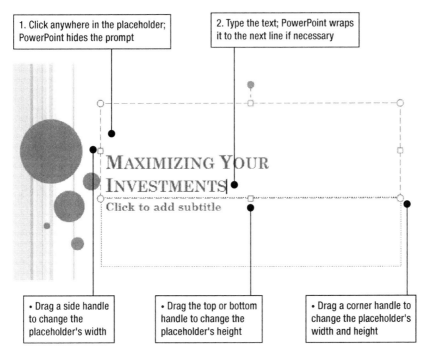

Figure 19–9. *You can quickly add text to a placeholder by clicking in it and then typing or pasting the text.*

NOTE: To reset a slide's placeholders to their defaults, choose Home ➤ Slides ➤ Reset. To change the layout of a slide, click the slide in the Navigation pane, choose Home ➤ Slides ➤ Layout, and then click the Layout you want on the Layout panel.

To move a placeholder, click to select it. Then move the mouse pointer over a border so that the pointer changes to a four-headed arrow. Then drag the placeholder to where you want it to appear.

Using Views to Work on Your Presentation

So far in this chapter, you've seen PowerPoint in Normal view, plus a brief visit to Slide Sorter view in the previous section. Altogether, PowerPoint provides four different views to help you work swiftly and easily on your presentations: Normal view, Slide Sorter view, Reading view, and Slide Show view.

The easiest way to switch views is to click the appropriate view button in the View Shortcuts group at the right end of the status bar (see Figure 19–10).

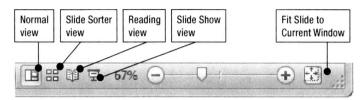

Figure 19–10. *Click a view button in the View Shortcuts group on the status bar to change views quickly. In Normal view, click the Fit Slide to Current Window button to make the slide fit neatly in the window.*

You can also switch views by clicking the View tab of the Ribbon, going to the Presentation Views group (see Figure 19–11), and then clicking the Normal button, the Slide Sorter button, or the Reading View button. To start a slide show from the current slide, choose Slide Show ➤ Start Slide Show ➤ From Current Slide.

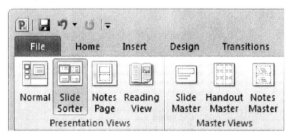

Figure 19–11. *You can switch to **Normal** view, **Slide Sorter** view, or **Reading** view by using the buttons in the **Presentation Views** group on the **View** tab of the Ribbon.*

Creating Your Slides in Normal View

As you've seen already, Normal view is the view you use to create your slides and work on their contents. Normal view is the view in which PowerPoint usually opens, and you can give yourself more space to work on a slide by hiding the **Navigation** pane and the **Notes** area.

Rearranging Your Slides in Slide Sorter View

When you need to rearrange your slides into a different order, use Slide Sorter view (shown in Figure 19–9, earlier in this chapter). By displaying each slide as a thumbnail picture in a grid layout, Slide Sorter view lets you easily see where each slide appears in relation to the other slides.

> **NOTE:** To select a slide in Slide Sorter view, click it. To select a range of slides, click the first slide, and then **Shift-click** the last slide; alternatively, click before the first slide and drag over the slides you want. To select slides that aren't next to each other, click the first slide, and then **Ctrl+click** each of the others.

Apart from rearranging slides, Slide Sorter view is also useful for finding the slide you need to edit. Once you've located the slide, double-click it to open the slide in Normal view for editing.

Viewing a Presentation in Reading View

When you want to read a presentation rather than edit it, use Reading view (see Figure 19–12). This view hides the Ribbon and most of the PowerPoint interface and displays a single slide as large as it will go in the window.

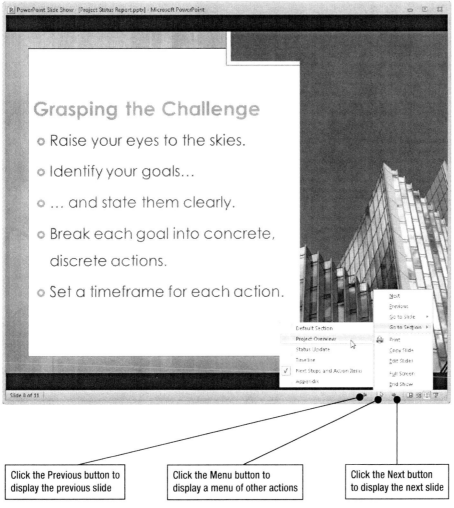

Click the Previous button to display the previous slide

Click the Menu button to display a menu of other actions

Click the Next button to display the next slide

Figure 19–12. *Reading view hides almost all of the PowerPoint interface to give you more space to read the slides. Click the **Menu** button to reach a menu of commands.*

TIP: The advantage of Reading view over Slide Show view is that Reading view displays the slide in a window that you can resize as needed rather than taking up the full screen. This is useful when you need to take notes on a presentation or put together additions for it.

Running a Presentation in Slide Show View

PowerPoint's fourth view, Slide Show view, is the view you use when running a presentation. Slide Show view displays the current slide full screen on the screen you're using for the presentation. If you have a secondary screen (for example, because you've connected your PC to a projector), you can choose to show your presenter notes on it to help you with the presentation.

You'll see Slide Show view in action in Chapter 22: "Delivering a Presentation in Person or Online," which covers running slide shows.

Opening Extra Windows to See Different Parts of the Presentation

Often, it's useful to be able to see two or more different slides at once, so that you can compare them or copy or move data from one to the other. You can do this by opening a new window on the presentation and then displaying the other slide in that window.

To open a new window, choose **View ➤ Window ➤ New Window**. You can then switch to another window either by clicking it (if it's visible) or by choosing **View ➤ Switch Windows** and then clicking the window you want.

To close an extra window, click its **Close** button (the ✕ button).

Creating the Outline of a Presentation

When you need to develop the outline of a presentation quickly, work in the **Outline** tab of the **Navigation** pane in Normal view. With the presentation open, click the **Outline** tab in the **Navigation** pane to display the outline.

The **Outline** tab (see Figure 19–13) shows the presentation as a sequence of collapsible slides. Each slide appears as a heading with its ordinal number and the text from the title placeholder (if there is any), together with text content, such as bullets.

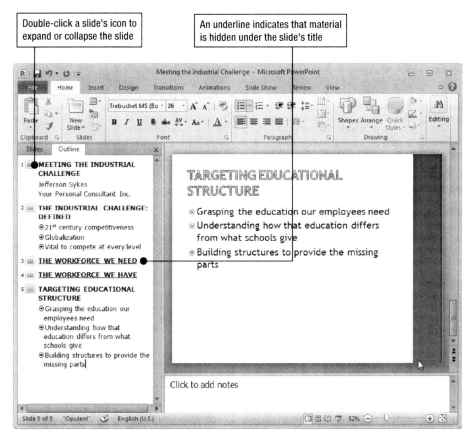

Figure 19–13. *You can quickly enter slide titles and text contents by using the* **Outline** *tab in the* **Navigation** *pane. As you work, PowerPoint enters the information with basic formating on the slide itself; you can fix it later.*

You can quickly build your presentation's outline on the **Outline** tab by using these techniques:

- *Create a new slide.* Press **Enter** at the end of a paragraph to start a new paragraph, and then press **Shift+Tab** one or more times (as needed) to promote the paragraph to a slide title.

- *Create a bulleted paragraph.* After typing a slide title, press **Enter** to start a new paragraph. Then press **Tab** to demote the paragraph to the first level. You can demote a paragraph to a lower level if needed (for example, to create second-level bulleted paragraphs).

- *Move a paragraph or selection up or down.* Click at the left end of a paragraph to select it, or click and drag to select multiple paragraphs. You can then drag the paragraph or selection up or down the outline to where you want it to be. For example, you can drag a bulleted paragraph from one slide to another.

- *Paste in text.* You can paste text into the **Outline** tab, and then promote or demote its paragraphs to the levels at which you want them to appear. So if you have text in a Word document or a OneNote notebook, you can paste it into the outline instead of retyping it.

Organizing Your Slides into Sections

When you add many slides to a presentation, it can become difficult to navigate through the presentation. To simplify matters, you can divide the presentation up into two or more sections. Each section can contain however many slides you need it to, and you can expand or collapse sections as needed.

To add a section, work as shown in Figure 19–14.

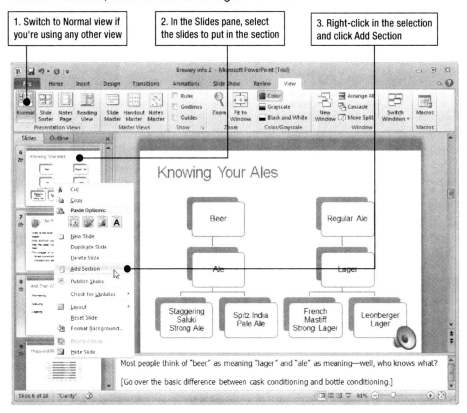

Figure 19–14. *To create a section, select the slides for the section in the **Slides** pane in the **Navigation** pane, and then give the **Add Section** command from the context menu. You cannot add a section from the **Outline** pane.*

Doing this creates a new section called Untitled Section. The name appears on the section bar across the top of the section in the **Slides** pane.

To rename the section, work as shown in Figure 19–15.

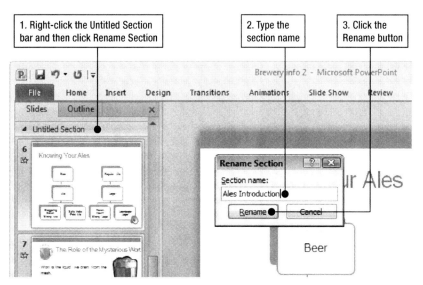

Figure 19–15. *Use the **Rename Section** dialog box to give the section a name.*

Once you've created your sections, you can manipulate them easily like this:

▪ *Expand or collapse a section.* Double-click its section heading. You can also click the triangle to the left of the section name.

▪ *Expand or collapse all sections.* Right-click a section heading, and then click **Expand All** or **Collapse All** on the context menu.

▪ *Move a section up or down the list of sections.* Either click the section heading and drag it to where you want the section, or right-click the section heading, and then click **Move Section Up** or **Move Section Down** on the context menu (see Figure 19–16).

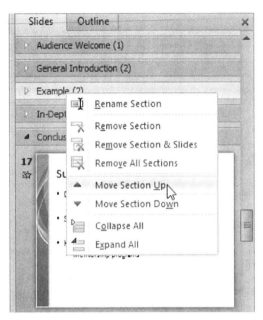

Figure 19–16. *After creating sections, you can use the context menu to rename them, rearrange them, or remove them.*

- *Remove a section but leave its slides.* Right-click the section heading, and then click **Remove Section** on the context menu. To remove all sections, click **Remove All Sections**.

- *Remove a section and its slides.* Right-click the section heading, and then click **Remove Section & Slides** on the context menu.

Summary

In this chapter, you learned how to start building a presentation in PowerPoint. We started by creating the presentation file from a template or theme and then customizing it as needed. We then covered how to add slides, put text on them, and rearrange or delete them. After that, we looked at using PowerPoint's four views efficiently and discussed how to create the outline of a presentation. Finally, you learned how to organize a presentation's slides into different sections for convenience.

In the next chapter, I'll show you how to create compelling slides for your presentation by introducing their components one at a time and adding animations as needed.

Chapter 20

Building Effective Slides for Your Presentation

In the previous chapter, you learned how to create a presentation and how to add slides to it. In this chapter, I'll show you how to create slides that convey your meaning clearly and powerfully to your audience.

Before you start creating your slides, it helps to plan which slides the presentation will contain and develop an idea of each slide's content. We'll touch on this first, and then examine which of PowerPoint's built-in slide layouts suits which type of content. Any time none of the built-in layouts is suitable, you can create your own custom layouts.

After that, you'll learn how to add text to your slides and format it to look good. Finally, we'll go through how to add tables, charts, SmartArt graphics, and hyperlinks to your slides, using the techniques you learned in Part 1 of the book and extra techniques specific to PowerPoint.

Planning the Slides in Your Presentation

As you plan your presentation, and as you create the slides for it, keep the audience in mind. Whether you'll deliver the presentation in person, via an Internet broadcast, or by distributing digital copies of the presentation, you'll want to make sure that your slides are easy to read, are attractive to look at, and convey your meaning clearly.

For most presentations, follow these general rules when planning and creating your slides:

- *Keep your text concise.* You can load any amount of text onto a PowerPoint slides—but you, your audience, and your message will benefit from concision. Try to keep between three and eight bullets per slide. Keep each bullet short so that the slide is easy to read.

- *Keep your slides uncluttered.* If you need to choose between fitting in more information on an existing slide and adding a slide, it's usually best to add the extra slide. Don't feel you need to fill up each slide— it's fine to leave blank space on a slide. You're not short-changing the audience by making the presentation easy for them to assimilate.

- *Illustrate your points.* When you make a point, drive it home by illustrating it with an example that catches your audience's imagination. For example, don't just say you've increased sales to 100,000 gallons of paint. Instead, spell out that this is enough to paint all the runways at Chicago O'Hare Airport twice over—first green for St. Patrick's Day, and then yellow to frighten away the Canadian geese.

- *Use your strongest material—not all your material.* Many presentations suffer from too much detail. Usually, you can convince your audience that you have the facts and figures with just a couple of well chosen examples; you don't need to numb them with a complete run-down of the data.

> **TIP:** You may find it useful to keep extra material in reserve by using hidden slides. See Chapter 20 for instructions on doing this.

- *Provide visual interest—but don't overdo it.* Even with the liveliest presenter, a text-only presentation can be dull as ditchwater. As you'll see in this chapter and the next, PowerPoint makes it easy to add tables, charts, graphics, videos, and animations to your slides, so it's a good idea to include visually interesting and relevant information to give the audience something to look at. You can also use audio in your presentations.

Choosing Slide Layouts to Suit the Contents

To get your material onto a slide, and to make it look good, you need to choose a suitable layout. You can either use one of PowerPoint's built-in slide layouts or create a custom layout of your own.

Using PowerPoint's Built-in Slide Layouts

For most presentations, the best way to start creating slides is by using the nine standard layouts that you can insert from the **Home ➤ Slides ➤ New Slide** drop-down panel (see Figure 20–1). Table 20–1 explains the layouts and what they're best for.

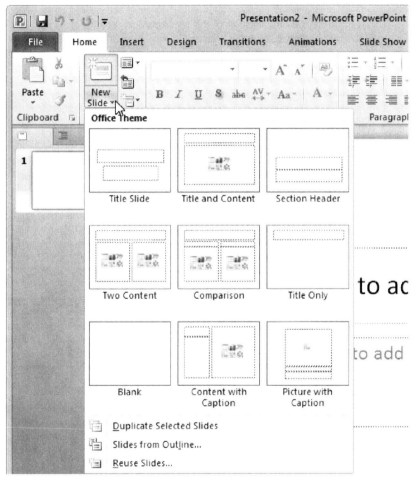

Figure 20–1. *From the **New Slide** drop-down panel on the **Home** tab of the Ribbon, you can quickly insert a new slide using any of PowerPoint's nine built-in layouts.*

Table 20–1. *PowerPoint's Standard Slide Layouts and When to Use Them*

Slide Layout	When to Use It
Title Slide	To start your presentation or to introduce a new section of it.
Title and Content	To display a content item, such as a table, chart, or picture.
Section Header	To start a new section of the presentation. In most designs, this slide has a substantially different look from other slides to suggest the change.
Two Content	To display two content items—for example, two pictures or two tables—but without necessarily comparing them to each other.
Comparison	To display two content items (for example, two charts) and compare them to each other. The Comparison layout is like the Two Content layout, but has an extra text box above each item that you can use to highlight the differences.
Title Only	To add only a title to a slide, or to have a title followed by content you place manually.
Blank	To create your own layout, or if you need to insert a blank slide as a pause in your presentation.
Content with Caption	To display a content item (such as a table or chart) over most of the slide, with a title and explanatory text alongside it.
Picture with Caption	To display a picture over most of the slide, with a title and explanatory text alongside it. The Picture with Caption layout is almost identical to the Content with Caption layout, but is customized for pictures rather than other content types.

You can change a slide's layout at any time by clicking the slide, choosing **Home ➤ Slides ➤ Layout**, and then clicking the layout you want. And you can snap a slide's layout back to its default settings by choosing **Home ➤ Slides ➤ Reset**. When you need just minor tweaks, you can drag the placeholders to different locations or adjust their sizes as needed.

> **NOTE:** If you change a slide's layout by applying a layout that has fewer placeholders than the number of containers you're currently using, PowerPoint leaves the extra containers on the slide so that you can deal with them.

Creating Custom Slide Layouts

When none of PowerPoint's built-in slide layouts is suitable for the slide you want to create, you can create a custom slide layout in either of two ways:

- Apply the closest slide layout to what you want, and then customize it. For example, you can delete a placeholder by clicking it and then pressing **Delete**, or copy a placeholder by clicking it and then **Ctrl**+dragging to where you want the copy.

- Start with a blank slide layout, and then add the objects you need.

> **TIP:** After you create a custom slide layout, you can reuse it by selecting the slide and choosing **Home ➤ Slides ➤ New Slide ➤ Duplicate Selected Slides**.

Formatting Text on Your Slides

You can format text on PowerPoint slides quickly by using the controls in the **Font** group and the **Paragraph** group on the **Home** tab of the Ribbon. You'll be familiar with most of these controls from the first part of the book, but Figure 20–2 points out several key controls and PowerPoint-specific controls that you'll use in this section.

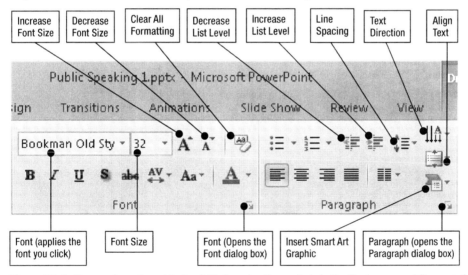

Figure 20–2. *You can format most text quickly by using the controls in the* **Font** *group and* **Paragraph** *group on the* **Home** *tab of the Ribbon.*

TIP: To change the formatting of all the text in a placeholder, select the placeholder itself. To change the formatting of just some of the text, select that text.

Changing the Font, Font Size, and Alignment

To make the text look the way you want, you'll often need to change the font, font size, or alignment.

Figure 20–3 shows you the easiest way to change the font—by using the **Font** drop-down list in the **Font** group on the **Home** tab of the Ribbon. Similarly, you can change the font size either quickly by clicking the **Increase Font Size** button or the **Decrease Font Size** button in the **Font** group on the **Home** tab, or by opening the Font Size drop-down list and clicking the size you want. And you can change the alignment quickly by clicking the **Align Text Left** button, **Center** button, **Align Text Right** button, or **Justify** button in the **Paragraph** group, also on the **Home** tab.

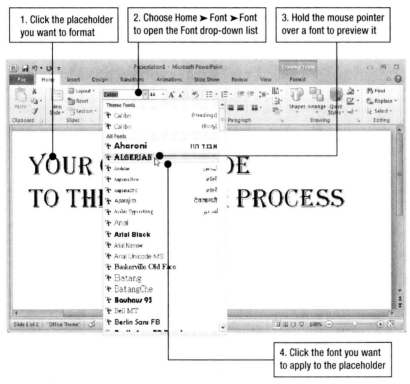

Figure 20–3. *The easiest way to change the font is to select the placeholder and use the **Font** drop-down list on the **Home** tab of the Ribbon. You can hold the mouse pointer over a font to preview it before applying it.*

> **NOTE:** When you need to reach the full range of font options, open the Font dialog box by choosing **Home ➤ Font ➤ Font**, clicking the little button with the arrow pointing down and to the right at the right end of the **Font** bar.

KEEPING YOUR TEXT EASY TO READ

Like most Windows programs, PowerPoint gives you such a wide variety of fonts that it's easy to make poor choices.

When choosing fonts and font sizes for your slides, put clarity foremost. If the audience can't read the text on a slide because you've chosen an unsuitable font or too small a font size, your words of wisdom will be wasted. After creating a slide, make sure that even the smallest text on it will be easy to read from the back of the audience—and by someone with less than perfect eyesight.

Often, it's tempting to use a striking or "design-y" font to look different. But in most cases, the best fonts are those that people barely notice because they're simply easy to read, such as the Calibri font used in the Office design. Unless you're presenting to designers, you're usually better off with straightforward fonts rather than fonts that set out to catch the eye.

Changing the Indentation and Line Spacing of Text

To make text look right on a slide, you'll often need to adjust its indentation and line spacing. For example, you may need to increase the indentation of some paragraphs to make clear that they are subordinate to the paragraphs above them. And if you create a slide with only a few short, easy-to-read bullet points, you may need to increase the line spacing so that the bullets occupy the whole slide rather than clumping at the top of it.

Changing the Indentation

To change the indentation quickly, click in the paragraph, and then click the **Decrease Indent** button or the **Increase Indent** button in the **Paragraph** group of the **Home** tab of the Ribbon.

To change the indentation a precise amount, click in the paragraph, then click the **Paragraph** button (the little button at the lower-right corner of the **Paragraph** group) to display the **Paragraph** dialog box (see Figure 20–4). Set the indentation using the controls in the **Indentation** area, and then click the **OK** button.

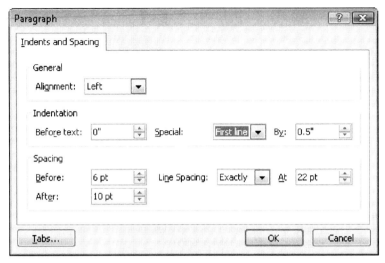

Figure 20–4. *Use the* **Paragraph** *dialog box when you need close control over the indentation and spacing of paragraphs.*

Changing the Line Spacing

To change line spacing quickly, click in the paragraph, click the **Line Spacing** button in the **Paragraph** group, and then make your choice from the panel: 1.0, 1.5, 2.0, 2.5, or 3.0. If you need to change line spacing for multiple paragraphs, select them first. To change line spacing for all the paragraphs in the container, click the container.

For greater control, click the **Line Spacing Options** item on the panel to display the **Paragraph** dialog box, and then use the controls in the **Spacing** area.

Rotating Text

For some slides, you may want to rotate text either in two dimensions or in three dimensions.

To rotate text simply, work as shown in Figure 20–5.

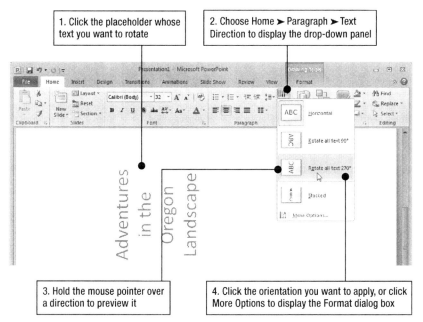

Figure 20–5. *Use the **Text Direction** drop-down panel panel in the **Paragraph** group on the **Home** tab of the Ribbon to turn text sideways or make it run in a stack down a slide. For other types of rotation, click the **More Options** button to open the **Text Effects** dialog box.*

For more complex rotations, click the **More Options** item at the bottom of the **Text Direction** drop-down panel to display the **Format Text Effects** dialog box. You can then work as shown in Figure 20–6.

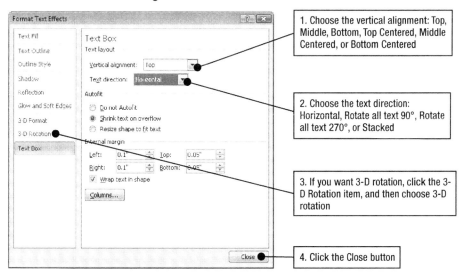

Figure 20–6. *Use the **Text Box** category in the **Format Text Effects** dialog box to specify the vertical alignment and text direction for the text in a placeholder. Click the **3-D Rotation** item in the left pane if you need to add 3-D rotation.*

If you need to add 3-D rotation to the placeholder, click the **3-D Rotation** item in the left pane, and then work as shown in Figure 20–7.

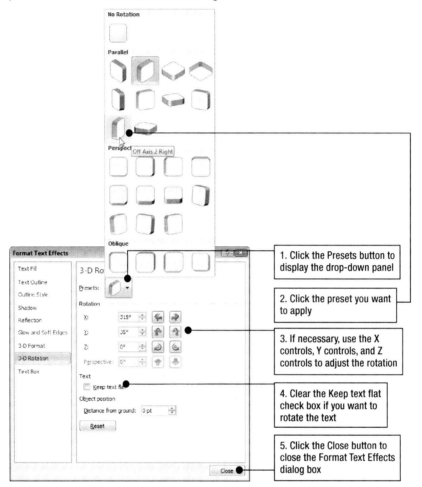

1. Click the Presets button to display the drop-down panel

2. Click the preset you want to apply

3. If necessary, use the X controls, Y controls, and Z controls to adjust the rotation

4. Clear the Keep text flat check box if you want to rotate the text

5. Click the Close button to close the Format Text Effects dialog box

Figure 20–7. *Use the **3-D Rotation** category in the **Format Text Effects** dialog box when you need to rotate text in three dimensions.*

TIP: If you need to display text upside down, put it in its own container, and then rotate the container so that it is upside down.

Using Bulleted Lists Effectively in Your Slides

Many PowerPoint slides use bulleted lists, as they can be a great way of presenting your content clearly. For bulleted lists to work effectively, you must keep the number of bullets on each slide under control, make the hierarchy plain, and ensure that the text is easy to read.

Creating a Bulleted List

Usually, PowerPoint creates bulleted lists for you. When you start typing text in a placeholder that has bullets applied, PowerPoint automatically gives the paragraph a bullet. When you press **Enter** to create the next paragraph, PowerPoint displays a bullet for that paragraph too.

To change the level of list paragraphs, work as shown in Figure 20–8.

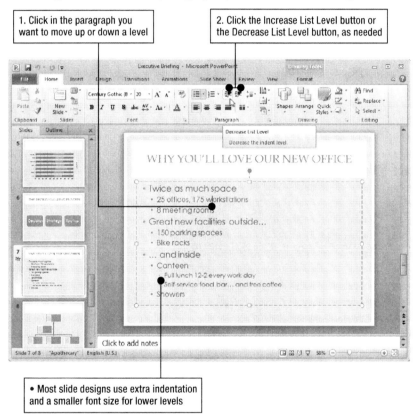

Figure 20–8. *You can quickly create different levels of bullets by using the **Increase List Level** button and the **Decrease List Level** button in the **Paragraph** group on the **Home** tab of the Ribbon.*

TIP: You can also move a paragraph down to the next lower level of bulleted list by positioning the insertion point at its beginning and pressing **Tab**. Similarly, you can move the paragraph up a level by positioning the insertion point at its beginning and pressing **Shift+Tab**.

Making Sure Your Bulleted Lists Are Readable

The fonts and font sizes PowerPoint uses for text depend on the slide design. Many bulleted slides start off in a small enough font size to enable you to type five or six bullets of two lines each. So if you have fewer bullets on a slide, or if each is less than a single line, you can increase to font size to make the words easy to read.

When you start a sub-bulleted list, PowerPoint reduces the font size. This makes the hierarchy of the bullet points clear, but it can easily make the text too small to read. You may need to increase the font size of the sub-bullets as well to keep them readable. The extra indentation and different bullets will still indicate the hierarchy.

> **CAUTION:** PowerPoint lets you create many levels of sub-bullets—just keep pressing **Tab** at the start of a line or clicking the **Increase List Level** button to go to the next level. But if you go past two levels of bullets, that should raise a red flag to indicate that your slide is becoming too complex. You can see this happening toward the bottom of the slide in Figure 20–8. If some content is that far subordinate, either cut it, or break the material up onto several slides.

Livening Up Your Slides with Custom Bullets

To give your slides an individual look, you can change the bullet characters they use. PowerPoint provides a wide range of bullet characters, but you can also create your own. To do so, click the text placeholder in which you want to use the bullets, choose **Home ➤ Paragraph ➤ Bullets ➤ Bullets and Numbering**, and then work as shown in Figure 20–9.

> **NOTE:** To apply custom bullets only to a particular paragraph rather than to a container, select that paragraph before applying the bullets.

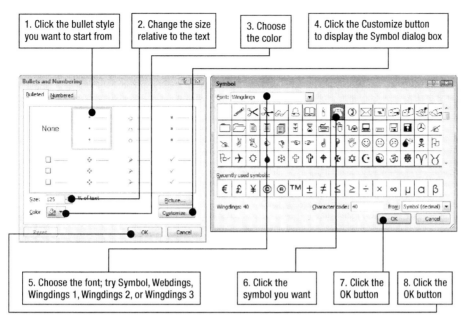

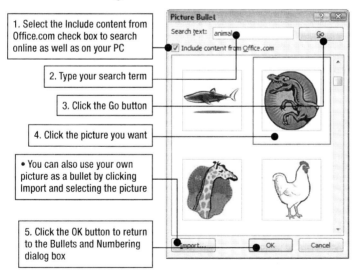

Figure 20–9. *Use the **Bulleted** tab of the **Bullets and Numbering** dialog box to set up custom bullets for a list To change the symbol, click the **Customize** button, and then select a suitable font and symbol in the **Symbol** dialog box.*

You can also use a picture as a bullet by clicking the **Picture** button on the **Bulleted** tab of the **Bullets and Numbering** dialog box and then working in the **Picture Bullet** dialog box as shown in Figure 20–10.

Figure 20–10. *Use the **Picture Bullet** dialog box to find a picture bullet that meets your needs or to import a picture you can use as a bullet.*

Adding Tables, SmartArt, Charts, and Hyperlinks to Slides

PowerPoint makes it as easy as possible to add graphical content to your slides. Click the appropriate icon in a content placeholder (see Figure 20–11), and then use the dialog box or pane that PowerPoint opens to identify the item you want.

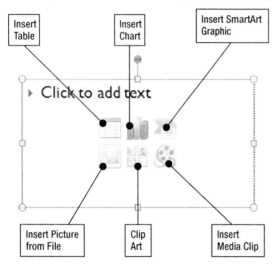

Figure 20–11. *Click one of the six icons in a placeholder to start adding that type of content, or click the* **Click to add text** *prompt to start typing text.*

Adding Tables to Slides

You can create a new table on a slide, but you can often save time by importing a table from Word or OneNote or by creating it from cells in an Excel worksheet.

Creating a Table from Scratch

You can create a table from scratch either by inserting it using the technique you learned in the section "Inserting a Table" in Chapter 3: "Working with Text" or by drawing it using the technique explained in the section "Drawing a Table," also in Chapter 3.

After creating a table, you can quickly change its design by choosing **Table Tools ➤ Design ➤ Table Styles**, and then clicking the style you want to apply.

TIP: When you create a table from scratch, you will often find that it occupies only part of the available area on the slide and that the font size is too small to read. You can enlarge the table by dragging the lower-right handle down and to the right, or by dragging the bottom handle downward. You can adjust the fonts easily by selecting the table's container (or selecting parts of the table, as needed) and then using the controls in the **Font** group on the **Home** tab of the Ribbon. For example, click the **Increase Font Size** button a few times to make the fonts easier to read.

Importing a Table from Word or OneNote

If the table you need to use in PowerPoint is already in a Word document or a OneNote notebook, you can quickly reuse it in PowerPoint—but you may need to reformat it.

To import a table from Word or OneNote, follow these general steps:

1. In Word or OneNote, open the document or notebook that contains the table.

2. Right-click in the table, and then choose **Table ➤ Select Table** to select all of it.

3. Right-click in the selected table, and then click **Copy** to copy the table to the Clipboard.

4. Switch to PowerPoint. For example, click the **PowerPoint** button on the taskbar.

5. Right-click the slide on which you want to place the table, and then click the appropriate icon in the **Paste Options** section. As you move the mouse pointer over the icons, PowerPoint shows a preview of how the table will appear, as you can see in Figure 20–12.

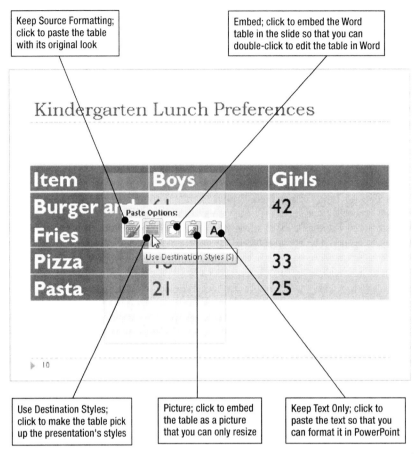

Figure 20–12. *Use the **Paste Options** icons on the context menu to control how PowerPoint inserts a table you've copied from Word or OneNote. When you move the mouse pointer over the **Paste Options**, PowerPoint makes the menu translucent so that you can see the table preview better.*

6. Format the table as needed in PowerPoint. For example:

   a. Resize the table's container to the size you need.

   b. Choose **Table Tools ➤ Design ➤ Table Styles**, and then click the style you want to apply.

   c. Still on the **Design** tab, choose options in the **Table Style Options** group. For instance, select the **Total Row** check box if the table needs different formatting for a total row at the bottom.

   d. If necessary, use the controls in the **Font** group on the **Home** tab of the Ribbon to change the font sizes. For instance, you may need to increase the font sizes to make the table readable in PowerPoint, because tables in Word and OneNote typically use smaller font sizes.

Creating a Table from Excel Worksheet Data

When a PowerPoint slide needs a table of data that you have in an Excel worksheet, copy the data across and paste it into a table. Follow these steps:

1. In Excel, select the cells you want.

2. Still in Excel, right-click the selection, and then click Copy on the context menu to copy the cells to the Clipboard.

3. Switch to PowerPoint. For example, click the PowerPoint button on the taskbar.

4. Click the slide on which you want to place the data.

5. Insert a table in one of these ways:

   - If the slide has a placeholder displaying the content icons, click the **Insert Table** icon. Either set the exact number of rows and columns your Excel selection will occupy, or insert a smaller table—for example, 2 columns by 2 rows. Click the **OK** button. PowerPoint automatically adjusts the number of columns and rows to fit the data you pasted.

   - Choose **Insert ➤ Tables ➤ Table**, and then click the table size. Again, either set the right number of rows and columns or (easier) create a smaller table.

6. Click to place the insertion point in the first cell in the table.

7. Right-click to display the context menu, and then click the appropriate button in the Paste Options area, shown in Figure 20–13.

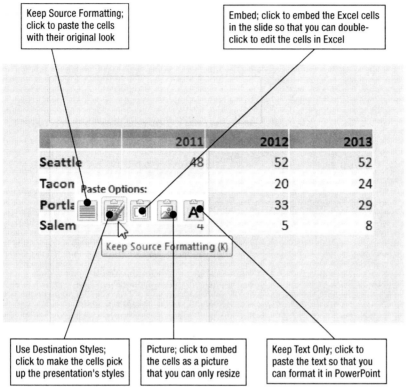

Figure 20–13. *Use the Paste Options icons on the context menu to control how PowerPoint inserts cells you've copied from Excel. When you move the mouse pointer into the Paste Options area, PowerPoint makes the rest of the context menu see-through so that you can see the preview clearly.*

8. Format the table as needed in PowerPoint. For example:

   ▓ Resize the table's container to occupy more of the slide.

   ▓ Choose **Table Tools ➤ Design ➤ Table Styles,** and then click the style you want to apply.

   ▓ On the **Design** tab of the Ribbon, choose options in the **Table Style Options** group.

   ▓ Open the **Home** tab of the Ribbon and use the controls in the **Font** group on the **Home** tab of the Ribbon to change the font sizes as needed. For most slides, you'll need to increase the font size considerably to make the data easy to read in PowerPoint.

Adding SmartArt Graphics to Slides

You can add a SmartArt graphic to a slide by using the techniques explained the section "Creating Illustrations by Inserting SmartArt Graphics" in Chapter 4: "Working with Graphics."

You can start adding a SmartArt graphic in either of these ways:

- If the slide has a standard placeholder, click the **Insert SmartArt Graphic** icon.

- If not, choose **Insert** ➤ **Illustrations** ➤ **SmartArt**.

After adding a S**martArt** graphic, you can animate it as discussed in the section "Animating a SmartArt Graphic" in Chapter 21: "Giving a Presentation Life and Impact."

Adding Charts to Slides

A chart can be a great way of presenting complex or detailed information in a way that's instantly clear on a slide. PowerPoint lets you add a chart to a slide in two ways:

- *Create a chart on an embedded worksheet.* Click the **Insert Chart** icon in a content placeholder, and then choose the chart type in the **Insert Chart** dialog box. PowerPoint then opens Excel for you and creates a new workbook so that you can enter the chart data and create the chart. The workbook is embedded in the PowerPoint presentation, so it becomes part of that file.

- *Copy a chart from an Excel workbook.* Create your chart in Excel using the techniques described in Chapter 14: "Creating Charts to Present Your Data." Then copy the finished chart and paste it into your PowerPoint slide. You can choose whether to embed the chart's workbook in the PowerPoint presentation, to link the chart back to its source data in the Excel workbook, or just to insert it as a picture.

Here's how to choose when to create a new embedded workbook, embed an existing workbook, link back to a workbook, or insert a picture:

- *Create a new embedded workbook.* Do this when you don't yet have the data for the chart in Excel and you need to keep the chart's data with the PowerPoint presentation—for example, you'll send the presentation to someone else who will need to work on the chart data too.

- *Embed an existing workbook.* Do this when you have the data for the chart, or the chart itself in a workbook in Excel and you need to keep the chart's data available in the PowerPoint presentation.

- *Link back to a workbook.* Do this when you want to be able to change the chart or its source data in Excel and then automatically bring those changes into PowerPoint by updating the chart. Linking requires the workbook to stay in the same relative place in the computer's file system to the presentation so that the presentation can find the updated data. Moving the presentation to a different computer breaks the link.

- ***Insert a picture.*** Do this when you don't need to keep the connection between the chart and its source data and you will not need to edit the chart in the presentation.

Creating a Chart in a New Embedded Workbook

To create a chart on a worksheet in a new workbook embedded in your PowerPoint presentation, follow these steps:

1. On the slide where you want to create the chart, click the Insert Chart icon in a placeholder or choose Insert ➤ Illustrations ➤ Chart. PowerPoint displays the Insert Chart dialog box (see Figure 20–14).

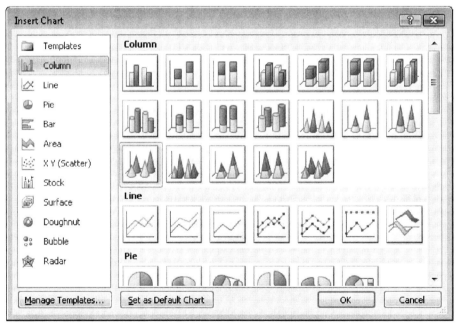

Figure 20–14. *In the **Insert Chart** dialog box, click the chart type you want to create, and then click the **OK** button. PowerPoint then launches Excel so that you can create the chart.*

2. In the left column, click the category of chart you want to create—for example, Column.

3. In the main area, click the chart type.

4. Click the OK button. PowerPoint creates a chart of that type on the slide and launches Excel, which creates a new workbook, embeds it in the presentation, and gives it a name such as Chart in Microsoft PowerPoint.

5. Change the chart range and the sample data (see Figure 20–15) to the data your chart needs. PowerPoint automatically updates the chart to match the data in the Excel worksheet.

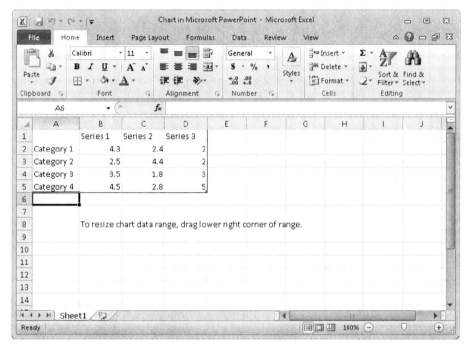

Figure 20–15. *Excel enters sample data on the first worksheet in the embedded workbook. Change this data to create your chart.*

6. When you have finished changing the data, click the Close button (the × button) to close Excel.

7. Use the controls in the Chart Tools section of the Ribbon to format the chart the way you want it. Figure 20–16 shows a slide containing a chart with formatting underway.

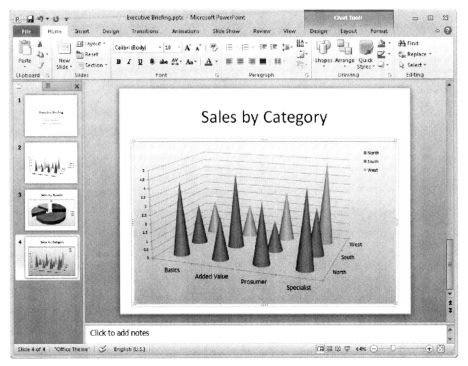

Figure 20–16. *Use the controls on the **Chart Tools** section of the Ribbon to format a chart you've created using an embedded workbook.*

8. When you save the presentation, PowerPoint makes Excel save the changes to the chart and its data source. You don't need to save them yourself.

> **NOTE:** To edit the data on your chart again, choose **Chart Tools ➤ Design ➤ Data ➤ Edit Data**. PowerPoint opens Excel, which displays the embedded worksheet.

Pasting a Chart from Excel into a PowerPoint Slide

If you have a chart already created in Excel, or if you have a workbook containing the data from which you will create the chart, you can paste the chart into PowerPoint. Follow these general steps:

1. Create the chart using the techniques explained in Chapter 14: "Creating Charts to Present Your Data."

2. Click the chart to select it.

3. Right-click in the selection, and then click Copy on the context menu to copy the chart to the Clipboard.

4. Switch to PowerPoint by clicking the PowerPoint window.

5. Select the slide on which you want to insert the chart.

6. Right-click the slide, and then click the appropriate button in the Paste Options section of the context menu (see Figure 20–17).

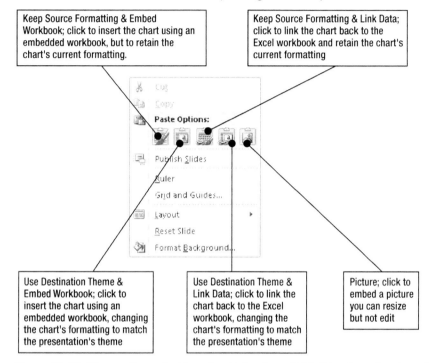

Figure 20–17. *When pasting a chart from Excel into a PowerPoint slide, choose how to paste the chart by clicking the appropriate icon in the **Paste Options** section of the context menu.*

7. Use the controls in the Chart Tools section of the Ribbon to format the chart the way you want it.

8. Save the presentation.

To edit the data in either an embedded or linked chart, choose **Chart Tools ➤ Design ➤ Data ➤ Edit Data**.

To update a linked chart, choose **Chart Tools ➤ Design ➤ Data ➤ Refresh Data**.

Adding Hyperlinks to Slides

You can add hyperlinks to PowerPoint slides by choosing **Insert ➤ Links ➤ Hyperlink**, and then using the **Insert Hyperlink** dialog box as explained in the section "Inserting Hyperlinks in Your Documents" in Chapter 3: "Working with Text."

In your presentations, you'll typically use hyperlinks on slides for two purposes:

- *Link to other slides in the presentation.* To make it easy for the presenter or someone browsing the presentation to move to another slide, add a hyperlink to it. Follow these steps:

  1. In the Link to box on the left of the Insert Hyperlink dialog box, click the **Place in This Document** button.

  2. In the **Select a place in this document** box (see Figure 20–18), click the slide you want to display.

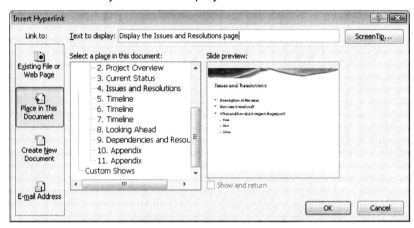

Figure 20–18. *From the **Insert Hyperlink** dialog box, you can quickly create a link to another slide in the same presentation. This is a great way of enabling the viewer to navigate quickly about the presentation.*

  3. Edit the text in the **Text to display** box as needed.

  4. If you need to provide additional information about the hyperlink, click the **ScreenTip** button, type the ScreenTip text in the **Set Hyperlink ScreenTip** dialog box, and then click the **OK** button.

  5. Click the **OK** button to close the **Insert Hyperlink** dialog box and insert the hyperlink.

- *Link to a web site.* You'll often want to include a link to your web site. With a live presentation, you can click the hyperlink to display your web site directly from a slide. In a presentation you share with others, they can click the hyperlink to go to the web site or to find out how to contact you.

Summary

In this chapter, you learned how to plan the slides for your presentation and create them using either PowerPoint's built-in slide layouts or custom layouts you create yourself. You now know how to add text to your slides and format it to look good. And you know how to add tables, charts, SmartArt graphics, and hyperlinks to your slides.

In the next chapter, I'll show you how to bring your slides to life by using animations and transitions.

Chapter 21

Giving a Presentation Life and Impact

By this point, you've almost certainly created a presentation, added slides to it, and populated those slides with compelling content. What you need to do now is add life and impact to the presentation so that it will wow your audience.

In this chapter, we'll look at how to add graphics, movies (from your PC or straight from YouTube), sounds, animations, and transitions to your presentation. You'll also learn to hide slides so that they don't appear during a slide show, allowing you to keep them in reserve.

Adding Pictures to a Presentation

You can give many slides greater impact by adding one or more pictures—graphics or photos—to illustrate or offset their text content.

You can easily add a picture in these ways:

- ▪ *Use a content placeholder.* If the slide includes a content placeholder, click the **Insert Picture from File** icon to display the **Insert Picture** dialog box. Click the picture file, and then click the Insert button.

- ▪ *Use the **Insert ➤ Images ➤ Picture** command.* If the slide doesn't have a content placeholder, choose **Insert ➤ Images ➤ Picture** to open the **Insert Picture** dialog box. Click the picture file, and then click the Insert button.

> **NOTE:** To add a clip art picture, click the **Clip Art** icon in a content placeholder or choose **Insert** > **Images** > **Clip Art**. In the **Clip Art** pane, locate the picture you want (for example, search for it by typing a term in the **Search for** box and clicking the **Go** button), and then click the picture to insert it.

Once you've added a graphic or photo to a slide, you can work with it using the techniques discussed in Chapter 4: "Working with Graphics." For example, you can resize the picture, drag it to a different position (see Figure 21–1), change its contrast and brightness by using the **Picture Tools** > **Format** > **Adjust** > **Corrections** command, or apply an artistic effect to it by using the **Picture Tools** > **Format** > **Adjust** > **Artistic Effects** command.

Figure 21–1. *After inserting a graphic or photo, resize it and reposition it as needed. You may also want to correct the picture's contrast and brightness or apply an artistic effect.*

Adding Movies and Sounds to a Presentation

Pictures can make a big difference to a presentation, but you may also want to add movies and sounds.

You can even add a video from YouTube to a slide, as long as the computer playing back the presentation will have an Internet connection.

Adding a Movie to a Slide

When you need to play a movie during a presentation, add the movie file to a slide. You can then not only format the movie file so that it appears the way you want but also adjust the way it plays back—for example, playing only part of it or making it loop.

Placing the Movie on the Slide

The first step is to place the movie on the slide, either by inserting the whole file or by linking it. Click the slide, and then open the **Insert Video** dialog box in one of these ways:

- ▨ If the slide has a content placeholder, click the **Insert Media Clip** icon.

- ▨ Otherwise, choose **Insert ➤ Media ➤ Video** (clicking the top part of the **Video** button).

Once you've opened the **Insert Video** dialog box, work as shown in Figure 21–2 to insert the movie.

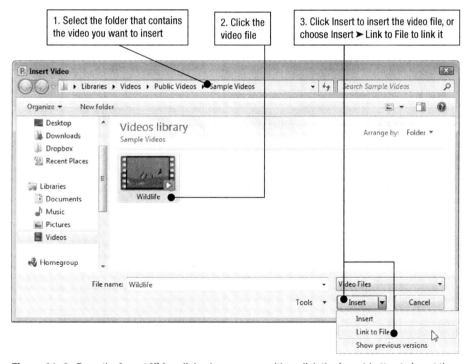

Figure 21–2. *From the **Insert Video** dialog box, you can either click the **Insert** button to insert the movie in the slide or choose **Insert ➤ Link** to link the file to the presentation.*

NOTE: Insert the movie file when you want to include it in the presentation so that you can move the presentation to another computer. Inserting the file increases the presentation's file size by the size of the movie file and a bit more. Link the movie file when you're sure you will give the presentation from this computer and you want to keep the presentation's file size down.

Changing the Movie File's Appearance

After inserting the movie file, you can adjust its appearance as needed by using the controls in the **Video Tools ➤ Format** tab of the Ribbon. Follow these steps:

1. If the **Format** tab isn't displayed, click it to display its contents (see Figure 21–3).

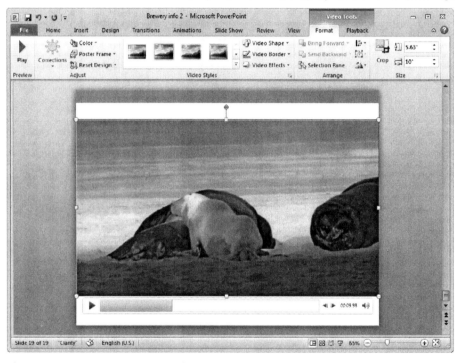

Figure 21–3. *Use the controls on the **Video Tools ➤ Format** tab of the Ribbon to make the video look the way you want—for example, by applying a video style or cropping the video.*

2. Click the video file to select it, and then drag it into the right position on the slide.

3. Resize the video frame as needed by dragging a corner handle. You can also crop it by choosing **Video Tools ➤ Format ➤ Size ➤ Crop**, and then dragging a corner handle with the cropping pointer.

4. To correct the video's brightness and contrast, choose **Video Tools ➤ Format ➤ Adjust ➤ Corrections**, and then click the balance of brightness and contrast you want.

5. To change the video's color balance, choose **Video Tools ➤ Format ➤ Adjust ➤ Color**, and then click the color option you want. For example, you can apply a sepia hue or make the video black and white.

6. To choose which frame of the video appears on the slide until you play the video, use the playback controls to move the video to the frame you want. Then pause the video and choose **Video Tools ➤ Format ➤ Adjust ➤ Poster Frame ➤ Current Frame**.

> **TIP:** Instead of using a frame from the video, you can use a still picture as the poster frame for the video. Choose **Video Tools ➤ Format ➤ Adjust ➤ Poster Frame ➤ Image File**, select the picture in the **Insert Picture** dialog box, and then click the **Insert** button.

7. To put the video in a frame, choose **Video Tools ➤ Format ➤ Video Styles ➤ More** (clicking the drop-down button on the **Video Styles** box), and then click the frame you want.

8. To change the video shape, choose **Video Tools ➤ Format ➤ Video Styles ➤ Video Shape**, and then click the shape you want.

9. To customize the border for the shape, choose **Video Tools ➤ Format ➤ Video Styles ➤ Video Border**, and then click the type of border you want.

10. To apply a video effect, choose **Video Tools ➤ Format ➤ Video Styles ➤ Video Effects**. On the menu that appears, click the type of effect, and then choose the specific effect from the panel that opens. For example, you can display a shadow under the video, or you can perform a 3-D rotation on it.

Choosing Playback Options for the Video

Click the **Playback** tab in the **Video Tools** section of the Ribbon to display its controls (see Figure 21–4). Then follow these steps to choose playback options:

1. To place a bookmark marking a point in the video that you want to be able to access easily, move the Playhead across the clip's control bar until you reach the right point in the video, then choose Video Tools ➤ Playback ➤ Bookmarks ➤ Add Bookmark. The bookmark appears as a dot that you can click.

> **NOTE:** You can remove a bookmark by clicking it and then choosing **Video Tools ➤ Playback ➤ Bookmarks ➤ Remove Bookmark**.

Figure 21–4. *On the **Video Tools** ➤ **Playback** tab of the Ribbon, you can set bookmarks, trim or fade the video, set the audio volume, and choose other options, such as looping.*

2. To trim the video so that only part of it plays, choose **Video Tools** ➤ **Playback** ➤ **Editing** ➤ **Trim Video**, and then work in the **Trim Video** dialog box as shown in Figure 21–5.

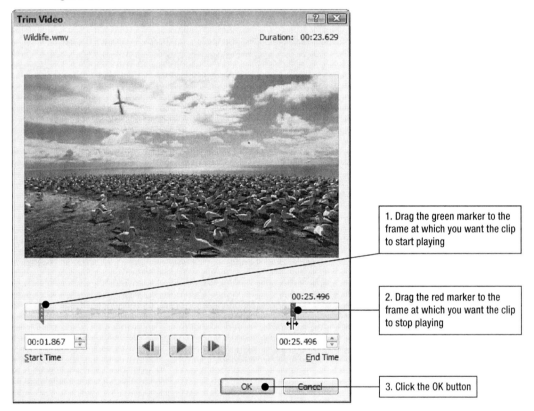

Figure 21–5. *In the **Trim Video** dialog box, move the start and end markers to set the part of the video clip you want to play.*

3. To fade the video in or out, set the timing in the **Fade In** box or **Fade Out** box in the **Fade Duration** area of the **Editing** group.

4. To choose how to start the video, choose **On Click** or **Automatically** in the **Start** drop-down list in the **Video Options** group.

5. To make the video play full screen rather than at the size you've given it on the slide, select the **Play Full Screen** check box in the **Video Options** group. This setting is useful for giving the video full impact without devoting a full slide to it.

6. To hide the video when it's not playing, select the **Hide While Not Playing** check box in the **Video Options** group.

7. If you want the video to keep playing in a loop until you stop it, select the **Loop until Stopped** check box in the **Video Options** group.

8. If you want the video to rewind to the beginning so that you can easily play it again, select the **Rewind after Playing** check box in the **Video Options** group. This setting can be useful for presentations you will run in a kiosk at a trade show.

9. If you want the video to rewind to the beginning so that you can easily play it again, select the **Rewind after Playing** check box in the **Video Options** group.

Adding a YouTube Video to a Slide

If you don't have a copy of the video you need to play, but it's available on YouTube, you can add it to a slide directly from YouTube.

> **NOTE:** For the YouTube video to play back correctly, the PC must be connected to the Internet. So if you'll give the presentation at a client's office, check that you'll have an Internet connection available.

To add a YouTube video to a presentation, find the video on YouTube, and then copy the embed code as shown in Figure 21–6.

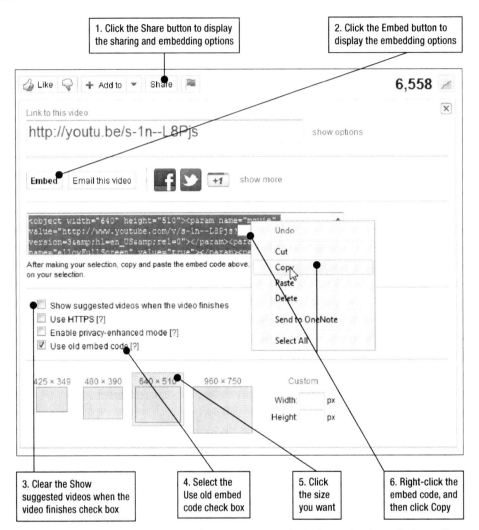

Figure 21–6. *After finding the YouTube video you want to embed, choose the size and other options, and then copy the embed code.*

After copying the embed code, add it to PowerPoint. Follow these steps:

1. Switch to PowerPoint. For example, click the PowerPoint window.

2. Select the slide you want to insert the video on. Create a new slide if necessary.

3. Choose **Insert ➤ Media ➤ Video ➤ Video from Web Site** to display the **Insert Video From Web Site** dialog box (see Figure 21–7).

Figure 21–7. *Right-click in the **Insert Video From Web Site** dialog box and click **Paste** to paste in the embed code for the YouTube video.*

4. Right-click in the box, and then click **Paste** on the context menu to paste in the embed code you copied.

5. Click the **Insert** button to insert the embed code.

6. Click the **Slide Show** button in the **View Shortcuts** group on the status bar to view the slide as it will appear in the slide show.

7. Select the video item on the slide, and then click the **Play** button. Make sure the video plays as you want it to.

8. Format the video item as discussed earlier in this chapter by using the controls on the **Video Tools ➤ Format** tab and the **Video Tools ➤ Playback** tab of the Ribbon.

Adding a Sound to a Slide

To add a sound to a slide, follow these steps:

1. Select the slide on which you want to add the audio.

2. Choose **Insert ➤ Media ➤ Audio ➤ Audio** (clicking the top part of the **Audio** button) to display the **Insert Audio** dialog box.

3. Navigate to the folder that contains the file you want to insert, and then click the file.

> **TIP:** You'll find various Windows sounds in the \Windows\Media\ folder on your PC's boot drive—usually drive C:.

4. Click the **Insert** button. PowerPoint inserts an audio icon (see Figure 21–8) representing the sound.

Figure 21–8. *PowerPoint inserts an audio item as a speaker icon. Click the icon to display controls for testing the audio and setting the volume.*

5. Select the icon by clicking it, and then drag it to where you want it to appear.

6. With the icon selected, use the pop-up controls to test the audio clip and set the volume at which you want it to play.

Adding Transitions to Slides

Instead of having a straightforward switchover from one slide to the next, you can set PowerPoint to play a *transition*—an effect that smoothes, animates, or dramatizes the change of slides.

You can set a different transition for each side if necessary. You specify the transition by selecting the slide and choosing the transition to play when the slide appears (as opposed to setting the transition for when PowerPoint changes the slide to the next).

NOTE: Depending on the presentation template or design you're using, some or all of the slides in the presentation may already have transitions applied to them. If so, you can leave them as they are, customize them, or replace them with other transitions.

PowerPoint's Three Types of Transitions

As you can see in Figure 21–9, PowerPoint's **Transitions** tab provides a wide range of transitions, broken up into three categories: **Subtle**, **Exciting**, and **Dynamic Content**.

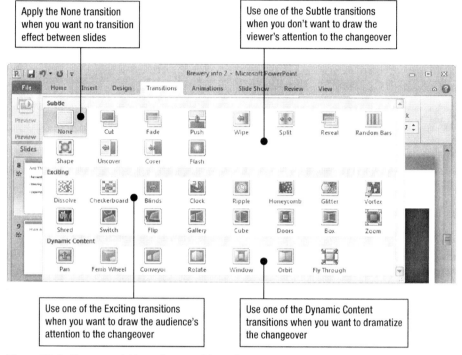

Figure 21–9. *You can quickly apply a transition using the **Transitions** drop-down panel on the **Transitions** tab of the Ribbon. Select the **None** transition option to remove an existing transition.*

> **TIP:** PowerPoint's transitions are easy and fun to apply, but don't go hog wild with them. In a typical presentation, not every slide benefits from a transition; and when you do use a transition, one of the **Subtle** transitions often gives the best effect. Keep the **Exciting** and **Dynamic Content** transitions for those rare occasions when you actually want to draw your audience's attention to the transition rather than to the content of the slides.

Applying a Transition to a Slide

To apply a transition, click the slide, click the **Transitions** tab, and then click the transition you want, either in the **Transition Scheme** box or on the **Transitions** drop-down panel.

You can preview a transition by holding the mouse pointer over it.

Choosing Options for a Transition

Some of the transitions have options, but others have none. If the transition you've chosen does have options, choose **Transitions ➤ Transition to This Slide ➤ Effect Options**, and then click the option on the drop-down panel. Figure 21–10 shows the options available for the **Ripple** transition.

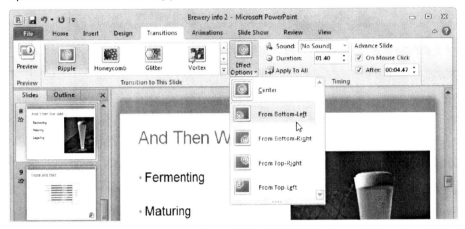

Figure 21–10. *If the **Effect Options** button is available, click it to view the available options for the transition. Then click the **Preview** button (choose **Transitions ➤ Preview ➤ Preview**) to view the change.*

Adding a Sound to the Transition

If you want to add a sound to the transition, choose **Transitions ➤ Timing ➤ Sound**, and then click the sound on the drop-down list.

You can make the sound keep playing until the next sound starts (click the **Loop Until Next Sound** item to place a check mark next to it), but this is not usually a good idea.

NOTE: To use a sound other than PowerPoint's built-in sounds, choose **Transitions ➤ Timing ➤ Sound ➤ Other Sound**, click the sound file in the **Add Audio** dialog box, and then click the **OK** button.

Changing the Duration of the Transition

If you want to change the duration of the transition, set it in the **Duration** box in the **Timing** group of the **Transitions** tab. PowerPoint automatically sets the duration to a suitable length for the transition you choose, but you may need to change it to make your presentation's timing work.

Choosing How to Advance to the Next Slide

In the **Advance Slide** section of the **Timing** group on the **Transitions** tab, choose how to advance the slide to the next slide:

- ■ **On Mouse Click.** Select this check box if you want to click the mouse to move to the next slide.

- ■ **After.** To display the next slide automatically, select this check box, and then set the timing in the text box.

Adding Animations to Slides

When you need to bring a slide to life, you can animate one or more of the objects on it by applying an animation to it. For example, you may need to make an object appear on a slide, draw attention to itself at a key point, or disappear from view when its role is over—or all three. Any object can have one or more animations, and you can arrange them into the order you need.

You can also use animations to reveal only part of a slide, or part of an object at a time, which can help keep the audience focused on your current point rather than reading ahead to the end of the slide

> **CAUTION:** As with transitions, it's easy to go over the top with animations. Resist the temptation: animations will have more effect in your slides if you use them sparingly and only at the appropriate times.

PowerPoint's Four Categories of Animations

To work with animations, you use the controls on the **Animations** tab of the Ribbon. As you can see in Figure 21–11, the **Animation Styles** drop-down panel contains four categories of animations—**Entrance**, **Emphasis**, **Exit**, and **Motion Paths**.

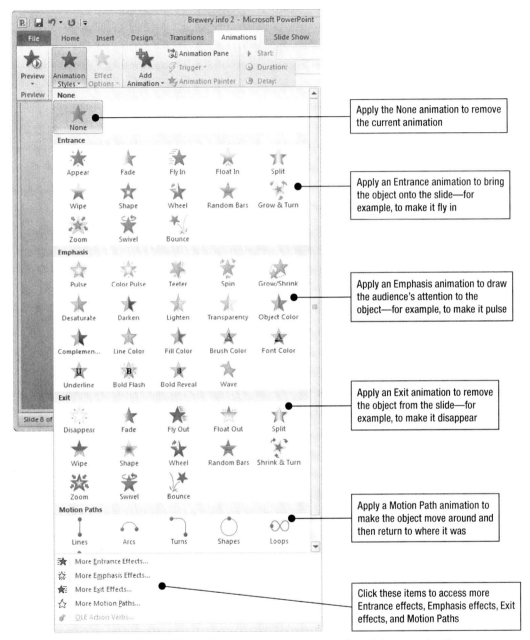

Figure 21–11. *From the **Animation Styles** drop-down panel, you can apply an **Entrance** animation, an **Emphasis** animation, an **Exit** animation, or a **Motion Path** animation. Click the **None** animation option if you want to remove the existing animation from the slide.*

Adding an Animation to an Object

To add a straightforward animation to an object on a slide, follow these steps:

1. Click the object to select it.

2. Click the **Animations** tab to display its controls.

3. Click an animation in the **Animation Styles** box, or click the **Animation Styles** drop-down button to display the drop-down panel.

4. Hold the mouse pointer over an animation style to preview its effect on the object.

5. Click the animation style you want to apply.

6. To choose options for the effect, choose **Animations ➤ Animation ➤ Effect Options**, and then click the option you want. The options available depend on the effect you've chosen. For example, the **Wheel** animation offers different numbers of spokes, as you see in Figure 21–12.

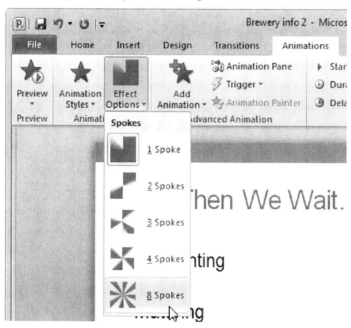

Figure 21–12. *To choose options for the animation effect, click the **Effect Options** button, and then click the option you want.*

To control when the animation runs, use the controls on the left side of the Timing group and follow these steps:

1. Open the **Start** drop-down list and choose when to start the animation: **On Click** (in other words, when you click the mouse), **With Previous** (at the same time as the previous animation), or **After Previous** (after the previous animation has finished).

2. In the **Duration** text box, set the number of seconds and hundredths of seconds you want the animation to run—for example, 1.50 for one and a half seconds.

3. In the **Delay** text box, set the delay before starting the animation (for example, after the previous animation finishes running). Again, use seconds and hundreds of seconds.

4. To change the order of animations, click an object, and then click the **Move Earlier** button or the **Move Later** button in the **Reorder Animation** area of the **Timing** group on the **Animations** tab. PowerPoint displays a number next to each animated item on the slide, so you can easily see the current order.

5. Click the **Preview** button in the **Preview** group to preview the animation and see if you need to make further changes.

Changing the Order of Animations

When you apply multiple animations to the same slide, you may need to change the order in which they occur. To do so, display the Animation pane by choosing **Animations ➤ Animation ➤ Animation Pane**, and then work as shown in Figure 21–13.

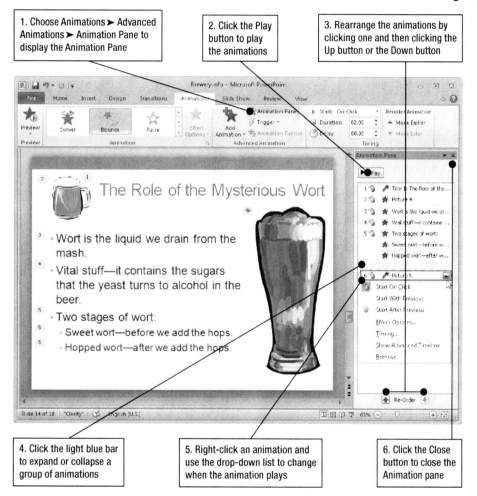

1. Choose Animations ➤ Advanced Animations ➤ Animation Pane to display the Animation Pane

2. Click the Play button to play the animations

3. Rearrange the animations by clicking one and then clicking the Up button or the Down button

4. Click the light blue bar to expand or collapse a group of animations

5. Right-click an animation and use the drop-down list to change when the animation plays

6. Click the Close button to close the Animation pane

Figure 21–13. *Use the **Animation Pane** to examine the animations and to control which plays when.*

Using Animation to Display Bulleted Paragraphs One at a Time

When you have several bulleted paragraphs in a text placeholder, you can use animation to display them one at a time. This helps prevent the audience from reading ahead of you and missing the point you're explaining.

To display bulleted paragraphs one at a time, click the container the bulleted paragraphs are in, and then apply an animation from the **Animation Styles** drop-down panel. Then choose animation options as shown in Figure 21–14.

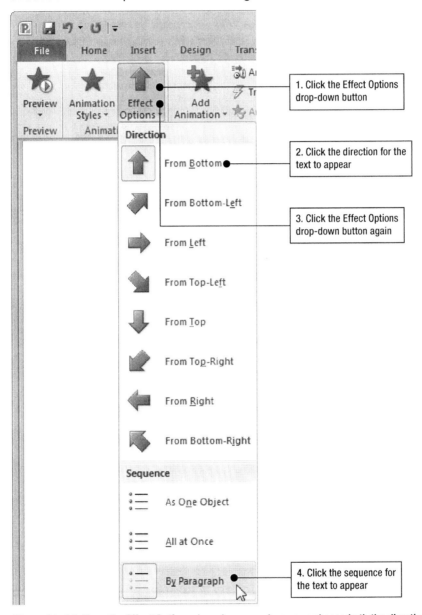

Figure 21–14. *From the **Effect Options** drop-down panel, you can choose both the direction for the text to appear and the sequence in which its components appear.*

NOTE: The **Sequence** animation option you'll usually want to use for text is **By Paragraph**, which animates each top-level paragraph separately. The **As One Object** option animates the whole object at once. The **All at Once** option animates each top-level paragraph separately but runs all the animations at once.

Choose **Animations ➤ Preview ➤ Preview** to preview the effect of the animation. If you need to control different levels of text separately, work as shown in Figure 21–15.

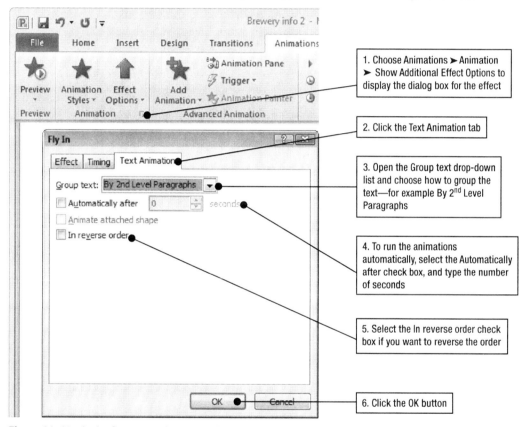

Figure 21–15. *In the **Group** text drop-down list on the **Text Animation** tab of the animation's dialog box, choose the level of paragraphs by which you want to animate the object.*

Animating SmartArt Graphics and Charts

You can apply animations to SmartArt graphics and charts. Animations are especially useful when you want to reveal only part of a SmartArt graphic or a chart at a time, gradually building up to showing the whole object.

Animating a SmartArt Graphic

PowerPoint enables you to animate the component parts of a SmartArt graphic in sequence, so you can choose between displaying the whole object at once, displaying all the objects at a particular level, or displaying one object at a time.

To choose how to display a SmartArt graphic, follow these steps:

1. Select the SmartArt graphic by clicking it on the slide.

2. Apply the animation to the graphic as a whole from the Add Animation box or panel. For example, apply the Fade animation. This makes the whole graphic appear at once with the animation.

3. Choose Animations ➤ Animation ➤ Effect Options, and then click the way you want to animate the graphic:

   ▓ **As One Object**. This option displays the graphic as a single object, so it all appears in one animation.

   ▓ **All at Once**. This option treats the graphic as separate objects, but runs the animation on all the objects at once.

   ▓ **One by One**. This option treats each component of the graphic as a separate object. In many cases, this is the most useful option.

   ▓ **Level at Once**. This option treats each level of a hierarchical SmartArt graphic as a separate object. Choose this option when you want to display one level of the graphic at a time.

   ▓ **Level One by One**. This option treats each level of a hierarchical SmartArt graphic as a separate object, and treats each object within the level as a separate object. Choose this option when you want to display the graphic one object of a level at a time.

4. Click the **Preview** button (choose **Animations ➤ Preview ➤ Preview**) to preview the effect.

5. If you need to change the order, choose **Animations ➤ Animation ➤ More**, clicking the little button in the lower-right corner of the **Animation** group. PowerPoint displays the dialog box for the effect.

6. Click the **SmartArt Animation** tab to display its contents. Figure 21–1 shows the **SmartArt Animation** tab for the **Fade** animation.

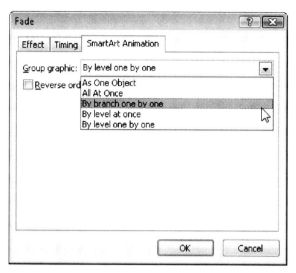

Figure 21–16. *Use the **Group graphic** drop-down list on the **SmartArt Animation** tab of the dialog box for an animation to control how the components of a SmartArt graphic appear.*

7.   Open the **Group graphic** drop-down list, and then click the option you want. The options available depend on the type of SmartArt graphic, but these ones are typical:

▪   **As One Object**. Choose this option to display the whole SmartArt graphic at once.

▪   **All At Once**. Choose this option to display all the components of the SmartArt graphic at once.

▪   **One by one**. Choose this option to display one component at a time

▪   **By branch one by one**. Choose this option to display each branch of a graphic such as an org chart separately, showing one component at a time.

▪   **By level at once**. Choose this option to display each level of a graphic separately, showing the whole level at once.

▪   **By level one by one**. Choose this option to display each level of a graphic separately, showing one component at a time.

8.   If you want to reveal the SmartArt graphic in reverse order, select the **Reverse order** check box.

9.   Click the **OK** button to close the animation's dialog box.

Animating a Chart

When you're displaying a chart, it's often helpful to use an animation to show part of it at a time rather than displaying the whole chart at once. To do this, follow these steps:

1. Click the chart to select it.

2. Apply the animation to the chart as a whole from the **Add Animation** box or panel. For example, apply the **Appear** animation.

3. Choose **Animations ➤ Animation ➤ Effect Options**, and then click the way you want to animate the chart:

   - **As One Object**. This setting displays the chart all at once, so you probably won't want to use it.

   - **By Series**. This setting displays one full data series at a time and is good for contrasting the data series to each other.

   - **By Category**. This setting displays one whole category at a time and is good for comparing the categories.

   - **By Element in Series**. This setting displays each element in a series at a time, then the next element in the series, and so on until the series is finished. This setting is great for focusing on the individual elements in the series.

   - **By Element in Category**. This setting displays each element in a category at a time, then the category's next element, and so on. Use this setting to zero in on the individual elements in the categories.

> **NOTE:** If you insert a chart as a picture, you can't animate its components.

4. If necessary, choose **Animations ➤ Advanced Animation ➤ Animation Pane** to display the **Animation** pane, and then adjust the settings. For example, if you've chosen the **By Element in Series** option, you can set the elements in a series to display automatically one after the other, using a short delay between them.

5. Preview the animation and make sure that the objects appear as you want them to.

Keeping Extra Information Up Your Sleeve with Hidden Slides

In many presentations, it's useful to have extra information that you can summon up to deal with points you don't want to cover unless the audience raises them. To cover this need, PowerPoint lets you hide any slide so that it doesn't appear unless you specifically choose to display it.

To hide a slide, right-click the slide in the **Slides** tab of the **Navigation** pane or in **Slide Sorter** view, and then click **Hide Slide** on the context menu.

PowerPoint indicates a hidden slide by showing around its slide number a box with a diagonal strikethrough (see Figure 21–17) in the **Slides** tab in **Normal** view and in the slides area in **Slide Sorter** view. On the **Go to Slide** menu in **Reading** view and **Slide Show** view, a hidden slide appears with parentheses around its slide number.

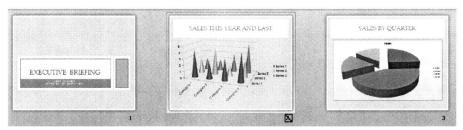

Figure 21–17. *In **Slide Sorter** view and on the **Slides** tab of the **Navigation** pane, a box with a diagonal strikethrough indicates a hidden slide.*

To change a slide back from hidden to normal, right-click the slide, and then click **Hide Slide** again, turning off the hiding.

Summary

In this chapter, you learned how to add life and impact to a presentation by using graphics, audio and video, animations, and transitions. You also learned how to hide extra slides so that they don't appear in the slide show unless you choose to display them.

At this point, you've probably got a presentation ready to deliver. In the next chapter, I'll show you how to deliver it, either in person or online.

Chapter 22

Delivering a Presentation in Person or Online

In this chapter, I'll show you how to deliver a presentation to your audience. You can deliver the presentation live, by showing the slides on a screen, or by broadcasting it on the Web. You can also publish the slides from a presentation to a slide library so that your colleagues can work with them.

First, I'll cover preparing to deliver a presentation—setting up the display, arranging Presenter view, practicing your presentation, and (if you need to) recording automatic timings. I'll then go through delivering the presentation to a live audience.

After that, I'll show you how to create a handout for a presentation, how to record narration into a presentation, and how to export and share a presentation with others.

Preparing to Deliver a Presentation in Person

In this section, we'll look at how you set up your presentation displays, how you use PowerPoint's Presenter view to keep your notes and controls on screen, how to practice your presentation, and how to record timings for slides that you want to advance themselves automatically.

Setting Up Your Display and Choosing the Resolution

Your first step is to connect your PC to the display or projector on which you'll give the presentation, and then get the displays set up. This example use a laptop and Windows 7:

1. Connect the projector to the laptop's external display port.

2. Turn on the projector.

3. Turn on the laptop and log on.

4. Right-click the desktop, and then click **Screen Resolution** on the context menu to display the **Screen Resolution** window (see Figure 22–1).

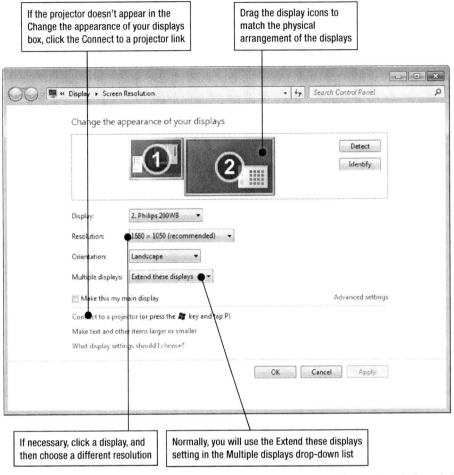

If the projector doesn't appear in the Change the appearance of your displays box, click the Connect to a projector link

Drag the display icons to match the physical arrangement of the displays

If necessary, click a display, and then choose a different resolution

Normally, you will use the Extend these displays setting in the Multiple displays drop-down list

Figure 22–1. *Start by setting up the projector or the external display in the **Screen Resolution** window in the **Control Panel**.*

5. Make sure both the displays appear in the C**hange the appearance of your displays** box. If not:

■ *Projector.* Click the **Connect to a projector** link. In the **Projector** panel that appears (see Figure 22–2), click the **Extend** button to extend your desktop onto the projector (usually best), the **Duplicate** button to show the same material on the projector as on your PC's screen, or the **Projector only** button if you want to use only the projector.

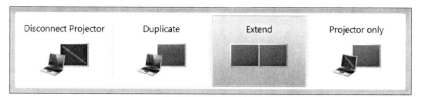

Figure 22–2. *In the **Projector** panel, you'll normally want to click the **Extend** button so that you can use **Presenter** view on your laptop's screen while showing the slides on the projector.*

> ▪ *Display.* Click the **Detect** button. If you can't tell which icon represents each display, click the **Identify** button to flash a large number on each display.

6. Drag the display icons to match how the displays are physically positioned. For example, if **Display 1** is to the right of **Display 2** rather than to the left, drag the **Display 1** icon to the right of **Display 2**.

7. If you need to change the resolution, click the display you want to change, choose the resolution in the **Resolution** drop-down list, and then click the **Apply** button.

8. Make sure the **Multiple displays** drop-down list has the right setting. Normally, you'll want the **Extend these displays** setting.

9. Click the **OK** button when you've finished making changes in the **Screen Resolution** window.

Choosing the Presentation Display and Turning on Presenter View

Now that you've got both displays working, tell PowerPoint which display you want to use for the presentation. If you're using two displays with your desktop extended, also turn on Presenter view for your other display. To make these changes, click the **Slide Show** tab of the Ribbon, and then work as shown in Figure 22–3.

> **NOTE:** Presenter view greatly helps you give an effective presentation. While the audience sees only the slide you're currently displaying in **Slide Show** view, Presenter view shows your current slide, the sequence of slides around it in the presentation, and the slide's notes. Normally, you'll use Presenter view on your laptop's screen, so you're the only one who can see it.

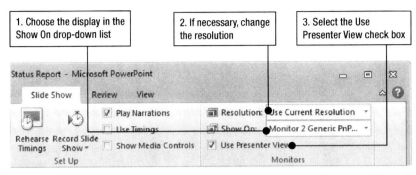

Figure 22–3. *Use the* **Monitors** *group on the* **Slide Show** *tab of the Ribbon to tell PowerPoint which display to show the slides on, to set the resolution, and to turn on Presenter view.*

TIP: The **Resolution** drop-down list in the **Monitors** group on the **Slide Show** tab of the Ribbon lets you change the resolution PowerPoint uses when showing the presentation. Until you start showing the presentation, PowerPoint uses the resolution you set in the **Screen Resolution** window.

Using Presenter View

Once you've turned on Presenter view by selecting the **Use Presenter View** check box in the **Monitors** group on the **Slide Show** tab of the Ribbon, when you start the slide show, PowerPoint displays Presenter view on the monitor that's not showing the slides to the audience. Figure 22–4 explains the main features of Presenter view.

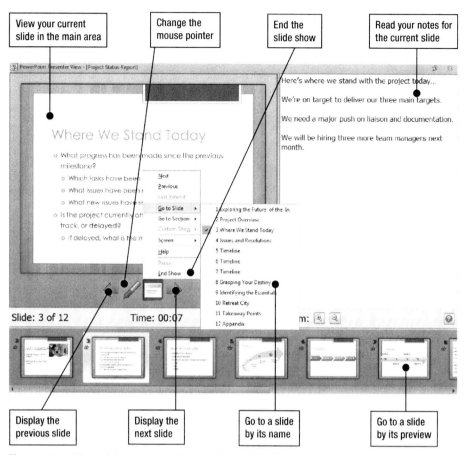

View your current slide in the main area

Change the mouse pointer

End the slide show

Read your notes for the current slide

Display the previous slide

Display the next slide

Go to a slide by its name

Go to a slide by its preview

Figure 22–4. *When giving a presentation, use* **Presenter view** *on a second screen to control the presentation, display your notes, and navigate quickly from slide to slide. Click the menu button to display the control menu shown here.*

NOTE: If you don't have a second monitor for Presenter view, you'll need to fall back on traditional means of handling your notes—memorizing them, printing them in Notes Pages print layout or on note cards, or writing them on the palm of your hand or on your cuff.

Practicing Your Presentation

To make sure that your presentation goes well on the day, practice it until you're confident you know your material and you can speak fluently from the notes you've given yourself. If you find your notes need more detail, rearranging, or other improvements, work on them, too.

> **TIP:** If you will give the presentation at your place of work, practice in the room in which you will deliver the presentation. This will help you not only plan how to arrange your equipment but also speak to the right size of room. If someone else will run the presentation while you speak, practice from the position in the room you will use for presenting rather than from the location of the equipment.

To practice your presentation, use Presenter view (if you'll use it during your presentation) or your notes. You may also want to set timings for slides, as discussed next.

Rehearsing Timings for Slides

For some presentations, you may need to set automatic timings for slides so that you don't need to cue them manually. To set timings, set up Presenter view as described earlier in this chapter. Then choose **Slide Show ➤ Set Up ➤ Rehearse Timings** and use PowerPoint's **Rehearse Timings** feature as shown in Figure 22–5.

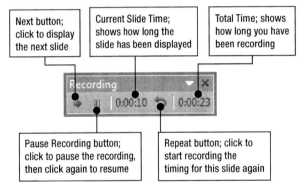

Next button; click to display the next slide

Current Slide Time; shows how long the slide has been displayed

Total Time; shows how long you have been recording

Pause Recording button; click to pause the recording, then click again to resume

Repeat button; click to start recording the timing for this slide again

Figure 22–5. *Use the controls on the **Recording** toolbar to set automatic timings for slides or to control the recording of your narration.*

When you finish going through the presentation, PowerPoint displays a dialog box (see Figure 22–6) giving the total show time and asking if you want to apply the timings to the slide show. Click the **Yes** button to apply the timings, and then save the presentation by clicking the **Save** button on the Quick Access Toolbar.

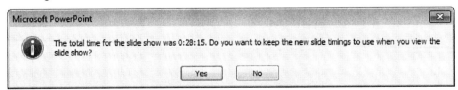

Figure 22–6. *Click the **Yes** button in this dialog box to apply the timings you've recorded to the slide show.*

Delivering a Presentation to a Live Audience

When you're ready to deliver the presentation live (or when you're practicing), use the commands and techniques explained in this section to start the presentation and display the slides. If necessary, you can annotate the presentation or display a black screen or white screen instead of your slides. You can also run the presentation from the keyboard rather than using a mouse.

Starting a Presentation

When you're ready to launch the presentation, start the slide show by choosing **Slide Show ➤ Start Slide Show ➤ From Beginning** or by pressing **F5**.

> **NOTE:** If you need to start from a slide other than the first, select that slide, and then choose **Slide Show ➤ Start Slide Show ➤ From Current Slide**. You can also press **Shift+F5** to start from the current slide.

Displaying the Slides You Need

When giving the presentation, you'll need to display slides in the right order. That may mean starting at the beginning of the presentation and running straight through to the end, but in many cases, you'll need to change the order—for example, you may need to go back to an earlier slide, skip ahead to a particular slide by name or number, or display a hidden slide.

PowerPoint provides plenty of different ways to move from slide to slide. The following ways are usually the most convenient:

- *Run the next animation or display the next slide.* Click the mouse button or press Spacebar.

- *Return to the previous slide.* Press **P**; or right-click the current slide, and then click **Previous** on the context menu.

- *Go to a slide by name or number.* Right-click the current slide, click or highlight **Go to Slide** on the context menu (see Figure 22–7), and then click the slide on the submenu.

> **NOTE:** Parentheses around a slide's number on the **Go to Slide** submenu indicate that the slide is hidden.

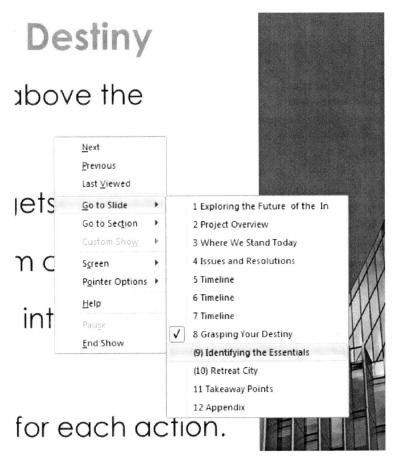

Figure 22–7. *The context menu for a presentation includes commands for going quickly to a different slide by name or number, going to a different section of the presentation, or returning to the last slide viewed.*

■ *Go to a section.* Right-click the current slide, click or highlight **Go to Section** on the context menu, and then click the section on the submenu.

TIP: To return quickly to the first slide in the presentation, hold down both the left and right mouse buttons together for two seconds.

■ *Return to the last slide viewed.* Right-click the current slide, and then click Last Viewed on the context menu.

Annotating the Slides

When giving a presentation in person, you may want to add annotations to slides—for example, to emphasize your key points visually, or to insert fresh information or details from the audience. To add an annotation, click the **Pointer Options** submenu on the **Slide Show** menu in Presenter view or on the context menu (see Figure 22–8), and then click the annotation tool you want.

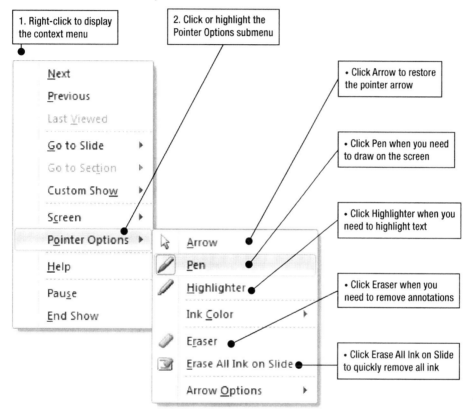

Figure 22–8. *You can quickly add annotations by using the tools on the **Pointer Options** submenu.*

For example, click Pen to activate the **Pen** tool, and then draw on a slide as shown in Figure 22–9.

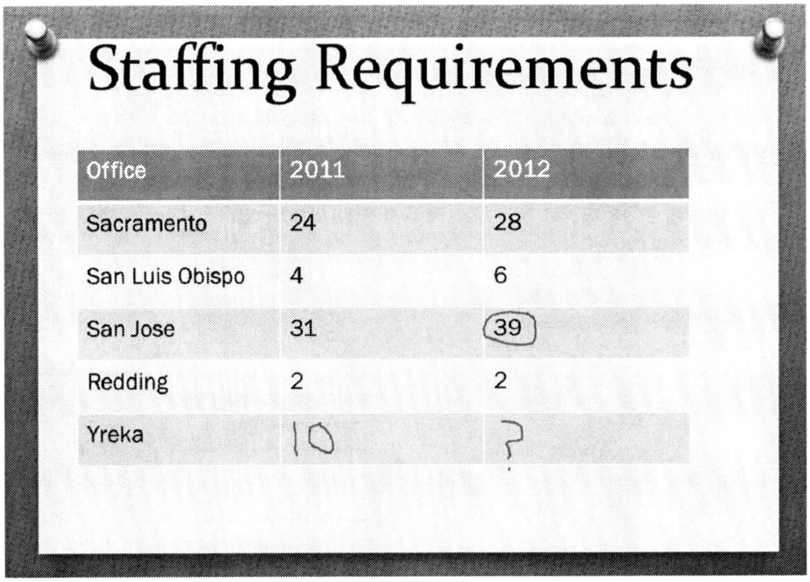

Figure 22–9. *You can use PowerPoint's annotation features to mark up slides during a presentation. You can save the annotations afterward if you want.*

> **NOTE:** To hide ink markup, display the context menu or the **Slide Show** menu, and then choose **Screen ➤ Show/Hide Ink Markup**. Repeat the command when you want to display the ink markup again.

When you end a slide show that you've marked up with ink annotations, PowerPoint displays a dialog box asking whether you want to keep them. Click the **Keep** button or the **Discard** option button as appropriate.

Controlling a Presentation Using the Keyboard

If you stay at your PC when you're giving the presentation, you can control the presentation by using keyboard shortcuts. Table 22–1 explains the keyboard shortcuts you can use. Several of the actions have two or more keyboard shortcuts. Each works the same; the one I've listed first is usually the easiest; but try them all, and use whichever you find most convenient.

Table 22–1. *Keyboard Shortcuts for Running a Presentation*

Action	Keyboard Shortcut
Run the presentation from the first slide	F5
Run the presentation from the current slide	Shift+F5
End the slide show	Esc, Ctrl+Break, or – (numeric keypad)
Display the next slide or trigger the next animation	N, Enter, Spacebar, Page Down, Down Arrow, or Right Arrow
Display the previous slide or trigger the previous animation again	P, Backspace, Page Up, Up Arrow, or Left Arrow
Display the next slide if it's hidden	H
Toggle on or off a white screen with no content	W or , (comma key)
Toggle on or off a black screen with no content	B or . (period key)
Display the All Slides dialog box for picking a slide	Ctrl+S
Go to a slide by specifying its number	*number key* followed by Enter (for example, 8, then Enter)
Start or stop an automatic slide show	S
Change the mouse pointer to a pen	Ctrl+P
Restore the normal mouse pointer	Ctrl+A
Toggle the display of ink markup on and off	Ctrl+M
Change the mouse pointer to an eraser	Ctrl+E
Erase all annotations from the current slide	E
Hide the mouse pointer	Ctrl+H
Open the context menu	Shift+F10
Select the first or next hyperlink on the current slide	Tab
Select the last or previous hyperlink on the current slide	Shift+Tab
Click the selected hyperlink	Enter
Display the Windows Taskbar (click the slide to hide the Taskbar again)	Ctrl+T

Displaying a White Screen or Black Screen

When you need to focus your audience's attention on you rather than on your slides, display a white screen or a black screen. A white screen works best in a lighted room and a black screen in a darkened room.

To display a white screen or black screen, open the context menu or the **Slide Show** menu (in Presenter view), and then choose **Screen ➤ Black Screen** or **Screen ➤ White Screen**. You can also press **W** or **,** (comma) for the white screen, or **B** or **.** (period) for the black screen.

Press **Esc** or click with the regular mouse pointer to go back from the black screen or white screen to the slides. (Don't click with a pen pointer—that draws on the black screen or white screen instead.)

Creating a Handout for a Presentation

When you're delivering a presentation live, it's often useful to create a handout that provides your audience with material to browse before you start, to scribble notes on as you proceed, and to take home afterward. To create a handout, PowerPoint uses Word, to which it automatically exports the slides and other material you choose.

To create a handout, first open **Backstage** view and give the **Create Handouts** command, as shown in Figure 22–10.

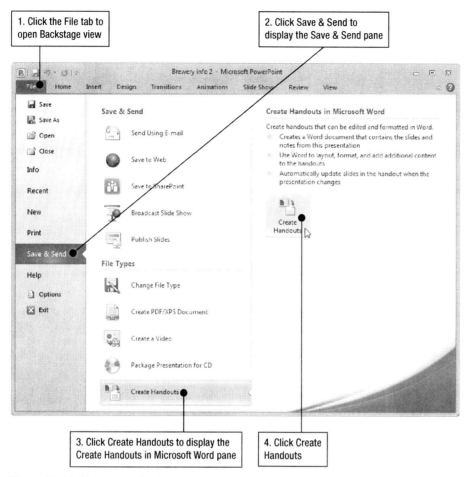

1. Click the File tab to open Backstage view

2. Click Save & Send to display the Save & Send pane

3. Click Create Handouts to display the Create Handouts in Microsoft Word pane

4. Click Create Handouts

Figure 22–10. *To start creating handouts, open the **Create Handouts** in **Microsoft Word** pane in Backstage view, and then click the **Create Handouts** button.*

PowerPoint then displays the **Send To Microsoft Word** dialog box, in which you choose options as shown in Figure 22–11.

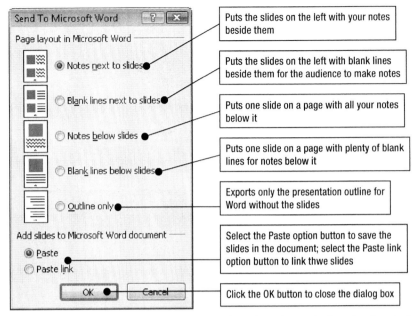

Figure 22–11. *In the **Send To Microsoft Word** dialog box, choose the layout and content you want for your handout.*

> **NOTE:** In the **Add slides to Microsoft Word** document area of the **Send To Microsoft Word** dialog box, you can choose whether to paste the slides into the document or paste link them. Paste the slides when you want to be able to move the Word document to a different computer than the presentation is on. The disadvantage to pasting in the slides as graphics is that the Word document becomes large. Paste link the slides when you will keep the handout document on the same computer as the presentation. Paste linking makes Word pull in the slides from the presentation when you open the document, so if you've updated the presentation, Word will update the slides automatically.

When you click the **OK** button to close the **Send To Microsoft Word** dialog box, Word creates the document containing the slides. This process may take several minutes, especially if the presentation contains many slides. If Windows shows the Word window as **Not responding**, give it time to finish creating the document; normally, it will start responding normally again.

Click the **Word** window's icon on the **Taskbar** to switch to the Word document. Check that the document has come out the way you want it, add any text needed (for example, add headers and footers with the details of the presentation), and then save the document.

Recording Narration into a Presentation

When you can't deliver a presentation in person, you can record your narration for the presentation and create a file that your audience can play back. This is great for creating a presentation that you will share on the Web or on a CD or DVD.

> **NOTE:** To record narration, you'll need a suitable microphone. In a pinch, you can use a microphone built into your laptop or your desktop PC's monitor, but such a microphone will usually pick up ambient noise. Usually, you'll be better off using a microphone that you can position freely, such as a handheld microphone or one on a stand, and best off with a noise-canceling microphone mounted on a headset.

Checking That Your Microphone Is Working

Before trying to record narration, check that your microphone is working and has a suitable input level set. Figure 22–12 shows you how to do this.

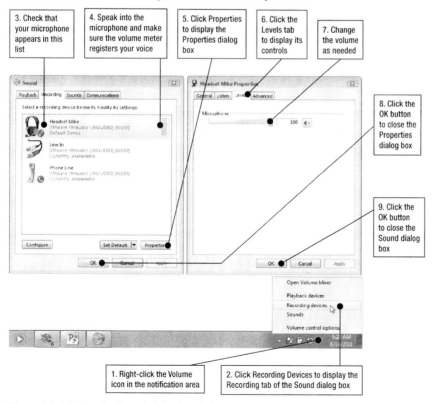

Figure 22–12. *Use the **Sound** dialog box (left) to make sure your microphone is picking up sound as it should. Use the **Levels** tab of the microphone's **Properties** dialog box (right) to adjust the input level.*

Starting to Record Narration

To start recording narration, work as shown in Figure 22–13.

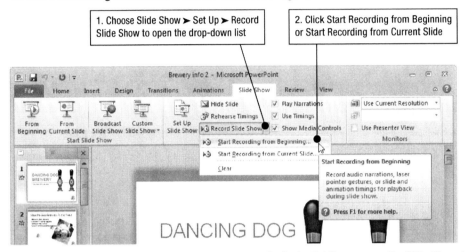

Figure 22–13. *From the **Record Slide Show** drop-down list in the **Set Up** group on the **Slide Show** tab of the Ribbon, you can start recording either from the beginning or from the current slide.*

When PowerPoint displays the **Record Slide Show** dialog box, choose settings and start recording as shown in Figure 22–14.

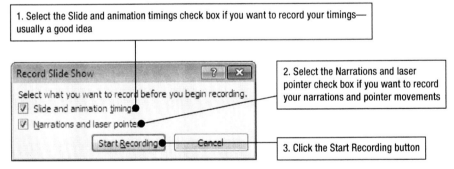

Figure 22–14. *In the **Record Slide Show** dialog box, you will normally want to select both the **Slide and animation timings** check box and the **Narrations and laser pointer** check box.*

When you click the **Start Recording** button, PowerPoint displays the **Recording** toolbar, and the recording starts. Speak your narration for the presentation, advancing the slides and animations as needed, using the controls on the **Recording** toolbar (shown in Figure 22–5).

When you reach the end of the presentation, PowerPoint automatically stops recording the narration.

Checking Your Narration and Rerecording if Necessary

Check how the narration sounds by playing the presentation in either Slide Show view or Reading view. If the narration has come out well enough, save the presentation (for example, press **Ctrl+S**).

If you find the narration isn't good enough, you can start over either on the current slide or at the beginning. Choose **Slide Show ➤ Set Up ➤ Record Slide Show ➤ Clear** to display the **Clear** submenu, and then click the **Clear Narration on Current Slide** item or the **Clear Narrations on All Slides** item, as needed. You can then record your replacement narration.

Exporting and Sharing a Presentation

Apart from delivering a presentation in person, you can deliver the presentation to other people across the Internet in several ways:

- *Send the presentation via e-mail.* The most direct way to get a presentation to somebody else is to e-mail it to them, as discussed in Chapter 5: "Coauthoring in Real Time and Sharing Documents." E-mail works well for small presentations, but many presentation files are too large for mail servers to handle. In this case, you're better off using a different means of distribution.

- *Save the presentation to SkyDrive.* You can save the presentation to a shared folder on Windows Live SkyDrive, also discussed in Chapter 5. Anyone with permission to view the folder can then download the presentation and view it. This is an effective way to distribute presentations across the Internet.

- *Save the presentation to a SharePoint site*. If you have a SharePoint site, you can save the presentation to it. Anyone with permission to view the folder on the SharePoint site can then view the presentation. In many cases, this is the best way to distribute a presentation within a company or organization that uses SharePoint.

- *Broadcast a slide show.* In broadcasting, you give the slide show live on the Web. Beforehand, you create a link to where you will broadcast the slide show. You send this link to the potential audience, and any of them can click the link to tune in to the slide show at the appointed time. The next section explains how to broadcast a slide show.

- *Publish slides.* When you need other people to be able to work with the slides in your presentation rather than just view them, you can publish the slides to a SharePoint site or to a slide library. People with access to the site or library can then open the slides, view them, and edit them as needed. The second section below shows you how to publish slides.

Broadcasting a Slide Show

When you need to share a slide show with a large audience over the Internet, you can broadcast it. To broadcast, you either give the presentation live or play back a recorded presentation at a scheduled time. Your audience tunes in to watch the presentation in their web browsers.

To broadcast a slide show from PowerPoint, you use Microsoft's PowerPoint Broadcast Service or an equivalent service. The PowerPoint Broadcast Service is free to anyone who has a Windows Live ID, so you'll probably want to try it unless you have a different broadcast service available (for example, one your company or organization runs on its own network).

> **NOTE:** A Windows Live ID is the identifier that Microsoft uses for Windows Live Mail, Hotmail, MSN, and other services. If you have an account with one of these services, you already have a Windows Live ID that you can use for the PowerPoint Broadcast Service. If not, you can sign up for a Windows Live ID using your existing e-mail address; go to `http://signup.live.com` and fill in the form.

Preparing the Slide Show Broadcast

To prepare your slide show for broadcast, open the presentation and then give the **Broadcast Slide Show** command from **Backstage** as shown in Figure 22–15.

1. Click the File tab to open Backstage view

2. Click Save & Send to display the Save & Send pane

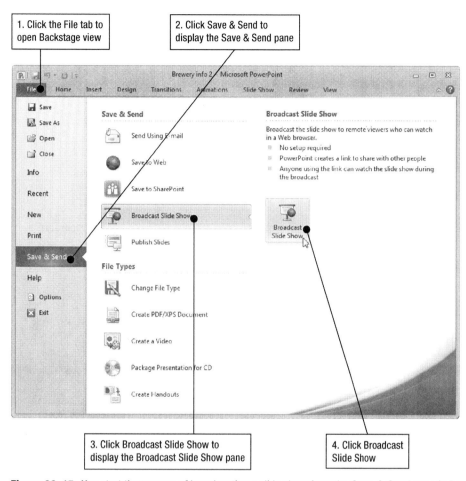

3. Click Broadcast Slide Show to display the Broadcast Slide Show pane

4. Click Broadcast Slide Show

Figure 22–15. *You start the process of broadcasting a slide show from the* **Save & Send** *pane in Backstage view.*

When you click the **Broadcast Slide Show** button, PowerPoint displays the **Broadcast Slide Show** dialog box (see Figure 22–16). Here, you normally just need to click the **Start Broadcast** button. If you need to use a different broadcast service than the PowerPoint Broadcast Service, click the **Change Broadcast Service** button, and then use the dialog box that opens to choose the service.

Figure 22–16. *Click the **Start Broadcast** button in the **Broadcast Slide Show** dialog box to start your slide show broadcast.*

If you're using the PowerPoint Broadcast Service, PowerPoint prompts you for your Windows Live ID. Type your e-mail address and password, select the **Sign me in automatically** check box if you want to use automatic sign-in from now on, and then click the **OK** button.

PowerPoint then prepares the slide show for broadcast and displays the **Broadcast Slide Show** dialog box shown in Figure 22–17 when it is ready.

Figure 22–17. *From this **Broadcast Slide Show** dialog box, you can copy the slide show's link or create an e-mail message containing it.*

Sharing the Slide Show Link with Your Audience

Share the link to the slide show with your audience in either of these ways:

- *Instant message.* Click the **Copy Link item** to copy the link so that you can share it—for example, by pasting it into an instant message.

- *E-mail.* Click the **Send in Email** link to create an e-mail message containing the link and canned text inviting the recipient to view the presentation. You can then add other details as needed, address the message, and send it.

Leave the Broadcast Slide Show dialog box on screen until you're ready to deliver the presentation.

Delivering the Presentation

When you're ready to start giving the presentation, click the **Start Slide Show** button in the **Broadcast Slide Show** dialog box. PowerPoint switches to Slide Show view (and displays Presenter view on your second screen if you're using it), and you can start giving the presentation.

> **TIP:** Until you start giving your presentation, viewers see a blank screen telling them that the presentation will start soon. Instead of leaving them in suspense, create a first slide that shows the time and time zone the presentation will start and gives some useful information (for example, the URL of your web site). Click the **Start Slide Show** button in the **Broadcast Slide Show** dialog box to display this first slide, and leave it on screen until you're ready to start the slide show for real.

Deliver the presentation as usual. When you have finished, choose **Broadcast ➤ Broadcast ➤ End Broadcast** to tell the broadcast service that the presentation is over. PowerPoint displays a confirmation dialog box (see Figure 22–18). Click the **End Broadcast** button. Viewers then see a message saying that the broadcast is over.

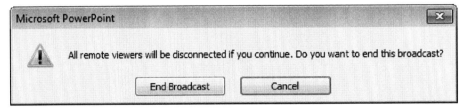

Figure 22–18. *Click the **End Broadcast** button in this dialog box to confirm that the broadcast is over.*

Publishing Slides to a Slide Library or a SharePoint Site

To make slides available to your colleagues so that they can update them, edit them, or reuse them, you can publish the slides to a SharePoint site or to a slide library.

To publish the slides, choose File ➤ Save & Send ➤ Publish Slides ➤ Publish Slides, and then work in the Publish Slides dialog box as shown in Figure 22–19.

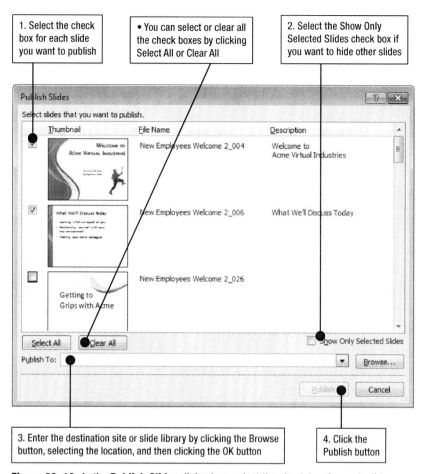

1. Select the check box for each slide you want to publish

• You can select or clear all the check boxes by clicking Select All or Clear All

2. Select the Show Only Selected Slides check box if you want to hide other slides

3. Enter the destination site or slide library by clicking the Browse button, selecting the location, and then clicking the OK button

4. Click the Publish button

Figure 22–19. *In the* **Publish Slides** *dialog box, select the check box for each slide you want to publish, and then choose the site to which you want to publish the slides.*

Summary

In this chapter, you learned how to deliver a presentation either live to an audience or by broadcasting on the Web. You now know how to set up your computer and displays for a presentation, use Presenter view, and record automatic timings if you need them. You can control a presentation using either the mouse or the keyboard, add annotations to your slides as needed, and blank out your slides with a white screen or black screen. You can also create a handout using Word and export and share a presentation with others.

This is the end of the PowerPoint part of the book. In the next (and last) part, I'll show you how to use Outlook.

Part VIII

Chapter 23

Setting Up Outlook and Meeting the Interface

In this part of the book, you'll learn to use Outlook, Office's heavy-duty e-mail and organizer program.

Outlook covers four main areas:

■ *Mail.* Outlook calls it Mail, but most of us call it e-mail—and it's the most important part of Outlook. We'll cover e-mail in Chapter 24: "Sending and Receiving E-mail."

■ *Contacts.* Outlook provides a powerful digital address book for storing the details of your contacts and keeping in touch with them. Chapter 25: "Managing Your Contacts with Outlook" explains how to work with contacts in Outlook.

■ *Calendar.* Outlook can help you keep tabs on your appointments, whether they occur once only or at regular intervals. Chapter 26: "Organizing Your Schedule, Tasks, and Notes." shows you how to manage your calendar with Outlook.

■ *Tasks.* Outlook provides a robust task list that you can use not only to track your own commitment but also offload them onto your colleagues. Chapter 26 also teaches you how to organize your life with tasks.

In this chapter, we'll set up Outlook to work with your e-mail account or accounts. To do this, you need to know your e-mail address and password. Depending on the details of your e-mail setup, you may also need to know which types of mail servers your ISP uses and their addresses—so if possible, arm yourself with this information ahead of time.

After setting up Outlook, we'll take a tour of the Outlook interface, because Outlook packs a host of controls into its window in order to handle all its different roles and tasks.

Set Up Your E-mail Accounts in Outlook

To set up your e-mail accounts in Outlook, follow these steps:

1. Choose Start ➤ All Programs ➤ Microsoft Office ➤ Microsoft Outlook 2010 to launch Outlook. If this is the first time you've run Outlook, the program displays the Microsoft Outlook 2010 Startup dialog box.

> **TIP:** If you find Outlook vital to your computing life, either pin the Outlook icon to the Taskbar (or the **Start** menu) or set Outlook to launch automatically on startup. See Chapter 1: "Meeting the Office Programs and Learning What They Do" for instructions on pinning a program or setting it to launch automatically.

2. Click the Next button to launch the **Account Configuration** wizard, which displays the **E-mail Accounts** pane (see Figure 23–1).

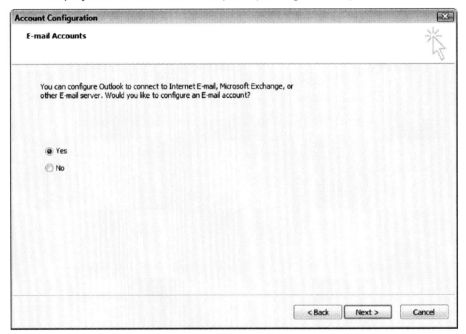

Figure 23–1. *To set up your first e-mail account with Outlook, click the* **Yes** *option button on the* **E-mail Accounts** *screen of the* **Account Configuration** *wizard, which runs automatically when you first open Outlook.*

3. Select the **Yes** option button, and then click the **Next** button. The wizard launches the **Add New Account** wizard, which displays the **Auto Account Setup** screen.

> **TIP:** Normally, the best way to set up an e-mail account in Outlook is to use the **Auto Account Setup** process. If this process doesn't work, you can try again, but this time select the **Manually configure server settings or additional server types** option button on the **Auto Account Setup** screen.

4. Choose settings as explained in Figure 23–2.

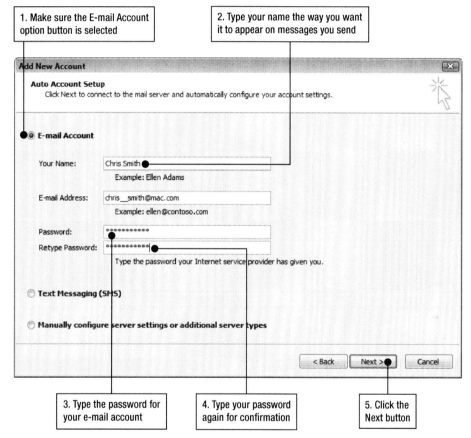

Figure 23–2. *On the **Auto Account Setup** screen of the **Add New Account** wizard, select the **E-mail Account** option button and fill in the details of your e-mail account.*

5. Click the **Next** button. The wizard displays the **Configuring** screen as it checks the settings you've provided, logs on to the mail server, and sends a test message. If all is well, the wizard then displays the **Congratulations!** screen. From this screen, shown in Figure 23–3, you can choose extra settings, start setting up another account, or simply close the **Add New Account** wizard.

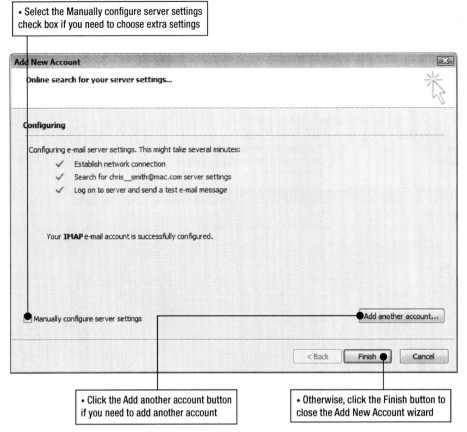

Figure 23–3. *If the **Add New Account** wizard displays the **Congratulations!** screen, your e-mail account is set up and functional.*

Changing the Default Settings for an E-mail Account

If you need to change the default settings for an e-mail account, select the **Manually configure server settings** check box on the **Congratulations!** screen of the **Add New Account** wizard. Click the **Next** button (which replaces the **Finish** button when you select the check box), and then work as shown in Figure 23–4.

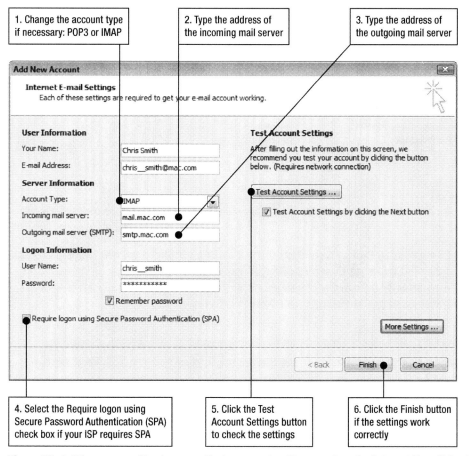

1. Change the account type if necessary: POP3 or IMAP

2. Type the address of the incoming mail server

3. Type the address of the outgoing mail server

Add New Account

Internet E-mail Settings
Each of these settings are required to get your e-mail account working.

User Information

Your Name: Chris Smith

E-mail Address: chris__smith@mac.com

Server Information

Account Type: IMAP

Incoming mail server: mail.mac.com

Outgoing mail server (SMTP): smtp.mac.com

Logon Information

User Name: chris__smith

Password: ***********

☑ Remember password

☐ Require logon using Secure Password Authentication (SPA)

Test Account Settings

After filling out the information on this screen, we recommend you test your account by clicking the button below. (Requires network connection)

● Test Account Settings ...

☑ Test Account Settings by clicking the Next button

More Settings ...

< Back   Finish   Cancel

4. Select the Require logon using Secure Password Authentication (SPA) check box if your ISP requires SPA

5. Click the Test Account Settings button to check the settings

6. Click the Finish button if the settings work correctly

Figure 23–4. *When you need to change particular account settings, work on the* **Internet E-mail Settings** *screen of the* **Add New Account** *wizard.*

NOTE: POP3 is the acronym for Post Office Protocol, a widely used communications protocol for handling incoming mail. IMAP is the acronym for Internet Mail Access Protocol, a newer protocol, which providers such as Gmail, Hotmail, and Apple use. If you're not sure which account type you have, ask your ISP or e-mail provider. The biggest difference between the two is that with IMAP your e-mail program keeps the messages on the server, which makes it easy to use various computers to manage your e-mail. By contrast, POP3 normally downloads messages to your PC, which enables you to work with messages even when your PC is offline.

Click the **Test Account Settings** button when you're ready to test the settings. Outlook displays the **Test Account Settings** dialog box (see Figure 23–5), which displays first the progress of the tests and then the result. Click the **Close** button when you've finished testing.

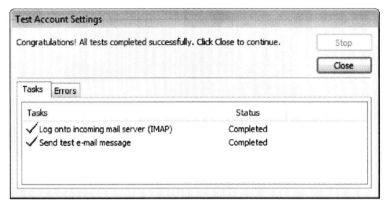

Figure 23–5. *The **Test Account Settings** dialog box lets you see at a glance whether your e-mail settings are working.*

If you need to customize further settings for the e-mail account, click the **More Settings** button to display the **Internet E-mail Settings** dialog box. This dialog box has several tabs of settings (exactly how many depends on the account type). Figure 23–6 shows the two tabs that contain the settings you'll most often need to change.

> **NOTE:** Normally, you'll need to set up different authentication for an outgoing server only if you have to send e-mail using a different ISP than you're using for your incoming mail. For example, some ISPs allow you to send e-mail through their servers with standard authentication only when your computer is connected to the Internet via that ISP. When you connect via another ISP (for instance, when you're on the road), you need to provide extra authentication so that the ISP knows it's you sending the messages rather than a spammer.

When you've finished choosing settings in the **Internet E-mail Settings** dialog box, click the **OK** button to close it. Click the **Finish** button to close the **Add New Account** wizard. The main Outlook window then opens.

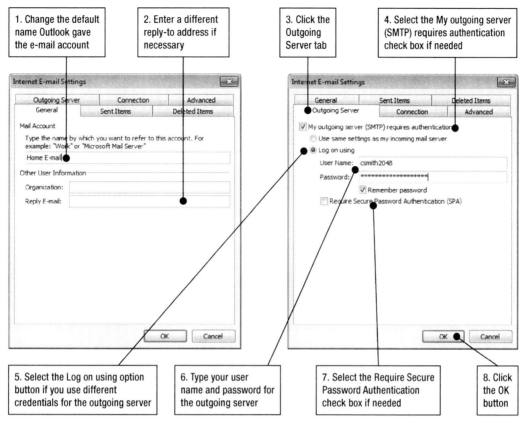

1. Change the default name Outlook gave the e-mail account

2. Enter a different reply-to address if necessary

3. Click the Outgoing Server tab

4. Select the My outgoing server (SMTP) requires authentication check box if needed

5. Select the Log on using option button if you use different credentials for the outgoing server

6. Type your user name and password for the outgoing server

7. Select the Require Secure Password Authentication check box if needed

8. Click the OK button

Figure 23–6. *On the **General** tab of the **Internet E-mail Settings** dialog box (left), you can change the name that Outlook displays for the e-mail account. You can also set a different reply-to address—the address to which a reply automatically goes. On the **Outgoing Server** tab (right), you can set up Outlook to use use different credentials for sending e-mail than for receiving it.*

Meeting the Outlook Interface

When Outlook opens, you'll see a window such as Figure 23–7. Outlook normally displays your Inbox at first, on the basis that you'll want to start by checking your e-mail. If Outlook is displaying a different item, click the **Inbox** item in the **Favorites** category in the pane on the left. (If the **Favorites** category is collapsed to a heading, click the white triangle to its left to expand it.)

NOTE: This chapter introduces you to Outlook using the Mail aspect of the interface. You'll learn to use the Calendar aspect, the Contacts aspect, and the Tasks aspect in subsequent chapters.

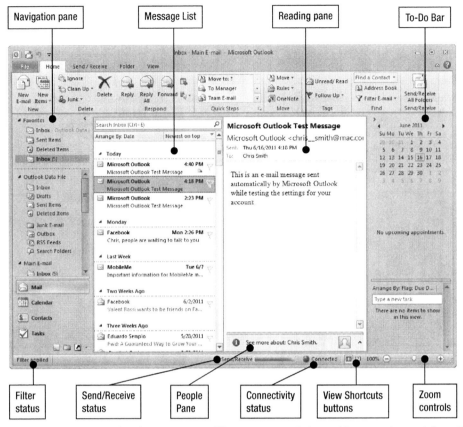

Figure 23–7. *Outlook's interface uses many different components to provide access to your information and its features.*

The following sections explain how to use the main components of the Outlook interface—and how to change those you're most likely to want to change.

Using and Customizing the Navigation Pane

The **Navigation** pane appears on the left side of the Outlook window by default. You use this pane to navigate to the items you want to work with.

Normally, your first navigation move is to display the Outlook area you want to work in: **Mail**, **Calendar**, **Contacts**, **Tasks**, **Notes**, **Folder List**, or **Shortcuts and Journal**. To do so, you click the appropriate one of the four buttons at the bottom of the Navigation pane.

Once you've displayed the area, the upper part of the Navigation pane displays controls for navigating about that area. For example:

- *Mail*. The Navigation pane displays your e-mail folders, so you can quickly click the folder whose contents you want to display.

▓ *Calendar.* The top of the Navigation pane displays a date picker that gives you instant access to the days of the current month (or whichever month you choose to display). Below this, the Navigation pane displays a list of your calendars, so that you can easily switch from one calendar to another.

▓ *Contacts.* The Navigation pane displays a folder of your contacts, enabling you to choose the group of contacts you want to work with.

▓ *Tasks.* The Navigation pane shows the **My Tasks** list, so you can pick the task you want to manipulate.

> **TIP:** You can switch quickly among Outlook's areas by using keyboard shortcuts. Press **Ctrl+1** to display Mail, **Ctrl+2** to display Calendar, **Ctrl+3** to display Contacts, **Ctrl+4** to display Tasks, **Ctrl+5** to display Notes, **Ctrl+6** to display the Folder List in the Navigation pane, and **Ctrl+7** to display Shortcuts in the Navigation Pane.

Normally, you use the Navigation pane all the time in Outlook, so it's a good idea to spend some time setting the Navigation pane up so that you can work quickly in it.

First, choose whether to display the full Navigation Pane most of the time or whether to display it in its minimized size, in which the Navigation Pane appears as a vertical strip at the left side of the Outlook window. Figure 23–8 shows you how to make these adjustments.

• Click and drag the right
border to change the
Navigation pane's width

• Click the Minimize the
Navigation Pane button to
minimize the Navigation pane

• Click the Expand the
Navigation Pane button to
expand the Navigation pane

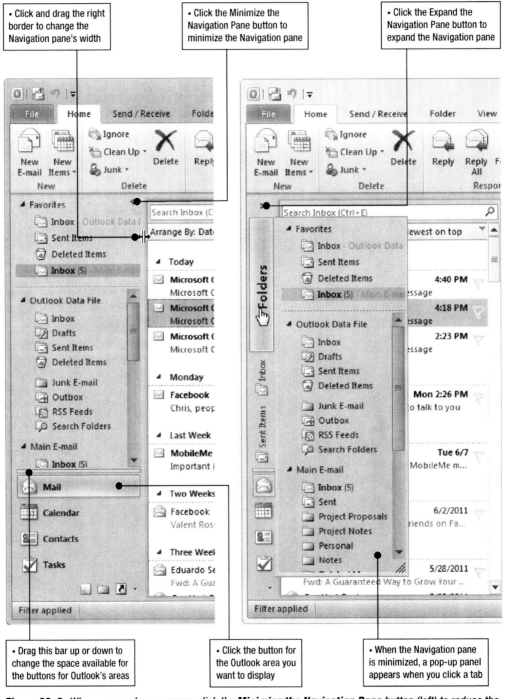

• Drag this bar up or down to
change the space available for
the buttons for Outlook's areas

• Click the button for
the Outlook area you
want to display

• When the Navigation pane
is minimized, a pop-up panel
appears when you click a tab

Figure 23–8. *When you need more space, click the **Minimize the Navigation Pane** button (left) to reduce the Navigation Pane to a narrow strip at the left side of the **Outlook** window (right). When you click an item that needs more space, a pop-up panel appears.*

As you can also see in Figure 23–8, you can adjust the size of the button area at the bottom of the Navigation Pane by dragging the divider bar up or down. To have all the buttons appear at their smaller size , drag the divider line down until the buttons appear in a single row at the bottom of the Navigation Pane. This gives you that much more space for working with the other items in the Navigation Pane, and is especially useful on small screens.

To have the first buttons appear at their full size but have the last buttons appear at their smaller size, drag the divider line down or up part of the way.

To choose which buttons appear at the bottom of the Navigation Pane, work as shown in Figure 23–9.

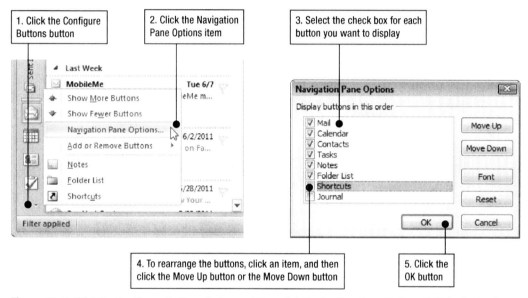

Figure 23–9. *Click the* **Configure Buttons** *button and then click* **Navigation Pane Options** *(left) to display the* **Navigation Pane Options** *dialog box (right), in which you can choose which buttons to display and the order in which they appear.*

> **NOTE:** you need to restore the buttons to their default order, click the **Reset** button in the **Navigation Pane Options** dialog box.

Using and Customizing the Message List

To the right of the Navigation Pane is the **Message List**, which shows the messages in the selected mailbox (for example, the **Inbox**). To the right of the Message List is the **Reading Pane**, which shows the contents of the selected message (or part of the contents). To view a message in the Reading Pane, you simply click it in the Message List.

> **NOTE:** Outlook provides the Reading Pane to help you plow through your messages quickly. But you can also open a message in a separate window if you prefer. To do so, double-click the message in the Message List.

Arranging and Sorting the Message List

To enable you to quickly find and read the messages you need, Outlook lets you sort the Message List in several different ways. This section runs you through the main ways of sorting the Message List, but you will want to spend some time experimenting with the various options to see which types of sorting you find most helpful for the tasks you perform with e-mail and the ways you prefer to approach them.

To set up the Message List, you use the controls in the **Arrangement** group on the **View** tab of the Ribbon (see Figure 23–10).

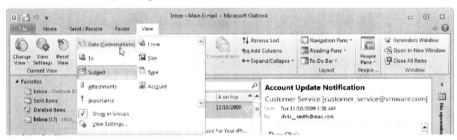

Figure 23–10. *Use the controls in the **Arrangement** group on the **View** tab of the Ribbon to set up the **Message List** the way you want it. Usually, you'll want to use the **Arrange By** control (shown open here) first to choose the overall sort order.*

Start by using the **Arrange By** control on the left of the Arrangement group to choose the overall arrangement. This control appears as a drop-down list if the **Outlook** window is narrow and as a box with a drop-down panel if the **Outlook** window provides enough space.

> **NOTE:** You can also configure the **Message List** in two other ways. First, you can click the **Arrange By** bar in the Message List, and then click the setting you want on the pop-up menu. Second, if you can find blank space in the Message List, you can right-click it and then use the **Arrange By** submenu on the context menu.

In the **Arrange By** control, choose from the following arrangement settings:

- **Date (Conversations).** Sorts the items by date and into conversations. (You'll learn about conversations shortly.)

▓ **To**. Sorts the items by the recipient's name or e-mail address. This setting is useful if you have Outlook checking different e-mail accounts, as it lets you separate the messages by account. Items sent to you by name (for example, Chris Smith) appear separately from those sent to the e-mail address.

▓ **From**. Sorts the items by the sender. This setting is good for locating messages from important people.

▓ **Size**. Sorts the items by their size. This setting is handy for quickly locating messages with large attachments. You can also use the **Attachments** setting (discussed shortly) to locate all messages with attachments.

▓ **Subject**. Sorts the items by their subject lines. This setting is useful for locating an item whose subject line you can remember but whose other details you can't. (You can also search for the item, as described shortly.)

▓ **Type**. Sorts the items into their different types, such as messages and news posts. This setting is helpful for separating e-mail messages from news feeds.

▓ **Attachments**. Sorts the items into a **With Attachments** group and a **No Attachments** group. This setting is good for locating messages with attachments that you need to deal with.

▓ **Account**. Sorts the items by the e-mail account to which they've been sent. This gives a similar effect to the **To** arrangement, but it uses only e-mail account names rather than your name.

▓ **Importance**. Sorts the items by their Importance tag into **High**, **Normal**, and **Low** groups. This setting can be useful if your colleagues use the **Importance** tag sensibly and consistently, but you may find so many people give their messages **High** priority that the result is meaningless.

Changing the Sort Order

Within each arrangement, you can change the sort order by clicking the right column heading in the Message List and choosing the order you want. For example, if you sort by **Date**, you can choose between **Newest** on top and **Oldest** on top, as shown in Figure 23–11; if you sort by **Subject**, you can choose between **A** on top and **Z** on top; and if you sort by **Attachments**, you can choose between **With** on top and **None** on top. You can also reverse the current sort order by choosing **View ➤ Arrangement ➤ Reverse Sort**.

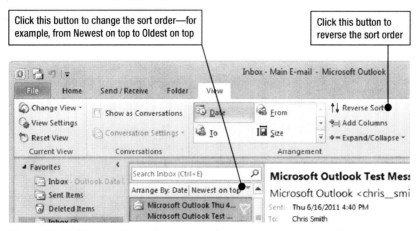

Figure 23–11. *You can change the sort order inside the arrangement you've chosen by clicking either the column heading or the* **Reverse Sort** *button.*

Choosing Whether to Group Items

For each arrangement, you can choose whether to show the items in groups or as a series. The groups vary depending on the arrangement. For example, when you sort by **Date**, Outlook uses groups such as **Today**, **Yesterday**, **Last Week**, and **Last Month**; when you sort by **From**, the groups are the senders (by name when it appears, and by e-mail address when it doesn't); and when you sort by **Size**, the groups are **Tiny**, **Small**, **Medium**, **Large**, and **Enormous**. Figure 23–12 shows you how to turn groups on or off.

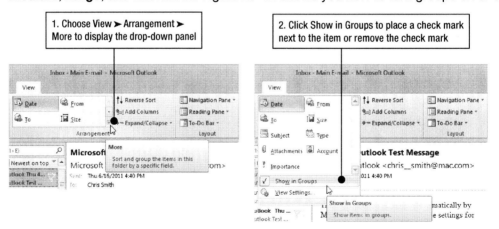

Figure 23–12. *You can quickly turn grouping on or off from the* **Arrangement** *drop-down panel on the* **View** *tab of the Ribbon.*

Viewing Conversations

When you've sorted the Message List by **Date**, which is often the most useful way for regular use, you can view your e-mail messages as conversations. When you do this, Outlook presents each exchange of e-mail messages as a separate section, enabling you to see the sequence of messages clearly and to determine who said what when.

To view messages by conversation, choose **View ➤ Arrangement ➤ Arrange By ➤ Date** to switch to Date order. Then choose **View ➤ Conversations ➤ Show as Conversations** to place a check mark next to this item. Once you've done this, each exchange of messages appears as a conversation, and you can expand a conversation by clicking it, and then clicking the white triangle to its left. In Figure 23–13, the **Today** category contains two conversations, of which the first is collapsed and the second is expanded.

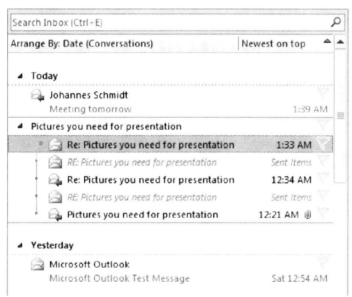

Figure 23–13. *When you need to see the sequence of an e-mail exchange, display the messages in conversations. It's usually best to use the **Show Messages from Other Folders** option and the **Show Senders above the Subject** option to make the conversation clear, as in this example.*

To see the details of a conversation, it's often useful to see the messages you've sent, plus any messages from earlier in the conversation that you've filed in folders. To see messages in other folders, choose **View ➤ Conversations ➤ Conversation Settings ➤ Show Messages from Other Folders**, placing a check mark next to this item. Clear the check mark when you no longer need to see messages from other folders.

To make the conversations clearer, display the sender above the subject by choosing **View ➤ Conversations ➤ Conversation Settings ➤ Show Senders Above the Subject**, placing a check mark next to this item.

If you want Outlook to automatically expand a conversation when you click it, choose **View ➤ Conversations ➤ Conversation Settings ➤ Always Expand Conversations**, placing a check mark next to this item. This behavior lets you work more quickly in the Message List, so you may well want to try it.

If you prefer to have the messages indented to show the different stages of the conversation, choose **View ➤ Conversations ➤ Conversation Settings ➤ Use Classic Indented View**, putting a check mark next to this item. Figure 23–14 shows a conversation that uses indented view.

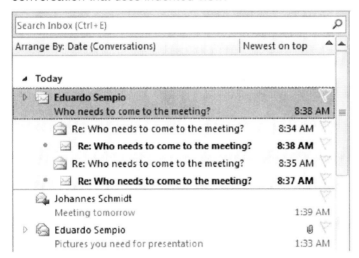

Figure 23–14. *Use* **Classic Indented** *view when you want to see the different stages of a conversation indented to different levels, as in the selected conversation here.*

Using and Customizing the Reading Pane

When you click a message in the Message List, Outlook displays the message's contents in the Reading Pane so that you can read it.

At first, Outlook displays the Reading Pane to the right of the Message List. If you prefer, you can position the Reading Pane below the Message List by choosing **View ➤ Layout ➤ Reading Pane ➤ Bottom**, as shown in Figure 23–15. (To put it back, choose **View ➤ Layout ➤ Reading Pane ➤ Right**.) You may prefer this layout, as it gives you a better view of the Message List (but not as much of it).

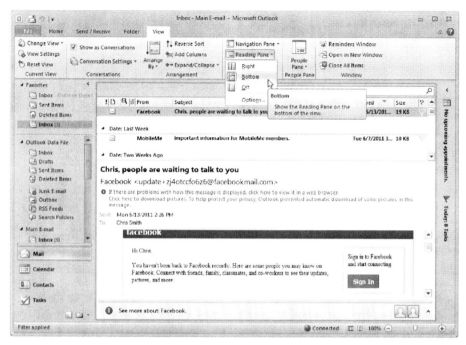

Figure 23–15. *Choose* **View ➤ Layout ➤ Reading Pane ➤ Bottom** *to move the Reading Pane below the Message List. This layout can make the Message List easier to navigate.*

> **TIP:** If your PC has a small screen, or if you need more space for the Message List, you may prefer to turn off the Reading Pane and read messages in a separate window instead. To turn off the Reading Pane, choose **View ➤ Layout ➤ Reading Pane ➤ None**. To read a message in a separate window, double-click the message in the Message List.

Normally, when you open a message in the Reading Pane and view it for a few seconds, Outlook marks the message as having been read. You can change this behavior by choosing **View ➤ Layout ➤ Reading Pane ➤ Options** and then working in the Reading Pane dialog box as shown in Figure 23–16.

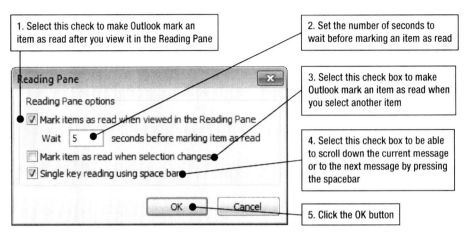

1. Select this check to make Outlook mark an item as read after you view it in the Reading Pane

2. Set the number of seconds to wait before marking an item as read

3. Select this check box to make Outlook mark an item as read when you select another item

4. Select this check box to be able to scroll down the current message or to the next message by pressing the spacebar

5. Click the OK button

Figure 23–16. *Use the Reading Pane dialog box to tell Outlook whether to mark items as read when you view them in the Reading Pane.*

NOTE: You can select either the **Mark items as read when viewed in the Reading Pane** check box or the **Mark item as read when selection changes** check box, but not both. If one of these check boxes is selected, Outlook clears it when you select the other check box.

Using and Customizing the To-Do Bar

When you're viewing your messages (or your contacts or tasks), the **To-Do Bar** appears on the right side of the Outlook window, giving you quick access to your appointments and to-do items.

To give yourself more space for your messages, you may want to minimize the **To-Do Bar** to a strip on the right side of the window. Figure 23–17 shows you how to do this and how to control which items appear in the **To-Do Bar**.

1.Choose View ➤ Layout ➤ To-Do Bar to display the To-Do Bar drop-down list

2. Click Minimized to minimize the To-Do Bar to a narrow strip

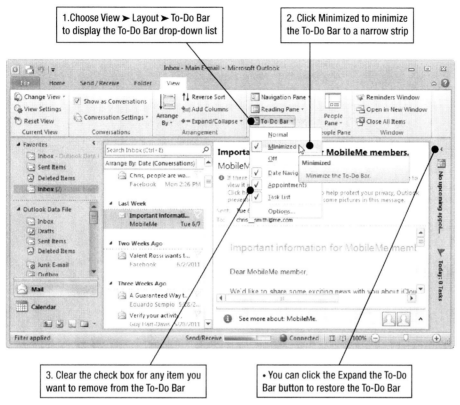

3. Clear the check box for any item you want to remove from the To-Do Bar

• You can click the Expand the To-Do Bar button to restore the To-Do Bar

Figure 23–17. *By using the **View ➤ Layout ➤ To-Do Bar** drop-down list, you can minimize the **To-Do Bar** to a strip at the right side of the Outlook window. You can also choose which items appear on the **To-Do Bar**.*

NOTE: If you want to hide the **To-Do Bar** altogether, choose **View ➤ Layout ➤ To-Do Bar ➤ Off**. When you want to restore it, choose **View ➤ Layout ➤ To-Do Bar ➤ Normal** or **View ➤ Layout ➤ To-Do Bar ➤ Minimized**, as needed.

To choose how many months and which appointments the **To-Do Bar** shows, choose **View ➤ Layout ➤ To-Do Bar ➤ Options**, and then work in the **To-Do Bar Options** dialog box as shown in Figure 23–18.

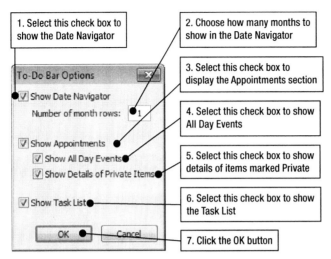

Figure 23–18. *Open the **To-Do Bar Options** dialog box when you want to change the number of months or the types of appointments that appear in the **To-Do Bar**.*

TIP: Showing two months in the date navigator is especially useful toward the end of the month, when you may want to start working with the next month.

Using and Customizing the People Pane

Outlook's **People Pane** gives you quick access to information about the people you work with or exchange messages with. These people can be either on a SharePoint site on your network or on a public network such as LinkedIn or Facebook.

To set up the People Pane, choose **View ➤ People Pane ➤ People Pane ➤ Account Settings**. Click the **Next** button on the introductory screen to display the **Microsoft Outlook: Social Network Accounts** dialog box. You can then set up your social networks as shown in Figure 23–19.

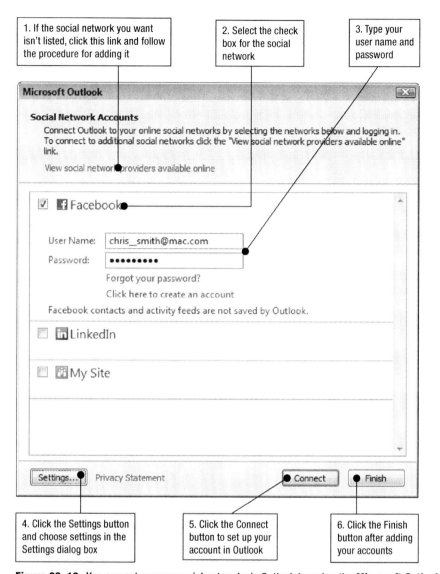

1. If the social network you want isn't listed, click this link and follow the procedure for adding it

2. Select the check box for the social network

3. Type your user name and password

4. Click the Settings button and choose settings in the Settings dialog box

5. Click the Connect button to set up your account in Outlook

6. Click the Finish button after adding your accounts

Figure 23–19. *You can set up your social networks in Outlook by using the **Microsoft Outlook: Social Network Accounts** dialog box.*

NOTE: If the social network you want to use doesn't appear in the main box, click the **View social network providers available online** link. In the Internet Explorer window that opens, follow through the process of downloading and installing the connector software for the network. You may need to close the **Microsoft Outlook: Social Network Accounts** dialog box, exit Outlook, and then restart Outlook before you can proceed.

When you click the Finish button to close the **Microsoft Outlook: Social Network Accounts** dialog box, Outlook displays a **Congratulations!** screen confirming that you've added the social networks. Click the **Close** button.

You can now expand the People Pane by choosing **View ➤ People Pane ➤ People Pane ➤ Normal** or by clicking the **Expand the People Pane** button (the ^ button) in the lower-right corner of the **Outlook** window. Figure 23–20 shows the People Pane open for the sender of an e-mail message.

Click the tabs on the left of the People Pane to display the different types of information about the contact:

- **Home**. Click this tab to display a summary of information. This is often the best place to start.

- **News**. Click this tab to see news about the contact—for example, updates to their social-networking profiles.

- **E-mail**. Click this tab to see recent messages from this contact. You can click a message link to open the message in a separate window.

- **Attachments**. Click this tab to see files you've received as attachments.

- **Meetings**. Click this tab to see details of the meetings you had with this contact.

- **Status Updates**. Click this tab to see details of updates to the contact's social networks.

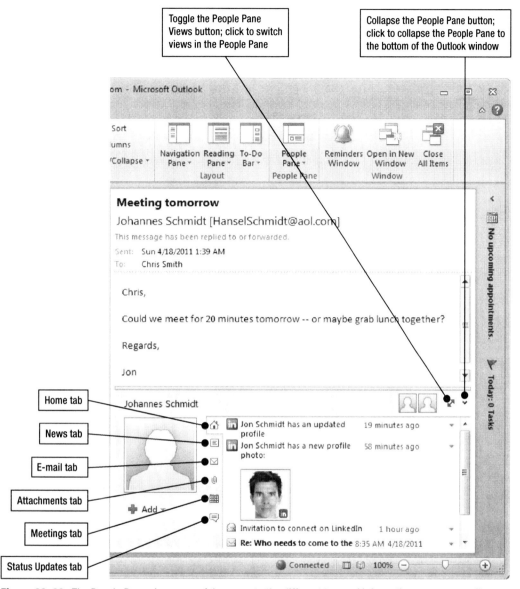

Figure 23–20. *The People Pane gives you quick access to the different types of information—news, e-mail messages, attachments you've received, and meetings you've had—about a contact.*

Using the Ribbon

Like the other Office programs, Outlook uses the Ribbon across the top of the window as its main control area.

The main part of the Ribbon contains five tabs: the **File** tab for accessing **Backstage**, the **Home** tab, the **Send/Receive** tab, the **Folder** tab, and the **View** tab. Outlook displays other tabs as needed; for example, when you select an e-mail attachment, Outlook displays the **Attachment Tools** section, which contains the Attachments tab.

The tab contents change depending on the area of Outlook you're using. Outlook displays the same tabs no matter which area (for example, **Mail**, **Calendar**, or **Contacts**) you're working in, but it changes the groups and controls. For example, when you're working with **Mail**, the **Home** tab includes the **New** group, **Delete** group, the **Respond** group, the **Quick Steps** group, the **Move** group, the **Tags** group, and the **Find** group. When you're working with **Calendar**, the **New** group and the **Find** group are still there, but the other groups are the **Go To** group, the **Arrange** group, the **Manage Calendars** group, and the **Share** group.

Summary

In this chapter, you set up Outlook to work with your e-mail account or accounts. You also met the Outlook interface, learning how to use the **Navigation Pane**, the **Reading Pane**, the **To-Do Bar**, and the **People Pane**, as well as the Ribbon.

In the next chapter, I'll show you how to send and receive e-mail using Outlook.

Chapter 24

Sending and Receiving E-mail

After setting up Outlook as explained in the previous chapter, you're ready to start using its Mail component to send and receive e-mail.

In this chapter, you'll learn first how to send and receive messages and attachments; reply to messages and forward them to others; and delete the messages you don't want to keep and file those you do. Then we'll look at how to quickly add standard closings to your messages by creating and using signatures. Finally, you'll learn how to deal with spam, or unwanted e-mail.

Sending an E-mail Message

To send an e-mail message, you create a message, address it, and add contents. You may also want to choose options for the message, such as setting its reply-to address to a different e-mail address than the one you're sending from.

Creating a New Message

When you need to write a new message, you can create a blank message, a message based on a theme, or a message based on a stationery design.

> **NOTE:** A *theme* is a coordinated look featuring colors, fonts, and graphical styles that work together. A *stationery design* is a background image that appears in the message, as if you were writing on a piece of paper that bore a design.

You can create a new blank message in any of these ways:

- *From the Taskbar.* Right-click the **Outlook** button, and then click **New E-mail Message** on the context menu, as shown in Figure 24–1.

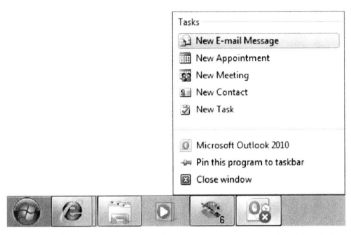

Figure 24–1. *You can quickly create a new e-mail message by right-clicking the* **Outlook** *button on the Taskbar and then clicking* **New E-mail Message** *in the* **Tasks** *area.*

- *From the Ribbon.* Choose **Home ➤ New ➤ New E-mail**.

- *From the keyboard.* With the Mail component active in the Navigation bar, press **Ctrl+N**.

> **TIP:** The **Ctrl+N** shortcut creates a new item in the area of Outlook you're using: in **Mail**, pressing **Ctrl+N** creates a new message; in **Calendar**, pressing **Ctrl+N** creates a new appointment; in **Contacts**, pressing **Ctrl+N** creates a new contact; in **Tasks**, pressing **Ctrl+N** creates a new task; and in **Notes**, pressing **Ctrl+N** creates a new note.

Whichever way you give the command for creating the new message, Outlook opens a new message window. The message window's title bar at first shows **Untitled**, but then it displays the subject line you give the message. Figure 24–2 shows a message window with a new message open. As you can see, the Ribbon in the message window contains the **File** tab and five other tabs: the **Message** tab, the **Insert** tab, the **Options** tab, the **Format** Text tab, and the **Review** tab.

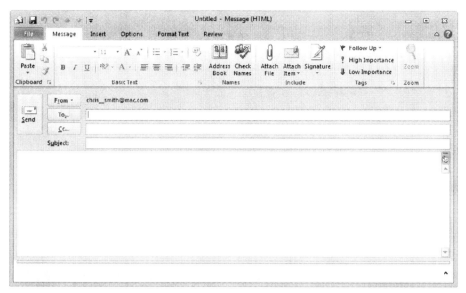

Figure 24–2. *A new message opens in a window named **Untitled** at first. The title changes to what you type in the **Subject** box.*

To create a message based on a theme or stationery, choose **Home ➤ New Items ➤ E-mail Message Using ➤ More Stationery** to display the **Theme** or **Stationery** dialog box, and then work as shown in Figure 24–3.

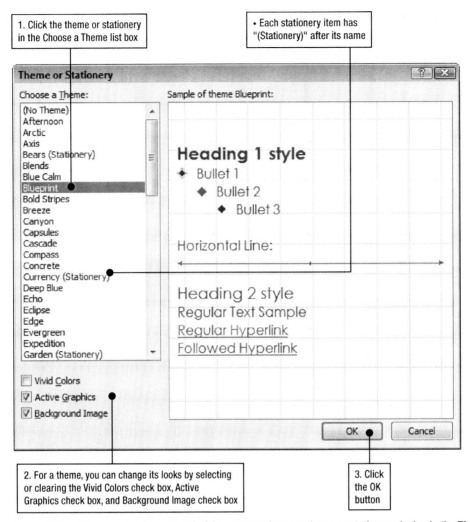

1. Click the theme or stationery in the Choose a Theme list box

• Each stationery item has "(Stationery)" after its name

2. For a theme, you can change its looks by selecting or clearing the Vivid Colors check box, Active Graphics check box, and Background Image check box

3. Click the OK button

Figure 24–3. *When you need a more colorful message, choose a theme or stationery design in the **Theme** or **Stationery** dialog box. Select the **Active Graphics** check box only if you want the message to include animated graphics.*

Choosing Which Account to Send the Message From

If you have set up Outlook to use multiple e-mail accounts, check which account appears next to the **From** button. Outlook uses the account you're working in, but sometimes you may need to change accounts. To do so, click the **From** button to display the drop-down list of accounts, and then click the account you want.

Addressing the Message

You can add the components of a message in any order that suits you, but what you'll usually want to do is address the message first. To do so, you enter the primary recipients in the **To** box and any Cc (carbon copy) recipients in the **Cc** box.

You can enter the e-mail addresses in three main ways:

▪ *Type or paste in an e-mail address.* If you know the e-mail address, you can click in the box (for example, the **To** box) and simply type it in. Or if you've copied from a document or a web page, you can paste it in.

▪ Type the name and have Outlook complete the address for you. Click in the box and start typing the name. When Outlook suggests a match (see Figure 24–4), press **Enter** to accept it. If Outlook suggests several matches, move the highlight to the right one by pressing **Down** arrow or **Up** arrow, and then press **Enter**; or click the right address.

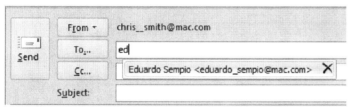

Figure 24–4. *Outlook automatically suggests matching contacts for names you start typing.*

▪ *Use the **Select Names** dialog box.* Click the **To** button or the **Cc** button to display the **Select Names** dialog box, and then work as shown in Figure 24–5.

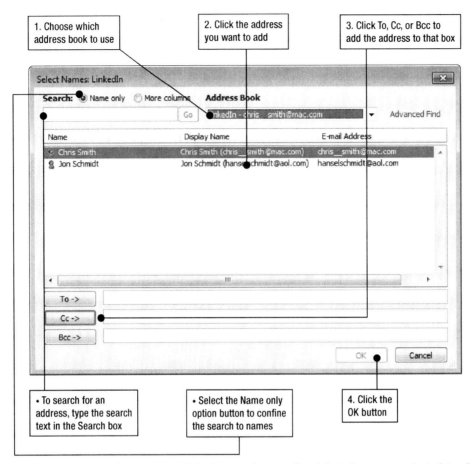

Figure 24–5. *Use the **Select Names** dialog box to select e-mail recipients from your contacts list or from a social network you've added to Outlook (as shown here). Use the **Cc** box to add recipients of carbon copies or the **Bcc** box to add recipients of blind carbon copies—messages in which the recipient does not see any Bcc addresses other than his own.*

Outlook enters the recipient's name in the **People Pane** at the bottom of the message window. You can click the **Expand the People Pane** button (the ^ button in the lower-right corner of the window) to expand the **People Pane** (see Figure 24–6) so that you can refer to information about this contact while writing the message to him or her.

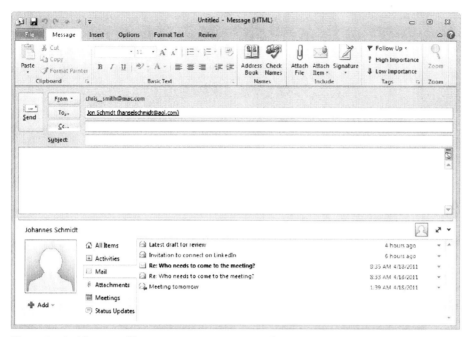

Figure 24–6. *After you address a message, you can use the **People Pane** for reference about the addressee.*

Adding the Subject Line and Message Contents

In the **Subject** box, type the subject of the message. This is the text that appears in the recipient's inbox to help them identify the message.

> **TIP:** Make your subject lines as clear as possible while keeping them short enough to fit in the short columns that appear in a typical e-mail program window. Your message will most likely be competing for the recipient's attention with many other messages, so making the subject clear will help it get read.

In the main box of the message window, enter the text of the message. Many e-mail messages require only plain text, which you can enter by typing as normal (or by using other standard text-entry techniques, such as pasting text or expanding **AutoCorrect** entries). Other messages need formatted text, pictures, or other graphical items.

The **Message** tab of the Ribbon in a message window provides essential formatting controls, such as font formatting and bulleted lists, as you can see in Figure 24–6. To reach the full range of formatting, display the **Format Text** tab of the Ribbon (see Figure 24–7), which contains everything from font formatting to styles.

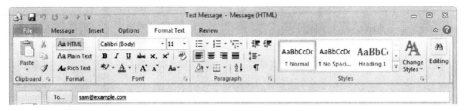

Figure 24–7. *The **Format** tab of the Ribbon in a message window provides a full range of formatting, including styles.*

> **NOTE:** Outlook lets you format the message content as plain text, as HTML, or as rich text, by clicking the appropriate button—**HTML**, **Plain Text**, or **Rich Text**—in the **Format** group on the **Format Text** tab of the Ribbon. Choose **Plain Text** when you want the text to have no formatting. Choose **HTML** when you want to use formatting that is compatible with most e-mail programs. Choose **Rich Text** for formatted messages only when you're sending to someone you know uses Outlook, as the results may be inconsistent in other e-mail programs.

The Insert tab of the Ribbon in a message window (see Figure 24–8) includes controls for inserting tables, illustrations, hyperlinks, and other objects—even charts and equations if you need them.

Figure 24–8. *From the Insert tab of the Ribbon in a message window, you can insert tables, illustrations, shapes, hyperlinks, and other objects.*

> **NOTE:** You can mark a message as being important by choosing **Message ➤ Tags ➤ High Importance** (or you can choose **Message ➤ Tags ➤ Low Importance** to mark a message as being unimportant). But be warned that high importance has been so widely abused in e-mail messages that many people ignore it.

Choosing Options for a Message

The **Options** tab of the Ribbon in a message window (see Figure 24–9) contains a range of options for making a message look and behave differently from normal.

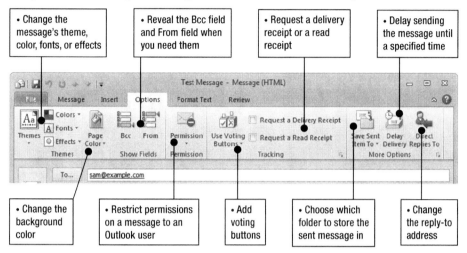

Figure 24–9. *The **Options** tab of the Ribbon in a message window lets you change the message's look and behavior.*

Most of these options are straightforward. Here are notes on those that aren't:

- *Permission group.* The **Permission** drop-down panel in the **Permission** group lets you set restrictions on a message you're sending to another Outlook user on your e-mail system. For example, you can set the **Do Not Forward** restriction on a message to prevent the recipient from forwarding the message.

CAUTION: Many of the options on the **Options** tab of the Ribbon work well—or work at all—only with Outlook. For example, many e-mail programs routinely ignore requests for delivery receipts and read receipts, because these features otherwise are useful to spammers who want to find out which e-mail addresses are live and which are not.

■ *Use Voting Buttons* *drop-down panel.* The **Use Voting Buttons** drop-down panel in the **Tracking** group lets you include a pair or group of option buttons to enable the recipients to respond quickly to a message. For example, you can choose **Approve;Reject** to have an **Approve** button and a **Reject** button, or **Yes;No;Maybe** to have a **Yes** button, a **No** button, and a **Maybe** button. To create your own buttons, click the **Custom** item, and then enter the text in the **Use voting buttons** box in the **Properties** dialog box (see Figure 24–10), separating the button names with semicolons (for example, **Tuesday;Wednesday;Thursday**).

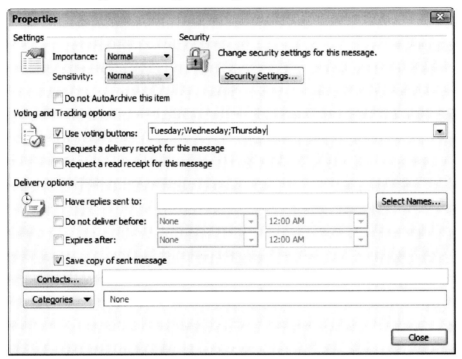

Figure 24–10. *The **Properties** dialog box gives you one-stop access to many of the options for a message, including creating custom voting buttons and directing of replies to a different e-mail address.*

NOTE: To reach the full set of voting, tracking, and delivery options for a message, choose **Options ➤ Tracking ➤ Message Options** (the **Message Options** button is the little button in the lower-right corner of the **Tracking** group). Outlook displays the **Properties** dialog box, which gives you access to all the settings.

- *Save Sent Item To.* Click this button to display a panel that lets you choose among saving the sent item to the default folder (**Use Default Folder**), not saving it (**Do Not Save**), and another folder (**Other Folder**). In most cases, **Other Folder** is the most useful choice; in the **Select Folder** dialog box that appears, select the destination folder, and then click the **OK** button.

- *Delay Delivery.* Click this button to display the **Properties** dialog box, and then use the controls on the **Do not deliver before** line to set the earliest delivery date and time. (Outlook uses this date and time if your PC is awake and online then; otherwise, it sends the message as soon after the date and time as possible.) Click the **Close** button to close the **Properties** dialog box.

- *Direct Replies To.* Click this button to display the **Properties** dialog box, and then enter the delivery address in the Have replies sent to box. This setting is useful when you need the reply to go to a different address than you're sending the message from, or when you need the reply to go to multiple addresses. Click the **Close** button to close the **Properties** dialog box.

Checking the Spelling in a Message

Outlook checks spelling and grammar as you type unless you turn off the **Spelling** checker and **Grammar** checker, so you can easily resolve spelling and grammar queries as you create the message.

If you choose not to check spelling and grammar as you work, you can start a check by pressing **F7** or by choosing **Review ➤ Proofing ➤ Spelling & Grammar**. The **Review** tab of the Ribbon (see Figure 24–11) also includes commands for researching the current word or looking it up in the Thesaurus, getting a word count, translating text, and setting the proofing language.

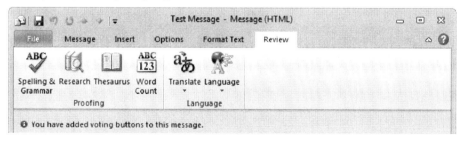

Figure 24–11. *From the **Review** tab of the Ribbon in a message window, you can check the spelling and grammar, research words, or get a word count for the message.*

> **NOTE:** See Chapter 2: "Using the Ribbon, Backstage, and Common Tools" for instructions on configuring the **Spelling** checker and the **Grammar** checker to check only the items you want.

Sending the Message

When you're ready to send the message, click the **Send** button below the left end of the Ribbon.

Receiving and Reading Messages

Normally, Outlook automatically checks your incoming mail server for messages, and collects those sent to you. You can also force Outlook to check e-mail at any point by pressing **F9** or choosing **Send/Receive ➤ Send & Receive ➤ Send/Receive All Folders** (to get all incoming mail and send all outgoing mail) or by clicking the **Inbox** and choosing **Send/Receive ➤ Send & Receive ➤ Update Folder** (to get the mail for this account).

> **NOTE:** To control how frequently Outlook checks for new mail, choose **File ➤ Options**, and then click **Advanced** in the left pane. Scroll down to the **Send and receive** heading, then click the **Send/Receive** button to display the **Send/Receive Groups** dialog box. In the **Setting for group** "**All accounts**" area, make sure the **Include this group in send/receive** check box is selected. Select the **Schedule an automatic send/receive every *N* minutes** check box, and then enter the number of minutes in the text box. You can also select the **Perform an automatic send/receive when exiting** check box if you want Outlook to send and receive when you close the program; this is useful for making sure you don't leave messages unsent. Click the **Close** button to close the **Send/Receive Groups** dialog box, and then click the **OK** button to close the **Outlook Options** dialog box.

Once you've received your messages, click the **Inbox** to display them. You can then read the messages either in the **Reading Pane** or in a separate window. The **Reading Pane** is often easiest, as it's designed to enable you to quickly triage your messages. Open a message in a separate window when you need more space to concentrate on it or when you need to compare the contents of two or more messages side by side.

Click the message you want to read, or press **Down** arrow or **Up** arrow to move the highlight to the message so that Outlook displays it in the **Reading Pane**.

TIP: When reading messages in the **Reading Pane**, press the spacebar to display the next screen of the message. When you reach the end of this message, press the spacebar again to display the next message. You can also press **Shift+spacebar** to display the previous screen of the current message or (from the beginning of the current message) to display the previous message.

To read a message in a separate window, double-click the message in the **Message List,** and then work as shown in Figure 24–12.

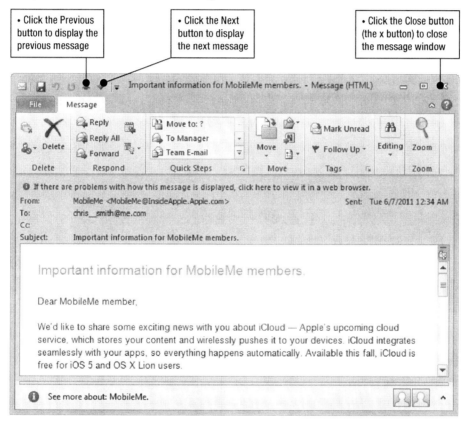

Figure 24–12. *Open a message in a separate message window when you want to concentrate on it or when you want to compare messages side by side.*

After reading a message, you can reply to it, move it to a folder, or delete it, as discussed later in this chapter.

Sending and Receiving Attachments

E-mail is a great way of sending messages quickly, but it's also useful for transferring files from one computer to another. To send a file via e-mail, you attach it to a message that you then send as usual; and when someone sends you a file, it comes to your **Inbox** as part of the message that brings it. You then detach the file from the message and store it in a folder.

Sending a File as an Attachment

To send a file as an attachment, start a message as usual. Then choose **Message ➤ Include ➤ Attach File** to display the **Insert File** dialog box, click the file you want, and click the **Insert** button. Outlook adds an **Attached** box below the **Subject** box in the message window showing the file's name and its size (see Figure 24–13). You can then add other files by repeating the process.

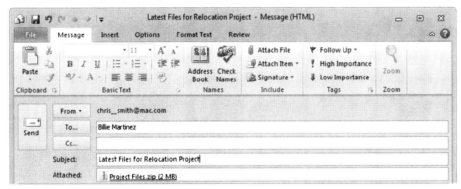

Figure 24–13. *Outlook displays the **Attached** box below the **Subject** box when you attach one or more files to a message.*

> **TIP:** You can also attach a file to a message by dragging the file from a **Windows Explorer** window to the message window.

Receiving a File as an Attachment

When you receive a file as an attachment, it arrives in your Inbox with its message. You'll see a paperclip icon on the message's listing in the **Message List** and the attachment's filename at the top of the **Reading Pane** (see Figure 24–14).

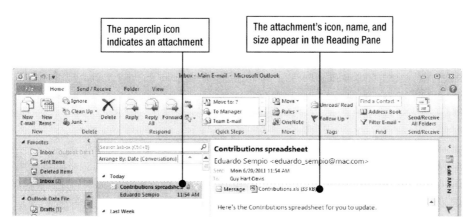

Figure 24–14. *The **Message List** displays a paperclip icon to indicate that a message has an attachment. The attachment's name appears at the top of the **Reading Pane**.*

Click the attachment's name to see a preview of the attachment and to display the **Attachment Tools** section of the Ribbon (see Figure 24–15).

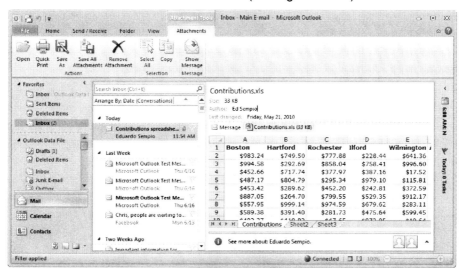

Figure 24–15. *Click the attachment's name in the **Reading Pane** to display a preview of the attachment. Outlook displays the **Attachment Tools** section of the Ribbon, which gives you access to commands for working with the attachment.*

To save the file to a folder, choose **Attachment Tools ➤ Attachments ➤ Actions ➤ Save As**. In the **Save Attachment** dialog box that opens, select the folder in which you want to save the file, and then click the **Save** button. You can then open the file either from a **Windows Explorer** window or from the program you use for that type of file—for example, **Word** for a word processing file or **Excel** for a spreadsheet file.

> **CAUTION:** The **Attachments** tab of the Ribbon includes an **Open** button, but don't open an
> attachment directly from Outlook. This is because the file opens in read-only mode, in which you
> cannot save changes you make to the file. You then need to use a **Save As** command to save the
> file under a different filename or in a different folder. Saving the file from Outlook and then
> opening it saves time and confusion.

After you save an attachment to a folder, you can either remove it from the message or
leave it in the message for reference. Removing attachments is usually a good idea
because otherwise your mailbox can become huge, but you may sometimes need to
keep attachments in messages as a safety net.

To remove an attachment from a message, follow these steps:

1. Click the attachment in the message.

2. Choose **Attachment Tools ➤ Attachments ➤ Actions ➤ Remove Attachment**.
    Outlook displays the dialog box shown in Figure 24–16.

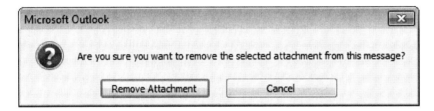

Figure 24–16. *Outlook confirms your removal of an attachment from a message.*

3. Click the **Remove Attachment** button. Outlook removes the attachment.

Replying to and Forwarding Messages

To reply to a message you've received, choose **Home ➤ Respond ➤ Reply** or press
Ctrl+R. To reply to all the recipients of a message you've received, choose **Home ➤
Respond ➤ Reply All** or press **Ctrl+Shift+R**.

Outlook opens a message window for the reply, adding **RE:** to the subject line to
indicate that it is a reply, and showing the original message and sender information
below the insertion point (see Figure 24–17). You can then enter the text of the reply—
and any other objects needed—and then click the **Send** button to send it.

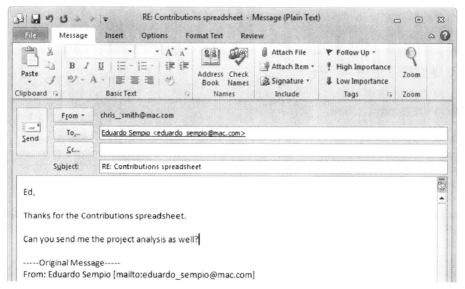

Figure 24–17. *Outlook adds **RE:** to the subject of a reply and includes the original message.*

To send a message you've received on to someone else, forward it by choosing **Home ➤ Respond ➤ Forward** or pressing **Ctrl+F.** Outlook opens a message window containing the forwarded message, adding **FW:** to the subject line to indicate that the message is forwarded, and placing the original message below the insertion point. You can then address the message, type whatever information you need to add to the forwarded message (for example, why you're forwarding it), and then click the **Send** button.

Deleting, Storing, and Organizing Messages

When you don't need to keep an e-mail message, you can delete it by selecting it and pressing **Delete** or choosing **Home ➤ Delete ➤ Delete**. But chances are that you'll need to keep many—perhaps most—of the messages you receive. That means creating a structure of folders in which you can place the messages, and then moving each message to the appropriate folder.

Moving a Message to a Mail Folder

The quick way to move a message to a mail folder is to drag the message from the **Message List** to the folder in the **Navigation Pane**. This technique works well when you have few enough folders to fit easily in the **Navigation Pane**; if you have a longer list of folders, you can drag down to the bottom of the **Navigation Pane** to make it scroll further, but even so, getting to the folder you want can be awkward.

When you have a long list of folders, use the **Move Items** dialog box to move the message to the folder you want. Follow these steps:

1. Select the message or messages you want to move.

2. Choose **Home ➤ Move ➤ Move ➤ Other Folder** to display the **Move Items** dialog box (see Figure 24–18).

3. Click the destination folder. If necessary, click the **New** button to create a new folder in the current folder.

4. Click the **OK** button.

Figure 24–18. *Use the **Move Items** dialog box to quickly move messages to a folder that's part of a long list. You can click the **New** button to create a new folder inside the current folder.*

NOTE: You can also create a new folder by working in the **Navigation Pane**. Right-click the folder in which you want to create the folder, and then click **New Folder** on the context menu. In the **Create New Folder** dialog box that opens, type the folder name, select the **Mail and Post Items** item in the **Folder** contains drop-down list, and then click the **OK** button.

Adding Consistent Closings to Your Messages with Signatures

When you send a message, you often need to let the recipient know standard information about you—for example, your name and phone numbers, or your company name and address, plus your position in it. To save you having to retype the same information over and over again, Outlook provides a feature called *signatures* that lets you set up one or more standard closings for inserting in your messages.

TIP: If you find signatures awkward, you can create a signature as an **AutoCorrect** entry and enter it by typing its abbreviation. See Chapter 2: ""Using the Ribbon, Backstage, and Common Tools" for coverage of AutoCorrect.

To set up your signatures, follow these steps:

1. Choose **Home ➤ New ➤ New E-mail** to open a new message window.

2. Choose **Message ➤ Include ➤ Signature ➤ Signatures** to display the **Signatures and Stationery** dialog box with the **E-mail Signatures** tab at the front.

3. Click the New button to display the **New Signature** dialog box (see Figure 24–19), type the name for the signature (for example, **Business Signature – Standard**), and then click the **OK** button.

Figure 24–19. *To start creating a signature, type its name in the **New Signature** dialog box, and then click the **OK** button.*

4. Outlook adds the signature to the **Select signature to edit** box.

5. Set up the signature as shown in Figure 24–20.

1. Click the signature you want to edit, or click the New button and use the New Signature dialog box to start a new signature

2. Type or paste the text for the signature

3. Add your business card if necessary

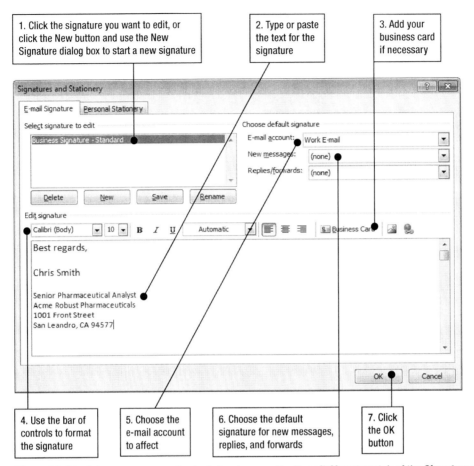

4. Use the bar of controls to format the signature

5. Choose the e-mail account to affect

6. Choose the default signature for new messages, replies, and forwards

7. Click the OK button

Figure 24–20. *Set up one or more standard signatures on the **E-mail Signature** tab of the **Signatures and Stationery** dialog box.*

NOTE: Replies and forwarded messages generally don't need a signature. If a particular reply or forwarded message would benefit from a signature, you can add it manually by choosing **Message ➤ Include ➤ Signature** and clicking the signature you want.

Dealing with Spam

E-mail monitoring companies report that more than nine out of ten e-mail messages are *spam*, or unsolicited commercial messages. ISPs and e-mail providers generally do a great job of preventing most spam from reaching us, but even so, plenty of spam messages evade the filters and make it to inboxes.

To help you deal with spam, Outlook automatically monitors your incoming mail and puts any suspected spam in the **Junk E-mail** folder. It's a good idea to visit this folder every day or two to rescue any messages that Outlook has falsely accused and to get rid of the rest.

Removing Non-Spam Messages from the Junk E-mail Folder

If your **Junk E-mail** folder contains a message that's not junk, click the message in the **Message List**, and then choose **Home ➤ Delete ➤ Junk ➤ Not Junk**. Outlook displays the **Mark as Not Junk** dialog box (see Figure 24–21). If this sender is safe, select the **Always trust e-mail from *sender*** check box; otherwise, clear it. Then click the **OK** button to close the dialog box. Outlook moves the message to the **Inbox**.

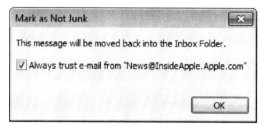

Figure 24–21. *When you mark a message as not being junk, you can choose whether to always trust the sender in the future.*

After checking that all the messages in your **Junk E-mail** folder are spam, select them, and then press **Delete** to delete them.

Marking Spam Messages as Junk

If you receive a spam message in your Inbox, click it, and then choose **Home ➤ Delete ➤ Junk ➤ Block Sender**. Outlook adds the sender to the **Blocked Senders** list, moves the message to the **Junk E-mail** folder, and then displays a dialog box (see Figure 24–22) telling you that it has done so. If you don't want to see this message box when you block other senders, select the **Do not show this message again** check box. Click the **OK** button to close the dialog box.

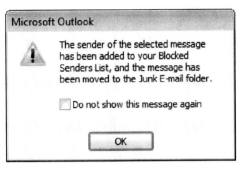

Figure 24-22. *When you block a sender, you can choose whether to have Outlook display this message again in the future.*

Summary

In this chapter, you learned to use Outlook's Mail component to send and receive e-mail. You now know how to create and send messages, how to receive messages, and how to read the messages you've received. You also know how to attach files to messages you send, how to deal with incoming attachments, and how to organize your messages. You learned how to create signatures and how to deal with spam.

In the next chapter, I'll show you how to use Outlook to manage your contacts.

Chapter 25

Managing Your Contacts with Outlook

In this chapter, I'll show you how to use Outlook to manage your contacts.

First, we'll go through how to create contacts either from scratch or by importing your existing contacts from sources such as address books or spreadsheets. After that, we'll examine how to work with contacts: viewing and sorting your contacts to reveal the ones you need, editing contact information when necessary, and quickly creating communications to your contacts.

Creating Contacts

You can create contacts either from scratch, entering data in a contact record manually, or by importing data from electronic files. In this section, we'll look at each method in turn.

Creating a Contact from Scratch

If you have a contact's information on a physical business card or a piece of paper rather than in an electronic file, create a contact record from scratch. Figure 25–1 shows you how to start creating a contact.

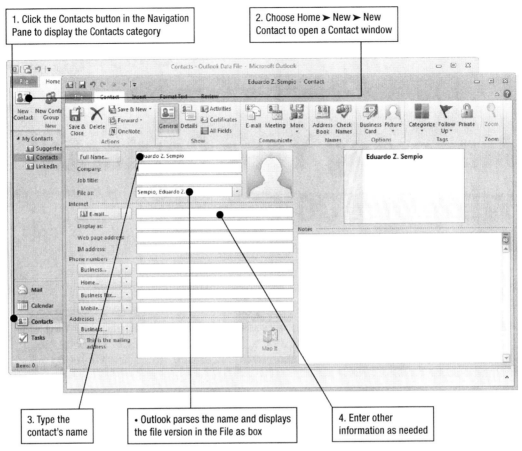

1. Click the Contacts button in the Navigation Pane to display the Contacts category

2. Choose Home ➤ New ➤ New Contact to open a Contact window

3. Type the contact's name

• Outlook parses the name and displays the file version in the File as box

4. Enter other information as needed

Figure 25–1. *With the **Contacts** item selected in the **Navigation Pane**, choose **Home** ➤ **New** ➤ **New Contact** to open a **New Contact** window. You can then type in the contact's details.*

> **TIP:** You can also start creating a new contact by right-clicking the **Outlook** button on the Taskbar and then clicking the **New Contact** item in the **Tasks** area. When you're in other areas of Outlook, you can add a contact by choosing **Home** ➤ **New** ➤ **New Items** ➤ **Contact**.

Correcting the Contact's Name

When you enter the contact's name in the **Full Name** text box and move to another field (for example, by pressing **Tab**), Outlook parses the name and enters it in the **File as** box. If you prefer to control exactly how the parts of the name are entered, click the **Full Name** button, and then work in the **Check Full Name** dialog box (see Figure 25–2).

Figure 25–2. *Use the* **Check Full Name** *dialog box to sort out any problems in parsing the contact's name, to add a title or suffix, or simply to enter a contact name the way you want it.*

If the **File as** box shows a different version of the name than you want to use for filing, click the drop-down button, and then click your preferred version.

> **NOTE:** If Outlook can't parse the name into its separate components, it automatically displays the **Check Full Name** dialog box to prompt you to fix the problem. This behavior is usually helpful, but if you don't want Outlook to do this, clear the **Show this again when name is incomplete or unclear** check box. If you prefer, you can use the **Check Full Name** dialog box to enter each contact name—just click the **Full Name** button instead of typing the name into the **Full Name** box.

Adding a Photo to the Contact

If you have a photo of the contact, click the **Add Contact Picture** placeholder to display the **Add Contact Picture** dialog box. Navigate to the folder that contains the picture, click the picture, and then click the **OK** button.

Entering the Contact's E-mail Address

If you have an e-mail address for the contact, enter it in one of these ways:

- *Type the address*. If Outlook can detect an obvious problem with the address, it displays the **Check Names** dialog box (see Figure 25–3) to prompt you to examine the address. If the **Select the address to use** box has the right version of the name, click it. Otherwise, click the **Cancel** button, and then revisit the address and fix the problem.

Figure 25–3. *Outlook displays the **Check Names** dialog box if there's an obvious problem with an e-mail address you try to enter. This address is missing the @ sign.*

▨ *Paste the address in*. If you have the address in a document or on a web page, copy it, and then paste it into the **E-mail** box.

▨ *Use the Select Name dialog box*. Click the **E-mail** button to display the **Select Name** dialog box. Navigate to the contact's name, click the e-mail address you want, and then click the **OK** button.

TIP: You can start creating a contact quickly by right-clicking the sender's name in an e-mail message and then clicking **Add to Outlook Contacts** on the context menu.

Whichever way you add the address, press **Tab** or click in the **Display as** box to move the insertion point there. Outlook automatically inserts in the **Display as** box a suggested way to display the name in messages: usually the full name followed by the e-mail address in parentheses. Having both the name and the address is usually clearest, but you can type a different description if you want; for example, **John Q. Smith (work e-mail)**.

NOTE: If you need to add another e-mail address for the contact, click the drop-down button to the right of the **E-mail** button, click **E-mail 2**, and then enter the address.

Entering the Contact's Phone Numbers

You can enter the contact's phone numbers by typing (or pasting) them straight into the four boxes in the **Phone Numbers** area. At first, these boxes are labeled **Business**, **Home**, **Business Fax**, and **Mobile**, but you can change any of them by clicking the drop-down button to its right, and then clicking the label you want on the drop-down list, which includes **Primary**, **Assistant**, **Car**, **Pager**, and other labels.

When you enter a number that Outlook can recognize, Outlook divides it into its components. For example, if you enter **5105551212**, Outlook displays it as **(510) 555-1212**.

When you need to enter a complex phone number, click the button to the left of the phone number's box, and then work in the **Check Phone Number** dialog box (see Figure 25–4).

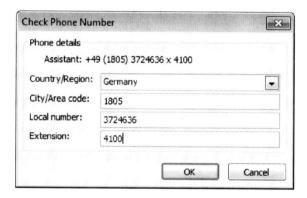

Figure 25–4. *Use the* **Check Phone Number** *dialog box when you want to enter a complex phone number (for example, including an extension) or have Outlook automatically insert the country code for you.*

Entering the Contact's Address

To enter the contact's address, open the drop-down list next to the button in the **Addresses** area, and then choose the address type: **Business**, **Home**, or **Other**. Then type or paste the address in the text box. For a complex address, click the button (which is labeled **Business**, **Home**, or **Other**, depending on your choice), and then work in the **Check Address** dialog box (see Figure 25–5).

Figure 25–5. *Open the **Check Address** dialog box when you need to make clear to Outlook which part of a complex address is which.*

Adding Notes about the Contact

In this field, enter any notes about the contact (or your dealings with the contact) that don't fit into the other fields. You can format the text in this field by using the controls on the **Format Text** tab of the contact window (see Figure 25–6). Start by applying styles from the **Styles** group, and then add direct formatting (such as boldface or different line spacing) only for special needs.

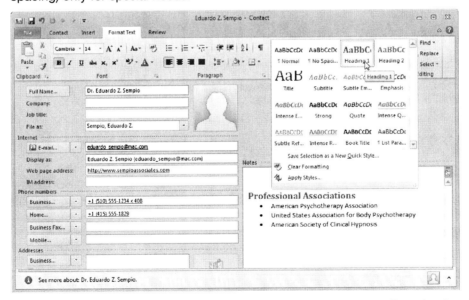

Figure 25–6. *You can enter any extra information in the **Notes** box. Use the **Format Text** tab to format your notes, starting with styles and then moving to direct formatting only if necessary.*

Entering Further Details for the Contact

Choose **Contact ➤ Show ➤ Details** to display the Details page of the contact window (see Figure 25–7), and then fill in the information: **Department**, **Office**, **Profession**, and so on.

> **TIP:** When you need to enter extra information for the contact, choose **Contact ➤ Show ➤ All Fields**. You can then pick a field in the **Select from** drop-down list and enter data for it.

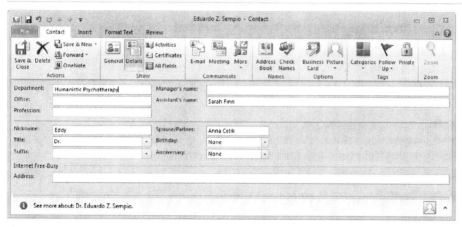

Figure 25–7. *The **Details** section of the contact window includes fields for further information about the contact's work and personal life.*

> **NOTE:** The **Internet Free-Busy** box is for entering the URL (the Internet address) of a file server that lets you check whether the contact is free or busy at any given point. You get this URL from the contact (or the contact's company). You can provide your own Free-Busy information to people who have you as a contact by choosing **File ➤ Options**, clicking **Calendar**, clicking the **Free/Busy Options** button, and then specifying the details in the **Free/Busy Options** dialog box in the **Calendar** options area. You'll probably need to ask an administrator for the URL.

Save the Contact—and Start Creating Another Contact If Necessary

When you've finished entering the contact's details, choose **Contact ➤ Actions ➤ Save & Close** to save the contact record and close the window.

If you want to create another contact immediately, you can click the **Save & New** button instead. If that contact is from the same company or organization, open the **Save & New** drop-down list and then click **Contact** from the **Same Company**. Outlook then copies the company information to the new contact for you.

Importing Contacts from Other Address Books

As you saw in the previous section, entering contact data manually gives you total control of which piece of information goes where—but it takes considerable effort. If you've already got some contact data stored in an address book, you can import it into Outlook and create contacts automatically.

This section shows you how to import data from the data sources you're perhaps most likely to have: **Windows Contacts**, an Excel worksheet containing contacts, **Yahoo! Contacts**, and **Google Contacts**.

Outlook gives you three main options for importing contacts:

- **Import an existing address book**. If your addresses are in an address book format such as Outlook Express (the e-mail program that Windows XP and older versions of Windows used), you can import the address book into Outlook.

- **Create a comma-separated values (CSV) file, and then import it**. Comma-separated values, abbreviated to CSV, is a standard format for exchanging data between spreadsheets or databases. The values are separated from each other with commas.

- **Create vCard files, and then import them**. A vCard file is a file that contains the virtual address card of one or more contacts. Outlook works only with vCard files that contain a single contact each.

Importing Windows Contacts to vCard Files

If you have contacts in the Windows Contacts folder, you can add them to Outlook by making vCard files from them. Follow these steps:

1. Create a folder somewhere convenient to put the vCard files. For example:

    a. Right-click your **Desktop**, click **New** on the context menu, and then click **Folder** on the submenu.

    b. Type a name such as **Exported Contacts** in the name box for the folder.

    c. Press **Enter** to apply the name.

2. Click the **Start** button, and then click your user name on the **Start** menu to open your user folder.

3. Double-click the **Contacts** folder to open it.

4. Select the contacts you want to export. For example, press **Ctrl+A** to select all the contacts, or drag a selection box around those you want.

5. On the toolbar, click the **Display additional commands** button (the **>>** button), and then click **Export** (see Figure 25–8).

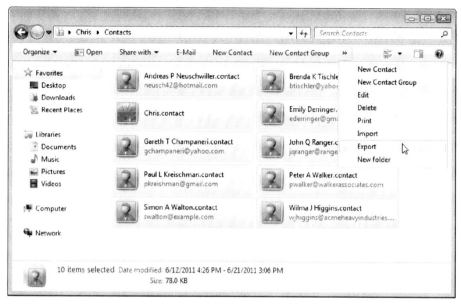

Figure 25–8. *In your **Contacts** folder, select the contacts you want to export, click the **Display additional commands** button, and then click **Export**.*

6. In the **Export Windows Contacts** dialog box that opens (see Figure 25–9), click the **vCards** item.

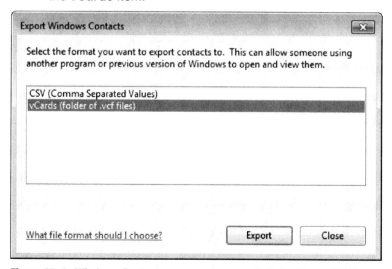

Figure 25–9. *Windows Contacts can export your contacts to either a CSV file or to vCard files. Usually, vCards are easier.*

7. Click the **Export** button. Windows Explorer displays the **Browse For Folder** dialog box.

8. Click the folder you created in step 1.

9. Click the **OK** button to close the **Browse For Folder** dialog box. Windows Explorer exports the contacts and displays a **Windows Contacts** dialog box telling you it has done so.

10. Click the **OK** button to close the **Windows Contacts** dialog box.

11. Click the **Close** button to close the **Export Windows Contacts** dialog box.

Exporting Yahoo! Contacts to a CSV File

To get your contacts from **Yahoo! Contacts** into Outlook, export them to a CSV file. Follow these steps:

1. Sign into Yahoo! and go to **Contacts**.

2. Click the **Tools** button, and then click **Export** on the drop-down menu to display the **Export** screen.

3. On the Microsoft Outlook line, click the **Export** button.

4. On the **Please answer the following to verify you are not a robot** screen, type the text of the captcha test, and then click the **Export Now** button. Yahoo! exports the contacts to a CSV file in your **Downloads** folder.

You can now import the CSV file as described in the section "Importing Contacts from a CSV File" later in this chapter.

Exporting Google Contacts to a CSV File

If you use Gmail or Google Mail, you can export your contact data to a comma-separated values (CSV) file that you can then import into Outlook. Follow these steps:

1. Sign into Gmail or Google Mail, and then go to the **My Contacts** area.

2. Click the **Export** link to display the **Export** screen.

3. In the **Who do you want to export?** area, select the **Everyone (All Contacts)** option button if you want to export all your contacts. Otherwise, select the **Only** option button, and then choose the appropriate group in the drop-down list—for example, **Friends**.

4. In the **Which export format?** area, select the **Outlook CSV** option button.

5. Click the **Export** button. Google exports the contacts to a CSV file in your **Downloads** folder.

You can now import the CSV file as described in the section "Importing Contacts from a CSV File" later in this chapter.

Importing vCard Files to Outlook Contacts

To import vCard files to Outlook contacts, follow these steps:

1. In Windows Explorer, open the folder to which you exported the vCards.

2. Press **Ctrl+A** to select all the vCard files.

3. Drag the vCard files to the **Outlook Contacts** window. Outlook creates a new contact for each of the vCard files and opens a **Contact** window showing it. Figure 25–10 shows an example.

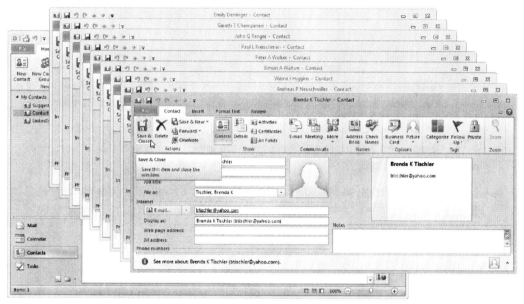

Figure 25–10. *Outlook opens a separate* **Contact** *window for each vCard you drag in. Add any extra information necessary to each card in turn, and then click the* **Save & Close** *button in the* **Actions** *group on the* **Contact** *tab.*

4. For each contact, fill in any other details you want to add (for example, notes), and then choose **Contact ➤ Actions ➤ Save & Close** to close each contact window.

Importing Contacts from a CSV File

When you've created a CSV file containing your contacts, follow these steps to import them into Outlook:

1. In Outlook, click the **File** tab to open Backstage.

2. Click the **Open** item in the left column to display the **Open** pane.

3. Click the **Import** button to launch the **Import and Export Wizard** (see Figure 25–11).

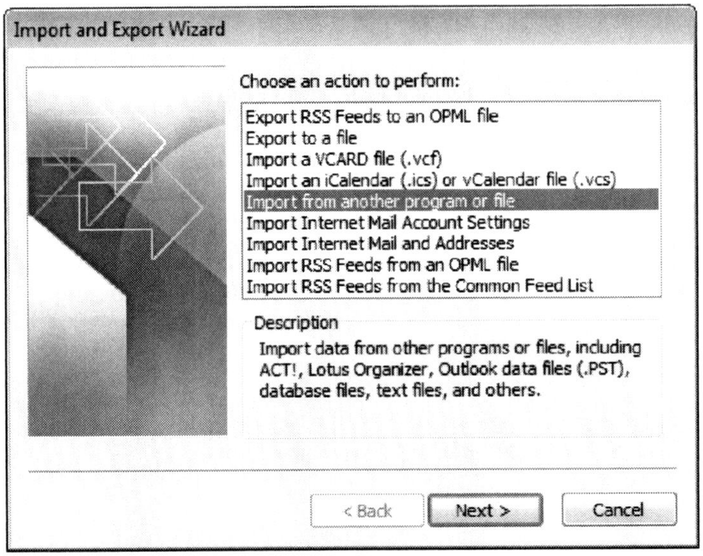

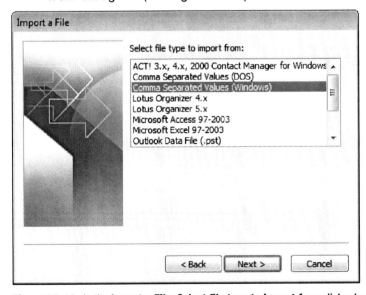

Figure 25–11. *On the opening screen of the* **Import and Export Wizard,** *click the* **Import from another program or file** *item to import a CSV file.*

4. In the **Choose an action to perform** box, click the **Import from another program or file** item.

5. Click the **Next** button to display the **Import a File: Select file type to import from** dialog box (see Figure 25–12).

Figure 25–12. *In the* **Import a File: Select file type to import from** *dialog box, click the* **Comma Separated Values (Windows)** *item.*

6. In the **Select file type to import from** box, click **Comma Separated Values (Windows)**.

7. Click the **Next** button to display the **Import a File: File to import** dialog box (see Figure 25–13).

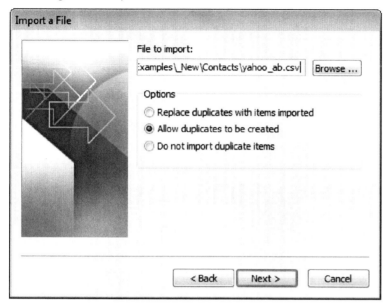

Figure 25–13. *In the **Import a File: File to import** dialog box, browse to the file you want to import, and then choose how to handle duplicate entries.*

8. In the **Options** area, choose how to handle duplicate entries by selecting the appropriate option button:

    ▪ **Replace duplicates with items imported.** Select this option button to replace any existing duplicates with new items created from the data you're importing.

    ▪ **Allow duplicates to be created.** Select this option button to allow Outlook to create duplicates by importing records with the same names. You'll need to go through your contacts afterward and integrate the duplicates (or remove them).

    ▪ **Do not import duplicate items.** Select this option button to avoid importing records that duplicate existing names.

9. Click the **Next** button to display the **Import a File: Select destination** folder dialog box (see Figure 25–14).

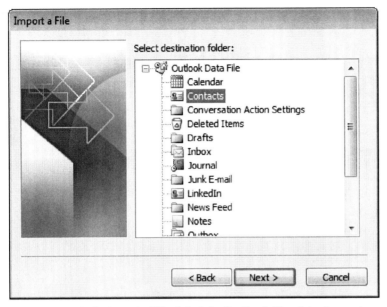

Figure 25–14. *In the **Import a File: Select destination folder** dialog box, make sure the **Contacts** folder is selected.*

10. Make sure the **Contacts** folder is selected in the **Select destination folder** box.

11. Click the **Next** button to display the **Import a File: The following actions will be performed** dialog box (see Figure 25–15).

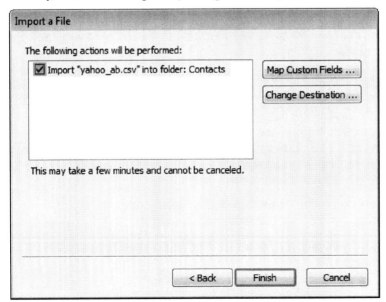

Figure 25–15. *In the **Import a File: The following actions will be performed** dialog box, select the check box for the contacts you want to import. In this case, you have only one option.*

12. In the box called **The following actions will be performed**, make sure the check box is selected for the contacts you want to import. When you're importing a CSV file, you'll normally have only one choice here.

> **NOTE:** From **The Import a File: The following actions will be performed** dialog box, you can click the **Map Custom Fields** button to display the **Map Custom Fields** dialog box, which enables you to customize which field from the CSV file goes to which field in the Outlook contacts. When you've exported a CSV file of contact data as described in this chapter, the fields have the correct name and order for mapping to Outlook, so you need to change the mapping only if you want to send a field to a destination other than its normal one. See the section "Mapping Custom Fields When Importing Contact Data" later in this chapter for details.

13. Click the **Finish** button to close the dialog box. Outlook imports the contacts and adds them to your contacts list.

Mapping Custom Fields When Importing Contact Data

When you import data that you've exported to a vCard or another standard format, the fields have standard names that Outlook can map to its fields—**Last Name to Last Name**, **First Name to First Name**, and so on. But when you import data that you have laid out in a spreadsheet or a similar tool, you may need to map the custom fields manually in order to get the data in the right places.

To map the custom data, click the **Map Custom Fields** button in the **Import a File: The following actions will be performed** dialog box (shown in Figure 25–15). Outlook then displays the **Map Custom Fields** dialog box, and you can work as shown in Figure 25–16.

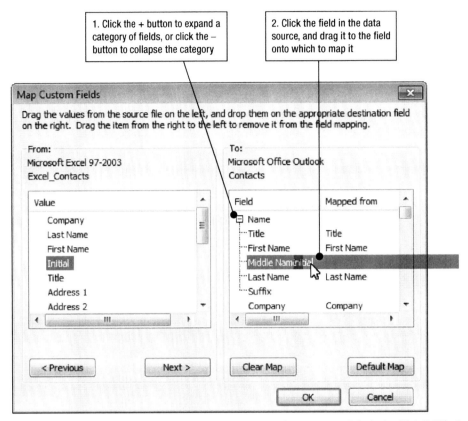

Figure 25–16. *Use the controls in the **Map Custom Fields** dialog box to tell Outlook which field in the incoming data to map to which field in each Outlook contact.*

NOTE: If your contact data has a header row, you'll see the field names from the header row in the left box in the **Map Custom Fields** dialog box. If your contact data has no header row, you'll see the values from the first row of data—the details of the first contact you're importing. You can click the **Next** button to display the next record or the **Previous** button to display the previous record (once you've gone forward from the first record).

When you've finished mapping each field, click the **OK** button to close the **Map Custom Fields** dialog box. You can then click the **Finish** button to finish the process of importing the data.

Working with Contacts

After creating contacts or importing them into Outlook, you can work with them. Outlook makes it easy to view and sort your contacts in different ways, edit the information in a contact record, organize your contacts into groups, and communicate with them.

Viewing and Sorting Your Contacts

To view your list of contacts, click the **Contacts** button in the **Navigation Pane**. You can then expand the **My Contacts** list by clicking the white triangle next to it, and click one of the groups of contacts that it contains. For example, the **Contacts** screen in Figure 25–17 shows two groups of contacts: the **Contacts** group in Outlook, and a **LinkedIn** group imported from the LinkedIn social network.

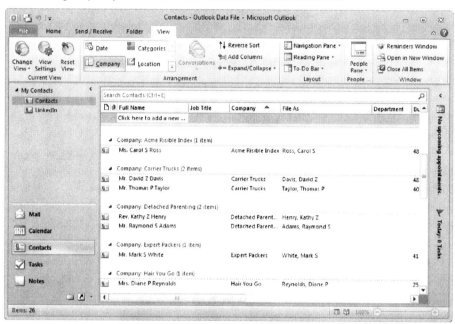

Figure 25–17. *Click the* **Contacts** *button in the* **Navigation Pane** *to display your contacts. You can then expand the* **My Contacts** *listing in the* **Navigation Pane** *and click the group of contacts you want to display. This screen uses* **List** *view.*

Changing the View

Figure 25–17 uses Outlook's List view. Outlook gives you four built-in views, which you can switch among by using the **View ➤ Current View ➤ Change View** drop-down panel:

- **Business Card** *view*. This view (see Figure 25–18) shows each contact's details on a virtual business card.

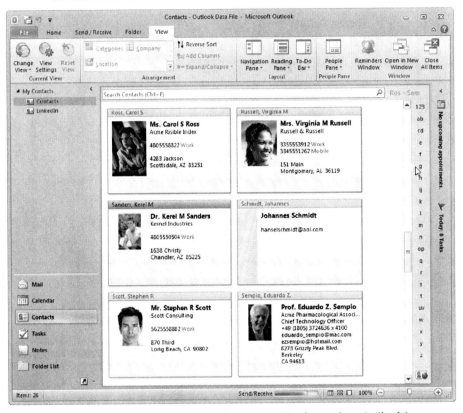

Figure 25–18. *Switch to **Business Card** view when you want to view each contact's picture.*

■ *Card view.* This view (see Figure 25–19) shows each contact's information laid out on a rectangle with all the fields clearly identified.

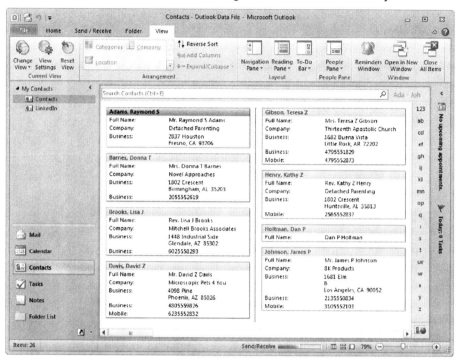

Figure 25–19. *Card view labels each item of contact information clearly.*

■ **Phone** *view.* This view displays the contacts as a phone list (see Figure 25–20).

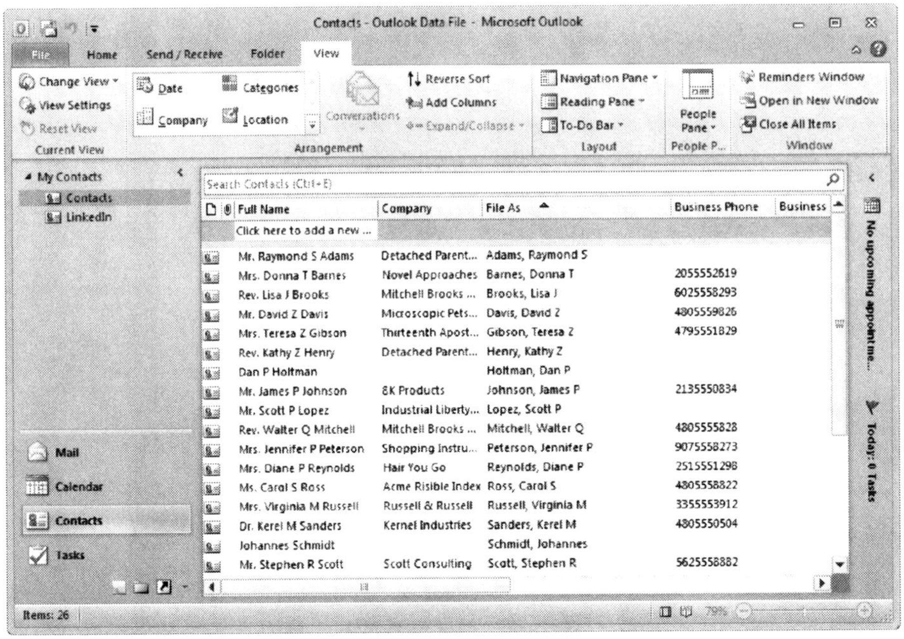

Figure 25–20. *Display your contacts in **Phone** view when you need to quickly find a phone number.*

Changing the Arrangement and Grouping

In **Phone** view and **List** view, you can use the **Arrange By** box or drop-down list in the **Arrangement** group of the **View** pane to change the way that Outlook arranges your contacts. When the **Arrange By** box appears, as in Figure 25–20, click the item by which you want to arrange the contacts: **Date**, **Categories**, **Company**, or **Location**.

For these two views, you can choose whether Outlook displays the contacts in groups within the arrangement. To turn grouping on or off, choose **View** ➤ **Arrangement** ➤ **Arrange By** (if the **Arrange By** drop-down list is displayed) or **View** ➤ **Arrangement** ➤ **More** (clicking the drop-down button at the right of the **Arrange By** box), and then click the **Show in Groups** item to either place a check mark next to it or to remove the check mark.

TIP: For a quick sort, click the heading of the column by which you want to sort.

Searching for a Contact

To search for a contact, click in the **Search Contacts** box at the top of the **Contacts** pane, and then type your search term. Outlook adds the **Search Tools** section to the Ribbon and displays the **Search** pane. Figure 25–21 shows you how to use the search results.

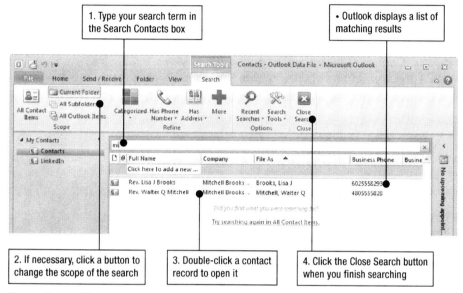

Figure 25–21. *When you start a search, Outlook adds the* **Search Tools** *section to the Ribbon and displays the* **Search** *tab, which contains controls for refining the search.*

Editing Contact Information

As you interact with your contacts and learn more about them, you'll often need to take notes, add further details, or change the information you've already entered.

To edit a contact's information, double-click the contact record in the list of contacts. Outlook opens the contact in a contact window, where you can edit the information freely.

When you've finished editing a contact record, choose **Contact > Actions > Save & Close** to close the contact record.

Communicating with Your Contacts

When working in a contact window, you can quickly start a communication with one of your contacts by giving the appropriate command:

■ *E-mail*. Choose **Contact** ➤ **Communicate** ➤ **E-mail** to create a new message to the contact.

■ *Meeting*. Choose **Contact** ➤ **Communicate** ➤ **Meeting** to start a meeting invitation to the contact.

■ *Phone call*. Choose **Contact** ➤ **Communicate** ➤ **More** ➤ **Call**, and then click the appropriate phone number (for example, **Business** or **Home**) on the submenu.

■ *Task*. Choose **Contact** ➤ **Communicate** ➤ **More** ➤ **Assign Task** to start a task request to the contact.

You can also start a communication by right-clicking a contact in the contacts list, and then making the appropriate choice on the context menu (see Figure 25–22); for example, choose **Create** ➤ **E-mail** to start a new e-mail message.

Figure 25–22. *You can start a communication by right-clicking a contact in the contacts list, and then making the appropriate choice from the context menu.*

Summary

In this chapter, you learned how to use Outlook to manage your contacts. You now know how to create contacts from scratch or import your existing contact data from **Windows Address Book**, **Yahoo! Contacts**, **Google Contacts**, or other sources into Outlook by creating either vCard files or CSV files. And you know how to view and sort your contacts, edit their contact information, and quickly and easily create communications to them.

In the next chapter, I'll show you how to use Outlook to manage your schedule and tasks.

Chapter 26

Organizing Your Schedule, Tasks, and Notes

In this chapter, I'll show you how to use Outlook to schedule your appointments, keep your calendar in order, and manage your tasks and notes.

First, you'll meet the Calendar interface and learn to display the dates you want. I'll discuss the different types of time commitments Outlook uses—appointments, events and meetings—and then I'll show you how to use the Calendar's different views.

After that, we'll go through how to create one-shot appointments (or events) and ones that repeat on a regular schedule. You'll learn to use Outlook to schedule meetings and respond to meeting invitations you receive.

Next, we'll work with Outlook's features for defining tasks you need to complete and tracking your progress on completing them. You can create either one-shot tasks or recurring tasks, record your progress on them, and keep your colleagues informed about what you're doing. You can also delegate a task to someone else and follow her progress with it, even receiving an automatic notification when she marks the task as complete.

Finally, you'll meet Outlook's Notes feature, which is useful for jotting down information as you work and then sharing your notes with other programs.

Organizing Your Schedule with the Calendar

To get started working with the Calendar, click the **Calendar** button in the **Navigation Pane** or press **Ctrl+2**. Outlook first displays the Calendar in **Day** view (see Figure 26–1).

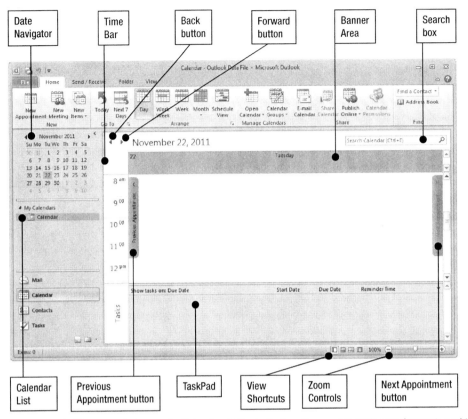

Figure 26–1. *When you first open the Calendar, Outlook displays the current day's appointments and tasks.*

These are the main parts of the Outlook window:

▪ **Date Navigator**. This area shows the dates in the current month. You can move to the previous month by clicking the left-arrow button or to the next month by clicking the right-arrow button. To see more than one month at a time, drag the line underneath the calendar down.

> **NOTE:** When you need more space to work on your appointments, you can click the **Minimize the Navigation Pane** button (the **<** button at the top-right corner of the Navigation Pane) to reduce the Navigation Pane to a thin strip at the left side of the Outlook window. You can then click the **Folders** button to display a pop-up panel showing the **Date Navigator** and the **Calendars List**. To restore the Navigation Pane, click the **Expand the Navigation Pane** button (the **>** button at the top of the strip).

▨ *Calendar List.* This area shows the list of your calendars under the heading **My Calendars**. Normally, Outlook starts you off with a single calendar named simply **Calendar**. You can expand the **My Calendars** list by clicking the white triangle to its left or collapse it by clicking the black triangle that replaces the white triangle when you expand it. You can add other calendars of your own to the **Calendar List** if needed, or you can add calendars that other people are sharing.

▨ *Time Bar.* This vertical strip shows the times of day, with the hours marked. At first, Outlook displays each hour divided into two 30-minute slots. You can change these intervals by right-clicking the **Time Bar** and choosing your preferred interval: **60 Minutes – Least Space for Details**; **30 Minutes**; **15 Minutes**; **10 Minutes**; **6 Minutes**; or **5 Minutes – Most Space for Details**.

▨ *Back* button. Click this button to display the previous time unit—the previous day when the Calendar is in **Day** view, the previous work week when the Calendar is in **Work Week** view, and so on.

▨ *Forward* button. Click this button to display the next time unit—the next day, the next work week, the next month or whatever.

▨ *Previous Appointment* button. Click this button to display the previous appointment.

▨ **Next Appointment** *button.* Click this button to display the next appointment.

▨ *Banner Area.* This area displays the day name (in Day view) or names (in other views).

▨ *Search* box. Click in this area and type a search term to search the Calendar.

▨ *TaskPad.* This area shows your list of tasks from the **Tasks** folder. You can create a new task by clicking a blank line in the TaskPad and typing the details of the task.

▨ *View Shortcuts.* Click these buttons to switch among Outlook's four views. See the section "Understanding and Using the Calendar Views" later in this chapter.

▨ *Zoom* controls. As with the other Office programs, click the – button to zoom out, click the + button to zoom in, or drag the zoom slider to zoom either in or out.

Displaying the Dates You Want to Work With

To display the dates you want to work with, click the appropriate button in the **Arrange** group on the **Home** tab of the Ribbon, as shown in Figure 26–2.

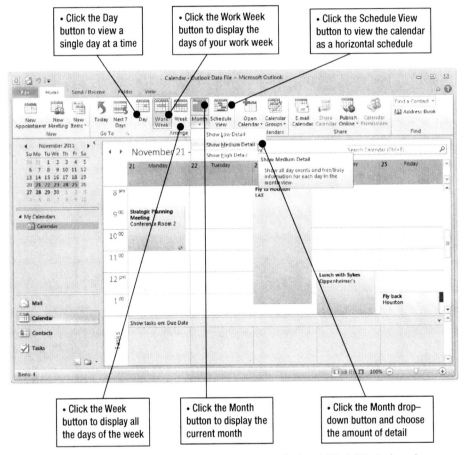

- Click the Day button to view a single day at a time
- Click the Work Week button to display the days of your work week
- Click the Schedule View button to view the calendar as a horizontal schedule
- Click the Week button to display all the days of the week
- Click the Month button to display the current month
- Click the Month drop-down button and choose the amount of detail

Figure 26–2. *Use the **Arrange** buttons to change the dates displayed. **Work Week** view gives you an overview of your commitments for the working week.*

> **TIP:** To change the start time and end time for work, change the days of the work week, or change the day on which the week starts, work in the **Calendar** category of the **Options** dialog box. The quickest way to reach this category is to choose **Home ➤ Arrange ➤ Calendar Options**, clicking the tiny button in the lower-right corner of the **Arrange** group.

Understanding Appointments, Events, and Meetings

Outlook's Calendar uses three different types of time commitments:

▨ *Appointment.* An appointment is an item on your schedule that requires only you, not other people you need to invite or resources (for example, a conference room or projector) that you need to reserve. The Calendar creates appointments by default unless you choose to create an event or a meeting. An appointment occupies the appropriate time slots in your schedule. For example, if you create a three-hour meeting starting at 10 AM, Outlook displays the appointment taking up the time slots from 10 AM to 1 PM.

▨ *Event.* An *event* is simply an appointment that lasts for 24 hours or more. Instead of taking up all of a day's time slots by displaying an event right across them, Outlook displays events in the banner area at the top of the schedule.

▨ *Meeting.* A meeting is an appointment to which you invite other people or for which you schedule resources.

> **NOTE:** You can change any of the three types of time commitments to another type by editing its details. For example, you can change an appointment to a meeting by inviting someone else to it.

Understanding and Using the Calendar Views

Outlook gives you four different views for viewing the Calendar:

▨ **Normal** *view.* This view (shown in Figure 26–1), displays the **Date Navigator** in the **Navigation Pane** and shows the **TaskPad** below the calendar listing.

▨ **Calendar and Task** *view.* This view (see Figure 26–3) automatically minimizes the **Navigation Pane** to provide more space for displaying the calendar listing and the **TaskPad**. Use this view when you need more space for working on your appointments and tasks.

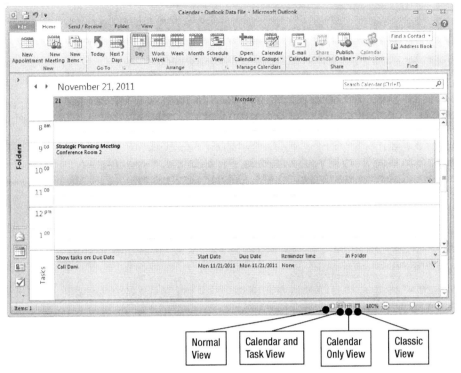

| Normal View | Calendar and Task View | Calendar Only View | Classic View |

Figure 26–3. *Calendar and Task view collapses the **Navigation Pane** to provide more room for working with your appointments and tasks.*

- *Calendar Only* view. This view (which looks like Figure 26–3, but without the **TaskPad** displayed) automatically minimizes the **Navigation Pane** and hides the **TaskPad** to give you as much space as possible for working in the calendar listing.

- *Classic* view. This view (see Figure 26–4) shows the **To-Do Bar** on the right of the **Outlook** window with the **Date Navigator**, **Appointment** list, and **Task** list in it. This view is useful when you need to see two or more months in the **Date Navigator**.

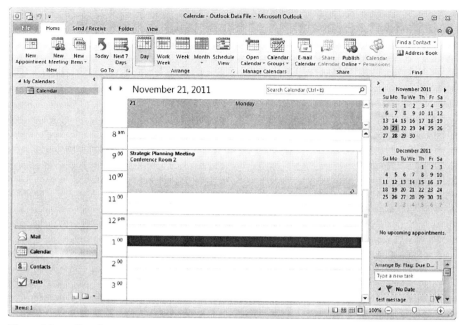

Figure 26–4. *Classic view displays the **To-Do Bar** on the right of the Outlook window. You can customize the contents of the **To-Do Bar** by right-clicking it and then clicking **Options**. For example, you can change the number of months displayed.*

Creating Appointments and Events

When you have an appointment that occurs only once, you can create an appointment either by working directly in the Calendar or by opening an **Appointment** window and entering full details.

Creating a One-Shot Appointment Directly in the Calendar

To create a one-shot appointment directly in the Calendar, work as shown in Figure 26–5.

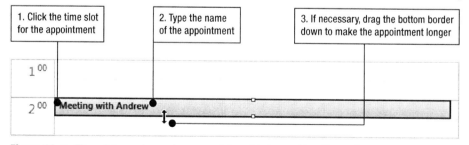

Figure 26–5. *The quick way to create an appointment is by working directly in the Calendar.*

Creating a One-Shot Appointment or Event with Full Details

When you need to create a one-shot appointment or event with full details, double-click the time slot for the appointment, and then work in the **Appointment** window, as shown in Figure 26–6.

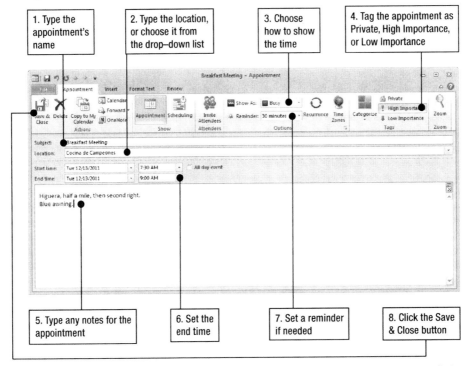

1. Type the appointment's name

2. Type the location, or choose it from the drop–down list

3. Choose how to show the time

4. Tag the appointment as Private, High Importance, or Low Importance

5. Type any notes for the appointment

6. Set the end time

7. Set a reminder if needed

8. Click the Save & Close button

Figure 26–6. *Open an **Appointment** window when you want to specify the appointment's details beyond the subject and the times. In the **Show As** drop-down list, you can choose to show the time as **Busy**, **Free**, **Tentative**, or **Out of Office**.*

> **NOTE:** If the event will last all day, select the **All day event** check box in the **Appointment** window.

If you need to change the time zone for the appointment, click the **Time Zones** button. Outlook displays a time zone drop-down list on the **Start** time line and the **End** time line (see Figure 26–7). Choose the time zones you need.

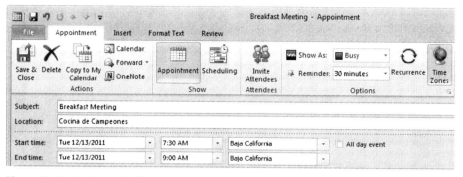

Figure 26–7. *To change the time zones for an appointment, choose* **Appointment** ➤ **Options** ➤ **Time Zones**, *and then use the time zone drop-down lists on the* **Start time** *line and* **End time** *line.*

Creating Repeating Appointments

To create a repeating appointment, set up the appointment as described in the previous section, choose **Appointment** ➤ **Options** ➤ **Recurrence**, and then work in the **Appointment Recurrence** dialog box as shown in Figure 26–8.

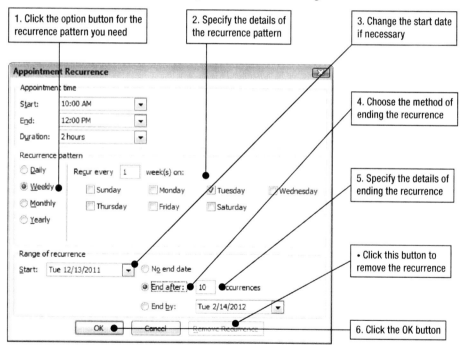

Figure 26–8. *Use the* **Appointment Recurrence** *dialog box when you need to create a repeating appointment.*

When you click the **OK** button to close the **Appointment Recurrence** dialog box and return to the **Appointment** window, which is now called **Appointment Series**. The **Recurrence** button in the **Options** group now appears pressed in to indicate that recurrence is turned on, and the **Recurrence** line appears below the **Location** box giving the details of the recurrence (see Figure 26–9). The **Appointment Series** tab replaces the **Appointment** tab.

Figure 26–9. *To indicate that the appointment recurs, Outlook selects the **Recurrence** button in the **Options** group of the **Appointment Series** window. The details of the recurrence appear on the **Recurrence** line below the **Location** box.*

Scheduling Meetings

If an event involves inviting other people or scheduling resources, it's a meeting rather than an appointment. This section shows you how to schedule meetings of your own and respond to meeting invitations that other people send you.

Setting Up a Meeting

To set up a meeting, follow these steps:

1. In the Calendar, click and drag through the time slots for the meeting. If the meeting needs just a single time slot, click it.

2. Choose **Home** ➤ **New** ➤ **New Meeting** to open a Meeting window (see Figure 26–10).

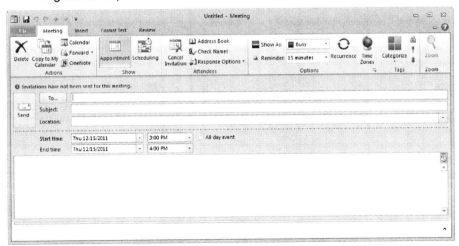

Figure 26–10. *To schedule a meeting, use the **Meeting** window to set up your meeting request, and then send it.*

3. Click the **To** button to display the **Select Attendees and Resources** dialog box (shown in Figure 26–11 with some settings chosen).

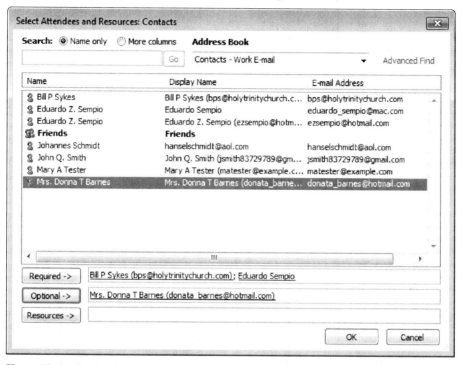

Figure 26–11. *Use the **Select Attendees and Resources** dialog box to specify which attendees you require for the meeting, which attendees are optional, and which resources you need.*

4. In the **Address Book** drop-down list, choose the contact list with which you want to work.

5. In the main list box, click the contact or contacts you want to add as required attendees, and then click the Required button to add them to the **Required** box.

6. In the main list box, select any contacts you want to add as optional attendees, and then click the **Optional** button to add them to the **Optional** box.

7. If your address book includes resources, select those you need, and click the **Resources** button to add them to the **Resources** box. For example, you may want to book a conference room or reserve a projector for a presentation.

8. Click the **OK** button to close the **Select Attendees and Resources** dialog box. Outlook returns you to the Meeting window, in which it has entered your chosen contacts in the **To** box.

9. Type the meeting's name in the **Subject** box.

10. Type the meeting's location in the **Location** box.

11. Type any message about the meeting in the main box. For example, you may want to make clear what the meeting will cover, what attendees need to prepare, and so on.

12. To check schedule information, choose **Meeting ➤ Show ➤ Scheduling** to display the **Scheduling** pane (see Figure 26–12). Here, you can see the information available about each participant's schedule, which should help you pick a suitable time for the meeting.

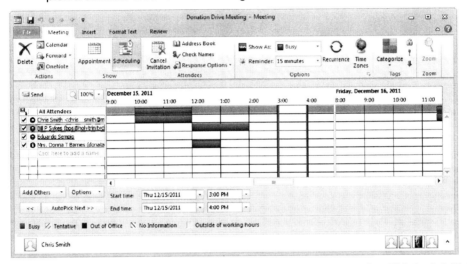

Figure 26–12. *Use the **Scheduling** pane to identify a suitable time for the meeting. Click the **AutoPick Next** button to pick the next time available to all required participants.*

13. When you've finished setting up the meeting invitation, click the **Send** button to send the meeting invitation.

Tracking the Status of Meeting Invitations You've Sent

After you send a meeting request, you receive the responses that the invitees send. Outlook tallies the acceptances and refusals for you. To see a summary of the responses, double-click the meeting in your calendar to open it in a **Meeting** window, and then choose **Meeting ➤ Show ➤ Tracking** (see Figure 26–13).

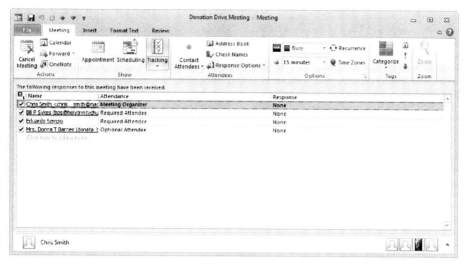

Figure 26–13. *Open the* **Tracking** *pane of the* **Meeting** *window when you need to check the responses you've received to the meeting request.*

> **NOTE:** To remove an attendee from the meeting, clear the attendee's check box in the **Tracking** pane. When you save the meeting, Outlook displays a dialog box noting that the attendees for the meeting have changed. Select the **Save changes and send update** option button, and then click the **OK** button. In the **Send Update to Attendees** dialog box, select the **Send updates only to added or deleted attendees** option button or the **Send updates to all attendees** option button, as needed, and then click the **OK** button.

Dealing with Invitations to Meetings

When someone sends you an invitation to a meeting, you receive an e-mail message with the details of the message and with a built-in mechanism for replying. Double-click the meeting message to open it in a **Meeting** window, and then click the **Accept** button, the **Tentative** button, the **Decline** button, or the **Propose New Time** button, as appropriate. Complete the resulting message with any more information needed, and then send it.

> **CAUTION:** In theory, invitations to meetings work consistently across different e-mail programs. In practice, various problems occur. If your invitations receive no response, follow up with conventional e-mail messages.

Working with Tasks

In this section, you'll learn how to work with Outlook's **Tasks** feature. You'll meet the interface Outlook provides for working with tasks, create new tasks, and manage your tasks. You'll also see how to assign tasks to other people and deal with the tasks they assign to you.

Meeting the Tasks Interface

To get started with tasks, click the **Tasks** button in the **Navigation Pane** or press **Ctrl+4**. Outlook displays the **Tasks** folder (shown in Figure 26–14 with several tasks added).

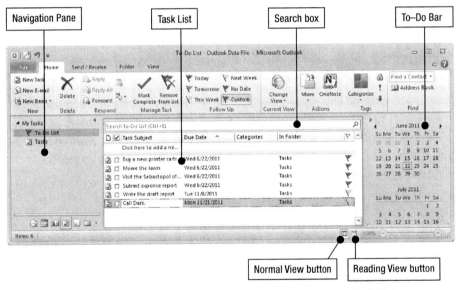

Figure 26–14. *Click the **Tasks** button in the **Navigation Pane** to display the **Task List**.*

By default, Outlook opens the **Task List** in **Normal** view, which shows the **Navigation Pane** on the left and the **To-Do Bar** on the right. If you want more space to work with your tasks, click the **Reading View** button on the status bar to switch the **Task List** to Reading view (see Figure 26–15), which minimizes the **Navigation Pane**, the **To-Do Bar**, and the Ribbon. You can also minimize the Ribbon only by pressing **Ctrl+F1** or by clicking the **Minimize the Ribbon** button at its right end.

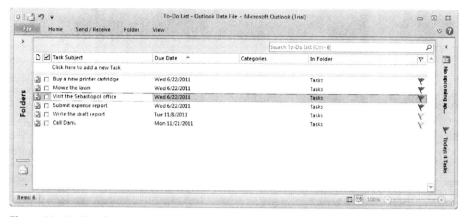

Figure 26–15. *Reading* view minimizes the Ribbon, the *Navigation Pane*, and the *To-Do Bar* to give you more space to work on your tasks.

Viewing the Task List

Apart from **Normal** view and **Reading** view, Outlook lets you arrange your **Task List** in nearly a dozen different ways. You can change view by opening the **Change View** drop-down panel, which you'll find in the **Current View** group on both the **Home** tab (see Figure 26–16) and the **View** tab of the Ribbon, and then clicking the view you want. These are the views:

- **Simple List.** This view shows all tasks, including those you've completed, with a minimal level of detail. This view is useful for general work.

- **Detailed.** This view shows all tasks, including completed tasks, with more detail than **Simple List** view provides. This view works well if you can widen the Outlook window far enough to make space for each column; on narrower screens, this view tends to be too squashed. You can remove any column you don't need by right-clicking the column heading and clicking **Remove This Column** on the context menu.

- **To-Do List.** This view displays tasks in your **To-Do List**. You can arrange them in different ways (for example, first by flag and then by start date) by clicking the column headings.

- **Prioritized.** This view shows tasks arranged by priority. This view is good for focusing on your key tasks rather than spending time on unimportant tasks scheduled for today.

- **Active.** This view shows tasks that you haven't marked as complete.

- **Completed.** This view shows tasks you've marked as complete. Normally, you'll use this view to review the tasks you've performed.

- **Today.** This view shows tasks scheduled for the current day.

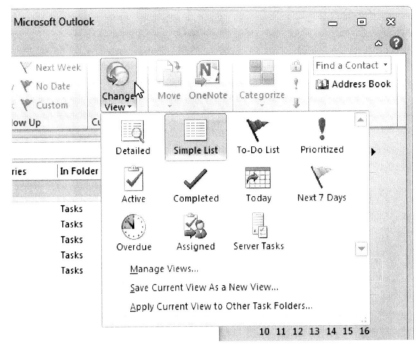

Figure 26–16. *You can change view by using the **Change View** drop-down panel in the **Current View** group of the **Home** tab and the **View** tab of the Ribbon.*

- **Next 7 Days**. This view shows tasks scheduled for the next seven days.

- **Overdue**. This view shows tasks whose due date has passed.

- **Assigned**. This view shows tasks you've assigned to others.

- **Server Tasks**. This view shows tasks assigned via Exchange.

Creating a One-Shot Task by Working in the Task List

When you need to create a task quickly, entering only a few details, create it in the **Task List**. Click the **Click here to add a new Task** prompt, type the task name (see Figure 26–17), and add any details needed in the other columns.

Figure 26–17. *You can quickly enter brief details for a new task directly in the **Task List**.*

Creating a One-Shot Task Using a Task Window

When you need to specify more detail for a task than the Task List allows, double-click blank space in the **Task List** or choose **Home ➤ New ➤ New Task** to open a **Task** window. You can then work as shown in Figure 26–18.

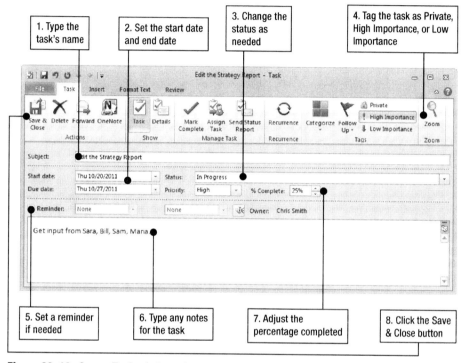

Figure 26–18. *Open a Task window when you need to specify the details of a task.*

> **TIP:** You can enter as much text as needed in the notes box. Format the text by using the controls on the **Format Text** tab of the **Task** window's Ribbon; start your formatting with styles, and add direct formatting only where strictly necessary. To insert a table, picture, chart, or other object, work on the Insert tab. To check the spelling, get a word count, or use the Thesaurus or other reference tools, work on the **Review** tab.

Creating Recurring Tasks

If your job includes tasks that repeat at regular intervals, you can set up recurring tasks to have Outlook remind you of them. Create the task as described in the previous section, click the **Recurrence** button in the **Task** window, and then work as shown in Figure 26–19.

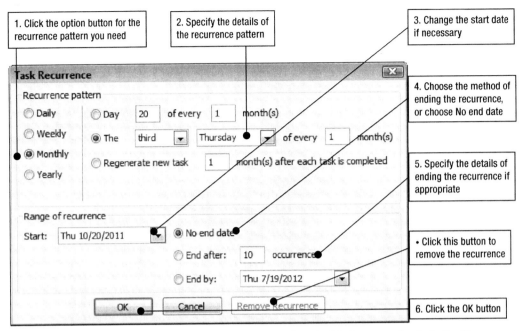

1. Click the option button for the recurrence pattern you need

2. Specify the details of the recurrence pattern

3. Change the start date if necessary

4. Choose the method of ending the recurrence, or choose No end date

5. Specify the details of ending the recurrence if appropriate

• Click this button to remove the recurrence

6. Click the OK button

Figure 26–19. *Use the* **Task Recurrence** *dialog box to set up the schedule for a repeating task. The* **Recurrence** *pattern options change depending on whether you select the* **Daily** *option button, the* **Weekly** *option button, the* **Monthly** *option button, or the* **Yearly** *option button.*

NOTE: Select the **Regenerate new task** option button when you want to create a new task a specific amount of time after the previous instance of the task was completed rather than sticking to a rigid calendar schedule for the tasks.

When you click the **OK** button to close the **Task Recurrence** dialog box and return to the **Task** window, the **Recurrence** button in the **Recurrence** group on the **Task** tab of the Ribbon appears pressed in to indicate that recurrence is turned on, and the schedule appears above the **Subject** box (see Figure 26–20).

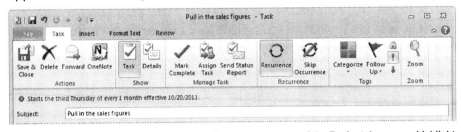

Figure 26–20. *The* **Recurrence** *button in the* **Recurrence** *group of the* **Tasks** *tab appears highlighted to show that recurrence is turned on. The recurrence schedule appears above the* **Subject** *box.*

Adding Details to a Task

To add details such as mileage or working hours to a task, double-click it in the **Task List** to open it in a **Task** window, then choose **Task ➤ Show ➤ Details**. In the **Details** pane (see Figure 26–21), enter the details in the boxes, and then choose **Task ➤ Actions ➤ Save & Close**.

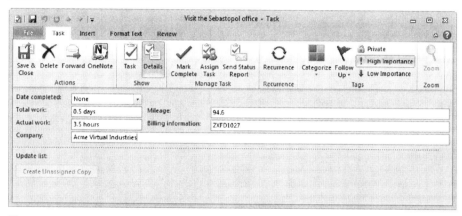

Figure 26–21. *In the **Details** pane of a **Task** window, you can enter details such as mileage, working hours, or the company involved.*

Marking a Task for Follow-Up

If a task needs further action, you can mark it for follow-up at the appropriate time in either of these ways:

- *Task List.* Click the task, go to the **Follow Up** group on the **Home** tab of the Ribbon, and then click **Today**, **Tomorrow**, **This Week**, **Next Week**, **No Date**, or **Custom**, as shown in Figure 26–22.

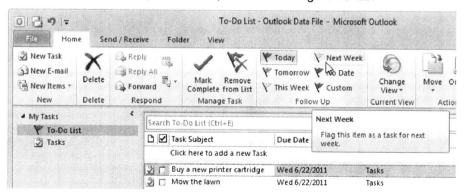

Figure 26–22. *You can quickly mark a task for follow-up by using the buttons in the **Follow Up** group on the **Home** tab of the Ribbon.*

■ *Task window.* Choose **Task ➤ Tags ➤ Follow Up**, and then click **Today**, **Tomorrow**, **This Week**, **Next Week**, **No Date**, or **Custom**.

When you need to set a different date than any of the preset buttons offers, click the **Custom** item, and then use the **Custom** dialog box (see Figure 26–23) to set the details of the follow-up.

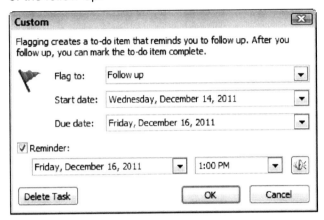

Figure 26–23. *Use the **Custom** dialog box to set a follow-up flag using the exact date and time you want.*

Sending a Status Report on a Task

To give a colleague an update on a task you're working on, follow these steps:

1. In the **Task List**, double-click the task to open it in a **Task** window.

2. Make any updates needed to the status.

3. Choose **Task ➤ Manage Task ➤ Send Status Report**. Outlook creates a message containing the details of the task status and displays it in a **Task Status Report** window (see Figure 26–24).

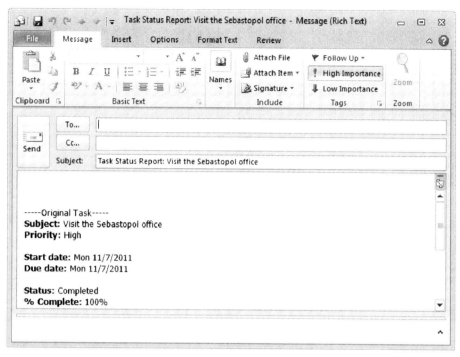

Figure 26–24. *You can quickly send a message containing a status report on a particular task to a colleague.*

4. Address the message, add any information needed, and then click the **Send** button to send it.

5. Choose **Task ➤ Actions ➤ Save & Close** to close the **Task** window.

Assigning Tasks to Other People

To assign a task to someone else, follow these steps:

1. Open the task in a Task window.

2. Choose **Task ➤ Manage Task ➤ Assign Task**. Outlook adds a **To** field to the top of the **Task** window (shown in Figure 26–25 with settings chosen).

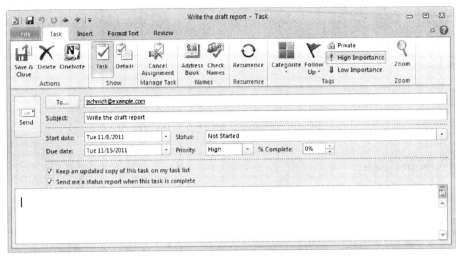

Figure 26–25. *To assign a task to a colleague, enter his e-mail address in the **To** box, choose options, and click the **Send** button.*

3. Enter the recipient's address in the **To** box. For example, click the **To** button, and then use the **Select Task Recipient** dialog box to choose the recipient.

4. Choose tracking options:

   ▪ **Keep an updated copy of this task on my task list**. Select this check box to have Outlook keep this task on your task list and update it so that you can see what (if anything) the recipient has done. This is usually a good idea.

   ▪ **Send me a status report when this task is complete**. Select this check box to make Outlook automatically send you a status report when the recipient marks the task as complete. This too is usually helpful.

5. Type any message needed in the box at the bottom of the **Task** window.

6. Click the **Send** button to send the task request.

When the recipient accepts or declines the task request, his e-mail program sends a response that you receive in Outlook. If you yourself need to remove the task from whomever you've assigned it to, click the **Cancel Assignment** button.

Dealing with Tasks Other People Send to You

When someone else sends you a task request, it arrives in your Outlook Inbox like any other incoming mail. From here, you can view it either in the Reading Pane or in a Message window, and click the **Accept** button or the **Decline** button as appropriate.

If you accept the task request, Outlook adds the task to your **Task** List, where you can work with it just like a task you've created.

Taking Notes

When you're working in Outlook, you'll often find it handy to have a place to jot down scraps of information that you need to deal with later. To do this, you can use Outlook's **Notes** feature.

Meeting the Notes Interface

To start using Notes, click the **Notes** button in the **Navigation Pane** or press **Ctrl+5**. Outlook displays the **Notes** pane (shown in Figure 26–26 with two notes created).

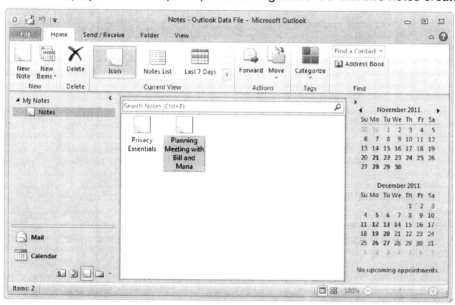

Figure 26–26. *Use Outlook's Notes feature to take quick notes as you work.*

Outlook opens the **Notes** pane in **Normal** view by default. To give yourself more space, you can click the **Icons Only** button on the status bar (the right button in the **View Shortcuts** group) to switch to **Icons Only** view, which minimizes the **Navigation Pane** and hides the **To-Do Bar**.

Creating a Note

To create a new note, work as shown in Figure 26–27.

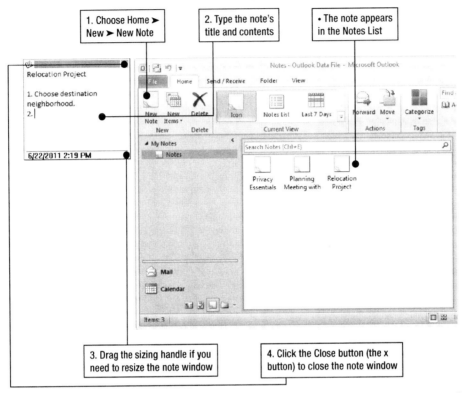

Figure 26–27. *Choose* **Home ➤ New ➤ New Note** *to create a new note, and then type the information in the free-floating window that opens.*

Viewing and Using Your Notes

By default, Outlook displays each note as an icon with its first line beneath it, as in Figure 23-15. When you need to see the text of each note, choose **Home ➤ Current View ➤ Notes List** to display the notes as a list including their contents (see Figure 26–28).

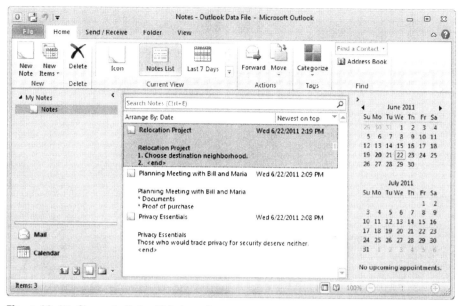

Figure 26–28. *Change to **Notes List** view when you want to see the contents of your notes at a glance.*

TIP: When you want to view only your recent notes, choose **Home ➤ Current View ➤ Last 7 Days**. Outlook displays only the notes you've created in the last seven days.

You can use the information you've saved in a note in either of these ways:

■ *Copy and paste a note's contents.* Copy the contents of the note, and then paste them into whichever program you want to use them in—for example, Microsoft Word or OneNote.

■ *Forward a note.* Click a note, and then choose **Home ➤ Actions ➤ Forward** to open a **Message** window with the contents of the note attached. Address the message as usual, type any covering message needed, and then click the Send button to send the message.

Summary

In this chapter, you learned how to use Outlook to schedule your appointments, keep your calendar in order, and manage your tasks.

You now know how to create appointments, events, and meetings, schedule meetings and respond to meeting invitations, and use the Calendar's views. You can manage your commitments by creating tasks, recording your progress on them, and keeping your colleagues informed about what you're doing. And you can use Outlook's Notes feature to jot down information as you work, and then share it with other programs.

Index

CPSIA information can be obtained at www.ICGtesting.com
Printed in the USA
243044LV00004B/6/P